J. HARDIE

Modern Perspectives

Guernica, by Pablo Picasso (1881-1973). Oil on canvas, 777 cm x 336 cm, painted in Paris, 1937. On extended loan from the artist to the Museum of Modern Art, New York. Reproduced by permission of SPADEM, Montreal.

In early 1937, Picasso was commissioned by the Republican government to paint a mural for Spain's pavilion at the Paris World's Fair. After several months of procrastination he had not even begun the work. On April 26, 1937, during the Spanish Civil War, the ancient Basque town of Guernica was devastated with heavy loss of life. It is generally believed that the attack was made by German bombers supporting the rebel leader, General Franco. However, a post-war controversy arose over an alternative explanation claiming that the devastation was caused by, or aggravated by Republican ground forces seeking to arouse the passions of the Basques and to give anti-Franco forces an international propaganda issue. Whatever the true cause of the tragedy, it provoked a memorable reaction.

Picasso, in his Paris studio, was galvanized by the news and immediately set to work. In less than two months the huge mural, titled simply *Guernica*, was completed. When it was put on display in the Spanish Pavilion it evoked strong criticism, both political and artistic.

The angular, almost theatrical setting in which the action of the mural takes place is a group of buildings. It is dark, but the central scene is lit by a strange sunlike lamp that resembles an eye. The subjects fall into two categories. The protagonists include a woman who leans from a window and thrusts a lamp, a traditional symbol of truth, towards a bull on the left. The bull, which Picasso has said represents "not fascism, but brutality and darkness," turns its head away. In the centre is a horse, mortally wounded, with its head upraised in a cry of agony. The artist has said that the horse represents "the people." On the ground is the battered form of a soldier. His dismembered body looks more like the plaster cast of a statue than a real human body. Just visible on a ledge in the background is a bird. It may be intended to symbolize the wounded spirit of humanity. The three remaining female figures do not participate directly in the action, but seem to serve as a Greek chorus, providing comments on the significance of the central action. One, holding the broken body of a child, cries out in despair. Another, with a look of horror and disbelief, rushes onto the scene from the right. The third woman, her garments aflame, cries out as she falls from a burning building. The mood of anguish, horror, and despair is unmistakably emphasized by the predominant colours used —severe blacks, deep greys and dead whites.

In *Guernica* Picasso expresses what one critic has described as a "monumental outcry of grief at its most anguished." In the distortion of familiar subjects—a screaming horse, grizzly animals, a broken child, tormented adults, displaced eyes, ears, profiles and limbs—Picasso has made a more stunning portrait of war's cruel reality than even a camera could record. (It is ironic that in a sense the painting has defeated photography, for it has proved impossible to photograph successfully on colour film.)

The story is told that during the Nazi occupation of Paris, the German Ambassador visited Picasso in his studio, where he noticed a photograph of *Guernica*. With ingenuous surprise he exclaimed, "Ah, Monsieur Picasso. So it was you who did that?" "No," Picasso retorted, "it was you." When asked about the story, Picasso laughed and said it was "more or less" true. "The Boches used to visit me on the pretext of admiring my pictures. I gave them postcards of my canvas *Guernica* and told them, 'Take them away! Souvenir; Souvenir!'"

Guernica is more than a cry of outrage against the Spanish Civil War, or even against war in general. It is an apocalyptic vision, a portrayal of the evil the artist has seen in the world about him, and a prophecy of the impending day of wrath and doom, the day of judgment.

Modern

Perspectives

John Trueman, Ph.D.,
Professor of History,
McMaster University,
Hamilton.

H. J. P. Schaffter, M.A.,
Head Master,
St. Michaels University School,
Victoria.

R. J. Stewart, B.A.,
History Teacher,
Birchmount Park Collegiate Institute,
Scarborough.

T. Murray Hunter, A.M.,
Associate Professor,
Department of History,
Carleton University,
Ottawa.

Maps by

S. A. Sauer, B.A.,
Map Curator,
Department of Geography,
University of Western Ontario,
London.

Contributing Editors:

D. Scollard
V. P. Seary

MCGRAW-HILL RYERSON LIMITED

Toronto   Halifax   Montreal   Vancouver

©The Ryerson Press, 1969. ©McGraw-Hill Ryerson, 1979.

6 7 8 9 0 D 8 7 6 5 4

Printed and bound in Canada

Canadian Cataloguing in Publication Data

Main entry under title:

Modern perspectives

Bibliography: p.
Includes index.
ISBN 0-07-082984-5

1. History, Modern. I. Trueman, John H., date.

D209.M63 1979　　　　　　909.08　　　　　　C79-094681-5

ACKNOWLEDGEMENTS

Beacon Press—*The Scientific Revolution 1500-1800,* by A.R. Hall, 1956.
British Printing Corporation—*The History of the 20th Century.*
Collier—*Europe in the Seventeeth Century,* by D. Ogg, 1962.
Harper and Row—*The Age of the Baroque,* 1610-1660, by C.J. Friedrich, 1962.
　　　—*The Establishment of the European Hegemony,* by J.H. Parry, 1961.
Heinemann—*Science Past and Present,* by F.S. Taylor, 1945.
Alfred Knopf—*A History of the Modern World,* by R.R. Palmer and J. Caton (3rd. ed., 1965).
Lippincott—*The Western World: Renaissance to the Present,* by J.R. Major, 1966.
　　—*Bold Men, Far Horizons,* by H.M. Mason, 1968.
Frederick A. Praeger—*Concise History of World War I,* by V.J. Esposito.
Queen's Printer, Ottawa—*Napoleon in Victory and Defeat,* by T.M. Hunter, 1964.

Authors of the source materials are acknowledged at the bottom of each reading.

PICTURE ACKNOWLEDGEMENTS

Alpenland: 221. Ashmoleon Museum: 19. L'Assiette au Beurre: 371 right. Associated Press: 544, 704. Aux Ecoutes, Paris: 634. Bettman Archives: 39, 186, 274, 286, 299, 316, 455. Biblioteca Nacional, Madrid: 199. Bildarchiv des Osterreichische Nationalbibliothek: 215 top. Bonn Museum: 215 bottom. Bradley Smith: 3. British High Commission: 748 lower right. British Printing Corporation/ History of the 20th Century: 403 top left, 503, 673 top. Brown Brothers: 283 top, 436, 487 centre. Bundesarchiv, Koblenz: 525, 527. Cambridge University Library: 93. Central Bibliothek, Zurich: 392. China Reconstructs: 675. Collection Potter-Palmer, Chicago: 216. Culver Pictures: 285 top, 314, 586. Daily Herald: 464. Daimler Benz Gmbh: 283 bottom. Deutsche Fotothek Dresden: 104. Die Nieuwe Amsterdammer: 403 top right. Editions Rencontres, Paris: 429 top. Ford Motors Ltd.: 452. Gernsheim collection: 311, 340. Hachette: 260, 324. Historical Pictures Services, Chicago: 285 bottom. Illustrated London News: 248, 270, 548. Imperial War Museum: 379, 406 top, 406 bottom, 407 bottom, 408 top, 408 bottom, 519, 522, 572, 583. Jugend: 331. Karsh, Ottawa: 592 top right, 592 left, 592 bottom, 593 top, 617, 669. Keystone: 561. Friedrich Krupp Gemeinschaftsbetriebe, Essen: 282 top, 329. Los Alamo Scientific Laboratory: 586 inset. The Louvre: 215 left. Mansell Collection: 35, 42, 51, 54, 55, 56, 58, 59, 64, 88, 88 inset, 92, 95, 99, 156, 165, 191-193, 214 centre, 226, 246, 262, 264, 279 bottom right, 282 bottom, 287, 336, 352, 371 left, 404, 421, 425. Météorologie Nationale: 753. Miller Services Inc.: 707, 747, 748. Minneapolis Star: 695. Mirrorpic: 533. Moro, Milan: 498. Mt. Wilson and Palomar Observatories: 459. Musée de la Guerre, Paris: 403 bottom. Musée des Beaux-Arts, Lyon: 132. Musée Royale des Beaux-Arts, Brussels: 164. National Archives, Ottawa: 580. National Archives, Washington: 407 top. National Galleries of Scotland: 114, 217. National Maritime Museum, Greenwich: 188. National Portrait Gallery, London: 214 top, 279 bottom left. New York Public Library: 67 top, 130. Oakland Museum: 448, 489. Photographie Bulloz: 160. Photographie Giraudon: 10, 15, 239. Pierre Seghers, Paris: 460. Radio Times Hulton: 42, 154, 159, 203, 261, 347, 364, 365, 451, 550, 582, 673. Reunion des Musées Nationaux: 167. Royal Academy of Art, London: 366. Science Museum, London: 285 centre. Dr. Landrum B. Shettles, Columbia Presbyterian Medical Centre: 756. Sigmund Freud Copyrights Ltd.: 288. Smithsonian Institute, Washington: 279 top, 404 bottom. Snark International: 344, 377 bottom left, 377 bottom right, 393. Sovfoto: 250, 429 bottom, 432, 437, 446, 508, 510, 512, 564, 570, 593, 753. Stata Maggiore Aeronautica, Rome: 408. Toronto Public Library: 2, 27, 60, 84, 127, 147, 179, 202, 214 bottom, 321, 353, 377 top, 405, 455 top left, 690. Toronto Star: 581, 595, 667, 710. Ullstein, Berlin: 18, 112, 309, 438, 444, 477. UNICEF: 655. United Nations: 640, 646, 655. United Press: 429 centre, 491. United States Atomic Energy Commission: 624. U.S.I.S.: 566, 578, 584, 750 bottom, 750 top. Victoria and Albert Museum: 207. Walker Art Gallery, Liverpool: 256. The Washington Post: 748. Weidenfeld and Nicholson: 64, 67 bottom, 97, 122, 137, 350. Wide World Photos: 628, 632.

PREFACE

The first edition of *Modern Perspectives* was published shortly after the Apollo XI astronauts landed on the moon. This act extended the reach of humankind beyond the protective womb of our small world. The awesome, hostile universe held, and continues to hold, unknown measures of joy and sorrow, pain and pleasure.

At the time of the landing in the Sea of Tranquility, many pundits claimed that this space journey was perhaps the single most momentous event in history. But it will take history and historians to place it within the perspective of the web of human experience. Certainly historians will record that it was the culmination of a decade of intensive scientific research and technological development. More likely they will try to see it as the fulfillment of a dream as old as humanity itself. They will see a Phoenician astrologer bent over his charts and calculations; a Galileo humiliated but unbroken before the Inquisition; a Kepler; a Newton; an Einstein; a Werner von Braun.

Historians may, however, also see the achievement against a background of tension and strife on earth. They may suggest that it was a symbol of monstrous immorality, the byproduct of a "weapons culture." Ultimately, however, historians will acknowledge that the goal of the astronauts was the same as their own, for human beings went to the moon not to learn more about it, but to learn more about themselves.

Historians seek to place the events of the past within a perspective, to discover some meaning, some order, in what often appears to be an arbitrary, chaotic experience. This is what the authors of *Modern Perspectives* have attempted to do. But it is clear that the authors do not share a single viewpoint. The reader, therefore, is challenged to compare viewpoints, to discover the underlying values and interests that distinguish the authors. In doing so, you should learn more about your own values and interests. In *Modern Perspectives* the reader is also provided with some of the tools of the historian—illustrations, maps, and documentary readings grouped around themes. It is hoped that the reader will be able to use these tools to participate directly in the process of historical thought.

Modern Perspectives, in short, attempts to do what its title implies—to provide its readers with insights into the great events of the past four centuries, and to help them to see these events in a meaningful perspective. To paraphrase a great Canadian historian, historians pursue their craft in order to make life bearable, if that is their fate, or if they are so fortunate, to celebrate the joy of life.

CONTENTS

1. THE AGE OF ABSOLUTISM
1. Two Leaders of Europe — 1
2. Despots and Revolutionaries — 34
3. European and World Wars — 63
4. The Scientific Revolution — 83

2. THE AGE OF REVOLUTION
5. The Age of Enlightenment — 105
6. The Background of the French Revolution — 125
7. The French Revolution — 143
8. The Napoleonic Era — 170
9. Europe After Napoleon — 210
10. The Revolutions of 1848 — 234

3. THE AGE OF IDEOLOGY
11. Industrialism and Reform in Great Britain — 251
12. The Generation of Materialism — 278
13. Italy, France, and Germany (1850-71) — 304
14. France and Germany (1871-1914) — 327
15. The Age of British Greatness — 346
16. The Background to World War I — 374
17. "The War to End All Wars" — 396
18. The Russian Revolution — 420

4. WAR AND PEACE

19. Society and Technology after the War	449
20. Economic Forces	470
21. The Rise of Totalitarianism	495
22. The Twenty Years' Crisis	530
23. Global Warfare	553

5. THE WORLD IN TRANSITION

24. Cold War and Coexistence	589
25. The Evolution of the United Nations	639
26. New Nations in Old Continents	660
27. Towards the Twenty-first Century	719
SOURCE READINGS	759
BIBLIOGRAPHY	797
INDEX	805

MAPS, CHARTS, AND TABLES

Approximate European Populations in 1600	9
French Public Debt	13
French Revenue and Expenditure, 1626-1640	17
Europe 1648	20-21
Comparative Dates of European Rulers	24-25
French Tax Revenue 1661-1683	28
Acquisitions of Louis XIV and Louis XV 1648-1774	31
French Tax Income 1683-1715	32
Europe 1660-1795	37
Growth of the Prussian Army	38
The Growth of Russia	43
The Petition of Right	50
The Bill of Rights	62
European Standing Armies	77
The World in 1763	78-79
The First Four World Wars	80
Leaders of the Scientific Revolution	87
Kepler's Three Laws of Planetary Motion	90
Newton's Three Laws of Motion	94
Bacon's Four Steps to Knowledge	100
Battle of Austerlitz	191
Napoleonic Europe	196-197
Europe 1815	223
Revolutions: The First Wave 1820-1829	240
Revolutions: The Second Wave 1830-1833	241
Revolutions: The Third Wave 1848-1850	242
Inventions That Launched the Industrial Revolution	254

World Population 1850-1914	290
Coal Production 1850-1918	290
Iron and Steel Production 1850-1918	290
Foreign Trade 1850-1913	291
Merchant Shipping 1850-1912	291
Distribution of Manufacturing 1870-1913	291
Unification of Italy 1859-1870	310
The Unification of Germany 1815-1871	319
Europe 1871	334-35
The Balkans	394
World War I 1914-1918	400-01
Casualties From the First World War	411
Territorial Changes Resulting from World War I	416-17
Unemployment in the United States 1929-1941	493
Europe 1936-1939	541
World War II 1939-1945	574-75
World War II in Europe 1939-1945	566-77
The Cost of Modern War	590
Europe 1979	598
The Cold War	630-31
Imperialism in Asia	664-65
China	678-79
Vietnam	692
Africa 1914	698
Africa 1979	699
World Population	721

UNIT ONE | # THE AGE OF ABSOLUTISM

# 1 Two Leaders of Europe

Laws must be made for subjects, just as medicines are prescribed for the particular disease and complexion of the sick . . . If it be my pleasure, I shall annul the laws.
—Philip II

Kings are absolute lords and have full authority over all people, secular and ecclesiastical . . . God should not forget what I have done for him.
—Louis XIV

The road was dusty as it always was in June. The litter moved slowly in the heat, its occupant stoically bearing his pain alone behind the thick leather curtains. Barely a sigh escaped lips trained to give orders and interpret duties, until at last the torturous swaying ceased. The procession had entered the courtyard, and gentle hands bore the seventy-one-year-old monarch to his room. Philip the Prudent had come home to die.

Home was a palace, austere, tomb-like, savouring of the eternal as it stood in Spain's arid Castilian plateau a full day's journey from Madrid. Like a monastery it brooded, this "Pentagon of the 16th century" which Philip II built for work and meditation, for the living and the dead.

Sombre and vast, angular and unrelieved, made of blocks of granite meant to last forever, and with its highest spire rising ninety metres from the ground, the Escorial was designed not only as a palace but as a monastery and a mausoleum. The monks moved in before the king, who, when he installed himself, brought with him eight coffins, those of his father, his dead wives and his children, to remind him of his own. Here, in an atmosphere that could be painted only by El Greco, the king of Spain worked and lived, a slim figure dressed almost like a monk himself, always industrious, avid for detail, despatching his courtiers to Mexico, to Manila, to Vienna, to Milan, his troops and his bars of bullion to Italy and the Netherlands, his diplomats to all courts, and his spies to all countries. . . .

The Escorial still stands, in all its gaunt majesty, a memorial to the greatest monarch of his age.

The Royal Monastery of San Lorenzo of the Escorial was built in the shape of a gridiron complete with handle, because it was on a grid that the saint was martyred. It was here that Philip lived out the balance of his sad, overburdened life—vainly trying to know, to control, and to direct every detail of a great empire stretching over half the world.

Philip II of Spain is one of the best examples of the "absolute" monarch of early modern times. Such a monarch, as we shall see in the next two chapters, attempted to obtain absolute control over the military, political, legal, economic, and even the cultural affairs of his country. Indeed, he identified himself with the state. A similar outlook was demonstrated by the absolutist king of France, Louis XIV, who said of himself, "When you are working for the good of the state you are working for yourself; the good of the one constitutes the glory of the other."

In order for an absolutism to be effective it must control at least three groups in the state: the Church, the nobility, and the assembly of Estates or parliament. Often an absolute monarch would play off one against the other, or might even try to neutralize one group —such as the assembly of Estates, which often had certain strange

Philip II of Spain: ". . . grave, distrustful, incredibly industrious and self-righteous, in his narrow and bitter way he turned his back on all change in an effort to keep Spain as it had been. The drift to bankruptcy and decline begun by his father was accelerated, and he led his country well down the road to ruin."

ideas about taxation, and posed a clear threat to the royal power. "The more you rely on such bodies," wrote one ruler to his son, "the more you lose your authority, since the estates are always trying to weaken your sovereign power."

Of course it was not enough merely to weaken the opponents of absolutism; a counterpoise had to be set up. Consequently two new bodies—both essential—emerged. First there was a group of skilled administrators, men who owed their position to the king's favour rather than to noble birth and who could maintain their favoured place only by developing and exploiting the resources of the state. Second there had to be a permanent standing army to act as an effective weapon in the hands of the government.

We must not, however, equate this carefully bolstered absolutism with modern dictatorship—it was not nearly as efficient or totalitarian. Even if an absolute monarch had reliable people at the centre of the realm, he or she still had to try to get orders carried out in the far corners of the kingdom and empire. And not only were communications agonizingly slow, but there was no dearth of local officials who could cheerfully ignore orders when they finally did arrive. A more corrosive influence still was a new political theory which called into question that close identification of state and monarchy espoused by Louis XIV. This new theory is well epitomized by the philosopher who, in his belief that the king's pursuit of glory was ruining France, was emboldened to ask, "Is the flock made for the shepherd or the shepherd for the flock?"

Let us now turn to the shepherd and the flock. We shall begin our story with the leaders of Europe: Spain and France.

1. THE SPANISH CRUSADE

No one matched Philip II in his devotion to government. "No secretary in the world sees more paper than His Majesty," wrote one cardinal. But if the king were to insist on seeing and personally annotating all the despatches from his vast empire, it must follow that it would take an eternity to get a decision from Madrid. "If death came from Spain," joked one of Philip's viceroys abroad, "I should be immortal."

Philip's first allegiance was to his dynasty, the Hapsburgs, who, by a series of fortunate coincidences of birth and marriage, had acquired territory not only in Austria but also in the Netherlands and Spain. In 1519 all these territories (augmented by some parts of Italy and Hungary) had been finally united under Philip's father, the Hapsburg Emperor Charles V. It was the largest territory to be under the rule of one man since the time of Charlemagne seven centuries earlier, and its population totalled some thirty-five million in Europe alone.

Philip had inherited this empire upon the abdication of his father in 1556. It included Spain, the Low Countries, Luxemburg, Burgundy, Naples, Sicily, and Milan, and an overseas empire consisting of Spanish America and the Philippines. After 1580 it was further increased when the kingdom of Portugal and its vast empire also became part of Philip's inheritance. No wonder that the century after 1550 is known in Spanish history as the *siglo de oro*, the century of gold!

Combined with Philip's dedication to his dynasty was his fanatical devotion to the Roman Catholic Church. The fires of the Counter-Reformation burned brightest in 16th century Spain, and at least one-third of the total Spanish population of eight million was in the direct service of the Church. Yet though Philip was an ardent Catholic he had no intention of allowing the Spanish Church any more independence than Henry VIII had allowed the Church in England.

Philip believed that in order to maintain the power of his dynasty, the Church—no less than the monarch—ought to devote itself to the service of the State. Hence Church and State were inextricably entwined for purposes of mutual support. The State received the wholehearted backing of the clergy, who, in turn, expected Spain's ventures to further Catholic power. It was inevitable that Spanish foreign policy in the second half of the 16th century should be really a sort of world-wide crusade.

The Dutch Revolt

Despite the wealth and power of Philip's government, strong opposition was always present in many parts of his empire. His influence in France was lessened by civil war. And in the Netherlands particularly, open rebellion flared against Spanish rule. When anti-Catholic and anti-Spanish demonstrations swept over all seventeen Netherland provinces, Philip resorted to his one sure method of dealing with heretics: repression. He sent in the Inquisition and attempted to regain control of the Low Countries by a harsh policy of execution, confiscation of estates, and heavy taxation. But the policy failed badly. Led by William of Orange, the man who had once been Philip's *stadholder* or principal minister in the counties of Holland, Zeeland, and Utrecht, the oppressed Dutch stubbornly held out against Philip in a national opposition to Spanish rule.

William was declared an outlaw; but the "outlaw" proceeded to organize the resistance so successfully that eventually the northern provinces of the Netherlands were freed from Spanish control. At

A detail from the large painting *The Triumph of Death* by Pieter Breughel, the Flemish painter of peasant life who died in 1569. The picture shows a devastated landscape in which tortured mankind is hemmed in by the battalions of death. It is a not-too-subtle comment on the repression of his countrymen by Spanish armies and the Inquisition.

this point Philip made a wiser move. He sent as his governor-general to the Netherlands an able general and diplomat, Alexander Farnese, the Duke of Parma. With twenty thousand additional troops, Farnese broke the back of the rebellion. He was able to split the resistance by subduing the ten southern provinces, many of whose Catholic inhabitants had become fearful of William of Orange's increasingly Protestant sentiments. Moreover, the fact that by this time both sides had resorted to looting, burning, desecration of churches, torturing, and killing meant that Parma could not only use force to bring some southerners to his side but could also appeal to both Catholics and moderates against William's religious vandalism.

By 1581 the seven northern provinces broke decisively with the south and asserted their independence as the United Provinces of the Netherlands, sometimes called Holland after the strongest of the counties. Neither side was prepared to concede the permanence of the division, however, and each strove bitterly to conquer the other. In December, 1585, it appeared that the fall of Antwerp, a port in Holland, was imminent. Queen Elizabeth I of England—who had once rejected Philip in marriage and baited him for a lifetime—feared that Antwerp could be used by Spain for launching an invasion against England. Accordingly, she sent an expedition to aid the Dutch. The expedition, although ill-fated, was merely the last of many "cold war" incidents between England and Spain. The Spanish monarch, long since goaded by the attacks of Elizabethan sea-dogs on his New World commerce, had already ordered the seizure of any English ships lying in Spanish ports. Now the December incident confirmed Philip's suspicions: he would have to invade England.

The Battle of the Atlantic

It was another three years before Philip's plans could come to maturity. At the end of July 1588 one of the mightiest Armadas the world had ever seen was sighted moving up the English Channel to Dunkirk where the Spanish army and invasion barges of the Duke of Parma awaited it.

The disaster of the next ten days is known to every student. In September, 1588, the shattered fleet crawled painfully back into Spanish ports, and Philip II was forced to the realization that his great crusade against England had failed. While the English rang bells and struck commemorative medals bearing the legend *Deus afflavit et dissipati sunt* ("God blew and they were scattered"), it was likewise to God that the king of Spain and his loyal subjects attributed their terrible defeat. "Kings," said Philip, "must submit to being used by God's will without knowing what it is. They must never seek to use it."

Resolutely Philip determined to begin all over again, but it was too late. Spain had lost the financial ability to support her claims to lead Europe. Despite the revenue from her empire, there was never sufficient income for the expenses of government—even the gold and silver of the New World provided only one-quarter of the crown's annual revenues. Consequently large amounts had to be borrowed or raised by heavier and heavier taxation, while prices rose more rapidly in Spain than anywhere else in Europe. On no fewer than four occasions in his reign Philip was forced to repudiate his debts.

Collapse did not, of course, come all at once: until the middle of the 17th century the Spanish military power was still one to be reckoned with. But as Philip II lay dying in agony in the Escorial in 1598, his plans for Europe and the Church were in ruins. Catholicism had not triumphed either in France or in the Netherlands, and England was more solidly Protestant than ever. Not only that, but she was increasing in strength and about to embark on the seven seas.

On the Continent itself, a France that had long been torn by civil and religious wars was preparing to assume the leadership of Europe for the next century and a half. As she, too, flexed her muscles, Spain's military power wilted and her internal unity was threatened. Moreover she remained economically backward. What has been called "the hardening of Spain's social and political arteries" in the 17th century slowly but surely removed her from the first rank of European monarchies.

2. THE LEADERSHIP OF FRANCE

The France that was to lead Europe for the next century and a half had been slow to develop as a single unified country. In the Middle Ages, the French kings had imposed a degree of consolidation, but had never managed—as in England—to submerge localism.

Part of France's difficulty was the very size of the country. France comprised three times the area and almost four times the population of England, with certain provinces such as Brittany, Burgundy, or Provence almost as large as some European kingdoms. At least three hundred districts had their own legal systems. A further complication was the religious cleavage that divided the country. On the one hand were the Roman Catholics, who, both king and clergy, insisted on maintaining a measure of independence from Rome and the papacy. On the other hand were the Protestants, mostly a radical branch called Calvinists, who strongly disapproved of bishops and even smashed religious images and stripped churches of any trappings which smacked of "popery."

APPROXIMATE EUROPEAN POPULATIONS IN 1600	
(IN MILLIONS)	
Prussia	2
Netherlands	2½
England	4½
Austria	5½
Spain	8
Russia	10
Italy	13
France	16
European Total	100

A State within a State

The Huguenots, as French Protestants were called, were concentrated in the south of France. This part of the kingdom was a centre of staunch independents who had been the last to come fully under the royal authority. Therefore the embracing of Protestantism was, at least in part, one way of protesting against being taken over by the Crown. Nor was the austere moral code of Calvinism a drawback to the ambitious townsmen (*bourgeois*) of the southern cities. Their religion emphasized a devotion to work which fitted in nicely with industrial aspirations.

By the last quarter of the 16th century the Huguenots made up about one-fifth of the country's population of sixteen million. Not all of these were weavers and craftsmen; the Huguenots by this time numbered among their adherents some of France's proudest families and a large part of the lesser nobility. Many of these nobles had been employed as soldiers in a long series of wars waged for the control of Italy between the Spanish and the French monarchs. When the struggle ended in 1559, however, with the signing of a peace treaty between Spain and France, these nobles found themselves in dire straits. Not only were they out of a job, but a decline in the value of money meant that they faced ruination as landlords. Disillusioned with an apparently ungrateful monarchy, and itching to take up arms again, these men found in the Huguenot opposition to the Catholic establishment just the opportunity they were seeking.

The prolonged wars with Spain had had a disastrous effect on the French monarchy, with the result that after 1559 it was both impoverished and increasingly unstable. When the French king Henry II died as a result of an accident at a tournament, it was his widow Catherine de' Medici who really exercised the royal power on behalf of her three sons—Francis II, Charles IX, and Henry III. While Catherine had no desire to see the Huguenots rule France, neither did she wish to see Philip II of Spain (who was her son-in-law), intervene in French affairs to the extent of bringing France within the Spanish orbit. Hence she played off one group against the other, pitting the Catholics led by the Duke of Guise against the Huguenots led by Henry of Bourbon, the king of the small independent kingdom of Navarre.

These struggles tore France apart. There were no fewer than nine separate wars between 1562 and 1598, with both Catholics and Huguenots guilty of atrocities. "I have often heard my mother say," wrote one Huguenot, "that just before I was born she several times had the greatest difficulty to save herself from being drowned like others of all ages and sexes by a great lord of the country, a persecutor of religion. He had them thrown into a river close by his house, saying that he would make them drink out of his big saucer." Brutality reached a climax in the summer of 1572 when a great company of Huguenots assembled in Paris to celebrate the marriage of Henry of Navarre to Catherine de' Medici's daughter. Catherine, fearful of the growing influence of the Huguenot leader Admiral de Coligny over her son Charles IX, saw an opportunity to strike hard. In the early morning of St. Bartholomew's Day (August 24)

Guise and other Catholic nobles began a systematic slaughter of the Huguenots. The news of the Massacre of St. Bartholomew's is said to have resulted in a rare event. Philip II smiled.

Among those murdered was the Huguenot leader Coligny. Henry of Navarre, however, managed to preserve his life by the very practical action of becoming a Catholic. It was only a temporary conversion. At the earliest opportune moment he once again declared himself a Huguenot.

Bloodshed rarely solves any problem, let alone a religious one, and the massacre of 1572 was no exception to this rule. The wars were renewed more savagely than ever, with Henry III heading a Catholic League pledged to work with Spain to destroy Protestantism in France once and for all. Finally in 1585 the Huguenots were offered the choice of conversion or exile, at which news Henry of Navarre is said to have remarked that one-half of his moustache turned white. But fate was to alter the balance in favour of the Huguenots. Henry III was assassinated in 1589, whereupon Henry of Navarre found himself the direct heir to the throne. He became Henry IV of France. France was now ruled by a heretic king.

Though a Protestant, Henry IV was well suited to bring peace to a tired France. A gallant soldier with a ready wit, he rivals the 13th century St. Louis as the most popular of all French kings. Moreover, Henry's virtues were matched with enough defects to make him seem a good deal more human than St. Louis. "He was," writes one historian, "an enthusiastic hunter, and equally persistent in his quest of the ladies of the court." This was the man destined to bind up the nation's wounds and lay the foundations for the absolutism of the mighty Bourbon dynasty.

A King Gains a Kingdom

In a sense Henry IV was a king without a kingdom, for the Catholic League refused to recognize him, and even shut the gates of Paris against him. But the king's charms, combined with good sense and some judicious bribery, eventually won over his opponents. Yet France was fundamentally Roman Catholic, and could never really be reconciled to a Protestant ruler. Henry was astute enough to recognize this fact, and calculating enough to act on it. "Paris is well worth a mass," is the matter-of-fact observation attributed to him. The next year, in 1594, he was crowned at Chartres as a Catholic king.

The Huguenots were, naturally, alarmed that their champion should seem to suit his own convenience by changing his religion. So in 1598 Henry sought to win back their confidence by drawing up the Edict of Nantes, a document which recognized the religious stalemate. Henceforth French Protestants could practise their religion. Every noble (*seigneur*) who was a manorial lord was granted the right to hold Protestant services in his own household, and despite the fact that in Paris and some two hundred other towns Protestant services were prohibited, they could now be held not only in every town in which Protestantism was the predominant faith but in at least one town in each district where there was a Catholic majority.

Now, too, Huguenots were to enjoy the same civil rights as Catholics: they could hold office, have their own courts, and be admitted to Catholic universities. Nor were they without physical means to maintain their gains, boasting about a hundred fortified towns which could be held by Protestant garrisons. They comprised virtually a state within a state. But Henry wanted to avoid any provocation for the use of these garrisons, and when some Roman Catholics objected to his toleration he made this eloquent reply: "I must insist on being obeyed. It is time that we all, having had our fill of war, should learn wisdom by what we have suffered." Accordingly the power of the central government imposed on France a religious settlement which demonstrated a degree of toleration unknown either in England or Germany at this time: it provided for the protection of the minority. It is a tribute to Henry IV that a substantial number of France's statesmen in the 17th century were Protestants.

With a king on the throne of France who had managed to heal its divisions and produce a new sense of national pride, Philip II's Spanish crusade there was doomed to fail, and in 1598 he renounced all claims against French territory. Now the foes from both within and without had been neutralized, but the rocky road to recovery lay ahead. The long civil wars and the campaigns against Spain had practically bankrupted the country, and it was the exacting task of Henry IV to restore economic stability. "Every peasant," he is supposed to have remarked, "should have a chicken in the pot for Sunday dinner."

The man who actually did the work of drawing up the policies of recovery was probably Henry's chief minister, the Duke of Sully. Sully could not revolutionize the financial administration, but he did try to remove some of its abuses in order to make the system work more efficiently. Certain taxes were lowered, and throughout France canals were extended, marshes drained, and bridges and roads rebuilt. Some old industries were revived, and some new ones —especially silk manufacturing—were promoted. In addition, tax collectors were required to hand over not only the current taxes but also (to the dismay of many) the ones they had collected in the past.

A few features of the antiquated French financial system, too, were extended. The salt tax (*gabelle*) on the peasants was increased, and the *paulette,* a ten per cent tax on the incomes of numerous office holders, was also levied in 1604.

Whether it was because of the success of Sully's financial policies or, as many historians now believe, the fact that prosperity had returned to France on the wings of peace, France's financial situation achieved the remarkable improvement demonstrated in the table below.

FRENCH PUBLIC DEBT (in *livres**)	
1560	43½ million
1576	101 million
1598	350 million
1610	224 million
*The old French equivalent of the later franc.	

In fact by the late years of the reign France had so recovered that Henry and Sully proposed a "Great Design" for Europe, a plan which is rather difficult for us to assess since our information about it comes from scattered passages in Sully's own *Memoirs. Le Grand Dessein* was in many ways a radical conception, proposing to arrange Europe into monarchies and republics, to grant toleration to Roman Catholics, Lutherans, and Calvinists alike, and to arrive at a common European foreign policy by means of international councils. The Great Design was of course never realized; it was never even clearly thought out. It was, in fact, little more than the noble dream of the Duke of Sully. But it was surely a noble dream.

In 1610 the great Henry died, struck down by the knife of a demented Catholic schoolmaster. His son Louis XIII was only a boy of nine and, for an interlude, fresh civil disorders broke out as Henry's widow attempted to act as regent. Finally in 1614 the French Parliament or Estates-General—a body which Henry IV had never called into session—was summoned. But now that the urgency of the situation had at last necessitated its meeting, the assembly found that it was no longer capable of acting. So many antagonisms developed that, after three weeks, the members were locked out of the halls and sent home by the queen regent, who said that she needed the rooms for a dance. The Estates-General had sealed its own death warrant by its impotence. It was its last meeting until 1789.

The King's First Minister

There was, however, a certain member of the 1614 meeting of the Estates-General who was not doomed to obscurity. A young bishop named Armand Jean du Plessis de Richelieu had been chosen to compose the address to the throne, and in his speech he advocated creating a government of "authority." This so impressed the queen regent that the young man was made Minister for Foreign Affairs in the Council of State. A few years later, at the age of thirty-seven, he became a cardinal, and in 1624 he was made the king's "first minister." Cardinal Richelieu was now the real head of the French government, a position he was to hold for the next eighteen years.

By any standards, the Cardinal was an amazing man. Neither rich nor handsome (he was a slight figure of a man), and subject to frequent bouts of ill health and agonizing migraines, he was nevertheless capable of unremitting industry, and by his single-minded devotion to duty managed to stay in the king's favour. With chilling candour he set forth his objectives in a statement to the king: "I promise to devote all my energy and all the authority that it may please you to put into my hands to destroying the Huguenots, abasing the pride of the great nobles, restoring all your subjects to their duty, and raising the name of your majesty among foreign nations to its rightful place." Any man who aimed at curtailing the strength of so many powerful groups was bound to make enemies, and there was no lack of people who resented

Cardinal Richelieu said France suffered from two diseases—liberty and heresy—and he did everything he could to cure them. His foreign policy concentrated on the defeat of the House of Hapsburg and he pursued it with persistence and skill. He was a connoisseur of art and music; he loved jewels and antiques; and he considered himself second to none as a critic of drama and the theatre. He even dabbled in poetry. He was a despot who was at the same time a brilliant statesman, perhaps the greatest France ever had.

Richelieu and tried to pull him down. "The four square yards of the King's cabinet," he once said, "are more difficult for me to conquer than all the battlefields in Europe."

Politics rather than religion made Richelieu pit himself against the Huguenots. He felt that France was dangerously weakened by the presence of a state within a state. "So long as they have a foothold in France," he wrote, "the king will not be master in his own

TWO LEADERS OF EUROPE   15

house, and will be unable to undertake any great enterprise abroad." Meanwhile, the Huguenots tried to force the Cardinal to acknowledge and confirm their privileges by displaying their strength in a revolt against the monarchy. So determined was their resistance that on one occasion they battled against the royal fleet, on another encouraged an English invasion of France, and finally seemed on the verge of calling in the Spanish to help them! At this frightening reminder of the wars of religion the Cardinal clamped down hard, subduing the rebels by seizing their strongholds and depriving them of their political assemblies. Nevertheless he proved enough of a statesman to leave them free to worship as they chose. It was a wise move. The Huguenots valued the tolerance of a throne that allowed them to continue to worship as Protestants, and their subsequent history reveals them to have been strong supporters of the monarchy.

Richelieu had also vowed to "abase the pride of the great nobles," and in this too he was as good as his word. He systematically clipped their wings by destroying their châteaux, thereby depriving them of private fortunes, and by appointing an *intendant*, a new middle class official who was to supervise tax collection and the administration of justice in each of thirty districts. These intendants were to Richelieu what the *missi dominici* had been to Charlemagne —the eyes and ears of the king. As the nobles' power diminished, of course, the king's increased.

Subjects were "restored to their duty" by being taxed heavily and efficiently. "All politicians agree," wrote Richelieu, "that when the people are too comfortable it is impossible to keep them within the bounds of their duty . . . . they must be compared to mules which, being used to burdens, are spoiled more by rest than by labour." The fact that the nobility, clergy, and officials were largely exempt from taxation meant that the other three-quarters of the population, and especially the peasantry, bore the brunt of assessment. Most of the antiquated taxes—the *taille* (a direct tax paid by non-nobles), the *aides* (sales tax), and the *gabelle* (salt tax)—came out of the pockets of the lower classes. Richelieu frankly confessed his "ignorance of finances," and indeed his neglect of the vexed question of taxation was his greatest failure. Unlike Sully, Richelieu seemed incapable of running affairs so that the government did not chalk up a huge yearly deficit. "For no sum of money is the safety of the state too dearly bought" was one of his favourite maxims.

The appalling deficits that swelled the public debt are only too evident from these figures:

	REVENUE	EXPENDITURES
1626	18 243 045 *livres*	44 657 161
1636	23 471 254	108 256 236
1640	43 454 166	116 208 911

Richelieu's failure to be realistic in financial matters was so serious that it has been said that the Revolution of 1789 was of his making.

The Cardinal had his limitations, and some of these were serious. But he is still no less than the founder of the modern French monarchy. To exalt that monarchy—to strengthen it and raise its international status—this was his constant ambition.

One of the ways in which Richelieu raised France's prestige was by intervening, in 1635, in the Thirty Years' War. This complicated series of wars between 1618 and 1648 is important not because of its events, which we shall barely outline here, but because of its consequences.

The fighting began in Germany as a religious struggle between Roman Catholics and Protestants, coupled with an attempt by the princes to be independent of the German emperor; yet before it was over not only Germany, but Spain, the Netherlands, Denmark, Sweden, and France were all involved. The war soon developed into a struggle for power, with Richelieu encouraging any alliance that would promise to oppose the Hapsburgs of Spain and Austria. His diplomacy was to achieve its end. Though he died six years before hostilities ended, Richelieu was the real architect of the final settlement which brought France to the pinnacle of power in Europe: the end of the Thirty Years' War saw the Madrid-Vienna axis go down to defeat and France replace Spain as Europe's greatest power.

The Peace of Westphalia (1648) ensured that the ideal of a medieval "Holy Roman Empire" would be shelved, for by it over three hundred German territories became sovereign states, and various borderlands went to the French, Dutch, and Swedes. The war had wrecked Germany. In some districts as much as one-third of the population perished, the total, it is calculated, dropping from

The Defenestration of Prague, 1618. A gathering of nobles, gentry, and citizens from all over Bohemia, angry at the loss of some of their religious privileges, threw three of the Emperor's officials out of the windows of the castle. They escaped because they landed on heaps of dung; one of them, Slavata, during the rest of his life used to tell how many times he bounced! This trivial incident helped start the Thirty Years' War.

twenty-one million in 1618 to thirteen and a half million in 1648. In fact the Thirty Years' War may have resulted in an even greater depopulation of Germany than that suffered as a consequence of the Second World War.

It was, writes a modern historian, a war unique in its dreariness and ferocity:

> . . . The narrative is relieved by few stirring episodes: there were few great personalities involved; the generation ending it had long since outlived the quarrels and hatreds that began it. Gathering momentum as it proceeded, considered interminable by those who suffered from its ravages, it was ended only by the exhaustion of the combatants and the perpetuation of injustices and resentments breeding future wars; for this melancholy struggle gave birth to the

Wandering peasants driven from their homes by war. In the later years of the Thirty Years' War opposing armies created wastelands so that the enemy could not maintain its troops. The suffering of the civilian population was thereby multiplied. Hunger and epidemics took their toll, and a barbarism from which death was the only escape enveloped Germany.

first of modern peace congresses which, in attempting to stabilize the frontiers of Europe, brought into prominence a great cause of unrest in modern times—the Rhine frontier. The Thirty Years' War retarded the civilization of Germany by more than a century, and the destinies of Europe have been profoundly influenced by that fact.

But the Thirty Years' War had some positive results too. It brought an end to the fruitless religious conflicts on the Continent, as well as finally shattering the illusion that any universal European monarchy was still possible. Moreover it produced in many a complete revulsion against such conflicts. Could not future wars be limited ones? Hugo Grotius, a Dutch humanist, thought so.

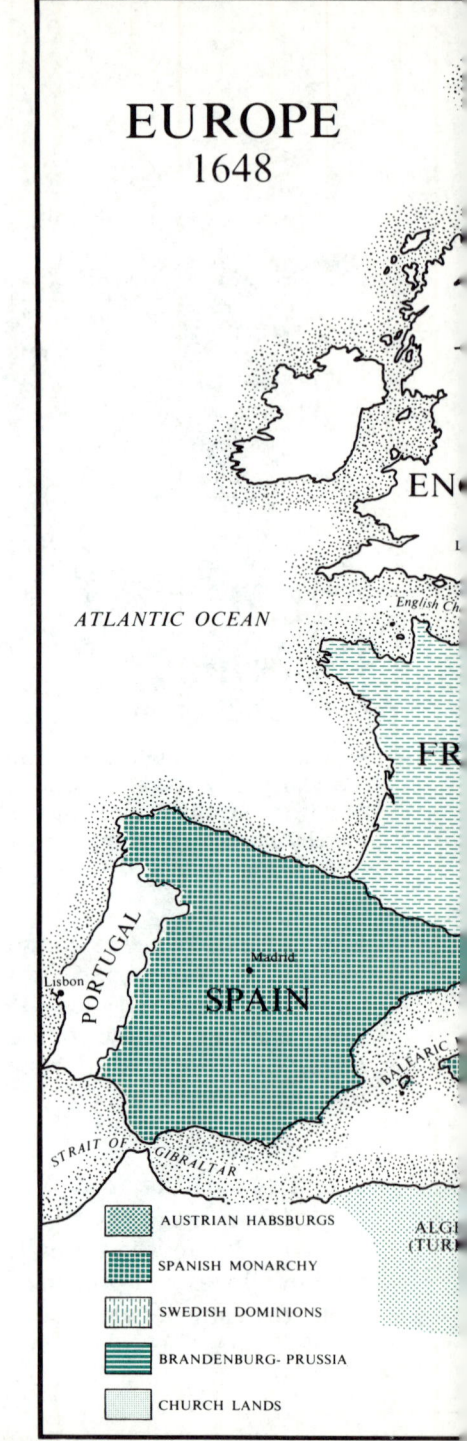

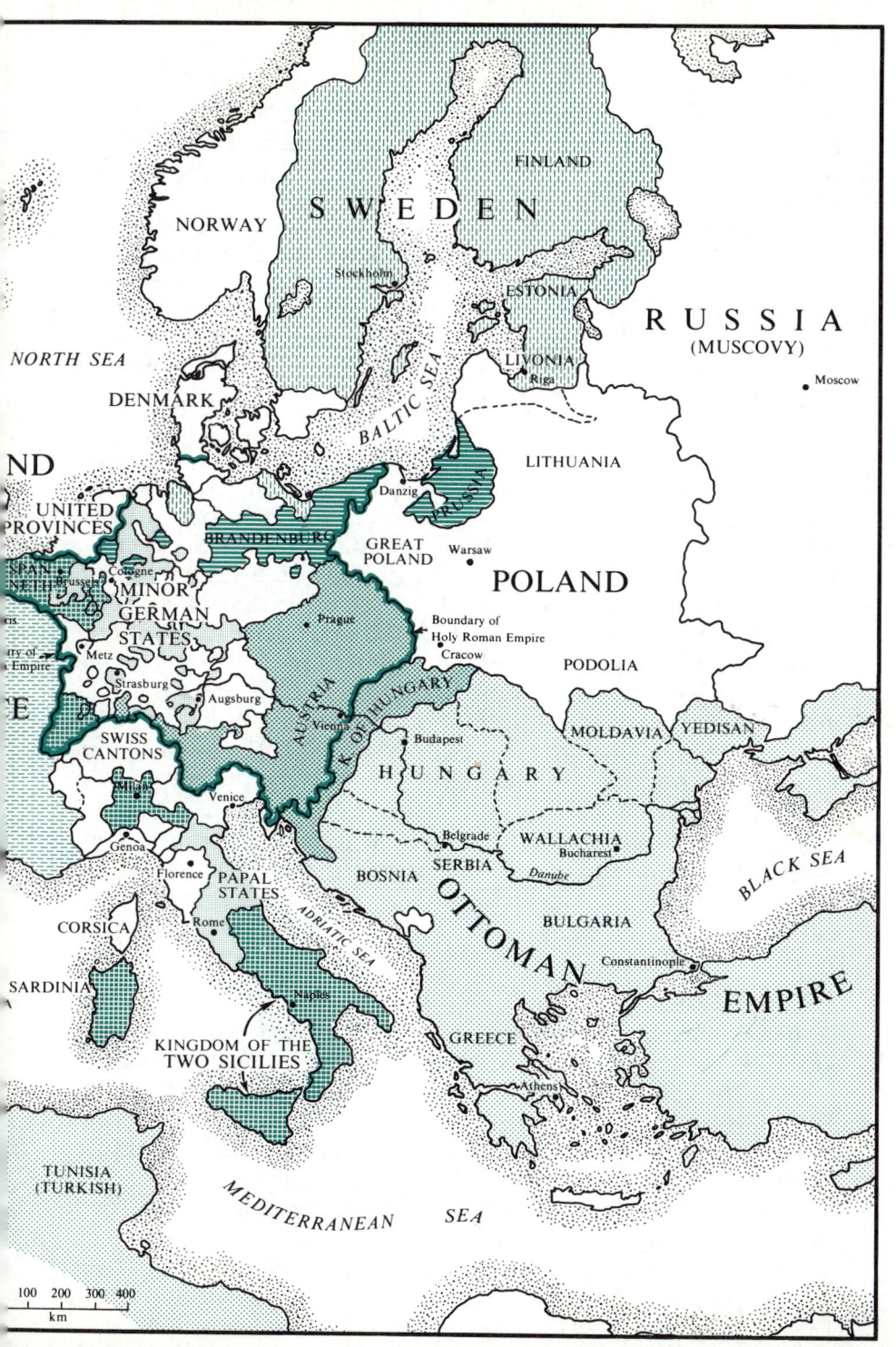

Sickened by the slaughter of the Thirty Years' War he published in 1625 a treatise *On the Law of War and Peace*, with the avowed purpose of formulating some sort of international law. Grotius wrote that he was convinced a common law existed among nations:

> . . . which is of force with regard to war and in war. . . . For I saw prevailing throughout the Christian world a licence in making war of which even savage nations might be ashamed; recourse being had to arms for slight reasons or none; and when arms were taken up, all reverence for divine or human law being thrown away, as if men were thenceforth authorized to commit all crimes without restraint.

The high-minded concepts of Hugo Grotius were not, of course, adopted. Nevertheless, the close of the Thirty Years' War marked the end of a phase in European history in that the long struggle between Catholic and Protestant was at last declared a draw. Henceforth the Calvinist faith was recognized as fully as the Roman Catholic or Lutheran. Moreover, the Peace of Westphalia accepted and extended the principle that had been established a century earlier by the Peace of Augsburg: each ruler could choose the subjects' religion, and the right of dissidents to emigrate was recognized. As the various German princes declared for their own faith, a boundary line between a Catholic South and a Protestant North became stabilized, a boundary that remains largely unaltered in Germany to this day.

After 1648 religious quarrels were no longer the primary considerations of the rulers of Europe. It was not the Church but the sovereign national State which was exalted by the Peace of Westphalia.

The Grand Monarch

Richelieu's hand-picked successor was Cardinal Mazarin, who served as the king's adviser for one year until Louis XIII's death, and then held the reins of power during the long minority of Louis XIV. Mazarin was a complete contrast to the austere Richelieu. A native of Italy, he surrounded himself with elegance—tapestries, works of art, perfumed pets, and, not least of all, a collection of beautiful nieces. He first came to prominence one day in 1632 during the Thirty Years' War when, as a papal ambassador, he galloped between opposing French and Spanish armies waving a crucifix and proclaiming a papal truce. Later he entered Richelieu's service, and eventually was made a cardinal. By this time he had also deemed it politic to become a French citizen.

Mazarin was as devoted to the royal power as Richelieu had been, but unfortunately equalled Richelieu in his indifference to the need for an overhaul of the state's financial structure. The condition of the peasantry remained deplorable, as one of the young king's officials made clear:

> For ten years now the country has been ruined, the peasants reduced to sleeping on straw, after their furniture has been sold to pay taxes which they cannot raise—to maintain the luxury of Paris, millions of innocent souls are forced to live on bread, bran, and oats, and cannot hope for any protection. . . . These unfortunates do not possess anything but their souls, and then only because they cannot be auctioned off.

With the peasantry thus impoverished, the crown in desperation at last had to turn for funds to those who were able to pay, namely the nobility. Resentment against the king's extravagant Italian-born minister flared into a series of civil uprisings instigated by the nobles and known as the *Frondes* (*fronde* was the name of the sling used by Paris urchins to pelt passersby with mud). The insurrections lasted from 1649 to 1652 and amounted to a minor civil war. Feeling against Mazarin rose so high that for a time he had to flee the country. But the selfishness of the *Frondeurs* did not gain them widespread support, nor was France ready to return to days of anarchy. The conspirators eventually fell out among themselves, and in 1653 Mazarin returned to reassert his authority.

Disillusioned with the blatant opportunism and incompetence that the rebels had displayed, the bulk of the nobility turned once more to their monarch. The king might not be able to give them prosperity, but royal absolutism was entrenched more strongly than ever. Louis XIV, for his part, was determined that no such show of power would be repeated. To this end he did all he could to debilitate the nobles, making them into court dandies whose power was only nominal. Moreover he determined to protect himself from the rude realities of Paris by making his home in Versailles, an idyllic retreat free from the clamour of the mob.

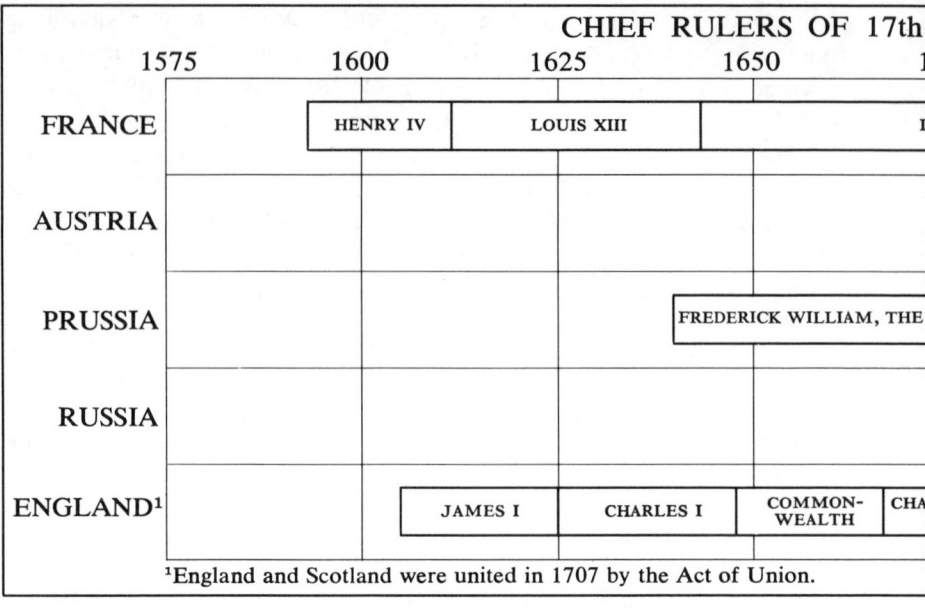

On March 7, 1661, Cardinal Mazarin died. The next day the Archbishop of Paris put a significant question to Louis XIV. "To whom shall we address ourselves?" he asked. "To me," replied the twenty-three-year-old king simply. The words betrayed no qualms, but in his *Memoirs* he wrote, "It was the moment for which I had waited and which I had dreaded." Louis proved equal to that moment. During the next fifty-four years he was the undisputed master of France. His contemporaries called him *Le Grand Monarque*, and the influence of this grand monarch, like that of his great-grandfather, Philip II, was so far reaching that the second half of the 17th century came to be known as the "Age of Louis XIV."

Never, it has been said, was there a more kingly king than Louis XIV. A contemporary described him as having "an exterior so unique and incomparable as to lend infinite distinction to his slightest actions . . . proportions such as a sculptor would choose to model, a perfect countenance and the grandest air ever vouchsafed to man, a natural grace and singular charm which has never perhaps been equalled." Nor was this kingly king only noble with

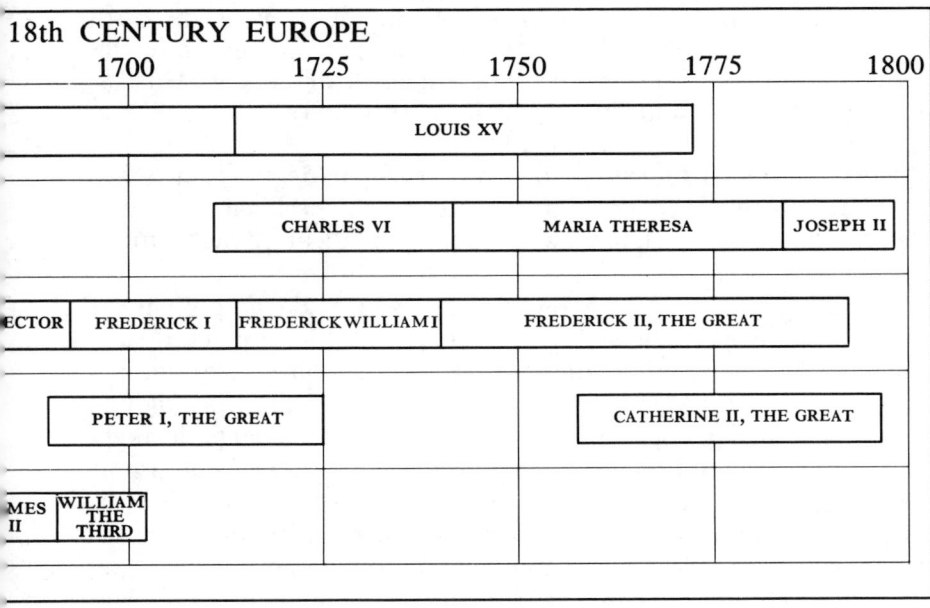

the nobles. His beautiful manners extended even to servants—a rare occurrence in days when the nobility often proved their superiority by treating underlings like dirt. Praise for Louis XIV was not unmixed with criticism, however. The contemporary philosopher Fenelon criticized him sharply, and a modern English historian has described him as "the most criminally stupid man in history."

What practices and policies could evoke such opposite poles of praise and criticism?

To begin with, it must be understood that Louis XIV believed implicitly in his own absolute authority. Early in his reign he selected as tutor for his son the learned Bishop Bossuet, who produced in his *Politics Drawn from the Very Words of Holy Scripture* an argument for Louis XIV's absolutism. Here are a few sentences from that amazing book:

The service of God and the respect for kings are bound together. . . . The royal power is absolute. . . . The prince need render account of his acts to no one. . . . As all perfection and all strength are united in God, so all the power of individuals is united in the

TWO LEADERS OF EUROPE   25

person of the prince. . . . Should God withdraw his hand, the earth would fall to pieces; should the king's authority cease in the realm, all would be in confusion. . . . Something of divinity itself is attached to princes and inspires fear in the people. . . .

These statements, buttressed by countless quotations from Scripture, held high the theory of the divine right of kings. It was a theory that was to dominate European political thought for a century.

The king who held such theories as these could hardly entrust power to another Richelieu or Mazarin. Instead he organized such ministries as those of finance, the army, the navy, and foreign affairs, whose ministers would carry out the royal will—although by the time policy got down to the level of the intendants, it might have undergone substantial alterations. The fact was that Louis had attempted a task which was simply too big for him: he was no radical innovator who could scrap outworn institutions, nor was he enough of an organizing genius to co-ordinate all governmental activities. The result was that a century later another Louis was told by his finance minister: "Sire, in its present state France is impossible to govern."

Louis XIV was certainly not a man afraid of work. "One reigns by work and for work," he said. But along with work went a top-heavy court, the outward manifestation of the king's divinity. At the little village of Versailles, ten miles from Paris, Louis built himself a whole new city centering around the tremendous royal palace. Here amid orange groves, fountains, and marble halls lined with mirrors, this monarch, who in his grandeur was known as the Sun King, held court. Even his daily routine of rising, eating, and going to bed (*lever, dîner,* and *coucher*) was, as you may see by referring to Source Reading I-1, a matter of minute and exact court ritual.

Louis' policy, like Richelieu's, stressed four main themes: curbing the power of the nobles, revamping the administrative machinery, restoring religious uniformity, and increasing the glory of France.

To make certain of the loyalty of his counsellors, Louis chose them from men of a humbler background than that of the nobility. He even set up special courts to hear complaints against nobles. Further inroads on the sanctity of the nobility were made when

Louis XIV, the "Sun King." This is a small model of the bronze equestrian statue by the sculptor François Girardon erected (1699) by the city of Paris on the Place Louis le Grand. The original was melted down during the French Revolution.

patents of nobility were sold to commoners (patents which were, by the way, revoked on no fewer than nine occasions during the reign, and their grantees forced to repurchase them each time—a very sharp practice indeed!). In addition, the nobles were trimmed of some of their wealth by being subjected to a head tax and, eventually, to a ten per cent income tax. The economic pressures on some nobles now became severe, for their income was falling at the same time as the expenses of court life were increasing. Many were reduced to vying for pensions that were dispensed in return for attendance at Versailles. No wonder one noble said to his king, "Sire, away from Your Majesty one is not only miserable, but ridiculous."

Another of Louis' ambitions was to bring order out of the administrative chaos. In his desire to rule efficiently, he perfected the Supreme Council, a body which met three times a week but whose members were not formally appointed as ministers. Consequently they were completely dependent on the king's pleasure and could be dismissed by the simple expedient of not being asked to attend future meetings. There were also other councils which met less frequently than the Supreme Council. But in all of them the king's voice was absolute—though his dependence on his ministers' specialized knowledge must often have caused him to choose a path that they had already marked out for him.

The decisions of the central government were carried out in the provinces by thirty intendants. These men, who were drawn from the middle classes, were empowered to take over the complete control of local government in time of war or other crises. It is, then, easy to see why they would become much more important than the provincial governors, who were drawn from the old nobility.

A Tireless Administrator

Of all Louis' ministers the most talented and most devoted was Jean-Baptiste Colbert, a man whose cold personality earned him the nickname of "The North." This tireless administrator prided himself on never taking a vacation, and certainly the tasks facing him required gargantuan labour. Of all the jobs tackled, none was more challenging than the reorganization of the fiscal system.

The tax collection machinery that Colbert inherited was both unjust and irregular. And although throughout his twenty-two years of power Colbert was not able—try as he might—to work out any uniform system, he did make a valiant attempt to see that such taxes as were collected did find their way into the royal treasury. Furthermore, he exposed large numbers of people who had hitherto been avoiding taxation by falsely claiming to be nobility, a status which exempted them from payment. How great was the problem facing Colbert, and how much success he achieved in grappling with it, may be judged from the following table.

	TAXES DUE	AMOUNT RECEIVED	LOSS
1661	85 000 000 *livres*	22 000 000	53 000 000
1683	116 000 000	93 000 000	23 000 000

But reorganization of the fiscal system was only part of Colbert's total programme to put France on her feet. As early as 1653, while he was serving under Cardinal Mazarin, Colbert had drafted a statement for a comprehensive economic policy:

We must re-establish or create all industries, even luxury industries; a system of protection must be developed by means of a customs tariff; trade and traders must be reorganized into guilds; financial hindrances which burden the people must be lightened; transport of commodities by land and sea must be restored; colonies must be developed and commercially bound to France; all barriers between France and India must be broken down; the navy must be strengthened to afford protection to merchant ships.

Colbert was determined to revive old industries and to create new ones, and to this end he introduced a system of monopolies, subsidies, tax reductions, loans without interest, and other measures designed to stimulate production. He also encouraged the immigration of hundreds of skilled foreign workers: tapestry-makers, dyers, and paper-makers from the Netherlands; silk workers, glass-blowers, embroiderers, and lace-makers from Italy; leather-workers and naval constructors from England, Germany, and Scandinavia. The manufacturers were closely controlled by a series of edicts enforced by government inspectors. But though such regulation did improve the production of textiles, it unfortunately stifled experimentation and innovation in other industries.

To promote French industry, tariffs on raw materials entering France were lowered while goods manufactured abroad were heavily taxed. The importation of some products—for example, Venetian glass and lace—was even forbidden. Trade within France itself was promoted by the improvement of roads and bridges, heavy transport in particular being aided by the construction of canals. A drastic reduction of the numerous tolls and taxes hitherto levied on goods travelling between various areas of France also stimulated internal trade.

Colbert firmly believed in the principle of mercantilism whereby colonies traded only with the mother country, supplying raw materials and buying finished goods. Naturally, then, he encouraged the import of gold and silver and such other raw materials as France did not possess, and stressed the export of manufactured products. Transportation of such goods was effected by the creation of a merchant marine, and a French East India Company—following the English and Dutch leads in 1600 and 1602—was established in 1664. Although other companies were chartered to trade with the West Indies, northern Europe, and the Levant, because of Colbert's lack of any practical experience in foreign trade they soon foundered. Nevertheless these companies did serve a useful purpose: they began a revival of overseas trade for France, and the men who financed the ships and sailed them received invaluable training as traders and seamen. Not least important, the trading companies inspired Colbert to create the foremost navy of its day, one that could hold its own against both the English and the Dutch.

Yet despite his vigorous programme, Colbert failed. Why? Because to put French finances on a sound basis he required peace, and he served an aggressive master. War took all the profits.

Louis XIV was greedy for territory. In Europe he cast covetous eyes on Holland, Hapsburg Germany, and Spain, while in North America and Asia he sought to outdo his English and Dutch colonial rivals. In a series of European wars—really one long interrupted war—France made herself the mightiest power on the continent, with the result that her fearful neighbours, England, Holland, and the German states, joined against her in a "Grand Alliance."

In all these wars Louis was the aggressor, although not an aggressor in a class with Napoleon or Hitler. Louis' wars were limited, more humane, more inefficient, and far less fanatical. War was an art, carried on by professionals and exemplified by the ideal of another 18th century ruler who said that when he was engaged in war the civilian population ought not to know it.

The tragedy of Louis' wars was that they exhausted the treasury which Colbert had laboured so hard to fill. Louis XIV created the

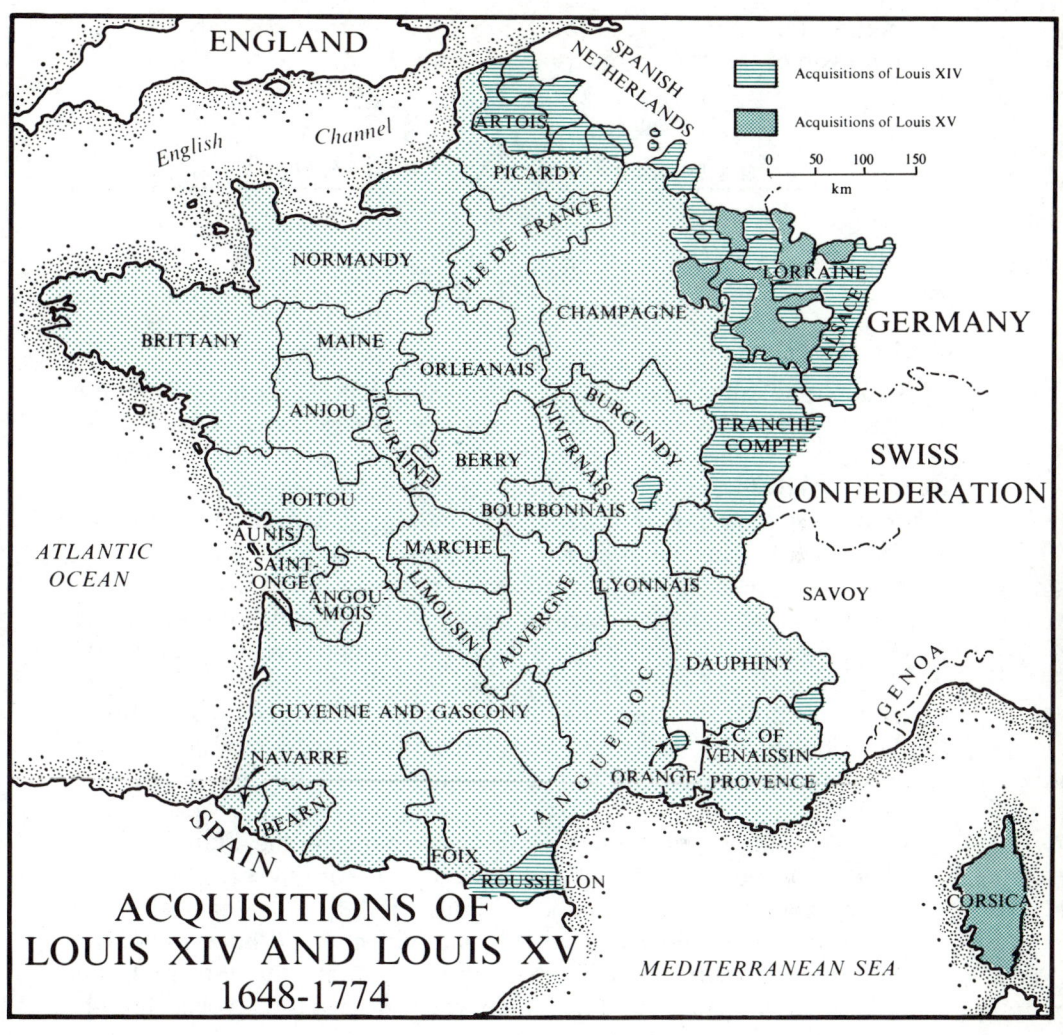

ACQUISITIONS OF LOUIS XIV AND LOUIS XV 1648-1774

first great standing army of modern times. In 1660 the army numbered seventy-two thousand; by 1700 it had risen to three hundred thousand. The expense of creating and maintaining such a vast army was crushing. After Colbert's death in 1683, Louis' ministers lacked his determination and ability, so that the collection of taxes lagged. This decline of revenue, coupled with the staggering costs of the army and the wars, crippled the state. The depressing trend exhibited in the following table contrasts sharply with the optimism of the earlier one on page 29.

	TAXES DUE	AMOUNT RECEIVED	EXPENDITURE	DEFICIT
1683	116 000 000 *livres*	93 000 000	109 000 000	16 000 000
1715	152 000 000	74 000 000	119 000 000	45 000 000

A Colossal Failure

Though he might be hailed as the Sun King around whom the entire universe revolved, and though he was alleged to have said, "*L'état c'est moi*," Louis failed on a colossal scale. He himself recognized this failure, as witness his last admonition to his great-grandson: "Do not imitate me by making war. Try to keep the peace with your neighbours, to comfort your people as far as possible, which I have unfortunately not been able to do. . . ."

Louis made another serious error when he revoked the Edict of Nantes in 1685. The result was that two hundred thousand Huguenots fled the country, talented "displaced persons" who contributed much to their new homelands in England and North America. By this one step Louis undid much of the good that was accomplished by his policy of bringing skilled foreign workers to France.

Above all, Louis had tried to make himself the State. "Never as long as you live," Colbert warned his son sternly, "send out anything in the King's name without his express approval." But it was an impossible ambition. No one person could hope to control the whole machinery of French administration, and though Louis XIV is called an "absolute" monarch his absolutism was limited in practice if not in theory.

What elements hampered Louis' pretentions to absolutism? For one thing, communication was so difficult that local officials could safely ignore royal orders which filtered through to them gradually from some far distant capital. These officials knew that it might be a matter of years before the central government could determine whether or not its orders were being carried out—or had indeed even arrived at their destination. When orders did arrive, they were probably not acted upon by competent officials: the monarch had nothing comparable to our modern civil service. Most policies were carried out (or ignored) by local officials whose efficiency—or even integrity—could not always be checked upon even by the intendants.

Finally, Louis was thwarted by the very nature of the society which he attempted to dominate. France consisted of no homogeneous mass which would easily mould itself to the desires of a strong monarchy. Instead, there were all sorts of privileged groups who jealously guarded their rights against even their monarch. The result was that in the final analysis Louis XIV did not have nearly the power of a modern dictator. The apparent strict control of absolutism, weakened as it was by administrative confusion, was more a façade than a reality in France.

A 19th century historian rendered this verdict on one of his country's most colourful kings:

Louis XIV carried the principle of monarchy to its utmost extent, and abused it in all respects to the point of excess. He left the nation crushed by war, mutilated by banishments, and impatient of the yoke which it felt to be ruinous. Men were worn out, the treasury empty, all relationships strained by the violence of tension, and in the immense framework of the state there remained no institution except the accidental appearance of genius. Things had reached the point where, if a great king did not appear, there would be a great revolution.

There were other portents of revolution. The real France was not reflected in the mirrors of Versailles, but could be seen in the French countryside of which the bourgeois La Bruyère wrote with bitter exaggeration:

One sees certain sullen animals male and female, scattered about the country, dark, livid, scorched by the sun, attached to the earth they dig up and turn over with invincible persistence; they have a kind of articulate speech, and when they rise to their feet, they show a human face, and, indeed they are man. At night they retire to dens, where they live on black bread, water, and roots; they save others the toil of sowing, ploughing, and garnering in order to live, and thus deserve not to lack the bread they have sown.

Louis XIV turned France in the wrong direction. Many of the causes for the ruin which eventually befell the French monarchy can be traced to the reign of the Sun King.

2 Despots and Revolutionaries

Salvation belongs to the Lord;
everything else is my affair.
—Frederick William I

In many respects the monarchies of central and eastern Europe lagged about a century behind that of France. Of these we must examine three: the Austrian, Prussian, and Russian. Here was nurtured the strictest absolutism. And yet at the same time, across a narrow channel of water to the north of Europe, a small country was to present the greatest challenge to absolutism. That country was, of course, England.

1. AUSTRIA

As the German Empire disintegrated in the wake of the Thirty Years' War, the Hapsburg dynasty of Austria built up a rival "empire," a collection of states along the Danube governed from Vienna. Then the War of the Spanish Succession (1710-13) added Belgium and parts of Italy to the Hapsburg domains of Austria, Hungary, Bohemia, and Silesia. It is a tribute to the Hapsburgs that they were able to consolidate such a conglomeration of peoples and tongues—a diverse collection of states hammered together in adversity by the pressure of the Moslems.

A Disputed Succession

The Austrian Archduke Charles VI spent most of his reign attempting to persuade his disconnected empire to accept his daughter, Maria Theresa, as his successor. Nevertheless when Charles died in 1740 the German princes chose to oppose his daughter's claim, and the War of the Austrian Succession (1740-48) broke out, becoming world-wide as England and France ranged themselves on opposite sides.

Maria Theresa, Archduchess of Austria, Queen of Hungary and Bohemia, wife of the Holy Roman Emperor Francis I, mother of sixteen children, and for forty years one of the central figures in the politics and wars of Europe.

By the Treaty of Aix-la-Chapelle Austria lost Silesia to Prussia, but Maria Theresa was confirmed as Empress. She immediately set about consolidating her realms by establishing German as the official language of the empire, imposing heavier taxation, and setting up a strong central council in Vienna while suspending the meetings of local diets. The net result was that she strengthened absolutism throughout the Hapsburg Empire. In fact she achieved in a decade the strength of monarchy that it had taken France a century and a half to create.

2. PRUSSIA

Stretching across north Germany from the Rhine in the west to east of the Vistula were the sandy, swampy lands of Maria Theresa's chief rival, Prussia. Prussia was a part of that shadowy collection of principalities known as the Holy Roman Empire. Not since the Treaty of Westphalia in 1648, however, had the venerable institution had any real political significance. Why? Because the treaty had recognized the sovereignty of some three hundred German territories, and although the states were loosely federated under an elected emperor they could for all practical purposes act independently of him. They could even formulate their own foreign policies. Moreover, each German ruler could exercise complete—and autocratic—control over the subjects of his own little state.

Early in the 17th century the German state of Brandenburg was augmented by the dukedom of Prussia. The rulers of Brandenburg-Prussia came from the ambitious Hohenzollern family, and they worked hard at building up their power. In 1648, it is true, Brandenburg-Prussia did not seem to have the potential for a great state: the total population was only 750 000, and the capital, Berlin, boasted a mere 6 000. Yet this state of Prussia (as it came to be known in 1701) was destined to become the rival of Austria.

The Sparta of the North

The first of the Prussian rulers to begin the consolidation of his power was Frederick William (all were called Frederick), the Great Elector. He built up a small but efficient standing army, which he then used to intimidate local assemblies into voting him a permanent tax. This step reduced his dependence upon the eastern landed gentry (the Junkers) for financial and military support, thereby reducing in turn the independence and power of the gentry themselves. In the end he set up a taxation system administered by his own picked civil servants, independent of local control. "A ruler is treated with no consideration if he does not have troops and means of his own," he observed shrewdly.

The Great Elector's son, Frederick I, boasted the proud title of "King" of Prussia, a title officially conferred on him by the German emperor in 1701. Frederick I did not follow the Great Elector's policies, preferring instead to try to imitate the splendour of Versailles. But his son Frederick William I reverted to his grandfather's type. A contemporary epigram clearly underlined the contrast: "Under Frederick I Berlin was the Athens of the north; under Frederick William it became the Sparta."

Frederick William I directed his energy toward strengthening the army and the administration. A board of civil servants administered the provinces under the king's close supervision, while the army was increased to a total of eighty-three thousand men

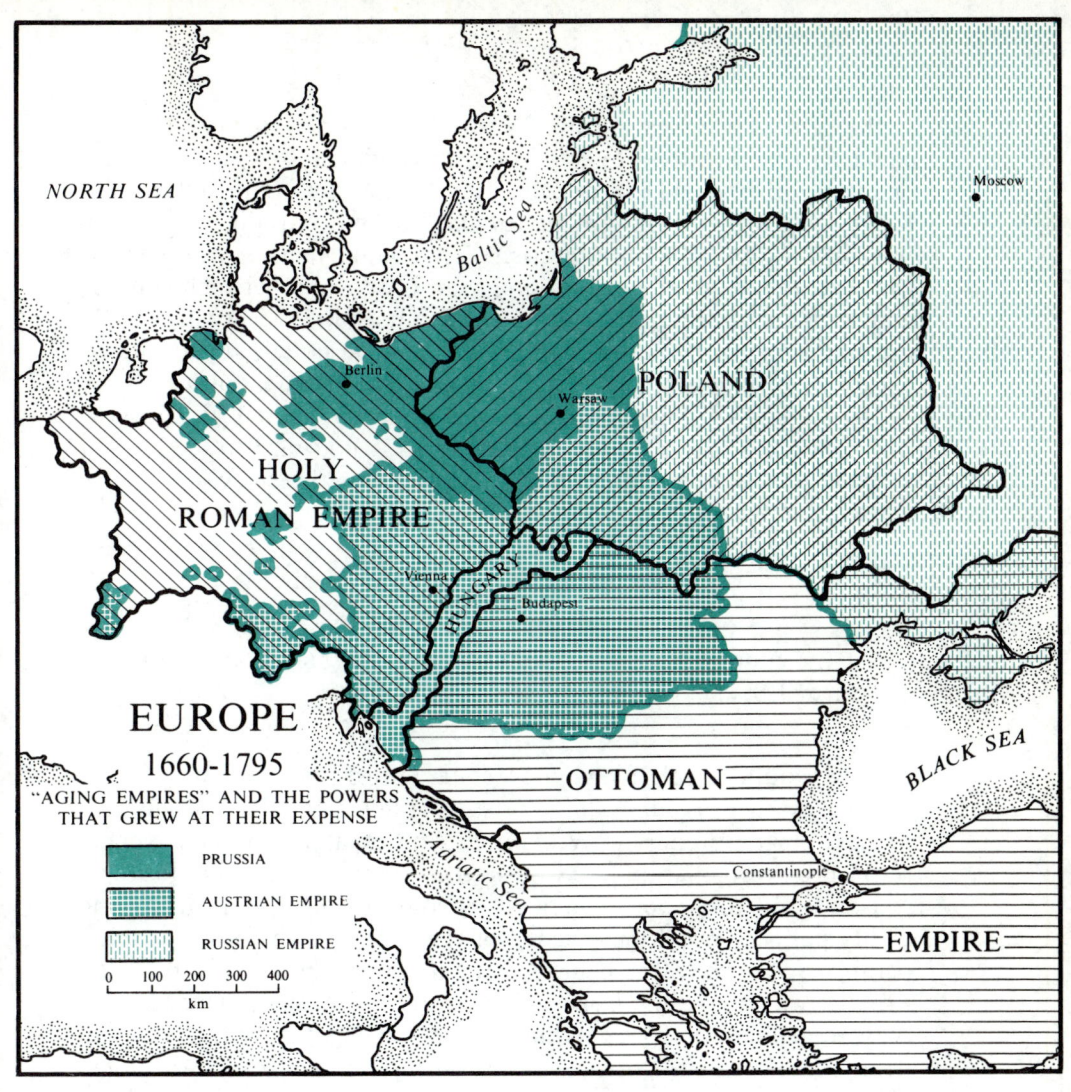

(remarkably large for such a small state—almost as large as the Austrian army). In the capital city of Berlin alone there were twenty thousand soldiers out of a total population of a hundred thousand. The army became Frederick William's extravagance, his first love. He organized a regiment of grenadiers, one hundred and eighty to two hundred and fifteen centimetres tall, employing agents to gather them from all over Europe and trading royal musicians and prize stallions for them. If tall men would not enlist or could not be bought, they were sometimes simply carried off by force.

In 1740 Frederick William's son, Frederick II (the Great), came to the throne. He had quarrelled violently with his domineering father—had even been imprisoned by him; but on his accession to the throne he carried on the family tradition of absolute rule combined with militarism. That same year, Maria Theresa came to the Austrian throne and war broke out between Austria and Prussia. Frederick's military machine flattened Austria without bothering to declare war, and, as we have noted, seized Silesia, a rich Austrian territory lying southeast of Brandenburg.

By the end of the reign of Frederick the Great in 1786, Prussia had become a major Power in Europe. It is not hard to see how or why: a glance at the accompanying table tells the story.

GROWTH OF THE PRUSSIAN ARMY

	1648	1740	1786
Population of Prussia	750 000	2 500 000	5 000 000
Size of Standing Army	8 000	83 000	200 000

How could a relatively poor state afford such an army? The answer is a Prussian characteristic: efficiency. "No profits, no Prussia," said Frederick William I. And so the country's meagre resources were manipulated with the utmost skill. The Prussian peasant paid forty per cent of his income to the government, and eighty per cent of all the revenue of the state was spent on the army (France spent sixty per cent, Austria fifty per cent). Yet by 1750 Prussia was the only larger continental state that managed not only to balance its budget but to show a healthy profit. A great deal of the credit for this surplus was due, once again, to Prussian efficiency, which ensured that the all important functions of the collection and distribution of taxes were carried out promptly and without graft. In fact it was really Prussia's superb civil service that set her apart from other continental states. In France public offices might be purchased or inherited. Not so in Prussia. There they went to the most capable, earned through competitive examinations.

Over this highly centralized government presided Frederick the Great. *All* business had to be reported to him in daily memoranda, to be dealt with by him personally, a burden of paper work which

Frederick the Great of Prussia, the cynical philosopher-king who was both a military genius and a man of letters. "My people and I have come to a satisfactory understanding," he said. "They say what they like and I do what I like."

required the king to get up at 03:00 each day (04:00 in the winter). "If the ruler does not concern himself directly with the army and set an example therein," he wrote, "all is lost." No wonder an Italian traveller reported that he found Prussia "a great barracks"!

Yet Frederick the Great was more than a soldier. He was aware of the intellectual currents of his time, and loved to play his flute while thinking up ways to outwit Maria Theresa. He was a blend of contradictory tendencies, as this English diplomat, who knew him well, fully realized:

I have seen him weep at tragedy, known him to pay as much care to a sick greyhound as a fond mother to a favourite child; yet the next day he has given orders for the devastation of a province or by a wanton increase of taxes made a whole district miserable. He is so far from being sanguinary that he scarce ever suffers a criminal to be punished capitally; yet in the last war he gave secret orders to . . . his army surgeons rather to run the risk of a wounded soldier dying than by the amputation of a limb increase the number and expense of his invalids.

3. RUSSIA

It was not until the 16th century that Russia first entered upon European affairs. What events had retarded the development of this huge and backward country?

In the early Middle Ages the eastern European (Slavic) peoples had been converted to Christianity by Byzantine missionaries from Constantinople. Then in the 9th century the Viking invasions of Europe spread eastward across the vast plains between the Baltic and Black Seas. These invaders, known as *Rus* (whence the name "Russia"), settled down and formed various states which centred on trading towns such as Kiev in the Ukraine.

Other European countries, of course, had also been affected by these two experiences. In the 13th century, however, there occurred an event with vast consequences, which, while not unique to Russia, affected her far more severely than the rest of Europe. This was the invasion of a savage people known as the Tartars, led by the great Mongol conqueror Genghis Khan. About the middle of the 13th century a Tartar state was founded close to the modern city of Volgograd (Stalingrad). The new state, which was called the "Golden Horde" after the army that had conquered it, was merely a satellite of the central Mongol government in Peiping, China. The local Russian princes were left completely under the Tartar yoke.

But gradually the princes of Moscow began to take advantage of Tartar weakness, and with the support of the Russian Church proceeded to form a rudimentary nation state. The result was that by the 16th century there was a new state in eastern Europe which was completely autocratic—a combination of three traditions: delayed feudalism, almost constant warfare, and a militant Church in alliance with the monarchy. The ruler was the Czar, the new Caesar, and when Constantinople finally fell to the Turks in 1453

Russian churchmen further embellished the theory of descent from Rome:

The Church of Old Rome fell because of its heresy; the gates of the Second Rome, Constantinople, have been hewn down by the axes of the infidel Turks; but the Church of Moscow, the Church of the New Rome, shines brighter than the Sun in the whole Universe. . . . Two Romes have fallen, but the Third stands fast; a fourth there cannot be.

Windows on the West

In 1689 a one hundred and ninety-eight centimetre tall youth of seventeen became "Czar and autocrat of all Russia," Czar Peter the Great. He is the father of modern Russia.

When Peter came to the throne Russia was largely isolated from the rest of Europe. Nevertheless, foreign manners were already beginning to affect the country. Few Russians travelled abroad, it is true; but foreigners had for some time come to Russia to trade, and many Russians—such as this 17th century writer—decried their influence:

Acceptance of foreigners is a plague. They live by the sweat and tears of the Russians. The foreigners are like bear-keepers who put rings in our noses and lead us around. They are gods, we fools, they dwell with us as lords. Our Kings are their servants.

Peter the Great, however, early came into contact with foreigners in the "German" quarter of Moscow and on Dutch ships in Russia's Arctic port of Archangel, and he had no intention of fostering this fear of them. Instead, he was the first Russian ruler in over six hundred years to leave home for anything except a military campaign, when he made a tour of Europe in 1697-98—even working for a week in a Dutch shipyard! On his return home he put down a revolt of the royal bodyguard (beheading a number of the mutineers himself), then set out to westernize Russia and extend her territories both north and south.

Though Peter recruited technical experts from the rest of Europe in his drive to modernize his homeland, his purpose was not to further western influence in Russia, but, on the contrary, to enable her to stand up to the West. For Peter's main objective was a military

Peter the Great, Czar of Russia, ordering the construction of St. Petersburg (Leningrad) in 1703. So many workman lost their lives in the building of the city, which was on piles driven into the marshes, that it was said to have been "built on bones."

one: to obtain warm-water ports on the Black and Baltic Seas. To acquire these ports he launched a series of calculated aggressions.

First he allied himself with Poland and Denmark in order to seize Sweden's Baltic colonies. To begin with it seemed that the enterprise was fated for disaster, for in 1700 a Swedish army of eight thousand routed a Russian one five times as large. But "General Winter" eventually came to Russia's aid. Employing a strategy later copied against Napoleon and Hitler the Russians fell back before the invading Swedish army, until finally in 1709 the enemy perished, frozen to death in the merciless snow and mud of the endless wind-swept Russian plains. Ultimately Peter the

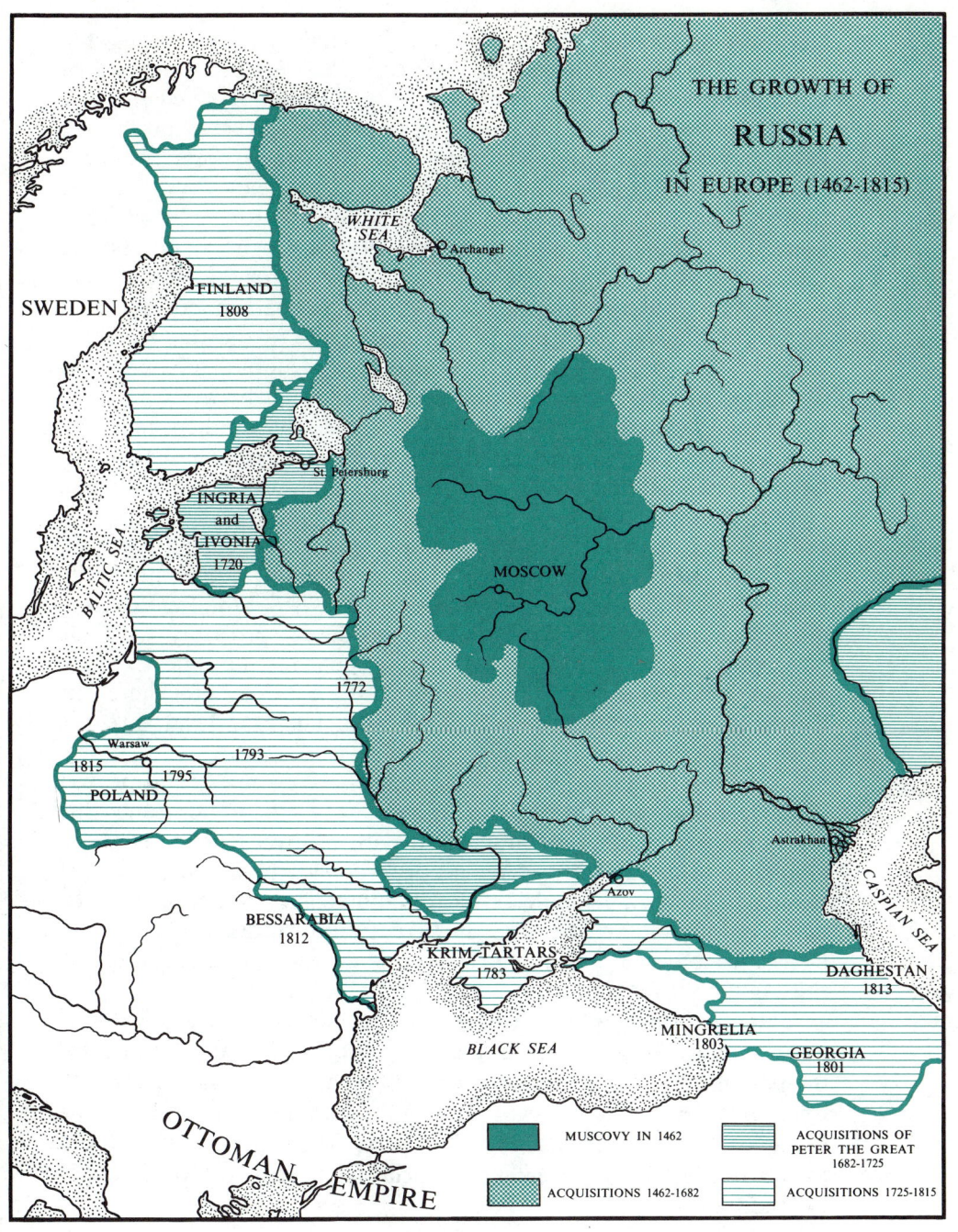

Great's plan succeeded: he obtained a strip of coast along the Baltic where he established the new capital of St. Petersburg (now Leningrad) as one of his "windows on the West." The second calculated aggression was launched against the Turks. But though Peter never succeeded in wresting any Black Sea ports from the Turks, all told he had made Russia a European Power to be reckoned with. Yet in reality he neither revolutionized nor westernized the country. While families of those who distinguished themselves in the army were ennobled, the mass of the people were beaten down into serfdom: the peasantry formed ninety per cent of the population, sixty per cent of them serfs in the full medieval sense of the word. Moreover, the assembly of nobles (*Duma*) was abolished in favour of a council of state selected by the Czar, and when the Patriarch of the Russian Orthodox Church died, in 1700, no successor was appointed. Peter, unlike Louis XIV, had achieved an absolutism that was no mere façade. The Czar was now head of both Church and State.

But Peter, like Louis XIV, had no strong successor. Between 1725 and 1762 Russia was ruled by a series of seven autocrats, none of them dominant personalities. The seventh, Peter III, a neglectful and worthless ruler, was murdered, probably with the connivance of his wife. This calculating lady now became Czarina, and in 1762 emerged as Catherine II (the Great) to share the European stage with Louis XIV, Maria Theresa, Frederick the Great, and George III of England.

Catherine the Great was a most remarkable woman, and proved a masterful ruler. During the thirty-four years of her reign she terrorized her court, and suppressed with an iron will the slightest challenge to her authority. A big boisterous woman with masculine manners, she was hard-drinking, dissolute, and immoral. Yet she had considerable artistic taste and great administrative ability. Her enormous physical appetites, it was said, were matched only by the vigour of her mind.

Catherine did accomplish some reorganization of provincial governments. However, as might be expected, she did nothing for the peasantry except increase their misery by stamping out a rebellion. Her foreign policy was the logical continuation of Peter the Great's: she won lands along the Black Sea from the Turks and joined Frederick the Great and Maria Theresa in the partition of Poland.

Catherine the Great: "A woman quite out of the ordinary, the empress possessed high intelligence, a natural ability to administer and govern, a remarkable practical sense, energy to spare, and an iron will. . . . Above all the empress was a supreme egoist."—from Nicholas V. Riasonovsky, *A History of Russia.*

Russia's rise to power in Europe was thus accomplished at the expense of her neighbours. Even so, it is only fair to note that both before and after this expansion of the 17th and 18th centuries Russia was less often the aggressor than the victim of aggression.

A Matter of Degree

In the 18th century the strength of the European monarchies varied from the Russian at the top of the scale to the English at the bottom. In Russia the ruler's powers were unlimited in theory and very great in practice because no group or institution in the land was capable of mounting an effective opposition. Only the great size of the country, the scantiness of the population, and the slowness of communications limited the power of the Czar. Nothing else could.

The Prussian monarchy was far less absolute than the Russian, because various Estates could not be disregarded. Yet the monarchy was very strong, and was supported by the incomparable Prussian army. As a Prussian general said of his homeland, it was "not a country with an army, but an army with a country that served as its headquarters and food supplier."

In France, on the other hand, the monarchy which in theory appeared more powerful than the Prussian was in reality weaker. The fact was that a country so large and populous as France could be governed only by an exceptional man—and then far from efficiently. Louis XIV *was* exceptional, but his successors certainly were not. Moreover, the courts of appeal (*parlements*) challenged the central government, and the Church still retained enough privileges to impede centralization.

In the Hapsburg empire, as one might expect, the task was impossible: the rulers were required to govern the ungovernable. Nevertheless they did manage to increase their authority by improving the army, by reducing the control of the Diets over taxation, and by building up a central civil service.

The rulers whose political careers we have summarized—notably Maria Theresa, Frederick the Great, and Catherine the Great—were cast in a different mould than the French or Spanish divine-right monarchies. The Austrian, Prussian, and Russian rulers of the second half of the 18th century all liked to think of themselves as "enlightened," as monarchs who ruled not through any divine sanction but through the exercise of reason and intelligence. Their philosophical assumptions and the results of those assumptions are more properly dealt with, therefore, in the later chapter on the Enlightenment.

4. ENGLISH LIMITED MONARCHY

There was one notable exception to the autocratic trend in Europe: England. Whereas the central and eastern European monarchies lagged a century behind the French, the English forged a century ahead. Although English monarchs might claim to rule by divine right, in the long run their divinity would extend only as far as Parliament decreed. For Parliament enjoyed one critically important control—without its consent and approval, the king was virtually unable to raise revenue. It was this power that in the long run gave Parliament the upper hand. And whereas in France the result of a declining monarchy was eventually chaos, in England this decline was accompanied by a great improvement in the efficiency and power of the central government.

The Power of the Purse

In 1603 the son of Mary Stuart, Queen of Scots, became James I of England. He had already ruled Scotland as James VI, and, like other 17th century monarchs, had an exaggerated concept of the power of the throne. "As for the absolute prerogative of the crown," he once declared, "that is no subject for the tongue of a lawyer, nor is it lawful to be disputed. It is atheism and blasphemy to dispute what God can do . . . so it is presumption and high contempt in a subject to dispute what a king can do, or say that a king cannot do this or that."

Such exalted sentiments were by no means limited to the Stuarts. James's Tudor predecessors had held similar views, but they had been clever enough to yield gracefully when they got into disputes with their parliaments. Moreover, they did without parliaments whenever they could, calling them only as a last resort when it was necessary in order to gain more revenue. Elizabeth had actually, by the latter part of her reign, sold nearly half of the Crown lands in order to pay for the heavy expenses of warfare; but of course when large portions of the Crown lands were sold the revenue from them was reduced accordingly—which meant a sharply curtailed royal income. Eventually the queen was forced to rely on parliamentary subsidies. But if Parliament was in an ugly mood Elizabeth was forced to improvise, as in 1599, when she borrowed sixty thousand pounds from the City of London. Parliament could be obstinate, yet it forgave Elizabeth much, partly because she was a woman and partly because in the last years of her reign she seemed to Englishmen to be the living symbol of a sort of Golden Age.

The pressures in England had been increasingly against absolutism. From the middle of the 16th century onward, the country gentry, the knights and squires, began to play an increasingly larger role in the House of Commons. These new Commoners were not easily overawed by the monarchy, particularly since the Crown's ability to reward their services was decreasing (by 1588, the year of the Armada, most of the Crown's honours and pensions had already been distributed). Now, too, the Commons felt the impact of lawyers, men able to lead an attack on the Crown's prerogatives, and of merchants, men who hated trade restrictions and wanted aggressive foreign policies.

Elizabeth called parliaments only when she absolutely had to: ten times in the forty-five years of her reign. Yet with every one she clashed over some question. Nevertheless she deemed it prudent to assent to 429 bills all told, rejecting only 36.

But while Elizabeth fought for the Crown's prerogatives in Parliament, she never tried to destroy the partnership of Crown, Lords, and Commons, or suppress what she felt were Parliament's rightful functions. Under the Tudors the Commons became the recognized voice of public opinion. And it was an increasingly strong voice. Membership of the House of Commons rose from 298 to 462. Elizabeth was not only a strong monarch; she was an exceedingly astute and tactful one. What would happen when the Commons no longer met its match?

Elizabeth's successor was a man who misjudged the strength of England's newly aggressive Parliament. For this error his upbringing was partly to blame. As James VI of Scotland he had dealt with the Scottish Parliament, a body which merely approved what the king and his Privy Council had already done. James's experience in Scotland had convinced him that if he himself did not rule, a gang of nobles would—hardly the proper training for a ruler who would have to deal with the most highly developed governing body in all Europe!

Thus it was almost inevitable from the beginning that James should regard any questioning of his policies by the Commons as highly presumptuous. As king, he believed, he was God's lieutenant on earth; as king he ruled by "divine right." "The House of Commons," he protested vehemently,

is a body without a head. The members give their opinions in a disorderly manner. At their meetings nothing is heard but cries, shouts and confusions. I am surprised that my ancestors should ever have permitted such an institution to come into existence. I am a stranger, and found it here when I arrived, so that I am obliged to put up with what I cannot get rid of.

How different from the attitude displayed towards Parliament by Henry VIII and Elizabeth!

One of James's legacies from Elizabeth was a large national debt, approximately four hundred thousand pounds. And so, like it or not, he was obliged to assemble Parliament on four occasions during his twenty-two year reign to raise desperately needed revenues. His parliaments sat for a total of 181 weeks, and he quarrelled with all of them—quarrelled so bitterly, in fact, that in the end he himself ripped from the journal of the Commons the record of their "Great Protestation," the bold assertion written to remind the king of the ancient privileges of the Commons that gave every member freedom of speech and freedom from arrest when discussing the important affairs of the kingdom. No wonder James warned his son Charles that he would live to have his "bellyful of parliaments."

Nor were financial troubles all that plagued James. He thoroughly detested the Calvinist Puritans, who wished to "purify" the Anglican Church of what they considered its Roman Catholic elements and who suspected the king of "popery." James equally distrusted the stubborn Scottish Presbyterians, who had withdrawn the control of the church from bishops when James insisted on reinstituting an episcopate that was to be appointed by himself.

There remained only one field for James to star in—the field of foreign affairs. But here, once again, he met with failure. Though he pursued the reasonable policy of ending the Spanish war in 1604, friendship with Spain was not popular with the majority of Englishmen. Parliament especially was clamouring for a naval campaign, and in the end there was little alternative but resumption of war with the ancient enemy—a war which was to end, some five years after James's death, in England's complete humiliation.

When James I died in 1625 the strains and stresses were plain for all to see: Parliament in a resentful mood, the English Church increasingly antagonistic, and the country at war. It was an ironic legacy from a man who had styled himself *Rex Pacificus*.

Downfall of the Monarchy

The new king, Charles I, was a handsome, high-minded man, a welcome contrast to James in his degenerate last years. Yet, because the son had grown up in his father's shadow, he was painfully aware of his own shortcomings. He always limped (he had probably had poliomyelitis as a child) and spoke with a stammer. Accordingly, he was ill at ease in the company of those who were fluent conversationalists—a self-consciousness that was interpreted as haughtiness.

As it turned out, Charles fared even worse with Parliament than his father had. It has been calculated that it would have cost him a million pounds a year to fulfil all the promises he made! One war—the one with Spain—was not enough for this indiscreet monarch. He must involve England in a second one, with France, by trying, unsuccessfully, to aid the Huguenots fighting against Richelieu at La Rochelle. Charles was desperate for money, but Parliament was determined to resist all his devices, even though resistance might lead to imprisonment. One very unpopular device was the forced loan, whereby each taxpayer was made to hand over the amount he would have paid had Parliament granted a tax. By 1628 the king was even more desperate. For want of money to pay his troops, or even to provide quarters for them, he adopted the practice of billeting them in private houses. And to make matters worse, any claims for damages committed by these troops were submitted to royally appointed commissioners who judged by martial law and who, therefore, were hardly apt to award redress.

Frustrated and embittered, the Commons attempted to bolster its position by drawing up the Petition of Right.

THE PETITION OF RIGHT

(1628)

1. No man shall hereafter be compelled to make or yield any gift, loan, benevolence, or tax, except by Act of Parliament.
2. No man shall be imprisoned or detained without any cause being shown.
3. No soldiers or sailors shall be billeted in private homes.
4. No commissions for proceeding by martial law shall be issued in the future.

A triple portrait of Charles I by Van Dyck, to be used as the basis for a marble bust by Bernini. When the sculptor saw the portrait, it is recorded that he shouted aloud: "the man is doomed!"

The king, forced by his empty purse, had to accept the document, a document of such importance in English constitutional history that it ranks with Magna Carta. Once again the principle had been set forth that even the Crown must be subject to the law.

It had taken Charles just five years to fulfil his father's prediction: he had had his bellyful of parliaments. More angry debates followed, until in 1629 the king—in utter exasperation—adjourned Parliament, not to summon it again until 1640. Charles's reaction was not surprising. After all, were not the other monarchs of Europe ruling their subjects in the tradition of divine right? Why should the Stuarts be any different? Charles had missed one vital aspect of his situation: there was a vast difference between the ineffective assemblies of the Continent, and the vigorous English Parliament in which the Commons had gained the initiative in legislation.

The period when Charles chose to rule without Parliament was termed by the king's enemies the "Eleven Years' Tyranny." Yet compared with Henry VIII or Elizabeth I, Charles was neither a tyrant nor a despot. On one point, however, he was adamant: he could and would rule without Parliament.

In order to dispense with Parliament Charles needed to cut his expenses. Accordingly the war with France was ended in 1629, and the one with Spain in 1630. Then various royal levies long since discontinued were revived. In this connection Charles's most lucrative source of revenue was the ancient tax known as ship money, the old Plantagenet custom by which seaports and maritime counties had been held responsible for supplying ships—or the money to provide those ships—for the navy. But Charles not only extracted ship money from ports, he even levied it on inland counties!

Not surprisingly, the tax raised a storm of protest. In all fairness to King Charles, however, it should be noted that almost every penny of ship money levied was spent on the navy. Charles I was convinced that a permanent state-owned navy was an absolute necessity at a time when both Holland and France were increasing their fleets. But unfortunately for the king the public saw in this tax only one more example of his determination to collect revenue without resorting to Parliament. The tragedy of the ship money controversy is that both sides were partly right. Regardless of who was right or wrong, however, the tax proved financially successful, so much so that by 1638 Charles was almost free of debt.

Now, however, Charles made a fatal error: he tried to force the English Church on Scotland. At one stroke he accomplished the remarkable feat of uniting his enemies, both in Scotland and in Parliament. Fearful of humiliating loss of face in Scotland, the king was determined to reassert his authority there. But this required a military campaign, and a military campaign required money. Charles had no alternative. In April, 1640, he found himself (for the first time since 1629) once again forced to call Parliament. Three weeks of wrangling followed; then the so-called "Short Parliament" was dissolved.

Charles still managed to scrape together enough money for his campaign in Scotland, but the campaign failed. Scotland then refused to make a peace not ratified by the English Parliament, so once again Parliament had to be called in. In November, 1640, the "Long Parliament" began, so named because theoretically it sat for twenty years (until 1660) without new elections.

This time, Parliament was in no mood to be trifled with. It had four specific goals: to remove the "evil councillors" of the king; to eliminate certain courts, such as the Star Chamber, that had proved dangerous to liberty; to forbid unparliamentary taxation; and to make sure that henceforth Parliament would meet regularly and that sessions would be of reasonable length.

Months of tension and fiery debate were climaxed in 1642 when Charles tried—and failed—to arrest five members of the House of Commons. Civil war was imminent. That summer Charles recruited an army in the north, mainly from the lords and the conservative gentry, gentlemen accustomed to handling weapons—the dashing cavalrymen known as Cavaliers. The parliamentary forces, on the other hand, were composed of the Puritan squires, city merchants, and professional people—the unwigged, close-cropped Roundheads.

When the war began in 1642 the Member of Parliament for Cambridge, Oliver Cromwell, recruited a voluntary cavalry force and joined the parliamentary army. Though he had been a prominent committee man he was certainly not looked upon as an outstanding opponent of King Charles. But now warfare forged his character. He quickly became second-in-command, and the army's most popular leader.

The battle lines were drawn. The north and west were mainly royalist and the south and east were mainly parliamentary in sympathy; yet there were exceptions. And although most nobles and gentry fought for the king and most townsmen for Parliament, there were a few groups of nobles and gentry on the parliamentary side and some townsmen on the royalist side. The country was split right up the middle. Son fought against father and brother against brother in the worst of all kinds of war, civil war. Finally in 1646 Charles, outnumbered and defeated by both Scots and English, surrendered and was imprisoned.

He was an awkward prize. No agreement could be reached on the vexed question of what to do with him, and the victorious groups began to quarrel among themselves. A second brief civil war flared up in 1648 when Charles tried playing off the army against Parliament and the Scots against the English—but Cromwell soon ended it. Determined at last to deal with both Parliament and the king, Cromwell's grip tightened into a vise. England found that she had only exchanged taskmasters. The army proceeded to turn on the Commons, by this time shrunk to about half of its pre-war total of

"I desire you would use all your skill to paint my picture truly like me, and not flatter me at all; but remark all these roughnesses, pimples, worts, and everything as you see me, otherwise I will pay never a farthing for it."
—Oliver Cromwell.

493 Members. Some 166 Presbyterian Members still willing to work for a reconciliation with the king were simply refused admittance to the Commons by the army. The fifty or sixty who remained set up a high court of justice to judge their king. By this illegal tribunal Charles I was tried, convicted, and executed in 1649. For the next five years England was a "Commonwealth," a republic in which there was neither king nor House of Lords.

The new Commonwealth waged successful wars in Ireland and Scotland, and also became involved in hostilities with Holland and

"He nothing common did, or mean, upon that memorable scene." Charles I was beheaded outside the palace of Whitehall before a great many spectators and surrounded by a strong body of troops. His head fell at the first blow, and as the executioner held it up for all to see, the crowd, hitherto silent, gave a great groan of horror and pity.

Spain. But ironically enough Cromwell could not work harmoniously with what was left of Parliament. In short, he failed to bring stability to England. Why? Because his government was really a military dictatorship.

In 1653 Cromwell was made Lord Protector of the realm. Two years later he dismissed the first Parliament of the Protectorate (as his government was called), and replaced it with new administrative arrangements. The country was divided into eleven districts, each under a Major-General who, at the head of five hundred cavalrymen, presided with such an iron hand that the "eleven years' tyranny" of Charles I looked pale by comparison. A second Parliament was similarly dismissed in 1658. Cromwell died before another was assembled.

Despite all his professions of belief in constitutional and parliamentary government Cromwell ruled as a dictator. Yet Englishmen still honour him as a great man. For despite his limitations he did

Oliver Cromwell dismissing Parliament in 1653. The English people quickly found that they had exchanged a weak and inefficient despotism for a powerful and capable one. Cromwell, the simple country squire, soon became a dictator who crushed all opposition.

use the arbitrary power of the army to curb the arbitrary power of the monarchy. Thanks to him, absolute divine right monarchy was no longer tolerated in England.

Restoration and Reaction

Within two years of Cromwell's death Charles Stuart, the thirty-year-old son of the executed king, was invited back from exile on the Continent, and it was solemnly declared that "the government of England is and by rights ought to be by King, Lords, and Commons." It was now 1660. Twenty years of searching for a political solution had brought England back to the House of Stuart.

Charles II, England's "Merry Monarch," soon became famous for his witty charm and his easy-going nature. But although he was a shrewd man he tended to be lazy, spending too much of his time in the gay extravagance of court life. The frivolity and lack of restraint practised by the king were mirrored in the social standards of the time as countless Englishmen exuberantly threw off the shackles imposed on them by the stern hand of Puritanism.

During the twenty-five years of his reign Charles II managed to conduct affairs with considerable skill—a skill very much needed, since a rather uneasy balance of power existed between the Commons and Lords on the one hand and the king on the other. Moreover, Charles now had to contend with a relatively new phenomenon, political parties. The Tories ("Tory" originally meant an Irish outlaw) were mainly conservative squires and gentry drawn from former Cavaliers and their descendants. The Whigs (a "Whig" was a Scottish cattle-thief) were financiers, city merchants, and Puritan and Presbyterian squires, and were drawn from former Roundheads and their descendants.

Actually Charles II would have liked to do two things: to regain for himself the authority that the king had once held, and to reestablish Roman Catholicism. But he had enough common sense to realize that he would never gain anything if he met Parliament head on. Instead he would have to be devious in pursuing his aims. One of his schemes for getting money without having to resort to Parliament involved a subterfuge with the French king, Louis XIV. Charles made a secret treaty with Louis (which Louis later leaked to the English Parliament) under which he was to receive two hundred thousand pounds in return for his promise to assist the French monarch in attacking Holland. Although these arrangements were not known in England there was such a general suspicion of Charles's desire to aid the French and the Catholics that in 1673 Parliament took preventive measures in the form of the Test Act, a bill which required all office-holders to take communion in the Church of England and made it impossible for Catholics to serve either in the government or in the army and navy.

Parliament's next act of defiance was directed towards the heir apparent, the king's brother James, Duke of York, who was a Roman Catholic. But Charles was able to withstand the efforts to bar his brother's succession to the throne by the simple expedient of dissolving Parliament. Before the members dispersed, however, Parliament did manage to pass one important piece of legislation,

James II was a royal misfit. Although tolerant of religious differences in advance of his time, he was lacking in political judgment and never learned to understand his fellow-men. Tactless and impatient of advice, he mismanaged every political problem with which he was faced, being rigid when concessions were called for and giving way when he should have been firm.

the Habeas Corpus Amendment Act (1679) by which any loopholes left by the old writ of habeas corpus were plugged. Henceforth judges could issue the writ even when courts were not in session; the court must produce the prisoner within three days; a statement of the reason for imprisonment must be given; and consequently release on bail was assured.

For the last four years of his reign, then, Charles II ruled alone. And surprisingly enough, when he died in 1685 there was no

The Fearefull Summer:

OR,
Londons Calamitie, The Countries Discourtesie, And both their Miserie.

Printed by Authoritie in *Oxford*, in the last great Infection of the Plague, 1625. And now reprinted with some Editions, concerning this present yeere, 1636.

With some mention of the grievous and afflicted estate of the famous Towne of New-Castle upon Tine, with some other visited Townes of this Kingdome.

By IOHN TAYLOR.

"The greatest scourge of man, more feared than war—the plague!"

William III was brought up among enemies and learned early to hide his feelings behind a mask that made him seem cold and remote. Obstinately opposed to Louis XIV, he made the defeat of French ambitions his aim in life, and though often defeated, he never despaired, and his policy and ideas continued to be followed long after his death.

dispute over the succession. The people's memories of civil war were sharper than their fear of Catholicism, and James II, a Roman Catholic convert, mounted the throne almost unopposed.

Unfortunately, it took James less than four years to provoke a revolution. Although he may very well have been genuinely tolerant, the majority of his subjects preferred not to think so, and feared, not unnaturally as events were to demonstrate, the same fate as Louis XIV was reserving across the Channel for the Huguenots. Thus when James sought to repeal the Test Act and Habeas Corpus, when he kept a standing army of twenty thousand men poised on the outskirts of London, and when he tried to force the Church of England to declare from all its pulpits his suspension of the laws against Roman Catholics, he virtually sealed his fate. Seven prominent peers—three Tories and four Whigs—decided to take the revolutionary step of inviting a foreign monarch to come to England to usurp their own king. William of Orange was contacted and assured that nineteen out of twenty Englishmen would rally to him. This able ruler of Holland had a celebrated ancestor in his great-grandfather, that William of Orange who had fought against Philip II of Spain. He appealed to Englishmen on two other counts: he was a famous Protestant leader who had rallied Europe against Louis XIV, and he could lay claim to the English throne by virtue of Stuart blood (his mother was a daughter of Charles I) as well as by marriage (his wife Mary was James II's daughter).

So it was that the Dutch son-in-law came, in 1688, at the head of an army of some fifteen thousand to his English father-in-law's land. And James, who might have made a stand, simply ran away to France. To the unpopularity of his policies James had added the ignominy of his flight. He had bowed to a revolution in which not one shot was fired. Small wonder that, on the heels of the bloody Civil War of 1642, it is enshrined in English history as the "Glorious Revolution."

Parliament was not going to take any chances of losing the power it had acquired so painfully throughout the 17th century. To make certain that in offering the crown to William and Mary they were safeguarding their rights, the members of Parliament passed the famous Bill of Rights—a model for all future bills of this kind. Its main provisions (which mostly restate old constitutional principles) are indicated in the table on the following page.

England was not yet a parliamentary democracy, for the Cabinet system, universal suffrage, and the abolition of the power of the House of Lords lay ahead in the 18th, 19th, and 20th centuries. But there could be no further doubt that Lords and Commons were supreme over the king.

The monarchy that emerged from the Glorious Revolution of 1688 no longer possessed a divine sanction. But it had the sanction of men: it was above all a parliamentary monarchy. Henceforth

> ## THE BILL OF RIGHTS
>
> (1689)
>
> 1. No law may be enacted or suspended
> 2. No taxes may be levied
> 3. No standing army may be maintained in peace time
>
>   without parliament's consent.
>
> 4. There must be frequent sessions of parliament, free elections, and freedom of debate.
> 5. There must be fair jury trial, no excessive bails or fines, and no unusual punishments.
> 6. No special courts may be created.
> 7. Subjects may petition the sovereign for justice without fear of retaliation.
> 8. Protestant subjects may carry arms for their own defence.
> 9. No ruler may be a Roman Catholic, or marry a Roman Catholic.

there could be no English absolutism. A shrewd Frenchman saw clearly what had happened in England when he described that country as "free because the sovereign, whose person is controlled and limited, is unable to inflict any imaginable harm on anyone."

As the 17th century drew to a close, England not only led Europe in the evolution of government but she was recognized as a first-class Power. We must now retrace the steps by which she achieved this status, and see, as well, just how she became involved with France in a great duel for empire. The results of this study will herald modern times, for we will for the first time observe European wars escalating into worldwide conflicts.

3 European and World Wars

> ...the greatness of the British nation is not owing to war and conquest, to enlarging its dominions by the sword, or subjecting the people of other countries to our power, but it is all owing to trade, to the increase of our commerce at home, and the extending it abroad.
> —Daniel Defoe, *The Complete English Tradesman* (1726)

> Of all States, from the smallest to the biggest, one can safely say that the fundamental role of government is the principle of extending their territories.
> —Frederick the Great, *History of My Time* (1742)

The prosperity of those modern nation-states whose development has been traced in the previous chapters was not just a matter of auspicious fortune. It was built on new business techniques which were the foundation stones for their commercial empires. Around the birth of these empires swirled changes so far-reaching, so sweeping, that they constitute what is known as the "Commercial Revolution." At the same time, the traditional methods and machinery of the military world were undergoing radical reappraisal. The combined impact of these revolutionary changes transformed society and marked the clear beginning of the modern world.

1. THE COMMERCIAL AND MILITARY REVOLUTIONS

In the 16th, 17th, and 18th centuries Western Europe developed financial, political, military, and scientific techniques which gave it the leadership of the modern world. Let us first examine the changes that now began to revolutionize the conduct of business.

In the great cities of Venice, Genoa, Milan, and Florence, Italian businessmen—following the precept of the Moslem merchants of the medieval Mediterranean—had perfected negotiable credit instruments in order to make the conduct of business easier. Once only cash could seal a bargain; now there was the *bill of exchange*, a document developed by the Genoese, which was a signed agreement to pay a certain price before a certain date (a technique we would today label "buying on time"). Eventually this simple bill of exchange developed into a complicated type of negotiable instrument called a *draft*. The draft involved three parties: the person owing the money (the drawer), the person paying the money (the

The Bourse of London, where merchants and bankers met to transact business. Samuel Pepys, the diarist, wrote late in 1667, "Sir W. Pen and I went into London and there saw the King with his kettle drums and trumpets going to lay the first stone pillar of the new building of the Exchange . . ."

The illustration shows a typical merchant of the period, richly dressed in expensive materials and with a well-filled purse hung from his belt. With the growth of trade and the development of trading companies, a new middle class of merchants and traders grew to power and influence through the possession of wealth.

drawee), and the person being paid (the payee). Today we have a form of draft in the modern bank cheque. The drawer is the possessor of the bank account who signs the cheque; the drawee is the bank; and the payee is the person to whom the cheque is made out.

These new techniques were soon to force a different method of business accounting called double-entry book-keeping—a key innovation which by 1500 was beginning to spread from Venice to business centres all over Europe. Double-entry book-keeping considered every transaction as either a debit or a credit. By adding up the credit side of the ledger and checking this figure against the total on the debit side it was possible at any time to take a trial balance. Yearly balances showed the overall state of the business concerned.

The 15th and 16th centuries also witnessed a rapid development of trading companies. Similar companies had, of course, existed during the Middle Ages in such associations as the 12th and 13th century *compagnia* of Italian cities. But by the 15th and 16th centuries the trading companies had far outstripped their medieval counterparts in the scale of their operations. Indeed, they became so esteemed that even kings chartered them, delegating to them some part of their own royal powers such as that of negotiating treaties or making wars. Alongside these *chartered companies* there developed *joint-stock companies*. Such ventures were run by a single management who handled the company's "stock"—that is, all the money (capital) put in by the members—and individuals were able to buy shares in this stock. The person with money to invest could now buy stock and let the elected managers of a company take the risk of running ships and selling goods.

As the scale of operations of joint-stock companies increased, it was only natural that the Italian merchants should align themselves with the companies with the most financial security, these being, of course, the ones who were backed by national states. Large fleets now became necessary for commercial supremacy, fleets which simply could not be managed by city-states such as Venice or Genoa but which were quite possible for maritime nations such as Portugal, Spain, the Netherlands, England, and France. In this way financial and military techniques were joined; in this way, might begat wealth.

The Professional War

At the same time as modern financial techniques were being perfected, a revolution was taking place in the art of warfare. The bowman was giving way to the musketeer. Gunpowder was, of course, no new thing. It had been known in medieval Europe from as early as the middle of the 13th century, although it had had surprisingly little effect on the battlefield since most medieval wars were fought with arrows, swords, lances, and siege machines. By the 15th century there were hand guns available, but these were clumsy affairs more effective as short-range clubs than long-range weapons. Now, however, at the end of the 15th century, cannon began to be produced in sufficient quantity—and to acquire sufficient mobility—to be a decisive factor in battle. Mounted on horse-drawn gun carriages or installed in warships, and forged out of brass, bronze, and eventually iron, they became deadly weapons. Hollow iron balls filled with gunpowder could explode on targets with a decisive effect which foreshadowed the shattering power of modern shells. Small arms also were greatly improved, and became less expensive when interchangeable parts were developed for them, so that by replacing a cog a damaged or broken musket could be made as good as new.

Warfare was becoming a professional affair, one in which it was more and more important to be able to predict how many would take part. It was necessary, then, to make use of specific numbers of men in standard units, and to rehearse the troops thoroughly in manoeuvres so that when they were plunged into battle they were in effect performing a mammoth-sized drill. Accordingly, the military units we call regiments, battalions, and companies, became essential, and generals now found they had to depend on heavy shock troops accompanied by fast, lightly-armed infantry and cavalry. In short, the day of the small skirmish was over and the smoke of world wars could already be sighted on the horizon. Henceforth only rich states could afford to equip and train armies.

Navies, too, developed specialized sailing ships to replace oared galleys. These warships—large, powerful galleons—were built to carry heavy guns, one and a half to three and a half metres, with a mass of as much as two tonnes and fire cannon balls of two to twenty-seven kilograms. The best place to locate the gun battery was between decks, where thirty or forty guns could fire through

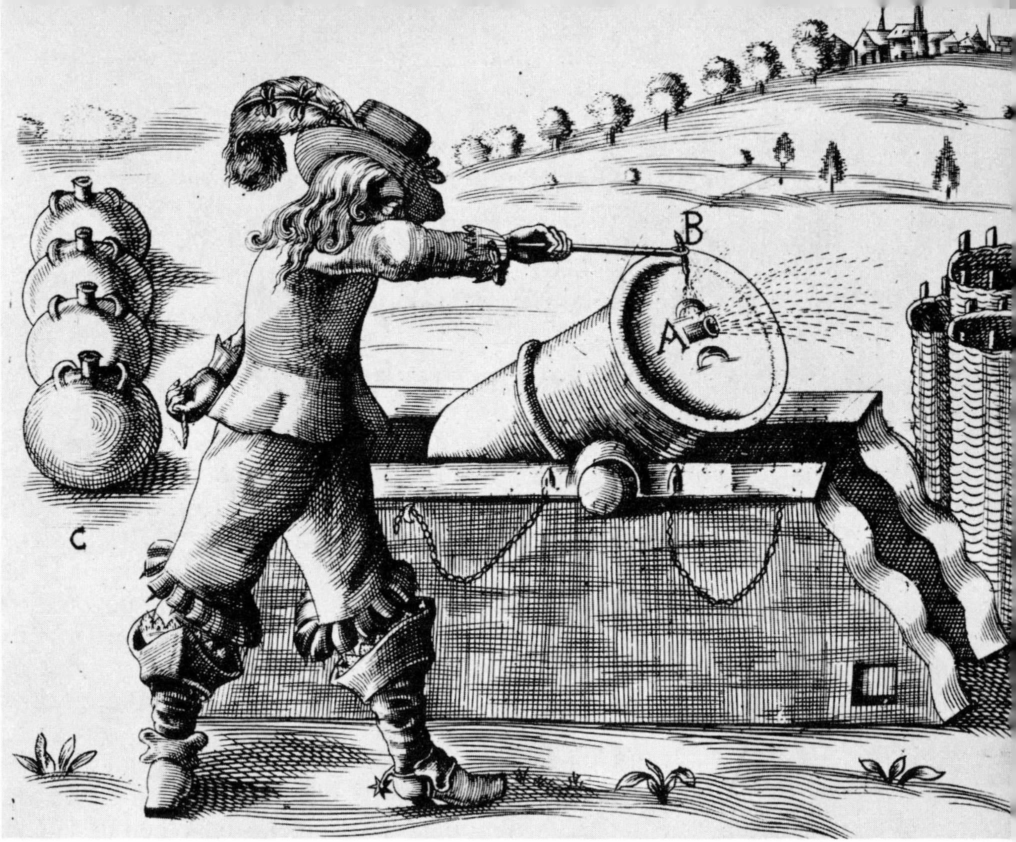

Although Europe had known gunpowder since the 13th century, the use of cannon and firearms was slow to develop. One of the the first appearances of cannon was at Crécy, in 1346, where they contributed to the English victory by frightening the horses of the French knights, though they appear to have done little damage otherwise. Muskets were not much better. So slow and difficult to use were these weapons that in the eight hours it took to fight the Battle of Nordlingen (1645) a musketeer only fired seven times!

square ports. Obviously, from now on to attack a ship by boarding it would be a very hazardous business. Instead, it was much simpler to concentrate such a heavy fire on the enemy that he might quite literally be blown out of the water. With such formidable ships and guns, the navies of the European Powers were more than a match for any non-European fleets they might encounter.

2. THE EARLIEST EMPIRES

With new lands being discovered in abundance and the gleam of gold to light the way, the race for empire was certain to be keen. First off the mark were the Portuguese. Thanks to the inspiration of a remarkable man, Prince Henry the Navigator, the Portuguese created what has been called an institute for navigation: a body of sailors, geographers, instrument makers, and merchants devoted to research that would aid exploration. Their foremost project was to find a way to reach India by sailing south along the west coast of Africa in the belief that sooner or later it would be possible to turn north and east.

Finally in 1488 Bartholomew Diaz did succeed in rounding the Cape of Good Hope, and India itself was reached by Vasco da Gama ten years later. The feat paid off handsomely. When da Gama returned to Lisbon in 1499 his cargo was worth sixty times the cost of his expedition—a very tidy profit! It was to be through Lisbon that the riches of the Orient were to flow into Europe for the next hundred years.

But the Portuguese purse was not filled only by the luxuries of India. Trade was also established with the East Indies, China, and Japan. Portugal also claimed Brazil, which was an important stopover for fresh water and vegetables. Portugal based her claim on a declaration by Pope Alexander VI dividing the overseas world between Spain and Portugal, the demarcation line being a hundred leagues west of the Azores. (The following year the Treaty of Tordesillas moved the Portuguese sphere 270 leagues farther still to the west.) Consequently when Pedro Alvares Cabral touched the coast of Brazil on his way to India in 1500, he could claim for Portugal an area almost as staggering in its size as it was in its apparent lack of riches.

Meanwhile Spain, too, had made some important moves in the imperial game of chess. Eight years before Cabral landed on the

South American mainland, a man fired by visions of discovering the fabled riches of India set sail for Queen Isabella of Spain. That man was Christopher Columbus. But the country Columbus reached was not India; it was the West Indies, and the only gold he was able to find was "in the ears and noses of occasional Indians." Although he made three other voyages, he never fulfilled his dream of reaching India, and died an embittered man.

Other explorers also made voyages which required great courage, but with no more success than Columbus. Finally, however, Spanish fortunes improved. In 1519 Hernando Cortes marched on the Aztec Kingdom of Mexico with only four hundred infantrymen, fifteen horses, and six small cannon, a force that had to be augmented by many more men from Indian nations hostile to the Aztecs before the great kingdom fell in 1521. Here at last was the beginning of riches. The next year the first large shipment of treasure reached Spain.

The Spanish now spared no effort in wresting the New World's fortune from its rightful owners. By 1532 Francisco Pizarro had crushed the Inca empire in Peru, and within a few years most of the rest of South America came into the Spanish orbit. By 1575, there were at least two hundred Spanish towns and 175 000 settlers in the New World. Nor was Spain's domain limited to one hemisphere, for in 1521 she had acquired a base in the Far East when Magellan discovered the Philippines.

Spain regarded her overseas possessions as vast plantations in which to nurture her cherished transplants: her religion, her language, and her political and economic institutions. The Empire itself disintegrated after three centuries, but its culture still colours much of both North and South American civilization.

The Diminutive Giant

The Spanish Crusade had been, as we have seen, partly frustrated by the hardy Dutch. The determination which had helped the Dutch oppose one of Europe's greatest Powers on land also showed itself on the sea, where they were destined to make a name for themselves as the greatest shipper of cargoes for Europe. So successful were they that in the first three-quarters of the 16th century they turned Holland into the emporium of the Continent.

The new demands of trade required new types of ships. For the coastal trade the Dutch developed a remarkable vessel called the "flyboat," a craft almost, it was said, "as warlike as a coal-scuttle," but capable of carrying up to nine hundred tonnes of cargo along the Atlantic coastline or into the Baltic Sea. These unromantic vessels were so thoroughly dependable that they themselves became a staple export, with Dutch shipyards sweating out an average of one craft per day to supply the French, English, Scandinavian, and Spanish demands for shipping.

At first the Dutch were content to profit indirectly from the eastern trade through the trans-shipment of oriental wares from the Portuguese ports of Lisbon or Cadiz. In 1580, however, Spain incorporated Portugal into her empire, and since Spain and Holland were at war, access to shipments in Portugal was cut off. Henceforth Dutch profits were to come either by piracy or by sailing directly to the East Indies from Holland. In the 1590's a whole series of voyages to the Indian Ocean took place, and as Portugal's power withered so did her settlements in the Far East—leaving the field open to a burgeoning Dutch trade. A new commercial dynamo had emerged.

In 1602 the powerful Dutch East India Company was formed to exercise exclusive trading rights over an immense area which stretched eastward from the Cape of Good Hope to the Strait of Magellan. For the next two centuries the Company paid its investors annual dividends ranging anywhere from ten to fifty per cent, and the Bourse at Amsterdam became the 17th century world stock exchange.

Dutch ambitions, fed by hardy courage and canny speculation, knew no bounds. It was said that Dutch captains would have sailed into hell to trade with the devil were it not for the fear that their sails might catch fire! And so from a colony at Capetown, where Dutch and Huguenot farmers (Boers) raised food to supply merchant ships, their commercial empire stretched to Mauritius in the Indian Ocean and ever eastward to Ceylon, Java, India, Malaya, Indonesia, China, and Japan.

Of course the western world, too, was regarded as fair game by the Dutch. There was, for example, Henry Hudson, who in 1609 explored the river that today bears his name. Then a few years later Dutch traders established a settlement on Manhattan Island which eventually became the site of New Amsterdam, and a large area along the Hudson and Delaware Rivers was claimed and named New Netherland. Certain West Indian islands were seized from Spain. At one point there was even a Dutch invasion of Brazil.

The extent of Holland's trade was truly amazing. In the 1660's the French estimated that the Dutch mercantile marine was double the size of the French and English combined. Englishmen recognized the Dutch success by coining a phrase to describe any extraordinary feat: "that beats the Dutch!"

But the economic shadow Holland cast was huge in comparison with her actual size. She could claim a population of only two and a half million; such a small nation could not afford to extend herself too far for too long. By the end of the 17th century the western bases had mostly been lost. Two other nations whose population and resources far outstripped Holland's now wrested the position of predominance from her, and though she remained a thriving commercial nation into the 18th century she was never again a world leader. New demands of a new era were putting her out of the competition. In the 18th century coal and iron, not spices and herring, were to be of ultimate importance. These France and England had in abundance. So it was that those mighty nations, equipped with the resources to develop the new century's industrialism, displaced their enterprising competitor and became the chief rivals in the duel for empire.

3. THE FRENCH EMPIRE

France's internal troubles in the 16th century had left her little energy for colonial expansion. There were, of course, dozens of voyages made by Norman and Breton fishermen to the Grand Banks off Newfoundland; it has been estimated that by 1600 there were at least six hundred French craft engaged in North American fisheries. And the fishermen did, it is true, set up shelters along the Newfoundland coast during the summer months in order to repair their nets and smoke and salt their catch. Since these camps also served as centres of barter with the natives, a profitable sideline in furs grew up. But the fishermen did not want traders to entrench themselves in North America. Permanent settlers, they feared, would compete with them. Consequently no settlements were made, and the most important result of the fisheries on the Banks, as far as the New World was concerned, was that much experience was gained in long and hazardous ocean voyages by men whose names are lost to us.

There were, however, two men who did immortalize themselves by their voyages: Verrazano and Cartier. In 1524 Giovanni Verrazano, sailing for Francis I, skirted the Atlantic coast from Cape Hatteras to Newfoundland in search of a northwest passage to Cathay. Then in 1534 the St. Malo navigator Jacques Cartier landed on the Gaspé peninsula. On his second voyage, in 1535-36, he sailed up the St. Lawrence as far as the Indian village of Hochelaga at the confluence of the Ottawa and St. Lawrence Rivers. But when a third voyage (1541-42) failed to establish a permanent settlement, the French authorities lost interest in Canada for another two generations.

It was 1604 before the *fleur de lis* was again to be raised on Canadian shores. In that year, under authorization from Henry IV, a Huguenot soldier named Pierre du Gua, Sieur de Monts, planted a little settlement on St. Croix Island. Among the 125 people who settled there was the geographer royal, Samuel de Champlain. In the spring, those settlers who survived the hard winter moved across the Bay of Fundy to Port Royal in Nova Scotia. Here they stayed, and from these humble beginnings grew the colony of Acadia. In no time Acadia became an area of constant dispute between England and France, until finally it passed to England in 1713 by the Treaty of Utrecht.

The most significant of all French contributions to Canada, however, was initiated in 1608 when Champlain founded a settlement at Quebec. Then over the next three-quarters of a century French explorers fanned out across the vast North American wilderness, first on behalf of Richelieu's Company of New France and later of Louis XIV's Company of the West, until their canoes had traversed waters from the Great Lakes to the mouth of the Mississippi.

The French settlements did not prosper greatly: they were choked by the extreme restrictiveness of Colbert's mercantilism and pummelled by the cruel winters of New France. It is small wonder that the combination of these two factors discouraged emigration. Moreover, the French habit of forming a single company for both trade and colonization meant that trade, which yielded quick profits, was emphasized at the expense of colonization, which might not yield returns for decades. Even a frequent motivation for emigration, the search for religious freedom, was missing. Dissenters often would gladly exchange the repression of the mother country for the hardships of a liberal colony. Yet after 1627 only Roman

Catholics were allowed to settle in New France. In view of such impediments to colonization it is not surprising that by 1700 the total French population in North America stood at only fifteen thousand settlers, whereas that of the English colonies numbered two hundred thousand.

In the West Indies, however, it was a different story. There, settlements flourished until French dominance extended over three times as many people as it did in Canada. So prosperous was this economy that in the 18th century the French Antilles became known as the sugar bowl of Europe. Other continents, too, were subjects for French speculation. At the same time as a foothold was being gained in the West Indies, the French African or Senegal Company was inaugurating a profitable slave trade in Africa. And in India a French East India Company established important trading posts. Henceforth, rivalry with the English was not confined to the West Indies and North America; it had spread to India as well.

The storm warnings were out. Both France and England were in a race to capture the bulk of the new wealth, and the time when they ran out of elbow room and started jostling one another could not be far off. In the East as well as in the West it would be sea power which would decide the outcome.

4. THE ENGLISH EMPIRE

About 1488 a Genoese named Bartholomew Columbus came to the court of Henry VII of England with an extraordinarily bold scheme. He wanted a backer to finance him in his attempt to establish a sea link with Cathay, so that the spices of the East could be brought directly to Southampton in English ships rather than by Venetian middlemen; and to this end he tried to interest the Tudor monarchy. Henry, unfortunately, took some time to make up his mind about the risks involved, and when he did decide to support Bartholomew and his brother it was too late. Christopher Columbus had already agreed to sail as an agent of Spain.

Yet even as Columbus sailed, another Italian, John Cabot, was living in Bristol. When the news of Columbus's epoch-making voyage reached England in 1493, Cabot believed that it was not Asia which had been discovered but rather some islands part way across the Atlantic. Cabot therefore proposed to sail to the nearest point of Asia by keeping to the northern latitudes. This time Henry

VII did listen. He authorized John Cabot and his three sons to sail into the "eastern, western, and northern seas," and an expedition set out from Bristol in 1497. It landed not in Asia, but on the rugged coast of either Newfoundland or Nova Scotia. The next year a further expedition explored the Atlantic seaboard of North America. But once again the explorers failed to find the riches of Cathay, discovering instead only native populations. After 1498 the English documents always refer to "the New Found Land," never to Cathay.

Mixed Motives

The voyages of the Elizabethans opened up the seas to Englishmen, yet they were no more successful in establishing colonies or stimulating trade than those of the Cabots. It was not until the 17th century that the English economy could really support active colonization. And when colonization did begin in earnest the motives for it were, as usual, mixed.

There was the religious argument: "The gaining provinces addeth to the King's Crown; but the reducing heathen people to civility and true religion bringeth honour to the King of Heaven." There was the strategic argument, namely "the inestimable advantage that would be gained to this State of England in case of war, both for the easy assaulting of the Spaniards' West Indies from these parts, and for the relieving and succouring of all ships and men-of-war that should go on reprisals." There was even the argument of over-population at home:

This main business is to be promoted in regard of the general populousness of Great Britain, which is the chief cause that charity waxeth cold. Every man hath enough to do to shift for his own maintenance, so that the greatest part are driven to extremities, and many to get their living by other men's losses; witness our extortioners, perjurers, pettifoggers at law, coney-catchers, thieves, cottagers, inmates, unnecessary ale-sellers, beggars, burners of hedges to the hindrance of husbandry and such like, which might perhaps prove profitable members in the New Found Land.

Above all there was the economic argument:

Behold then the true form and worth of foreign trade, which is, the great revenue of the king, the honour of the kingdom, the noble profession of the merchant, the school of our arts, the supply of our wants, the employment of our poor, the improvements of our lands, the nursery of our mariners, the walls of the kingdoms, the means of our treasure, the sinews of our wars, the terror of our enemies.

The colonies would, it was hoped, provide luxuries such as precious metals, fish, and wine. But equally important in the mother country's eyes was the acquisition of naval stores, that is, fir poles, fir masts, pitch for caulking seams, and hemp for cordage. Hitherto these had come mostly from the Baltic and could, therefore, be denied England by whichever power controlled that area at the time. Hence alternative supplies were vital to the maintenance of English sea power.

It was from a variety of motives, then, that the English founded colonies in the New World, and one by one they began to dot the map with red. A charter to the Virginia Company led to the first permanent English settlement at Jamestown in 1607. In 1620 the *Mayflower* carried a small band of religious dissenters—Puritans, the "pilgrims" as they were called—to New Plymouth near Cape Cod. And a few years later in 1632 Lord Baltimore founded the colony of Maryland as a haven for another group of dissenters, this time Roman Catholics. Other colonies were founded over the next century, until in 1732 the thirteenth, Georgia, was established. For the most part they soon graduated from simple trading posts into permanent areas of colonization, with the citizens developing constitutions and claiming "the rights of Englishmen." Indeed it was as early as 1619 that the first representative assembly in the Americas met at Jamestown, Virginia.

By 1700 the English in North America had so prospered that they could boast a total population approximately thirteen times greater than that of New France. Even in Canada they were inching themselves in. Newfoundland was colonized in 1610, and in 1670 England's flag flew as far north as the Hudson Bay area when Charles II granted a charter to Prince Rupert and his associates as the "Governor and Company of Adventurers trading into Hudson's Bay."

Nevertheless, for 17th century Englishmen the mainland colonies of the New World seemed a relatively poor investment. By far the most important were those in the West Indies where, between 1609 and 1655, England acquired eight islands. These were most profitable, first for the raising of tobacco and cotton and later for the production of sugar. As the "sugar islands" they quickly became England's prize colonies, for sugar yielded a value per acre three times that of tobacco and its price remained steadier.

Meanwhile on the other side of the world more English ventures were prospering. On the last day of 1600 Queen Elizabeth I issued a charter to "The Governor and Company of Merchants of London Trading to the East Indies"—the mighty East India Company. At first the Company, whose shares brought a steady annual profit of twenty to twenty-five per cent, traded with Java, Sumatra, and the Moluccas; but soon it concentrated its efforts on India. Between 1612 and 1687 strategic trading posts were set up at Surat (north of Bombay), Madras, and Calcutta, a great triangle from which all of India might be dominated. The whole of Europe felt the effect of England's new link with the East as exotic products—coffee, tea, raw silk, and cotton—flooded the West. In 1650 the English were importing one hundred thousand pieces of Indian cotton; within a generation they were importing two million pieces a year.

By the end of the 17th century, then, the colonial picture had changed drastically. Portugal's power was generally confined to Brazil,[1] the Spanish Empire had passed its peak, and the Dutch were about to drop out of the race. But France and England each wanted a monopoly of too many areas. A conflict of interest was inevitable, and a series of colonial and world wars clouded the horizon. Which empire was the stronger? On the one hand the French colonies had a measure of unity and discipline, whereas the English suffered from a lack of both. Nevertheless the English empire had two great advantages: sea power and population. In the end these were to prove decisive.

5. THE WARS FOR EMPIRE

The European wars of the late 17th and 18th centuries not only buffeted the continent, but had repercussions in the colonies as well. Let us see how they affected both Europe and North America.

---

[1] Even when Philip II absorbed Portugal in 1580 the Portuguese empire had remained independent. In 1668, Portugal herself was again recognized by Spain as independent and separate.

The Sport of Kings

Warfare during the first three-quarters of the 18th century was, as far as the civilian population was concerned, more humane and civilized than it had been during the Thirty Years' War. This change was due to economic and social circumstances. For one thing, armies and navies had become more expensive to operate as they increased in size. A measure of this increase can be seen in the following table:

	STANDING ARMIES	
	1740	*1784*
French	190 000	300 000
British	18 000	58 000
Austrian	108 000	282 000
Russian	130 000	290 000

Navies grew at a similar rate.

If the taxes were to be raised to support such large military establishments, then the productive part of the population could not be disrupted. War was not yet a patriotic affair. Officers were drawn mostly from the nobility; privates and ordinary seamen, on the other hand, were not even drawn from the working classes, but were conscripted or impressed from the ranks of the unemployed, or, in many instances, hired from abroad. In these circumstances, loyalty and discipline could hardly be expected:

To camp near a large woods, to conduct a night march, to send out a foraging party, or to grant sailors shore leave was to invite wholesale desertion. Sailors had to be kept aboard ship and soldiers had to march in close order by day and carry their supplies with them. As a result, armies could not travel more than five days' march from their base of supplies, military objectives had to be limited, and wars tended to degenerate into sieges.

Frederick the Great did not mince words on the matter:

If a soldier during an action looks about as if to flee, or so much as sets foot outside the line, the non-commissioned officer standing

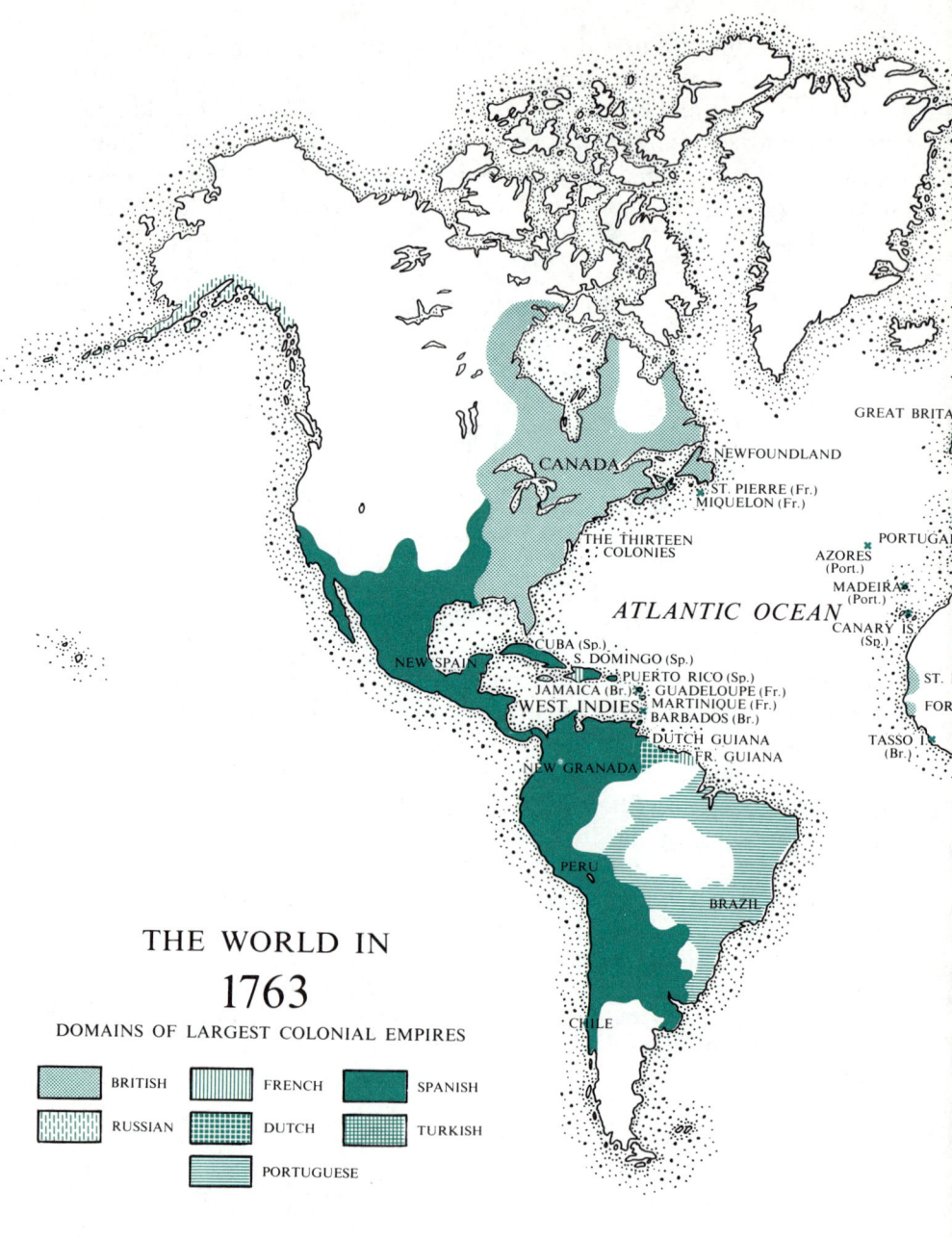

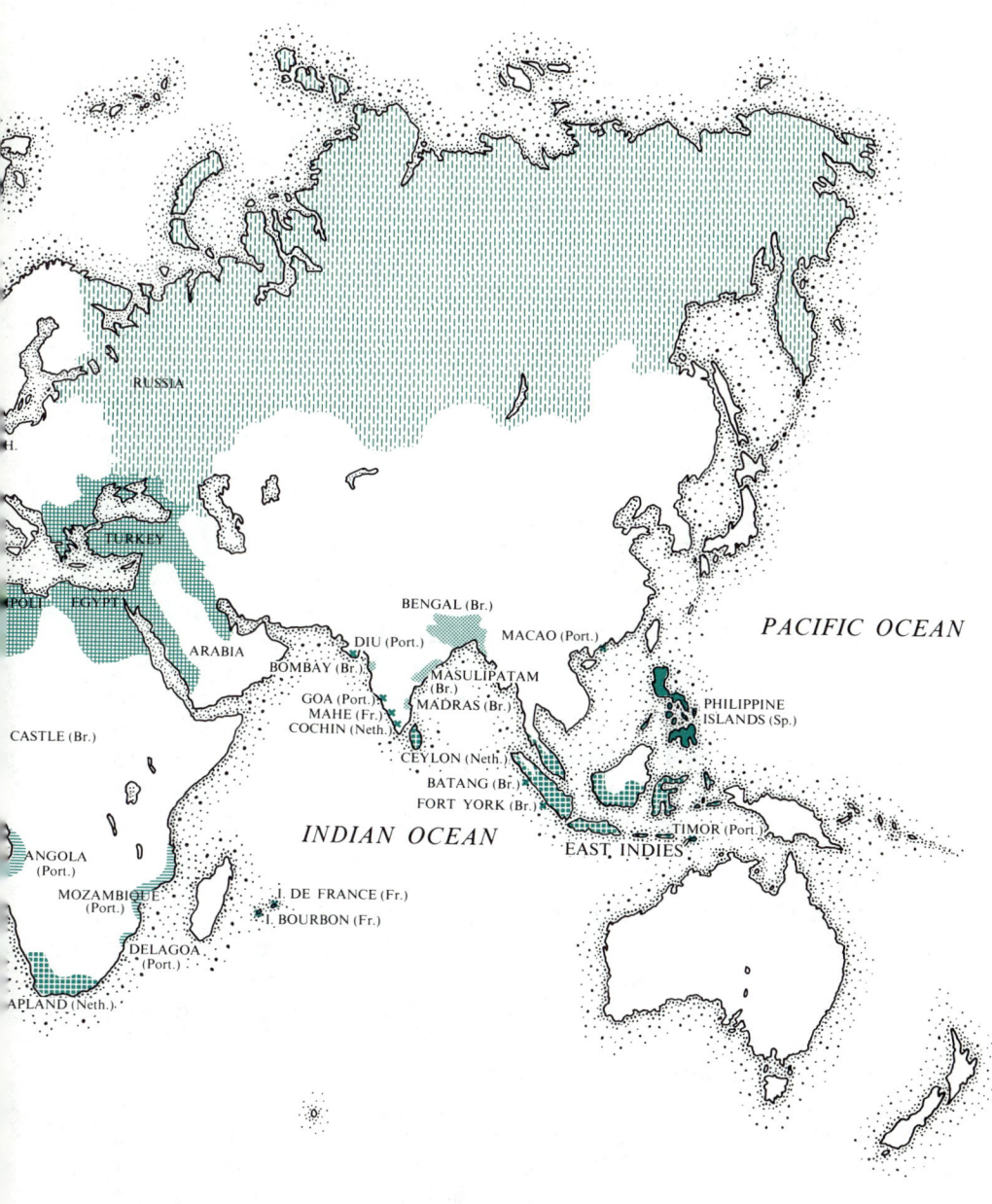

behind him will run him through with his bayonet and kill him on the spot.

Eighteenth century warfare was fought mostly by men who had no interest in the outcome, and there was, therefore, a good deal of truth in the description of it as a sport of kings. It was only in the American and French Revolutions of the last quarter of the century that war again fired the masses and became a thing of fanaticism.

France Loses the Leadership of Europe

Now began a series of wars in which England and France lined up on opposite sides, and backwashes of the European struggles struck shores around the world. The first three wars spread to America from Europe, but the fourth had its beginning right in the Ohio River Valley.

THE FIRST FOUR WORLD WARS			
In Europe		*In America*	
1688-97	War of the League of Augsburg	King William's War	1689-97
1701-13	War of the Spanish Succession	Queen Anne's War	1702-13
1740-48	War of the Austrian Sucession	King George's War	1744-48
1756-63	Seven Years' War	French and Indian War	1754-63

The first two of these "World Wars" were not fought simply over commercial rights in the Atlantic basin, or to decide the disposition of the Spanish lands, or even because of the personal ambitions of Louis XIV. Rather they involved the whole question of the balance of military power in Europe. Before 1688 France towered over all the other nations on the continent, but by the end of the 17th century there were two challengers to her military power: England and Austria. In the 18th century there followed a third and fourth "World War." These, as always, were caused by a collision of interests—in this case the expanding economic preserves of England and France who were now competing all over the world. This friction was coupled with a radical disturbance of the balance of power in Europe, a disturbance triggered by the desire of Prussia to gain more land to support her army—the very army which was the means of obtaining more land.

The War of the League of Augsburg forced Louis XIV to give up plans to incorporate certain German territories into France, and to abandon his support of the exiled James II against William and Mary. For although Louis won land battles, the combined Dutch and English fleets were too much for the French navy. In this war the colonies—India and the Americas—saw fighting, with the New Englanders, for example, capturing Port Royal in Nova Scotia.

Four years later Louis again girded himself for action. This time he was determined to put his grandson on the Spanish throne, and the resulting War of the Spanish Succession raised up a "Grand Alliance" of England, the Netherlands, Austria, and Prussia against France. It was a humbling experience for Louis. On the battlefields of Europe English troops under the Duke of Marlborough (an ancestor of Sir Winston Churchill) chastised the French armies, while an Anglo-Dutch fleet wrested Gibraltar from Spain. In America French-led Indians massacred New Englanders, who retaliated by again taking Port Royal. The war ended by the Treaty of Utrecht (1713), which recognized Louis' grandson as the Spanish king but gave England Nova Scotia, Newfoundland, and the area around Hudson Bay. France's North American colonies now had good reason to feel threatened.

Next came the War of the Austrian Succession. Touched off by Frederick the Great's seizure of Silesia in 1740, it also reverberated along the frontiers of North America. The New Englanders, supported by the British navy, managed to capture Louisbourg, the great French fortress that commanded the Gulf of St. Lawrence from Cape Breton Island—only, to their disgust, to have it handed back to France by the peace terms.

Finally came the mightiest struggle of them all. Although English colonial speculators had secured grants in the Ohio Valley, the French decided to build the strong outpost of Fort Duquesne (modern Pittsburgh) there in order to back their claims to this rich valley. In 1754 Lieutenant-Colonel George Washington, commanding a force of one hundred and fifty Virginia militiamen, met some French troops in the forests about sixty-five kilometres from Fort Duquesne. Shots were exchanged—shots that ricocheted around the world. The next year at the urging of New England the British ordered the cruel but understandable deportation of several thousand French Acadians from Nova Scotia lest they become a "fifth column."

This small French and Indian War should have stayed small; but it was to become entangled with the mother countries' struggles in Europe. By 1756 war between England and France was officially declared, and soon another state, Prussia, became inextricably involved, with telling effect in the great Anglo-French duel for empire. In the end, France was so pinned down in Europe by Prussian activities that the British war minister, William Pitt the Elder, made this shrewd observation: "America was conquered in Germany."

Prussia's involvement in the whole affair had sprung from a deep-seated distrust of Russia's new strength. Fearful of encirclement and a two-front war, Frederick the Great had turned to England for an ally. Then without waiting to be attacked by Austria, Russia, and France, he marched into Saxony. A "diplomatic revolution" had thus turned these erstwhile enemies into new-found friends. On the other hand, England and Austria, who had fought France in the three previous world wars, now fought each other. But England and France, who had already been at war for two years in North America, as usual found themselves on opposite sides. The Seven Years' War went on to infect the West Indies, the Philippines, Africa, and India.

In Europe, Frederick managed to beat back France, Austria, and Russia, three first-class Powers whose combined populations were ten times that of Prussia. Meanwhile, after some initial defeats, it appeared victory would come to the British in America. Louisbourg fell in 1758, Quebec in 1759, and Montreal in 1760. The war dragged out for three more years before the Treaty of Paris (1763) provided Britain with a completely victorious settlement. France was left some West Indian possessions, and two fishing islets off Newfoundland's south shore, St. Pierre and Miquelon. England acquired New France and—from Spain—Florida. All America east of the Mississippi was now in the orbit of the English-speaking world.

Britain emerged from the Seven Years' War the greatest naval and colonial power in the world. By the same token France ceased to be the arbiter of Europe.

The Scientific Revolution

> Our century has more history in its hundred years than had the whole world in the previous four thousand years; more books have been published in the last century than in the five thousand years before.
> —Campanella, *The City of the Sun* (1602)

In 1543, three years before Michelangelo became chief architect of St. Peter's and three years before Luther died, there was published a book with the provocative title *On the Revolutions of the Heavenly Spheres*. Its author was a Pole, Nicholas Copernicus, the man who is usually considered to have set the first pebble rolling in the avalanche of ideas which was to produce the most marked change in the course of western civilization since the birth of Christ. We are speaking, of course, of the Scientific Revolution.

The new ideas which added up to that revolutionary change were introduced between the middle of the 16th century and the beginning of the 18th. What were they? Who introduced them, and what was their effect?

1. THE NEW UNIVERSE

Contrary to popular belief, scientific observation had existed during the later Middle Ages. But such observation was strictly limited, and there was little questioning of the traditional Aristotelian picture of the universe. It was characteristic of the medieval mind to seek answers through preconceived concepts, rather than by the inductive method of observing and then attempting to explain the observation. Thus the question "What kind of an orbit does a planet follow?" would be answered "circular" on the grounds that the circle was the perfect pattern and God would surely cause the heavenly bodies He had created to move only in perfect patterns! If we are to appreciate the magnitude of the achievement of 16th and 17th century scientists, we must begin by examining the universe as the men of the Middle Ages conceived it to be.

Nicholas Copernicus had virtually finished his great work on astronomy ten or more years before it was finally published. "The scorn which I had to fear," he said, "in consequence of the novelty and seeming unreasonableness of my ideas, almost moved me to lay the completed work aside."

The Centre of the Universe

First of all, the earth was thought of as a solid globe at the centre of the universe. This globe was enfolded in layers of water, air, and fire, which, along with earth, formed the four elements that composed all material substances. Secondly, above the earth was the sky. Medieval men believed that there was a whole series of invisible spheres, ten in all, to which the moon, planets, and stars were fixed. These crystalline spheres, transparent and impenetrable, turned round the motionless earth once every twenty-four hours, while stuck to them like jewels were the stars, radiating their own light.

By the later Middle Ages astronomical observations had led to data that had to be fitted in with Aristotle's original pattern of spheres. Nothing daunted, theorists had by the 16th century arrived at more than eighty spheres, some riding on the backs of others, in order to account for the revolutions of the heavens. Yet despite its complexity, the system was capable of making accurate predictions about the future locations of stars. The earth, so the theory held, was the centre of the universe, and while the skies turned it remained motionless. In fact, the reason bodies fell earthward when they dropped was simply that they sought out the place of ultimate heaviness in the universe—the earth. This, strange though it may seem to us, was the picture of the earth and the universe that dominated astronomical thought from the 4th century B.C. to the 16th century A.D.

But there were those who questioned some of Aristotle's ideas. One man felt that a universe of eighty and more cumbersome spheres was a rather ugly thing for God to make, so for a generation he worked at devising a simpler universe which would still adequately explain the movements of earth, planets, and stars. This man was Copernicus.[1]

To contrive his new universe Copernicus turned back to the old idea of Aristarchus of Samos (3rd century B.C.) that the earth rotated on its axis and moved about the sun. Copernicus' plan still required rotating spheres, but a mere thirty-four of them! And they rotated not around the earth but around the sun, to form a *heliocentric* universe. The earth was fixed to the third sphere and revolved on its own axis every twenty-four hours, while the moon

[1]For dates of some of the leading figures of the Scientific Revolution see the table on p. 87.

rotated around the earth. Copernicus' theories were well known during his lifetime and were circulated by some of his disciples, though his final statement, *On the Revolutions of the Heavenly Spheres*, was not published until the year of his death (the first copy, it is said, was brought to him the day he died).

Although the Copernican theories provided a tidier plan for the heavens they failed to answer two questions. Why must there be spheres at all? And why do bodies, when dropped, fall toward the earth if it is no longer the centre of the universe? Copernicus' answers to both questions marked him as a conservative. The sphere, he said, was essential because a circle was regarded as the perfect form of motion, while articles fell earthward because all spheres tended to draw their outside bodies to them in order to form more perfect spheres, just as water forms into drops. Such old-fashioned reasoning illustrates the extent to which Copernicus' system was based on philosophical deduction rather than on astronomical observation.

The truth was that though Copernicus moved the earth and put the sun at the centre of things, his reasons for doing so were hardly what we would call scientific. He had the right idea for the wrong reasons: his heliocentric universe required a new theory of motion.

Many Christians were seriously disturbed by the new idea that the earth moved; for did not Psalm 93, verse 1, read: "the world also is stablished, that it cannot be moved"? Luther scorned Copernicus as "the fool who would overturn the whole science of astronomy," and most other 16th century references were equally uncomplimentary. There were also certain upsetting events. In 1572 an incident occurred which has been described as "a greater shock to European thought than the publication of the Copernican hypothesis itself." The shocking event? A new star appeared in the sky and shone for two years before disappearing. Why was this so disturbing? Because all stars were supposed to be fixed on spheres, and to have been created by God in seven days. Where, then, had this new star come from? And where did it go?

An even more startling event occurred a few years later, in 1577, when a new comet streaked across the sky cutting a path straight through the "impenetrable" crystal spheres. It was a shattering experience. The famous Danish astronomer Tycho Brahe roundly declared that he did not believe in the existence of spheres, though he did believe that the earth stood still. Clearly some more satisfactory universe than the Copernican was required, and it would have to be based on astronomical observation.

LEADERS OF THE SCIENTIFIC REVOLUTION

1473-1543—Nicholas Copernicus
1514-1564—Andreas Vesalius
1537-1619—Fabricius of Aquapendente
1546-1601—Tycho Brahe
1561-1626—Francis Bacon
1564-1642—Galileo Galilei
1571-1630—Johann Kepler
1578-1657—William Harvey
1596-1650—René Descartes
1608-1679—Alfonso Borelli
1642-1727—Isaac Newton

A Mighty Mechanism

Before 1609 Galileo Galilei, a Florentine, made a great discovery that changed the course of his life. He describes it here:

About ten months ago a rumour came to our ears, that an optical instrument had been made by a certain Dutchman, by aid of which visible objects, though very distant from the eye of the observer, were seen distinctly as if near to him. . . . The same was confirmed to me a few days later by a letter written from Paris by the noble Frenchman Jacob Badovere of Paris, and so I set myself to inquire into the principles and means by which I might be able to arrive at the discovery of a similar instrument, in which a little later I succeeded by a study of the theory of Refraction. And so I prepared a leaden tube, at the ends of which I fixed two glass lenses, both plane on one face, one of them being spherically convex, the other concave on the other face. Then applying my eye to the concave end, I saw objects as quite large and near, for they appeared three times nearer and nine times larger than before . . . . At length, sparing no labour and no expense, I succeeded in making an instrument so excellent that things seen through it appeared nearly a thousand times larger and more than thirty times nearer, than if viewed by natural vision alone.

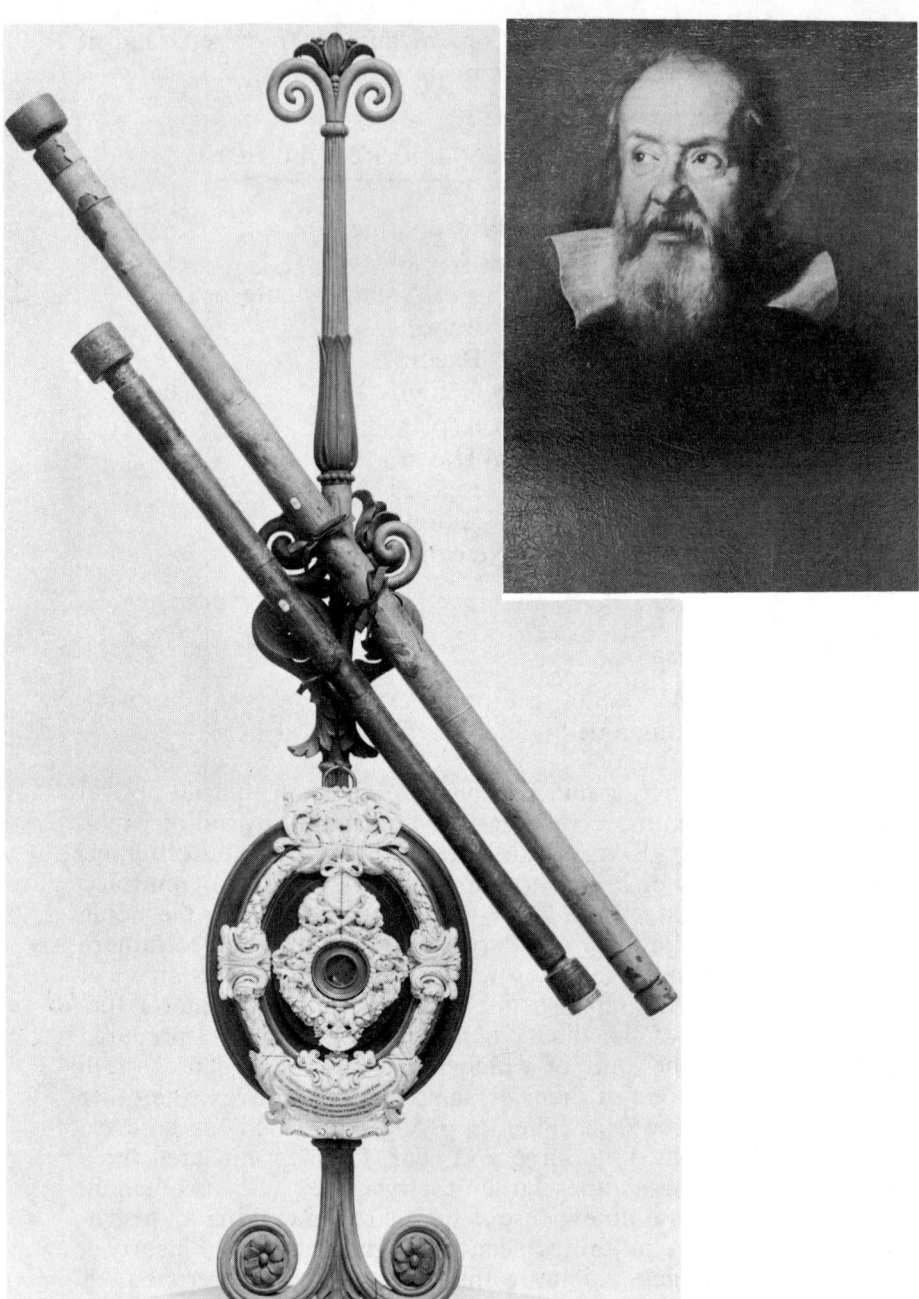

"My dear Kepler—what would you say of the learned here, who, replete with the pertinacity of the asp, have steadfastly refused to cast a glance through the telescope? Shall we laugh, or shall we cry?"—Galileo, writing to Johann Kepler.

The writer of these words was a great scientist learned in mathematics, physics, mechanics, optics, astronomy, and the classics. When this brilliant teacher, so popular that a hall seating two thousand was necessary for his lectures at the University of Padua, turned his telescope on the heavens he discovered some amazing things. He saw Jupiter had four moons of its own (astronomers now see eleven), and formed, therefore, a sort of miniature solar system revolving around the sun. He also turned his telescope on the moon, and his description of what he observed may be read in Source Reading III-3. He saw Venus as a round object whose outline altered like the moon's, and which must, therefore, be dependent on the sun for its illumination. And—most amazing of all—he discovered that the sun, the unchanging and immaculate sun, was spotted. So enraged were the Aristotelians by this last discovery that they suggested that the sun-spots were an intervening cloud, or that Galileo was looking at flaws in his own lenses. But there they were, nonetheless, sun-spots whose movement suggested the rotation of the sun itself.

Galileo put all this evidence and more into a book called *Dialogues on the Two Chief Systems of the World* (1632). The book was an attempt to demolish Aristotelian and Ptolemaic astronomy, but Galileo's greatest concern was to establish Copernican views. He seems to have accepted the theory of spheres so completely that he used fallacious arguments to demonstrate the rotation of the earth.

Galileo's enthusiastic advocacy of the heliocentric system brought him into disfavour with the Roman Catholic Church. In 1616 the Inquisition declared the proposition that the sun was the centre of the universe "absurd in philosophy, and formally heretical, because expressly contrary to Holy Scripture," while the proposition that the earth rotated once every twenty-four hours on its axis was "open to the same censure in philosophy, and [was] at least erroneous as to faith." The Church proceeded to put Copernicus' book on the *Index*, and Galileo was ordered by Pope Paul V not to "hold, teach, and defend" these theories. Nevertheless he eventually published his *Dialogues*, whereupon he was tried by the Inquisition, recanted, and was confined to his house for life.

Though most famous as an astronomer, Galileo also founded the science of mechanics. He proved Aristotelian ideas of motion to be false, invented the thermometer, tried to measure the velocity of light, and succeeded in finding the mass of air, probably being the first to produce a partial vacuum.

Yet, remarkable as he was, Galileo did not really improve on Copernican astronomy or solve the problem of the earth's movement. It was left to a brilliant German contemporary, Johann Kepler, to discover the laws of planetary motion.

Kepler was so impressed with the order and harmony of the universe that he set about trying to find the mathematical formulae that must govern the whole system. Any such generalizations, he reasoned, would have to be based on astronomical observations, not philosophical concepts. "The celestial machine," said Kepler, "is to be likened not to a divine organism but rather to a clockwork." And so he began with observations of the planet Mars. Because Kepler held the Aristotelian theory that any moving body would stop unless it was continually being pushed along, he originally accounted for the movement of the planets by assuming that rays of force coming from the sun, like spokes in a wheel, propelled the planets forward as the sun revolved. Yet his observations of Mars showed him that the planet did not move along a circular path but rather in an oval or ellipse. Furthermore, he found, a planet's rate of orbit varied.

From these observations Kepler deduced two laws of planetary motion, laws which were to have radical repercussions when they were announced in his book, the *New Astronomy or Celestial Physics* (1609). Ten years later he added a third law.

KEPLER'S THREE LAWS OF PLANETARY MOTION

1. Planets describe ellipses about the sun, the sun being in one focus.
2. Planets move so that the line joining the sun to the planet sweeps out equal areas of the ellipse in equal periods of time.
3. The squares of the periodic times of the planets are proportional to the cubes of the major axes of their orbits.

These laws simply mean that planets move in elliptical orbits, speeding up as they near the sun and slowing down as they recede from it, and the size of a planet's orbit is proportional to the time required for one revolution around the sun.

What Kepler, assisted by others' observations, had done was to smash once and for all those persistent crystalline spheres which had spun unchallenged from Aristotle through Copernicus, and about which even his great contemporary Galileo was ambiguously silent. Kepler firmly denounced the belief in spheres, or "orbs" as he called them:

Neither indeed is to be feared that the lunar orbs may be forced out of position, compressed by the close proportions of [other celestial] bodies, if they are not included and buried in that orb itself. For it is absurd and monstrous to set these bodies in the sky, endowed with certain properties of matter, which do not resist the passage of any other solid body. Certainly many will not fear to doubt that there are in general any of these Adamantine [i.e., impenetrable] orbs in the sky, that the stars are transported through space and the ethereal air, free from these fetters of the orbs, by a certain divine virtue regulating their courses by the understanding of geometrical proportions.

Kepler's observations checked and his laws held; but he did not know why. The man who was to make the grand synthesis of Galileo and Kepler, and who was to provide the answers as to why the universe operated as it did, was Isaac Newton. So great was Newton's work that for a century and a half after him astronomers and mathematicians did little more than develop the theories that he had initiated.

Born in Woolsthorpe, England, in 1642 (the year Galileo died), Newton's fondness for books and mechanical contrivances overruled his mother's early determination to make a country squire of him, and made his parents decide to send him to Cambridge University. The year after Newton's graduation the Great Plague (1665) broke out in London and the surrounding country, with the result that the university closed and Newton went home to spend the next two years in retirement. It was during these years that most of Newton's great ideas first came to him, and it is to this period of his life that the famous story of the apple belongs.

When the plague receded Newton returned to his university and eventually became professor of mathematics. After years of careful

"Isaac Newton combined a unique brilliance in mathematics, physics, and philosophy, with a fine skill for experimentation, which together, enabled him to contribute more to human knowledge than perhaps any other person in history." FACING: a page of calculations from Newton's manuscript to determine the orbit of Halley's comet.

deliberation he published his theories, which were summed up in what has often been called the greatest scientific book ever written, his *Mathematical Principles of Natural Philosophy* (1687).

Newton selected from among the many current theories regarding the structure of the universe and combined those he judged to be correct into one coherent system. A number of these theories of motion had already been put forward: the theory that heavenly bodies were floating in space, that they exerted an attraction or "pull" on one another, and that a body once set in motion would continue in motion until stopped by friction or some other agency. Newton demonstrated mathematically that if such theories of motion were true, the earth and the other planets would describe an ellipse around the sun—and an ellipse was what Kepler's observations had proved that they in fact did follow. At last the whole universe could be explained by mathematical laws: it was a mighty mechanism that ran like clockwork.

Newton's laws of motion became classics and his fame was

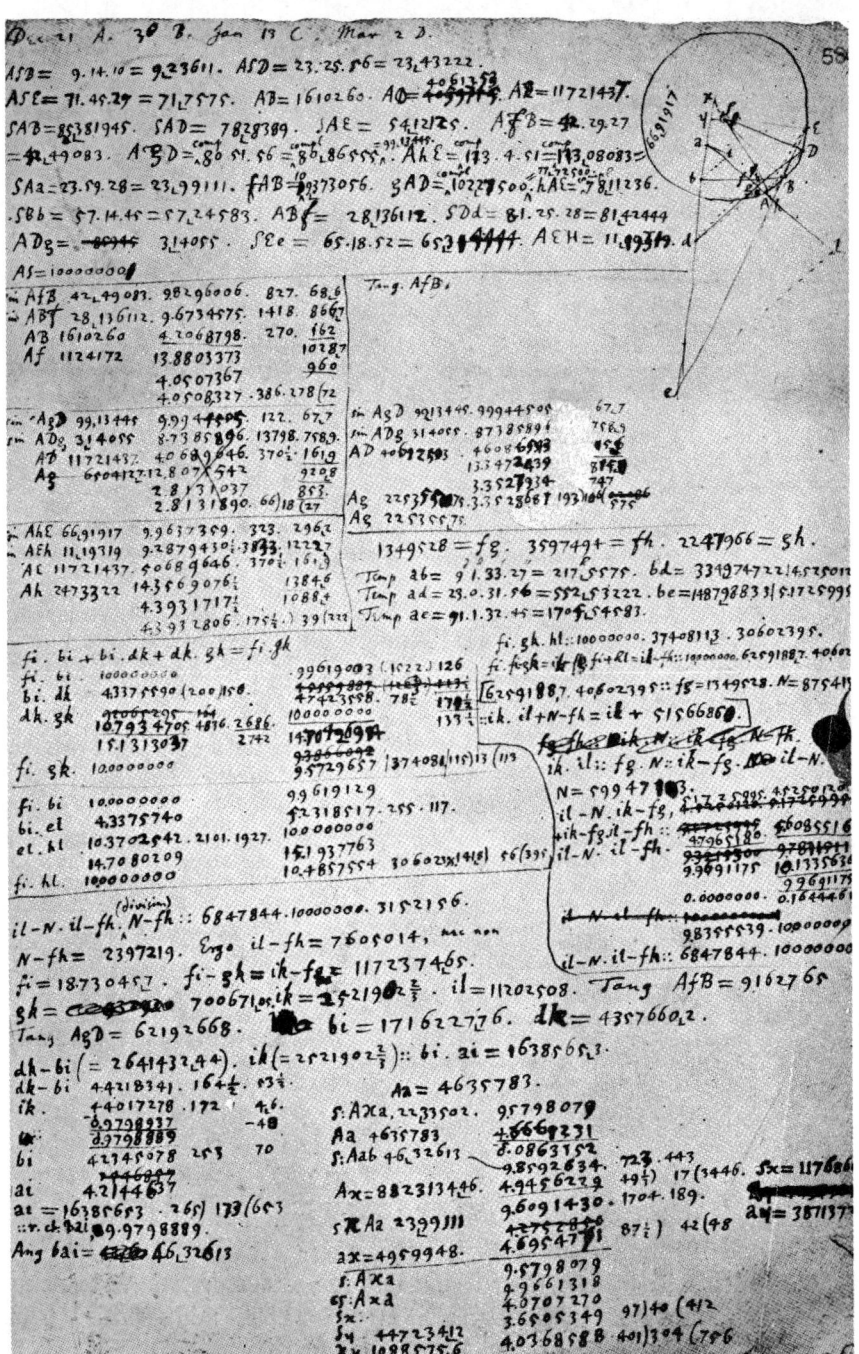

assured. By 1789 there had been at least seventy-three books published about the *Principles,* forty in English, seventeen in French, three in German, eleven in Latin, one in Portuguese, and one in Italian, many of which went through edition after edition. And he had other claims to fame, among them his work on optics and the theory of prismatic colours. But although loaded with honours in his old age, Newton himself never lost his humility: "I know not what the world will think of my labours, but to myself it seems that I have been but as a child playing on the sea-shore; now finding some pebble rather more polished, and now some shell rather more agreeably variegated than another, while the immense ocean of truth extended itself unexplored before me."

NEWTON'S THREE LAWS OF MOTION

1. A body will continue in a state of rest, or of uniform motion in a straight line, until compelled to change its state by some external force impressed upon it.
2. Every change of motion or acceleration of a body is directly proportional to the force that makes the change.
3. To every action there is always an equal and opposite reaction.

---

2. THE NEW PERSON

The only other science in which there was progress comparable to that made in astronomy was anatomy, and curiously enough the beginning of the revolution in this field coincided with that in astronomy. It was only a month after Copernicus published his epoch-making book that Vesalius published *On the Structure of the Human Body,* a treatise that laid the foundations of modern anatomy.

Vesalius had begun by accepting the teachings of Galen of Pergamum, who had summed up the knowledge of the late 2nd century A.D., and he set out to prepare editions of Galen's work. Yet he came, very reluctantly, to disagree with Galen, who had never dissected an adult human subject, and whose deductions from animal dissections led him into errors concerning human anatomy.

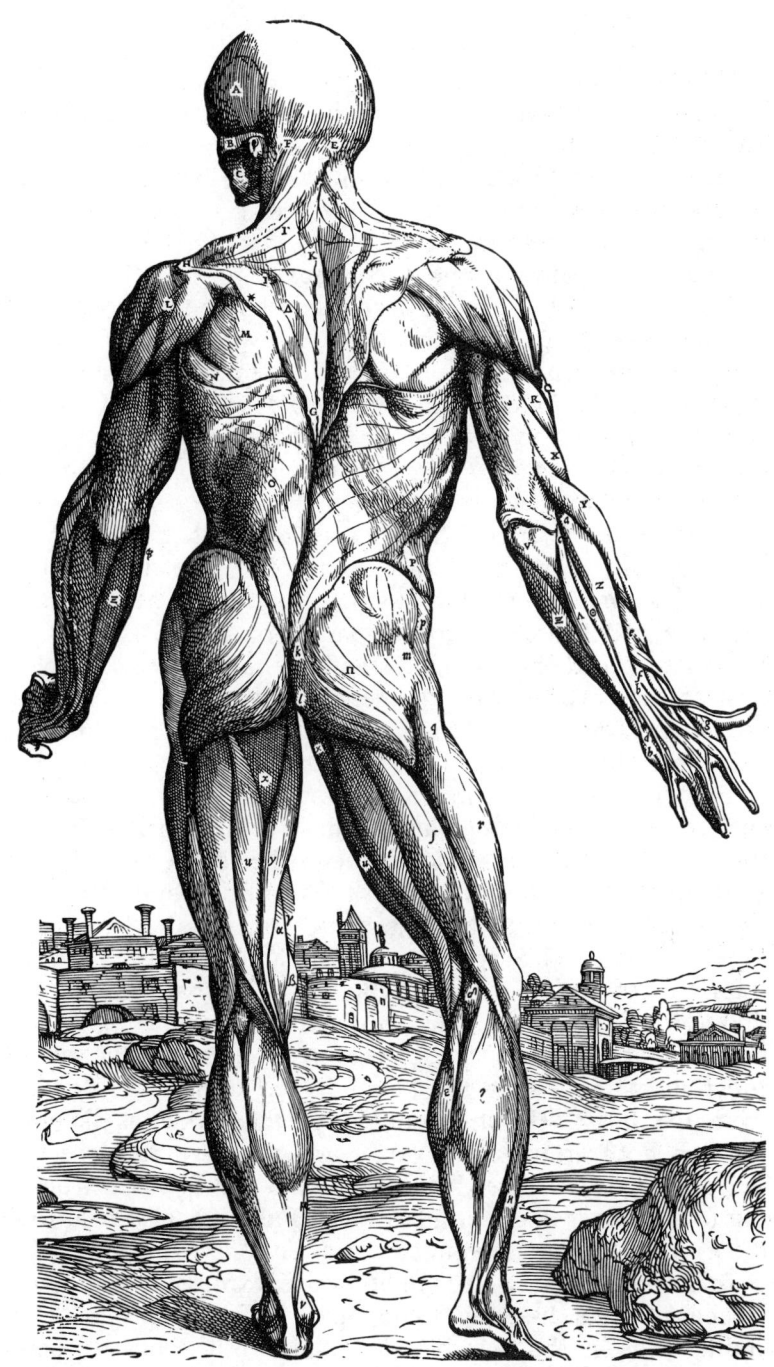

An illustration from *On the Structure of the Human Body*, written by Vesalius in 1543.

Human dissection was a relatively new technique. True, the Moslems had earlier encouraged it, but only in the 14th century had it been practised on any scale by western Europeans. Even then, such dissection as Leonardo da Vinci performed in the 15th century was not for the sake of furthering medical knowledge but to analyse the structure of the body in order to portray it more accurately in painting and sculpture.

Vesalius, however, made a science of human dissection. He set to work to explore the human body, layer by layer and bone by bone. But though he was an expert dissectionist Vesalius was still much under the influence of Galen, and was guilty of modifying at least one drawing to fit Galen's words. He also completely accepted Galen's theory regarding the functions of the heart. According to Galen, there were two kinds of blood in the body, that in the veins and that in the arteries. The venous blood was drawn into the right chamber of the heart, whence some of it seeped through a thick wall (*septum*) into the left chamber, where it was enriched by the "vital spirits" from the air and passed on to the arteries. Vesalius merely recorded that in his dissections he had been unable to find any passageway through the septum. It was a demonstration of the mighty power of God, he added, that He should be able to make blood pass through an apparently solid septum.

But there was born in 1578 a man who was not satisfied with such a pious conclusion, and who set out to discover "not from books, but from dissections" how the heart actually worked. William Harvey was educated at Cambridge and Padua, and on his return to England became a professor in the London College of Physicians and Surgeons. At Padua he had been the pupil of Fabricius of Aquapendente, who, in 1574, had written a treatise about the valves in the veins (though he was not the first to detect them). Fabricius did not, however, understand the valves' real function in preventing the blood in the veins from flowing away from the heart. He still thought of the blood as flowing away through both arteries and veins, and surmised that the valves of the veins existed merely to prevent too much blood from flowing out to the hands and feet all at once. Fabricius also held to Galen's theory that the lungs pumped air directly into the heart.

In London, Harvey began intensive explorations of the heart's mechanism. He dissected some eighty different species of animals, finding that in the cold-blooded ones—fish, frogs, serpents—the

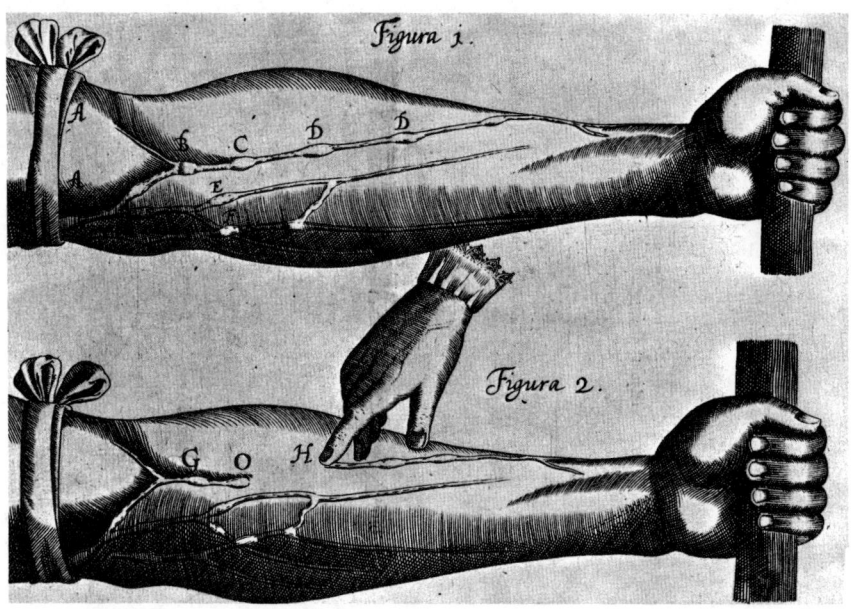

An illustration from the first edition of Harvey's treatise *An Anatomical Treatise on the Heart and the Blood.* Along with the accompanying text, it explained how blood in arteries and veins can flow in only one direction.

beating hearts could be exposed even after the subjects were dead. Harvey did not really "discover" the circulatory system, since various earlier theories had suggested certain aspects of it. What he did was, like Newton, take various theories and produce a generalization that correctly related them in a single synthesis. The resulting synthesis was published in 1628 in *An Anatomical Treatise on the Movement of the Heart and the Blood.*

Harvey's theory is familiar to all of us today. He thought of the heart as a pump rather than a filtration plant, and discovered that in a single hour a heart pumped out more than the person's own mass in blood. The arteries would burst, the veins empty unless somehow this vast flow of blood could get from the tissues into the veins and back to the heart. "I began to think," he wrote, "whether there might not be a motion, as it were a circle." In other words, the blood must *circulate.* Harvey did not, however, understand the action of the lungs; he thought they prevented the blood from boiling because of excessive heat. Nor could he trace the blood from the arterial to the venous system through the capillaries. It was not until 1661 that the microscope (which had not been available to Harvey) showed the capillaries in the lungs of the frog.

Mechanically satisfying though it is, Harvey's discovery of the circulation of the blood took up to half a century to win acceptance. Its importance was that it opened up a whole new series of problems and questions about the blood. In one particularly interesting instance, a scientist combined Harvey's work on the heart with the implications of Galileo's mechanics. Alfonso Borelli's book *On the Motion of Animals* (1680) applied mechanics to muscular movements, calculating, for example, that the power of the wing muscles of a bird is "greater by ten thousand times than the weight of the bird." The human heart was compared to a piston or a wine-press, exerting at each beat a force equal to at least sixty thousand kilograms of pressure. But Borelli, like so many others, pushed his theories too far in trying to reduce the human body to nothing more than a complex machine.

3. THE NEW METHOD

Had these successive discoveries about people and the universe in which they lived resulted in any agreement on a new method of scientific inquiry? To answer this question we must briefly consider two men: Francis Bacon and René Descartes.

Francis Bacon was the son of one of Queen Elizabeth's senior civil servants. He went to Cambridge University at the age of thirteen, stayed two years, and then entered the profession of law, becoming Lord Chancellor under James I. Unfortunately, however, he was tried and convicted for corruption, and ended his life in disgrace and banishment from the court.

We remember Bacon not for his pursuit of wealth and political power but for his views regarding scientific investigation as set forth in his treatise *Novum Organum (The New Instrument)*, published in 1620. In it he rejected the knowledge of the ancients because it divorced theory from observation and experiment, attacking, in particular, too great a dependence on the authority of Aristotle. But Bacon recognized that modern man, too, was led astray by his own idiosyncracies in thinking, and he detected four of these "idols," as he called them: the tendency to accept the statements

The title page of Sir Francis Bacon's book *Novum Organum*, the second part of his great work *Instauratio Magna*. The picture shows a ship under full sail passing between the Pillars of Hercules out of the Mediterranean into the open Atlantic. This is symbolic of Bacon's aim to replace Aristotelean (closed) logic with the free thought of the "New World" based on experiment and science. The Latin motto below the ship is translated, "Many will pass through and knowledge will be increased."

of a prominent person as authoritative; mental quirks common to the whole human race; errors carried over without question from age to age; and the personal bias of each individual.

How could both ancient and modern sources of error be avoided? By scientific investigation, said Bacon, investigation "laborious to search, ignoble to meditate, harsh to deliver, illiberal to practice, infinite in number, and minute in subtlety." In other words knowledge could be attained by following four steps:

BACON'S FOUR STEPS TO KNOWLEDGE

1. Collect reliable, tested information — for example that gained by experiment.
2. Classify and compare this material.
3. From such classification and comparison adduce generalizations and scientific laws.
4. Test these laws by further application to the phenomenon in question.

The fact, however, that Bacon approached science as a philosopher rather than as a practising scientist meant that his scientific views carried little weight. Moreover Bacon's work was limited by his times, for his contemporaries Galileo and Kepler were only just beginning to transform the universe, and Newton had not yet been born. More influential and more subtle was the work of the Frenchman René Descartes, who was thirty when Bacon died. Descartes was a strange combination of diverse characteristics. Born into a noble family and educated by the Jesuits, he served as a soldier in the Netherlands, Bavaria, and Hungary. He retired from the army to pursue his studies, first in France and then in Holland, eventually becoming the tutor of the queen of Sweden. So assiduous was he in this post that he rose each day at 04:00 to teach his royal student mathematics, as a reward for which dedication, it is said, he contracted pneumonia and died.

Descartes, who is the inventor of co-ordinate geometry, believed that the key to the universe was mathematics. His *Discourse on the Method of Rightly Conducting the Reason and Seeking for Truth in the Sciences* (1637) was written, not in Latin (as all other scientific works had been), but in the vernacular, and was an exposition of the way to find out the principles on which all of nature is based. Descartes was far better known than either Galileo or Bacon, and his Cartesian method was immensely influential.

One must begin, said Descartes, with what is certain, and from that deduce mathematically the rest of the universe. What *is* certain? For Descartes, his own existence: *I think, therefore I am*. From this initial certainty he proceeded to deduce the absolute necessity of God's existence, and from that premise went on to work out a whole system for the universe by setting up a chain of argument as precise as a geometrical proof. "You can," he once said, "substitute 'the mathematical order of nature' for 'God' wherever I use the latter term."

Once again it was the genius of Newton to unite the Baconian emphasis on experimentation with the Cartesian emphasis on the mathematical interpretation of nature, just as he had combined Galileo's telescopic observations and theories of mechanics with Kepler's laws of motion.

4. THE EFFECTS OF THE SCIENTIFIC REVOLUTION

Though we have said nothing about a whole galaxy of scientific subjects—chemistry, zoology, psychology, surgery, and geology—perhaps we may sum up from our discussion the immediate effects of the Scientific Revolution.

In the beginning, the discoveries of the Scientific Revolution were a shock to many people. Their traditional picture of the universe was shattered. Aristotle was overthrown. Even the Bible was openly questioned as doubt extended to a religion that had been anchored to hitherto unshakable physical facts. This loss of certainty is well expressed by the English poet John Donne:

> *And new philosophy calls all in doubt;*
> *The element of fire is quite put out;*
> *The sun is lost, and th' earth, and no man's wit*
> *Can well direct him where to look for it.*

Yet Donne himself wondered if adaptation to the Copernican universe might not be possible: "Methinks the new astronomy is thus applicable well, that we which are a little earth should rather move towards God, than that He which is fulfilling, and can come no wither, should move toward us." In fact the discrediting of some traditions could provide a challenge to work out a new set of beliefs more in accord with proven scientific knowledge.

As the 17th century wore on, doubt began to be replaced by a sense of both confidence and exhilaration, a feeling very pithily expressed in Alexander Pope's epitaph on Newton:

> *Nature and Nature's laws lay hid in night;*
> *God said,* Let Newton be! *and all was light!*

Indeed it seemed to many that the task of science was not to attack religion but rather to show how great a mechanic God was; for if the universe was a machine there had to be a mechanic to build it and start it going, after which it ran along pretty much on its own in accordance with certain mathematical laws. Moreover man, too, was a machine, a combination of pumps, levers, and lenses. The way in which scientific laws affected religion was something to be worked out in the second half of the 18th century.

It was to be expected that methods of science, which had not been carefully defined in the 17th century, should steadily improve. Learned societies where scientists could meet to discuss their latest theories and pool their knowledge were formed, the earliest being the Florentine Academy of Experiment (1657), followed by the Royal Society of England (1660), the French Academy of Sciences (1666), the Berlin Academy (1700), the St. Petersburg Academy of Russia (1724), and others. The attention given by such organizations to experiment and precision helped prepare the way for the inventions of the Industrial Revolution.

And so the new science sprang into being—a science that knew no nationality: Polish, Italian, German, and French scientists had their discoveries synthesized by two Englishmen, Newton and Harvey. And the confidence it bred knew no bounds, a confidence which ought to be easy for our 20th century, with its perpetual scientific competition, to understand. So great was this faith in science, so avidly did learned societies pursue its techniques, that men had the feeling they were witnessing a new age—as indeed they were. Perhaps the Scientific Revolution is more characteristic of modern times than any changes of the Renaissance or the Reformation. It was far richer than the scientific development of the Medieval Transition, far more specialized than the Renaissance science of a Leonardo. No earlier civilization had experienced anything like it: it was peculiarly western, peculiarly European, peculiarly modern.

The men of the Scientific Revolution felt that, at the very least, history had made a new beginning.

UNIT TWO | # THE AGE OF REVOLUTION

5 The Age of Enlightenment

I disapprove of what you say, but I will defend to the death your right to say it.
—Attributed to Voltaire

If we were to pick a single dominant figure to symbolize the 18th century it would not be a king or a churchman, a great statesman or a victorious general, but an intellectual—a thinker—for the 18th century was above all "the age of the arisen intellect." Everywhere, thought was awakened and genius flourished. It was in this period that Bach made his great contribution to the development of modern music, that Richardson and Fielding launched the modern English novel, and that practical geniuses applied the new scientific knowledge to improve man's health, wealth, and comfort. It was an age, too, in which autocratic kings and queens read the books (and sought the company) of Europe's most eminent thinkers and took pride in introducing "enlightened" reforms.

1. THE IMPACT OF "SCIENTIFIC" THOUGHT

We have already traced the beginnings of modern science in the 17th century and the way in which men came to look at the world, and each other, from a new "scientific" point of view. But it was in the 18th century, often called "The Age of Enlightenment," that scientific ideas first began to be applied widely to everyday life. It was in this period that men began to experiment with electricity, made their first tentative aerial flights by balloon, and discovered effective ways to fight smallpox and scurvy. Farmers with a "scientific" outlook revolutionized methods of agriculture that had been accepted without question and practised without change for centuries. Within a few decades they had doubled and tripled the average mass of livestock and increased by almost 2.5 times the grain yield of a hectare of land. Engineers invented factory machines to mass-produce cloth and, most important of all, by learning how to harness the energy of steam they made available one of the greatest new sources of power developed since the invention of the windmill, the water wheel, and the horse collar.

As science and technology gained widespread acceptance and prestige, bold thinkers attempted to apply "scientific methods" to every aspect of life. If a person's intellect could bring about such startling improvements in farming and industry, then why not also in politics and economics or even in ethics and religion? With a new and unbounded confidence in human reason, men and women questioned, as never before, old-established traditions and ideas. They re-examined every venerable institution and each blindly-accepted belief, asking "Is it rational? Is it natural?" At the same time they developed a deep, non-religious faith that human life was becoming progressively better and better. People of this era believed that reason alone, when applied in all areas of human activity, could lead to perfection and happiness in both society and the individual. This 18th century faith in progress can be contrasted with both the medieval attitude, which never thought of perfection divorced from God, and the attitude of the Renaissance person who still felt inferior to the ancient Greeks and Romans. The Age of Enlightenment was both a period of confident inquiry and a time of surging optimism. For educated men and women it had this in common with our present era—it was an exciting time to be alive.

Atheists and Deists

One result of the elevation of rational thought was an erosion of former religious loyalties, and a greater concern with the material affairs of this world. What need was there for a God of Love, for forgiveness and salvation, when human nature was not only basically good but perfectible? A few extreme radicals denounced all religion and espoused atheism. Others, known as Deists, renounced orthodox religion while continuing to believe in God as the "First Cause" or "Supreme Intelligence." A popular Deist image, arising from Newton's description of the ordered physical universe, pictured God as an almighty watchmaker who had created the universe, set it in motion, and then left it to run by itself according to natural laws. That God should be Redeemer as well as Creator was considered both unnatural and unnecessary.

Important social consequences resulted from the new approach to religion. While the great bulk of ordinary people still adhered to traditional religious institutions, churchmen definitely declined in influence and prestige, and businessmen, the nobility, and rulers, as well as a considerable number of ordinary people, threw off restraints imposed by religion. At the same time, as people wavered in their religious beliefs or cast them aside, they became less inclined to persecute those whose beliefs differed from their own. Moreover, with the increased confidence in reason and intellect, superstition declined; the spirit of secularism was spreading throughout society with increasing rapidity. It was well said that in the Age of Enlightenment, people had "never argued so much about religion and practised it so little."

The Prestige of England

Although rational thinking was to reach its full flower in France, it was England and the English system of government that provided the initial inspiration. Europeans were deeply influenced and impressed by England's revolution of 1688 that had established parliamentary government, accompanied by freedom of the press and a large measure of religious toleration. Admiration for Britain was unbounded.

The "Glorious Revolution" of 1688 triumphantly vindicated the great English philosopher, John Locke. Locke championed the rights of the individual. He condemned religious intolerance as being both ineffective and immoral. He stated that it was the prime duty of a sovereign to defend the rights of each one of his subjects to life, liberty, and property, for he claimed that it was only in return for the protection of these rights that subjects submitted to be ruled. Locke called this agreement between a sovereign and his people a "social contract," and stated that if a ruler broke his trust by failing to protect the liberty of his subjects, then they in turn had the right to rebel and seek another ruler. What Locke had done was to declare that just as surely as Newton's law of gravity governed the physical universe, so there existed "natural rights" and laws that ruled society.

2. THE SPREAD OF NEW KNOWLEDGE

In France this novel, exciting, "scientific" way of looking at the world was enthusiastically taken up and developed by a group of radical thinkers, known collectively as the *philosophes*. These men turned upon 18th century society the cold, clear light of rational thought, and exposed much that was unjust, outmoded, and rotten. Their weapon was the pen, and the spread of education amongst the growing middle class provided them with a ready audience.

Throughout western Europe there was an insatiable demand for reading matter of all kinds. Pamphlets, periodicals, and news sheets —forerunners of the modern daily paper—were avidly read and discussed. There was also an eager demand for dictionaries, encyclopedias, atlases, and reference books of all kinds, by readers who were growing increasingly thoughtful and well-informed. The *philosophes* were brilliant popularizers and propagandists who catered to the public demand by developing a style of writing that was clear, readable, and often extremely witty. Moreover, since French had replaced Latin as the common language used by educated people throughout Europe, the stimulating views of the *philosophes* quickly spread across Europe. "Enlightened" ideas were soon being quoted and discussed as avidly at the Russian court in St. Petersburg as in the fashionable drawing rooms of Paris. Their effect was felt even in the distant British colonies of North America.

Between 1751 and 1772, Denis Diderot, a French novelist and playwright, with the aid of Jean d'Alembert, performed the prodigious task of collecting and summarizing the new ideas and new knowledge in a thirty-five volume Encyclopedia, published in Paris. *L'Encyclopédie* contained articles by the most distinguished scientists, historians, and philosophers of the day. Diderot himself contributed over a thousand articles, and there was even a discourse on cosmetics submitted anonymously by the king's mistress, Madame de Pompadour. To avoid censorship, *L'Encyclopédie* ostensibly accepted the orthodox religious view of the world, but scattered throughout the volumes were merciless, if indirect, attacks on traditional Christian beliefs, and its whole tone reflected the skeptical, inquiring, and scientific outlook of the age. In article after article the encyclopedists proclaimed their faith in

Two illustrations from *L'Encyclopedie*, which serve the double purpose of informing readers about the manufacture of glass and at the same time of contrasting the slow, almost primitive, methods used in France with the "scientific" technology that was carrying Britain into the Industrial Revolution.

THE AGE OF ENLIGHTENMENT

human nature and in the natural rights of man, and denounced the cruelties, the superstitions, and social inequalities that marred European society. Not surprisingly, this work was officially suppressed and "Encyclopedist" became a term of abuse to describe any "rationalist" or liberal thinker.

3. IDEAS THAT CHANGED THE WORLD

Among the many eminent contributors to *L'Encyclopédie* were three of the most famous *philosophes* of the period, Montesquieu, Voltaire and Rousseau. They came from different backgrounds, and often disagreed vehemently in their views, yet they were unanimous in their condemnation of society as it existed and were certain that life could be made very much better for the great majority of humanity. All three were literary geniuses, and their views—brilliantly expressed—opened the way for the sweeping changes that were to come with the American and French revolutions.

Montesquieu

Montesquieu, an aristocrat by birth, made an exhaustive study of many forms of government and published his conclusions in a famous work entitled *The Spirit of the Laws* (1714). There was, he decided, no one ideal form of government. On the contrary, a government should be adapted to the size, the climate, and the social maturity of the people for whom it was intended. He considered, for instance, that a republican democracy was most suitable for very small states, a limited monarchy ideal for nations of a middle size (such as his own France), and despotism best for vast countries with tropical climates.

But Montesquieu's most important doctrines stemmed from a two-year visit to England which filled him with enthusiasm. "England," he declared, "is the freest country in the world." As Montesquieu saw it, power in Britain was cleverly divided among the executive (the monarch), the legislature (parliament), and the judiciary (the courts). These separate powers checked and balanced each other so that no one branch of government could enjoy unlimited power and so become oppressive. His analysis of the British constitution was mistaken, for he failed to recognize the great powers of Parliament, but nevertheless his views had widespread influence. Montesquieu compared the unlimited power of the French king unfavourably with the limited monarchy of Britain where, "the sovereign . . . is unable to inflict an imaginable harm on anyone." When the Americans came to draw up a constitution, they incorporated into it these checks and balances that Montesquieu regarded as a sure safeguard against despotism.

Voltaire

Even more influential than Montesquieu was François Marie Arouet whose pen name, "Voltaire," is perhaps the most famous in history. Born in Paris of respectable, middle class parents, Voltaire was constantly in trouble as a young man for writing scathingly witty satires on members of the royal government. At the age of thirty, after twice being imprisoned without trial in the infamous Paris fortress, the Bastille, he left France for three years' exile in England. There he was immediately struck by the Englishman's freedom of speech, his tolerance of many religious sects, and his general prosperity. "An Englishman," he wrote, "goes to heaven by the road he pleases. There are no arbitrary taxes. The peasant eats white bread and is well clothed and is not afraid of adding to his land for fear that the taxes will be raised next year."

When Voltaire returned to Paris he described his impressions in *Letters on the English*, which circulated widely in manuscript form among his friends and were later published in English and then in French. French authorities were infuriated, for his praise of England was so lavish that it implied criticism of France with its tyrannical regime, its unjust courts, its pampered aristocracy, and its religious intolerance. Once again, Voltaire was forced to leave Paris.

Having by good luck made a large sum of money in a business venture, Voltaire had no need to struggle for a living. For most of the remaining forty years of his long life he lived in the country and devoted his brilliant literary gifts to the struggle for individual freedom. With prodigious energy he produced novels, plays, pamphlets, essays, poems, and historical works and dictated or wrote twenty or more letters a day. He gave open-handed hospitality to eminent writers and thinkers who travelled from all parts

Frederick the Great visiting Voltaire in the palace at Potsdam. Frederick's views on society and life—his philosophy—were so greatly influenced by Voltaire and other French thinkers, that he too became a *philosophe*, and poured out his thoughts in a stream of writings on philosophy, politics and history; and in poetry. None of these, unhappily, made valuable contributions to scholarship.

of Europe to see him, and indeed, referred to himself as the "hotel-keeper of Europe." He corresponded not only with the most powerful rulers of the day but with scores of ordinary men and women who wrote to him for advice. No great writer has ever been easier to read; his style was witty, sarcastic, and incisive. Always his aim was "by speech and pen to make men more enlightened and better." Before he died, Voltaire had become the greatest and most influential literary and intellectual figure in Europe.

Voltaire became the champion of religious toleration, though he himself was bitterly intolerant of any organized church. Orthodox Christianity, he felt, encouraged superstition, cruelty, stupidity, and intolerance and therefore was the greatest enemy of humanity. Next to religious toleration, he cherished freedom of speech. "I disapprove of what you say," he wrote to a fellow *philosophe*, "but I will defend to the death your right to say it."

Voltaire poured scorn on government corruption and tyranny, but he was less fearful than Montesquieu of the "over-powerful ruler" or despot. He was, in fact, afraid of democracy, probably because of his exceedingly low opinion of the masses. His political ideal was rule by an enlightened or rational despot who, while safeguarding the basic rights of each individual to "life, liberty and property" would govern for the general good. It did not matter, thought Voltaire, how powerful a ruler was so long as he was "enlightened" in outlook. In fact, an enlightened ruler might well *need* great powers to carry through his policies in the face of ignorant, "unenlightened" opposition. An enlightened ruler would allow subjects full freedom of thought, would oppose sloth, religious bigotry, and intolerance; would encourage industry, art, and science; and would use his governing powers to help create a just, efficient, and modern state.

Rousseau

The views of Jean-Jacques Rousseau, the champion of the common person, were very different from those of Voltaire and Montesquieu. Rousseau, whose parents were French Huguenots, was born in near-poverty in the Swiss city of Geneva. His mother died soon after his birth and his father, a watch-maker, left him to the care of relatives. His childhood was desperately unhappy. At the age of sixteen Rousseau ran away and after a lonely time wandering from job to job, settled for ten years in the home of a wealthy and cultured

Jean-Jacques Rousseau. Rousseau wrote much that was foolish and superficial, but he also wrote *The Social Contract*, which supplied the French Revolution with its text; as its author, he changed France and the world.

widow. Here the moody young man took long walks in the country and came to love nature. He also had the chance to meet brilliant people, to read Voltaire, and to study Latin.

In 1741, Rousseau drifted to Paris. There he became secretary to a government minister. After suffering an injury, he attempted to sue his master but quickly found there was no equal justice between an aristocrat and a common citizen. This bitter experience was a turning point in the life of a man already morbidly oversensitive. For the next fifteen years, Rousseau became a passionate critic of government and society.

Rousseau's most famous book, *The Social Contract*, opens with these challenging words: "Man is born free, yet everywhere he is in chains." His romantic mind pictured a primitive and bygone Golden Age in which man once lived close to nature. It was a paradise in which property did not exist and all men were equal. Political power, said Rousseau, was purely man-made, for no man had any natural authority over his fellows. Governments, which had been established originally by men for their own benefit, had grown to be tyrannical and cruel. They had destroyed liberty by means of unjust laws, crushing taxes, police, prisons, and armies—all of which Rousseau felt were simply devices by which the strong ruled the weak. Man, who was naturally good, had been made bad by civilization, which was basically evil and corrupt.

For men to be good and happy, Rousseau wanted society itself to be changed and improved. He longed for a levelling of class distinctions which he saw everywhere, and he challenged men to recapture the simple, noble existence of their primitive ancestors. Then, he claimed, the natural goodness and brotherhood of man would triumph. There would be justice and equality for all.

Rousseau also wrote two romantic and widely-read novels, *Emile* and *The New Héloise,* which evoked new respect for the individual human being and for the simple, everyday things of life. He punctured the pride of an aristocracy obsessed with outward appearances and with an artificial social status. He shook the faith even of the French aristocracy in their own inborn superiority. Influenced by Rousseau, the queen of France and her bored courtiers attempted for a time to capture the joys of the simple life by playing milkmaids on a model farm, erected without regard to expense, in the palace gardens at Versailles.

Rousseau taught that the basis of society should be the "general will" of the people, that authority should rest on the consent of the governed, and that government officials should be, in effect, not the masters but the servants of the public. The people alone should be sovereign. Each individual would have his rights safeguarded, but he in turn should respect the common interest that unites the people of a society. Perhaps because he himself was an unhappy misfit in society, Rousseau longed for a system of government in which each individual might have a sense of his own worth by taking a direct and personal share in government. This ideal form of democracy would only be practical in a very small state and, in fact, it was his native city of Geneva that Rousseau had in mind as he wrote. But his ringing phrases inflamed men's minds. They inspired idealists and revolutionaries who dreamed of government "by the people" extended to territories far larger than Geneva. Its greatest appeal was to the downtrodden disenfranchised masses of France.

Rousseau's ideas have influenced history down to the present day, inspiring both democratic and nationalist-totalitarian states. Nationalist dictators of the 20th century have claimed—and still claim—to epitomize in themselves the "general will" of their subjects, while in democracies there has developed from Rousseau's doctrine a belief in the almost divine authority of the wishes of the majority—"the will of the people." Rousseau would probably have condemned both these uses of his ideas.

The Physiocrats and Economists

Other thinkers of the Age of Enlightenment questioned the generally accepted economic belief of the 18th century known as mercantilism. Among them were the physiocrats of France, such as Quesnay and Turgot. Mockingly dubbed "economists," the physiocrats felt that economic activities were controlled by natural laws just as valid as those put forward by astronomers, physicists, or *philosophes*. They attacked the high tariffs, the trading prohibitions, the navigation acts, and other regulations by which governments had for centuries controlled and regulated trade. They coined the phrase *laissez-faire* (leave alone) to describe their policy of freeing trade and investment from government control. Like Montesquieu and Rousseau, the physiocrats were eager to see the powers of government reduced, in the belief that the greatest prosperity could result only when natural laws were allowed to operate freely.

The most eloquent and influential champion of the new economic thought was a brilliant Scottish professor, Adam Smith. Going considerably beyond the physiocrats, he argued compellingly in his masterpiece, *The Wealth of Nations* (1776), that if the law of supply and demand were allowed to operate and that if countries were allowed to produce and trade freely the goods they were best suited to manufacture or grow, then all countries would benefit. He derided the idea that if one party grew rich in trade the other must necessarily grow poor. He declared it nonsense to think that wealth consisted basically of gold and silver or that a nation should endeavour solely to export goods and import bullion. Ironically, in the very year that Adam Smith's book was published, the Americans signed the Declaration of Independence, effectively putting an end to the British "mercantile" system of colonial trade.

The Ferment of Ideas

The ideas of the great *philosophes* and thinkers of the 18th century swirled like powerful currents and eddies in many different directions. While there was a general faith in the benefits of reason, science, technical progress, and civilization, thinkers differed in their opinions as to how these benefits could be brought to the common man. Rousseau rejected civilization in favour of his "noble savage"—a simple primitive man, uncorrupted by the trivialities of civilization and a brother to his fellow human beings. Voltaire, however, believed civilization infinitely preferable to a primitive state in which men would be little more than savage beasts of prey. He claimed that reading Rousseau "makes one long to go on all fours." He was willing to forgo a certain degree of political liberty in order to enjoy freedom of thought, freedom of speech, and freedom from persecution under an "enlightened" monarch. Montesquieu, on the other hand, wanted political liberty with stringent safeguards against despotism. Yet all thinkers of the period were agreed on their goal—they wanted men to enjoy a greater degree of freedom.

It was Voltaire's views, however, which won the support of most of the *philosophes* and which most widely influenced European governments of the 18th century. Not surprisingly, many monarchs were strongly attracted to Voltaire's ideal of "enlightened despotism," which advocated that they impose reforms without suggesting that they should relinquish any of their royal privileges or powers.

4. ENLIGHTENED DESPOTISM

Prussia

After 1740, experiments in enlightened despotism were made by a number of European rulers—in Prussia, Austria and Russia, Sweden, Spain, Portugal, and several of the smaller German and Italian states. The most famous "enlightened" monarch was Frederick II of Prussia (Frederick the Great) who was also studied in Chapter Two. Frederick had begun to correspond with Voltaire when still only a prince, twenty years old, and when he came to the throne of Prussia in 1740, he was already steeped in the ideas of the French Enlightenment. He was a rationalist, a religious sceptic, a patron of culture and art, and a composer of French verse. He was also a man gifted with tireless energy and determined to make his people prosperous by promoting industry and trade. "The Monarch," he declared, "is not the absolute master but only the first servant of the state." And to Voltaire he wrote:

My chief occupation is to fight ignorance and prejudice in this country. . . . I must enlighten my people, cultivate their manners and morale, and make them as happy as human beings can be or as happy as the means at my disposal permit.

It was no wonder that, when Voltaire came by invitation to the Prussian court in 1750, he felt he had entered a *philosophe's* paradise.

In many ways Frederick the Great was indeed the living embodiment of Voltaire's ideal monarch who set a pattern that other monarchs sought to follow. In order to restore the prosperity of his people after the ravages of the Seven Years' War, Frederick had canals built, forests cleared, and new industries started. He induced thousands of skilled immigrants to settle in Prussia by offering them exemptions from taxes and from military service. New crops and modern farming methods were introduced from England, and thousands of acres of sandy wasteland were reclaimed and made productive. The civil service was made more efficient, the courts more honest, and the practice of applying torture to obtain evidence was forbidden. Plans were even made to provide elementary education for the children of all, whether rich or poor. Like a true disciple of Voltaire, Frederick also enforced religious toleration, shocking his devout, Lutheran subjects by declaring that Roman Catholics might build churches "as high as they please," and he added that if the Turks were to migrate to Prussia, he would himself build them mosques. Frederick, in short, did much to make his people enlightened and prosperous. There was a limit, however, to his willingness to undertake reform. He maintained a firm belief in social rank and privilege, gave the nobility almost unlimited power over the peasants, and retained serfdom even on his own estate. What was more unfortunate, was that his motive was less the happiness of his subjects than aggrandizement of his own power. He regarded a thriving industry and a fast-growing population as essential for war, and as we have seen, proved himself a ruthless dictator, a wily diplomat, and an ambitious and aggressive warrior. Moreover, although Frederick was enormously able and energetic, he attempted to direct personally all government business, delegating no responsibility and training no successor. When, twenty years after his death, a leaderless Prussia fell swiftly to Napoleon's army, men wondered if autocratic monarchy, however enlightened, was a lasting solution to the problems of government. Frederick demonstrated that the weaknesses as well as the strengths of enlightened despotism lay in the fact that everything depended on the monarch.

Austria

In Austria, Maria Theresa strove earnestly to strengthen and modernize her empire, though, being a devout Roman Catholic and averse to the more radical ideas of the *philosophes*, she qualified only partially as an "enlightened despot." Afraid of arousing opposition she satisfied herself with partial reforms, introduced cautiously. However, her son Joseph II, who had been co-regent with his mother for fifteen years, accepted eagerly the idea of "enlightened despotism" and determined to sweep away all vestiges of the old order. A serious, high-minded man, he was aware of the miseries and injustices suffered by the poor. He felt it his duty to consider only "the greatest good for the greatest number" and he used the full weight of his authority to force a complete and radical reform of the country. Serfdom, which his mother had modified, he abolished outright. He decreed equal justice and equal taxation for all, complete freedom of the press, and toleration for all religions except for a few sects that he regarded as too outrageous to be permitted. To the Jews he gave full citizenship, with the right to receive aristocratic titles and the obligation to perform military service. At the same time, disregarding the fact that most Austrians were Roman Catholics, Joseph made Roman Catholicism completely subject to the state. He insisted upon nominating bishops and tried to use the clergy to teach respect and obedience for the government. Using money from expropriated monasteries, he financed secular hospitals that were later to make Vienna famous as a medical centre.

Joseph's reforms inevitably aroused widespread opposition, not only from the clergy and nobles but even from the serfs who were baffled by the freedom thrust upon them. They had "grown accustomed to their chains" and longed for the return of their ancient customs. Ironically, it was in order to establish his advanced and "enlightened" regime that Joseph created a network of secret police to spy out and denounce "unenlightened" opponents of the new order. Thus, a high-minded idealist—the paternal, well-meaning Joseph—created the police state later associated with some of the most infamous regimes of modern times.

Joseph, in fact, proved to be a revolutionary ahead of his time, a leader whose followers could not keep up. It was not enough to impose reforms from above without a broad base of popular support, and there were too few civil servants and administrators sharing his views to help him carry out his enlightened policies. Two great provinces of the empire, Hungary and the Austrian Netherlands, rose in revolt against autocratic "government by decree." Before Joseph died, aged only forty-nine, he already knew that few of his reforms would outlast him. Bitterly, he commented: "After all my trouble I have made few happy and many ungrateful." He ordered this epitaph to be cut upon his tombstone: "Here lies a man who, with the best of intentions, never succeeded in anything."

Russia

Catherine the Great of Russia, who had had a French education, also aspired to be an enlightened, "progressive" monarch, at least during the earlier part of her reign. She invited Diderot, editor of *L'Encyclopédie,* to visit her and—like so many European monarchs of the day—she exchanged long letters with Voltaire. Under her influence the French language and French culture became dominant at the Russian court and amongst the aristocracy. At the capital of St. Petersburg, French architects, painters, dancing masters, and chefs became fashionable, and for the rising generation of Russian noblemen, French supplanted Russian as the first language. As a result, the already wide chasm separating the sophisticated Russian nobility from the great mass of illiterate and down-trodden peasants became still wider.

Catherine was responsible for a number of significant reforms that inspired Voltaire to remark approvingly: "Light now comes from the north." She improved the machinery of government, codified the laws, limited the use of torture by the courts, and introduced a greater degree of religious toleration (though she would not allow Dukhobors,[1] a sect that had split from the Orthodox Church in 1785, to build their own chapels). She also founded a university and a number of secondary schools, bettered hospital conditions, and introduced vaccination.

None of Catherine's reforms, however, was as sweeping and whole-hearted as those that Joseph II tried to impose on Austria, for Catherine's authority rested on the support of a deeply conservative nobility. When Diderot suggested further reforms, Catherine commented: "You write on paper but I have to write on human skin, which is incomparably more irritable and ticklish." Catherine's concern was for the thin skins of army officers and great landowners—members of the aristocratic class that had acclaimed her own accession and had deposed or murdered more than one of her predecessors. And the Russian aristocrats were totally unwilling to abolish serfdom, to develop new industries, or to encourage the growth of a healthy middle class.

After a widespread and fearful peasant uprising in 1773, which was put down only after the rebel host had been scattered by famine, Catherine dropped all pretence of enlightenment. Her regime henceforth was based on undisguised repression. Backed whole-heartedly by the great landowners, she was able to wield absolute authority over the civil service, the courts, the army, and

[1] Many Dukhobors emigrated to Canada in the 1890's to avoid military conscription, which they regarded as sinful.

A certain insight into peasant life in Russia.

foreign affairs. In return, she allowed the landowners to enjoy unlimited power over the lives and labours of their luckless serfs, who were often treated no better than slaves. A serf could be arbitrarily punished by whipping, imprisonment or exile; he might be sold away from his family or put to forced labour in the forests or the mines. Catherine's reign, far from being renowned for its enlightenment, became notorious for the strengthening of serfdom throughout Russia.

To please the nobility, Catherine also followed an aggressive foreign policy, giving her favoured supporters huge estates and large numbers of serfs in the conquered territories. During her reign Russian armies, under the brilliant but callous leadership of General Suvorov, extended the borders of Russia south to the Black Sea and west to the frontiers of Germany. Suvorov's conquests became Catherine's proudest boast and earned for her the title "The Great," yet they were bought at the terrible cost of untold thousands of Russian lives.

5. ENLIGHTENED MONARCHY: SUMMARY AND ASSESSMENT

The wars of Catherine's reign illustrate the gap that often appeared between the ideals of the *philosophes* and the practices of their royal admirers. Voltaire had declared that a truly enlightened monarch would follow a pacifist policy towards other lands, and he poured scorn on the "glories" of war and bloodshed. Yet both Frederick of Prussia and Catherine the Great, despite their eager reading of the French *philosophes*, recklessly squandered money and lives in costly wars of aggression. Prussia, as we have seen, had for its size the largest standing army in Europe, and it was the three most famous of the so-called "enlightened" monarchs, Frederick of Prussia, Catherine the Great, and Joseph of Austria, who perpetrated "the crime of the century" by cold-bloodedly seizing half of Poland and dividing it among themselves (1772).

In domestic affairs, "enlightened despotism" was proof that most rulers in the 18th century acknowledged the need for reform, and usually meant some degree of improvement in the lives of the common people. There was a growth of religious toleration, which meant a lessening of persecution of minority faiths, and especially of the more odious uses of torture to enforce acceptance of religious doctrine. Similarly, the more barbaric forms of torture by the state against persons suspected or convicted of crimes or political offenses began to diminish. In some countries, notably Prussia, there was a reform of the legal system to make the law courts "cheaper, more expeditious, more honest." In Austria, Joseph II's reforms made all subjects, peasant or noble, equal before the law and subject to equal punishment for equal crimes. These reforms were unenduring, being mostly repealed by Joseph's successor Leopold, but the peasants did emerge considerably better than they had been before, and laws against the abuse of peasants' rights remained in force.

Another positive result of the Age of Enlightenment was the substantial growth of literacy among the educated middle class, especially in France. With increasing literacy came a parallel concern with the affairs of state among businessmen and professionals, who assiduously read newspapers, magazines, pamphlets, and *L'Encyclopédie*. Those who were unable to read these materials at home could find them in coffee houses or reading rooms established for that purpose. Yet another accomplishment of the period was the construction of much useful social capital, with the building of roads and bridges, and the draining of marshes.

Perhaps the greatest failure of the enlightened despots, however, was their inability to establish a more equitable and rational system of taxation. In virtually every country of continental Europe the burden of financing the state was born to an excessive degree by the lower classes. In France, Turgot planned to abolish certain taxes that were paid only by the peasantry and to spread the burden more fairly, but pressure from the nobles resulted in his dismissal and the blocking of the reform. In Austria, Joseph II tried to alleviate the burden on the peasants by implementing an absolute equality of taxation for all classes, but this reform too was annulled after his death. Consequently, in the context of economic welfare, there was but slight improvement in the sacrifice of the peasant masses, who benefited little, if at all, from living in the age of progress. In every case, the resistance of the nobles and those who sought to obstruct reform was too great to be overcome. Nor could any ruler be expected to carry through reforms to the point of surrendering his own lofty authority and status. Thus every despot, however enlightened, reached a point beyond which he could not go.

Despite this limitation, however, enlightened monarchs, secure in their own authority, often tolerated or even encouraged the development of ideas. This toleration was to prove their undoing for, as Voltaire pointed out, "When once a nation begins to think, it is impossible to stop it." It was only to be a matter of time before subjects sought to substitute Rousseau's "will of the people" for the authority of kings.

6 The Background of the French Revolution

Revolutions are not trifles, but spring from trifles.
—Aristotle

While other nations in 18th century Europe, both large and small, experimented with enlightened monarchy, France itself—the home of progressive ideas—suffered from an outdated and inefficient administration, chronic social injustice, and grave economic problems.

The financial troubles of France were in many ways the most obvious. While the French royal court and aristocracy indulged in reckless extravagances (the queen herself would bathe in milk for the sake of her complexion), whole sections of the population lived in appalling squalor and periodically rioted in face of acute, recurrent shortages of food. At the same time the government of France, administering probably the richest and certainly the most populous country in all Europe, was crippled with mountainous debts and teetered on the edge of financial collapse.

The economic ills of France, were, however, only dramatic symptoms of a far more evil and deep-rooted cancer—privilege—that gnawed its way into every part of French national life, until the whole was made rotten and corrupt. Privilege, by which small numbers of Frenchmen enjoyed special rights, favours, and advantages at the expense of the great majority, was a prime cause of French economic difficulties. Privilege split French society into many mutually hostile parts; it perverted justice; it wasted the abilities of the most intelligent middle class in Europe and, most harmful of all, it threw the heaviest burden of taxation onto the shoulders of those who could least afford to bear it—the peasants.

For over a century grievances of all kinds festered and grew in France, until it became clear to all thinking men that only the most sweeping and enlightened reforms could avert a disaster. But after the death of Louis XIV, France had the misfortune to be saddled with two monarchs, neither one of whom had the strength, the foresight, or determination to alter the fatal drift of events. The outcome was the French Revolution of 1789, a political and social upheaval of such magnitude that it shook Europe to its foundations and profoundly altered the subsequent history of the western world.

1. THE FAILURE OF ENLIGHTENED DESPOTISM IN FRANCE

Louis XV, the grandson and heir of Louis XIV, was far too preoccupied with trivial amusements to play any steady or effective part in politics. Decisions were left to court favourites, especially the sprightly and talented Madame de Pompadour. When forced to step aside briefly from his hunting, gambling, or amorous affairs, in order to preside over government business, Louis XV "opened his mouth, said little, and thought not at all." He lived only for the pleasures of the moment, cynically dismissing the future with the remark, *"Après moi le déluge."*

He was succeeded by his twenty-year-old grandson, Louis XVI, an amiable and pious youth without clearness of mind or strength of character. Though genuinely well-meaning and anxious not to appear despotic, Louis XVI was easily swayed by anyone who could catch his ear. "No one trusts him," it was said, "for he has no will of his own." Twice he appointed ministers who attempted to carry through enlightened and much needed financial reforms but he quickly withdrew his support when their proposals met opposition. The first of these ministers, Turgot, was a *philosophe* and an economist who wished to free trade from antiquated restrictions and to make the wealthy pay their share of the taxes. He lasted thirteen months. The second, a hardheaded Swiss Protestant banker, named Necker, was dismissed when his stringent economies offended the personal friends of the gay and frivolous queen, Marie Antoinette. Thereafter, Louis XVI increasingly found escape from his cares in the enjoyment of manual hobbies, in hearty eating and drinking, and such sports as shooting deer from a palace window. "How fortunate you are," he remarked to a minister who resigned, "I wish I could resign too."

Meanwhile the Old Regime (as the pre-Revolutionary French society later came to be called) continued very much as it had in

Louis XVI was slow. He moved slowly. He thought slowly. He was slow to make up his mind. It is said that even his eyes moved slowly. He fell asleep at inopportune times, but he liked unexpected jokes, provided they were not too elaborate. In an age when most men were skeptics he was devotedly religious. Simply, he was not a man of his time.

the days of Louis XIV, the autocratic "Sun King." There was no political, religious or economic freedom. The monarchy was based on the idea of Divine Right, with legal power strongly concentrated in the hands of the king. (Louis XIV had been able to declare without exaggeration, "The State—it is I.") The weakness of the king was particularly unfortunate, as the monarchy, over a period of several centuries, had become virtually the only source of executive power in France. The French Bourbon kings had gradually whittled away the power of the lords and made the nobles, as well as the clergy, subject to royal authority. Legislative power also came to be concentrated in the monarchy. Once it had lain with an Estates-General, or Parliament, representing the people of

France, which had met at irregular intervals over a period of three hundred years. But the Estates-General had been dismissed in 1614 —as was described in Chapter One—and it had not been summoned since. There was, then, no appeal against the arbitrary decisions of the king's government; ordinary citizens might be imprisoned without trial "for any reason or no reason, without knowing why, on whose accusation, or for how long." Even the courts were suppressed if they failed to support the royal decree.

2. SOCIETY UNDER THE OLD REGIME

Beneath the king all Frenchmen were legally divided into three Estates, or orders of society. The First Estate, made up of the clergy, and the Second Estate, consisting of the nobility, enjoyed many privileges. The Third Estate, which had no special rights, included all the remaining citizens, from wealthy and educated city lawyers and businessmen to the poorest and most illiterate peasants.

At one time, each of the three Estates had sent representatives to a parliamentary body, known as the Estates-General. But with the dismissal of the last Estates-General in 1614, this division of society into Estates had become politically meaningless. The divisions were also outdated as a gauge of men's usefulness and worth because, while the clergy and nobility had declined in influence, a new important middle class had grown up in France within the Third Estate, thriving on the discovery of new worlds overseas and the growth of industry and trade. It was the middle class that provided the intellectual leadership of 18th century France and helped to develop the ideas of the *philosophes* and the economists. It was the middle class also that filled the ranks of the civil service and came to the rescue of an impoverished government with handsome cash loans. Nevertheless, though these social divisions were entirely outmoded, the Estate to which an individual belonged was enormously important, for upon it depended his social status and his legal rights.

The First Estate

Within the First Estate, which by 1789 numbered around one hundred thousand clergy (or a half of one per cent of the population), there was a wide gulf between the higher clerics such as cardinals, bishops, and abbots, and a much larger number of common priests. The higher Church positions were all but monopolized by members of noble families who often enjoyed huge incomes, gathered from Church properties and tithes, while leading scandalously worldly and vicious lives. Louis XVI is said to have protested as he rejected one high-born candidate for Church office, "Let us at least have an Archbishop of Paris who believes in God." At the other extreme within the Church were humble parish priests who frequently lived on a tiny and uncertain income and worked devotedly to advise, instruct, and comfort the common people.

The clergy as a whole enjoyed great privilege. They represented the only legally permitted religion; they had their own courts of law; they enjoyed a complete control over education, and they had the right to censor any printed article or book. Moreover, although they controlled far more than their share of all the land in France—besides much other wealth in the form of fine buildings and art treasures—the clergy were exempt from all direct taxes, paying the king instead periodic "free gifts."

The Second Estate

The Second Estate was made up of some four hundred thousand men, women, and children of noble birth; like the First Estate, it was broadly divided into two categories. At the top were the "nobles of the sword." The ancestors of this group had once formed a warrior aristocracy, the highly trained armoured knights who, in the disordered Middle Ages, had brought to their serfs a measure of security. Under all-powerful monarchs, in a consolidated nation state, the nobles were no longer necessary as a specialist warrior class. Yet, although they had long outlived their social usefulness, the titled aristocracy enjoyed great wealth and many social privileges which they guarded jealously. They monopolized the most coveted positions not only in the Church but also in the government, the army, and the fleet. (Even while France was helping the American colonists in their struggle for democratic rights, no citizen could gain a commission in the French forces without proof of noble blood for four paternal generations.) The wealthiest nobles spent much of their time in sumptuous idleness at the royal palace at Versailles, dancing, gambling, or cultivating their courtly manners. Meanwhile, they were supported by the money wrung from peasants toiling on the vast country estates.

A French nobleman dressed as an "American savage" for a royal pageant. The pageants were as lavish and extravagant as possible, and participants were expected to dress and behave accordingly. The duke, who had heard that the Indians wore head feathers, overdid his part a bit! Spectacles such as this did little to ease the financial problems undermining the regime, or to reconcile the oppressed common people to the upper class.

Below the haughty nobles of the sword were the "nobles of the robe"—so called since they were entitled to wear an ostentatious gown—whose ancestors had bought a title or earned one for services to the monarch. They were scorned and snubbed by the older nobility as *nouveaux riches,* but in fact they formed the most progressive and intelligent part of the Second Estate, and included in their number Montesquieu and some, like Lafayette, who were to play an active part in the Revolution.

The nobility as a whole shared with the clergy the enviable privilege of being exempt from most direct government taxes. All nobles were excused from the burdensome land tax (*taille*) and many, in addition, managed through influence at court to win total exemption from the income tax (*vingtième*) and the poll tax (*capitation*). To pay taxes at all came to be regarded as socially degrading and, often as not, the nobles refused point blank to do so. Their attitude was, as Voltaire described it, "Let those pay taxes who work; we should not pay because we do not work."

The Third Estate

The Third Estate, which did pay taxes, was by far the largest, forming over ninety-six per cent of the population of France. Its most prominent members were bankers, merchants, lawyers, and other professional men, often intelligent, articulate, and widely read. This *bourgeoisie,* or middle class, was centred mostly in the cities and towns and grew rapidly in numbers, influence, and wealth during the 18th century as a result of a massive increase in foreign trade. Some of the bourgeoisie accumulated great fortunes and lived in homes scarcely less grand than the nobles. Others, less well-to-do, lived closely intermixed with the common people, often living in better parts of the same houses. This close contact of the bourgeoisie with less educated members of the Third Estate enabled them to provide the real leadership of the Revolution when it came, and it was through them, by word of mouth, that the radical views of the *philosophes* spread down through the population. In time, even the poorest and least educated city workers formed political opinions which they aired in heated arguments on harbour wharfs, in back alleys, and on street corners.

The educated bourgeoisie had every reason to want drastic changes in the Old Regime. With their growing numbers and prosperity, their ability and education, they had become increasingly ambitious. For a long time they had envied the aristocracy and tried to force their way into its ranks. In the past a few had succeeded, becoming nobles of the robe, but for most the way was blocked. No matter how much money they made, they were excluded from any share in the making of government policy, barred from all leading

"A Woman of the Revolution," typical of those who marched to Versailles to bring the royal family back to Paris, or who invaded the Tuilleries in 1792. Painting by Jacques David.

positions in the state, and denied all social prestige. In England, the daughter of a shrewd and wealthy businessman or banker could, and often did, marry the blue-blooded offspring of an ancient, titled family. But in France even this road to social advancement was denied to the bourgeoisie. The nobility held itself disdainfully aloof—a closed, superior caste. If, as very occasionally happened, a

French nobleman did permit his son to marry the heiress of a wealthy merchant, he might scornfully explain that he was "manuring his land." Faced with a denial of their intelligence and worth, and smarting with injured pride, the French bourgeoisie yearned for the destruction of the closed, caste system. In place of the old aristocracy, dependent solely on birth and inherited privilege, the bourgeoisie wanted a new, open aristocracy based on merit and hard-earned wealth. It was the bourgeoisie which was to be the driving force of the Revolution.

3. THE GRIEVANCES OF THE PEASANTS

In the late 18th century, France was still largely an agricultural country, and the great majority of the Third Estate, and therefore of the total population, was made up of peasant families. Relatively few peasants were still tied to the land as their forebears had been in the middle ages or as many peasants still were in Eastern Europe. Most French peasants were sharecroppers, cultivating another man's land for a half share of the harvest. Others farmed their own or rented land, or hired themselves out for cash wages. Yet there were very few peasants who did not still owe to a neighbouring lord some feudal obligations dating from centuries past. These dues, which varied from district to district, were itemized in written documents *(terriers)* and were renewed whenever ownership of the land changed. Each time, the legal expenses involved were borne by the peasant and the document was carefully filed away in the archives of the lord's chateau. These archives were bitterly hated, for they came to represent a loathesome and humiliating burden from which the peasants felt they would never be free.

In many districts peasants were still liable to the *corvée,* a form of tax paid in personal labour to the king, to the local lord, or to both. It was doubly galling since it was a tax that no other citizen had to pay. Generally it demanded two weeks' hard labour on the roads.

Other burdensome and out-dated taxes were *banalités,* originally taxes that peasants in the middle ages had paid for the use of their lord's flour mill, bake oven, or wine press. When only a local lord could provide such facilities, *banalités* were not especially resented, but by the 18th century, many peasants had their own mills, ovens, and presses—yet the *banalités* still had to be paid.

Some land, even though paid for in full, continued to carry with it an obligation for the peasant owner to hand over a share of every crop produced. If a peasant decided to resell land that had been bought outright, he still had to pay his lord a percentage of the selling price. In cases where a peasant's land passed to an indirect heir, such as a nephew, the lord might claim the entire first year's income from the new owner. These and other similar rights meant that lords, in effect, could collect rent in perpetuity from any land that their ancestors had had the good fortune to control in feudal times. The peasants, considering the land as rightfully theirs, came to look upon their lords as useless and loathsome parasites.

Perhaps most hated of all were the special privileges, held by the nobles alone, to hunt, to shoot, and to fish. A peasant was liable to savage punishment if he shot a pigeon pecking his grain, a fox raiding his chicken house, or a rabbit nibbling his vegetable patch. Woe betide a peasant, too, if his dog chased a game bird, or if he scythed his grass during the partridge nesting season. Worse still, the lord and his hunting companions had the right at any time to gallop roughshod across a peasant's land regardless of the growing crops.

In addition to bearing these burdens—a bitter hangover from the feudal past—the peasant had to pay his full share and more of government taxes. These included such indirect taxes as those on wine and cider *(aides)* and the hated salt tax *(gabelle)*. The latter was especially unfair, for salt was a government monopoly, and every man, woman, and child over seven had by law to buy three kilograms a year, in some districts at a price of fifty or sixty times above its actual value. Direct government taxes such as the *taille,* the *vingtième,* and the *capitation* also fell especially hard on the peasant since those who could best afford to pay—the nobles and the clergy —did not have to do so.

On top of all else, it fell to the peasant to support the church by handing over a tithe (originally a tenth, but by the 18th century, around one-thirteenth) of all he produced on his land. Had the tithe been used simply to support the local parish priest and to help needy widows and orphans, there might have been little complaint, but much of the wealth from the tithe went to sustain the palaces and the luxuries of the noble higher clergy.

Thus the peasants, the largest and poorest of the Third Estate, paid three times over. To the nobles they gave feudal dues, to the state, direct and indirect taxes, and to the Church, tithes. While it is true that during the 18th century peasants in most parts of Europe were even worse off than those in France (with the major exception of England), the French peasants were miserable and they knew it. The peasants of France were too oppressed and too unorganized to start a revolution, but once a revolution had begun they backed it with their overwhelming numbers and with a ferocity born of generations of despair.

4. GOVERNMENT UNDER THE OLD REGIME

Even at its best, under an able and untiring ruler such as Louis XIV, the absolutist system of government in France was cumbersome and inefficient. Under monarchs who found politics a bore, the administration fell into gross and chaotic disorder.

Over the years one new government department after another had been created, only to conflict with older departments, which continued to flourish and grow. Politically France consisted of forty long-established provinces, each cherishing its own privileges, traditions, and loyalties. Superimposed on the provinces and cutting across their boundaries were some thirty administrative *départements* of the central government, known as *intendancies*; to further complicate administrative affairs, there were numerous cities and towns that had an important voice in local matters of trade. Jurisdictions were seldom clear and a host of government agencies became hopelessly entangled. Petty officials, fearful of responsibility, constantly referred matters to higher authorities or to another department. Decisions as minor as repairing a church steeple or as important as replacing a bridge on a major highway were delayed for months or even years. Officially nothing of consequence could be done, no disputes between rival departments settled, without a time-consuming appeal to the monarch. The most effective way to cut through bureaucratic red-tape was to pass bribes, and in time every level of the administration of the Old Regime became riddled with corruption.

Legal matters bogged down in a court system that had developed and proliferated haphazardly over the centuries. Of royal courts alone there were twenty-three varieties; there were also manor courts, church courts, and courts run by the provinces. Almost every province had its own code of laws, so that a serious offence in one locality might be of no legal significance sixteen kilometres away. Voltaire commented wryly that in riding across France, "one changed laws as often as one changed horses." For merchants trying to do business between provinces the legal complexities were exasperating.

Throughout France privilege corrupted justice. Any noble might have a civil case against him transferred from one court to another more favourable or, as a last resort, he might appeal to the king whose word was the ultimate law. Nobles were spared, too, the painful indignities of torture, though torture was an approved means of obtaining evidence in criminal cases from members of the Third Estate.

Intensely annoying to businessmen and manufacturers was a tangled growth of government regulations covering every aspect of business. Manufacturing monopolies were given to selected companies, wages were set, and prices (at least in theory), were fixed. At the same time foreign trade was restricted by taxes not only on imports but also on exports. Internal trade was even more severely handicapped by customs barriers that divided province from province and by tariffs levied on goods entering city walls. The latter taxes, by sharply raising the price of food and other goods, brought suffering to the poor town-dwellers, while they did nothing for the profits of the merchants. Thus economic freedom —the *laissez-faire* ideal of the economists—became a dream that French businessmen would make almost any sacrifice to gain.

The Old Regime contained a mixture of ingredients that made revolution almost certain: monarchs, weak-willed in everything, save clinging to their royal prerogatives; church leaders, too often faithless and dissolute; aristocrats living idle and parasitic lives; a middle class, restless and ambitious; a peasantry over-taxed and downtrodden; an administration at once inept, chaotic, and corrupt. When the inevitable explosion took place, many Frenchmen wondered only why it had not occurred earlier.

5. THE ADVANCED CIVILIZATION OF FRANCE

Underlying all else was a further intangible but important factor which made revolution likely—the high level of civilization in France. Paris boasted the most advanced and sophisticated society in all Europe. Its art, its architecture, its manners, its language,

Marie Antoinette entertains the court with her harp. Married at fourteen, the change from her mother's austere and pious upbringing to the corrupt surroundings of Louis XVI's Versailles gave her problems she was too young to solve. Her friends were chosen unwisely, and favoured too openly. She made enemies and set malicious tongues wagging. Maturity came too late to save her, and the political changes she hated and misunderstood took her eventually to the guillotine.

and its ideas were everywhere admired and influential. For example, it was said that every civilized person had two countries—his own and France. No rich young Englishman's education was considered finished without some months' enjoyment of Parisian society. Wealthy Parisian hostesses vied with each other in inviting the most brilliant conversationalists to gatherings, known as salons, held in elegant and spacious drawing rooms. Here, intelligence and charm counted for more than mere nobility, and nimble minds matched wits, to the delight of the assembled company. Some hostesses especially patronized philosophers, others economists, while some held salons on successive days of the week for moralists, chemists, physicians, or artists and writers. Often hostesses would arrange concerts of chamber music, or exhibitions of sculpture or painting, but the prime purpose of salons was stimulating talk, and conversation ranged over the whole field of ideas that obsessed men and women in the Age of Enlightenment.

Though politics could be a dangerous subject, men like Voltaire and Rousseau, the physiocrats and encyclopedists, became masters of "the art of saying everything without being sent to the Bastille" —or, for that matter, to any one of the other medieval fortresses used as royal prisons.

Under the Old Regime, censorship by Church and State tended to be clumsy and haphazard, with none of the chilling efficiency of the modern police state. Books banned in Paris were published abroad and smuggled into France to be circulated from hand to hand. Censorship merely gave to subversive ideas the tempting succulence of forbidden fruit. In books, in plays, and in conversation the *philosophes* made their criticisms of the regime clear through subtle jokes, sly innuendoes, and satirical remarks. Unable openly to criticize the government, instead they commented scathingly on the absurd customs of the Hindus, the Hottentots, or the Iroquois. They admired extravagantly the religious liberty of Pennsylvania and the political freedom of Britain. They "annihilated with laughter." When for economy half the royal horses were sold, it was whispered, "how much more sensible it would have been to dismiss half the asses that fill the royal court." And even noblemen were amused to see one another lampooned in a famous play, *The Marriage of Figaro*. The king protested that the comic hero went perilously far in asking, "What has a noble done for all his privileges except to give himself the trouble of being born?", but a courtier carelessly replied with another of Figaro's lines, "It is only little minds that fear little writings."

The truth was that French civilization was too advanced, French citizens too thoughtful, to be able to tolerate the Old Regime in silence. After the revolution had come, Louis XVI pointed sadly to the volumes of Rousseau and Voltaire in his prison quarters with the remark, "These two men have destroyed France." They had not—but their words had, indeed, played a vital role in undermining the structure of the Old Regime.

6. THE FINANCIAL PLIGHT OF THE OLD REGIME

A thoroughly bad government can survive if it has the backing of age, tradition, and wealth, but even a popular regime is in trouble if it has no funds. The Old Regime in France was not only appallingly bad and detested by its most enlightened citizens, it was also chronically hard-up. Throughout the 18th century it outspent its income recklessly and persistently. Time and again it resorted to heavy borrowing to stave off disaster, only to plunge ahead once more on its fateful course toward bankruptcy.

Taxation

Part of the government's financial difficulties were a result of its grossly inefficient methods of collecting taxes. Without the aid of any sort of budget, the King's Council periodically fixed upon a sum to be raised by direct taxation. This sum was then divided among the intendants, who in turn allotted a tax quota to each town and parish. The actual task of collection was carried out by individuals who, if they failed to gather their quota, had to make good the deficit out of their own pockets on pain of imprisonment. As a further incentive they had the right to retain for their own profit any sum they could extort over the stipulated amount. Sometimes a tax collector could, by bribery, have the tax quota for his own region set artificially low, at the expense of a neighbouring district, thereby reducing his risks and making his profits more certain. But whatever his quota, a collector would extort the most ruinous taxes, and resort to ruthless means, rather than suffer personal loss or imprisonment.

Indirect taxes, if collected efficiently, might have brought the royal treasury a huge annual income. The government, however, was frequently so desperate for a large and immediate lump sum that it sold the right to collect such taxes, generally on a six-year contract, to the highest cash bidder. (It was a method of tax collection that had been proved inadequate in Roman times.) Holders of tax contracts, known as tax-farmers, made full use of royal authority to squeeze the taxpayers dry. In the process, they not only recovered the price they had paid the government but also amassed monstrous profits which, by rights, should have gone into the royal treasury. Not surprisingly, tax-farmers came to be among the wealthiest as well as the most hated members of the French bourgeoisie. Even if taxes had been systematically and efficiently collected, however, there remained the unalterable fact that under the Old Regime the richer a man was the fewer taxes he had to pay. And, in time, those less fortunate, however hard pressed, could pay no more.

War, a Drain on the Treasury

A second and even more important cause of France's chronic insolvency was her costly participation in the wars of the 18th century. The pattern had been set earlier by Louis XIV, who squandered huge sums to little advantage fighting four wars in quick succession. On his death-bed Louis gave to his heirs a solemn warning: "Endeavour to live at peace with your neighbours; do not imitate me in my fondness for war, nor in the exorbitant expenditure which I have incurred." His advice went unheeded. Between 1733 and 1783, France fought four more major wars, none of which she could afford and each of which led the government more deeply into debt. It was the third of these conflicts, the Seven Years' War (1756-1763), that directly paved the way for the French Revolution: this war resulted not only in the loss to France of virtually the whole of her rich, overseas trading empire, but brought with it a succession of military disasters galling to a proud nation. Defeat exposed, too, the corruption and incompetence of the administration—and of officials like Bigot, the avaricious intendant of New France—so that even in the eyes of Frenchmen hitherto loyal, the regime came to be despised and discredited.

Involvement in America

Peace found the Old Regime struggling under mounting annual deficits. Then, in 1775, the outbreak of the American Revolution presented France with yet another fatal temptation to make war. Here was a seemingly golden opportunity for the nation to avenge itself on Britain for the peace of 1763. French manufacturers, too, nursed the hope that with the breakup of Britain's North American empire their wares would gain entry to a rich market long denied them by British mercantile policy. Though Turgot warned Louis XVI, that "the first gun shot will drive the state into bankruptcy," other ministers persuaded the king in 1778 that intervention was imperative in the best interests of France.

Militarily the war was a success. For a brief spell the French navy regained command of the seas and threatened Britain itself with invasion, and it was a French fleet and French troops that enabled Washington to force the surrender of a British army at Yorktown. But financially the war was a disaster. French military forces and fleets which, together with great quantities of money and supplies, helped launch the American republic, could be raised only by floating further huge cash loans at interest rates of up to ten per cent.

Politically, too, the War of American Independence had dire consequences for the Old Regime. The Declaration of Independence with its ringing phrases on liberty, equality, and fraternity was hailed ecstatically in France. Here were Voltaire's ideals in practice: the people asserting their will, human equality established by law. Benjamin Franklin, sent to France as an American envoy and lionized by Parisian hostesses, proved an eloquent propagandist for republican beliefs. French officers, like the wealthy, young Marquis de Lafayette, who fought with Washington's army, helped transplant into France American ideas, "sufficient to subvert every European state." Lafayette, who had volunteered his services perhaps with no higher motive than a desire for glory and adventure, after his return to France hung prominently in his mansion a framed copy of the Declaration of Independence. Thousands of ordinary French soldiers returned home, too, having seen with their own eyes a revolution succeed.

Bankruptcy or Reform?

But it was the King's pressing financial needs that led to the breakdown of the regime and opened the way for sweeping changes. So badly strained were government finances that, by 1788, one-half of all state expenditure went solely to pay interest and other charges on the public debt. At the same time fully another quarter of all government spending was swallowed up by the costs of maintaining an army and navy for peacetime defence.

The government, faced with bankruptcy, found itself with no easy way of escape. It could neither repudiate the public debt without ruining its credit, nor cut expenditure on the armed forces for fear of imperiling the national safety. Yet only limited savings could be made by reducing the royal establishments. While French court life, centred in the royal palaces at Versailles and Fontainbleu, dazzled visitors with its extravagance, it represented only a twentieth part of government spending—a small portion compared with the heavy drain of debts accumulated in successive wars. One solution remained: to make all men pay their fair share of taxes.

In 1786, Calonne, who had succeeded Necker as Minister of

Finance, proposed drastic reforms. These included a complete overhaul of the administrative machinery of government, the sweeping away of internal customs duties, and a sharp reduction of the feudal obligations of the peasants. Moreover, he proposed to reduce—though not to do away with—the tax exemptions of the privileged classes, and he specifically urged "a direct tax on all landowners without exception." Most revolutionary of all, he recommended the establishment of local government assemblies in which all the old distinctions between members of the three Estates, or orders of society, would be abolished. These proposals, if carried out, would have done much towards transferring the Old Regime into an efficient and enlightened autocracy. But did Louis XVI have the strength to force through such reforms in the teeth of resistance from the privileged orders?

The following year, to avert political and financial collapse, the king had no choice but to act. He summoned an "Assembly of Notables" in the desperate hope that they would sanction Calonne's proposals. Instead, they condemned outright every proposal that affected their interests and angrily demanded—and obtained—the dismissal of Calonne. His successor, the Archbishop of Brienne, then turned to the *Parlement* of Paris, a body of magistrates that formed the most powerful appeal court in the country. It, too, defied the king's wishes and refused to sanction either new taxes or further loans. New taxes, it claimed, might rightfully be granted only by the Estates-General, the national assembly that represented the three Estates of France. Its stand was hailed enthusiastically as a blow struck for the rights of man, though in truth the magistrates were aristocrats determined only to protect their own interests and to force the king into surrendering to them a share of his power. The king saw the threat to his position. The *Parlement* was at once dismissed and orders given for the arrest of its leaders. Immediately there were popular protests throughout France and excited mobs clamoured for a summoning of the Estates-General. Meanwhile, bankruptcy loomed.

In July, 1788, Louis XVI called on the Estates-General to meet at Versailles in May of the following year. It was to be the first gathering of the representatives of the people of France in 175 years.

7 The French Revolution

> The major advances in civilization are processes which all but wreck the societies in which they occur.
> —Alfred North Whitehead

During the hot summer of 1789, while the financial and political crises of state were coming to a head, the great mass of the French people—the labourers of the countryside and towns—had still more pressing worries of their own, for starvation and unemployment stalked the land. For more than a decade the cost of living had steadily risen, and the wages of the poor had been left far behind. In 1786, a free-trade treaty with Britain, though highly approved by the economists, brought further hardships. France was flooded with cheap, mass-produced English cotton goods. French textile mills could not compete, and there was heavy unemployment followed by a general business depression. Then, in 1788, there was a disastrous grain harvest, and the following winter the price of grain began to soar. By July, 1789, the price of bread was higher than it had been at any time in eighty years—and bread was the staple food of every French working man.

In previous hard times the government had subsidized the price of wheat and taken measures for public relief, but, in the fateful summer of 1789, the government was in no position to help. All across France there were ugly incidents—grain stores were pillaged, grain dealers were mobbed and lynched, and in several places troops had to open fire to restore order. In desperation the king recalled Necker—who had earlier been dismissed for proposing stringent economies of government spending—to grapple with the financial crisis. But while the privileged and the well-to-do argued over problems of taxation and politics, tens of thousands of angry and frightened French men and women thought only of their empty stomachs, nursed their hatreds, and longed for change.

1. REVOLUTION AT VERSAILLES

It was against this background that the Estates-General gathered at Versailles, some sixteen kilometres from Paris, on May 5, 1789. Almost at once there was a heated wrangle over voting procedures. Traditionally each Estate was entitled to one vote, which meant that on every issue the clergy and the nobles could outvote the Third Estate by a majority of two-to-one. The delegates of the Third Estate naturally insisted that the three Estates meet as one body, and that each member cast one vote. In theory, the nobles and the clergy, each group casting 300 votes, would be able to balance exactly the 600 votes of the Third Estate. But in practice some liberal-minded noblemen and a large number of the clergy (two-thirds of whom were poor parish priests) might be expected to vote with the Third Estate. Thus, voting "by head" would give the Third Estate a clear majority and open the way for the sweeping reforms so dreaded by the privileged orders. On this key issue a majority of the clergy and nobles refused to give way. The Commons for their part refused to act until the other two Estates had joined them. For five tense weeks there was deadlock.

During this period two men emerged as leaders of the Third Estate, each elected under a rule which allowed members of other Estates to sit for the Commons. The first was a free-thinking priest, the Abbé Siéyès. Small and intense, he was a poor speaker but a man with brilliant ideas. Probably every delegate in the Third Estate was influenced by a famous pamphlet in which Siéyès asked and answered the following questions:

> What is the Third Estate? Nothing.
> What should it be? Everything.

This dry, donnish priest time and again was able to express exactly the feelings of the delegates.

The second leader, the Comte de Mirabeau, was a broad-minded aristocrat, by nature a rebel and a profligate. He was conceited, quarrelsome, and overbearing, but he had great courage and a burning belief that the most desirable form of government was constitutional monarchy. Repeatedly, Mirabeau swayed the assembly by his forceful and eloquent speeches, just as Siéyès influenced it with his ideas. Each man tried to direct and control the revolution. Mirabeau died prematurely less than two years later; Siéyès was swept away by the flood.

In mid-June, guided by Siéyès and Mirabeau, the delegates to the Third Estate seized the initiative. Without asking leave of the king ("had the United States asked for the sanction of the king of England?") they declared themselves to be the "National Assembly"—in effect the representatives of the people of France. It was the first open act of rebellion.

The National Assembly

Frightened by their own boldness, but grimly determined, the delegates of the Third Estate then called upon the clergy and nobles to join them. At the same time, afraid that at any moment they might be dismissed, they urged all Frenchmen to cease paying taxes if the National Assembly should cease to exist.

The clergy and the lords debated angrily in their separate chambers whether or not to join the defiant commoners. On June 19, by a majority of 149, the clergy voted to do so and there was "applause like thunder" as the count was announced. The conservative bishops had been decisively out-voted by the humble priests. Among the nobles the debate was equally stormy but the issue never came to a vote, for Louis, belatedly, had decided to act.

When the representatives of the Third Estate met to resume their meetings, they found that the king had ordered the doors of their assembly hall locked against them. For some minutes, baffled and angry, they stood around in the drizzling rain. Suddenly one of their number found an open doorway nearby, leading into a large, indoor tennis court. Moving on impulse, the nearly six hundred delegates crowded in, followed and cheered by an excited crowd of soldiers and spectators. There were rousing speeches. Then, within the four walls of the court, all the delegates but one uncovered their heads, raised their right arms, and swore a solemn oath not to disband until they had given France a constitution. It was June 20, 1789.

Not long after, when a uniformed messenger solemnly ordered the Assembly in the name of the king to retire, Mirabeau thundered, "Sire, go tell your master that we are here by the will of the people and nothing but bayonets shall drive us out!" For a full week Louis XVI hesitated, uncertain of the loyalty of the troops he had available. Then he weakly gave way, ordering the three Estates to sit as one body and to vote "by head."

One delegate wrote ecstatically, "The revolution is over," and Necker advised the king to take no further action against the Assembly. But Louis was not yet ready to be relegated to the position of a constitutional monarch. Troops and artillery were called in from all parts of the country until Versailles looked like an armed camp. The courageous delegates who had started the revolution could do no more. They appeared totally at the mercy of the king's bayonets and were afraid that at any moment they would be arrested or dispersed. Some even slept in the assembly hall, not daring to leave. They were saved by the decisive intervention of the people of Paris.

The Fall of the Bastille

On July 11, news reached the capital that Necker, whom the people considered to be their champion, had been dismissed. Necker's bust, draped in black, was borne shoulder high through the city. Troops who tried to intervene were pelted by paving stones, and when a unit from the French Guards was ordered to fire on the crowd, it refused. Word spread that foreign mercenaries were about to massacre the citizens. Fear swept the city. There was no longer any order. Food stores were looted, gunsmiths' shops and an army depot were ransacked for arms, and toll-gates—symbols of a hated tax— were burned to the ground.

On the morning of July 14, rumour had it that royal troops were approaching Paris and that the guns of the Bastille had been pointed down a city thoroughfare. For four hundred years the grim fortress, with its frowning towers, had stood within the city as a symbol of royal authority. Many had been tortured or held captive within its walls. Although by 1789 the Bastille had almost ceased to be used as a royal prison, its very name still aroused hatred and dread. As mobs gathered in every corner of the city, the cry went up, "To the Bastille, to the Bastille!" The garrison consisted only of some hundred and twenty military pensioners and Swiss mercenaries. The crowd cut down a drawbridge and surged through an outer guard house. The garrison opened fire and in four hours' fighting nearly one hundred civilians were killed. Then a company of the French Guards joined the assault with cannon. As the garrison surrendered, on honourable terms, several hundred infuriated citizens surged inside. While some toppled stones from the battlements

"Blood and wine are the same colour, but today, blood is far more intoxicating than any wine."

and smashed everything breakable, others ran down dark, underground passageways, hammered open dungeon doors and ostentatiously freed the seven remaining prisoners in the fortress. One of them had been there since 1759. Only the French Guard prevented the entire garrison from being lynched. The governor, less fortunate, was set upon by the mob and hacked to pieces. The mayor of Paris met the same fate. While "women and children danced and cried," the victims' heads were borne through the streets on pikes.

All over Europe the fall of the Bastille was hailed as the dawn of a new era of liberty and, to this day, July 14 is celebrated in France as a national holiday. It was an event of great symbolic value, but its immediate significance was that the king had lost control of Paris and had little chance of regaining it. The people of Paris stood wholeheartedly behind the National Assembly. Whether Louis himself realized the seriousness of the situation is doubtful. When late that night he was told of the fall of the Bastille, he exclaimed incredulously, "It is a great revolt." "No, Sire," was the reply, "it is a great revolution."

In Paris, the bourgeoisie took firm hold of the leadership. A new city government, or commune, was established and a hastily-formed people's army, the National Guard, was placed under the command of Lafayette. Its insignia, combining the red and blue colours of the city of Paris with the white of the French monarchy, became the emblem of the revolution. Frightened by the turn of events, Louis attempted to soothe public feelings. He entered the capital and publicly pinned a tricolour cockade to his hat. The crowds, which at first had been sullen, burst into shouts of "*Vive le Roi!*"

Le Grand Peur

Though the king had tacitly accepted the situation, no one expected a mild reaction from the aristocracy. Already, the king's second brother, the Count of Artois, and a number of wealthy nobles, had fled the country with wagon-loads of possessions. They were only the first of many groups of *émigrés* who were to foment anti-revolutionary feeling abroad. Inside France, alarming rumours spread that the aristocrats planned to blow up the Assembly, and it was said that thousands of jobless men and brigands had been hired by the nobles to restore order. Panic among the peasants swept through the provinces. "The Great Fear" intensified their hatred for the "aristos" and resulted in spontaneous peasant uprisings throughout France. Landlords and their agents were driven out, and hundreds of chateaux ransacked or burned to the ground. With them were destroyed the hated *terriers* (legal documents) which recorded the feudal obligations of each peasant. In the provincial cities and towns, as news came of the fall of the Bastille, citizens' committees sprang up, determined to safeguard the Revolution. Units of the National Guard were formed and in many places were joined by royal troops. Local bastilles were seized, and government officials everywhere were forced to take orders only from the National Assembly. No one any longer paid taxes. The king had lost all authority.

The End of Feudalism

In almost three months the Assembly, with its predominantly middle class membership, had paid little attention to the grievances of the peasants. Now, spurred on by the peasant uprising, the National Assembly, in a single all-night sitting (August 4-5), abolished hundreds of feudal laws, while deputies of all orders hastened to renounce their most cherished privileges. All tithes and manorial dues were abolished and it was decreed that henceforth all men were to pay their fair share of taxes. Feudalism was at an end.

On August 26, the Assembly issued an historic "Declaration of the Rights of Man," which proclaimed that "all men, being born equal, should have equal rights." The Declaration destroyed forever the old theory that France was the personal property of its monarchs. By it the Assembly declared its support for "liberty, property, security and the right to resist oppression." Liberty it defined as "the right to do whatever does not harm another." All men were to be equal before the law. There was to be liberty of opinion, "even in religion." All citizens were to share in the making of laws, either "in person or by their representatives." No man was to be barred from high office by birth. Finally, it declared (as Montesquieu would have wished) that the powers of government were to be separated. The Declaration was truly "the death certificate of the Old Regime." Thousands of copies were printed, distributed, and read in all parts of Europe. "Liberty, Equality, Fraternity" became the rallying cry of the Revolution.

Bread and Riots

Meanwhile, the scarcity and high cost of bread continued to produce riots. In Paris, more people than ever were out of work, and long lines of starving men and women formed outside the bakers' stores. Coupled with the shortage of food came rumours that the king was plotting to flee. The news spread that troops which had recently reached Versailles from Flanders had trampled a tricolour flag. The result was a further outbreak of violence. On October 4, an unkempt crowd of market women gathered, chanting "Bread! Bread!" Arming themselves with clubs, they marched on Versailles, followed by a horde of their menfolk and children, as well as units of the National Guard led by Lafayette. The National Assembly was invaded and Louis XVI, amidst the uproar, was forced to sign the decrees of August 4 and the Declaration of the Rights of Man. The next day the crowd, in wild-eyed triumph, dragged the king and the royal family to the old Tuileries palace in Paris, where it was felt they would be safely under the eye of the people. "We have the baker and the baker's wife and the baker's boy," cried a voice from the mob. "Now we shall have the bread!" For the next three years Louis XVI was to live in terror for his life.

Ten days later the National Assembly also moved to Paris. No one thereafter dared challenge the control which the Paris mob held over the Revolution. Some of the more moderate revolutionaries, including many who had fervently taken the tennis court oath, grew fearful of the course of events. They quietly left the Assembly, and emigrated from France.

2. THE NATIONAL ASSEMBLY

During the next two years (October, 1789–September, 1791), the National Assembly completed the work of destroying the Old Regime and, in lengthy debates, set about the task of devising a new form of government to take its place.

The Constitutional Monarchy

The creaking administrative machinery of the Old Regime, with its overlapping provinces and intendencies, was swept away, and the entire country was divided into the eighty-three, roughly equal *départements*, which are still to be found in modern France. Local officials, even judges and tax-collectors, were no longer to be appointed by the king but elected by the people. Henceforth the nation was to be ruled by a single chamber, to be known as the Legislative Assembly. The king's powers were to be reduced to a shadow; in future he could merely suspend legislation for a limited period, not veto it. However, despite the earlier bold declaration that all men were "equal in rights," the National Assembly showed its essentially middle class outlook. The delegates felt they had to be practical. Since most Frenchmen were uneducated, how could they hold sensible political opinions? Only "active" citizens, that is those over twenty-five, who paid direct taxes equivalent to three days' wages a year, were to be eligible to vote or to hold office. Thus the new constitution was far from establishing a government of the people. It established, instead, a constitutional monarchy, in which the reins of power would be held by the well-to-do bourgeoisie.

These changes did nothing to solve France's problems, which had only grown worse since people had stopped paying taxes. Desperate for money, and influenced by the anti-clerical outlook of the *philosophes*, the National Assembly decreed that the enormous landed wealth of the Roman Catholic Church be forfeited and used as security for a new issue of paper money. Thousands of hectares of Church (and later Crown) lands were sold to the bourgeoisie and the peasants. To compensate the Church for its losses, but also to bring it still more closely under State control, the clergy in future were to be paid by the government. Further drastic steps to secularize the Church followed. All monasteries were closed and in July, 1790, the "Civil Constitution of the Clergy" was enacted, decreeing that bishops and priests were henceforth to be elected by the people in the same way as public officials—regardless of the fact that a voter might be a Protestant, a Jew, or an atheist. At the same time all clergy were ordered to take an oath of loyalty to the State.

These measures were a deep affront to all devout Roman Catholics, including Louis XVI, and they were roundly denounced by the Pope. To the many plain, parish priests, who had given active and valuable support to the Revolution in its opening stages, the Civil Constitution meant an agonizing struggle of conscience. A minority, known as the "juring" clergy, took the state oath, but more than half the clergy, the "non-jurors," refused to do so. Some of the latter joined the *émigrés* in exile but others, risking imprisonment and death, stayed behind and actively encouraged the faithful in opposition to the Revolution. The Civil Constitution of the Clergy not only created inside France the first sizeable movement of opposition, but it also had lasting repercussions in European politics. Throughout the 19th century the official outlook of the Roman Catholic Church tended to be anti-liberal and anti-democratic, while those who were liberal in politics tended to be fiercely anti-clerical.

The Flight of the King

It was a question, now, of how long the constitutional monarchy could survive. It received one serious setback in April, 1791, when

Mirabeau, its most forceful champion, died; it received a still worse setback when the king made an inept attempt to flee France in order to seek foreign help in crushing the Revolution. On the night of June 20, Louis slipped out of Paris in disguise, accompanied by his unpopular Austrian queen, Marie Antoinette, their two children and a handful of loyal retainers. All that night their heavy coach lumbered towards the eastern frontier. Early the following morning, at a stop to change horses, the king momentarily showed his face at a window. The postmaster's son immediately became suspicious, for the face he had glimpsed was similar to the royal portrait on every bank-note. Word sped ahead and at the little village of Varennes, only thirty-two kilometres from the frontier, the road was blocked by a crowd of villagers with farm wagons. The royal fugitives were ignominiously carried back to Paris and the king was suspended from his duties.

Despite Louis' obvious lack of sympathy, the National Assembly were still determined to have a constitutional monarchy, and for that they still needed the king. When, on September 14, 1791, the constitution was completed, Louis XVI reluctantly swore to uphold it, and was restored to his throne. At last the king and the Revolution appeared to be reconciled. Although a minority of Frenchmen felt the Revolution had gone too far, and others that it had not gone far enough, most greeted the new constitution with genuine approval. In Paris there was a joyous celebration with flags, fireworks, and dancing. The king was even hailed as "*notre bon roi*," and a pardon was issued to all *émigrés*.

It was just twenty-seven months since the National Assembly had taken its defiant oath in the tennis court at Versailles, and the weary delegates felt their task was done. They had abolished absolute rule and swept away privilege and feudalism. They had transformed France into a bourgeois republic, and in effect, reduced the king to being little more than "chief clerk to the state." The Revolution was over—or so it seemed.

Before dissolving, the National Assembly, in a misguided act of self-denial, decreed that none of its members should be eligible to take part in the new Legislative Assembly. France was thus robbed of all the experience gained by several hundred delegates in two years of intense political activity.

3. THE LEGISLATIVE ASSEMBLY

The Legislative Assembly, which was elected by "active citizens," and first met in October, 1791, was filled with ardent, idealistic young men, full of eloquence and ideas but totally lacking experience in government. Almost at once a power struggle began between the monarchists, anxious for the new constitution to work, and radical groups who wished to see the monarchy abolished and France become a truly democratic republic, with every adult male citizen given the right to vote.

The Radicals

The radicals had the backing of the Paris mob—the working men and women who still looked in vain for steady prices, steady jobs, and the right to vote. They also had the support of an increasing number of well-organized political clubs, which flooded the country with propaganda in the form of letters, newspapers, and pamphlets. These clubs had originally been formed in 1789 as political luncheon clubs, in which members could exchange views and plot strategy. Most influential was the *Jacobin Club* (so named from the monastery in which it met). In its early months the Jacobin Club had charged substantial dues and was limited in membership to such well-to-do, "moderate" revolutionaries as Siéyès, Mirabeau, and Lafayette. In time its dues were reduced and the Jacobin Club, through affiliated clubs formed in virtually every town of any size in France, gained a nation-wide influence. Later, under the leadership of Maximilien Robespierre, the Jacobins became increasingly radical. The *Cordelier Club*, another radical club, charged low dues from the start and became a rallying point for working men. There were also a number of conservative clubs but their membership declined as more and more of their members fled the country.

In the new Legislative Assembly the most radical delegates, the Jacobins and the Cordeliers, sat to the left of the speaker. They were referred to as "the Mountain" because their seats were in the highest part of the hall. Close to them sat another strongly republican faction named the Girondins, after the south-eastern district of France from which many of them came. In the "plain," the level, centre section of the hall (sometimes scornfully referred to as "the marsh" or "the belly") sat a majority of delegates who voted as independents. Finally, to the right of the speaker—it was at this time that the terms "right" and "left" entered politics

"But now if Mirabeau is the greatest, who of these Six Hundred (members of the Third Estate) may be the meanest? Shall we say, that anxious, slight, ineffectual-looking man . . . that greenish-looking individual whose name is Maximilien Robespierre."—Carlyle, *The French Revolution*

—there sat the *Feuillants,* a relatively conservative group that had broken with the Jacobins to support constitutional monarchy. Significantly, it was the Feuillants who had been considered radical in the old Assembly.

The Girondins

The Girondins soon became the dominant group in the Assembly. They knew next to nothing about administration, but had a passionate, infectious enthusiasm for republican ideals and made eloquent speeches comparing themselves with the republican heroes of ancient Greece and Rome. Holding an almost sentimental affection for their fellow men, they cherished a romantic dream of establishing throughout Europe a republican heaven on earth. But, while fiercely uncompromising in demanding the overthrow of the monarchy, they were not extreme democrats. Their opponents of the Mountain hated their middle class bias and called them "aristocratic republicans."

The Girondins knew that revolutionary France faced many enemies. There were *émigrés* tirelessly agitating for foreign intervention; non-juring priests at home, inciting the peasants to oppose a godless regime; and the foreign rulers, who viewed with horror the growth of social equality and mob violence. Moreover, the queen (as they suspected) was secretly sending imploring letters to her brother, the Emperor Leopold of Austria. "We no longer have any recourse," she wrote, "but in the foreign powers. At all costs they must come to our aid."

Foreign Threats to the Revolution

In August, 1791, Leopold joined with Frederick William II of Prussia to issue the Declaration of Pillnitz. It was a carefully-worded manifesto in which they declared it was "of common interest to all sovereigns" to restore order and the monarchy to France. Further, they declared that they would themselves take military action if all the other great military Powers would do so. It was an empty threat (for they well knew that Great Britain would not join them) perhaps intended as a sop to Marie Antoinette and the importunate *émigrés*.

The declaration, however, alarmed and infuriated all patriotic Frenchmen, and as war hysteria swept the country, the Girondins, whose power was swiftly growing, angrily demanded the expulsion of all *émigrés* from the lands bordering France. At this moment the prudent Leopold died. His reactionary young successor, Francis II, promptly joined forces with the king of Prussia, and eighty thousand Austrian and Prussian troops were mustered for invasion on the eastern frontier of France. When they refused to withdraw, the Girondist ministry that had taken power in April, 1792, as a result of Pillnitz, declared war.

In France patriotic fervour became intense. The monarchists welcomed a war which they mistakenly believed would rally the French people behind the throne and the constitution. The working classes, aroused by the fiery speeches of radical politicians, rallied to the defence of the Revolution, though they cared little enough for the king or the middle class Legislative Assembly.

The threat of the Duke of Brunswick that he would put Paris to the sword if the King were molested infuriated the Parisians already stirred by the oratory of Danton and Marat. On August 9-10, 1792, reinforced by the newly-arrived Marseilles battalion of republicans, the Paris mob attacked the royal palace, the Tuileries. Its defenders, the Swiss Guard, were slaughtered, the palace was looted and set afire, and the Royal Family fled to the Assembly for protection.

Volunteers flocked to the capital. Among them were a group from Marseilles, "five hundred fanatics, three quarters of them drunk, all wearing red bonnets, marching bare-armed and dishevelled." They brought with them the *Marseillaise,* a revolutionary song whose rousing words and martial music were to transform the ragged soldiers of the Revolution into frenzied zealots.

The End of the Monarchy

France was totally unprepared for war. Thousands of officers had emigrated, discipline among the troops was chaotic, and arms were inadequate. The three French armies in the field suffered a series of reverses; one general was lynched by his own troops for "treason." As word of these setbacks reached Paris, and public anger mounted, a political re-alignment began to develop. Both peasants and lower class workers in Paris had long felt that the government of the constituent assembly had favoured the propertied interests over them, a feeling intensified by steadily rising prices. Now, popular discontent, seeking an outlet, turned against the royal family. Did not everyone know that the king and queen were in league with the enemies of France? Indignation and hatred were still further aroused when the Duke of Brunswick, leading the Austro-Prussian armies, threatened to destroy Paris if any harm should come to the king. As a consequence, the political parties of the Plain, who favoured a constitutional monarchy, were discredited and lost power, while conversely the radical anti-royalist republicans were bound to profit. It was a situation almost made to order for radical orators who roused the people to a fury against the foreign enemies, against the king, and against the monarchist system. On the night of August 9-10, 1792, a mob stormed and set fire to the royal palace of the Tuileries, massacred many of the Swiss Guard, and forced the king in the early morning to fly for his life to the Legislative Assembly. The terrified deputies, now virtually under the complete control of the radical Paris Commune (civic government) and the Jacobin clubs, agreed to depose the king and ordered the immediate election of a National Convention to draw up another—this time republican—constitution for France. The vote was to be given to every adult male. The Feuillants, once the vanguard of the Revolution, crept into hiding.

The Fury of Extremism

During this critical time two men had risen to power on the crest of the mob. The first, Georges Danton, was a towering, heavily-built man with a "rough, loud voice," striking, pockmarked features and a bull neck. He was a lawyer by training but had grown up on a farm, and all his life retained the simple, down-to-earth tastes of a countryman. He liked nothing better than to escape from the clamour of politics to the quiet of his home and garden. Politically, his influence stemmed from his humble background, his deeply sincere republicanism, and his extraordinary talent as an orator. With his powerful voice and sweeping gestures he could whip a crowd into a frenzy, while his own able mind always remained cold and dispassionate.

Far less attractive was Jean Paul Marat, a conceited, quarrelsome little man, with quick birdlike movements, darting brown eyes and a "cadaverous complexion." Before the Revolution he had been a physician of some eminence, but a quarrel with the Academy of Science soured his outlook and gave him deep feelings of persecution. In 1789, he founded with Danton the left-wing Cordelier Club and gained influence as the editor of a scurrilous and vitriolic newspaper, *Friend of the People*. Its motto became, "Let us tax the rich to subsidize the poor," and in it Marat gleefully maligned virtually every leader of the bourgeois class. He became the idol of the Paris mob, denouncing moderation and proclaiming violence to be the most effective road to a democratic paradise. In a voice described by an English observer as "croaking" and "hollow," Marat said, "I believe in the cutting off of heads."

Danton and Marat both played a large part in the August uprising, which led to the deposition of the king, and in the tumultuous events of the six weeks which followed. France was in a state of virtual anarchy. The royal family was flung into jail under foul and humiliating conditions. Lafayette, commander of the French armies and a known monarchist, fled to the Austrians. Trade was at a standstill and prices rose higher than ever. Meanwhile, as voters went to the polls to elect the National Convention, the invading Austrian and Prussian armies kept advancing. At this critical time it was Danton, eloquent and bold, who became "the voice of the revolution and of France." In a series of speeches he rallied Frenchmen to the defence of the nation and called for "audacity, more audacity and still more audacity."

"We must be daring and more daring and always more daring—and France is saved!" was the roar of defiance from the young lawyer Georges Danton as the Austro-Prussian Army moved toward France. Robespierre, reaching for dictatorship and seeing him as a rival, contrived his fall and execution. "I have lived," said Danton, "entirely for my country. I am Danton till my death; tomorrow I shall sleep in glory."

Jean Paul Marat: "... belonging to no party, he always stood alone, always attacking with mad violence all those in power. Equality within the state and government by the people were his aims, and he would go to any lengths to destroy those who even delayed or debated their attainment."

On the home front, radical leaders employed terror to crush disunity. While Marat plastered Paris with posters calling for the blood of "traitors," Danton ordered house-to-house searches for hidden weapons and royalist sympathizers. A "Revolutionary Tribunal" was set up to try "crimes against the state." Old scores were settled as men denounced their neighbours. Hundreds were arrested "on suspicion."

On September 2, fear turned to outright panic, as word reached the capital that the key fortress of Verdun was on the verge of surrender. Spurred by Marat, the Paris mobs again erupted into violence. Organized groups broke into the prisons in a bestial hunt for "enemies of the revolution." Over 1 100 men, women and children were dragged out and butchered. Many of them were liberal aristocrats who, rather than flee, had remained to share the future of their country. Abroad—and particularly in Britain—news of the September massacres turned public opinion against the Revolution.

Lafayette's command had been taken by Dumouriez, a fearless and brilliant commander. On September 20, 1792, to the astonishment of France as well as of all Europe, Dumouriez's tattered, half-trained, revolutionary army met and turned back the renowned regiments of the Prussian army at Valmy. Although it was less a battle than a gun duel, fought in drizzle and fog, Valmy ranks with the decisive military engagements of history. In the words of one historian: "After Valmy every Frenchman who held sword or musket looked upon himself as the champion of a cause which was destined to triumph."

4. THE NATIONAL CONVENTION

On September 21, the same day that the electrifying news of Valmy reached Paris, the National Convention gathered for its first session. The Girondists, the middle class republicans once considered radical, now sat on the right, in place of the vanished constitutional monarchists. In the high seats to the left sat the Mountain, made up of the Jacobin and Cordelier club extremists. Most numerous were the independents of the Plain, seated in the centre. The independents attempted to avoid extremes and to vote on each measure according to its merits, but they came to be dominated first by the Girondists and later by the Mountain. The extremists, by appealing to the crowded public galleries and through them to the mob outside, were now in a position to force through any measures by threats of violence.

The first act of the Convention was to abolish the monarchy and declare France a republic. There was now no turning back. Every reminder of the past had to go: the *émigrés* were condemned to perpetual banishment; churches were ordered to be turned into "Temples of Reason;" all titles were banned. Henceforth, every French subject was to be hailed as *"citoyen"* or *"citoyenne."* Even the old calendar was abolished. September 22, 1792, became the first day of the Year One of the French Republic. Months, the days of the week, and holidays—all were renamed.

In December, 1792, Louis XVI, now plain "Citizen Capet," was dragged before the Convention for trial. In January he was voted guilty of treason and by a vote of 387 to 334 was condemned to death. He died bravely in public, beneath the guillotine. The queen nine months later, travelled "through the little door to heaven," while their ten-year-old son (Louis XVII) died an unrecorded death in captivity.

The execution of Louis shocked the outside world, but in the Convention Danton roared, "Come all the kings of Europe against us and we will hurl at their feet in defiance, the head of a king." Hard after Valmy, in September, 1792, the jubilant French armies won a series of short-lived successes, overrunning Flanders, occupying the left bank of the Rhine, and annexing Savoy and Nice. From Paris, the Convention encouraged its troops with Girondin propaganda, declaring its intention to make war "against all kings on behalf of all people." But already lofty, republican professions of "brotherhood for all men" were beginning to give way to nationalist dreams of conquest. Intoxicated by the taste of military glory, the French revolutionaries revived Louis XIV's old policy of extending the eastern boundaries of France to the Rhine.

At first, the great Powers of Europe had been delighted to see their old rival, France, weakened by internal upheavals. But they became alarmed by a revolutionary creed which leapt all national barriers to proclaim the rights of man. They were shaken, too, by the increasingly bloodthirsty and aggressive tone of the Revolution. In Great Britain there was a traditional concern over French control of the Flanders coast. Early in 1793, England formed a coalition with Austria, Prussia, Spain, Savoy, and Holland to make war on France. Of the great Powers, only Russia held back, busy with her own ambitions in Poland. Belgium and the Rhineland were retaken by the allied forces; Dumouriez, out of sympathy with a Convention of "three hundred scoundrels and four hundred imbeciles," deserted to the Austrians. Before long, five allied armies threatened France herself with invasion.

5. THE COMMITTEE OF PUBLIC SAFETY

The military crisis and the treachery of Dumouriez enabled the Jacobin and Cordelier club extremists of the Mountain to gain control of the National Convention, in April, 1793. Emergency, dictatorial powers were given to Danton and a small group of able and determined men, known as the Committee of Public Safety.

The Girondins were driven from power and many of their delegates were placed under arrest. The rest fled to the provinces. In July the monstrous Marat was stabbed to death by a young Girondin sympathizer, Charlotte Corday; twenty-one Girondin leaders were subsequently guillotined.

From April to July, 1793, Danton again proved himself an inspiring war leader. He called on France to become "a nation in arms" and worked ruthlessly to enforce unity and to speed the flow of men and munitions to the front. But the plight of France remained desperate. Insurrections blazed as the allied armies advanced from south and east. In the Vendée, in western France, Catholic peasants, incited by non-juring priests, rose against conscription. In Lyons, Marseilles, and other provincial centres there were revolts led by surviving Girondins against Parisian domination. In Toulon, royalist rebels welcomed the British fleet into the harbour.

Robespierre and "The Reign of Terror"

Early in July, 1793, after a fierce struggle for power, control of the Committee of Public Safety began to fall into the hands of Maximilien Robespierre. Danton was ousted and, weary at last of politics and of the terror which he himself had instigated, retired to the country.

Robespierre, who for over a year was to wield vast power, was a dapper, bespectacled, little lawyer, with a sharp voice, a prim

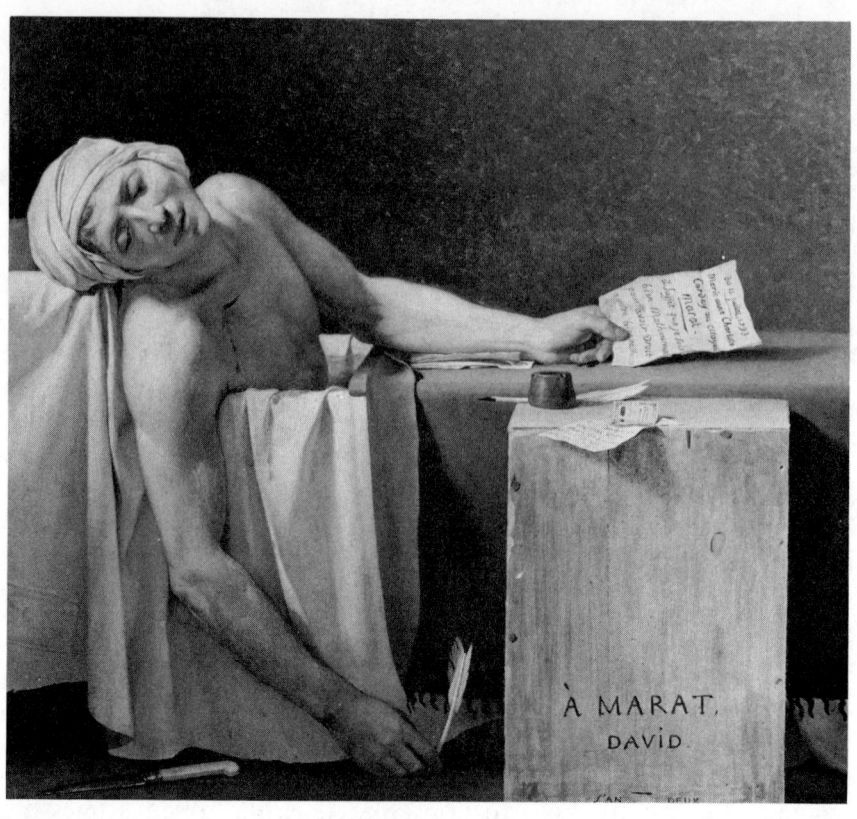

" 'What is going on in Caens?' was Marat's question.
'Eighteen deputies from the Convention rule there in collusion with the Department,' Charlotte Corday replied.
'What are their names?' Marat asked.
She gave them as Marat wrote them down.' They will be guillotined!' he said. With that, she rose and plunged a knife into his lungs. He was able only to cry for help before he died."—from L. R. Gottschalk, *Jean Paul Marat*

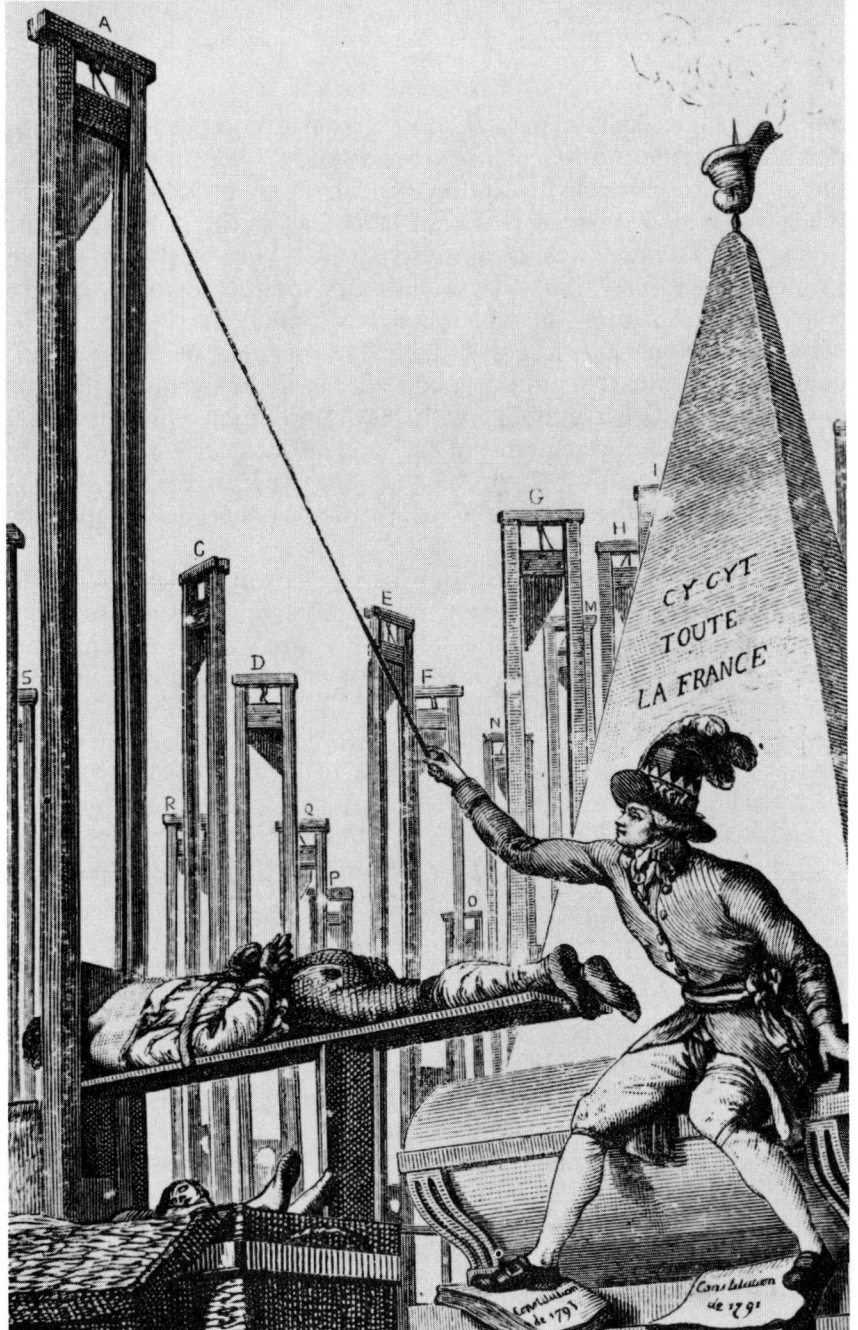

"Here lies France." This bitter caricature of Robespierre is said to have cost the cartoonist his life. Robespierre, having guillotined all the French nation, is shown sitting on a coffin operating a guillotine in the midst of a forest of the machines. Each of them represents a category of victims, including the Committee of Public Safety, the Girondins, the Cordeliers, the nobles and priests, the generals and soldiers, the people of talent, and old men, women, and children.

manner, and a sickly, pale, almost greenish complexion. He appeared altogether "a man unfit for revolution," yet he was perhaps the greatest of French revolutionary leaders, as blindly devoted to the writings of Rousseau as Lenin later was to the gospel of Karl Marx. Robespierre was a burning idealist, who yearned to see France transformed into the world's first perfect democracy—"a Republic of Virtue"—in which the basic goodness of man, proclaimed by Rousseau, might flourish. He dreamed of every citizen being devoted to the public good, filled with a burning love for his country and for equality with his fellow man. Unfortunately, in his blind, fanatical pursuit of an ideal, Robespierre would spare neither friend nor foe. Terror became "the order of the day." Anyone opposed to the "Republic of Virtue" (either deliberately or unwittingly) deserved to die.

During Robespierre's "Reign of Terror," from September, 1793 to July, 1794, between twenty and twenty-five thousand suspects died beneath the guillotine (the "official" figure was seventeen thousand). Anyone who in any way had been contaminated by the monarchy, or the Girondin party, was liable to summary execution. "No one feels safe; no one is safe," wrote a contemporary. "If not a suspect, one may be suspected of being a suspect." Years later, when Siéyès was asked what he had accomplished in those days, he answered with a wry smile, "I lived." Even Danton, after all his services to the Revolution, was put to death, together with most of his followers. He was accused of unseemly moderation (had he not said, "I would prefer being guillotined to guillotining"?). By the law of the Twenty Second of Prairial (or June 10, 1794, by the conventional calendar), revolutionary tribunals were empowered to convict and execute without even listening to evidence. And throughout France heads continued to "fall like slates."

To those, like Robespierre, who believed the Revolution worth any sacrifice, the Terror was justified as a measure of national defence. It gave to France, in a time of national danger, an administration far stronger and more centralized than any under the Old Regime. The Terror blocked any general uprising; one after another the insurrections were crushed. The period of Robespierre's power was memorable also for its military triumphs. Under Carnot, "the organizer of victory," the army grew till it had over three-quarters of a million men. Devastating new military tactics were devised to exploit the sheer weight of numbers and the revolution-

On 9th Thermidor (July 27), 1794, Robespierre hesitated when addressing the National Convention. A voice cried "It is the blood of Danton which chokes you!" and tumult broke out. Robespierre and his followers left the meeting to draw up a proclamation of insurrection against the Convention. Robespierre was sitting pen in hand ready to sign when troops burst into the room. According to some versions, Robespierre was shot by a young man named Merda; according to others, he shot himself. At any rate, the wound was not fatal, but the next day, Robespierre was dragged to the guillotine and executed along with twenty-one of his followers. "The Revolution had finished devouring her children."

ary zeal of the troops. On the field of battle the French soldiers advanced in dense masses, "roaring the Marseillaise," while swarms of sharp-shooters advanced in front and on either flank to throw the enemy off balance. Generals who faltered were executed. "Forced loans" provided the cash. A new system of semaphore signals sped messages from Paris to the Front in fifteen minutes. In two and a half years of fighting (1793-1795), every enemy was driven from the soil of France. Flanders was retaken, and in Holland the revolutionary armies established the new "Batavian Republic." By March, 1795, only Britain, Austria, and Savoy remained at war with France. But the foundation of all these victories was laid in the reign of Robespierre. At terrible cost, his regime saved France from conquest and ended for years to come any prospect of counter-revolution or civil war.

Robespierre's own end was as ghastly as any he had meted out to others. In time, even his closest supporters in the Convention began to fear for their lives. Others were offended by his introduction of a preposterous new state religion, centred on the worship of a "Supreme Being," with himself as its chief prophet. On July 27, 1794, Robespierre was surprised by a small group of armed men, bent on his arrest. He attempted to kill himself but only succeeded in blowing off his jaw. Half dead, and with his face bound in a rough bandage, he was hustled to the scaffold, where he died without a trial. Within days, over ninety of his Jacobin club supporters had met a similarly abrupt end, meted out, not by another club or organization, but by "disparate elements" who had been personal enemies of Robespierre.

6. THE CONSTITUTION OF 1795

One after another, each of the great revolutionary fanatics, like their more moderate predecessors, had been swept away in the flood—first Marat, then Danton and, finally Robespierre. Thereafter the Revolution lost its impetus and became altered in character. The National Convention, purged by the guillotine of extreme radicals, was rejoined by those Girondin delegates who still survived, and by numbers of moderates who returned from exile. Political control moved back to the middle class.

On August 22, 1795, the National Convention drew up a conservative, republican constitution—the third constitution to be produced by the Revolution. Executive power was vested in five men (the Directory) and legislative power was given to two chambers (the Council of Elders and the Council of Five Hundred). But the Convention delegates, to safeguard their own interests, decreed that two-thirds of the members in each new chamber were to be chosen from among their own number. This led to a dangerous outbreak of rioting, instigated by the Royalists, who had hoped to gain a majority in the coming elections. France seemed on the verge of another wave of anarchy and civil war. The National Guard, some thirty thousand strong, prepared to remove the Convention by force, while the Convention, though it had many fewer troops under its control, was ready to resist. It gave the command of its forces to Paul Barras, a profligate former noble who had been prominent in the group which overthrew Robespierre. Barras was not a trained soldier, so he gave wide responsibility for the protection of the Convention to a young artillery officer whom he had seen in action at the siege of Toulon. The officer, without hesitation, ordered his guns to be fired point-blank into the rebel mobs. This "whiff of grapeshot" (in fact it killed or wounded over five hundred persons), saved the Republic and altered the course of history. The name of the artillery officer was Napoleon Buonaparte.

 The Napoleonic Era

> Napoleon! Always enlightened by reason, always clear and decisive . . . his life was the stride of a demigod from battle to battle and from victory to victory . . . his fate was more brilliant than the world has ever seen or is likely to see after him.
> —Goethe

> . . . a moral monster, against whom every hand should have been lifted to slay.
> —Thomas Jefferson

When the army of the Republic laid siege to Toulon in the summer of 1793, its artillery commander was wounded and had to be replaced. Trained professional officers were hard to find since most of them had been royalists and had left France. A young Corsican officer, Napoleon Buonaparte, was available, and it was proposed that he take charge of the guns. His furious energy, courage, and resourcefulness were immediately apparent, as was his military skill and his ability to inspire his men to tremendous efforts. Largely because of his ability and leadership, the besiegers were successful, and Toulon was captured.

Bonaparte—he was now using the French spelling of his name—was promoted to Brigadier-General and sent to Italy to reconnoitre the ground over which the war against France's enemies would probably be fought. Then, in the spring of 1795, he arrived in Paris during a lull in the fighting. Once again, his remarkable gift for being in the right place at the right time stood him in good stead. Paris, throughout the summer of 1795, was tense with uncertainty. The government, its very life endangered by the threat of rioting, gave command of the troops to General Bonaparte. Ruthlessly and efficiently he dispersed the rebel mobs with cannon (this was the "whiff of grapeshot" incident described on the last page of the last chapter). Paul Barras, at whose suggestion Bonaparte had been given command of the troops, was made one of the five new Directors. For his services, Bonaparte was given command of the Army of the Interior. The career of Napoleon, sometimes regarded as the greatest man in modern history, had begun.

"Unkempt in appearance, with a sallow complexion almost as noticeable as his brooding glance. . . ." — Napoleon Bonaparte as a young man.

1. THE EMERGENCE OF A MILITARY GENIUS

The European scene in 1795 was one of tremendous turmoil and uncertainty. France had been at war with her European neighbours for nearly four years.[1] The aim of revolutionary France was to extend its borders from the Rhine to the Alps to correspond with those of ancient Gaul. Under a succession of able generals these "natural boundaries" had practically been gained in a series of military triumphs such as Europe had scarcely seen before. Holland and Belgium were conquered, the Germans pushed beyond the Rhine and forced to ask for peace, and Spain neutralized.

By 1796, peace had been made with all but Austria and Britain. The British were prepared to fight forever to drive the French out of the Low Countries, because of their fear that French control of the Scheldt waterway and the magnificent port of Antwerp could damage the commercial importance of London. But while the British would continue to fight, they had no army on the Continent even though they appeared supreme at sea. Russia, while hostile to France, was busy with its own conquests in Poland. Austria, therefore, remained the principal enemy. Victory against the Austrians would be a valuable achievement for an ambitious general.

War Against Austria

Bonaparte felt that Austria could best be attacked through Italy. When he had served in Italy with the army two years before, he had drawn up plans for a campaign which he believed would result in victory over the Austrian armies now occupying the northern areas of that country. The Directors approved Bonaparte's plans, and put him in command of the Army of Italy—even though he was not quite twenty-seven years old!

He now astonished Europe by the brilliance of his campaign. Bonaparte never in his entire career gave the army any new ideas. He introduced no new tactics or formations, no innovations in drill, no improved weapons and, though an artillery expert, no new types of gun. All he gave it was victory. He relied on speed, and the French army carried no heavy baggage trains. It "lived off the

---

[1]France had declared war on Austria and Prussia (the First Coalition) in April, 1792, on Piedmont in July of that year, and on Britain, Holland, and Spain in February, 1793. Russia, while hostile to the Revolution, did not take an active role against France.

country." In less than three weeks he drove the Austrians across the Po River and forced Piedmont out of the war.

Next he turned his full attention to the Austrians and laid siege to Mantua. The smaller French forces were handled with such skill and rapidity as to give them superiority in numbers at the critical time and place to bring victory. Four times the Austrian armies came into Italy to relieve Mantua and four times they were beaten back.

After a fifth battle, at Rivoli in January, 1797, in which the Austrian army was again badly beaten, the garrison of Mantua surrendered the great fortress that blocked the road to Austria. The way was now open to the French to march on Vienna.

Before pushing into Austria, Bonaparte turned aside to deal with the Pope. The Vatican was opposed to the anti-clerical French Republic, and had supported Austria in the war. With victory imminent, however, and French troops occupying the papal territories in northern Italy, the Pope signed a treaty agreeing to pay France thirty million francs; to close all ports in the papal territories to the allies, especially the English; and to acknowledge the republic made up of its former possessions in northern Italy. Another interesting provision in the treaty obliged the Pope to turn over to France one hundred works of art.

The rest of the story is soon told. The French army was now accustomed to victory, their opponents to defeat. While one French force pushed into southern Austria, Bonaparte with another drove steadily toward Vienna. On April 7 Austria gave up and asked for peace terms.

It was now that Bonaparte made one of the deals which gave him the reputation for heartless cynicism. Instead of halting the war, he offered Austria the Republic of Venice in return for Belgium (the Austrian Netherlands) and Lombardy. Venice had been neutral in the war but it was weak—and to be weak was to invite the contempt of General Napoleon Bonaparte.

A pretext was found for attacking Venice. An *agent provocateur* was paid to publish a proclamation—which conveyed the impression that it was issued by Venetian authorities—urging the people everywhere to rise and massacre the French. The Doge, as head of the Republic of Venice, at once officially denied the proclamation, but the damage was done. A few days later the people of the Venetian city of Verona rose in fury against the French. In reply,

Bonaparte poured in troops, and Venice had no choice but to submit to his will. First, her art treasures were shipped to France; this done, the once-proud Republic was forced to accept Austrian sovereignty as part of Napoleon's deal.

Genoa was the next victim, succumbing to a similar method of provocation and threat, to become the "Ligurian Republic" under the protection of France. In October, 1797, the Treaty of Campo Formio ended hostilities with Austria. The principal terms gave Nice and Savoy and Belgium to France, and Venice to Austria. By additional arrangements, Ferrara and Bologna were taken from the Pope and united with Lombardy, which in turn became the "Cisalpine Republic." The Papal States themselves shortly were transformed into the "Republic of Rome" and Naples, too, was made a republic. Not surprisingly, all these newly-fashioned republics were patterned after the French model.

The Egyptian Campaign

With Austria defeated and Italy redesigned to French advantage, the only enemy left was England. Would not the conquest of France's traditional enemy be a suitable project for the conqueror of Austria? Bonaparte went to the English Channel coast, looked at the cold grey seas and the dilapidated French fleet and, in spite of having fifty thousand men under his command, decided the idea was impractical.

Instead, he suggested an alternative invasion—Egypt. It was an idea that he had long contemplated. Even before the war in Italy was finished he had written, "Through Egypt we shall reach India, we shall re-establish the old route through Suez and cause the route by the Cape of Good Hope to be abandoned . . . in order truly to destroy England, we must occupy Egypt."

Money was needed to finance the expedition but that was a simple matter. Switzerland was invaded on a pretext that the democratic peoples of certain Swiss cantons should be freed from the oppressive rule of Berne. The unhappy Swiss were obliged to pay France an enormous sum of money, three million francs of which went straight to defray the cost of the Egyptian expedition.

The expedition set sail from Toulon on May 19, 1798. In addition to an army of over thirty-five thousand troops, a brilliant group of artists and engineers, mathematicians, geologists, antiquarians, and chemists was also included. Among the official aims of the expedition were the acquisition of scholarly knowledge and "the improvement of the condition of the natives of Egypt." These praiseworthy objectives were offset somewhat by another of the official reasons for the expedition, which was "to assure the free and exclusive use of the Red Sea to the French Republic." The isthmus of Suez was to be cut through and the English were to be driven from "all their possessions in the East to which the general can come."

Moving with his customary speed, Bonaparte captured Alexandria within a day of landing. A forced march across the desert toward Cairo ended in a crushing victory over the Mameluke army near the Pyramids, while, as he told his soldiers, "Forty centuries looked down upon you."

The victory at the Pyramids had scarcely been won, however, when terrible news came from Alexandria. A small British fleet commanded by Sir Horatio Nelson, had surprised the French fleet at anchor in Aboukir Bay forty kilometres east of Alexandria. Unable to manoeuvre, the French ships were pounded to splinters.

Despite the disaster, and a considerable amount of discontent from his officers and men, Bonaparte himself was in fine spirits. The learned men he had taken to Egypt with him were urged to make the army independent of Europe. They planted crops, built mills and ovens, set up foundries, brewed beer, made gunpowder, and engaged in research. French soldiers in Upper Egypt made the treasures of ancient Memphis available to Western eyes. A French officer found near Rosetta at the western mouth of the Nile a basalt slab engraved in Egyptian hieroglyphic, demotic (or ordinary "popular" writing), and in Greek, three versions of the same statement. This gave his fellow-countryman, Champollion, "the father of Egyptology," the key to translate the Egyptian inscriptions still plentiful at the many ruins in the country and hitherto indecipherable.

But in spite of all the intellectual activity of the scientists and philosophers and the practical achievements of the experts, Egypt was still a vast prison in which the French army was caged. Turkey had declared war and two Turkish armies were on the way to recapture Egypt—if the French waited they might have to face both at once. Certainly it was never Bonaparte's way to await attack, and he set off at once with the Army of Egypt through Syria to Constantinople.

With his small, compact force of experienced veterans he quickly captured El Arish from the Turkish advance guard and plunged onward to Jaffa which was stormed after a short siege. Some three thousand prisoners were shot because the French were short of food and had nowhere to keep them. Bonaparte, who is said to have given the order for the massacre with reluctance, commented that it would serve as a warning for others not to resist.

Only one obstacle, the little fortified port of Acre, remained blocking the coast road into Syria. There, an eccentric but brilliant Englishman, Sir Sidney Smith, was in command of a small British naval squadron. Earlier, his ships had luckily captured seven French vessels carrying Bonaparte's siege artillery, which Smith installed in the crumbling, almost unarmed fort. He stiffened the Turkish garrison with British sailors from his ships, and helped put the fort into a state of defence.

Bonaparte tried to rush Acre as he had carried Jaffa, but every attack failed with heavy losses. There was little hope of starving out the garrison because the British navy could supply the town from the sea. In the meantime, a deadlier enemy than the Turks had appeared. Plague broke out in the French camp and spread with alarming rapidity. Nine weeks had been spent hammering at Acre which by all the rules should have fallen at the first push. Now there was no alternative but to admit defeat and begin the long, terrible march back into Egypt, leaving behind many of the wounded and the sick, although every effort was made to carry them along.

Back in Egypt, French morale began to plummet. Bonaparte and his men were tired of Egypt, tired of fighting enemies whom they despised. It was at this period of low morale that the brilliant Sidney Smith struck another blow. He had some unimportant negotiations with the French about an exchange of prisoners, and with cunning malice sent Bonaparte a packet of English and German newspapers.

The news they contained was nearly all bad. A new Coalition of Britain, Austria, Russia, Portugal, Naples, and Turkey was winning one battle after another.[1] The Italian conquests had been nearly all lost, there were French defeats on the Rhine and, in Switzerland, Masséna, an ex-smuggler and France's best general after Bonaparte, stood ready to ward off an invasion thrust at France itself.

[1]This was the Second Coalition, formed in December, 1798.

It was time to go home. On the night of August 22, 1799, with his chief of staff, some of his best officers, and a few of the scientists who had accompanied him to Egypt, he slipped quietly away on a fast frigate bound for France. The army and its new commander, Kléber, did not know he was gone until the next day, when that astonished and furious officer got the letter Bonaparte had left appointing him to the command of the imprisoned army.[1]

2. THE SEIZURE OF POWER

In France, the situation was critical. With the ring of foreign enemies on the point of invasion, the Directory was proving untrustworthy, fumbling, weak, and totally unable to produce solutions in answer to the crisis. France badly needed leaders who could shape events, but the only man who came forward was the Abbé Siéyès.[2] He was elected a Director in May, 1799, and immediately began to intrigue with Barras, who was still a Director, with the Royalists, and with other discontented groups. It was his plan to overthrow the Directory and substitute a new form of executive with himself as head. While he had the highest regard for his own abilities he knew he was not a man of action. If the dismissal of the Directors called for the use of force, he would need "a sword," some general to whom the army might rally, and who was strong enough and tough enough to strike hard if the Paris mobs tried to rise to the defence of the Directors.

His original choice was Joubert, but Joubert had been killed at the battle of Novi in August. Bernadotte, the Minister of War, was the next choice, but Bernadotte vacillated, unable to decide. At this point Bonaparte arrived in Paris, the conquering hero back from the mysterious East with a string of new victories to his credit—perfectly timed as always. Here was the sword Siéyès had been seeking.

In his usual decisive manner, Bonaparte calculated the best course of action to follow. Obviously, the decision would be critical.

---

[1] Within a year the unfortunate Kléber was assassinated.
[2] It was Siéyès who had led the Third Estate in the opening days of the French Revolution, and who had written the famous pamphlet, "What Is the Third Estate?" As the Revolution became more radical, he had been displaced by the extremists, and spent the decade following the Tennis Court Oath in relative obscurity.

The prospects of almost unlimited power lay ahead, but even one false move could ruin everything.

Actually, as early as 1797, after his victory at Mantua, Bonaparte had considered a *coup d'état,* but decided against it: "the pear is not ripe," he remarked to a friend. Instead, he took pains to dispel the fears of the Directory that he might be a threat to their power. On his return from Italy, he made a point of wearing civilian dress, seeking the company of scientists and other learned men, and avoiding military pomp and public appearances. Indeed, he even came to the Directors' assistance when the elections went against them, and the Councils became more royalist and moderate: he sent General Augereau, a swashbuckling swordsman and hot-headed Jacobin, to clear the Royalists out of the Councils. Many of them were packed off to the fever-ridden swamps of French Guiana; it was brutal and it was illegal, but it kept the way clear for Bonaparte whenever he felt the pear was ripe.

Now returning from Egypt, Bonaparte found himself welcomed everywhere as a hero, while the Directory, on the other hand, was obviously unpopular. He realized, however, that it was still too soon for a direct seizure of power. Momentarily, he considered the idea of becoming a Director himself, but the minimum age was forty and the incumbent Directors would not agree to change the rule. Therefore, when Siéyès appeared with his plan for a takeover, the opportunity seemed ideal. Siéyès, in Bonaparte's eyes, was a weak man with an undeserved reputation for political wisdom, who could be easily disposed of when the right moment came.

Accordingly, Bonaparte agreed to work with Siéyès, suggesting that there be a provisional government of three men, himself, Siéyès, and Roger Ducos, a former Girondin who could be counted on to join the winning side. Siéyès agreed, still believing that he could use the "sword" and throw it away.

Siéyès arranged that the Council of the Five Hundred and the Council of Elders move to St. Cloud, away from possible interference by the mobs of Paris. He also arranged that Bonaparte be given command of the armed forces in and near the capital.

When the Councils assembled on 18 Brumaire (November 9), Bonaparte arrived with two regiments led by the dashing Murat. The deputies were in an angry mood, and when Bonaparte appeared before the Council of Elders and gave a stumbling, poorly

The British view of Bonaparte's overthrow of the Directory. To most British observers *Brumaire* was only another sordid Paris revolution in which one group treacherously betrayed and attacked former colleagues.

worded speech denouncing the Directors, he was badly heckled, and retired in confusion. He then went alone into the hall where the Five Hundred were meeting, and before he could speak found himself surrounded by angry deputies who actually attacked him.

Four soldiers came to his rescue and carried him semi-conscious from the hall. Once safely outside he harangued the troops telling them that a Jacobin minority was terrorizing the Council of Five Hundred and had attacked him with daggers (an exaggeration bordering on outright falsehood). Murat promptly led a company of grenadiers with fixed bayonets into the hall. The deputies fled, many of them jumping from the windows. The Council of Elders and a few deputies of the Council of Five Hundred were rounded up by Bonaparte's younger brother, Lucien (who was President of the Council of Five Hundred), to give the shadow of legality to the whole affair by decreeing the establishment of a provisional executive of three Consuls.

Almost immediately Siéyès was outmanoeuvred by Bonaparte, so completely, in fact, that he even voted for his own displacement (and that of Ducos) as Consul, and nominated two supporters of Bonaparte to replace him! The overly elaborate constitution he had drawn up was brutally altered to suit Bonaparte's desires. Siéyès was given a seat in the powerless Senate and an estate in the country with a strong hint, which he took, that he should go there and leave politics to abler men. His "sword" had turned in his hand.

The new Constitution of the Year VIII (1799) which was set up a month later kept an appearance of political liberty, but in reality placed the supreme power in the hands of Bonaparte, who was made First Consul for a period of ten years. The other two consuls acted as advisers, and actually were minor officials who neither opposed his policies nor offered themselves as his rivals for power. There were various governing bodies: a Tribunate to debate bills, a Senate to guard the constitution, and a Council of State composed of experts—"fifty of the least stupid Frenchmen"—to draw up laws. But these organizations had no real power—they simply provided the appearance of democracy to a government that was really a dictatorship.

Because Bonaparte believed that government should have a broad base of support, the new constitution was presented for the approval of the people of France in a plebiscite early in 1800. It was approved by a vote of over three million, while fewer than two thousand opposed it.

3. THE FIRST CONSUL

As First Consul, Bonaparte's first task was to organize and pacify France. "We have done with the romance of the Revolution. We must now commence its history. We must have eyes only for what is real and practicable. . . ." Such were his words to one of his first meetings with the Council of State.

Foreign Policy

By far the most urgent problem facing the new First Consul was to secure France from its enemies. An Austrian army was besieging Genoa and the French garrison led by Masséna was in serious trouble. Another Austrian force was pressing closer to the "natural frontier" of the Rhine. Bonaparte gathered an army quickly and entered Italy by crossing the Alps over the Great St. Bernard Pass. Some twenty-five kilometres of this route were impassable for wheeled vehicles so that the cannon had to be put in hollowed logs and dragged by ropes. The French painter David depicted the First Consul heroically riding over the pass on a spirited, prancing charger. Actually he did nothing quite so romantic, but rode a sure-footed mule.

The Austrians remained quite unaware of his advance and were thrown into confusion when his army came down out of the mountains and stood between them and their base. The two armies met on a plain near the village of Marengo on June 14, 1800. The battle lasted all day and the outnumbered French only turned defeat into victory when reinforcements reached them late in the day and a charge by French cavalry started a panic among the tired Austrian attackers. Six months later Moreau defeated another Austrian army at Hohenlinden in Germany. Austria asked for peace terms, while Czar Paul withdrew from the Second Coalition and actually became mildly pro-French. Naples and Portugal gave up the war. Only Britain, helpless on land but supreme at sea, remained to carry on the struggle.[1]

Then, on March 27, 1802, came the Treaty of Amiens, by which peace was declared between Britain and France. The terms were exceptionally favourable for France. She retained Belgium and the left bank of the Rhine as an integral part of her territory, and won recognition for her "satellite" republics. In addition, all conquests made by England were returned to France with minor exceptions. Thus, from a position perilously near disaster, France emerged farther ahead than ever. Napoleon's star was high indeed.

---

[1] Actually, the last of the Second Coalition powers formally to end hostilities with France was Turkey, who did not agree to peace terms until June, 1802. Turkey, however, was militarily too ineffective to carry on a war unaided against France.

Internal Policy

The first internal matter Bonaparte turned to after becoming First Consul was to establish control over local government. The *departements* into which France had been divided by the Assembly in 1790 were each given a prefect appointed by the First Consul. Mayors were appointed in communes of more than five thousand in population.

A settlement in the matter of religion was also made. The antireligious feeling so widespread in the early years of the Revolution was dying down. Bonaparte had no very deep religious beliefs of his own but he held religion to be necessary for a stable society and as a support for morality. Moreover, he always tried to satisfy the peasants and the simple soldiers because he believed his strongest support came from them. All through the troubled years of the Revolution, the peasants had clung with deep affection to their religion and to their orthodox priests. Therefore, one of his first acts after *Brumaire* (as his *coup d'état* came to be called) was to free the priests from the necessity of taking the oath to support the constitution.

One result of these measures was the ending of strong opposition in Brittany and La Vendée, where the peasants, led by royalist aristocrats, had fought for nine years against the Revolution. By a mixture of diplomacy and force he split this opposition and made it ineffective. The peasants no longer had religious grounds for continuing their opposition, the nobles were placated by flattery and reassurances, and the really stubborn leaders who remained were driven into exile in England, or, in one case, convicted on a trumped-up charge of treachery and shot.

The new Pope, Pius VII, was informed that Bonaparte was anxious to settle France's differences with the Church. The political advantages to the Pope of such an agreement would be to show that Catholicism was not the religion of royalism alone. Bonaparte, on the other hand, sought to strengthen French influence on neighbouring countries whose religion was Catholic. He also argued that "Fifty *émigré* bishops in English pay are the present leaders of the French clergy. Their influence must be destroyed and for this I must have the authority of the Pope." A further motive was to consolidate the support of the French bourgeoisie and peasantry by relieving the minds of those who had acquired, legally or otherwise, lands formerly owned by the Church.

A year of hard bargaining produced the Concordat, or religious agreement, which was completed in 1801. Bonaparte gained everything he wanted. All bishops were asked to resign, so that the constitutional, or juring ones and the non-jurors might no longer continue to divide the Church. Bonaparte would nominate bishops while the Pope would consecrate them. The Church gave up all claim to lands taken from it, and relinquished its right to collect tithes. Henceforth the State would pay salaries to the clergy. France recognized that the Catholic faith was the faith of the great majority of the French people, but refused to declare it to be the state religion. It could be freely practised in France but like the other public organizations was subject to police regulations governing public behaviour.

The Jacobins, who included many high ranking officers of the army, were bitterly opposed to the Concordat, and some generals showed their displeasure by tumbling priests out of the pews at church services. The publication of the Concordat was delayed until Easter, 1802, so that it would be covered up by the announcement that peace had been made with Britain by the Treaty of Amiens. Bonaparte had ended France's war with her neighbours and her dispute with the Church. His popularity was immense.

Having organized his country's government and its religion, the First Consul took another bold step. This was the establishment of the Legion of Honour, to be composed of men who had given great services to the state, or who had "by their learning, talents and virtues" contributed to the life and defence of France. The Legion indicated a sharp reversal of official French attitudes towards aristocracy: whereas only eight years earlier the mere possession of a title was enough to send its owner to the guillotine, now various ranks of distinction were deliberately being reintroduced. Frenchmen who feared Bonaparte's organization of the country was depriving men of liberty now worried that equality, too, was in danger. When one of those opposed to the new order of merit remarked contemptuously that crosses and ribbons were the toys of monarchy, Bonaparte replied, "Well, men are led by toys. I don't think that the French love liberty and equality. They have one feeling—honour. We must nourish that feeling: they must have distinctions."

Still another reform was being prepared during the early years of the Consulate. This was the great task of organizing the laws of France into a code or systematic arrangement. Old French law had been a tangle of laws and customs going back to Roman and Frankish times, feudal customs, ecclesiastical privileges, local rights, and royal decrees. Bonaparte appointed four experts to do the work, which when finished was taken before the Council of State. There, in over one hundred sessions, with Bonaparte himself as chairman at more than half of them, the new French Civil Code, later called the *Code Napoléon*, took final form.

The Code was moderate in tone, and combined much that was good in the old laws of France with the basic ideas of the Revolution—equality of all men before the law, freedom of conscience, freedom of work, and the separation of Church and State, although it drew back here and there from the liberal positions adopted in the early enthusiastic years of the Revolution. It tried to strengthen the family by giving the father real authority. A father's consent was necessary for the marriage of sons up to the age of twenty-five and daughters up to twenty-one. The father was even permitted to put his children in jail if he wished—one month for those under sixteen, six months for those over sixteen but under twenty-one. Women, too, were given an inferior status. A single woman could not act as a guardian nor witness a legal document. A wife owed obedience to her husband, who was also given almost complete control over the family property even though it might originally have belonged before marriage to the wife.

In spite of these flaws, and the great emphasis the Code gave to the rights and protection of property—a feature that satisfied the middle class which had originally expected to benefit from the Revolution—the adoption of the Code in 1804 is one of the most notable events in legal history. Nothing else that Napoleon Bonaparte did has had as lasting and as beneficial effect for France and for the world. During the 19th century it served as a model for the laws of many countries of Europe and elsewhere in the world, in Egypt, in Latin America, and in Japan. The civil law of the Province of Quebec is based to a large extent on the *Code Napoléon*. In France the Civil Code was supplemented during the Empire by several other codes dealing with commerce, and with crime and punishment, but these were neither as successful nor as widely copied as the *Code Napoléon* itself.

4. THE EMPEROR

In the spring of 1802 Bonaparte had reached the highest point of his career. He controlled France with the full support, as he was soon to prove, of the middle class and the vast majority of the people. He controlled the newspapers and suppressed those likely to oppose him. He commanded the army. He had weeded his Jacobin or republican opponents out of the Tribunate, the only legislative body likely to cause him trouble. He had made peace with the Church and with Britain. He had regained the colonies France had lost without making any concessions or giving up any French territory. Therefore, when his supporters suggested that his achievements deserved the reward of being Consul for life, he fully agreed. The people of France approved in a plebiscite in which the vote was three and a half million in favour and only eight thousand opposed. From that time onward he referred to himself as *Napoleon*. Now all that remained was that Napoleon establish a *dynasty*—in other words, that his position become hereditary—for the new monarchy to be complete in form as well as fact.

The final move was soon to come. In February, 1804, a combined Jacobin-royalist attempt to overthrow the government, probably to assassinate Napoleon, and to bring back a Bourbon to the French throne, was discovered. Several generals were involved, including Moreau, the victor of Hohenlinden, but the whole affair had been well known to the French police, who arrested its leaders as soon as the time was ripe. Rage swept France against royalist assassins, Moreau's treachery, and the British, who had helped in the conspiracy. Arguing that if Napoleon's office were made hereditary, plots to murder the head of state would become useless, his supporters whipped up public opinion in favour of this new change in the constitution. The appropriate legal motions were passed by the Senate and the Tribunate, and on May 14, 1804, Napoleon became the hereditary ruler of France. Georges Cadoudal, one of the leaders of the plot, made the wry comment while awaiting execution in prison, "We came to give France a king and we have given her an emperor!"

Jacques David's painting of Napoleon's coronation, showing him about to place a crown on the head of Josephine. The picture shows Napoleon's mother looked on approvingly. This was to save face for the new Emperor, since his mother had remained in Rome with Lucien Bonaparte, then at odds with Napoleon, and was not present at the ceremony. David also painted his own family, his friends, and himself in the gallery, even though they were not in attendance. And long after the painting was finished, Napoleon instructed David to alter the portrait of the Pope, so that his hand would be raised as if to bless the event—something the Pope had refused to do! Thus is history made.

The new Emperor was crowned in Notre Dame with pomp and circumstance. The Pope on Napoleon's invitation came to Paris to assist, but when the time came for him to place the crown on the new Emperor's head, Napoleon took it from his hands and donned it himself. He had risen by his own efforts and did not owe his crown and title to the Church.

The Wars of the Third Coalition

Napoleon was supreme in France, but France was not to be left unchallenged by the other nations of Europe, especially Britain. Despite the Treaty of Amiens in 1802, the peace between Britain and France had never been secure. The real reasons for which Britain had fought were not changed. The French still held Belgium and Holland and thus threatened Britain's commercial life. Napoleon was extending French power by interfering in the affairs of Switzerland. Piedmont was incorporated into France. The official French newspaper *Moniteur,* much of whose subject matter was written or dictated by Napoleon, reported that a French mission to Egypt believed that country might easily be reconquered. It was obvious that Napoleon had no intention of keeping peace, and consequently the British declined to surrender Malta as they had promised to do at Amiens. With Malta in British hands the central Mediterranean could be closed to the French and their route to Egypt and India blocked. On May 13, 1803, war was declared by Britain.

On the same day Napoleon was made Emperor, William Pitt (the Younger) again became British Prime Minister.[1] He at once gathered together another alliance, the Third Coalition, to oppose Napoleon. Russia, Austria, and Britain agreed to act together against new French adventures. Russia was to lead an armed League to enforce peace and would insist that the French withdraw from Italy, Switzerland, Holland, and North Germany. Pitt hoped that the Coalition could put half a million men in the field against the French. The attack on France would come from two directions, an Austro-Russian one from the East and an Anglo-Russian one from Southern Italy.

Napoleon was already at work preparing a counter-attack. Initially, his plan had been to strike at Britain directly, by launching an invasion. With this purpose in mind he concentrated his forces at Boulogne and other places along the north coast of France opposite England. Flat-bottomed boats were constructed for the transport of an army with its horses, guns and equipment across the English Channel. These preparations went on from late in 1803 to the summer of 1805, but there was no chance of mounting an attack on

---

[1]Pitt, among the most militant of English statesmen in his opposition to Napoleon, had previously been Prime Minister from 1783 to 1801, resigning when his government refused to continue the war.

"The Manning of the Navy." Press gangs theoretically were allowed only to impress those who were sailors already, but in practice they took anyone they could find.

England without gaining control, even for a short time, of the Strait of Dover on the Channel. Napoleon said that all he needed was control of the Channel for eight hours, but this proved impossible. The British navy blockaded French naval ports and refused to be lured away. And the French navy, even when strengthened by that of Spain, with whom France was allied, was no match for the British. The British ships were masterpieces of construction, and the officers and crews, some of whom were at sea for such long periods that they became strangers to their children, had developed skills unequalled by those of any other navy before or since.

By the middle of August, 1805, Napoleon realized that an invasion of Britain could not be managed. He was also aware, however, of the net Pitt was trying to draw about France. He decided to hit first and to hit hard at the Austrians before they could be joined by their Russian allies.

The great camps at Boulogne and the other coastal areas were emptied as five armies poured south at thirty-two kilometres a day to meet the leisurely advance of the Austrians in South Germany. By mid-October in a series of battles near Ulm a large Austrian army was badly beaten. The Russians who were marching to join the Austrian army turned back in retreat. Six weeks later on December 2, 1805, Napoleon won what was to be his greatest victory, the Battle of Austerlitz, over a combined Austro-Russian army.

Austria, helpless from two crushing defeats, had no alternative but to accept a humiliating peace treaty. All Austrian territory in Italy, as well as some in Germany, was lost; the rulers of Bavaria, Wurtemburg and Baden, who had formerly been subject princes of the House of Hapsburg, were rewarded with lands and titles for having sided with Napoleon. Napoleon's Italian kingdom, formerly the Cisalpine Republic, had Venice added to it. Masséna was sent south to drive the Bourbons out of Naples and the Pope was ordered to close his ports to British shipping.

Germany received Napoleon's attention next. By playing off the minor German states against each other, France was able to extend her influence to dominate most of Germany, with the notable exception of Prussia. Under French auspices, the so-called Confederation of the Rhine was established, an organization made up of fifteen German states whose princes promised to give military support to the French Empire.

As usual, Napoleon was unscrupulous in his diplomatic manoeuvring. Hanover, which had belonged to the king of England, was first occupied by French troops, and then offered to Frederick William III of Prussia as an inducement against having a possible alliance with England. At the same time, in the hope of arranging a peace treaty with Britain, Napoleon offered to restore Hanover to the English Crown in exchange for the French colonies seized by the British. Word of this remarkable double-dealing reached Frederick William who, with a weak man's sudden firmness, mobilized the Prussian army and demanded that the French leave Germany. He called on Russia for help as well; but before help could reach him, Napoleon had completely defeated the Prussian army on one foggy autumn day in the twin battles of Jena and Auerstadt (October 14, 1806). Two weeks later Napoleon made a triumphal entry into Berlin accompanied by his marshals and brilliant staff and surrounded by the Imperial Guard.

THE MASTERPIECE — THE BATTLE OF AUSTERLITZ

(December 2, 1805)

Napoleon's military genius was fully displayed in his great victory over the Russians and Austrians at Austerlitz. Balked in his plans for a cross-Channel invasion of England, the Emperor began his 1805 campaign by rapidly concentrating the *Grand Armée* on the Rhine and invading southern Germany. The capture of a large Austrian force at Ulm prepared the way for a quick thrust to Vienna and a northern advance into Moravia (now part of Czechoslovakia).

At Austerlitz, Napoleon took up a deceptive position *behind* high ground, facing a combined Russo-Austrian army of more than 80 000 men (see map). Critics of the battle have frequently commented on the subtlety of his dispositions—since normal tactics would have been to occupy the high ground in force. Napoleon, however, was intent on luring his opponents to destruction. He was able to create an impression of apparent indecision and concern for his communications, with the result that the Allies thought they could boldly cross his front and envelop his right wing. In doing so, they exposed their own flank to a sudden, devastating assault launched by Napoleon across the plateau on his front. So confident was the Emperor that, on the eve of the conflict, he issued a proclamation to his soldiers telling them exactly how he would win the battle.

The Allied Army marched blindly into the trap and was overwhelmingly defeated with total casualties of about 30 000. A captured Russian artillery officer, overcome by the dishonour of losing his guns, begged the Emperor to shoot him—receiving the truly imperial reply: "Calm yourself, young man. It is no dishonour to be defeated by *my* army".

Austerlitz re-established Napoleonic domination in central Europe. In England, news of the defeat of her allies caused the death of William Pitt, the British Prime Minister who had organized three successive coalitions against Napoleon. Still in the future lay the wasting Peninsular War, the disastrous Russian campaign of 1812, and Waterloo.

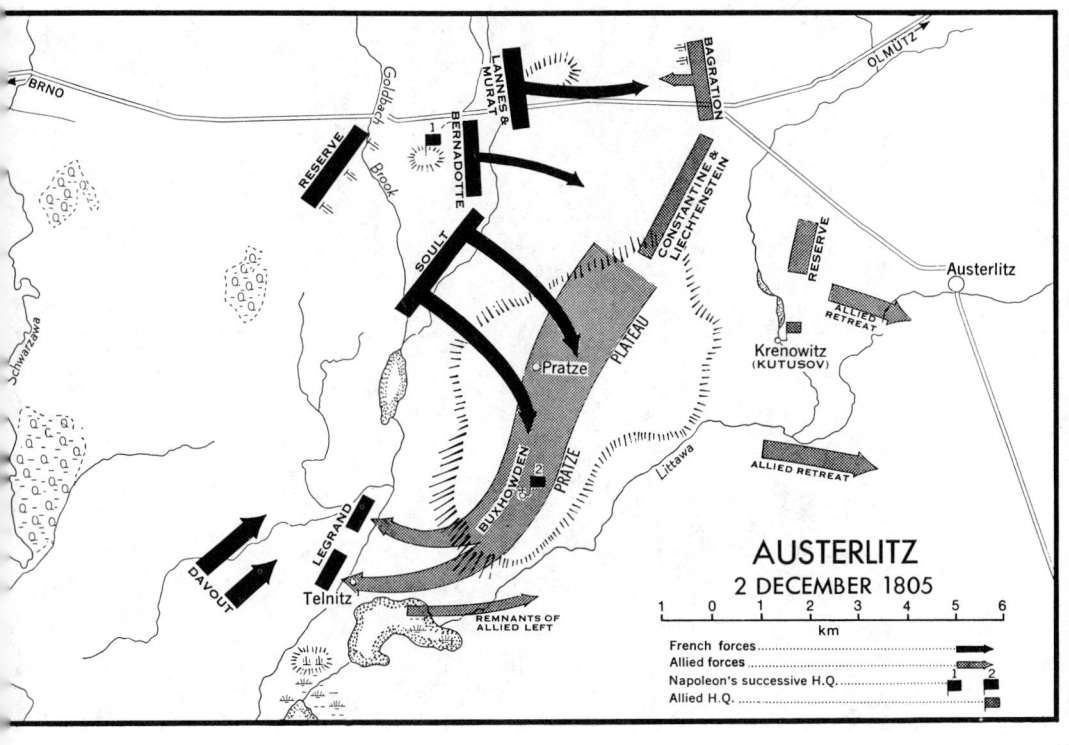

Not all the victories of 1805 were French ones, however. On the morning of October 21 thirty-two kilometres off the Spanish coast near the shoals of Cape Trafalgar, the British fleet under Lord Nelson attacked a combined French and Spanish fleet almost twice its size. The battle that followed was such a crushing defeat for the French that their navy and that of Spain ceased to have much importance in the long years of war that followed. In England the news of Trafalgar, arriving just after word of the French victory at Ulm, caused almost as much gloom as jubilation, for Nelson had been killed aboard H.M.S. *Victory* as the battle was ending.

Trafalgar was one of the greatest naval victories of all time, setting limits on Napoleon's activities which he was never able to exceed. His plan to invade Britain or Egypt or India had become an empty dream. He might march his conquering armies back and

THE NAPOLEONIC ERA 191

The death of Nelson at Trafalgar. Dressed in his Admiral's uniform, replete with decorations, he presented an irresistible target for French sharpshooters.

forth across Europe but he could neither build up an overseas empire nor interfere with Britain's ocean-borne trade. The British henceforth in the war controlled the Mediterranean, and had the power to strike at the French Empire at any part of the European coast that seemed to offer advantages.

The Continental System

The setback at Trafalgar only served to confirm that, for Napoleon, the greatest enemy was always Britain.

The Industrial Revolution was making Britain very wealthy, and British gold was freely provided to her allies so that they might equip and pay their armies. The British fleet, steadily growing in size and power, blocked his path to overseas conquests. But to remain prosperous, maintain the navy, and be able to carry on the

struggle against him, Britain had to export her manufactured goods. This suggested that Britain might best be attacked through a form of economic warfare. Accordingly, in November, 1806, Napoleon issued from Berlin a decree that the British Isles were to be considered in a state of blockade. All commerce with them was forbidden. British goods found on the Continent were to be seized and those possessing them imprisoned. No ship that had touched a British port would be permitted to enter a port in France or in any country allied with France. This was the foundation of the *Continental System,* the name given to the measures aimed at ruining Britain by excluding her goods from the Continent.

The British reply was to pass *Orders in Council,* decrees issued by the government, forbidding neutrals to trade with the French or their allies or between ports that observed the Berlin Decree. The British claimed the right to seize both ships and cargoes if they disobeyed the Orders. Napoleon in turn replied with his *Milan Decrees* that promised capture and seizure to any neutral ship that obeyed the British Orders. Neutral countries, such as the United States of America, were caught between the combatants. Neither side could make its blockade completely effective, nor could Europe at that time get along without British manufactured goods. A year or two after establishing the Continental System Napoleon had to shut his eyes while his agents in a roundabout way got fifty thousand greatcoats made in Yorkshire and two hundred thousand pairs of English boots with which to equip a French army shivering through a Polish winter.

Master of Europe

The next member of the Third Coalition to receive Napoleon's attention was Russia. As a first step, the Poles were encouraged to revolt against their Russian overlords, but without waiting for the results of a Polish uprising, Napoleon attacked a Russian army advancing into eastern Prussia to aid the beleaguered Prussians. The opposing armies met at Eylau, December 7, 1807, in one of the bloodiest battles of the war, with both sides claiming the victory. Six months later a second great battle, at Friedland, was a heavy defeat for Russia and the Czar decided it was time to ask for peace terms. Napoleon and Alexander met on a raft moored in the middle of the river Niemen at Tilsit and agreed to proceed with a peace treaty.

The Treaty of Tilsit (July 8, 1807) which followed this meeting made France the master of Europe, and left Britain friendless once again. Prussia lost about half its territory and, but for the influence of the Czar, would probably have disappeared altogether. Russia, whose foreign trade was mostly with Britain, became an ally of France. Russia agreed to try to persuade the British to make peace and also return to France all the conquests they had made overseas. If the British refused, Russia was to go to war on the side of France. Russia and France would also compel Portugal, Denmark, and Sweden to close their ports to British shipping. In return Russia was to be allowed to deal with Turkey and to win from Sweden, if she could, additional territory.

To consolidate his power, Napoleon placed his relatives and friends in key positions of power throughout Europe. One brother, Louis, was king of Holland, another, Joseph, was king of Sicily, and a third, Jerome, was king of the newly created State of Westphalia. His stepson, Eugène de Beauharnais was Viceroy of Italy. Some of his marshals had been made princes, as had certain of his close advisers. His military victories and diplomatic successes had made him the most powerful ruler in the world.

Education Under the Empire

Now that Napoleon had established a dynasty he took steps to ensure its future. Education in France was organized so that it supported the emperor and his form of government. Before the Revolution education had been entirely in the hands of the Church; Napoleon was content at first to leave primary education to the priests, provided they taught certain things. A new Catechism approved by a majority of the bishops in 1806 asked the question "What would one think of those who failed in their duties to the Emperor?" The answer was that they would be resisting the order established by God.

Gradually the Emperor tightened his control of education. In 1808 the "University of France" was established. This was actually a ministry of education, whose head was directly responsible to the Emperor. It controlled all teachers in all schools, their licenses, pay, and promotion, and decided what subjects might be taught and what books might be used. Each *lycée*, or secondary school, was to have a library of fifteen hundred volumes; the police made sure there were no books other than those favourable to the imperial rule. Napoleon wanted the school system to provide him with officers and civil servants, and designed the curriculum accordingly, but he hoped that it would also train French youth to be reasonable and reasoning people. This highly centralized educational system, though modified from time to time, continues in use in France today, just as does the *Code Napoléon*.

The Structure Develops Faults

Just when the Emperor felt that he had Europe at his feet, trouble broke out in an unexpected quarter. The Iberian Peninsula, embracing Spain and Portugal, had been outside the arena of war and revolution that swept the rest of Europe for the past fifteen years. Spain, it is true, as a rather reluctant ally of France had seen its navy destroyed at Trafalgar, but the government of the country and the life of the people remained little changed by the effects of

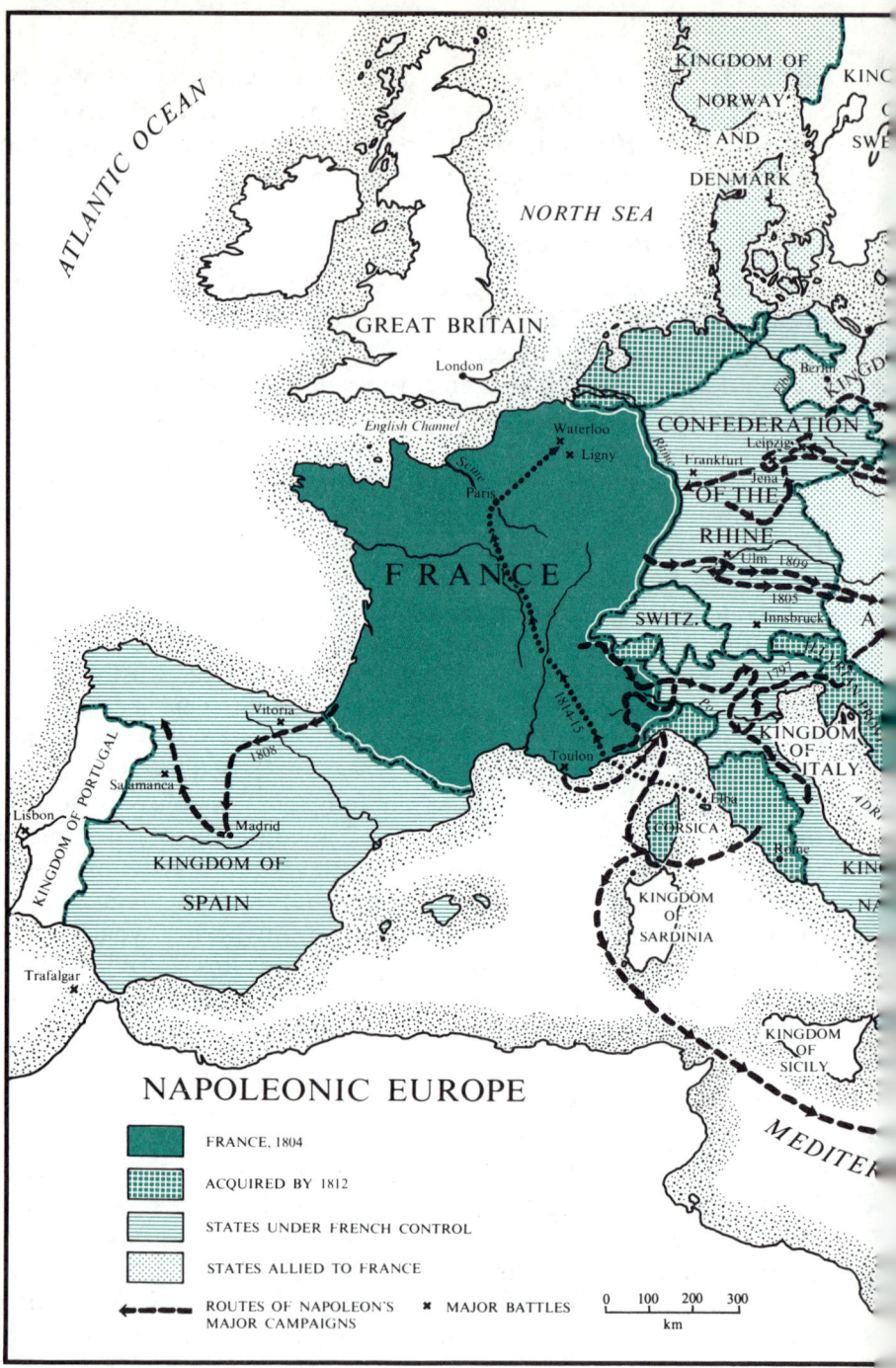

the French Revolution or by the marching armies of the Emperor.

The government of Spain was pitifully weak. The Bourbon king, Charles IV, was feeble and senile, the queen wanton, and their son, Ferdinand, prince of Asturias, irresponsible and rather stupid. The real control of the country was in the hands of Manuel Godoy, the queen's favourite, an unpopular nobleman who had given himself the magnificent title Prince of the Peace.

Napoleon, who disliked weakness, treated the Spanish government with the contempt it deserved. To weld Spain and Portugal into his Continental System, he took fifteen thousand of Spain's best soldiers to serve in Germany. Then he sent General Junot with a considerable army through Spain to seize the Portuguese royal family and the national treasure, on the grounds that Portugal, Britain's ally, had refused to obey the rules of the Continental System. Next, by a combination of trickery and threats he persuaded Charles IV to abdicate. Ferdinand became king only long enough for Napoleon to terrify him into giving up the crown in his turn. The Emperor thereupon gave Spain a new king; his older brother, Joseph, was promoted from being king of Naples to become king of Spain and the Indies, and large bodies of French troops were sent to make sure that he was well received by the Spanish.

It was now that things began to go wrong. Junot arrived in Lisbon to find that while Portugal was still in French hands, the Portuguese royal family, the treasure, and the fleet had been rescued by the British navy and were safely on their way to Brazil. And worse, in the Spanish capital of Madrid the people, proud, ignorant, brave, and filled with hatred for the swaggering French soldiers and their arrogant officers, had risen in a fury and killed every Frenchman they could find. All over the country the people sprang to arms and attacked the French.

Napoleon was determined to conquer Spain, now changed from an ally to a bitter enemy. The Spanish armies, badly trained and equipped and poorly led, should have proved easy for the veteran French troops to defeat. Some of them were, but at Baylen (July, 1808) one of these tattered Spanish armies forced the French General Dupont to surrender with twenty thousand men. The news that a French army had been beaten in Spain sent a thrill across Europe. The French were not invincible after all. The victory inspired the Spanish to even higher feats of courage. They cooped

"Fiercely individualistic, intensely proud, and heroically stubborn, the Spanish fought with such savage passion that the French could only move with safety . . . in strong parties, and even then were often fiercely attacked." The painting is entitled "The Heroic Resistance of the Town of Arbos."

up French garrisons. They defended their towns from street to street and from house to house. In the countryside they formed bands that fought *guerrilla* (Spanish: "little war") warfare, ambushing convoys, killing stragglers, destroying supplies, and hindering communications. For the next five years they harassed the French and made it unsafe for troops to move except in strength.

A few weeks after Baylen, a compact British army led by Sir Arthur Wellesley, an Irish soldier who had made a reputation in India as a skilful general, landed on the Portuguese coast and marched on Lisbon. During the next five years the British were to win a series of battles in Portugal and Spain that kept the French slowly retreating toward their homeland as one after another of Napoleon's best marshals were beaten. Spanish, and particularly Portuguese, soldiers trained by British officers proved they could stand up to the best French troops. During all this time Napoleon was obliged to keep a large army, more than three hundred thousand men, in Spain. The losses in battles and by guerrilla action drained off many of his best troops. Every country in Europe occupied by the French paid large sums of money into the Emperor's treasury. The war in Spain drained away much of this money, which, like the men wasted there, might have been used to better advantage elsewhere. When he was in exile on St. Helena Napoleon once remarked, "It was the Spanish ulcer which ruined me."

5. DOWNFALL

By the end of 1808, Austria, stubborn and unforgiving—and encouraged by British promises of help—was once more preparing for war.

Nor was it just Austria that was stirring. Czar Alexander was beginning to doubt the wisdom of his alliance with Napoleon. The Germans, too, were growing restless; the *Code Napoléon* which some German states had adopted or had had forced upon them worked very well, but the Continental System meant nothing but hardship.

The war with Austria resembled the earlier struggles between Napoleon and the Austrians. He moved with speed and precision, the Austrian army was slow and fumbling. Once more Austria had to ask for peace and once more she was shorn of great slices of territory and obliged to pay to the French vast sums of money. This time there was a further humiliation for the Austrian Emperor. Napoleon demanded and got his daughter Marie Louise in marriage. Arrangements had previously been made for his divorce from his first wife Josephine, and on April 2, 1810, France had a new Empress.

In the lull that followed the Austrian surrender, Napoleon worked even harder to perfect his Continental System and to plug any loopholes through which British goods might leak into Europe. These repressive measures, however, were beginning to have an adverse effect; the general alarm and resentment caused by the blockade were making French rule unbearable over much of Europe. Napoleon's expectation that the Continental System would force Britain to surrender was based on a misunderstanding of the source of British wealth. Her prosperity came not from commerce, important though that was, but because Britain was the world's most advanced manufacturing country. Her population, crowded into growing industrial cities, could only be fed if food, mostly wheat and other grains, could be imported. If this supply of food had been cut off Britain would have been in serious trouble, but Napoleon, not realizing the true state of affairs, permitted European, even French, traders to ship grain to Britain under a system of licenses.

So while the Continental System failed to strike down his enemy, it did succeed in alienating friends. The Czar, who disapproved of Napoleon's marriage and who resented his support of Polish yearnings for independence, saw Russian trade being strangled by the Continental System. He opened Russian ports to neutral ships, most of which carried British goods, and put a high duty on imported French luxuries.

Napoleon decided that the Czar's resistance could not be tolerated. Now the ruler of seven kingdoms and thirty principalities, an empire far exceeding that of the Czar in wealth, Napoleon began to prepare over the next year for the invasion of Russia.

On June 23, 1812, three great columns of the Grand Army began to cross the Niemen River on pontoon bridges to invade Russian territory. No one opposed them, nor did crowds of oppressed people rush forward to thank them for "liberation." Only the empty cart tracks that passed for roads in Russia stretched before them in the sultry heat.

It had been Napoleon's hope that the Russian armies would be encountered near the frontier and crushingly defeated, one by one, so that the Czar would be obliged to ask for peace terms. Nothing of the sort happened. The Russians simply drew back as the Grand Army advanced, losing men and horses with every kilometre to the Cossacks who hung off on either side of the French columns, picking off stragglers, wiping out foraging parties, and threatening constantly with unexpected raids. At Borodino, about one hundred and fifteen kilometres west of Moscow, the Russians made a stand on September 7, 1812. It was the bloodiest battle of the century and its description forms one of the finest passages in Tolstoy's great novel *War and Peace*, but it was a heavy defeat for the Russians. It was not sufficient, however, to force them to give up the war. They retreated once more, leaving the way open to Moscow.

The French entered Moscow on September 14, only to find the city empty. Troops, officials, nobles, merchants, and most of the

"Russian peasant, French emperor"
—a Russian anti-Napoleonic cartoon.

population were gone. The military depots were burning and the fire engines had been broken. Fires broke out continually among the wooden buildings. Napoleon waited for Czar Alexander to ask for peace but the Czar had vowed never to talk with Napoleon as long as a French soldier stood on Russian soil. For five weeks while the autumn days lost their warmth and gave signs of winter's approach Napoleon waited. When he could delay no longer he set out with an army now reduced to a little over one hundred thousand men back toward Poland. A more southerly route home was barred by strong Russian forces so that they were obliged to return along the northern route by which they had come, which was already stripped bare of food, forage, and shelter. By November the icy storms of the Russian winter fell on the stumbling army and completed the destruction begun by the Russian forces, which harried it every step of the way. While still in Russia, Napoleon turned the command over to his brother-in-law, Marshal Murat, and hurried back to Paris to crush a revolt that had broken out. By the middle of December, 1812, only twenty thousand starving, frost-bitten survivors of the Grand Army struggled out of Russia to safety. The rest had vanished.

6. DEFEAT

Throughout 1813 shadows gathered around the Empire. At forty-three, Napoleon was beginning to tire. He no longer studied the facts of a situation from which to draw brilliant conclusions. He had been a conqueror, a master of men and events, for so long that facts no longer seemed to matter. Only his will, his desires, mattered, and the facts had better fit them.

France, too, was tired and when Napoleon raised a new army, one hundred and fifty thousand of the new conscripts were boys under twenty, to be hurried into battle untrained. An officer asked one of them why he was not firing his musket and the boy answered that he would shoot as well as the next man if only someone would show him how to load! Many Frenchmen worried about the cost of maintaining an empire constantly at war, surrounded always by enemies.

The enemies, however, realizing that Napoleon's star was finally in decline, found new strength and courage. In Germany a new spirit of national pride, a fiery patriotism, was arising; Prussia, and

"Retreat from Moscow" painted by Meissonier.

the rest of Germany, were finding a national purpose just as Spain had done. When the Russians crossed into Germany in pursuit of the retreating French, Prussia, too, rose in arms, and the French garrisons were again forced to retreat westward. Napoleon, still the incomparable general, defeated the enemy in a series of battles, but he did not follow up his victories with the same effectiveness as at Marengo or Austerlitz, so that the results were indecisive.

In October, at the Battle of Leipzig, Napoleon was beaten and his Empire had begun to crumble. Bavaria, long an ally of France, reversed allegiance. Holland declared her independence from France. Naples made a treaty with Austria and the king of Naples who signed it was the former Marshal Murat, who thus turned his back on Napoleon, his brother-in-law and friend of many years.

Now it was the territory of France herself that was at stake. The allied armies of the Russians, Austrians, Prussians, and Swedes were massing in the north and east, and Wellington and the British were swinging up from Spain and Gascony in the south. From January to March, 1814, Napoleon fought a brilliant series of battles, beating first one enemy commander, then another. But it was of no use.

On April 1, 1814, a provisional government was formed, that persuaded the Senate to depose the Emperor. Realizing that the army would neither obey him nor fight, Napoleon wrote out his abdication and on April 11 at Fontainebleau signed a treaty with the Allies. He was to keep the title, an empty one now, of Emperor, and he was given as his kingdom the little island of Elba just off the coast of Italy, together with an income and a bodyguard of four hundred men. The journey south to Fréjus, the port where he had landed to the cheers of the crowd fifteen years ago on his return from Egypt, was terrifying and dangerous. Mobs cursed him and threw stones at the windows of his coach and he was obliged to disguise himself, even wearing the despised white cockade of the Bourbons. On April 28, he boarded H.M.S. *Undaunted* to sail into exile.

7. THE HUNDRED DAYS

Europe now began to put its house in order. The new king of France, Louis XVIII, fat, gouty, and nearing sixty years of age, promised to accept the results of the Revolution that had executed his brother Louis XVI. The Treaties of Paris (May, 1814) left France with little to complain about. All her captured colonies, except three small islands, were returned by Britain. Even the art treasures snatched by Napoleon all over Europe, were, with few exceptions, retained.[1] A final settling of borders was still being worked out, but there were no indications that the agreement would be unduly hard on France.

Before long, however, the pleasure Frenchmen had felt at the return of the Bourbons changed to dismay. Louis XVIII seemed benevolent and soft, but his brother and heir, the Count of Artois, who had been detested before the Revolution, was rapidly making himself as unpopular as before. He was the leader of those royalists who would try to undo the results of the last twenty-five years. Resentment against the Bourbons was especially prevalent among the officers and men of the army. The officers were put on half pay, which soon fell in arrears, while the "other ranks" were left to get on as best they could, or to starve. They had nothing but contempt for those, including fat Louis the king and his haughty, arrogant brother, who had lived out the war years in smug comfort far from the roar of gunfire. Anxiety, too, gripped the peasants and others who held land or property that once had belonged to the Church or to the nobility.

A few months before, Napoleon had been cursed as the cause of France's defeat, humiliation, and misery. Now the "old moustaches" who had fought at Jena and Wagram whispered to one another that the Emperor would return in the spring when the violets were in flower. It was obvious that something was being plotted. On the afternoon of March 1, 1815, the corpulent little man in the familiar grey greatcoat stepped ashore on the French mainland. "I shall reach Paris," he said, "without firing a shot."

He was as good as his word. Troops sent to stop his progress joined him in thousands, the orders of their royalist officers to shoot drowned in the thunderous cheers of *"Vive l'Empereur!"* Marshal Ney, sent south by the king to stop his advance, promised to put him in an iron cage, but signed his own death warrant by joining him instead. Later that year the Bourbons, who understood very little about loyalty and courage, had Ney shot for treason.

[1]These settlements were later changed, at the Second Treaty of Paris; see p. 224.

For the present he marched with the Emperor at the head of a steadily growing army.

The Bourbons fled from Paris, Louis XVIII taking refuge in Belgium. In Vienna, the Congress issued a declaration that Napoleon, as an enemy and disturber of the peace of the world, was an outlaw, subject to "public prosecution." Napoleon in Paris protested that he had learned by experience, that he was a changed man who now longed only for peace. At the same time he gathered an army, a simple task since the veterans were flocking to his standard. Many of the famous marshals and generals were gone but there was a multitude of able younger men to take their places.

The combined allied armies moved to attack him, and Napoleon had to fight. His strategy was the one that had served him so well in the past. He would knock out the two enemy armies in the north before they could combine, and then turn to the east with the expectation of repeating the process. He himself attacked the Prussians under General Blücher while Ney attacked an English and German army commanded by Wellington. The results were not decisive. Napoleon beat Blücher, and the Prussians retreated, pursued in a careless manner by strong French forces under Marshal Grouchy. Ney was fought to a standstill by Wellington.

Wellington's army withdrew to a position near the Belgian village of Waterloo. It was his favourite position for a battle, a long ridge behind the crest of which he could position his men out of danger until the time came for them to come over the top, and in three long lines deliver shattering volleys into the advancing French columns. The rain which had fallen most of the previous day had softened the ground so that it was difficult to move the guns, and the roads were deep in mud.

The actual fighting began shortly before noon on June 18, 1815, with the French guns firing across the grain fields. From then until evening a furious battle was fought, with the French trying to dislodge Wellington's men and drive them back to Brussels a few kilometres away. By 18:00 the advance units of Blücher's Prussians were coming from the east to link up with the British. A final charge was made by the Old Guard led by Marshal Ney. It was turned back by the fire of the British infantry and tumbled back down the sloping ground. Grouchy had lost contact with the Prussians who were arriving in increasing numbers on the left of the British line. A great cheer welcomed Wellington as he rode

The Victor of Waterloo—Arthur Wellesley, the First Duke of Wellington, known to many as the "Iron Duke," and to his soldiers as "Old Hooky."

along the line and gave the order to advance. The Battle of Waterloo was won and Napoleon's career ended.

On July 7 the allied armies entered Paris and Louis XVIII was restored to his throne the next day, returning "in the baggage-train of the Allies." Napoleon, one hundred days after he reached Paris from Elba and three days after Waterloo, had abdicated again, some thought to try to escape to the United States. But his old enemy the British navy was blockading the French coast. He was unable to slip through its cordon, and eventually surrendered to Captain Maitland of H.M.S. *Bellerophon*. Shortly afterward another British ship, H.M.S. *Northumberland*, carried him to exile on St. Helena in the South Atlantic and there, old before his time, he died in 1821.

While in exile in St. Helena Napoleon pronounced what might have been his own epitaph. "If I had succeeded," he said, "I should have been the greatest man known to history."

What did he aim at and what did he achieve? If it was the unification of Europe under his rule, or, as he saw in his more ambitious dreams of glory, an empire that embraced the world, it is unlikely that even his energy and genius could have accomplished it for longer than a very brief period. The rise of nationalism and the spread of the Industrial Revolution released forces which he, with his essentially 18th century outlook, could neither have understood nor controlled. As it was, the political arrangements he imposed on Europe scarcely survived his downfall.

He carried the French Revolution beyond the boundaries of France. The Cisalpine Republic and the Confederation of the Rhine made men aware that they were Italians or Germans and that it was possible for them to rule themselves and take pride in their race, its history and achievements. Thus he planted the seeds of the nations of Italy and Germany, and gave their peoples an incentive and a sense of nationality that helped shape modern Europe.

The legal, administrative, and educational institutions which he conferred on France have remained as lasting reminders of his genius. Not trained in the law himself and therefore personally responsible for little or nothing in the *Code Napoléon*, he gave direction and force to the work of the jurists who made the codification. Without him it might never have reached completion. By introducing it in the countries conquered or occupied by his armies he gave it the impetus which spread its use over much of the western world.

While educationists will debate the value of his ideas as an educator—he did not believe, for example, in much education for girls or women—no one can find fault with the organization of his school system merely as an organization. It was an efficient machine for the production of the kind of citizen he believed France required. That there was about it something of the air of the barracks room was not, to his soldier's eye, anything but a merit. Modified by changing demands of the times, it remains the system in use in France, just as the political organization of the country is still largely that which he decreed.

Napoleon's real claim to fame thus lies in his abilities as an organizer and as an administrator. He had little grasp of economics, as the failure of his Continental System showed, nor did he appreciate or feel the need to encourage art and literature, even though he plundered art treasures in conquered countries. Great though his fame as a military genius, his skill lay rather in the clever use of men and materials available in a particular situation, rather than in the invention of new methods or in the use of new equipment. He was offered ships driven by steam engines, and even a submarine, but these products of the technology of the Industrial Revolution had no appeal for him and he rejected them. Before his military career ended at Waterloo his enemies had painfully learned the military lessons he had taught. He was beginning to suffer his share of defeats; victories, unlike the glorious days of Marengo and Austerlitz, were becoming harder to achieve.

And so it all ended with an ailing and complaining invalid slowly dying on a sub-tropical island of a disease never properly diagnosed, a man who filled his days with unsuccessful attempts to learn English composition ("Since sixt wek y leave the english and y do not any progress."), and with the writing or dictation of dreary memoirs which are unreliable about facts and intended to justify everything he did in the days of his power. Perhaps the final word about him was said by another great Frenchman, de Tocqueville: "He was as great as a man can be without morality."

9 Europe After Napoleon

My life coincides with an abominable period. I came into the world either too early, or too làte; at present I am good for nothing . . . I am spending my life propping up mouldering buildings.
—Prince Metternich

In contrast to the 18th or 20th centuries, the 19th century was a period of relative international calm. However, though wars were few and limited, European social and political development did not stagnate. This was a century of change, change that occurred more rapidly than during any previous century. These changes took place through the action of three major forces: liberalism, nationalism, and industrialism.

Revolutionary France unlocked the forces of liberalism and nationalism throughout Europe. The French Revolution had been the seed-bed of ideas that were to transform Europe. The long struggle with France ended in a military victory for the allied nations of Austria, Britain, Prussia, and Russia. But France had had more than military aims. She had been eager to export fresh ideas to every corner of Europe. In this she was more successful than she had been on the battlefield of Waterloo. The proof of this success was in the dramatic changes produced during the decades that followed in the political, social, economic, religious, and cultural life of Europe. Monarchy, for centuries the dominant political institution of Europe, was openly criticized. Feudalism, a way of life with roots in the Middle Ages, was abolished in France, altered in Prussia, and thrown open to question in Austria and Russia. The age-old agricultural economy of Europe began giving way to industry as inventions and technology brought about new methods of production. The Roman Catholic Church, which before the Reformation had seemed almost impervious to criticism, was again weakened in influence as the forces of change grew in strength.

The Great Powers, who favoured stability and continuity and opposed the forces of change released by the Revolution, were prepared to fight on the battlefield of men's minds as they had against Napoleon's *Grande Armée*. Their first tactic was to prevent renewed war. To accomplish this they agreed, for the first time in history, to maintain their wartime alliance even after the smoke of battle had vanished. This was the Congress System, developed by the Great Powers at the Congress of Vienna. Then, feeling secure against the possibility of another great European war, they began a peacetime assault on the forces of change, liberalism and nationalism. During the generation after Waterloo, the battle of ideas replaced the battle of arms, as reaction fought revolution, as the forces of the past fought the forces of the future.

1. THEORIES OF SOCIETY

During the 17th and early 18th centuries, European society underwent little basic change. But storm clouds began to appear on the horizon late in the 18th century when the *philosophes* dared to question and even ridicule traditional political, social, economic, and religious concepts. Suddenly the storm broke as the leaders of the French Revolution, and later Napoleon, vigorously assaulted the *ancien régime*. Despite the efforts of the forces of stability and continuity to restore the traditional European values after Napoleon's defeat, new ideas, or ideologies, had taken root throughout Europe, each of which attacked, in varying degree, the foundations of European society. The first major period of the conflict of ideas took place between 1815 and 1848; even today in the 20th century we are still very much in the midst of this conflict. Those forces which were and remain important are: liberalism, socialism, nationalism, romanticism, and conservatism.

Liberalism

Liberals were convinced that man was inherently good. He was born with the gift of reason, and if given freedom and the opportunity to develop his powers of reason through education, he would improve both himself and the society in which he lived. To the liberal, freedom was of fundamental importance. It was essential that men should have the liberty to speak freely and to criticize openly any ideas and institutions. He had to have the liberty to choose his religion or even to have no religion at all, if he wished. He had to have the liberty to choose the way in which he was governed and the people who would govern him. Liberals also believed in economic freedom—the right to engage in commerce and industry, free from the restraining and interfering hand of government. In order to gain these freedoms, which they considered to be fundamental rights, liberals demanded written constitutions. At the same time, they opposed the hereditary rights and privileges enjoyed by the nobility, and insisted that material and social advancement should come through education, individual hard work, and thrift. Liberalism found its greatest support among the rising middle class or *bourgeoisie*, which was composed of businessmen and industrialists.

If there is one phrase that became, and continues to be, identified with 19th century liberalism, it is *laissez-faire*, which means, roughly, leave alone. It was originally and most frequently applied to economic matters, and referred to the liberal belief that the greatest welfare and prosperity would result if the government did not interfere in business and commerce. Later it became a liberal watchword that could be applied to a wide range of issues, social as well as economic. Holding strictly to their concept of *laissez-faire*, liberals believed that governments existed only to preserve order, to protect a nation from external enemies, and to safeguard a free society in which the individual, through his own efforts, could achieve economic and social success.

As the European economy developed from an agricultural base to an industrial base, a fundamental problem of liberalism became apparent. The *laissez-faire* economy brought improved techniques and efficiency with greater prosperity for some, but produced many ugly effects as well. Unemployment increased as workers were displaced from their jobs by new processes and machines. Workers, exploited by industrialists, earned low wages and were forced by their poverty to live in appalling slums clustered around the growing industrial complexes.

As people became aware of these problems, there was a demand that improvements be made. But the ability of liberals to act was restricted by their adherence to the concept of *laissez-faire*. They maintained that if government were to intervene by passing legislation, it would be interfering with businessmen and business conditions, and could only result in matters getting worse. It was not that the liberals approved of the evils of industrialism, but that they were trapped by their rigid, though sincere, adherence to *laissez-*

faire. They failed to recognize that all people were not endowed with equal ability and opportunity to reach higher social and economic levels.

Some liberals, however, began to reconsider the value of *laissez-faire* since it so obviously permitted social misery. These liberals adopted the theories of socialism. Prior to 1848, socialism won few adherents. Later in the century, however, as liberal-dominated parliaments extended the franchise, thereby gradually increasing the working class vote, more socialists won seats in European parliaments. In time, as socialism became better organized and its ideological base gained more depth, it became a powerful force for social change. The socialists, therefore, will be discussed in Chapter 12.

Romanticism and Idealism

Romanticism was a disillusioned reaction against the failure of the Age of Reason to produce a better world. In the Age of Reason, men had questioned and denied; it was characteristic of the Romantic reaction that men sought a cause in which they could affirm their belief. The instincts and emotions were glorified, and reason and the intellect attacked. There was an intense veneration of nature, a sentimental fondness for the common and humble man, an interest in folklore and legend and the historical roots of culture, a concern for the many nationalist movements of subject peoples for liberation and, above all, a deep contempt for formalism.

The impact of Romanticism was strongly reflected in the art and literature of the period. Landscape painting that emphasized nature's beauty and tranquility came into its own as a major form of art, with the works in England of John Constable and others. The poetry of Wordsworth, Shelley, Keats, and Byron in Britain and of Goethe and Heinrich Heine in Germany, idealized the Romantic concept of nature, mysticism, and beauty. The Romantic spirit was also reflected in the novel. Victor Hugo savagely attacked social injustice in France, and depicted the poor people as heroes and heroines. The epics of Sir Walter Scott were sentimental interpretations of Scottish legend. In Goethe's masterpiece, *Faust*, the hero sells his soul to the devil in order to escape a life of barren intellectual pursuits for a more sensual existence. In architecture, the new interest in the Gothic and Romanesque styles of the past

"I am certain of nothing but the holiness of the Heart's affection and the truth of imagination. . . . What the imagination seizes as Beauty must be truth."—John Keats

"Grau, teurer Freund ist all Theorie
Und grün des Lebens goldner Baum."

"All theory, dear friend, is grey, but the golden tree of life springs ever green."—Goethe

"We declare to you that the earth has exhausted its contingent of master-spirits. Now for decadence and general closing. We shall have no more men of genius."—Victor Hugo

Romanticist musicians. Top: Franz Schubert. Left: Frédéric Chopin. Right: Ludwig van Beethoven. The portrait of Chopin, by Delacroix, is itself considered a classic example of Romantic art.

"Giaour and Pacha Fighting" by Eugène Delacroix. Almost the epitome of the Romantic spirit, the painting was inspired by Byron's poetry: "I recognize his pale forehead; it is he who stole Felia's love from me, he is the accursed Giaour."

produced such handsome buildings as the Houses of Parliament in London. In music also, there were excellent examples of the Romantic spirit. The soaring power of Beethoven's symphonies were based on such themes as emotion and heroism. Chopin was inspired by the folk music and folk themes of Poland in many of his *polonaises* and *mazurkas*. Even the names of these compositions provide a clue to their relationship with the Romantic period: both the *polonaise* and *mazurka* are traditional Polish folk dances. Wagner's interest in Germanic legends dominated his operas.

Closely related to Romanticism was Idealism, so named because it advanced the theory that only ideas were "real." Like Romanticism, Idealism was a rejection of the rationalism and excessive dependence upon reason of the previous age. Whereas people in the

"The Honourable Mrs. Graham" by Thomas Gainsborough. An excellent example of the Romantic concept of the aristocracy—beautiful, wealthy, cultured, delicate. Compare this portrait with Jacques David's painting "A Woman of the Revolution" on page 132.

Age of Reason believed that logic and reason alone could provide answers to all questions of philosophy, the Idealists argued that certain problems, such as the nature of truth, morality, or the existence of God, could not be solved by logic, but only by faith. The best presentation of this theory was the *Critique of Pure Reason,* a profound work by the German philosopher Immanuel Kant.

The political ideas of the Idealist period culminated in the writings of the German philosopher, Georg Wilhelm Hegel. Applying the thought of Kant and other idealist philosophers, Hegel developed an all-embracing theory of history. He believed that nations undergo an historical evolution, until they reach a highly developed stage in which the interests of every citizen fit perfectly with the interests of the state. Hegel felt a state that had reached this stage of development was "supreme," and was not bound by any laws of morality. He also held that only by submission to the will of the state could the individual achieve true liberty. The influence of this theory was enormous. The theories of Hitler and in particular, Mussolini, were directly descended from Hegel's concept of the "divine state." In another direction, Hegel was the greatest single influence upon the thought of Karl Marx.

As schools of thought, Romanticism and Idealism were less consistent than many of the other ideologies. In some aspects they were compatible with liberalism, in others, more with conservatism and nationalism. In many ways, Romanticism was more a literary movement, and Idealism more a technical philosophy, than an ideology. Nevertheless, the impact of both Romanticism and Idealism on subsequent periods has been strong and lasting.

Nationalism

Nationalism is a term that does not lend itself easily to definition; however, it can be explained as being an emotional awareness of the common ties of language, customs, race, and even religion that are possessed by a people. It manifests itself when a people unite to promote common political and cultural goals.

Nationalism had existed in western Europe at least since the Hundred Years' War (1338-1453), but its effects were only slight until the 18th century. At that time, improvements in transportation and communications began to bring people together more frequently. At the same time, widening educational opportunities were raising the cultural level of the populace, making them aware of their past glories, military, literary, and artistic. Not until the French Revolution, however, could people be so moved by nationalistic sentiments as to feel that the possession of one's country was worth defending with one's life.

The French armies that fought in the Revolutionary Wars were composed of citizens intent on saving and glorifying France and the French people. In contrast, former wars had been fought by feudal levies conscripted to save a dynasty (in France's case, the Bourbons), or the lands of the nobility. But during the Revolution, the democratic Jacobin belief in the sovereignty of the people stressed that the nation, and not the monarch, determined the form of government a people would have. Individuals were thus considered to be citizens of the nation, not subjects of the king. As this dynamic transfer of allegiance was made from king to nation, the vibrant force of nationalism unleashed hidden reserves of power unknown since the days of the Roman legions. Carnot, "the organizer of victory," enlisted the first citizen army that drove back the Prussians at Valmy in 1792. Napoleon later won many famous victories gained by his spirited troops who were eager to bring fame and glory to the French nation. And, ultimately, it was this same force that inspired his enemies and helped bring about his downfall.

Liberalism and nationalism combined to inspire peoples like the Poles, Czechs, Greeks, and Italians to throw off the governing chains of foreign powers and to establish their own forms of government. By 1848, nationalism had become a force more potent than liberalism, and by the 20th century led to the outbreak of two global wars. Even today it remains perhaps the most important ideological force in world politics.

Conservatism

Liberalism and nationalism were relatively new forces when the Congress of Vienna met in 1814-15. They were the principle ideological causes of revolution and change. Set against them was conservatism, the force that defended stability and continuity. The term conservatism, applied to describe a political and social attitude, was first used by the French counter-revolutionary writer, Chateaubriand. It was also used by Edmund Burke, the Irish writer and politician, in his famous work, *Reflections on the Revolution in France*. Both men believed in the necessity of maintaining continuity in social, political, and religious institutions, and making changes gradually with as little dislocation as possible. They agreed that the upheaval which had followed the storming of the Bastille was a denial of much that was good in the many centuries of tradition in Europe.

Conservatives in Europe believed in a strong monarchy, an established Church, and heredity rights. In their opinion, the mass of the people were not to be trusted, and the aristocracy, because of their education and upbringing, were the only ones qualified to govern and set the social and moral values of a society.

Apart from these common basic beliefs, though, there were variations in conservative thinking. One variety of conservative thought, the evolutionary and constitutional form, upheld traditional liberties. This type of conservatism was willing to accept change and was prepared to believe in constitutional guarantees of freedom. Burke and most English conservatives accepted this view. Other conservatives, however, who held a counter-revolutionary and reactionary outlook, upheld traditional authority and were often blindly resistant to change. These people were mostly to be found on the Continent.

The Congress of Vienna was dominated by conservative statesmen, who were determined to return European society and politics to the way it had been before the French Revolution. To maintain the reimposed *ancien régime*, they created the Congress System. One man was largely responsible for this and his name has become associated with the generation following the Congress of Vienna. He was Prince Metternich, Chancellor of Austria.

2. THE AGE OF METTERNICH

Some historians have rendered a harsh verdict on Metternich. Liberals have linked his name with all opposition to progress. The romantic English poet, Robert Browning, in his poem *The Italian in England*, described the attitude of liberal Italians toward Met-

"Error has never approached my spirit." — Prince Metternich

ternich. In the poem, an exiled Italian states that if he had three wishes:

> I know at least what one should be:
> I would grasp Metternich until
> I felt his red wet throat distil
> In blood thro' these two hands.

More recently, historians have softened somewhat the formerly harsh judgment of Metternich. Although they disagree on the purposes and effectiveness of his policies, they do agree on his importance.

Clemens Wenzel von Metternich-Winneburg was born in the Austrian town of Coblenz on the Rhine. His father had been in the diplomatic service of the Austrian Emperor; through him, the young Metternich became familiar with European political problems. As a student in Mainz, he followed closely the progress of the French Revolution. He spent the remainder of his life waging unsuccessful warfare with the twin products of that Revolution: liberalism and nationalism. To Metternich, the Revolution was

". . . the gangrene which must be burned out with the hot iron, the hydra with jaws open to swallow up the social order. . . ." When Napoleon was reaching the peak of his career in 1806, Metternich was named Austrian Ambassador to France and remained there until 1809 when he returned home to be named Foreign Minister and then Chancellor. Hardworking, a brilliant conversationalist, and a master of intrigue, he vainly believed that he alone could maintain peace and stability in Europe. Even after he had been forced to flee to London (in 1848) to save his life, he maintained his position on his life's work with the cryptic comment: "Error has never approached my spirit." At other times he was not so sure of the success of his decisions. In 1828 he wrote:

My life coincides with an abominable period. I came into the world either too early or too late; at present I am good for nothing . . . I am spending my life propping up mouldering buildings.

These "mouldering buildings" were the European balance of power and the multi-national Austrian Empire. In 1814, when the victorious powers met in Vienna to tackle the problems of a shattered Europe, Metternich presided over the Congress. All his efforts at Vienna were spent in an attempt to create a balance of power in Europe and to stifle liberal and nationalistic sentiment.

The Congress of Vienna

In the autumn of 1814, when the Congress of Vienna convened, the Austrian capital lived up to her reputation as a city of gaiety and elegance. Although nearly bankrupt, the Austrian court lavishly entertained the visiting heads of state, their ministers and numerous advisers, servants, and followers.

Three basic principles guided the deliberations at Vienna: compensation, legitimacy, and the security of Europe. In line with the first principle, the victorious powers were eager to obtain financial or territorial compensation for their sufferings after more than twenty years of war. By the principle of legitimacy, the delegates agreed to restore the system of monarchy in those countries where it had been overthrown since 1789, and return the legitimate or traditional ruling families that had been deposed. Ideas such as national self-determination, democracy, and the right of a people to name the form of government they desired, were little under-

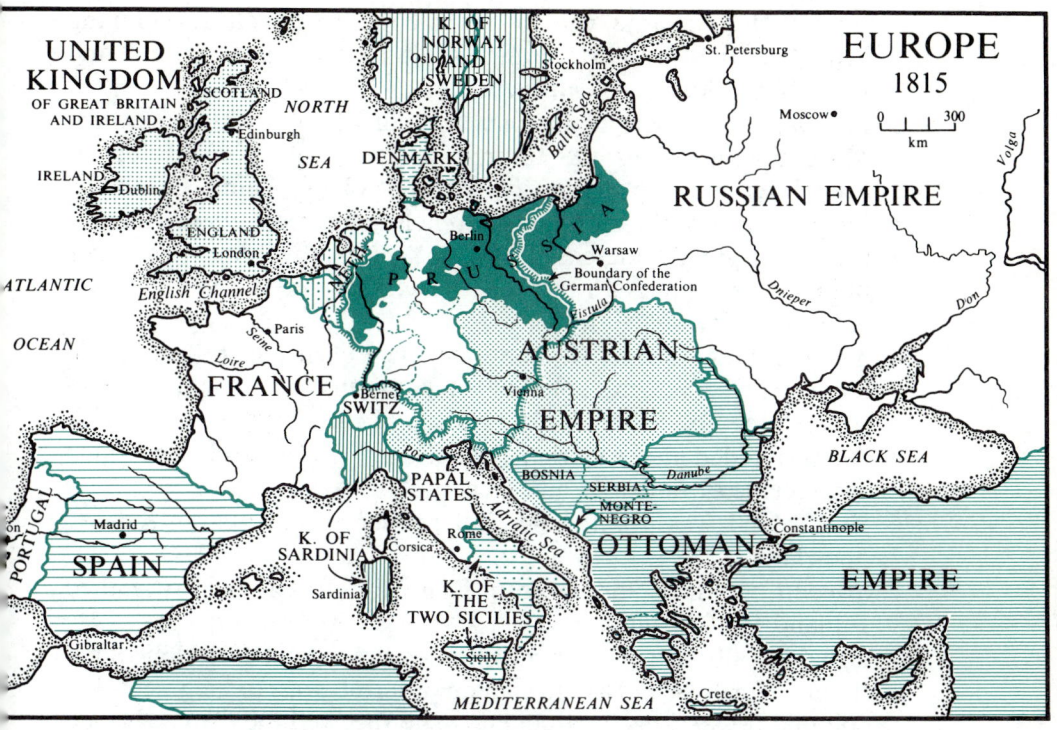

stood or trusted in 1815. Finally, to ensure the security of Europe, the four major powers, Austria, England, Russia, and Prussia agreed to back up the Vienna settlement, by forming a peacetime alliance. On June 8, 1815, a Final Act, codifying the arrangements of the Congress, was signed by all the powers.

CHIEF TERRITORIAL AGREEMENTS MADE AT VIENNA, 1815:

1. In Central Europe, Napoleon's Confederation of the Rhine was broken up. In its place was established the German Confederation. Although each of the thirty-nine member states was allowed self-government, Austria dominated the Confederation by holding the permanent presidency of the Diet or federal Parliament.

2. In Italy, Sardinia was granted Genoa, the Bourbons were restored to the throne of the Two Sicilies, and the Pope was returned to power in the Papal States. Lombardy and Venetia were placed under direct Austrian rule. Tuscany and Modena were given to Austrian princes, and Parma and Lucca to Marie

Louise, the Austrian wife of Napoleon. An effective beginning had been made on Metternich's plan to bring Germany and Italy under Austrian control.

3. Prussia gained part of Saxony and all of Swedish Pomerania. More significant for the future was her acquisition of former French territory on the left (west) bank of the Rhine. Originally intended as a bulwark against French aggression, these Rhenish provinces greatly increased Prussia's population and hence her military strength. As a result, she later became the most powerful of the German states.
4. The Congress decided to continue the Polish partition, and the large area of Poland not divided between Austria and Prussia was retained by Russia under the title of the Kingdom of Poland.
5. Austria ceded the Austrian Netherlands to Holland, for which she received Lombardy and Venetia.
6. Switzerland was granted her independence and guaranteed her neutrality.
7. Sweden obtained Norway from Denmark, Russia in turn gained Finland from Sweden.
8. Britain's only European acquisition was the island of Heligoland in the North Sea. Britain's main interest was to augment her colonial possessions; consequently she received the Cape of Good Hope, Malta, Ceylon, Mauritius, and some former French West Indian possessions.

At first the Congress had been willing to treat France with considerable fairness. By the first Treaty of Paris (May, 1814), the four major Powers together with Spain, Portugal, and Sweden, had signed a formal peace with France. The victors had ordered France to lay down her arms and had restored her boundaries of 1792. But after Napoleon's "One Hundred Days," from March 1, 1815, to June 22, the allies were not so lenient. The second Treaty of Paris (November, 1815) reduced France to her boundaries of 1790, forced her to restore the art treasures looted by Napoleon, imposed an indemnity of seven hundred million francs, and arranged for partial military occupation of her territory.

The Congress System

Having concluded the terms of the peace settlement, the major Powers turned their efforts toward the construction of a system to preserve peace in Europe. To this end two alliance systems were formed, one called the "Holy Alliance," the other the "Quadruple Alliance" (later expanded and called the "Quintuple Alliance").

The Holy Alliance originated in 1815, in a treaty between Austria, Russia, and Prussia. Inspired by Czar Alexander, the Holy Alliance was a pledge by the three nations to conduct their affairs according to "the principles of Christianity." Significantly, the Holy Alliance held no appeal for either the British or the French. Castlereagh, the chief British representative at Vienna, referred to it as "a piece of sublime mysticism and nonsense," and remarked sarcastically that it would "maintain the peace of Europe for at least seven years." The Holy Alliance never had a concrete effect upon European affairs, and simply revealed the wide differences in political outlook between the liberal western and the conservative eastern nations. In the popular mind, it was confused with the Quadruple Alliance, and was regarded as a "league of despots directed against liberty."

Much more successful than the Holy Alliance was the Quadruple Alliance, formed in 1815 by Austria, Russia, Prussia, and Britain. This unprecedented peacetime alliance was intended to deter any nation from imitating Napoleon's attempts to conquer Europe. To this end the members agreed to review international differences at periodic conferences. This arrangement has been called the Congress System. Because the members agreed to act together, or in concert, it has also been termed the "Concert of Europe." The Congress System succeeded in establishing a balance of power, a situation in which no single Power could disregard the wishes of the others combined.

In 1818 the Quadruple Alliance was expanded and renamed the Quintuple Alliance upon the admission of France. France! The common enemy of the monarchists, and home of the Revolution and Napoleon, who together had nearly succeeded in overturning Europe—invited by the victors to join the Congress System to restore order and stability to Europe! That such a turn of diplomacy should occur was a great tribute to the skill and ability of the French representative at Vienna, Charles Maurice de Talleyrand-Périgord. As early as the first Peace of Paris, Talleyrand had argued persuasively that to have a strong and stable French government would be in the best interests of all Europe. Then, he sensed a conflict between England and Austria against Prussia and Russia

Talleyrand: "His success in creating this combination (of Britain, France, Austria) constitutes one of the most useful achievements in all diplomatic history. For in Talleyrand, the sense of proportion and the sense of occasion transcended opportunism; they amounted to genius." — Harold Nicholson, *The Congress of Vienna*

over the issue of the future of Poland; by clever manipulation, he created a united front between France, Austria, and Great Britain through a secret alliance against Russia. By this means, he gained the gratitude of Britain and Austria, and their support for a more lenient treatment of France. It was in no small measure due to his diplomatic skill that France was so quickly re-established as a major European Power.

3. THE STRUGGLE WITH LIBERALISM AND NATIONALISM

With the problems of international relations thus solved, the Powers of Europe became increasingly preoccupied by the spread of liberalism and nationalism, which were regarded as anathema by most European leaders. Metternich continued to be the chief protagonist of conservatism in Europe. By exploiting the deep-seated fears of the leading European conservatives, he led the Congress Powers in a great struggle against these two forces. Initially, the task did not seem difficult. Europe east of the Rhine was still semi-feudal and agricultural. Because the Industrial Revolution had barely been felt there, the small middle class was timid and without power. The three major forces of reaction—the monarchy, the Church, and the landowners—seemed to offer an impregnable barrier to the winds of change. Despite Metternich's efforts, however, revolutionary ferment was beginning to spread.

The Congress powers held four formal conferences, at Aix-la-Chapelle (1818), Troppau (1820), Laibach (1821), and Verona (1822). Under Metternich's direction, attention was focused on liberal and nationalistic revolts in the German Confederation, Spain, Naples, Piedmont, Greece, and the Netherlands.

Liberalism and Nationalism Suppressed

The first signs of the nationalist-liberal ferment appeared in the German Confederation, when German soldiers returned from the Napoleonic wars bearing revolutionary ideas. Indeed, in Germany these ideas had begun to form even earlier. In 1807-08, J. G. Fichte, a Prussian university professor, had delivered a series of lectures, called *Addresses to the German Nation*. By tracing German history back to the period of the Roman Empire, Fichte had tried to show that the Germanic peoples had made a significant contribution to European civilization. Many Germans who agreed with him believed that their culture would develop better if the German states were politically unified. And so, even though no organized attempt at unification had been made, by 1814 the spirit of nationalism was already beginning to spread throughout the Confederation.

One group that gave vague expression to the spirit of German nationalism was the *Burschenschaft*, a national student fraternity that had chapters in several universities. The students adopted an emblem with the motto: "Honour, Liberty and Fatherland." In October, 1817, a giant rally of the *Burschenschaft* was held at Wartburg to celebrate both the defeat of Napoleon at Leipzig in 1813, and the 300th anniversary of the beginning of the German Reformation. After much beer-drinking and the singing of patriotic songs, the students formed a large torch-light parade, which concluded with the ceremonial burning of reactionary books. This display of student activity did not have popular backing; nor was it really intended to be more than a semi-serious student prank. But to Metternich the Wartburg festival was a disturbing omen. His fears were increased by two incidents: the murder of a reactionary spy in the pay of Czar Alexander, named Kotzebue, and an attempt upon the life of a minister of one of the Confederation states.

Metternich believed there was a growing conspiracy aimed at overthrowing Confederation governments. In 1819, therefore, he called a conference of the principal Confederation states, and persuaded them to adopt a series of restrictive rules to prevent conspiracies. These became known as the Karlsbad Decrees. By the Decrees, universities were placed under the strict surveillance of proctors. A central investigating committee was formed to uncover and destroy dangerous political organizations. All books, pamphlets, and newspapers were subjected to censorship. Foreign literature was stopped by custom guards. Even the books taken by professors and students from libraries were carefully recorded. Students were forbidden to discuss contemporary politics or religion. This early form of the police state was Metternich's response to liberalism and nationalism.

The Italian Peninsula and Spain

In the Italian Peninsula, Metternich faced a similar problem. The Vienna settlement had given Austria control over all the Italian States except the Kingdom of Sardinia (sometimes called Piedmont or Savoy). Austrian rule was harsh. All mail was routed through Vienna, where it was opened by the secret police. Even where direct rule was not possible, as on the island of Sardinia, Metternich employed spies. The callous and inhumane attitude of the Austrian bureaucrats deepened Italian resentment. In one case, a mother whose son had been hanged was sent a bill for the hangman's noose. There was also a natural resentment by the Latin Italians against being ruled by Germanic Austrians. Moreover, the Italians had earlier received a taste of freedom when Napoleon had encouraged liberal reforms and Italian nationalism. The main resistance to Austrian control took shape in the famous secret society, the *Carbonari* (the "charcoal burners"), whose organization extended from the Alps to Sicily.

The Outbreak of Revolt

Despite Metternich's rigidly repressive methods, revolts broke out in Europe in 1820 and continued until the great upheavals of 1848. The first serious revolt took place in Spain, where the army joined ranks with the liberals to force the Bourbon king, Ferdinand VII, to restore the Constitution of 1812, itself modelled on the French Constitution of 1791. For three years (1820-1823) a liberal *Cortes*, or Parliament, checked the king's absolute power. But in response to Ferdinand's pleadings, the Congress Powers meeting at Verona (1822) agreed to despatch French troops to disband the Parliament and suppress the liberals.

The early success of the Spanish liberals in 1820 inspired their counterparts in Italy. In the Kingdom of the Two Sicilies, the *Carbonari* compelled the Bourbon king, Ferdinand IV of Naples, to adopt a constitution. Rebellion then became contagious and spread to Milan and Sardinia. At the moment when revolution threatened to engulf all of Italy, the Austrians were given permission by the Congress of Laibach (1821) to intervene. Austrian troops streamed into Italy and ruthlessly suppressed the revolts.

Russia

Even distant Russia experienced revolutionary ferment. During the occupation of France, from 1814 to 1818, numerous impressionable young army officers had come into contact with Jacobin and other influences "that completely unsteadied them." Returning to Russia, the misery of the peasants and the despotism of the ruling classes seemed completely intolerable. By 1820, they had begun forming a number of secret revolutionary societies for the overthrow of the czardom and the establishment of a limited monarchy or even a republic. Then, in 1825, Czar Alexander died; this was the signal for a group of these officers to raise the standard of revolt. Believing that Constantine, one of Alexander's sons, was willing to support their liberal demands for a guarantee of fundamental rights, they rebelled in December, 1825. Using the slogan, "Constantine and constitution," they sought support from the Russian army. Nicholas, Alexander's oldest son and appointed successor, moved swiftly to crush the rebellion and to keep intact the power of landowners and the institution of serfdom. So failed the Decembrist Revolt, the only significant liberal uprising in Russia during the 19th century.

Greece

All of the attempted revolutions during the 1820's drew the attention of liberals throughout Europe. None, however, appealed so strongly as did the Greek struggle for independence against the Ottoman Turks. For several hundred years the Ottoman Empire had ruled the Greeks. After Greek nationalists had staged an abortive revolt in 1821, Europe became sentimentally attached to the Greek cause. The romantic revival had focused attention on the great contributions of ancient Greece to the western world. Now, the "heathen Turk" was enslaving the descendants of Plato and Pericles. Young liberals, such as the English poet, Byron, rushed to enlist in the Greek rebel armies. Intellectuals put pressure on the French and British governments to intervene. Russia offered to move against her ancient enemies, the Moslem Turks, and to aid her fellow Orthodox Christians, the Greeks. France and Britain, anxious to prevent Russian expansion in the Balkans, joined Russia in 1827 to defeat the Turkish fleet at Navarino, in the last great naval battle fought by sailing ships, and thereby to free Greece. In 1829, Greece was granted her independence, and in 1832 became a kingdom under the protection of Great Britain, France, and Russia.

Up to 1830, the Congress System and the forces of conservatism appeared to have been successful. With the exception of the Greek cause, Metternich had succeeded in putting down open revolt by force. Moreover, none of the significant revolts had taken place within the borders of the major powers. But strains had already begun to appear. Indicative of these problems was Britain's disenchantment with the Congress System.

British Attitudes towards the Congress System

Britain, whose government was slowly becoming more liberal, had objected to Congress intervention to destroy internal revolutions. Although the British protest had rested officially on the principle that the Congress System had been formed to prevent only international disputes, there was another reason. During the revolution in Spain, smashed by French troops at the behest of the Congress, the Spanish colonies in South America had taken advantage of turmoil in the mother country to declare their independence. As a result, the commercial door of South America had been opened to British merchants. A Bourbon restoration in Spain would have meant the renewal of the Spanish mercantile system and the loss of Britain's newly gained markets. After the Verona meeting (1822), Britain had unofficially withdrawn from the Congress. Britain's action demonstrated that internationalism was a difficult philosophy to maintain in the face of conflicting national interests.

The Congress System was further limited by the growing differences in political attitudes between East and West. Neither France nor Britain had entered the Holy Alliance, which they both regarded as being at best an empty agreement, and at worst, a tool for repression and reaction. Eventually France joined Britain in rejecting the reactionary policies of the three Eastern autocracies, Prussia, Russia, and Austria.

Europe learned from the Congress System. Although by treaty the Quadruple Alliance lasted only twenty years (1815-1835), its principles continued to guide general European conduct through most of the century. Moreover, the precedent of formal, peacetime international co-operation was later revived in the League of Nations (1919-1946) and survives today in the United Nations.

The Revolution Spreads

Despite the success of the Congress Powers in holding back liberalism and nationalism, by 1830 it was obvious that they had certainly not been able to destroy these two ideological forces completely. Indeed, events were soon to reveal that the development of liberalism and nationalism had already gone too far to be checked. The first of a new wave of revolts was to take place in France.

In 1814, Louis XVIII had granted a constitution known as the Charter, which recognized many of the changes produced by the Revolution, including the Napoleonic law codes and the settlement with the Roman Catholic Church. The Charter created a two-house legislature with a very limited franchise. Unlike many conservatives, Louis XVIII recognized that the clock could not be completely turned back to 1789.

In 1824, Louis was succeeded by his ultra-reactionary brother, Charles X, long admired by extreme conservatives. Charles felt that his brother had been too soft. He revoked the Charter, made sacrilege punishable by death, and restored some of the land taken from the nobles during the Revolution. He consistently tried to overrule the Chamber of Deputies, and when a hostile Chamber was elected in July, 1830, he dissolved it. In the election that followed, the voters returned a liberal majority. When Charles again dissolved the Chamber, it was the signal for revolt—the July Revolution. Barricades thrown up in the streets of Paris effectively held off royalist troops. Within three days, Charles, the last of the Bourbons, had fled to England. In a carefully arranged demonstration, the aging but respected Lafayette embraced Louis Philippe, the Duke of Orleans, before the Paris mob and declared him to be "Republican King."

Louis Philippe was the choice of the moderate liberals. A successful businessman and the son of a noble (Philippe Egalité) who had renounced feudalism, he was believed to be the type of ruler who would promote the best interests of the liberal *bourgeoisie*. Proclaiming the tricolour in place of the Bourbon *fleur de lis*, he granted a constitution and a representative Chamber of Deputies. With little bloodshed the July Revolution had been carried out. The July Monarchy had begun.

The success of the July Revolution sent a political tremor throughout Europe. The first area affected was France's northern neighbour, the Kingdom of the Netherlands. A creation of the Congress of Vienna, the Kingdom of the Netherlands was composed of both the Dutch and the Belgians and had been intended as a buffer to prevent French expansion. In forming this new state the Congress had ignored the concept of nationality. Consequently, for fifteen years the Belgians felt uncomfortable in their forced union with the Dutch. In 1830 they proclaimed their independence. While Russia and Austria were occupied elsewhere, France and

England threw their support behind the Belgians. The revolt succeeded and the Kingdom of Belgium was formed as a constitutional monarchy. In 1839, at a London conference, all the Powers, including Prussia, agreed to guarantee the perpetual neutrality of Belgium.

Meanwhile, revolts also broke out in Italy and in the German Confederation. Metternich sent troops to the Papal States to restore order to the Pope's kingdom, and used the German uprisings as an opportunity to issue a revised version of the Karlsbad Decrees. Thousands of German liberals fled to France and England.

In Poland, an uprising took place to protest the increasingly reactionary policies of Czar Nicholas. Russian troops squashed the revolt unmercifully. The Polish-Constitution was abolished and the leaders of the rebellion were deported to Siberia. No further attempt to throw off Russian control was made by the Poles for more than thirty years.

The areas of Europe not under Metternich's control or influence, largely Europe west of the Rhine, were developing into a pattern of liberal, constitutional, and parliamentary governments geared to the interests of the commercial and industrial middle class. But Europe east of the Rhine was still under the yoke of Metternich, and there the political and economic conditions of 1815 remained relatively unchanged.

10 The Revolutions of 1848

> 1848 was the turning point at which modern history failed to turn.
> —G. M. Trevelyan

In 1815 the Congress Powers had restored the Bourbons in France, and had also formed the Kingdom of the Netherlands. With the successful French and Belgian revolutions of the 1830's, however, both monarchies disappeared. Two blows had been struck against the Vienna settlement.

In the early 1830's, Metternich and his fellow conservatives might still have been consoled by reminding themselves that these political upheavals had taken place on the western fringe of Europe. A mere strengthening of the secret police and a revision of the Karlsbad Decrees would be sufficient to hold back the eastward-moving waves of liberalism and nationalism. As long as the forces of conservatism were vigilant, Europe east of the Rhine would remain within their control.

What conservatives failed to understand, however, was that economic changes were slowly reshaping Europe during the generation following the Congress of Vienna. The growth of industrialism in France and Belgium had brought about an increase in the size of the middle class. In 1830, as in 1789, it was this class that sparked the liberal revolution. When the same economic forces moved into the German Confederation, the Italian peninsula, and even the Chancellor's own Austrian Empire, they were closely followed by liberalism and nationalism. These developments led to the Revolutions of 1848 which began in France and quickly spread to Central Europe.

1. EUROPE'S CHANGING ECONOMY (1830-1848)

France

France, in the years prior to 1848, underwent a number of far-reaching economic changes which affected the social structure of the country, and which caused pressures that compelled an accompanying change in political organization.

The first years of the July Monarchy were relatively happy and stable for France. Louis Philippe, the "bourgeois king," seemed to have all the qualities demanded by liberals. He promised that, unlike the France of 1792, modern France would not export revolution to Europe; he only wanted the state to be prosperous and peaceful. The July Monarchy was created by and maintained for the middle class. During the 1820's a small class of manufacturers, bankers, and shipping owners had begun to enjoy the first benefits of industrialism. In 1830 it was these people who were eager to support Louis Philippe. In return, the king was willing to grant a constitution, which would provide a parliament that could legislate protective tariffs, and would guarantee the middle class their rights. And to the lower classes he was the "citizen king," who, unlike Charles X, had cast aside the ceremonial robes of the ancient Bourbon monarchs and instead walked down the boulevards wearing a trim business suit and carrying an umbrella.

During the 1830's, France experienced a railroad boom as transportation fingers stretched into every corner of the nation. This led to an increase of trade and a rapid urban development chiefly in the north where textile factories were being built. Banks, investment houses, and shipping firms joined in the prosperity as industrialism replaced the old agricultural economy.

As prosperity increased in France, however, so did the evils of industrialism and the factory system which created the recurrent cycle of boom and bust. During the latter periods, farmhands lured from the rural districts to the cities suffered from the misery of unemployment and hunger, and the growth of slums spread sickness and disease. During army recruitment in urban districts in 1840, nine out of every ten young men called up were considered physically unfit for military service. Demands for aid to the unemployed and unhealthy were consistently ignored. Most liberals believed that government aid in the form of social welfare was no less dangerous than intervention in the economy by way of restrictive tariffs. Radical insistence on the extension of the franchise brought the reply which later hounded François Pierre Guizot, Louis Philippe's chief minister: "If you want the vote, get rich!" To be an elector a citizen had to pay two hundred francs annually in direct taxes. This was a considerable sum and one paid only by a very few members of the upper middle class. (There were only about two hundred thousand voters in a population of nine million adult males). Most revenues were obtained by indirect taxes which bore heavily on the lower middle and working classes. It was a situation that offered every opportunity for revolutionary agitators to exploit.

The German Confederation

Central Europe responded more slowly to the challenge of industrialism. As in France, the railway-building boom was in the forefront. Railways greatly improved transportation and communication throughout the entire Confederation and by so doing served as a stimulus to manufacturing. Prussia took steps to eliminate the single remaining barrier to a rapid growth of trade by forming a free trade bloc or *Zollverein* to eliminate tariffs between Confederation states. Originally, each of the thirty-eight states had protected itself by a tariff wall. As early as 1818, Prussia had begun to persuade her neighbouring states to enter into a free trade bloc. By 1833, she had attracted seventeen member states to the Zollverein.

The railway boom, manufacturing growth, and the Zollverein led to gradual urbanization and the emergence of a middle class that wanted the same freedoms enjoyed by its counterparts in France and England. Yet two problems were present that did not exist, or were less formidable, in Britain or France. Despite the industrial growth of the 1830's and 1840's, two-thirds of the population remained rural and agricultural. A larger and more powerful bourgeoisie was needed before the absolutist Hohenzollern monarchy and the rural aristocracy could be persuaded to grant liberal reforms. The other problem was political disunity. Germany was still a collection of thirty-eight separate states even though railways and increased trade were bringing people from every corner of the Confederation into contact with one another. It was becoming obvious to many that political barriers were as weak as trade barriers. The Zollverein was developing a German economic nationalism and tied closely to this was a growing political nationalism.

The Austrian Empire and Italy

Industrialism had hardly taken root in either the Italian peninsula or the Austrian Empire in the 1840's. Railways were just being built and manufacturing concerns were small and supplied only a local market. Nationalistic movements would take place in Italy and the multi-national Austrian Empire, but they would have to await economic changes similar to those that had taken place in the German Confederation.

2. THE REVOLUTIONS

The February Revolution in France

Before the government of Louis Philippe had passed the first decade of its existence, it was obvious that he was unwilling or unable to take effective measures to cure the problems of industrial society. And as the growth of discontent increasingly became apparent, an accompanying growth of socialism and radicalism began as well. The French version of the *carbonari,* the *charbonnerie,* and other secret societies, began to flourish. One of the most romantic but bizarre was the *Seasons* formed by the revolutionist, Auguste Blanqui, who was once described as a man who ". . . seemed to have passed his life in a sewer and to have just left it." He spent nearly half of his life in prisons, including fifteen years in solitary confinement. The leaders of the society were named after the four seasons. Under them were leaders named after the twelve months and then others after the days of the week. It attempted a revolt in 1839, but it was a fiasco. Although the Paris police were successful in infiltrating most of these organizations, the very existence of revolutionary groups was sufficient to keep agitation stirred up among the poor and unemployed.

The severe crop failures and the subsequent business depression of 1846-47 increased tension. When public demonstrations were banned by the government, opposition members of the Chamber decided to hold banquets at which political speeches could be made and protests heard. The idea suddenly became popular. Banquets were held throughout the nation in large cities and small towns. When in February, 1848, a gigantic banquet was planned for Paris, Prime Minister Guizot moved to prevent it. With tension increasing in the capital, students and editors of radical newspapers fomented demonstrations. Mobs began to gather in the streets, paving stones were ripped out, carriages overthrown, and barricades hastily built. When police fired into a crowd killing more than fifty demonstrators the revolt began. The National Guard refused to support the government, Guizot resigned, and Louis Philippe abdicated; disguised as an English sea captain, the "citizen king" escaped to England. The July Monarchy had come to a swift and inglorious end.

The Monarchy had been overthrown as easily as in 1830 yet a new government was not installed so readily, for, unlike 1830, this was not simply a revolt of the middle class. It was backed by the new class created by the Industrial Revolution, the *proletariat* (roughly, the property-less class). The revolutionaries immediately proclaimed a republic, and Alphonse de Lamartine, a poet and popular liberal republican, was named its provisional President. Most of the members were moderates, but they included Louis Blanc, the socialist politician,[1] and Albert, a workingman, to appease the restive Paris mob. The provisional or temporary government called national elections for a Constituent Assembly to be held in April. Although every adult male had been given a vote, the results were bitterly disappointing to Blanc and his followers. Fear of socialism had gripped the provincial bourgeoisie and peasant landowners who believed that their land would be confiscated by a socialist government. While Paris returned socialist deputies, rural France made certain that the Assembly would be dominated by more moderate and conservative members.

The Constituent Assembly soon had its back against the wall. By June, the radical Paris mob was seething. The new republic had not provided employment for the thousands of hopefuls who had streamed into the capital seeking work. Under pressure, the provisional government had made an insincere attempt to introduce a scheme to provide work for the unemployed, which failed badly. Suddenly once again, and this time more violently, revolution began. Pitched battles broke out as the unemployed workers, desperate and infuriated, attacked the soldiers and the National Guards who were defending the government. As at the polls, the radicals were again unsuccessful. The army remained loyal and in

[1] Blanc's ideas are discussed on p. 298.

"La Barricade" painted by Meissonier. Paris, February, 1848.

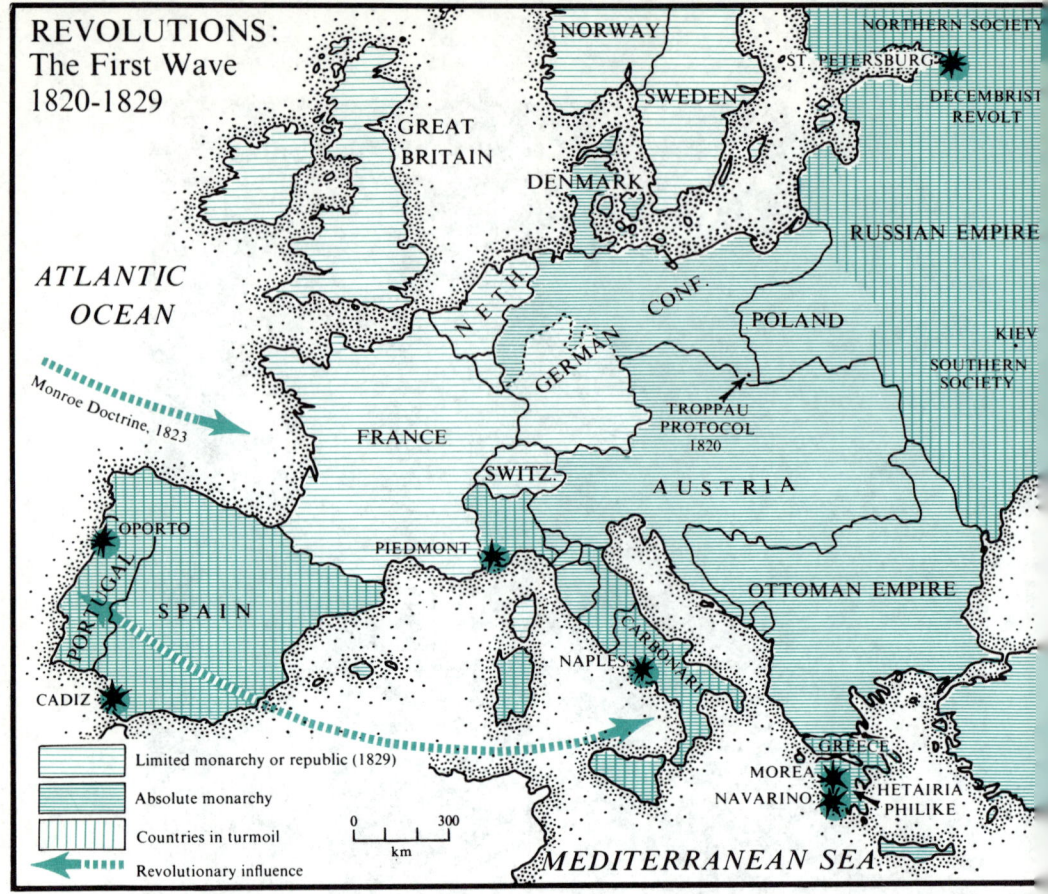

the three bloody June days (June 23-26), more than ten thousand people were killed. When the government regained control, almost eleven thousand people were deported to Algeria and other colonies.

Revolution in the Austrian Empire

The Austrian Empire and the German Confederation felt the first shock waves of the February Revolution in France. The Austrian Empire was divided into three main areas—Austria, Hungary, and Bohemia. The dominant peoples were the Germans in Austria, the Magyars in Hungary, and the Czechs in Bohemia. Scattered in pockets throughout these areas were Poles, Ruthenians, Slovaks, Serbs, Croats, Slovenes, Dalmatians, Romanians, and Italians. Metternich sat on a linguistic tinderbox which he feared the spark of nationalism could ignite.

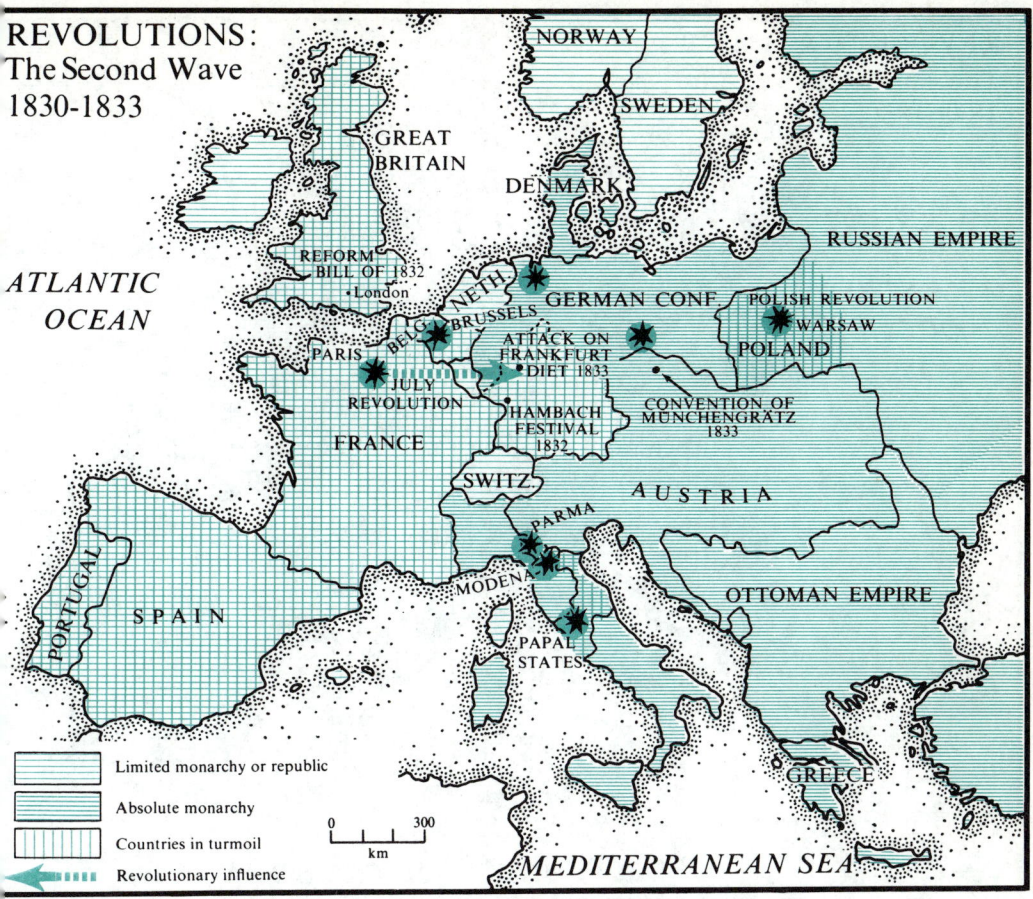

The revolt began in the Hungarian capital of Budapest, where Magyar radicals pressed the Hungarian Diet to enact sweeping liberal reforms. The demand was led by Louis Kossuth, a Magyar journalist and parliamentarian, who made an impassioned plea for Magyar nationalism. Spurred by Kossuth's oratory, the Diet, in a flurry of legislative zeal, passed a battery of reforms and finally agreed to seek self-government within the Austrian Empire.

Encouraged by the success of the Hungarians, Austrian liberals in Vienna pressed the Emperor for the resignation of Chancellor Metternich. With the autonomy movements unchecked and Vienna in open revolt, the feeble-minded Emperor, Ferdinand I, meekly gave in. Metternich resigned and hastily made his way to sanctuary in England. As a further concession, Ferdinand agreed to a Constituent Assembly to which all parts of the Empire would send

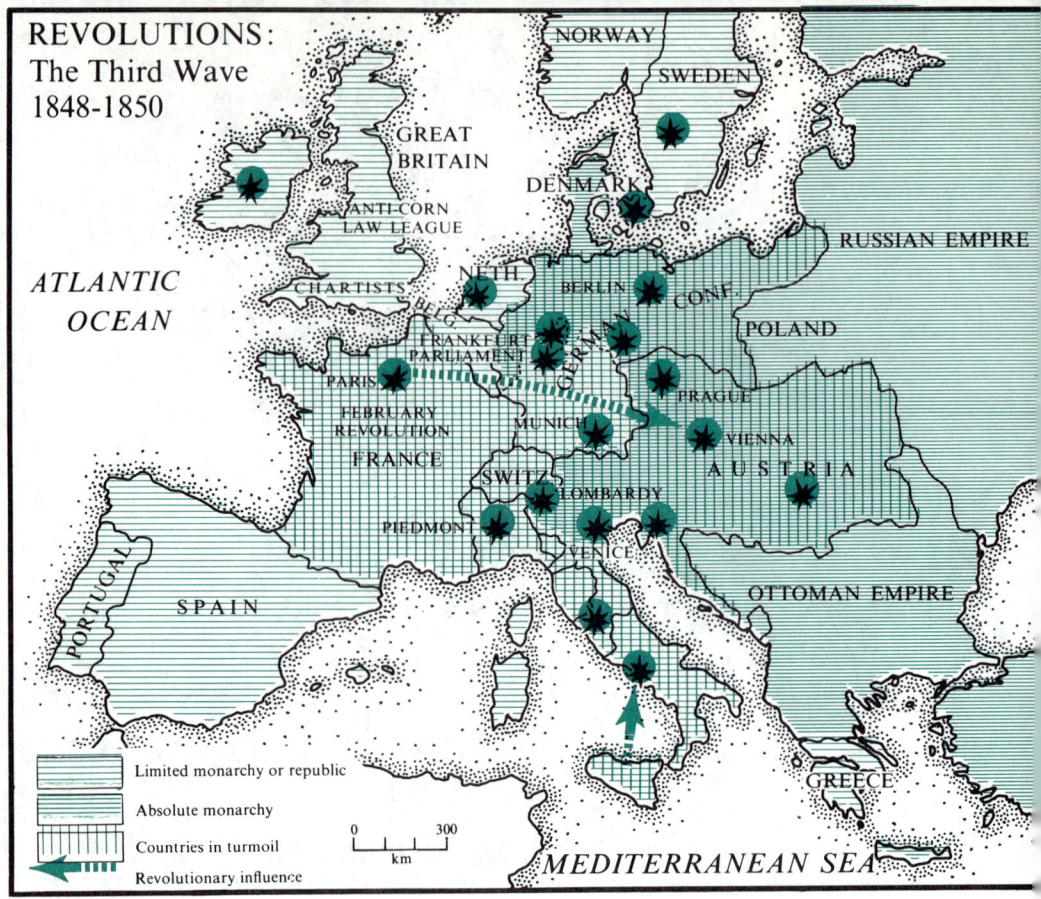

delegates. In the southern reaches of the Empire the Italians drove the Austrian army out of Milan and Venice. Everywhere Hapsburg control appeared ready to dissolve.

Then, unexpectedly, events began to favour the Hapsburgs. The turning point came in Bohemia, in the northern part of the Empire, now Czechoslovakia. There, two rival nationalist groups found their aspirations in direct conflict. On one hand was the force of **Pan-Slavism**, the ideal of a fusion of all Slav peoples in some form of political unity, which would include Bohemia. Opposed to this was Pan-Germanism, supported by those who wished to incorporate Bohemia into a predominantly German empire. As both Germans and Slavs would be minority groups in the other's empire—a situation both regarded as intolerable—their interests were fundamentally opposed. Both Germans and Slavs held independent congresses to discuss their positions in the spring of 1848. The Pan-Slav congress, held in Prague, a city where German-Slav tensions were particularly high, was thoroughly anti-German in character. Rioting broke out, which was soon aggravated by the animosity between the two groups. The situation invited repression by the military; the city was bombarded, the Pan-Slav congress crushed and dispersed, and a temporary military dictatorship established as the first step in restoration of government control. The Empire controlled the army, the insurrectionists did not; in the final analysis, it was this critical factor that made the difference.

As the next step to re-establishing control, the Emperor Ferdinand, whose weakness had been an important factor in allowing the revolts to begin, was coerced into abdicating, and was replaced by the young and resolute Franz Josef. At the same time Austrian troops regained strength and poured back into Milan, Venice, and Bohemia.

In Hungary, ironically, nationalism contributed to the revival of Hapsburg power. There, the defiant Magyars declared their complete independence from the Austrian Empire. But within the new state of Hungary was a small minority of Croats who feared Magyar domination more than Austrian. Thus the Croats were willing to listen to Austrian appeals for help to overthrow Hungary. Croat troops joined Austrian whitecoats in a joint attack upon Magyar forces.

With revolutionary turmoil isolated in Hungary and Hapsburg control restored elsewhere, the Constituent Assembly was dissolved. Its only lasting achievement was the Act of Emancipation by which the remaining feudal obligations were abolished and freedom of movement and equality before the law were granted to the peasants.

Revolution in the German Confederation

By March, 1848, the revolutionary ferment had spread to the German Confederation, where conservative governments were meekly granting liberal concessions. Inspired German liberals and nationalists called a conference of representatives from all the German states to meet at Frankfurt in March to create a constitution for a united Germany. A provisional government, or Pre-Parliament, called an election to be held immediately for that purpose. Almost everywhere the revolutionaries were successful. Even in Prussia, the Hohenzollern ruler, Frederick William IV, allowed the election of a legislative assembly and did not prevent the election of delegates to the Pre-Parliament. Elections held throughout the Confederation sent almost seven hundred men to Frankfurt to form the National Assembly of Germany. Almost all were from the middle class—businessmen, lawyers, and university professors. There was one farmer and not a single workingman. Unlike France, where industrialism had created both a sizeable middle class of businessmen and a large working class, these workers were not strong in the German States. This was not a revolt of the proletariat as in France.

As the sessions opened, the liberals prepared a Declaration of Rights of the German People modelled on the French Declaration of the Rights of Man. This was "the German 1789." But liberal aims were soon subordinated to nationalistic ones. How were the German states to be unified? Three choices were open. The new nation could be formed with only German people, including Austria but excluding her non-German nationalities; the new nation could exclude the Austrian Empire entirely; or it could include the complete Empire. Another problem concerned leadership of the nation. Since most delegates accepted the idea of constitutional monarchy, should the crown be offered to the Hapsburgs or to the Hohenzollerns? Both problems were settled by outside forces. While the National Assembly was deliberating at Frankfurt, the Pan-Slav Congress meeting at Prague demonstrated the Czech opposition to the proposed new German nation. The Hapsburgs, too, refused to consider the union. Uncertain and confused, the National Assembly stalled.

3. RETURN TO REACTION

The revolutionary fires had burned quickly and violently. They were extinguished as rapidly, and by August, 1849, the revolutions had collapsed. Yet in the early months of the year all seemed well. In the German Confederation, the National Assembly issued a federal constitution with a responsible parliamentary government. Then they turned hopefully to King Frederick William of Prussia and offered him the crown of a united Germany. But the Hohenzollern monarch would have nothing to do with the revolutionaries.

As word of William's refusal spread, support for the National Assembly fell off sharply. Within weeks, the delegates left Frankfurt or were driven out by Prussian troops. Without the support of an aroused working and peasant class, and hemmed in by a reviving aristocracy, German liberalism collapsed in the spring of 1849.

There is a postscript to the unification movement in the Confederation. Frederick William of Prussia became intrigued by the thought of reigning over a unified Germany. Early in 1850 before an assembly of German princes, he proposed a German union led by Prussia to replace the defunct Confederation. Yet the Hapsburgs would have nothing of this, and six months later the German Confederation was again cemented together at Olmutz under pressure from Vienna. Lacking support, Frederick William was ignominiously forced to back off and again accept Austrian leadership in central Europe. The "humiliation of Olmutz" was a goad which later inspired Prussian nationalism against Austria.

After the fall of the Napoleonic Empire in 1814, the Italian peninsula again came under the domination of Austria. Lombardy and Venetia were annexed outright by the Hapsburgs, and the remaining nine states effectively controlled by pro-Austrian governments supported by Austrian arms. By 1848-49, however, the revolutionary tempests that had swept Europe seemed to have reached Italy as well. Guiseppe Mazzini, an ardent republican, and Guiseppe Garibaldi, a romantic soldier of fortune, had staged a brilliant but only briefly successful attempt to unify the Italian states. Early in February they had combined to engineer a *coup d'état* in Rome. By proclaiming the Eternal City a republic the two revolutionaries hoped to rejuvenate the flagging spirit of Italian liberals. The call to arms was heard but not heeded. A renewed Hapsburg vitality inspired the Austrian whitecoats to a climactic victory over the Piedmontese in March. The finality of the military defeat was marked by the abdication of King Charles Albert in favour of his son, Victor Emmanuel II. By the summer of 1849, of all the Italian states only Rome had not surrendered to the revamped forces of reaction. Then in early July the final blow came as a conservative French National Assembly authorized French troops to destroy the Roman Republic and restore Pius IX, the ex-liberal turned reactionary, to the papal throne.

". . . Such was Louis Napoleon, the Man of Mystery. Conspirator and statesman; dreamer and realist; despot and democrat; maker of wars and man of peace; creator and muddler—you can go on indefinitely, until you begin to think that at the heart of him was a gigantic nothing. . . . Bismarck called him a Sphinx, and added: he was a Sphinx without a riddle. Was it not rather that he had too many riddles, and riddles to which he himself did not know the answer?"—A. J. P. Taylor

Revival of Bonapartism

By August, 1849, Vienna was tranquil, Budapest languished under Russian occupation (requested in 1848 by the desperate Hapsburgs), French troops protected Rome, and Berlin had expelled her liberal legislators.

Liberalism seemed dead. Even in France, the only part of Europe where revolution had been successful, there were ominous signs of disaster. Six months after the bloody June Days of 1848, the Assembly held a presidential election with results that staggered most Europeans. The President-elect of the Second French Republic was Louis Napoleon Bonaparte, nephew of the great Napoleon. More than the fear of a revival of Bonapartism gripped Europeans. Few had ever heard of Louis Napoleon and fewer still held him in high regard. His early career lent support to their opinions. Brought up in Switzerland, he had gone to Italy, joined the *carbonari* and became involved in the Italian uprisings of 1830-31. Yet he longed to return to France, and had twice failed miserably in comic-opera attempts to invade France during the July Monarchy. After the second venture he was imprisoned in the fortress of Ham for a short time but managed to escape quite easily by walking off the grounds in the guise of a stonemason. Footloose, though he found time to dash off a book called *The Extinction of Poverty,* he drifted to England early in 1848 during the Chartist demonstrations. In London he was hired as one of the Duke of Wellington's special constables. After the June Days he had travelled to Paris where he was nominated as a presidential candidate.

His timing was excellent. Frenchmen were tired and sickened by the bloodshed of the abortive revolution. Both the French peasantry and the middle class feared socialism. Moreover, the magic of the Bonaparte name conjured up images of stability as well as glory, while most Frenchmen forgot that a Bonaparte had brought military defeat to their native land a generation before. When the ballots were counted Louis Napoleon had been elected by a landslide.

Despite the spottiness of his early career, Louis Napoleon proved to be both a careful administrator and a clever politician. For three years he carefully cultivated the support of businessmen, farmers, and labourers. For a time the Second Republic and French liberalism seemed secure. Then, in 1851, the political honeymoon was

". . . about ten at night [December 6, 1851], five companies of infantry preceded by fifty of the secret police, appeared in the Rue de Constantine, where they arrested all the men they found in their apartments. The result was that some three hundred workmen left their homes and darted through the streets like hunted hares. To provide for such an escape, the transverse streets were well-posted with infantry and cavalry, and every one of the wretched men fell into the hands of the various guards. Those who resisted being captured were shot upon the spot, while the remainder were led before the court-martial, and being deemed dangerous characters, were shot at midnight in the Champ de Mars."—Report in the *Illustrated London News*, Dec. 20, 1851.

abruptly ended. Without warning the Assembly was dissolved and a plebiscite held which asked the electorate to extend Louis Napoleon's presidential term for ten more years. Now the idol of the masses, he received a margin of twelve to one in his favour. One year later he openly removed the last fabric of political disguise by terminating the Presidency and the Republic. In choosing the title of Napoleon III, he announced the formation of the Second Empire. French liberalism shared the fate of the movement throughout Europe. The Revolutions of 1848 were dead!

* * * *

"1848 was the turning point at which modern history failed to turn." This is an opinion typical of liberals who regretted the resurgence of conservatism in the aftermath of the early successes of 1848. Why did liberalism weaken and to what extent did it fail? In France the pattern of the great Revolution of 1789 was repeated. Rival groups united in the early stages of the February Days to overthrow the July Monarchy, and then turned upon one another. The struggle among socialists, republicans, and conservatives led to the blood-spilling of the June Days. Out of this came the simple solution developed in 1799—find a strong man. Thus emerged Louis Napoleon and the end of the Republic.

In the Austrian Empire, the German Confederation, and the Italian peninsula, all revolutionaries shared the French desire to establish liberal parliamentary governments responsible to an electorate protected by a written constitution. Originally these aims were quickly reached. At this point, however, liberalism and nationalism abruptly became incompatible. In the Austrian Empire rival national groups such as Magyars and Czechs were eager to secure legal and constitutional rights for themselves but not for others. Their own separate national existence became more hallowed than their earlier devotion to human rights. The observant and opportunistic Hapsburgs, whose real enemy was nationalism, were able to use that force to play one national group against the other. Thus the Empire was saved, and the revolutions destroyed.

In the German Confederation also, liberalism surrendered to nationalism. Liberal aims dimmed as the delegates at Frankfurt gradually became obsessed with the problem of a unified Germany. When the Hohenzollerns refused their offer, the National Assembly collapsed.

Yet there were gains for liberalism in 1848 as well as setbacks. In the Confederation and the Austrian Empire, the abolition of the remains of feudalism by liberal assemblies at the height of the uprisings was not rescinded by later administrations after 1849. In 1850, Frederick William of Prussia delivered a partially liberal constitution to his people, and in Piedmont Victor Emmanuel II retained the liberal constitution accepted by his father.

UNIT THREE | # THE AGE OF IDEOLOGY

11 Industrialism and Reform in Great Britain

> ... a nation of shopkeepers.
> —Adam Smith, *Wealth of Nations* (1776)

The great political and social upheavals that shook Europe during the revolutionary and Napoleonic eras sent only slight tremors to the British Isles. But although Britain was spared the extremes of violence that occurred across the English Channel, she, too, was undergoing changes. These changes, however, were evolutionary rather than revolutionary, and at first were economic rather than political. The 18th century witnessed the final stages of the Agricultural Revolution, which had been underway since the Tudor period, and the beginning of the Industrial Revolution. These developments, while eventually leading to a higher standard of living, originally carried in their wake great social and economic distress. The more unsavoury side of industrialization, which included unemployment and urban slums, led to important political, social, and economic reforms. By 1850, Britain had experienced, in her own fashion, as complete a revolution as had her continental neighbours.

1. THE CHANGING ECONOMY: THE AGRICULTURAL AND INDUSTRIAL REVOLUTIONS

Since feudal times, agricultural land in Britain had been held and cultivated by what was called the "open field system." Arable land was divided into three sectors—one to be planted in the spring, a second to be planted in the fall, and the third which was allowed to lie fallow. Each peasant or farmer was allotted numerous strips of land located in each of the three different sectors, and was also allowed to use the open pasture field that was available as common land for all.

Because of this system of landholding, the efficiency and output of agriculture was very low. The holdings of the peasants were scattered about the three sectors, instead of grouped in one compact unit, so that much time was wasted simply travelling from one strip to another. For the same reason, it was impractical for the peasant to use heavy implements, since these would be difficult to transport between the holdings. Another problem was that the strips of land were of an awkward shape that made ploughing difficult. The open fields, which were used by all but often cared for by none, were over-planted or over-grazed, and consequently much less productive than they might have been. With the resultant low productivity of the land, the peasant farmers generally were compelled to devote all their time simply to producing sufficient food for subsistence, and had no time for experimenting with innovations and better techniques.

As a consequence of all these factors, output of the open-field system was relatively low. For the Agricultural Revolution to take place, it was first necessary that the landholding system be transformed. The first signs of change came in the 15th century, with the beginning of the "enclosure movement." The landowning aristocracy enclosed the open fields, and consolidated the arable land into one holding, usually forcing out the peasantry in the process. By the 18th century, most of the agricultural land in Britain had been enclosed into large-scale holdings.

Immediately, a rise in efficiency resulted from the more compact land unit. The new landholders had become much more profit-conscious, and were anxious to raise their profits by increasing output. New and improved techniques were eagerly tried. One of the most significant improvements was the discovery that clover, planted in the field that had been allowed to lie fallow, would not only provide an excellent winter feed for livestock, but would actually make the soil more fertile. The significance of this discovery was enhanced by the innovation by Lord "Turnip" Townshend of the four-field system of crop rotation. With this system, the holding was divided into four fields. In the first field, there would be an autumn planting of a cereal crop, such as wheat, in the second field an autumn planting of a root crop, such as potatoes or turnips, in the third field a spring planting of another cereal, such as barley or oats, and in the fourth field clover would be planted. Each year the crops would be rotated from field to field in a four-year cycle. Another increase in the food supply resulted from the experiments of Robert Bakewell, who began scientific animal breeding. These experiments enabled him to produce larger beef cattle and sheep, and more powerful horses. The success of these experiments can be seen from the increase in the average size of animals between the beginning and the end of the 18th century: oxen grew from an average of 170 kg to 360 kg; calves from 23 kg to 68 kg; sheep from 17 kg to 36 kg. Still another agricultural innovator was Jethro Tull, a law student turned farmer, who introduced deep ploughing, drill sowing, and the horse-drawn hoes.

By the end of the 18th century, the Agricultural Revolution was developing at an ever-increasing speed. After 1793, the wars with France greatly increased the demand for British-grown food. Prices soared, thus attracting more profit-seeking farmers, who enclosed more land, and sought more ways of improving efficiency and output.

Largely because of these improvements in agriculture, as well as simultaneous improvements in medicine, the population in Britain showed an amazing growth, from five million in 1600, to seven million in 1700, to more than ten and a half million in 1800. This meant an enormously increased demand for manufactured goods, that strained the capacity of the primitive industrial system to the limit. Manufacturing traditionally had been undertaken by the "cottage industry" method, an inefficient system by which farmers and their families worked independently in their homes. It was clear that tremendous profits awaited anyone who could raise the output of industry. Indeed, by 1820, industrialization had become an absolute necessity for Britain. Her population had grown to the point that her domestic agriculture could no longer produce adequate supplies of food to meet the need. Food had to be imported, which meant that the equivalent value of exports was required—and exports meant manufactured goods.

It was this opportunity, and a set of ideal conditions in England, that led to the Industrial Revolution. The British Isles were abundantly rich in the raw materials needed for industrial development. Coal and iron were in large supply. Unlike continental Europe, feudalism had vanished, and hindrances such as internal tariffs did not exist. Similarly, Britain had enjoyed much greater stability and order than had the Continental countries. With the population growing and moving into the cities, there was a plentiful labour

INVENTIONS THAT LAUNCHED THE INDUSTRIAL REVOLUTION

1701	Seed-planting Drill	Jethro Tull
1709	Iron Smelting	Abraham Darby
1712	Steam Pump	Thomas Newcomen
1732	Threshing Machine	Michael Menzies
1733	Flying Shuttle	John Kay
1768	Spinning Jenny	James Hargreaves
1769	Steam Engine	James Watt
1778	Spinning Mule	Samuel Crompton
1781	Rotary-motion Steam Engine	James Watt
1784	Mill-rolled Iron	Henry Cart
1787	Power Loom	Edmund Cartwright

supply. A fair internal transportation system, good harbours, a strong merchant marine, and a growing overseas empire that provided both raw materials and a market for finished goods, were the final requirements for the growth of industry.

The foundation stones of the Industrial Revolution were coal, iron, and steam. Coal had always abounded although it had never proved to be a suitable fuel in the smelting of iron, so that iron masters had had to use charcoal for this purpose. A major development, therefore, was the replacement of charcoal by coke, which is simply dry-heated coal, as a fuel used in blast furnaces for the production of high-quality pig-iron. This innovation was made by Abraham Darby in 1709. Darby's success freed ironmakers from the need to locate near forests for their fuel supply, and allowed them to establish factories near coal fields. Although Darby had been able to produce a high quality iron, he had failed to discover how to remove the carbon which made his iron brittle. This discovery was made seventy-five years later by Henry Cort, a forge master, who developed the puddling and rolling process. Pig-iron was reheated with coke until it became almost a liquid. It was then stirred with iron rods until the carbon was burned off (the puddling process), and finally passed as molten iron between rollers which removed the remaining impurities. Cort's discovery achieved exactly the same results for the forge masters as Darby's had for the furnace owners who produced the raw iron. Both branches of the iron industry, no longer reliant on wood charcoal, could now locate around coal fields. Soon these two branches saw the advantages of merging production facilities. This was soon followed by the business marriage of the iron and coal industry. In this way began the process by which large amounts of capital were concentrated in few hands. Possessing money and a skilled labour force, iron makers were able to develop many uses for their product. In time, as iron production jumped forward, it replaced timber and stone in building and bridge construction. Manufacturers of farm machinery, the hardware industries, and ship builders all found uses for Cort's improved iron.

The next stage in the development of the Industrial Revolution was the substitution of machine for human or animal power. Prior to the 18th century, some rudimentary forms of mechanization had been implemented, utilizing water-power, but these had forced manufacturers to locate near rivers and streams.

As early as 1711 Thomas Newcomen, an engineer, had built a steam engine designed to pump water from flooded mine tunnels. Newcomen's machine remained the standard of its kind, and although it was able to drive a wheel, too much energy was wasted in its operation. In 1765 James Watt, a mathematical-instrument maker, discovered a method of improving Newcomen's machine by adding a condenser separate from the cylinder and thus saving much of the wasted energy. Watt's invention, the steam engine, soon found application in industry. With the steam engine using coal as fuel, industry could locate nearer to markets and the sources of raw materials. Its most obvious effect was to increase production and to substitute machine power for more elementary forms of power.

The iron and coal industries were relatively new in England, and while they enthusiastically applied steam power to their production methods, an older industry was truly revolutionized by Watt's invention. Since the early Middle Ages the textile industry had utilized the

An early-18th century mine. The countryside had not as yet been disfigured by industrialization . . .

"cottage industry" method of production. Even before the introduction of an effective steam engine, inventions had appeared in the industry. In 1770, James Hargreaves, a weaver and a carpenter, had produced a hand machine, called a "jenny," by which a spinner could spin as many as eighty threads at once. The same year Richard Arkwright, a barber and wigmaker, and John Kay, a clockmaker, had worked together to make a water-frame that accelerated the weaving process. In the same decade Samuel Crompton, a weaver, had combined the best features of the jenny and the water-frame to produce the "mule." All of these inventions were worked manually or by water-power, and it was not until 1787 that Edmund Cartwright, a clergyman, poet, and amateur inventor, devised a loom that could be operated by steam power. Because of these new inventions, it became possible to produce textile goods on a mass-production basis. Obviously, the greatest efficiency could be obtained by combining all the different machines, with their operators, in one location or factory. Soon the more enterprising cotton manufacturers were shifting their operations from the cottage industry to large factories situated in towns.

Before it was possible for this development to take place on a wide-spread scale, however, it was essential that entrepreneurs or manufacturers be supplied with adequate funds of capital, without which the machines and factories could not be purchased. Funds were also required for short-term needs, such as wages. Thus one of the prerequisites for the growth of industry was the development of a system of capitalism.

The Growth of Capitalism

Capital in the Industrial Revolution came from three main sources: the landed interests, the merchants, and the financial institutions.

Landed interests As farming developed into an increasingly large-scale enterprise, it became possible for landlords to accumulate increasingly large margins of profit. This could be used for acquiring farm machinery and undertaking research, which in turn would increase productivity and profit farther still. With these profits to use as an investment fund, a number of intelligent capitalist-landlords soon appeared, on the alert for new opportunities for making money.

The great landowners were not the only source of capital. Many small independent farmers, bewildered by the great social changes taking place in the countryside and unable to compete with their great neighbours, were glad to sell out and move to the cities. Those who invested the ready cash they received in industry often became very prosperous. For example, the Peel family came from the comfortable yeoman class; at first farmers, they became farmers and weavers, and then were drawn into industry. Thus a substantial fortune was left to Sir Robert Peel, who became a Prime Minister of England.

Merchants Not all funds came from the agriculturists. One of the principal sources of wealth in 18th century England was foreign trade, and the merchants who organized such trade were among the wealthiest entrepreneurs in the country. Foremost among these were the directors of the great chartered companies—the East India Company, the South Seas Company—who were "the merchant princes of England." These persons had close connections with the government, were often directors of the Bank of England, and were always keenly aware of the most profitable avenues for investing their capital. Similarly keen for profits, although organized on a smaller scale, were the merchants who traded with continental Europe.

There was a connection between merchant wealth and the Industrial Revolution. Many examples could be given. Richard Arkwright, one of the great entrepreneurs of the textile industry, was able to borrow capital from merchants. James Watt also received backing from them. Similarly, the first factories of Glasgow were financed by the tobacco merchants from the West Indies.

Financial Institutions The third major source of funds to promote manufacturing was that of the financial institutions. In business terms, financial institutions (such as banks) are really a means by which those who *need* capital for their business, and those who *have* capital to invest for profit, can efficiently come together for mutual advantage. The Industrial Revolution could flourish only as these were built up. There was not really a good banking system in the first half of the 18th century. The Bank of England had been founded in 1694, but it was really the Bank of London, and was unwilling to open branches in other centres. Other financial institutions dealt mainly in foreign exchange or in the raising of loans for the government. Consequently, there existed a need for banks willing to deal with private investors. This need was filled by the private country (local) banks, which were established independently by the industrialists themselves, partly to obtain short-term capital, but also to obtain an outlet for their funds. These were becoming common by 1760, and as they increased in number —and as the Bank of England came to establish branches outside the radius of London—the availability of cash for industrial enterprise expanded accordingly.

The part actually played in the Industrial Revolution by the banks is sometimes debated. While they did help with the extension of existing industries, it is often said that they were not a principal source of funds for the initiation of new industries, because they were not willing to incur the risks involved at that time in setting them up. An important function that they did perform, however, was the transferring of short-term funds from one part of the country to another—from an area where there was little demand to an area where there was great need. In other words, banks and other financial institutions helped increase the mobility of capital, an essential role in the Industrial Revolution.

At the same time as there was an accumulation of capital and an increasing mobility of capital in England, there was also investment from foreign sources. The Dutch invested in English securities, whether of the government, the Bank of England, or the East India Company. The rate of interest was higher in England than it was in Holland, and this encouraged large-scale investment. Foreign capital played an important role in the early stages of the Industrial Revolution; for example, Matthew Boulton, who backed James Watt, borrowed some of his capital from Amsterdam.

Capital was mobile, and was also cheap. The interest rate was forced down by the English government as a matter of policy: the government itself was a heavy borrower and did not like to face high interest rates. Within fifty years there was a reduction from eight per cent to three per cent. By the beginning of the Industrial Revolution, the industrialists could borrow at a relatively inexpensive rate.

English capitalism did not originate with the Industrial Revolution. It had previously been based on land, trade, or finance, and these sources had been drawn upon by the manufacturers of the 18th century. Nor was the movement of capital to industry a one-way street, for many of the industrialists immediately upon obtaining their wealth proceeded to invest in land. Nevertheless, the availability and mobility of capital were essential ingredients of the Industrial Revolution.

The concentration of factories that was facilitated by capitalist financing brought social consequences similar to those produced by the Enclosure Movement. As large factories were being established, farmers who had supplemented their income through domestic textile work were forced to move to the towns to find employment.

The growth of population, especially in urban areas, and the steady development of the iron and textile industries, made it necessary to find better transportation methods to reach both the growing domestic and foreign markets. From this need emerged the growth of railways. While canals had been in use for many years, they were more costly than railways. Through the use of steam power, and with a higher quality iron to make rails, railway

... but the blight was soon to set in. The illustration shows a 19th century copper factory.

development skyrocketed. In 1825 George Stephenson introduced the first railway in the world using a steam-driven engine; it covered the nineteen kilometres of the Stockton-Darlington railway line in one hour. Four years later on the Liverpool-Manchester railway, Stephenson's steam engine, "The Rocket," reached a speed of fifty-six kilometres per hour. Immediately businessmen saw the possibilities of railways. By 1850 more than eight thousand kilometres of railway had been laid throughout the British Isles, and a powerful new industry had been formed.

Shipbuilding was another gigantic industry that grew partially from the discovery of a better quality iron and partially from increasing foreign demand for British manufactured goods. By the end of the 18th century, British shipbuilders feared that their rapidly declining supply of local timber would cause them to lose their lead in shipbuilding to the forest-laden United States. The happy discovery of the application of iron to their industry was

A locomotive race held in 1829. George Stephenson's *Rocket* came in first.

revitalizing. At the same time, other nations were eager to trade their raw materials for British finished goods, which were the best in the world. Consequently, British shipyards turned out more ships than all other shipbuilding nations combined. By the 1830's, Britain enjoyed virtually a global manufacturing monopoly, and became known as "the workshop of the world."

2. CONSEQUENCES OF INDUSTRIALISM

The change from an agricultural to an industrial economy made the British people mobile. Until the 19th century, Britain had been a nation of small towns, inhabited by people who seldom travelled many miles from their native area. When textile and iron manufacturers began to locate their factories in or near cities located in the areas where raw materials were available, people were drawn from their farms and villages to find employment in the cities.

Since there was no government control of housing standards, sanitary facilities, or police protection, many early 19th century

"... wretched, defrauded, oppressed, crushed human nature lying in bleeding fragments all over the face of society. Every day that I live I thank Heaven that I am not a poor man with a family in England."—an American traveller in Britain, 1845. The illustration is entitled "Over London by Rail" by Gustav Doré.

cities developed large slum areas. A complete lack of sanitation was common. This brief description of a street in Manchester was made by a medical doctor:

A cottage row may be badly drained, the streets may be full of pits, brimful of stagnant water, the receptacle of dead cats and dogs. Yet no one may find fault.

Entire families were forced to live in a single room, and often because of unemployment were unable to find money for food, clothing, or rent.

If a factory worker found his home and his street unhealthy, he could also find just complaint in the factory system which often employed his wife and even his children. Employers soon learned that they could hire women for lower wages than men. Mothers sometimes took their children to work with them tying them to their machines to prevent them from wandering. Children, too, worked in factories under appalling conditions. A boy, aged twelve, reported to a commission of inquiry into factory conditions that he had ". . . seen the children much beaten ten times a day so that with some the blood comes, many a time." This same commission learned of the practice of mothers who repaid loans from employers by having their children work off the debt in the factories.

In the absence of laws to limit hours of work and establish minimum wages, women and children were paid poorly and forced to work as long as seventeen hours per day. In addition men were often forced to remain idle while their families worked. The Earl of Shaftesbury, a tireless advocate of factory reform, spoke in the House of Commons on the subject:

It has been the practice in mills, gradually to dispense with the labour of males, but particularly grown-up men, so that the burden of maintaining the family has rested almost exclusively on the wife and children, while the men have to stay at home, and look after household affairs, or ramble about the streets unemployed.

Factory conditions were bad enough but still those in coal mines were worse. A witness to a parliamentary commission made this report:

Labour very hard . . . sometimes above thirteen hours; some days nothing at all to eat; a good many children in the mines, some under six years of age; sometimes it is as hot as an oven, sometimes so hot as to melt a candle; . . . the girls wear breeches; beaten the same as the boys . . . work by candle-light; exposed to terrible accidents; children are plagued with sore feet. . . . It is wet under foot; the water oftentimes runs down from the roof; many lives lost in various ways; and many severely injured by burning.

Despite the appalling working conditions in factories and mines, most attempts to introduce reform through legislation were turned aside by the determined advocates of *laissez-faire*. While opponents of government intervention were usually willing to admit that many

The command they hold over it at every curve and angle, considering the pace, the unevenness of the floors and rails, and the mud, water, and stones, is truly astonishing. The younger Children thrust in pairs" (S. S. Scriven, Esq., Report, §§ 49—52: App. Pt. II., p. 65, 66).

John Marsden, aged eight and a half, Wike-lane Pit: " I hurry a 'dozen and twelve' corves a day, [that is 20 to the dozen]; my brother Lawrence helps me, and we have to hurry the corves about 200 yards" (S. S. Scriven, Esq., Evidence, No. 42: App. Pt. II., p. 113, l. 14).—Joseph Hellewel, aged ten years, Weigh Pit: " I hurry about 40 corves a-day; they weigh each

Fig. 4.

"Talk of serfs! Did feudal times ever see any of them so debased, so absolutely slaves, as the poor creatures who, in the 'enlightened north', are compelled to work fourteen hours a day, in a heat of eighty-four degrees, and who are liable to punishment for looking out at a window in the factory!" — William Cobbett. The illustration is a page from the Royal Commission on Children's Employment (Mines), 1842.

evils existed in cities and factories, they were unwilling to remedy them by acts of Parliament.

There was similar resistance to educational reform. Although there had always been schools operated by individuals and religious groups, there was no publicly controlled system. If children could not find jobs and were without schools, many became involved in crime in the city slums. Of the few schools in existence, many were of questionable quality. A committee investigating education in Manchester learned that in one working class area only 252 out of 12 000 children attended school. Moreover, one of the best schools:

. . . is kept by a blind man who helps scholars say their lessons. He is, however, liable to interruption . . . as his wife keeps a mangle (clothes-wringer) and he is obliged to turn it for her.

It would be incorrect, however, to suggest that the Industrial Revolution had *no* beneficial results for the great masses of the people in Britain. The new inventions and techniques brought a flood of useful new articles—clothes, bed-linen, even houses—which previously could never have been obtained by the average person. Even a varied diet was for many a very real improvement. Another benefit was a reduction in working hours. At first the improvement was scarcely apparent, with men often working more than eighty hours per week just to manage a bare living or to ensure their continued employment. As the use of machinery became more prevalent, however, and the productivity of workers increased accordingly, it was possible for substantial reductions in the working week to be made. By the end of the 19th century, productive labourers were working shorter hours than in almost any previous society in history.

The Industrial Revolution also changed the ageless pattern of traditional authority, by which the village squire and parson dominated the lives, even the thinking, of the simple country folk. It was a society of deep-set, ageless conservatism that stultified the growth of the individual. With the migrations to the city, however, the tight press of humanity meant a quickening of thought, a growth of new ideas, that in the long run was almost certainly beneficial.

The Industrial Revolution was a transformation from one form of society to another. Always in history, such transformations are harsh, producing dislocation, hardship, uprooting, misery. The Industrial Revolution was no exception, although most certainly it was less harsh than, say, the Bolshevik consolidation in the Soviet Union following the Russian Revolution. Unquestionably, in the long run the great majority of the populace gained from industrialization more than they suffered.

3. RESPONSE TO INDUSTRIALISM

Industrial growth and the movement of people to urban areas generated a social and political, as well as economic, revolution. While the Enclosure Movement had previously strengthened the power of the landowners, now two new urban social classes were being formed: a rising manufacturing, merchant, and professional, or "middle" class, and a large working class or "proletariat." The middle class was beginning to demand the political power it believed should go with its newly acquired wealth. This put it in conflict with the existing holders of power, the rural aristocracy. At the same time, the factory worker was just beginning to demand alleviation of his economic and social distress. Neither class was able to make much progress under the existing political system, which was tightly controlled by the Tories and Whigs.

The Tories

The Tory Party had been in power during most of the reign of George III. Tories found their support in the established Church (the Church of England), the universities, among the gentlemen farmers and the great landed families. They believed in continuity and tradition, and opposed changes in the political, social, economic, and legal systems. Dependent upon income from agricultural products raised on their vast estates, they were strongly opposed to the middle class policy of free trade, which would admit cheap foreign grain into the British Isles. Above all, they firmly resisted any attempt to widen the franchise to permit either the middle or working classes to obtain representation in Parliament.

The Whigs

The Whig tradition dated from the period following the Glorious Revolution of 1688 when many of the British freedoms were established. Yet, like the Tories, they too were largely wealthy landowners and Anglicans. In their ranks, however, were investment dealers, bankers, manufacturers, and the wealthier merchants. These people were willing to support cautious reform of the system of government and law. They were certainly interested in altering the commercial and financial policy that protected the landowners against imported agricultural products. While there were differences between Whigs and Tories, a contemporary compared them to two rival stagecoaches that splashed each other with mud but went by the same route to the same place.

The Radicals

Among those who accepted this definition of the traditional parties was a group known as Radicals. Not actually a party with a definite platform that was supported by a certain section of society, the Radicals were really a collection of individuals. The most famous was John Bright, a middle class manufacturer and ardent advocate of *laissez-faire*. Bright was so strongly against government intervention in the economy that he opposed state manufacturing of munitions, which he considered an invasion of free enterprise. Another Radical was Jeremy Bentham, whose penetrating and life-long study of the law led to many changes in the English legal system. His maxim, "the greatest good for the greatest number," formed the basis of his philosophical system known as Utilitarianism. Bentham asked of every law, "What is its use?" and urged the repeal of all laws that had no utility or did not serve the interests of most people.

Another important critic was William Cobbett. In his newspaper, the weekly *Political Register*, which he started in 1802, he criticized many abuses of the day, from the practice of flogging soldiers to the system of representation in Parliament. Constantly under government attack, he was fined and imprisoned for libel. Yet his journalistic attacks upon government and society continued and led to public awareness of the political and social problems that existed.

In the period immediately after the Napoleonic Wars, many

working men found themselves unemployed as demand for British goods declined. The severe effects of this economic depression reinforced the arguments of the growing number of critics. When agitators like Henry "Orator" Hunt, a fiery speaker, appealed directly to the working class, the response was immediate. Hunt and others marched at the head of skilfully organized torchlight parades to harangue huge outdoor meetings in the large industrial areas. After a particularly large meeting had been held at the Spa Fields in London, Parliament feared violence and possible revolution. To prevent further public demonstrations, so-called "Gagging" Acts were passed, prohibiting public meetings without a licence from a magistrate. Incensed by restrictions on their liberty, Hunt and others organized a gigantic meeting in St. Peter's Field in Manchester in 1819. When more than fifty thousand people turned out, the authorities panicked and sent the Manchester Yeomanry, an untrained volunteer unit, to arrest the leaders. Instead, they made a general attack to disperse the crowd. The results were chaotic. With drawn sabres, the troops charged at the crowd and before the meeting had been broken up eleven people were dead and more than four hundred wounded.

This tragic clash between the working class and the authorities was derisively called the "Peterloo Massacre." To the Tory government Peterloo was an excuse for added repression. It hastily passed the infamous "Six Acts." By this legislation, magistrates were given extensive powers to prevent agitation and sedition; they could order the searching of houses, the confiscation of weapons, the suppression of all drilling or training in the use of firearms, and they could forbid the holding of meetings. In addition, a heavy tax was placed on newspapers accused of spreading ideas designed to foment violence and opposition to authority.

The Six Acts marked the height of repression. During the 1820's, as the fear of working class agitation began to decline, advocates of moderate reform found support for their ideas.

A favourite target of the reformers and the source of much working class discontent was the factory system. An early attempt to limit hours of work, especially for children, had won small but hopeful success in 1802. The first Factory Act, passed by the Tory government in that year, placed a limit of twelve hours daily on child labour. The law covered only cotton mills, placed no minimum on the age of child workers, and applied only to children who were wards of the state. During the next fifty years, further legislation gradually placed restrictions on all factory owners. By mid-century no child under nine years of age could be employed in textile mills, and government inspectors were to be appointed to prevent factory owners from working children under thirteen more than six and a half hours daily. The Ten Hours Act of 1847, resulting from agitation led by Tories like Lord Shaftesbury as well as by Radicals and Liberals, was the first law that limited the working hours of adults. By it no woman was allowed to work more than ten hours daily. Even the mine owners were at last restricted by the Coal Mines Act (1842) which forbade the employment underground of children under ten years of age.

Another source of concern for the reformers was the penal system, which as late as 1823 contained more than two hundred capital crimes, including one for "wearing a mask" and another for "injuring Westminster Bridge." Robert Peel, a reforming Tory Prime Minister, drastically reduced the number of capital crimes. By 1838, only murder and attempted murder were crimes for which an accused might be hanged. Peel also established the first London police force in 1829, giving his name (Bobbie) to all English constables.

Working class people were hampered not only by low wages and inadequate working and living conditions but also by the educational system, which seemed to doom their children and grandchildren to live at the same social and economic level. There were private schools which were available only to the wealthy, and Church-operated schools for the less fortunate, but it was not until 1833 that Parliament gave the first public grant to these religious societies and so began a state-supported educational system.

Unemployment was an evil for which there appeared no remedy. In 1834 Parliament passed a Poor Law that established workhouses in which the poor could live. While Parliament was prepared to accept the existence of poverty and unemployment, the rules for poor relief indicate the attitude they took toward the poor and unemployed. A workhouse was to provide work that would be "less desirable than the most unpleasant means of earning a living outside." To prevent natural increase of the poor, husbands and wives were separated.

In many ways, the Poor Law and the workhouse were backward steps that retarded any meaningful improvement. There were still

Illustration from an article in the *Illustrated London News*, August 20, 1842.

thousands of poor and unemployed who gained no relief. For those who believed that many more changes were necessary, there was still one obvious answer: if laws were to be changed, they would have to be changed by the people who wanted reform—the middle and working classes. But Parliament was controlled by the upper class. It became clear to reformers, Radicals, and some Whigs as well, that the only solution lay in a thorough change in the system of parliamentary representation. Both middle and lower class representatives would have to hold seats in Parliament.

4. THE GREAT REFORM BILL

The British Parliament before 1832 has been described as "unreformed." The system of representation established centuries earlier had allowed two members in the House of Commons for each county or borough. No consideration had been made for the shifts in population created by the Industrial Revolution. With the growth of industry, thousands of people left the south and moved into the Midlands and northern England. The result was that southern England was over-represented and northern England underrepresented, and population and representation were often wildly disproportionate. In the south, for example, Gatton, once a populous borough, contained six houses and one voter, and one constituency, Old Sarum, was a deserted ghost town. Yet two Members of Parliament represented each of these "towns." These two and other similar towns were known as "rotten" boroughs. In contrast, the mushrooming population of such northern cities as Manchester, Birmingham, and Leeds had no representation at all.

The franchise qualifications were as confusing as the distribution of seats was unfair. In the counties anyone who owned or rented property valued at forty shillings could vote. This usually included well-to-do farmers and small landholders. In the boroughs, however, there was no uniformity. A "scot and lot" borough gave the vote to all ratepayers. In another kind of borough hereditary "freemen" were allowed to exercise the franchise. In still another, only the members of the local municipal council could select the Members of Parliament. Another kind of voter was the "pot walloper," a person who owned a hearth large enough on which to boil a pot.

The confusing variety of franchise qualifications, many of them originating in the Middle Ages, was condemned by all Radicals, most Whigs, and even a few Tories. But neither Whigs nor Tories agreed with the Radical demand for universal manhood suffrage. Opponents of the "one man, one vote" concept argued that a parliamentary seat represented property, not people. Seats were publicly sold and were sometimes valued as high as seven thousand pounds. In many boroughs a wealthy landowner controlled a majority of votes through bribery and was said to have the borough "in his pocket." "Pocket" boroughs assured a man and his descendants perpetual representation in Parliament.

To liberals within the Whig Party, reform of Parliament was

essential if legal and economic reforms were to be made. Among the Radicals there were some who saw parliamentary reform as the way to achieve working class representation. With this aim the Whigs had no sympathy, since they were as willing as the Tories to defend property representation. Lord Grey, the Whig Prime Minister, refused to introduce as part of the Reform Bill a measure allowing vote by ballot, since this would reduce a landlord's power over his tenants. To the Whigs, reform of Parliament in 1832 was meant to be the final reform measure rather than a beginning step on the road to democratic government. Their main aim was to gain representation for the manufacturing and commercial people who supported them.

The passage of the Reform Bill by the Whigs in 1832 was actually the turning point in the change from a rural nation ruled by landowners to an urban nation ruled by manufacturers. The Whigs had been in control of the House of Commons for almost a year when in 1831 they introduced the Reform Bill. Attempts were made to revise the Bill, which were unacceptable to Prime Minister Grey. He was aware that the debate in the Commons had awakened national interest, and decided to take the question to the voters. This judgment proved sound when the Whigs, campaigning on a platform of parliamentary reform, were swept back into power. This time, the Bill was passed with a comfortable majority. When the House of Lords firmly rejected it, the Commons reintroduced and again passed the Bill. By this time political interest had reached a fever pitch and mass demonstrations in favour of the Reform Bill were staged throughout the country. Grey warned King William IV that, since the Reform Bill had wide popular backing, another rejection by the Lords could spark a revolution. Yielding to pressure, the king agreed to Grey's request by promising to name to the House of Lords enough new members who would support the measure to enable it to pass. Faced with this possibility, the Lords backed down and allowed passage.

The First Reform Bill altered both franchise requirements and the system of the distribution of seats. The first change was to make voting qualifications uniform. As a result, the electorate was increased slightly from fewer than 478 000 to 814 000 voters. An extensive redistribution of parliamentary seats was also made. Fifty-six rotten boroughs were completely disenfranchised, and thirty boroughs had their representation reduced from two members to one. On the other hand, forty-three boroughs and sixty-five new county seats were formed.

The net result of the First Reform Bill was to diminish, though not completely destroy, the power of the rural aristocracy and to increase that of the wealthy manufacturers, bankers, and merchants. However, not all members of the urban middle class obtained the vote. The Bill began the transfer of power from the rural counties of the south to the cities of the north. The Bill's chief merit, however, was to alter the political centre of gravity, thereby opening the door to other reforms, social and economic as well as political. Furthermore, the decision to grant reform through legislation removed completely the potential cause of violence and revolution so common on the Continent. The moderate tradition of legislative reform began in 1832 was to characterize the peaceful evolution of the British parliamentary system in the following hundred years.

5. LABOUR UNIONS AND THE CHARTIST MOVEMENT

The First Reform Bill was a victory for the middle class. Because the political interests of the working class were largely ignored, workers turned their attention to the union movement. The first signficant development in British union history was the passage of the Combination Act (1799-1800), which forbade working men from combining to bargain for wage increases. Regarded as criminal bodies and conspiracies, unions were forced to operate secretively. Then, in 1824, Parliament was persuaded to repeal the Combination Acts. But the new freedom was short lived. Following a wave of strikes Parliament revived the conspiracy law in 1825 and unions were once more forced underground.

In the early 1830's an enterprising though unorthodox manufacturer stood up as a friend of labour. Robert Owen, a wealthy textile owner and the son of a Welsh tradesman, had risen by hard work to become a partner in one of Scotland's largest mills. He went on to establish model factories, which included safety devices to protect workers, shorter-than-average working hours, and on-site schools for his employees' children. In 1834 he formed the Grand National Consolidated Trades Union (G.N.C.T.U.). Owen tried to enrol all British workingmen in one big union which would give them control of the economy. Once this goal had been achieved, he argued, the step from economic power to political power would

"Gin Lane," an engraving by William Hogarth. One of the most alarming consequences of industrialism was the almost uncontrolled spread of alcoholism.

be simple. Owen's initial success in gaining thousands of followers startled the authorities and employers who then turned against the G.N.C.T.U. Lacking a thorough organization and facing a hostile Parliament, the movement collapsed within a year.

Owen's failure was only one of a number of setbacks for a working class that had experienced the Peterloo Massacre, the Six Acts, and the Combination Acts of 1825. They were still prepared, however, to follow new leaders who would promise them economic relief and political representation. Their demand for these objectives grew more intense when thousands of men were thrown out of work as a result of the world-wide depression of 1837.

Discontent led to a new working class organization known as the Chartist movement. The Chartists were led by William Lovett and Feargus O'Connor. Lovett, the son of a workingman, was the more conservative of the two men. O'Connor, the son of an Irish revolutionary, was a colourful orator who edited a radical newspaper, *The Northern Star*. Elected to the House of Commons—the first Chartist M.P.—his desire for power made his speeches and editorials more violent. Eventually he became insane.

In 1838 Lovett, O'Connor, and other workingmen drew up a "People's Charter." Essentially this contained a list of working class demands, including universal male suffrage, equal electoral districts, annual parliamentary elections, payment of M.P.s, vote by secret ballot, and removal of the property qualifications for M.P.s. In a few months the movement grew and a national convention was held in London in 1839. A petition containing more than a million signatures in support of the Charter was presented to Parliament. The Whig government was in no way prepared to endorse the Chartist proposals and rejected both the 1839 petition and an even larger one presented to the Commons in 1842. By 1848, lack of success and the increasing violence of O'Connor's speeches had substantially reduced the hopes of many workers in Chartist influence. In that year a final petition was prepared, which included names such as that of the Duke of Wellington and Victoria *Rex* (sic). This last act was an inglorious swan song; after 1848, the Chartist movement broke up. The aims of the Chartists were too revolutionary for the times, but every aim in the Six Points except that demanding annual parliaments was adopted by the early 20th century.

6. THE REPEAL OF THE CORN LAWS

During the 1840's another matter shared public attention with the Chartists. This concerned the "Corn Laws," a series of laws which placed a tariff on imported grains. Since the rural aristocracy depended for their wealth upon the sale of home-grown English grains, they were anxious to prevent the importing of cheaper European and American grains. With their control of Parliament, especially before 1832, they were able to pass tariff laws to protect their monopoly by maintaining a higher price on foreign grains. Opposed to them were the urban manufacturers, who saw the Corn Laws as a hindrance to their export market. European farmers, who were prevented from trading their agricultural products in the British market, were not willing to allow British manufactured goods to have free entry into Continental markets. Although Europeans wanted British manufactured goods, they were prepared to erect tariff walls until free trade agreements could be made. As long as Parliament was controlled by aristocratic, agriculturally-based landowners, the middle class manufacturers could not alter the Corn Laws. Once freed from the economic restraints that tariffs imposed upon them, the middle class manufacturers would soon become far more powerful. Thus, the first breakthrough in this struggle was represented by the Reform Bill which began to alter the political balance between the upper and middle classes.

The Anti-Corn Law League was formed in 1838 by a group of English manufacturers led by Richard Cobden and John Bright. From the beginning it was efficiently organized and made effective use of propaganda. Aided by railways and the recently introduced penny post (1841), League pamphlets carried their message to all parts of the nation. Trained League lecturers addressed large meetings in the northern urban industrial centres. They tried to appeal not only to the middle class but sought backing among Chartist supporters as well. They argued that Continental markets for English manufactured goods would increase manufacturers' profits. These profits would bring about higher wages and more employment. By permitting cheaper European grains to have free entry into the British market, bread, the staple of the working-man's diet, would be cheaper. Their final argument was one zealously maintained by liberal free trade advocates: countries which are freely exchanging goods are not prone to engage in war.

The League appeal to the Chartists generally fell on deaf ears, for Chartist leaders reminded the workingmen that the middle class had done nothing to help them enter Parliament in 1832. Many Chartists saw the competition of foreign agricultural products as a threat to their employment: rural labourers would lose their jobs and be forced to seek employment in the cities. The Anti-Corn Law League did, however, pre-empt much of the Chartists' appeal, and was a contributing factor in the latter's decline.

The tariff question, however, was settled by events outside

Britain. In 1845, a ruinous blight attacked Ireland's staple crop, potatoes, and it was feared that unless cheap, imported wheat were allowed into the British Isles, a national calamity would result. Peel, the Tory Prime Minister, denounced by his own party but supported by the Whigs, decided to act to meet the emergency. In 1846, the Corn Laws were repealed, although it was not until the 1860's that the last tariffs on grain were removed.

Contrary to the fears of the landowners, and the claims of the League, repeal did not lower the price of imported grain. This did not take place for more than twenty years, until transportation costs became substantially lower. Until that time British grain remained consistently cheaper than either European or American. The greatest significance of repeal was the harm it did to the actual power and prestige of the aristocracy. With British manufacturers now relatively free to trade in European markets, their economic, and eventually political and social, position became dominant. The growth of industry, and Britain's virtual monopoly of export manufacturing produced an era of free trade (1840-1870) throughout the world.

Between the end of the Napoleonic Wars and the repeal of the Corn Laws, the economic and political face of Great Britain was completely altered: population jumped from thirteen to twenty million; exports more than doubled to reach a value of seventy-one million pounds. She became the workshop of the world. Political change was no less significant. Before 1815 Britain had been a rural, agricultural nation strongly attached to tradition and resistant to change. Within a generation, she became an urban, industrial power, whose enlightened middle class with its belief in gradual social and political change had become the model for all European liberals.

Perhaps the most significant feature of British development was that, unlike Europe, her working class never resorted to revolution; nevertheless, her working class standard of living was the highest in the world. Liberalism through revolution failed in Europe; liberalism through peaceful legislative evolution succeeded in the British Isles.

12 The Generation of Materialism

"Dissatisfaction with the world in which
we live, and determination to realize
one that shall be better are the prevailing
characteristics of the modern
spirit."
—G. Lowes Dickinson, 1898

Liberalism and idealism were popular and powerful forces until 1848. Both withered and scarcely survived the failure of the revolutions of that year. To meet the new demand of Europeans for peace and stability, there emerged the forces of nationalism and realism. Where liberalism had meant freedom, nationalism stood for power. Where idealism had been identified with the abstract speculations of philosophy, realism was recognized in the concrete proofs of science. Science, at mid-century, gained a popularity never shared by philosophy. Not yet too complex to be appreciated by the masses, science could also be applied to industrial uses and thereby provide material benefits for almost everyone.

Enchantment with science and industrialism was brief. The very popularity of science produced new research which soon caused it to be understood by only a few specialists. Industry brought social and economic changes which quickly outweighed its early beneficial results for the masses. To challenge the rapidly changing social and economic order, men grouped together in associations or trade unions. Some, impatient and perhaps revived by the spirit of 1848, spurned unions. They advocated a revolutionary overhauling of society. To replace capitalism, they offered socialism.

1. SCIENCE

The first half of the 19th century saw the beginning of the tremendous surge of scientific discovery. Most scientists believed that man was on the verge of great discoveries. The interrelationship of the sciences became more clear to optimistic researchers and philosophers of science. By the century's end, however, scien-

"The principal result of Faraday's labours is our ability to use electricity. Prometheus, they say, brought fire to the use of mankind: electricity we owe to Faraday."—Sir William Bragg. LEFT: Michael Faraday. RIGHT: Dmitri Mendeleyev. TOP: Guglielmo Marconi.

tific research had broken ground in so many new fields that more unanswered questions had appeared than solutions. Scientists glumly admitted that a synthesis of all knowledge had become more remote.

The credit for the rash of laboratory finds after 1850 belongs to no particular nation. In the physical sciences, British scientists Michael Faraday and James Clerk Maxwell made significant discoveries in the fields of electromagnetism and thermodynamics that altered the scientific concept of energy. An international convention of chemists standardized the system of atomic masses, and when a Russian, Dmitri Mendeleyev, systematized the period table of elements and gave science a clearer understanding of molecular structure, a new concept of matter emerged. At the same time the Italian, Stanislao Cannizzaro, the Frenchman, Marcelin Berthelot, and Clerk Maxwell were forming the kinetic theory of gases.

The major advances in pure science formed a direct link with technology. One of the most important industries affected was steel. Improvements in the production of steel were introduced first by the Bessemer process (1856) and later by the Siemens-Martin or open-hearth process (1868). Both methods, however, could be used only with iron ore which did not contain phosphorus. In 1876, two chemists, Thomas and Gilchrist, found a way to remove phosphorus from the iron ore. This discovery had a particular political significance, for it meant that Germany was now able to accelerate its steel production largely through the smelting of phosphoric iron ore found in the Lorraine mines taken from France in 1871. But steel production shot forward across the Continent and by the turn of the century European mills were rolling out thirty-three million tonnes. In 1870 the total figure had been one million tonnes. A sister product of steel was coal. Production of this mineral increased during the same period from 218 to 965 million tonnes.

Steel and coal production led to a revolution in transportation. Distances seemed to shrink as railway networks spread like spiderwebs across Europe and into Asia. Between 1870 and 1910, railway mileage trebled from 55 000 to 165 000. The most spectacular line was the Russian Trans-Siberian, which could carry a traveller from St. Petersburg on the Baltic Sea east to Vladivostok on the Pacific Ocean. An equally important rail route was the Berlin-Baghdad Railway by which German political and economic influence was extended through the Balkans and into the Middle East. The longest railroad in the world—and in its own context one of the most politically significant—was the Canadian Pacific Railway, the construction of which was virtually a prerequisite to the formation of Canada.

Similar changes were taking place in water transport. The brief but romantic age of the sleek, picturesque clipper ship was ended by the introduction of steel-hulled ocean liners such as those of the British Cunard and the North German Lloyd steamship lines. Aided by the invention of the screw propellor, the marine turbine and Diesel's heavy oil engine, European manufacturers extended their markets throughout the world in the most modern vessels. Engineering achievements in canal building further reduced the length of ocean travel when the Suez Canal was opened in 1869 and the Panama Canal in 1914.

Other significant inventions in transportation included the bicycle in the 1870's, followed a decade later by the electric streetcar and the automobile. Having revolutionized land and sea travel, it was not surprising to find scientists attempting the conquest of the air. As early as 1809 Sir George Cayley of Britain was experimenting with a model that combined the features of the helicopter and the airplane. From the middle of the 19th century in Britain, France, Germany, and the United States, great progress was made in learning the principles of flight and aviation. Many experimental models using steam-powered engines were built which flew briefly and over short distances. It was not until the internal combustion engine, using gasoline as fuel, provided motive power that was both light enough and strong enough that heavier-than-air flying machines became possible. Building on the accumulated information and experience gained by many men before them, two American brothers, Wilbur and Orville Wright, flew at Kitty Hawk, in 1903, in an airplane powered with a gasoline engine. The flight lasted fifty-nine seconds at a speed of fifty-six kilometres per hour. In 1909, another milestone in aviation history was reached when Louis Bleriot piloted his airplane over the English Channel.

Side by side with the growth of transportation came developments in communication. In 1858, the first trans-oceanic telegraph message was transmitted through the Atlantic cable from Valentia, Ireland, to Heart's Content, Newfoundland. Less than twenty years later, a Scottish-Canadian inventor, Alexander Graham Bell,

TOP: The first Bessemer steelmaking plant on the Continent, put into operation by Krupp in 1862.
BOTTOM: The *Great Western,* the first steamship.

TOP: Construction of the Panama Canal, 1913.
BOTTOM: Gottleib Daimler, the inventor of the internal combustion engine and builder of the first automobile, photographed here in 1886.

invented the telephone and with the dawn of the 20th century, an Italian physicist, Guglielmo Marconi, inventor of wireless telegraphy, sent the first radio message across the Atlantic Ocean from Poldhu in Cornwall, England, to St. John's, Newfoundland.

Scientific research which had discovered relationships between chemistry and electricity provided the basis for the growth of electro-chemical industries. From these industries came many new products including dyes, fertilizers, explosives. The discovery of chemical fertilizers was only one of the many new developments in rapidly changing agricultural techniques. Inventions in farm machinery included reapers, binders, and tractors. Even the processing of agricultural products was dramatically changed with the introduction of the tin can, condensed milk, and even a partially successful food freezing machine invented in 1867.

Other inventions of the era were: the sewing machine, the typewriter, linotype machines, motion picture cameras, cheap soap, and more comfortable furniture.

While the physical sciences were producing revolutionary technological changes in industrial Europe, the biological sciences were having an equally important effect on society. If chemists and physicists were able to alter man's concept of energy and matter, then biologists were able to change man's concept of himself. The most significant biological theory of the 19th century was the development of the theory of evolution. This theory maintained that all beings were classified into orders and species. Over great periods of time, all life had gradually evolved through adaptations to changing environment. The evolution of these species had been brought about because of a competitive struggle for existence.

The theory of evolution was not novel to the 19th century nor was it the idea of a particular scientist. Many thinkers had made contributions to its development. Thomas Malthus, an English clergyman, had produced the dismal observation that human population increased at a geometrical ratio while the food supply increased at only an arithmetical ratio. Sir Charles Lyell, a Scottish geologist, had recorded that changes in nature occur gradually over extremely long periods of time. These and other theories were all synthesized by the English biologist, Charles Darwin, and first published in 1859 in what soon became an explosive book, *The Origin of Species.*

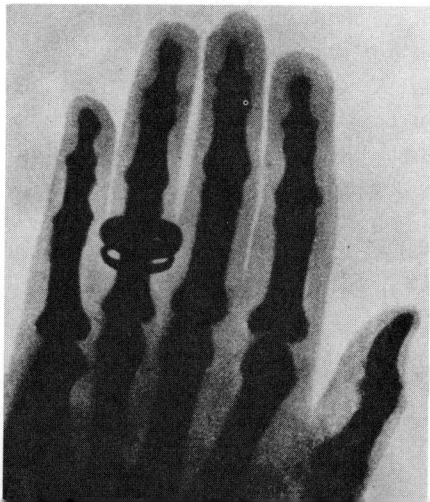

TOP: Marie and Pierre Curie, who together won a Nobel Prize, with their daughter Irene who herself won a Nobel Prize. After M. Curie died, Mme. Curie won *another* Nobel Prize. CENTRE: The first photograph ever taken. BOTTOM: The first x-rays ever taken, by William Roentgen, in 1895.

"I love fools' experiments. I am always making them."—Charles Darwin

Reaction to Darwinism, as it became known, was immediate and prolonged. Nearly everyone accepted or rejected what he wanted from Darwin's theory. In the age of nationalism some saw in the idea of "the struggle of the fittest to survive" strong justification for a belief in national rivalries. To both racists and imperialists, there was alleged proof for the relative greatness of societies. Freethinkers found new ammunition for their attacks on clericalism and dogmatic religious instruction. Supporters of *laissez-faire* found new bases for their belief that government intervention in national economics introduced an artificial restraint upon the natural laws of economics. Economic survival, like physical survival, should go to the strongest and most cunning. Just as delighted by their interpretation of Darwinism were socialists who strongly opposed *laissez-faire*. They believed that Darwin's emphasis on the importance of environment proved that government intervention could alter social and economic conditions to improve man and the society in which he lived. Karl Marx was so enthused by the English scientist's theories that he sought Darwin's approval to dedicate his famous book, *Das Kapital*, to him. Darwin quickly declined.

"... There are over a hundred medical institutes and international scientific centres bearing his name, and there can be but few men and women alive who have not heard that name uttered at least once. And everyone is indebted to Pasteur, more or less directly, for the successful treatment of some ailment or other."—from Hilaire Cuny, *Louis Pasteur*

While the great controversy over evolution continued into the 20th century, biological and medical sciences were making other, less-questioned, discoveries. In medicine the French chemist, Louis Pasteur, studying the process of fermentation for a wine producer, developed pasteurization and saved the lives of countless numbers of children. Joseph Lister, an English surgeon, through

Freud reading the manuscript of *An Outline of Psycho-Analysis,* 1938.

his "germ" theory developed aseptic and antiseptic surgery, thereby maintaining life for many surgical patients. The Curies, Pierre and Marie, French chemists and physicists, discovered radium later used in the treatment of cancer.

Another science which evolved in the 19th century was psychology, which was first believed to be related to biology and physiology. Significant research into the laws of heredity had been done by Gregor Mendel, an Austrian monk. Then Wilhelm Mundt, a German physician, established a relationship between the mind and the body. Other experiments performed by the Russian physiologist Ivan Pavlov into conditioned reflexes developed the theory of behaviourism. Pavlov's work seemed to indicate that mind, like body, was governed by certain mechanical laws. Psychologists soon began to reject this belief and began new research into the operation of the subconscious mind. By stressing the importance of the mind as independent of the body, they ended the marriage of physiology and psychology. The leading psychologist was the Viennese physician Sigmund Freud and his associates, the

Swiss Carl Jung and the Austrian Alfred Adler. Their researches led to the development of psychoanalysis as a treatment of mental illness.

2. IMPACT OF SCIENCE AND TECHNOLOGY

The deepening of scientific research had a great effect on every aspect of European life. One of its most immediate results was seen in the changes accompanying the organization of finance and industry. In the century between 1830 and 1929 world trade had doubled almost every two decades. To promote the growth of factories which manufactured these goods, domestic and international investment skyrocketed. One of the most far-reaching changes came in the organization of the business firm. With the prospect of large profits made possible by the widely increasing demand for consumer products, businessmen were forced to find larger supplies of investment capital. Until the 1850's any investor who put his funds in a business firm was legally liable for any losses suffered by the firm. Few investors were willing to risk capital on those terms until the concept of *limited liability* was accepted, first in England and later on the Continent.

Under the terms of limited liability, an investor could lose no more than the amount of money which he had invested if the firm met financial trouble. This development accelerated the growth of public investment and with it the mushrooming of giant corporations. The days of the small business firm were limited. Many small firms, forced to face the savage competition of price-cutting corporate giants, went under, sold out, or merged with other small firms.

The lure of giant profits transformed the face of the industrial community as trusts or monopolies were formed. These changes revealed themselves in different ways. *Vertical combination* was a method by which one business organization would obtain control of a product at every stage of its production from raw material to manufactured goods. In steel production, for example, giant corporations such as the German Krupp Works would control the iron ore mines, the steel mills, and the plants which manufactured products from railroad rails to cutlery. *Horizontal combination* was another method by which rival producers secretly agreed to share the existing market and to enlarge it by squeezing out any rivals

Population
(millions)

Year	Austria-Hungary	France	Germany	European Russia	United Kingdom	United States
1850	35.5	35.6	35.3	60.	27.2	23.2
1870	35.9	36.1	40.8	72.	31.8	39.8
1880	37.8	37.7	45.2	85.2	34.6	50.2
1890	41.3	38.3	49.4	93.7	37.5	62.9
1900	45.4	39.0	56.4	99.7	41.5	76.0
1910	49.2	39.6	64.9	115.6	44.9	92.0
1914	50.8	39.8	67.8	124.2	46.2	99.1

Production of Coal (Including Lignite)
(annual average, millions of tonnes)

Year	France	Germany	United Kingdom	United States
1850	4.4	5.8	40.	6.5
1870-74	15.	42.	123.	44.
1880-84	20.	66.	159.	85.
1890-94	26.	94.	183.	156.
1900-04	33.	157.	230.	286.
1910-14	40.	247.	274.	474.
1915-18	20.	250.	247.	545.

Production of Pig Iron and Steel
(millions of tonnes)

Year	France		Germany		United Kingdom		United States	
	Iron	Steel	Iron	Steel	Iron	Steel	Iron	Steel
1850	.4	—	.2	—	3.0	—	.6	—
1870	1.2	.2	1.4	.2	6.1	.2	1.8	.1
1880	1.7	.4	2.7	.7	7.9	1.3	3.9	1.3
1890	2.0	.7	4.6	2.2	8.0	3.6	9.4	4.3
1900	2.7	1.6	8.5	6.6	9.1	5.0	14.0	10.4
1910	4.0	3.4	14.8	13.7	10.2	6.5	27.7	26.5
1913	5.2	4.7	19.3	18.9	10.4	7.8	31.5	31.8
1918	1.3	1.8	11.9	15.0	9.2	9.7	39.7	45.2

Foreign Trade: Exports of Domestic Production Only
(millions of dollars, current prices)

Year	France	Germany	United Kingdom	United States
1850	200	—	357	135
1870	560	500	998	377
1880	694	765	1 115	824
1890	750	885	1 317	845
1900	825	1 150	1 455	1 370
1910	1 240	1 870	2 150	1 710
1913	1 360	2 410	2 625	2 428
(per cent of world total)				
1913	7.2	13.1	13.9	13.3

Merchant Shipping: Total Tonnage and Steam Tonnage
(thousands of gross tonnes steam tonnage in parentheses)

Year	France	Germany	United Kingdom	United States
1850	624 (13)	—	3234 (152)	1439 (41)
1870	972 (140)	891 (74)	5163 (1010)	1376 (175)
1900	942 (479)	1762 (1223)	8440 (6539)	750 (309)
1910-12	1327 (760)	2722 (2268)	10 614 (9 707)	842 (561)

Percentage Distribution of World's Manufacturing

Year	France	Germany	United Kingdom	United States
1870	10.3	13.2	31.8	23.3
1896-1900	7.1	16.6	19.5	30.1
1913	6.4	15.7	14.0	35.8

Compiled by Rondo E. Cameron

by a variety of tactics. Both horizontal and vertical combinations even extended across national boundaries. Organizations such as these were termed *cartels*.

The growth of corporations led to the formation of a small but powerful group of men who controlled the corporations. Known by different terms—captains of industry, entrepreneurs, robber barons—their wealth was almost legendary and their political power equally great. In effect they had replaced the landowning aristocracy who, only decades before, had controlled Europe.

The profit of manufacturing is dependent on the size of the market, and the European market grew steadily. Between 1870 and 1914 the population had increased at a rate of about one per cent annually from 293 million to 490 million. Even more important than the growth of population was its distribution. The industrialization of Europe uprooted people and sent them overseas or to the cities. It has been estimated that out of every seven Europeans between 1851 and 1871, one went abroad and four or five went to the cities. In all, more than twenty-five million emigrants left Europe, most having gone to North or South America.

The reasons for population growth were many. Least among these was a rising birth rate; after 1870, the birth rate began to decrease. Most instrumental was the decrease in the death rate which came as a result of better sanitation methods and from improvements in medical science.

The movement to the cities introduced new problems to European politicians. How were these densely populated and sprawling municipal areas to be controlled? How could these new governments provide public health and sanitation facilities and public order? Finally, how was the industrial worker to gain protection from disease and bad working conditions in the many factories surrounding the cities to which the rural masses had been drawn?

One of the most urgent tasks which government assumed was to provide popular education. How badly it was needed is revealed by the high illiteracy rate of a century ago. More than forty per cent of the people of England could neither read nor write. In France and Belgium, this figure rose a further ten per cent. In Russia and the Balkans it rose to ninety per cent. By the 1870's, however, popular education had begun. Industrialization brought a new harvest of tax money which paid for public schools. Urbanization, by bringing people together, made instruction of the masses easier than when families had been scattered in rural areas. Popular education, liberals had long argued, would provide equality of opportunity. Even some conservatives were moved to agree with Guizot's statement: "The opening of every schoolhouse closes a jail." Crime would be reduced by popular education.

In western Europe, there were added reasons for the growth of popular education. With an ever-widening franchise, it became more necessary to create an informed electorate. Disraeli's aphorism, "We must educate our future masters," reveals the attitude of yielding conservatives to the inevitability of popular education. It was also true that where industry took deepest root, the need for education was most recognized. The complexity of machinery and the growth of bureaucracy forced a demand for engineers and secretaries. Education also became a weapon of nationalists. The schoolhouse was the ideal place to emphasize the supreme virtue of patriotism. Anti-clericals began to weaken the hold on youth formerly held by the Church. The school desk became more familiar than the church pew to most European children.

The results of the spread of popular education were profound. Industrial society was more regimented and organized than rural society. The child was exposed to group discipline first in school, later in the factory, and finally in the barracks. Some feel that without this training Europe would have buckled from the convulsive shock to society brought by the First World War.

Industrialization, urbanization, and education all contributed to the weakening of two ancient influences of family and Church. Both parents and priests gradually exercised less control and influence over European children. They were now rivalled by the foreman and the teacher.

The Impact of Science

Organized religion was at first unable to adapt itself to the revolutionary changes in society. Many intellectuals, convinced of Darwinism, attacked theology, while nationalistic politicians challenged the internationalism of Churches, especially the Roman. With the Church still on the defensive and resistant to change, congregations became smaller. Many intellectuals, workers, liberals, socialists, and scientists fell out with organized religion. People now looked to the state for the fulfilment of needs formerly carried out by religious institutions. Schools and hospitals were two areas gradually coming under state control.

Eventually the Churches began to bend. Some clericals recognized the need to become better informed on political and social problems and to adapt themselves to the changing order. The Christian Socialism advocated by Charles Kingsley in England was an attempt by some to bring together Christian ideals and political realities. The Salvation Army founded by William Booth was an indication that some of the clergy had accepted the need of religion to attack vigorously the social problems of industrial Europe.

The Roman Church was the slowest to react. In the *Syllabus of Errors* (1864), Pius IX, whom the Revolution of 1848 had changed from a liberal to a reactionary, launched the Church on a crusade against "modernism" which included liberalism, socialism, and science. However, his successor, the scholarly Leo XIII, gradually reversed the Roman attitude toward modernism. In the encyclicals *Immortale Dei* (1885) and *Libertas* (1888), he contended that democracy and Christianity were compatible. In *Rerum Novarum* (1891) he urged the formation of Roman Catholic trade unions and socialist parties.

By the beginning of the 20th century, through adaptation to evolving conditions, the Churches of Europe began to regain lost ground.

3. LABOUR

The original purpose of the labour union was to allow men to band together for mutual protection. Better working conditions and higher wages could be obtained through collective bargaining with the employer. Employers, however, usually were able to control legislatures, and in most of Europe unions were illegal until well into the second half of the 19th century. Prevented from actively improving working conditions, workers developed the co-operative movement. The first really successful co-operative association was begun by the Rochdale Pioneers in England (1844). Twenty-eight workingmen each invested one pound each and opened a retail store. Purchases of goods by each member were carefully recorded and at year's end, dividends were paid according to the amount of each member's purchases. Thus by sharing costs and profits workingmen were able to gain some relief from high living costs. Consumer co-operatives grew quickly and by 1900 there were more than 1 400 retail shops in England based on the Rochdale model.

On the Continent consumer co-operatives were not so numerous as producer co-operatives. These included bakeries and small factories in which workers became capitalists on a cost and profit-sharing basis. In Germany, credit banking began, and by 1900 over thirty thousand co-operative credit societies existed in Europe. The co-operative movement spread to the countryside and Denmark took the lead in the establishment of co-operative agriculture. By the end of the century more than four-fifths of all Danish dairy produce came from co-operative farms. Co-operatives were formed in many areas: real estate, insurance, and banking. The English concept of "self-help" spread to non-economic organizations of workingmen such as the Workers' Educational Association, through which ambitious workers might obtain an education at night school.

The co-operative movement was not the total answer to the problem of the workingman. What was needed was the right to form labour unions, and to be able to bargain collectively. Gradually these rights were won, with the start made during the prosperous years after 1870. Liberals and democrats had long favoured laws allowing freedom of association and the right of collective bargaining. Unions were given legal recognition in Austria-Hungary in 1870, England in 1871, France in 1884, and Germany in 1890.

Most unions were formed by skilled tradesmen and were called trades or craft unions. Because they had a better education and were better able to organize themselves than unskilled workers, craftsmen made more headway. Early attempts to unionize unskilled workers, such as Owen's ill-fated Grand National Consolidated Trades Union, were complete failures.[1] By the 1880's, with greater concentration of workers in large factories, unskilled workers began to form industrial unions. Soon the number of organized industrial workers far outnumbered the craftsmen. Local and regional unions began to seek links with one another, and first national and then international organizations were formed.

[1] See pp. 273-274.

Most unions in the 1850's and 1860's urged their members to support liberal parties which were trying to obtain legal recognition for unions. In England, support was given to the radical, John Bright, in France to the radical republican, Jean-Joseph Bararet and in Germany to the progressive liberals, Hirsch and Duncker. By the 1880's, having won legal recognition, some unions were actively supporting political parties.

Two of the most powerful *international* unions had a firm ideological base. One was the Roman Catholic union movement designed by the Church to combat the influence of socialists and anticlericals. Another was the socialist and later communist union movement. In France, the largest union, the *Confédération Général du Travail* (C.G.T.) formed in 1895, refused to align itself with a single political party.

In England, the oldest and most influential labour organization, the Trades Union Congress formed in 1868, resisted political affiliation for years. Then in 1900, it radically changed its policy and laid the base for the British Labour Party.[1] In Germany, while the liberal Hirsch-Duncker unions and Catholic unions had some strength, the socialist trade union movement soon commanded the respect of the growing labour force.

By the turn of the century unionism in Europe had become "respectable." It had succeeded in persuading liberal legislatures to enact laws to improve working conditions and to shorten hours of work. In some cases it was partly responsible for urging governments to provide social security for workers. When the 20th century opened, labour was hungry for more gains. Many workers had become convinced that gradual piecemeal concessions from employers and legislators were not enough. A ten-hour day this year and sickness insurance perhaps next year was too slow and uncertain a rate of progress. They wanted the entire package immediately. To obtain this, it was necessary to change the political and economic system; the answer was to support socialist political parties. Many responded to the call. As a result, socialist parties were strengthened in most western European legislatures.

4. SOCIALISM

Socialism grew as the effects of the Industrial Revolution continued to become more oppressive. Most socialists were appalled by the

[1] See pp. 358-367.

widening gap between the wealth of the *bourgeoisie* and the poverty of the working class, or *proletariat*. Profits from industrial production were being concentrated in the hands of a few big businessmen, who used the parliamentary system to obtain laws that would benefit their own interests. At the same time, workingmen and their families failed to gain proportionate benefits and in most cases suffered from the industrial system. The solution proposed by the socialists generally was to substitute co-operation for competition. It was competition as advocated by liberalism, they believed, that had created the harsh economic inequalities between the growing slums of Paris and the fashionable châteaux of Versailles.

Early socialism was not a unified ideology or body of thought that all socialist thinkers agreed to and supported. The ideas of individual exponents varied widely and were often contradictory. Most socialists, however, shared the common belief that government intervention or control was necessary to cure the social evils of the day; it was this fundamental belief that distinguished them from liberals.

Many of the early socialists were French. One of these was an aristocrat, Comte de Saint-Simon, a philosopher and writer who had fought in both the American and the French Revolutions. The basis of his thought may be seen in a quotation from his book, *The New Christianity* (1825): "The whole of society ought to strive towards the amelioration of the moral and physical existence of the most numerous and poorest class." Society, he felt, ought to organize itself in the way best suited for attaining this end. Among his proposals were the abolition of class distinctions, of private capital, and the control of society by industrial experts. Another early socialist was Charles Fourier, who advocated the abolition of economic competition by the establishment of voluntary co-operative communities (called *phalansteries*) in which the members would engage in both agriculture and manufacturing, and pool their resources for the common good.

More influential than either Saint-Simon or Fourier was a third socialist thinker, Pierre Proudhon. Proudhon entitled his most famous book simply *What is Property?*; his brief answer was "property is theft." The remedy Proudhon suggested for the curing of social evils was the abolition of all private property. Eventually, Proudhon's thinking developed to a point where he wanted to abolish not just property, but all forms of government, assuming—

rather optimistically—that men, once free from the restraints of compulsion, would participate voluntarily in whatever activities were socially beneficial or necessary. In effect, therefore, Proudhon was as much an *anarchist* as a socialist, and as such attracted a considerable following throughout Europe, especially in Russia.

One of the socialists whose *immediate* influence was greatest, both through his writings and activities, was Louis Blanc, a journalist, historian, and active French politician. Blanc tried unsuccessfully to put into practice a scheme to support his belief that every man had the right to work. Unlike later socialists, he did not advocate government ownership of industry, but rather a scheme of "national workshops," in which the government should be prepared to finance worker-controlled factories. After repaying the government and contributing to the operation of the business, these co-operative ventures were to distribute the remaining profits among the members. This division was to be made on the basis of a formula later adopted by the communists: "From each according to his ability; to each according to his need."

There was a general weakness common to the approach of the early socialists, however; this was the lack of depth with which they analysed the problems they were criticizing. While they all recognized that industrial society had produced numerous undesirable features, they were often superficial in their understanding of how that society worked. Consequently, their proposals for improvement and change were generally over-simplified and unrealistic. They naively believed that a "harmony of the passions," to use Fourier's expression, that would cure all social evils, would naturally develop simply by making minor changes to the social structure. Why this would happen the early socialists could never adequately explain; nor did they apparently realize the difficulty of making "minor" changes to society without stirring up far-reaching complications. To use the French agitator Auguste Blanqui as an example: "I have no theories. What exists is bad, something else must take its place, and gradually things will come to what they ought to be." Because of this rather simple optimism, the early socialists were termed "Utopians" by those who thought themselves more sophisticated, more "scientific," in their insights.

The originator and most important exponent of "scientific" socialism was Karl Marx. It is Marx's philosophical thought which is the foundation-stone—in theory at least—of modern commu-

Karl Marx: as writer of "one of the major interpretations of western history, [his] was the most compelling prophecy of the age of the common man, and became the most powerful militant ideology of our times."—John C. Cairns, *The Nineteenth Century*.

Karl Marx: his theories "must always remain a portent to the historians of opinion—how a doctrine so illogical and so dull can have exercised so powerful and enduring an influence over the minds of men, and, through them, the events of history." — John Maynard Keynes, *The End of Laissez-Faire*.

nism. For this, Marx is sometimes regarded as one of the two most influential persons in the 19th century (the other being Charles Darwin).

Marx set himself the task of developing an entire philosophical "system" that would use logical proof in place of moral indignation to demonstrate his theories. He would prove, not that change *should* come, but that change *had to come*.

In formulating his system, Marx was deeply influenced by the period in which he lived. The prevailing ideas of the economists of the time stressed an "iron law" that income could never rise above subsistence level; from this, Marx concluded that the existing society was totally useless for the working class, and would have to be abandoned completely rather than modified. But how? The answer was *revolution*. Europe was still feeling the tremendous shock waves of the French Revolution; from this, Marx was convinced of the need of revolution for any total re-direction of human affairs. And how would the revolution come about? This was the crucial question; to answer it, Marx drew principally from the ideas of the most influential German philosopher of the time, Georg Hegel.

Hegel had developed a "deterministic" theory of history, by which the unfolding of historical events was thought always to follow a necessary, logical sequence of development. The path of this development Hegel called "dialectic," a Greek word meaning "to reach conclusions through the clash of opposite elements." By this theory, each element, or "thesis," had as its opposite an "antithesis"; when these came together, the resulting struggle would produce a "synthesis," a higher level of development combining the best of both elements. Or, regarded alternatively, the dialectic meant that every society contained within itself the seeds of its own destruction.

To Marx, this was the key to understanding revolution. The existing system (the "thesis") which Marx expected to see destroyed, was that of middle class capitalism. Because of the nature of the system, Marx believed, capitalism would be racked by chronic problems of overproduction and unemployment. Since the capitalists extracted profit, or "surplus value," the workers were paid less than the value of the products they created, which meant they would not be able to purchase these products. This would produce a glut. To obtain an adequate share of the diminished market, the producers would be compelled to compete ruthlessly among themselves. Continually, the least efficient capitalists would be driven to the wall, and be forced into the working class, or proletariat. Relentlessly, the working class would grow, and the ranks of the capitalists diminish. Ultimately, there would only be two classes—capitalists and workers. As the process continued, the workers would acquire not only the skills needed for production, but the ability to operate the controls of government. Inexorably, the living conditions of the working class would become more and more intolerable, until finally, in one great moment of revolution, the workers would seize control, and abolish the capitalist system. Thus the capitalists, compelled by the forces of historical development, would create the working class (the "antithesis") which would destroy them. "The expropriators would be expropriated."

In the new order that would follow (the "synthesis"), the control of the government would be in the hands of the workers; this phase was termed the "dictatorship of the proletariat." But this stage, too, would end. Since the workers would have assumed control of the state for their own benefit, there would be no one exploited and no one to exploit. This would mean that the government would be unnecessary, the state being principally a means used by the capitalists to oppress the workers (so the theory held) and keep them under control. With this exploitation gone, the state would become redundant, and, in time, would simply "wither away."

Marx's ideas have met with more rejection than acceptance, except, ironically, in countries such as China and Russia where the conditions were totally inappropriate for their application. Indeed, Marxism as a theory has substantial flaws. The basic idea of the dialectic, despite its ponderous complexity, is too vague to have any real value. The expectation that the living conditions of the workers would inevitably worsen was based on faulty economic reasoning and a badly oversimplified view of the functioning of capitalism. The assumption that the class struggle would automatically educate and prepare the working class to take over control of production and of government was scarcely less naive than the optimistic hopes of the utopian socialists whom Marx enjoyed criticizing.

Nevertheless, the theories had a certain strong appeal; the force of history seemed to be behind those who sought to overthrow society. The closing lines of the most famous revolutionary call to arms, the *Communist Manifesto,* were: "Let the ruling classes tremble at a Communist revolution. The proletarians have nothing to lose but their chains. They have a world to win. Working men of all countries, unite!"

In addition to his principal work of formulating his philosophy and theory, Marx was intermittently engaged in political activity, attacking the capitalist system, and trying to bring about the socialist revolution. As editor of a newspaper in Prussia, his radical and intemperate views resulted in the paper being suppressed. In short order, he moved to Paris, was expelled from France, joined the Communist League in Brussels, participated in the 1848 revolutions in Germany, was expelled from Prussia, and finally sought refuge in England, where he spent the rest of his life. In 1864, he helped organize the First International Workingman's Association, and soon became its leader. Partly because of its lack of common purpose, partly because of the sharp tempers of the various leaders —especially Marx!—the First International was less influential than it might have been in encouraging the advent of socialism. Nevertheless, its importance was considerable. Socialist parties in Germany and France were affiliated with the International, received assistance from it, and benefited from its ideas and encouragement. Strike funds were collected, and numerous benefits obtained for workers in several countries. By the end of the 1860's the International had a dues-paying membership of nearly a million, and through its alliances with different unions, a total strength of seven million. With the 1871 revolt of the Paris Commune[1] it appeared that the International was about to meet with success. But the Commune was bloodily suppressed, with a list of casualties in excess of twenty thousand. The socialists were blamed—somewhat unjustly—for the bloodthirstiness of the encounters, and the more moderate members of the International were frightened off. Within a year, the First International had faded into insignificance.

In 1889, the centenary of the French Revolution, a Second International was formed. Like its parent, the Second International was split by ideological wrangling which had already begun among socialist parties throughout Europe. The essential problem concerned the methods to be used to gain Marxist goals. Almost immediately the Second International was divided into two factions. One continued to believe in the literal application of Marxist principles. The other insisted that adaptation to changing conditions should guide socialist theory. The second faction, headed by Eduard Bernstein, were known as *revisionists*. Capitalism, they argued, was gaining, not losing strength. Socialists should therefore work with liberals to reform capitalist society. Believing in parliamentary democracy, revisionists were also called gradualists, reformists, or evolutionary socialists. Orthodox Marxists violently denounced revisionists as capitalist pawns. They argued in favour of total, revolutionary overthrow of existing society with no deals made with liberalism. After 1918, the distinction between those who wanted minimum and those who wanted maximum socialist gains was defined by use of the terms socialism and communism.

[1] See Chapter 14.

Communism made a strong appeal during periods of economic depression and in countries where liberalism and democracy had shallow roots. Examples of this were in Italy and Germany where the franchise had been narrowly restricted. This also helps to explain the complete triumph of Russian communism. Socialism, conversely, won adherents during periods when wages were rising and in countries where liberal-democratic traditions were relatively old. France and Great Britain responded more warmly to socialism than to communism. The British approach to socialism, being essentially different in its basic premises from Continental variations, will be discussed in Chapter 15.

One other major problem faced the socialist movement. Since one of the fundamental beliefs in socialism was the international solidarity of all workingmen, nationalism was its natural enemy. Meeting after meeting of the Second International witnessed the repeated assurances that all socialist parties would refuse to support declarations of war presented to European parliaments. As the fear of war increased before 1914, socialist parties with their strong union membership pledged themselves to general strikes, if war were declared. Wars were begun and waged by capitalists for capitalists. If workingmen refused to fight, war would be impossible. Yet in every parliament of the western European belligerents in 1914, including Germany where the Social Democrats were the largest single party in the Reichstag, socialists voted for war. One of the outstanding socialists who did oppose the war, Jean Jaurès, the leader of the French Socialist Party, was assassinated. The heady emotion of nationalism was still greater than the dreamy promises of socialism.

13 Italy, France, and Germany (1850-71)

> The Italians are wise before the deed; the Germans in the deed; the French after the deed.
> —George Herbert, *Jacula Prudentum*

As the smoke of revolutionary fire drifted slowly away from the ruins of the 1848 upheavals, most Europeans believed that liberalism and nationalism had been mortally wounded. In actuality, however, the very opposite proved to be true. By 1871, many of the goals sought by liberals and nationalists had been won. Italy and Germany had each been united under constitutional monarchs. Hungary had become a free and equal partner with Austria. France was again a republic.

These amazing political changes were achieved, not by revolution, but by the determined actions of realistic politicians. Louis Napoleon of France, Camillo di Cavour of Piedmont, and Otto von Bismarck of Prussia were all sensitive to the growing political consciousness of the European political masses. By identifying themselves and their governments with nationalism and the common good of their people, these politicians were able to construct powerful nation states.

The era following 1849 was marked by the emergence of a new approach to politics. Romantic idealism had withered on the barricades of Paris, Vienna, and Rome. The slogans of liberalism were all too hollow if liberals could not produce results. Ideas were meaningless and impracticable without power, and throughout Europe in 1849, power had strangled every revolutionary struggle. After 1849, astute politicians began to practise the new art known by the German term, *realpolitik,* or political realism. The three men who became identified with *realpolitik,* were Napoleon, Cavour, and Bismarck.

1. LOUIS NAPOLEON AND THE SECOND EMPIRE (1852-70)

Only France had given liberals any cause for hope in 1848 when the Second Republic was established. Four years later these hopes were dashed when Louis Napoleon formally abolished the Republic and became Napoleon III, Emperor of the French.

During the early days of the Empire, Napoleon held absolute power. As Emperor he nominated all officials of the French government including members of the Senate, the Council of State, the High Court of Justice, and the Cabinet. By extending the franchise to all adult males, he allowed the public to choose the Legislative Body, successor to the Chamber of Deputies, but this democratic "control" was simply an illusion. All legislation originated outside the Legislative Body, which actually had no law-making power at all. Official government candidates had the backing of the Emperor and were usually assured of election against any but the most popular opposition candidates through ballot manipulations by government prefects. The government was superficially democratic, while control rested in the hands of one person. The idealism of 1848 had given way to the cynicism of *realpolitik*.

Other forms of government control were less disguised. Restrictive censorship was imposed on newspapers and magazines. Public meetings had to be authorized and vigorous opponents of the Second Empire were either imprisoned or deported. A large colony of republicans, among them some of the leading French writers, lived in foreign exile. One of these was Victor Hugo, whose bitter pen attacked Napoleon savagely from abroad. The famous author derisively nicknamed the Emperor *le petit Napoleon*.

Despite mild opposition by die-hard republicans, the first years of the Second Empire were happy and prosperous, and Napoleon's popularity was high. A period of industrial expansion highlighted by the Paris Exhibition of 1855 found Napoleon giving government support to growing big business. The growth in the steel industry and railways brought France to a level just below Belgium and Great Britain, the leaders in the Industrial Revolution. Some of the money from industrial fortunes began to trickle down to the working classes. Napoleon added to his image of a benevolent dictator through the construction of state hospitals and asylums.

To provide employment and to remedy the poor health of Parisians he directed the demolition of many of the slums of Paris. In place of the rat-infested ghettos, he substituted wide, tree-lined boulevards along which stately mansions and modern buildings were constructed—and which, in case of public disorder, could easily be swept by gunfire.

Had the Emperor restricted his interest to domestic concerns, his reign might have been long and untroubled. Unfortunately, however, a spirit of adventure coupled with an obsession for intrigue led him into fatal foreign involvements. Although his famous declaration of *"L'Empire, c'est la paix"* suggested that he had no intention of following in his uncle's footsteps, his actions denied this.

Crimean War (1854-56)

Bonaparte's first venture into European politics came with the Crimean War. In 1853, Russia threatened to make war on the weak Ottoman Empire. Great Britain, traditionally conscious of the need of a strong buffer to Russian expansion in the Eastern Mediterranean, was prepared to support the Turks. France, with no prospects of territorial or strategic gain from entering a Russo-Turkish conflict, became involved because of Napoleon's meddling and a religious dispute. Both the Russians, on behalf of the Orthodox Church, and the French, on behalf of the Roman Catholic Church, claimed the right to protect Christian subjects resident in the Moslem Ottoman Empire. Finally in 1854, France and Great Britain declared war on Russia. Then in 1856, Czar Nicholas 1 sued for peace and a conference was arranged for Paris. By agreeing to meet in the French capital, the great Powers recognized the Second Empire and were prepared to accept another Bonaparte among the crowned heads of Europe.

Franco-Austrian War (1859)

Napoleon's next adventure involved France in Italian affairs. He was, no doubt, motivated by his own brief experience in the *carbonari* and through his knowledge of his uncle's abortive attempt to unify the Italian states. In 1858, Napoleon was invited by

Camillo di Cavour, Prime Minister of Piedmont, to meet secretly to discuss Italian affairs. Cavour, already familiar with the Emperor's romantic attachment to the cause of Italian unity, convinced him that peace in Europe could never be reached until Italy obtained her freedom. He had already cleverly taken steps to curry favour with Napoleon by having sent a detachment of Piedmontese troops to aid the French forces in the Crimean conflict.

Napoleon responded in true "cloak and dagger" fashion. The two practitioners of *realpolitik* met secretly in the French resort town of Plombières in 1858. Cavour was able to win a pledge of French support for Piedmont in a war that Cavour would stage with Austria—provided that Austria could be made to appear the aggressor. The promise was the release of the Italian provinces of Lombardy and Venetia from Austrian subjugation. The price was the surrender to France of the districts of Nice and Savoy at that time held by Piedmont.

Within a year Austria and Piedmont were at war. The Plombières agreement was honoured as French troops joined Piedmontese regulars. In the brief but bloody campaigns the Austrians were thrust back at Magenta (June 4, 1859) and Solferino (June 24, 1859). Suddenly, despite French military ascendancy, and upon Napoleon's initiative, a peace was negotiated at Villafranca (July 11, 1859) with the Austrian Emperor, Franz Josef. Napoleon was motivated by three concerns. First, the rapid and unforeseen French victories had concerned the Prussians, who began to mobilize troops along the Rhine—an obvious threat to French security. Then, clerical opinion, including that of the Empress, a devout Catholic, was actively hostile to Napoleon's declaration of war upon another Catholic power, so that the Emperor feared a possible *coup d'état* by opponents of the war. Finally, Napoleon, who had always been an armchair strategist, toured the battlefields, and was genuinely horrified by the sickening effectiveness of modern weapons.

Intervention in Mexico (1863-67)

The Austrian war of 1859 was Napoleon's last military triumph. From that point on, the diplomatic road led downhill to catastrophe as his foreign policy became increasingly confused and even contradictory.

By aiding Piedmont Napoleon had appealed to liberal opinion. His next move was undertaken partly to placate the ruffled clericals who had called for an end to the Austrian war. In 1862, he authorized French troops to join the English and Spanish forces sent to Mexico to overthrow the revolutionary government of Benito Juarez. The rebels, who were mildly anticlerical, had refused to repay debts made by the former government to various European creditors. When the British and Spanish, satisfied with exacting some payment from Juarez, agreed to withdraw their armies, Napoleon kept French troops on. He then agreed to support a Hapsburg, Archduke Maximilian, as Emperor of Mexico. Then, as in 1859, Napoleon did an "about-face." Under pressure, this time from mounting liberal opposition at home, and fearing threats of intervention by American troops, he ordered the withdrawal of French forces from Mexico, whereupon the Mexicans executed his puppet, Maximilian, at Querétero.

Napoleon's foreign policy was animated by a vague and romantic desire to restore France to the role of "arbiter of Europe," a status gained during the period of the First Empire. Several factors made this impossible. Napoleon III was neither the military nor political strategist that his uncle was. His policy decisions were based sometimes on impulsive actions. Moreover, he was troubled by domestic opposition that was constantly growing in strength during the 1860's. Another basic flaw was his failure to judge the strength of his enemies. All of these factors, plus worsening physical health, led him and France gradually downhill to military defeat.

The end came in 1870, when France unwisely declared war on Prussia. Thousands of Parisians in a gay, holiday mood lined the Champs-Elysées cheering the parading French troops with cries of "On to Berlin!" The Prussians, however, with better soldiers, better generals, and better weapons, were a superior fighting force. Within two months the French army had been routed at Sedan, and Napoleon himself was taken prisoner of war.

News of the French humiliation reached Paris within hours of Napoleon's surrender. This was the signal for revolution. While republicans were taking over the government without a shot fired in defence of the Second Empire, the Empress Eugènie escaped to England, where the Emperor joined her following his release by the Prussians. Two years later he died.

"A great unrecognized incapacity"—this was Bismarck's comment on Napoleon III. In their meeting at Biarritz in October, 1865, pictured above, Bismarck outmanoeuvred Napoleon completely; by offering "concessions," Bismarck obtained French connivance in the crushing of Austria.

In Paris a citizen army was formed, under the leadership of Leon Gambetta, a fiery young radical orator who was given the position of Minister of War. Gambetta dramatically escaped from besieged Paris by balloon to Tours, where he conducted the war until all hope was gone. He then moved to Bordeaux where the provisional government was set up. Despite the efforts of this modern Carnot, the citizen army was no match for the ruthlessly efficient Prussian war machine. The Prussian siege of Paris lasted over four months. The defence of the capital was nothing less than heroic; after the food supply ran out, rats, and even the elephant in the Paris zoo, were eaten. Finally, however, it was obvious there

Léon Gambetta preparing to escape from besieged Paris by balloon.

was no further hope. On January 28, 1871, Paris surrendered. France had been not just defeated but conquered by the Prussian enemy.

2. THE STRUGGLE FOR ITALIAN UNIFICATION

Napoleon's most constructive action may have been his intervention in Italian affairs in 1859. There is no doubt that he truly believed that the several states that made up the Italian peninsula should be unified as a single Italian nation. Yet Italy had not known political unity since the fall of the Roman Empire. Hampered by internal discord and frustrated by foreign conquest, she had remained a group of independent states until the era of the French Revolution. Napoleon Bonaparte's formation of the Kingdom of Italy briefly raised the hopes of Italian nationalists, but their enthusiasm was short lived when the Congress of Vienna once again politically fragmented the peninsula. But the dream lived on; between 1815 and 1848 a multitude of liberal-nationalist organizations, among them the *Carbonari* and *Young Italy*, waged unsuccessful rebellion against Austrian domination. Led by the republican idealist and founder of *Young Italy*, Giuseppe Mazzini, they answered Metternich's scornful description of Italy as a "geographical expression" with the rallying cry, *Italia fara da se!* (Italy will go it alone!).

Political Divisions of Italy

The 1848 revolutions had brought small comfort to Italian liberals and nationalists. Lombardy and Venetia remained under direct Hapsburg rule. The duchies of Parma, Modena, and Tuscany were controlled by Austrian puppet rulers. The Papal States were under the temporal rule of Pope Pius IX, an acknowledged foe of liberalism. In the very south of the peninsula the notoriously corrupt Spanish Bourbon, Ferdinand II, ruled the Kingdom of the Two Sicilies. Yet two significant developments emerged from the year of revolutions. First, Piedmont emerged as the only state in Italy ruled by Italians and with a freely elected parliament. King Victor Emmanuel II retained the constitution granted to the Piedmontese by his father Charles Albert. Piedmont thus became a haven for Italian liberals, more than one hundred thousand of whom fled to exile in this northern state. Second, Camillo di Cavour, one of the founders of the liberal newspaper *Il Risorgimento* (The Resurgence), and a deputy in the Piedmontese Parliament, resolved that Italy could not "go it alone." Only foreign intervention could drive out the detested Austrians.

One problem that remained, however, was that none of the other Italian states was happy with Victor Emmanuel's liberalism, nor did any of them want to sacrifice their independence for a wider scheme of Italian unity. The many years of dreaming of a unified Italy had naturally produced different ideas on the form the new state should take. Some supported the republicanism of Mazzini. Others believed in the scheme of Vincenzo Gioberti, a Roman Catholic priest, who suggested a confederation of the Italian states with the Pope as President. But gradually it became evident that the leadership in Italian unification was to come from the monarchy of Piedmont with its popular and liberal king, Victor Emmanuel. The slogan, "Italy and Victor Emmanuel," soon became the watchword of most liberals and nationalists.

Camillo di Cavour

If the symbol of Italian unity was Victor Emmanuel, the driving force behind the movement was the liberal and realistic Prime Minister of Piedmont, Camillo Benso di Cavour. Cavour was born near Turin of a highly respected artistocratic family. His reading of philosophy and history brought him early in life to reject his family's conservative outlook. After several years of military and academic training he resigned his army commission to manage his father's extensive estates. Several weeks spent in the visitors' gallery of the English House of Commons convinced him that social change could be implemented better by parliament than by revolution and conspiracy as advocated by Mazzini. A man of restless energy, he studied and experimented successfully on the family estates with modern agricultural techniques. With the profits thus gained he organized industries and founded two banks. He also formed agricultural societies and schools for the poor. In 1847 he became the editor of *Il Risorgimento*.

The same year Cavour was elected to the Piedmontese Parliament. Five years later he became Prime Minister. In that position he quickly took steps to modernize the state. Efforts were made to stimulate agricultural production and to give government support to growing industry. The state treasury was reformed and trade treaties were signed with most European countries. As a liberal, Cavour resented clerical interference in secular affairs; accordingly he dissolved the monasteries, expelled the Jesuits, and instituted state control of clerical incomes. For these measures, he was excommunicated by Pius IX.

Cavour's modernizing tendencies won him the attention and respect of British and French liberals. This was precisely what he needed as he planned for the day when he could call on them for help against Austria. This help was given when at Plombières in 1858 Napoleon agreed to support Piedmont against Austria.[1] The first stage of Italian unification was on the horizon.

Now Cavour began to plan for war with Austria in such a way that the Austrians would appear to be the aggressors. Within a year from his meeting with Napoleon, Cavour had set the trap. Austria accused Piedmont of fomenting disturbances in Lombardy and Venetia and demanded that Piedmont disarm. Piedmont's

---

[1] See above, p. 307.

"There is only one diplomat in Europe, but unfortunately he is against us—he is M. di Cavour."—Metternich

rejection of the Austrian ultimatum sparked an Austrian declaration of war.

When Austrian troops began to mobilize, Cavour called upon Napoleon for aid. The Emperor responded and French forces were sent to combine with Piedmontese armies. Two quick victories led Cavour to believe Napoleon's announcement that he intended to free Italy "from the Alps to the Adriatic."

Then, without approval from Cavour, the Emperor contacted Franz Josef of Austria and a truce was arranged at Villafranca. The terms included the granting of Lombardy to Piedmont, the retention of Venetia by Austria, and the formation of an Italian Confederation with the Pope as President. Cavour was livid with rage and urged Victor Emmanuel to carry on the war without France. But the king realized the necessity of French military aid and accepted the terms. Cavour resigned in frustration and anger.

The proposed Italian Confederation was never formed. In 1860 the militantly anti-papal duchies of Parma, Modena, Romagna, and

Tuscany held plebiscites that demonstrated an overwhelming desire to seek union with Piedmont. Only the threat of renewed French intervention would have stopped Austrian troops from marching into the northern duchies. At this point Cavour cleverly returned to his position as Prime Minister and bargained for Napoleon's approval of the union in exchange for ceding Nice and Savoy to France—a typical example of *realpolitik*. A dubious plebiscite was held in these two tiny territories to give the stamp of "popular consent" to the transaction. Austria, reluctantly, accepted the failure of the Italian Confederation.

Giuseppe Garibaldi

Now all of northern Italy except Venetia was in union with Piedmont. The next step was the acquisition of the Papal States and the Two Sicilies. However, with Roman Catholic opinion in France hostile to both Piedmontese pressure on the Pope and an invasion of the Sicilies, Cavour could not again count on Napoleon's support against Austria. At this point the unification movement was inspired by the actions of Giuseppe Garibaldi. Garibaldi was a sea captain, a merchant, and a guerilla chief, but most of all a restless enemy of tyranny who was prepared to travel the world to support the cause of freedom. Born in Nice, he became the captain of a merchant ship. Trading in Marseilles he met the exiled Mazzini who impressed him with his vision of a free and unified republican Italy. He gave up his sea career and became an active organizer for *Young Italy*. Constantly hunted by Austrian police, he fled to South America, where he formed a guerrilla band to help defend the tiny republic of Rio Grande do Sul against Brazil. News of the 1848 revolutions brought him quickly back to his native soil where, in 1849, he joined Mazzini in a desperate but unsuccessful bid to form a Roman Republic.[1] When French troops broke up the Roman Republic he retired to a farm for the next eleven years.

Conquest of Sicily (1860)

As plebiscites were being held in the northern duchies in 1860 a revolt broke out in Sicily. The Sicilian revolt drew Garibaldi from retirement. Within weeks he had gathered a band of almost a thousand Italian patriots known as the Redshirts. Within three months of landing in Sicily, Garibaldi's daring, combined with the

[1] See above, p. 245.

Giuseppe Garibaldi: "He evoked from the people and even from the politicians a personal devotion almost without parallel in modern history; again and again he chose the right course by instinct; and he showed himself the greatest general that Italy has ever produced." — A. J. P. Taylor.

military bungling of the Sicilians, allowed the Redshirts to reach the outskirts of Naples, the capital of the Kingdom of the Two Sicilies.

Flushed with success, Garibaldi was ready to enter Naples and then march into the Papal States and capture Rome. Cavour, who had secretly championed Garibaldi's invasion, while officially denying to Europe that Piedmont was in any way involved, now moved to stop the guerilla leader. If Garibaldi advanced on Rome, he would come into direct conflict with Napoleon's garrison guarding the Pope. In addition, Cavour feared a clash between Garibaldi's republicanism and his own scheme for a constitutional monarchy for unified Italy.

Kingdom of Italy (1861)

While Garibaldi was mobilizing his forces, two of Cavour's secret agents arranged with Napoleon one of the best examples of the diplomacy of the age. They agreed that Piedmontese troops led by Victor Emmanuel would meet and defeat the French forces outside Rome commanded by General Lamorcière, whom Napoleon detested. The king would then quickly march south to Naples to meet Garibaldi and forestall his march on Rome. Napoleon, plotting the destruction of his own troops, told the Piedmontese "to do it but do it quickly." The plan succeeded. The French troops were defeated though Rome was untouched. To Cavour's surprise, Garibaldi met Victor Emmanuel with open arms—and the two men toured Naples in triumph. Soon after, plebiscites were held in Sicily and in the Papal States except Rome. All voted for unification.

The triumph of Italian nationalism was not enjoyed for long by those who had made it possible. While Victor Emmanuel was being crowned King of Italy in 1861, Garibaldi, who had done so much to make Italian unification a reality, returned to his small farm and obscurity. Three months after the formation of the new state, Cavour, overworked and weakened by fatigue, died of typhoid fever. Mazzini, who retained his determined belief in republican principles, was an exile from the country his pen and organization had helped to create.

Acquisition of Venetia and Rome

The successes of 1859-61 were too strong to prevent Italy from forgetting Venetia and Rome. In 1866, Bismarck offered Venetia to the new kingdom in return for Italian help in an Austro-Prussian war. The war ended in a Prussian victory and although the Austrians had badly defeated the Italians, Bismarck carried out his pledge. Venetia was annexed by Italy.

Rome fell easily to Italy in 1870, when the French garrison stationed there was withdrawn to fight in the Franco-Prussian War. Despite the angry opposition of the Pope, a plebiscite was held and Italian unification was complete.

3. THE UNIFICATION OF GERMANY

In the aftermath of the 1848 revolutions unification of the German states seemed as unlikely as had that of Italy. Austria was the most powerful Germanic state and she had made clear her position on German unity when at Olmutz in 1851 she rejected Frederick William IV's proposal of a league of German princes. The "humiliation of Olmutz" demonstrated Austrian dominance in German affairs during the 1850's, and was a blow to the ambitions of Prussia. Prussia's weakness in foreign policy was matched by her internal problems. Conservatives were alarmed when Frederick William IV granted a constitution which established a Parliament in 1850. But their fears were baseless, since German liberalism had never been revolutionary, and the traditional German respect for authority was to weaken further the cause of democracy and the establishment of responsible parliamentary authority.

Germans before Olmutz and after have always shown remarkable ability to recover and seemingly gain vitality from defeat. This happened, for example, after the disastrous defeat at Jena in 1806 and in recent times after the Second World War. During the 1850's while the aging Frederick William lived out his life, Prussia played a subordinate role to Austria. One man was gaining experience during this time, waiting to take revenge for the Olmutz defeat. He was Otto von Bismarck.

Bismarck

Bismarck, the son of a Prussian *Junker*, was always influenced by the social superiority of his class. The *Junkers* were the rural nobility of East Prussia. Stubborn, proud, and intellectually and socially narrow, they treated other Germans as inferiors. Bismarck once told a politician: "I am a *Junker* and mean to have the advantages of that position." His mother, on the other hand, was not a *Junker*, and was determined to develop in her son a more broadly based outlook. To a certain degree she succeeded. As a young man, Bismarck attended the University of Göttingen, where he studied little, drank heavily, frequently engaged in duels, and became unsuccessfully involved in several romances. For a time he even strayed into the ranks of the illegal *Burschenschaft*. Managing to scrape through his examinations, he barely qualified for the Prussian civil service. Here he stayed only a short time, and like Cavour returned home to manage his father's estates. Later, after another unsuccessful stint in the civil service, he told a friend he would never have been happy at that level of government because he could not put up with superiors!

Junker loyalty to the monarchy was legendary and in the midst of the revolutionary crisis of the March days in 1848, Bismarck rushed from his estates to Berlin to offer his services to the king. As a reward for this patriotism, he was sent to represent Prussia at the German Confederation. Here he soon gained a reputation as an outspoken partisan of Prussian interests and as a severe critic of Austria. Later he was posted to St. Petersburg as the Prussian

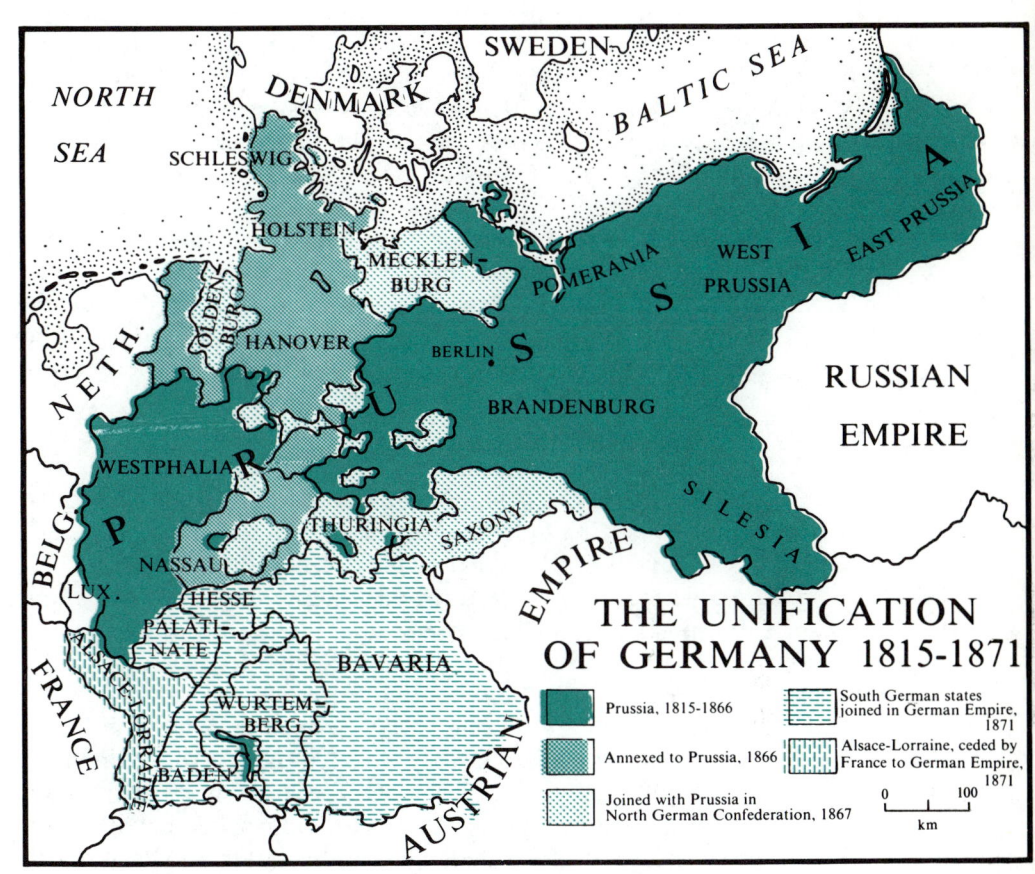

ambassador to the Romanov court. This was followed by a brief spell in Paris in 1862 as ambassador.

Bismarck was a clear-thinking political and diplomatic strategist whose class loyalty was exceeded only by devotion to Prussian interests. Although he was both the symbol and the architect of German nationalism and political unification, he achieved this goal only when he was certain of Prussian leadership in a greater Germany. The greatest practitioner of *realpolitik*, he calmly divorced personal morality from politics. Whatever was necessary to achieve a goal was good policy. "Great crises," he had once written, "provide the weather which favours Prussia's rise in so far as we use them fearlessly, perhaps even ruthlessly."

His acid tongue won him respect and fear, but never love. He had few friends and trusted no one. A tall man, grown stout from overindulgence in physical appetites, he once expressed a desire to repeat his life in order to drink more champagne. His large frame supported a small head whose bushy eyebrows were often fixed in a frown. Despite his size and the respect his appearance commanded in Parliament or at international conferences, his thin piping voice made him no orator. Although known as the Iron Chancellor, he was extremely high-strung and sensitive. He once admitted this by saying, "I am all nerves, so much so that self-control has always been the greatest task of my life and still is."

Bismarck was to dominate European affairs for twenty years. He first established his dominance in Prussia during a constitutional crisis. In 1862 William I was on the verge of abdicating because the Prussian Parliament had refused to grant him the funds necessary to increase the strength of the army. William, like Bismarck and von Roon, the War Minister, was convinced that Prussian supremacy in German affairs could not be obtained without a stronger army. With events reaching a head, von Roon telegraphed Bismarck, then Prussian ambassador in Paris, with the terse message: "Danger in delay. Hurry!" This was the pre-arranged signal and while the ambassador was rushing to Berlin, William was persuaded to accept Bismarck as Minister-President of Prussia.

Bismarck loathed representative institutions. Democracy, liberalism, and parliaments, had no place in monarchical Prussia according to his thinking. His response to the continued refusal of Parliament to vote funds was to rule without them. By using other

"... The great questions of the day will not be decided by speeches or by majority decisions ... but by blood and iron!"—Bismarck, 1862

"From a technical point of view the distinctive achievement of Bismarck is that few statesmen in modern history have achieved a revolution in the balance of forces in Europe with such an economy of blood and iron."
—L. C. B. Seaman, *Bismarck*

revenues outside legislative control, he secured the money to carry out von Roon's plans. He then turned to a project of long standing —the humbling of Austria.

The Danish War (1864)

An opportunity arose with a conflict over the duchies of Schleswig and Holstein. Largely German in population, they had been considered to belong personally to the king of Denmark since the 15th century. When the Danes moved to annex them in 1863, German nationalists raised a storm of protest. Bismarck quickly declared war on Denmark. Austria, fearing a Prussian gain at her expense, joined in the declaration. Without allies, the Danes were easily defeated and surrendered the two duchies to Austria and Prussia jointly.

Some historians differ, but many accept the theory that Bismarck planned all of his wars well in advance, as a seasoned chess player always thinks several moves ahead. He certainly did not enter the Danish war for the sake of conquest. His object was to find a vulnerable spot in the Austrian armour and then strike. While Austria and Prussia jointly administered the conquered duchies, Bismarck carefully manoeuvered to gain sole possession of them for Prussia. By a temporary agreement, the Convention of Gastein (1865), the administration of Holstein was granted to Austria and that of Schleswig to Prussia. But as Bismarck said, this arrangement only "papered over the cracks."

Seven Weeks' War (1866)

Realizing that an Austro-Prussian war was probable, Bismarck's next step was to secure the isolation of Austria. England's interest was increasingly centred on her colonies, and because she had failed to act during the Danish War, she was not expected to intervene now. Russia was cool to Austria, who had failed to help her during the Crimean conflict. Further, Bismarck had, with great foresight, gained Russian favour by offering the Czar military support during the Polish revolt in 1863. The new state of Italy, hungry for Great-Power status, accepted an alliance with Prussia. Bismarck held out Venetia as the reward for victory. His main fear was Napoleon's reaction to an Austro-Prussian War. His suggestion of "future compensation" for French neutrality, which the Emperor accepted, was another clever diplomatic move.

By 1866 Bismarck was prepared, and relations with Austria neared the breaking point. When Prussian troops were sent into

Holstein on a trumped-up excuse, Austria appealed to the members of the German Confederation, and the Frankfurt Diet voted the use of federal troops against Prussia. The Prussian military machine quickly destroyed the armies of the smaller German states in less than two weeks and then convincingly routed the Austrians at Sadowa (July 3, 1866).

The Prussian victory in the Seven Weeks' War produced several significant results. It demonstrated that the balance of power in central Europe had been completely altered. Prussia was now clearly the dominant German state and Bismarck was an obvious threat to Napoleon's position as "arbiter of Europe." Within Prussia the Minister-President was recognized as national hero. And finally, Prussia had come to prefer national honour and military glory to free speech and parliamentary responsibility; 1866 marked the death of effective German liberal opinion.

North German Confederation (1867)

To many Germans, including William I, the great enemy was defeated and Prussia could now exact vengeance from Austria. But Bismarck had other plans. Austrian friendship might be needed in the future. Holstein was annexed and Venetia was given to Italy, who had honoured her alliance, but at the Treaty of Prague, Prussia did not demand a square inch of Austrian soil. The lesser German states, however, were treated more severely. Hanover, Hesse-Cassel, Nassau, and the free city of Frankfurt were annexed to Prussia. One year later these states were officially united in the formation of the North German Confederation. The constitution made the king of Prussia the hereditary President. A legislature of two houses was formed—the *Bundesrat* (which represented the states) and the *Reichstag* (elected by universal manhood suffrage). All important executive power was given to the Chancellor (Bismarck) who was responsible not to the legislature but to the President (William I).

Only three large German states now remained outside of Prussian or Austrian control. Bavaria, Wurtemburg, and Baden, fearful of French retaliation, did not join the North German Confederation but signed secret military agreements with the Confederation when Bismarck revealed French plans for expansion into southern Germany.

Among the important factors in Prussia's uninterrupted series of military victories was her superior weaponry, which was perhaps the finest in the world. The illustration depicts an artillery test, just prior to the Franco-Prussian War.

The Ausgleich (1867)

The Seven Weeks' War ended Austria's dominant position in German affairs. Austrian interests became increasingly centred in the Balkans rather than in northern Europe. Other changes occurred within the Austrian Empire because of the still powerful effects of the 1848 revolutions. The nationalistic Magyars finally obtained recognition. In 1867 the *Ausgleich* (compromise) established the Dual Monarchy of Austria and Hungary. Each state was to control its own internal affairs but was to be united by the same ruler, army, and foreign policy.

Franco-Prussian War (1870-71)

The formation of the North German Confederation was a major diplomatic defeat for France. Napoleon, whose Mexican escapade had just collapsed, was being pressured on one side by liberal and on the other by clerical hostility. He desperately needed a diplomatic victory, and at Bismarck's expense. Bismarck understood Napoleon's weaknesses, and prepared the bait at which he knew the Emperor would strike. In 1870, he persuaded Leopold, a Hohenzollern prince, to agree to become a candidate for the vacant Spanish throne. Napoleon immediately sent the French ambassador in Berlin, Benedetti, to demand that William prevent Leopold from accepting the candidacy.

When the king agreed, Napoleon was elated and Bismarck dismayed. But the French failed to leave well enough alone. Without consulting Napoleon, Gramont, the French foreign minister, instructed Benedetti to insist upon assurances from William that he would never again promote the Hohenzollern candidacy in Spain. This time, the king was polite but firm. He turned down the ambassador's request and announced that the subject was closed. He then telegraphed Bismarck at Ems to inform the Chancellor of his actions. Bismarck, acting on inspiration, released to the press an edited version of the telegram. In its revised form the "Ems dispatch" suggested that Benedetti had been rebuffed by William.[1] Both Prussian and French opinion were incensed by the news and eager for war. Napoleon, suffering from a fatal illness and too weak to resist, reluctantly declared war.

Once again Bismarck was prepared and this time it was France who was without allies. To prevent British intervention, the Chancellor revealed Napoleon's interest in expansion into the Rhineland. Russia was bought off by Bismarck's rejection of the limitations on Russian access to the Black Sea imposed upon her by the Congress of Paris at the end of the Crimean War. Italy was a recent Prussian ally and the lenient Treaty of Prague assured Bismarck of Austrian neutrality.

[1] Bismarck's role in editing the Ems dispatch has been disputed by modern historians. Bismarck himself claimed that he had deliberately precipitated war by twisting the words out of context. The challenge to this claim is based on the proposition that even after Bismarck's changes, the telegram could still not be interpreted as an insult to France. The fact remains, however, that Napoleon, his advisers, and the French newspapers—which had just been relieved from censorship—all regarded the dispatch as an outrageous and unacceptable affront to French honour.

It took the superb Prussian army only two months to defeat the French, although final victory was not achieved until January, 1871.[1] On January 21, 1871, a week before the final end of hostilities, William I, King of Prussia, was crowned William I, Emperor of Germany, in the historic Hall of Mirrors at Versailles. All of the German states except Austria had been united under one government.

Between the March uprisings in 1848 and the proclamation of the German Empire in January, 1871, Europe witnessed several exciting transformations. A hesitating, groping society had idealistically built the barricades of 1848. By 1871, society had become distrustful of ideals and slogans. This change had been produced by the drive for power and was characterized by the use of *realpolitik*.

The map of Europe had been significantly altered. The five Powers which had controlled the Congress of Vienna were still powerful but the weakest, Prussia, had now become the strongest. The Age of Metternich had given way to the Age of Bismarck.

Metternich's chief enemies, liberalism and nationalism, had combined to destroy him. Bismarck discredited liberalism and enlisted nationalism to create Germany and the new Europe. Metternich's system had brought peace for thirty-three years. Bismarck as the arbiter of Europe would add ten years to that total. Yet the success of Germany caused many to imitate her with the inevitable result of conflict among rival Powers. The 19th century, which, in the political sense, began in 1815 when the Great Powers agreed at Vienna to govern Europe in harmony, ended in 1914, when agreement was no longer possible.

[1]See above, pp. 308-311.

14 France and Germany (1871-1914)

"Never tolerate the establishment of two continental powers in Europe."
—Adolph Hitler, *Mein Kampf.*

The victory of Prussia over France in 1871 led to the formation of the German Empire. Bismarck, supported by a booming industrial economy and Europe's most powerful army, became arbiter of Europe during the last generation of the 19th century.

In France military humiliation was followed by social and political turmoil. When a new Republic was formed it barely managed to gain national support.

1. IMPERIAL GERMANY (1871-1914)

The formal creation of the German Empire on January 18, 1871, took place on the 170th anniversary of the establishment of the Prussian kingdom. Indeed, for Bismarck the unification of the German states was a Prussian, not a German, achievement. During the next nineteen years while he remained Chancellor, he maintained one policy: to make Germany dominant in European affairs and to keep Prussia in control of Germany.

The Imperial Constitution

The Imperial Constitution was similar to that constructed by Bismarck for the North German Confederation. The Reichstag or lower house was elected by universal manhood suffrage and drew its members from the twenty-five states according to population. From Prussia came 236 of the 397 members. The Bundesrat or upper house, also called the Federal Council, represented the princes of the states. Here again, Prussia held control, having seventeen of the fifty-eight delegates. Bavaria, with the next largest representation, had only six delegates. Unable to exercise any legislative power except over money bills, the Reichstag could not control the executive whose head was the Chancellor. Bismarck, as Chancellor, presided over the ultra-conservative Bundesrat and could cast Prussia's entire seventeen votes. He was responsible to the Emperor who was the king of Prussia. Since the concept of parliamentary responsibility was not accepted, democracy was never given a chance in Germany.

Growth of Industry

Heinrich von Treitschke, a 19th century German political philosopher, declared that it was essential to have "faith in the God who made iron," and it was iron in industry as well as in politics that made Germany powerful. Initially, Germany had been slow to industrialize. There were several reasons for this. The existence until the mid-19th century of the traditional guild system of master, journeyman, and apprentice obstructed the efficient use of labour, and effectively prevented the organization of major business enterprises. The role of government was essentially counterproductive for encouraging industrialization. Regulations of all sorts discouraged initiative and enterprise: government permission was required to open a mine, for instance, and could be withdrawn at any time without explanation. Unlike Britain, Germany suffered from a severe shortage of capital, without which large-scale industrialization could not begin. German deposits of iron-ore contained large proportions of phosphorus, which, until the invention of new refining techniques in 1876, could not be used for making steel.[1] Perhaps the severest handicap, however, was the heritage of the Peace of Westphalia of 1648, by which Germany had been divided into a loosely-knit web of petty states, each following its own economic policy, and protecting its interests through regulations aimed against its neighbours. Laws affecting commerce varied, and even the currencies differed. In such circumstances, efficient economic enterprise was almost an impossibility.

As Prussia grew to a position of dominance, however, she was able to force through changes that would set the stage for an economic transformation. With the establishment of the German Empire, the problem of the multiplicity of small states was abruptly

[1]See p. 280.

"Fritz," the great hammer in the Krupp foundry, by the late 19th century the largest steel factory in the world.

eliminated. Restrictions on freedom of movement and enterprise were removed, and legislation enacted to permit the formation of large business corporations. The guild system was gone. The acquisition of Lorraine from France in 1871 provided a rich source of iron ore. Concentration of capital for industrial expansion was made not just by private sources, such as the enormous armaments manufacturer, Krupp, but also by the German government itself, which financed mines, railways, and other large-scale undertakings. As a result of all these changes, German industrial activity marched forward. Railway construction, shipbuilding, and chemical industries increased material prosperity. But it was the massive production of iron and steel that catapulted Germany into the position of Europe's second greatest manufacturing nation. In 1871, England had produced more than four times as much iron as Germany. By 1910 Germany had surpassed England and was producing three times as much as France.

Having done everything possible to encourage prosperity through *internal* changes, Bismarck also moved to advance Germany's economic strength as a major *international* power. Free trade was ended in 1879, and by the 1880's high tariffs were protecting infant industry and the precious grain markets coveted by the Prussian *Junkers*. By preparing the way for economic self-sufficiency, Bismarck planned for Germany to be independent of foreign industrial and agricultural supplies in time of war.

Political Parties

Bismarck had enemies. While the Reichstag was relatively powerless to control legislation, it was still a sounding board for public opinion. Political parties were formed and each of the five major parties at one time or another challenged the Chancellor's policies. The National Liberal Party found its support among the rising middle class who backed Bismarck until he no longer supported their free trade theories. The Progressive Party with its left-wing liberal leadership was the most democratic. Appealing to radicals, it consistently urged the constitutional change necessary to make the Chancellor responsible to the Reichstag, but attracted little support. The National Conservative Party drew its support chiefly from Bismarck's own class, the *Junkers* of East Prussia. Owners of large estates, they demanded tariff protection against cheaper imported grains. Since they were the most militaristic class (the cream of the German General Staff was Prussian) they warmly endorsed Bismarck's constant demand for a standing army of 400 000 men. The Centre or Catholic Party believed in states' rights, and was strongest in southern Germany where localist feeling died hard. During Bismarck's arduous struggle from 1871 to 1883 with the Roman Catholic Church, the Centrists were among his greatest foes. But the most bitter opponent of the Iron Chancellor was the Social Democratic Party. The Social Democrats combined a policy of democratic socialism with doctrinaire Marxist communism, and advocated, among other things, ministerial responsibility and a wide extension of government ownership. The Social Democrats were regarded by the government with "unspeakable wrath"; they were imprisoned, fined, intimidated, and ostracized, but nevertheless grew steadily to become the largest party in Germany. Their support came from the working classes in the growing industrial areas of the north and west.

Intellectual and religious freedom versus the Prussian state.

Domestic Policy

Bismarck's domestic policy was always related to his foreign policy. While he once said: "We Germans fear God and nothing else," he also believed that God marched with the biggest battalions. To insure that every soldier was a fervent patriot he believed in the need to develop an independent and forceful national outlook among the German people. Any organization which tried to share the loyalty of German citizens was subversive and had to be destroyed. One such organization was the Roman Catholic Church. Bismarck launched a *Kulturkampf* or "struggle for civilization" against this international religion in 1871, by closing the Catholic section of the Ministry of Education and forbidding Catholic supervision of schools. Two years later the Prussian Parliament passed the "May Laws." The state gained the power to veto all clerical appointments, and to supervise numerous internal functions of the Church. This was followed by the Reichstag's expulsion of the Jesuits from the Empire. The reaction was not pleasing to the Chancellor. The Centre Party gained strength, and resistance from Catholics throughout Germany stiffened. Even foreign opinion was hostile. In 1879, Bismarck felt it wise to repeal the laws, and by 1883 the *Kulturkampf* in effect had ended. Bismarck had suffered a defeat.

The second international organization that Bismarck felt compelled to destroy was *socialism*. The attack was two-pronged. On the one hand he assaulted the Social Democratic Party—which was affiliated with the Second International—with every weapon short of making the party illegal. On the other, he stole many parts of the Social Democratic platform to prove to the workers that the State would provide for them. Neither move stopped the growth of socialism. When two unsuccessful attempts were made on the life of William I, Bismarck saw his opportunity to blame the socialists, who actually were guiltless of the crimes. The so-called "Exceptional Laws" (1878) banned meetings and publications of the Social Democrats. Legal proceedings were taken against party officials and many were expelled from their homes. Despite these extraordinary measures German socialism continued to grow stronger.

To woo the workingman away from the socialists he enacted social welfare legislation which actually put Germany far in advance of the more liberal states of France and Great Britain. Laws were passed to provide insurance for workers against sickness (1883) and accidents (1884). Hours and working conditions in industry for women and children were regulated in 1887. Old age pensions and disability insurance were introduced three years later. Finally, trade unions were given more freedom.

Foreign Policy

Bismarck's main preoccupation was in the area of foreign affairs. He was well pleased with the powerful position Germany had won through the Franco-Prussian War. German ambitions, he believed, were now "satiated." For the remainder of his public life his one great aim was to safeguard the new, post-war balance of power.

In Bismarck's eyes, France was the one nation likely to challenge the *status quo*. Certain that she was an implacable foe, merely biding her time for revenge, Bismarck was careful to maintain a powerful German army. At the same time, he exerted all his diplomatic skills to ensure that France remained isolated and powerless. With her own strength alone, France could never hope to reverse the verdict of Sedan.

Isolation of France was only one side of Bismarck's foreign policy, however. Equally as important was the protection of Germany through diplomatic alliances with the other Powers. After lengthy diplomatic manoeuvres Bismarck brought Germany, Austria-Hungary, and Russia together in the League of the Three Emperors (*Dreikaiserbund*) in 1872. The treaty was later renewed (1881-1887). A secret understanding was reached, ostensibly no more than an agreement to preserve peace; if a fourth Power were to attack any one member of the League, the other two would maintain a "benevolent neutrality." As an alliance, the League was doomed from the start, since Austrian and Russian ambitions in the Balkans were irreconcilable. However, while the League lasted it served Bismarck's purpose by making it unlikely that either Austria-Hungary or Russia would form an alliance with France.

Meanwhile, in 1879, Bismarck had negotiated, in great secrecy, a Dual Alliance for defensive purposes between Austria-Hungary and Germany. Its most important clause bound each nation to come to the help of the other in case of attack by Russia. To the Iron Chancellor the agreement meant exactly that and no more; he was not prepared to see Austria-Hungary destroyed as a major Power but on the other hand he was determined not to back her in reckless adventures in the Balkans. The Austrians, however, assumed from the start that they could count on German backing should they come to blows with Russia, no matter *what* the circumstances. Thus there began "a diplomatic tug-of-war between Berlin and Vienna" which resulted ultimately in disastrous consequences, not just for Germany and Austria, but for the whole world. In retrospect, the Dual Alliance can be seen as an important precursor of the First World War.

"The Three Emperors." Puppet-master Bismarck, controlling the Emperors of Austria, Germany, and Russia.

In 1882, the Dual Alliance was secretly expanded into the Triple Alliance with the inclusion of Italy. This latter agreement, renewed at five year intervals, lasted until 1915. It stated that if any one of the allies were attacked by two or more Powers its partners should give immediate military aid. Italy's inclusion in the Alliance was indeed a masterpiece of Bismarck's diplomacy. Italy had no love for Austria but was enraged with France for having taken Tunisia. Yet French ambitions in North Africa had been deliberately encouraged by Bismarck, both to foment French rivalry with Italy and Britain and also to take French eyes off Alsace-Lorraine.

In 1887 Russia, provoked by Austrian policy in the Balkans, had withdrawn from the *Dreikaiserbund*, but Bismarck was determined not to allow her to drift into friendship with France. That same year, behind Austria's back, he negotiated a secret Reinsurance Treaty between Germany and Russia, agreeing to recognize Russia's claims in the Balkans—in direct opposition to the Dual Alliance that had been signed only eight years before! It was a cynical and dishonest act, but Bismarck was prepared to make almost any promise to achieve his aims. The only other nation with whom France might conceivably have become allied was Great Britain, but the British held themselves aloof from the Continent, satisfied with their traditional policy of "splendid isolation." To make doubly sure that Britain would not be tempted into an alliance with France, Bismarck took pains to cultivate good Anglo-German relations; he did all that he could to discourage German colonial expansion and was careful to avoid any challenge to Britain's supremacy at sea. There could never, believed Bismarck, be a serious quarrel "between a land rat and a water rat."

By 1882 Bismarck had achieved his ambition. He had woven a complicated web of alliances and counter-alliances which he hoped would preserve the peace indefinitely or, in the last resort, guarantee a German victory. Although France was neither conciliated nor disarmed, she appeared to have no hope of obtaining a powerful friend, and Germany stood unchallenged as the strongest single state on the European mainland.

Bismarck's Legacy

In 1888, the aged William I died, to be succeeded by his ailing son Frederick III, who himself died only three months later. William II, the new Emperor, was a young man of thirty-one who resented Bismarck's power, and regarded him as merely a foolish old man. Personal relations between the two became intolerable. In 1890, at the age of seventy-five, Bismarck was forced to resign. From his estate in retirement the old man tried to influence German policy, but without great effect. In 1898, he died. His less capable successors, and the excitable and unpredictable William II, proved unable to maintain his intricate system of alliances. Germany's foreign ambitions became increasingly aggressive, and would eventually bring her into conflict with Great Britain and France.

Domestic policy after Bismarck followed a rather ambiguous course. While more conciliatory attitudes were adopted towards "the masses", with the dropping of anti-socialist laws and the extending of social security legislation, the Prussian state remained virtually absolutist in its fundamental character. The prerogatives of the king were scarcely diminished, and above all, there was almost no control over the executive (the Chancellor) by the Reichstag, or Parliament. In summary, it must be said that while Bismarck preserved stability in Germany, his complete aversion to parliamentary democracy failed to prepare the German people for the political conditions of 20th century Europe. With the continued growth of reform-minded Social Democrats despite the severest measures of repression, it is quite likely that a constitutional crisis would have racked Germany had not the Great War come first. And in the years following Germany's defeat, the virtual absence of democratic roots made the rise of Hitler considerably easier.

2. THE THIRD FRENCH REPUBLIC (1871-1914)

The French defeat in the Franco-Prussian War completely upset the balance of power in Europe and displaced France from her position of "arbiter of Europe." For the next twenty-three years she remained friendless and alone until she became allied with Imperial Russia in 1894. Military defeat and loss of honour were hard for proud Frenchmen to bear; the desire for revenge became a national obsession.

Election of a National Assembly

With Bismarck's permission, national elections were held in February (1871) to choose a government to settle the peace terms. For Gambetta and the Republicans, who stood for continuation of the war, the election results were disheartening. The overwhelming sentiment in the nation, outside of Paris, was for a return to peace and order. Some four hundred Monarchists and Conservatives, who promised peace, were elected. Only two hundred Republicans and thirty Bonapartists gained seats. The head of the executive of the new National Assembly was Adolphe Thiers, a former Prime Minister under Louis Philippe.

Thiers met Bismarck to discuss settlement, at the Treaty of Frankfurt, 1871. The harsh terms startled Europe. France would pay an indemnity of five billion francs and would suffer partial military occupation until repayment had been completed. The mineral-rich provinces of Alsace and Lorraine would be ceded to Germany. The last term did much to develop the revenge sentiment in France, which later haunted Germany.

The Paris Commune

The announcement of the peace terms shocked France, and, most of all, the citizens of Paris, who had fought so hard for four months. Then Thiers made several unpopular decisions, which threw the capital into turmoil and finally rebellion. First he decided to convene the National Assembly in Versailles instead of in Paris, which the Parisians saw as a blatant insult. Then he removed the suspension of debts made during the siege of Paris, and disbanded the National Guard. Suddenly the frustrated Parisians could stand no more. In defiance of the National Assembly's authority they elected their own government, called the Commune. When similar rebellions began in other French cities, civil war broke out. What followed during the next two months was one of the blackest pages of French social history. The Commune leaders came from a variety of political backgrounds. Some were anarchists and followers of Proudhon, some Marxists from the First International, others were Jacobins, and still many others were radicals and simple working class people and patriots who felt that they had been betrayed by the surrender to the Prussians. As the occupying German troops watched, Paris again prepared for an assault, made this time by the French army. During the next several weeks barbarism and butchery knew no precedent. In the fighting on the barricades, women and children were massacred. Prisoners, including the Archbishop of Paris, were executed. Many of the French troops were illiterate Breton peasants who believed they were fighting in a Catholic Crusade. In one week twenty thousand or more Communards were executed and later thousands more were arrested and deported. Even the infamous "Terror" of 1793 had killed no more than this, and then over a period of fifteen months. By the end of May the army had ended the revolt in Paris and throughout France.

The Paris Commune has created a legacy in French political and social history. Throughout the Third Republic there remained a latent hostility among the working classes to the State. The class mistrust, brought into the open in 1789, revived in 1848 and honed to razor sharpness in 1871, has never been permanently blunted. Moreover, many legends, most of which lack any foundation in fact, have grown out of the Commune. Chief among these is that the Communards were directly controlled by the First International.

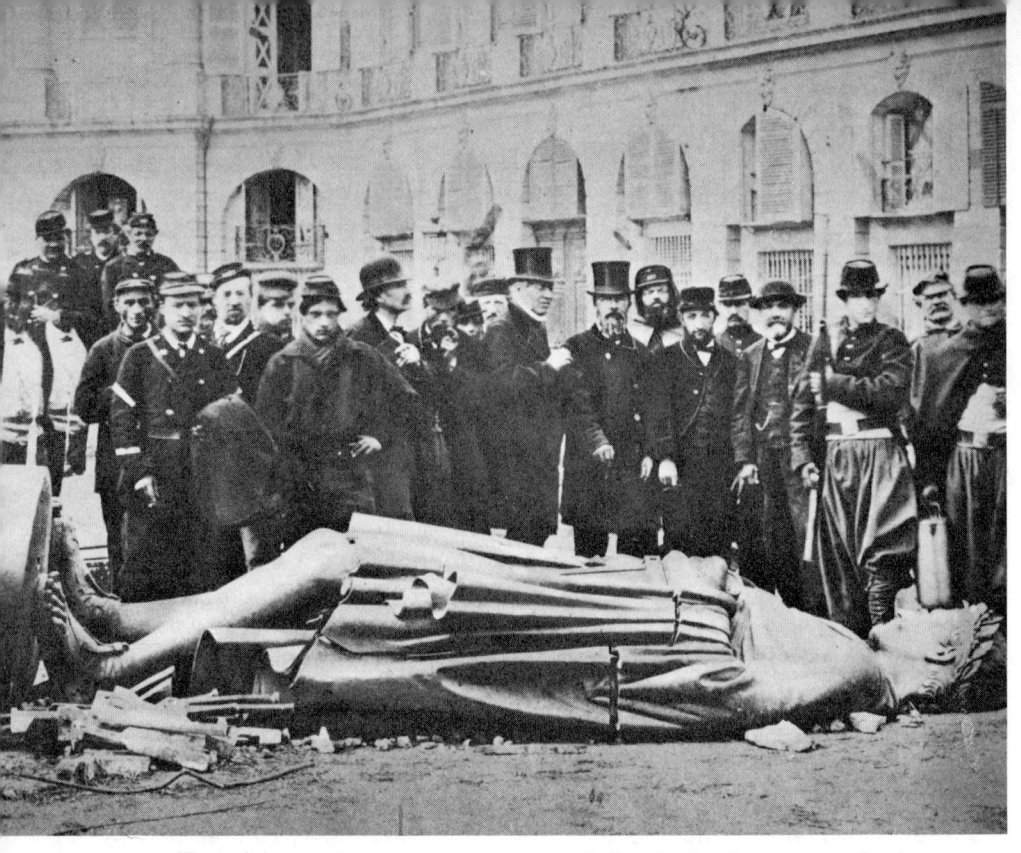

To celebrate the apparent success of the Paris Commune, the insurgents pulled over the Vendôme Column commemorating Napoleon I's victories. "Some of the onlookers were eager to be photographed with the Emperor at their feet, but had cause to regret their rashness after the insurrection had been put down, when those who were recognized were punished."

Karl Marx, who tensely watched the events in the London daily newspapers, was willing to propagate this theory, as were many of his subsequent followers. Few, very few, of the leaders and supporters of the Commune were socialists. Part of the misunderstanding can be traced to the French word *commune* which means *township*, not *communist*. Yet both communists and their opponents have regarded the Commune as one of the important events in the history of international communism.

Establishment of the Republic

With the National Assembly once again in control, it turned to the problem of governing. Although elected solely for the purpose of negotiating a settlement with Germany, it remained in power for four years. Because the Monarchists dominated the National Assembly it seemed likely that the monarchy would be restored. Yet they themselves were divided, between the Bourbons and the Orleanists. When a reconciliation between these two groups seemed at last possible the Bourbon candidate refused to accept the one condition for a restoration—the choice of a flag. He absolutely refused to become king under the Republican standard, the tricolour, and insisted on the white flag of the Bourbons. With the chances of a restoration slipping away, the Assembly replaced Thiers with Marshal MacMahon, a royalist, as President of the Republic. If France were not to become a monarchy it would at least have a monarchist President. Finally, in 1875, the Assembly passed a series of constitutional laws which have become known as the "Constitution of 1875."

By the 1875 Constitution, the legislative branch was made bicameral, as in England and Germany. A Chamber of Deputies or lower house was elected by universal manhood suffrage, and a Senate or upper house was chosen by indirect election. Both houses when meeting together (by definition, the National Assembly) elected the President for a term of seven years. As in England, but not in Germany, the executive was chosen from the majority party or parties in the Chamber and was responsible to it.

By 1879, Republicans had gained control of both houses, MacMahon resigned, and Jules Grévy, a Republican, was elected President. The electoral success of the Republicans not only destroyed all hopes of a royalist restoration, but also widened the gulf which separated them from the Monarchists. To the Monarchists, Republicans represented Jacobinism, mob violence, and vicious anticlericalism. To Republicans, on the other hand, Monarchists symbolized the privileged aristocrats of the *ancien régime*. It was natural then that the Republicans should use their legislative power to attack what they considered to be the stronghold of royalist propaganda—the Church-influenced system of education. Taking Gambetta's battle cry of "Clericalism, that is the enemy," they began by expelling the Jesuits from France (1880) and followed by eliminating religious supervision of all State primary schools (1882). The intensity of anticlerical feeling divided the nation for many years into two camps, the one represented by the republican village schoolmaster, and the other by the monarchist parish priest—respectively *le rouge* and *le noir*.

Despite their continued control, the Republicans remained constantly on trial. The first crucial test of strength developed in 1887 over the Boulanger Affair. General Georges Boulanger was a vain, handsome military hero with a great amount of personal charm and popular appeal. After winning a series of by-election victories (a candidate could stand for election in more than one constituency) he was appointed Minister of War in 1886. He immediately introduced some military reforms which made him the delight of the enlisted soldier. His well-publicized appearances at military reviews attracted large audiences. To many he became the symbol of French defiance against Germany and the man who would lead the nation in a war of revenge to regain honour and the lost provinces. For a time it was rumoured that he was plotting to lead a *coup d'état* to restore the monarchy. When he was quickly dropped from the Cabinet and tried to leave Paris by train, more than three thousand of his followers stood or lay on the tracks. While the supporters of the Republic trembled, Boulanger lost heart. Suddenly and unexpectedly he fled to Belgium where he committed suicide on the grave of his mistress.

Although the Republic survived the Boulanger Affair, many realized how shallow were its foundations. They soon lost more confidence when details of the Panama Affair were made public. Ferdinand de Lesseps, the builder of the Suez Canal, organized a company to construct a waterway through the jungle-infested Isthmus of Panama. Guilty of waste and extravagance, the company ran out of capital, and public appeals for more money to finance construction failed. In 1888, the government agreed to back some lottery bonds to raise the required revenue. Then, in 1892, an anti-Semitic newspaper dramatically accused a Jewish financier, Baron Reinach, of having bribed several Deputies to vote for government support of the bonds. Shortly after, Reinach was murdered and his blackmailer, Cornelius Herz, also a Jewish financier, escaped to England. Public inquiries were held and charges of corruption filled the courts. Enemies of the Republic were quick to point out that this type of morality was ruining France.

Dreyfus Affair

The Panama Affair brought great discredit to the Republic and also opened the wound of anti-Semitism, which soon became a bleeding sore in the third and most serious trial of the Republic—the Dreyfus Affair. Alfred Dreyfus, an Alsatian Jew, was a Captain in the French army. It was alleged that certain secret military documents which were found in a wastepaper basket in the German Embassy contained his handwriting. Dreyfus was court-martialled in secret, publicly degraded, and sent to the tropical penal colony of Devil's Island to solitary confinement. Only the Dreyfus family was convinced of his innocence until an intelligence officer, Colonel Picquart, discovered evidence to link the handwriting to a debt-ridden infantry officer named Esterhazy. Because Dreyfus' innocence would cause questioning of military justice, Picquart was sent to Africa and was replaced by a Colonel Henry.

By now the doubt of Dreyfus's guilt had become public, and pro-Dreyfus anticlerical Republican groups began to demand a re-trial. To oppose them, anti-Dreyfus monarchists, anti-Semites and pro-clericals supported the army and the original conviction. At this point, the popular French novelist, Emile Zola, wrote an open letter to the President of the Republic entitled *"J'accuse"* in which he roundly attacked the army and the enemies of the Republic. Finally, under pressure, the case was reopened and it was discovered that Colonel Henry had forged a document to frame Dreyfus. Henry was imprisoned and committed suicide. The re-trial was held in 1899 and Dreyfus was again found guilty with extenuating circumstances but his ten-year sentence was ended by a presidential pardon. The pro-Dreyfus faction refused to give up and in 1906 the case was reopened. The original judgment was declared "wrongful and erroneous," and Dreyfus was decorated with the Legion of Honour and promoted to Major.

Like the Commune, the Dreyfus Affair left a legacy of bitterness with faint memories that can still be felt in modern France. It brought the issue of anticlericalism to a head and led directly to the separation of Church and State in 1905, when Napoleon I's Concordat was abrogated. Moreover it greatly strengthened the Radical Party that had, in part, used Dreyfus as a tool in its struggle against monarchism and clericalism. The Radicals, supported by some moderates and socialists, entered office in 1899

An example of the non-too-subtle anticlerical propaganda that followed in the aftermath of the Dreyfus case.

and remained in power until the outbreak of the First World War. Zealous defenders of the Republic, their political success assured a wider acceptance of the republican form of government. Furthermore, they not only separated Church and State but carried out a sometimes senseless purge of anti-republican elements within the French army. Finally, the Affair was a fearful omen of the limits to which anti-Semitism might lead.

Social Welfare Laws

The precarious hold on power by the Republicans should not obscure the social welfare and liberal legislation passed during this period. Laws gave protection to women and children in industry and a ten-hour day to workers (1892). Workmen's compensation (1898) and old age pensions (1911) were introduced. Trade unions were legalized (1884) and freedom of association for all groups except monastic orders of the Catholic Church was permitted (1901). Freedom of speech and press was granted (1881).

France in 1914

France entered the 20th century as a modern industrial nation. Because of the loss of Alsace and Lorraine she had turned her efforts to the building of an empire in Asia and Africa. The products from her expanding overseas colonies increased her material prosperity and placed her just behind England or Germany in industrial development. Only one major problem still plagued her —the loss of honour and territorial possessions. In Paris the statue of Strasbourg was permanently veiled in black. No Frenchman was allowed to forget the humiliation of Sedan nor the loss of Alsace and Lorraine. The desire for *revanche* was riveted into the French character. Frenchmen were advised by Gambetta to "think always of it but to speak never of it."

In September, 1870, Napoleon III, Emperor of France, was taken prisoner at Sedan. From the ashes of an ignominious imperial defeat emerged the Third French Republic. A few months later, amid the glitter of the historic Hall of Mirrors in Versailles, William I, king of Prussia, was proclaimed Emperor of Germany. Forged from the iron of victory, the second *Reich* was born. While both these Powers successfully overcame their respective internal crises, the problem of their increasing mutual hostility was only resolved on the battlegrounds of the First World War, almost half a century later.

15 The Age of British Greatness

> If there be one test of national genius universally accepted, it is success; and if there be one successful country in the universe for the last millenium, that country is England.
> —Ralph Waldo Emerson

> A scientist says: Roast beef made England what she is today. Moral: Eat more vegetables.
> —Author unknown

In 1851, Great Britain staged the Great Exhibtion, the first world's fair. To the thousands of foreign visitors the Exhibition provided obvious proof of the global supremacy of British engineering and industrial skill. The industrialization of the British Isles had made Great Britain both wealthy and powerful.

Nevertheless, Britain was not without problems. The benefits of industrialization were largely confined to the upper and middle classes; the emerging urban working class, a social and economic by-product of industrialization, was not so fortunate. British workers suffered from poverty, unemployment, and sometimes unbearable living conditions. Gradually resentment against these hardships grew to militance, and led to the formation of powerful unions and later to the socialist movement.

Changing economic conditions were responsible for new political developments. More powerful trade unions and increasing prosperity aided in the growth of democracy. In the last half of the 19th century two reform bills were passed to extend the franchise to the common man. Finally, before the outbreak of the first World War, the Commons wrested the legislative authority of the United Kingdom from its senior House, the Lords.

1. WORKSHOP OF THE WORLD

The British Isles were naturally endowed with the chief raw materials for industrial production, and manufacturers made continued good use of them. Annual coal production at fifty million tonnes

London, *circa* 1865.

in 1850, had quadrupled by 1900. One-half of the world's supply of pig-iron came from Britain and by 1870 the value of exports of iron and steel had been increased twenty-three times since 1830. Raw materials, especially coal; and manufactured goods, such as textile products, shoes, furniture, and machines, were carried around the world in British ships. At mid-century sixty per cent of ocean-going tonnage was British. The advances in manufacturing had come as a result of practical scientific knowledge. As a result of the discoveries of Henry Bessemer and Thomas Gilchrist, for instance, a high quality of steel was produced. British railway companies financed and constructed a large part of the world's railway systems which were expanding at the rate of one hundred and sixty kilometres a day in 1850. The result of all these developments was the return to Great Britain of billions of pounds of profit. British investors ploughed much of this back into growing home industry as well as into foreign industrial development. London became the financial capital of the world, and by 1900 British overseas investment had reached two and one-half billion pounds.

Industrial Britain had been built by the middle class, whose prosperous members proudly boasted of their achievements. Prosperity was also beginning to trickle down to the lower classes as well, and between the Great Exhibition and the First World War, real wages doubled (by "real wages" is meant the actual purchasing power of income, measured in terms of goods and services, such as food, clothing, and housing, that can be bought). One reason for this advance was the steady rise of the productivity of labour. Another reason was the substantial reduction in the price of food that came after 1870, when improvements in the transportation and packaging of foreign foods enabled them to be sold more cheaply on the British market. Developments such as refrigerator ships, and even such a simple invention as the tin can, meant that perishable goods could be stored cheaply for long enough periods to be shipped to Britain. One of the results of these improvements was an amazing growth in population. England and Wales had grown from nine million in 1801 to twenty-one million in 1851, and by 1901 the figure had reached thirty-two million. These were statistics to which the middle class would point when attacks were made on the social consequences of the industrial system.

In the early 1870's, however, Britain saw its beautiful dream of unlimited industrial prosperity shattered. During the severe economic depression which dragged on intermittently between 1874 and 1896, British overseas markets began to decline. Having long held a great lead in industrial knowledge and production, British industrialists relaxed and failed to open adequate new markets. German and American companies, using aggressive salesmanship and offering products manufactured with British techniques and methods, began to compete in world markets. Foreign manufacturers, themselves protected by rapidly rising tariff barriers, were even underselling their British counterparts in Great Britain itself. When German pencils were found on the desks of Members of Parliament, Englishmen began to realize how stiff the competition had become.

Agriculture, too, began to decline. British farmers, unprotected since the repeal of the Corn Laws, finally felt the pressure of foreign competition. Ironically, the very improvements that made cheaper foreign agricultural goods available to the working class, now were instrumental in causing the decline of the British rural class. European and American competitors, using the railroad and shipping system that in many cases had been built and financed by Britons, began to acquire an increasingly large share of the British market. Eventually British farmers followed industrialists in releasing more and more workers from their jobs. By the end of the century, Britain's world supremacy in trade and industry had slipped away.

2. SOCIAL REFORM

Despite the unquestioned progress made by the working class, it was still this section of the population that suffered most severely during periods of economic decline. Low wages and recurring unemployment were an inescapable part of life. The rapidly increasing population was still shifting from the rural areas to the great cities, mushrooming up around the northern coalfields. At mid-century, one out of every two Britons lived in cities and towns; fifty years later, urban areas held three out of every four. Throughout most of the 19th century, city life meant poor housing, inadequate sanitation, and wretched poverty. One of the most reliable measuring sticks of social well-being, the infant death rate, actually *rose* in urban centres between 1858 and 1902. As a modern historian has observed, "the stagnant mass of poverty at the bottom of the social pyramid remained nearly as stagnant and as nauseous as before." As late as 1901, a committee revealed that in the city of York more than forty per cent of the working class did not earn enough to meet their bare physical needs. Other committees found similar results throughout Great Britain.

Nevertheless, in the second half of the 19th century progress began, slowly, very slowly, but surely, towards improving the living conditions of the working class. The growth of trade unions, the effects of the first sanitation improvements, the gradual extending of popular education, all were causes.

Despite the rigid insistence of the middle class on the virtue of *laissez-faire* economic policy, British politicians listened to the

ARE YOU READY TO DIE? "A hush pervades the hall of the (Salvation Army) in Whitechapel, wherein the destitute sit till bed time. Pinched, white, forlorn faces defiantly regard unwelcome intruders upon their misery. Late comers, finding the place full, beg very hard to lie on the forms in the hall until morning. Those who can afford it have the luxury of a penny supper, after which they wait for prayers . . ."

widespread demands for reform. The Factory and Workshops Act (1878) fixed a minimum working age at ten, and limited female factory workers to a sixty-hour week. By the turn of the century the minimum age was raised to twelve. However, no attempt to limit the length of a working day for men was made until 1908, when miners were prevented from working more than eight hours daily. The long delay in passing such legislation applicable to adult males reflected the *laissez-faire* outlook that measures should be taken to protect only those who were helpless, i.e. children and women; men, it was assumed, should look after themselves. For similar reasons it was not until 1896 that the first Workmen's Compensation Act was passed to provide payment to workers injured on their jobs.

The old evil of inadequate public sanitation and industrial slums also came under attack. In 1871 and 1875, public health acts were passed, which enabled each municipality to appoint a medical health officer and to regulate water, sewage, and disease control. Public housing acts were passed in 1875 and 1879 to give municipalities the authority to destroy slum dwellings and construct living quarters to house the poor.

In the field of public education, Forster's Education Bill of 1870 was a milestone, which remedied a chaotic situation. Until then, approximately one-half of the four million school age children had been unprovided for. Under the terms of the Bill, grants were made to the existing Church-operated, elementary schools, and in areas where there were no schools, public boards were formed and grants offered for the establishment of non-religious schools. Attendance was made compulsory in 1876 when the leaving age was set at fourteen. However, schools were not free until 1891, although the state paid the fees of poor children unable to afford them. Public secondary schools were created in 1902 with the passage of Balfour's Education Act, and attendance was finally made compulsory and free up to age fifteen, by Butler's Act of 1944. It should be noted that the Scottish educational system, long considered one of the finest in Europe, had provided free, compulsory education much earlier than the English.

Reform through what we now call welfare legislation had been carried out under both Liberal and Conservative ministries during the 1870's. More comprehensive and enduring legislation was not passed until the 20th century, in the last Liberal ministry in English history (1906-16).

3. THE DEVELOPMENT OF THE PARTY SYSTEM

Although it was certainly not apparent at the time, the passage of the First Reform Bill in 1832[1] was the beginning of the end for the two traditional English parties—the Whigs and the Tories. After 1832, political power began moving slowly but surely to the middle class, and away from the aristocracy. In the rapidly expanding new cities especially, where all tax-payers above a certain level became equal in their power to vote, a party more concerned with maintaining the special privileges of the landowning class than in providing

[1]See pp. 272-273.

"I am bound to furnish my antagonists with arguments but not with comprehension."—*Benjamin Disraeli*

facilities for education or sanitation, was not likely to receive widespread support. Particularly the Tories, who more than the Whigs were the party of privilege, suffered from the changing base of political power. Then, fourteen years later, the Tories suffered another blow when their leader, Sir Robert Peel, backed by the Whigs, supported the repeal of the Corn Laws. This decisive blow against the landholders was too great a strain for the old Tory party, and following Benjamin Disraeli, most of them renounced their leader. For the following two decades there were four major political groupings in British politics: protectionist Tories; Peelites (free trade Tories); Radicals (a small but influential body of manufacturers and intellectuals such as John Bright, Richard Cobden, and John Stuart Mill) and Whigs. The last three groups gradually merged during this period to form the Liberal Party, while the

"But you will deceive yourself if you think you have any real conception of Mr. Gladstone's genius till you sit beneath him or beside him, till that voice speaks to you, till you look into the face of the orator, till you feel the influence of a personality as persuasive as it is powerful; till, in one word, you are in his presence and subject to his sway."—*George Smalley*, LONDON LETTERS, 1890

Tories (who changed their name to the less reactionary-sounding "Conservatives"), spent these years in the political wilderness.

With party structure so confused and regrouping constantly taking place, leadership in the House of Commons fell to individuals whose personality and force of character could command respect. Outstanding among mid-Victorian politicians was the Liberal, Viscount Palmerston, who became Foreign Secretary in 1830 and then Prime Minister in 1855. A brash and outspoken champion of British nationalism, Palmerston's chief interest was Britain's position in world affairs.

By the mid-1860's, the two-party system gradually returned to British politics. For three decades following the death of Palmerston in 1865, the political scene was dominated by the epic struggle waged between the two titans of the era—Disraeli and Gladstone.

Benjamin Disraeli was the son of a Jewish man of letters who had his son baptized a Christian. Although prejudices dogged him all his life, his charm and personality carried him to the top of the

Conservative Party which he entered in 1837, after a brief flirtation with the Radicals. A romantic novelist who dressed flamboyantly, he gained a deserved reputation for his skill in debate. He had an acid wit which he used effectively both in the House of Commons and during private conversation. Once asked to define the difference between a misfortune and a calamity, he replied: "It would be a misfortune if Mr. Gladstone fell into the Thames. It would be a calamity if somebody pulled him out." Although he enacted important social welfare legislation, he devoted most of his energies to foreign affairs. Affectionately known as "Dizzy," he was Prime Minister briefly in 1868 and then from 1874 to 1880.

William Ewart Gladstone was in many ways the direct opposite of Disraeli. The son of a prosperous businessman, he entered politics in 1833 as a Tory. A deeply religious man, he regarded politics as a branch of morality. Although he lacked Disraeli's cleverness in debate, he was the greatest orator of his day. As Prime Minister for four terms (1868-74; 1880-85; 1886; 1892-94), he was the "G.O.M." (Grand Old Man) and was always referred to respectfully as Mister Gladstone.

Political Reforms

Between 1875 and 1894 the scene of British politics was virtually transformed. The most urgent task that required action at the beginning of the period was the extension of the franchise beyond the relatively narrow limits that had been set down by the Reform Bill of 1832.

Prior to 1865, one of the great obstacles to reform was the attitude of Palmerston himself. Although a liberal in foreign affairs —he was constantly concerned with European nationalities struggling for freedom, and actively aided the Italian bid for unification —in domestic affairs he was strongly opposed to progress. The extension of the franchise in 1832, he believed, had been daring enough. Shortly before his death in 1865 he confided to a young Member of Parliament on this subject of domestic legislation that "there is really nothing to be done. We cannot go on adding to the Statute Book *ad infinitum.*"

Palmerston's attitude to reform had destroyed several mild attempts by his more liberal colleagues to make electoral changes during the 1850's. By the time of his death, the demand for electoral reform had become urgent. Industrial growth throughout the country had exaggerated the anomalies remaining from the First Reform Bill of 1832. Only one man in six possessed the vote; the working class was virtually excluded from the franchise. The mood of the people throughout the country was aroused by what was now recognized as a gross injustice. In the north, John Bright was stirring working men almost to a fury, and in London there were signs of mob action.

Palmerston was succeeded as Prime Minister by Lord Russell, who in turn made Gladstone leader of the House of Commons. In 1866, Gladstone introduced a reform bill so weakly moderate as to infuriate Bright and the radical liberals. But *any* electoral reform apparently was unacceptable to the more conservative members of the Liberal Party, who bolted to the Conservative side. As a result, the reform bill was defeated. Russell and Gladstone resigned, and the Liberals were out of office.

The new government was formed by the Conservatives, with Lord Derby the Prime Minister and Benjamin Disraeli the leader of the House of Commons. Queen Victoria, alarmed at the growing unrest that was now evident everywhere, put pressure on Derby and Disraeli to pass a new electoral reform bill. Disraeli—who while in Opposition had staunchly opposed the Liberal reforms as a "leap in the dark"—promptly introduced and passed the Second Reform Bill in 1867, which was far more radical and progressive than the bill which had caused the Liberal defeat a year before.

In rural counties, all residents of houses rated at twelve pounds or more and all leaseholders with property valued at four pounds annually received a vote. In the boroughs the franchise was extended to all householders who, as owners or tenants, had lived in the borough for twelve months, and to all lodgers who paid ten pounds annual rent. In addition, forty-five seats were redistributed. The result was to give the vote to the middle class in the counties and to most skilled workmen in the boroughs. The electorate was approximately doubled, from roughly one million to two million voters.

The passage of the Second Reform Bill opened the door to a series of further political reforms. One such reform was the Ballot

Act of 1872, which virtually eliminated bribery, since the voter no longer needed to make public his political choice. In 1884, Gladstone's ministry passed the Third Reform Bill, which had the effect of granting the vote to agricultural workers. This was followed in 1885 with a redistribution of seats. Not until 1918, however, were all resident and property qualifications removed, and in that same year, for the first time, women over thirty were allowed to vote. Finally, in 1928, all men and women over twenty-one obtained the franchise.

The Irish Home Rule Bill

In 1881 Disraeli died. With no one of comparable stature to take his place, and Gladstone's popularity still strong, the Conservatives appeared to be headed for another string of politically lean years. Then in 1886, Gladstone made his fateful decision to introduce a Home Rule Bill for Ireland. Among other effects, this resulted in the Liberals' exclusion from power for seventeen of the following twenty years. It also brought to a head the most emotional issue of 19th century British politics, the problem of home rule for Ireland.

Gladstone was genuinely concerned with helping the Irish peasant class. The first step towards this end was the disestablishment of the Church of Ireland in 1869, and the redistribution of much of the Church's endowment to schools and charitable institutions. Then, in 1870 and 1881, the Irish Land Acts were passed, which contained a number of measures to alleviate the most extreme forms of distress suffered by the peasants, notably rack-renting by absentee (English) landlords, and eviction without compensation for improvements by the tenants. By this point, however, the Irish problem had become greatly complicated by the rapid growth of the "Home Rule for Ireland Party," which was dedicated to the establishment of an Irish government. The dominant figure soon became Charles Stewart Parnell, a brilliant orator consumed by hatred for England. The leader of a small group of Irish members in the British House of Commons, Parnell tried to focus attention on the Irish problem by obstruction tactics in the House, and succeeded in almost paralysing the functioning of government. Gladstone had hoped that the Land Act of 1881 might have an ameliorating effect on the Irish opposition, but was soon disillusioned when Parnell denounced the Act as a fraud. Gladstone then had Parnell imprisoned, and suspended civil liberties in Ireland. Not surprisingly, this made matters worse; resistance stiffened throughout Ireland, and almost fifty thousand soldiers and policemen were required to maintain order.

In 1886—"the most exciting year in the annals of nineteenth century England with the possible exception of 1832"—the affair reached its climax. A "Home Rule for Ireland" Bill was introduced which, by establishing an Irish Parliament in Dublin, would have brought the United Kingdom to an end as a legal entity. So bitter was the controversy that the Liberal Party was permanently split between those in favour and those opposed to Home Rule. Led by Joseph Chamberlain, a rising Liberal who saw the Bill as a step towards breaking away a piece of the Empire, a group called the Liberal Unionists left the Party. Their departure defeated the Bill and brought down Gladstone's ministry. Again, in 1893, Gladstone brought in another Home Rule Bill only to have it defeated this time by the House of Lords. Somewhat surprisingly, the turbulence of the Irish political scene subsided. The policy of "Killing Home Rule with Kindness" seemed to be succeeding. Two decades later it was apparent that the success had been an illusion. For the moment, however, the home rule problem ceased to be a pressing issue.

In 1895, the Liberal Unionists fused with the Conservatives, and for ten years the Conservatives held power. During this period of Conservative control the main interest was focused on international relations and colonial affairs. Chamberlain, as Colonial Secretary, gradually won over some of his new party colleagues to his scheme for Imperial Federation and a return to a protective tariff. The result, however, was an open break between Chamberlain and the Conservative Prime Minister, Arthur Balfour. The Conservatives were divided into three warring factions, and left helpless in the face of a resurgent Liberal Party under the leadership of Henry Campbell-Bannerman. In the election of 1906, the Liberals received the greatest majority in their history. Once again Chamberlain's policy had destroyed his party.

4. UNIONS, SOCIALISM, AND THE LABOUR PARTY

Despite their great election victory, despite the exceptional talent in their cabinet, despite the disarray within the ranks of the Conservatives, the Liberals were facing for the first time a serious new political challenge. This was the first British party organized specifically to appeal to, and represent, the workingman—the Labour Party.

The Labour Party was in a sense the combined product of two heritages, the first a series of labour struggles dating back half a century, and the second, a peculiarly British tradition of political thought that developed in the 1880's. Following the collapse of Robert Owens's short-lived Grand National Consolidated Trades Union in 1837, and the failure of the Chartists, the union movement finally gained a foothold in 1851[1], when the first enduring union was formed. This was the Amalgamated Society of Engineers, an organization comprising only skilled workers. Other skilled workers, inspired by the success of the engineers, soon followed their example. These new unions were formed by men dismayed by their inability to achieve parliamentary reform and aware that good times and higher profits made employers more pliable. In 1868 several of the unions met to form the Trades Union Congress, an organization designed to eventually represent all craft unions in England.

Unions and politics had always been related. One year after its formation, the Trades Union Congress established a Parliamentary Committee to encourage workingmen to interest themselves in political matters and to agitate for legislation to benefit unions. However, repeated efforts by socialists to have the Committee endorse their aims, such as nationalization of industry, were constantly defeated. Labour fell back on its practice of bargaining with the Liberal or Conservative parties and the Radicals to achieve its aims.

As prosperity increased, so did the number and influence of trade unions. Both the Liberal and Conservative parties became more aware of the need to cater to the demands of workingmen. This became more essential after the passage of the Second Reform Act in 1867, which gave the vote to most skilled labourers in English

[1] See Chapter 11.

towns and boroughs. In 1871, unions were given the right to be recognized as "legally constituted friendly and benefit societies." Five years later they were at last given real strength when Disraeli passed legislation permitting strikes. A new dimension was added to the union movement when non-skilled or industrial unions were formed. Even women's trade unions came into existence. An official from an industrial union wrote the Women's Trade Union League in 1889, saying, ". . . please send an organizer to this town as we have decided that if women here cannot be organized, they must be exterminated."

The first great victory for industrial unionism came in 1889, when the London dock workers went on strike for a minimum wage of sixpence an hour. The strike, which completely halted all shipping in the world's largest port, was extremely successful. The victory was a tremendous incentive to unskilled labour to join the ranks of the unions.

The Socialists

The unions and the working class had by this point reached a stage of *economic* power which, when exploited efficiently through an astute application of politics, would translate into enormous *political* power. It was the role of the socialist intellectuals to develop the ideas and guidelines by which this translation could be realized.

Socialism was still virtually unknown to British workingmen in the 1860's, even though its great intellectual leader, Karl Marx, had lived for years in London. The first important socialist organization, the Social Democratic Federation, was formed in 1884 by a wealthy, disillusioned Tory, H. M. Hyndman. Known as "the socialist in the top hat," Hyndman had been strongly influenced by Marx's *Das Kapital*. The Federation, which aimed at the nationalization of land and all means of production, exchange, and distribution, was a failure as a practical political party, yet it served to bring socialist ideas before the public.

One year earlier, another collectivist organization, the Fabian Society, made its appearance. At first the Fabians included among their members radicals, anarchists, and revolutionaries, but soon these began to drop out, and a core of progressive young intellectuals dominated the movement. These included historians Sydney

...e Webb, the dramatist George Bernard Shaw, and the ... G. Wells. Taking their name from *Fabius Cunctator*, ... general who chose delaying tactics rather than attack, ...ed a political program based on "the inevitability of ... ..." Their aims, which were continually explained in an endless stream of pamphlets, stressed the nationalization of land. Unlike many socialists they believed in compensation for landowners in cases where property would be expropriated by the state. They endorsed parliamentary methods, and, because socialism was in their opinion inevitable, they urged a cautious and gradual development. In the following passage, Sydney Webb explained how society, while still proclaiming the virtues of individualism and *laissez-faire,* was being slowly surrounded by socialistic practices:

The practical man, oblivious or contemptuous of any theory ... or general principles of social organization, has been forced ... into an ever-deepening collectivist channel. Socialism, of course, he still rejects and despises. The individualist town councillor will walk along the municipal pavement, lit by municipal light and cleansed by municipal brooms with municipal water, and seeing by the municipal clock in the municipal market, that he is too early to meet his children coming from the municipal school, hard by the county lunatic asylum and the municipal hospital, will use the national telegraph system to tell them not to walk through the municipal park, but to come by the municipal reading room, by the municipal museum, art gallery, and library, where he intends to consult some of the national publications in order to prepare his next speech, in the municipal hall in favour of the nationalization of canals and the increase of government control over the railway system. "Socialism, Sir," he will say, "don't waste the time of a practical man by your fantastic absurdities. Self-help, Sir, individual self-help, that's what has made our city what it is."

Particularly, the Fabians concentrated their writings and practical effort on the introduction of their ideas at the municipal level. There were many successful examples of socialist innovation in British cities that were inspired by Fabian ideas.

The pioneer effort in direct political participation was made by Keir Hardie, a Scottish trade unionist who won a seat in Parliament in 1892. Hardie, the first avowed socialist to enter Parliament, raised the eyebrows of many a "gentleman" member when he took his seat, his rough tweed miner's cap in his hand. In the following year he formed the Independent Labour Party with a program similar to the Social Democratic Federation and the Fabian Society.

The Labour Party

In 1900 representatives from the Trades Union Congress, the Independent Labour Party, the Social Democratic Federation and the Fabian Society held a meeting to try to bring together the growing but divided forces of socialism. The historic meeting produced the Labour Representation Committee. Designed to encourage trade union backing for candidates willing to support the interests of Labour, the Committee encountered organizational problems too great to allow them to be effective in the election of 1900, in which only two of their candidates were elected.

The future of the Committee was dramatically altered by the famous Taff Vale decision of 1901. The courts ordered the Amalgamated Society of Railway Servants to pay the owners of the Taff Vale Railway Company twenty-three thousand pounds to compensate them for loss of income during a strike. This decision meant that unions were deprived of effective strike action; the result was an immediate surge of support for the Committee. In the election of 1906, twenty-nine candidates were elected. After the election, the members changed their name to the Labour Party. The new Labour Party supported Campbell-Bannerman and the Liberals in Parliament; as a reward for their support, the Taff Vale decision was reversed by the Trades Disputes Act passed by the Liberal government in 1906. In 1913 the Trades Union Act allowed unions to deduct fees from willing members for the support of a political party. The Labour Party continued to increase its representation in Parliament and in 1924 formed its first (albeit brief) government.

Other acts passed by the reforming Liberal government between 1906 and 1914 indicate clearly how thoroughly the basic tenets of *laissez-faire* had been abandoned. The Old Age Pension Act (1908) gave every man and woman over seventy who earned less than ten shillings a week, a weekly pension of five shillings. A new Workmen's Compensation Act, an improvement on the original Act of a decade earlier, gave added protection to the workingman. In 1911 the National Health Insurance Act gave free medical treatment to anyone earning less than one hundred pounds sterling annually, and in the same year an unemployment insurance fund was established.

The Peaceful Revolution

Great Britain was the only European nation where the marriage between socialism and unionism had been so complete. As a result, British workers were often better protected by welfare legislation than were their counterparts on the Continent.

Great social changes can seldom be made, however, without complicated reactions and results. One result of the welfare legislation was a great increase in government expenditure, which, combined with the sharply rising costs of maintaining naval supremacy,[1] left the existing sources of tax revenue completely inadequate. In 1909, the Liberals decided to make a radical change in their approach to taxation by shifting the heaviest tax burden from the *producers* of wealth to the *possessors* of wealth. To this end, taxes were levied on income, especially unearned income, with a "supertax" on high income, and a further tax on inheritances. In addition, a twenty per cent tax was applied on increases in land value, with a special tax on unimproved rural property that was aimed at breaking up privately owned parks and hunting reserves.

Not surprisingly, the landowning upper class was appalled. Since this group dominated the House of Lords, the budget was thrown out when it came to the second chamber for passage, in 1910.

The Lords' rejection of the budget raised a serious constitutional question. In a democratic age, could they turn down a bill passed by representatives of the majority of Britons? It was even more doubtful if they had the right to interfere with a bill involving money, a matter recognized for centuries as the prerogative of the Commons. Many Liberals, such as the outspoken David Lloyd George, Chancellor of the Exchequer, felt that this was the moment to test the power of the Lords, and an election was called on the issue of the budget. The Liberals lost seats, but the Labourites and Irish Nationalists were (for different reasons) prepared to support them.

Finally, the Lords accepted the budget. Immediately, the Liberals introduced the Parliament Bill, which was designed to limit and

[1]See Chapter 16.

contest the power of the Upper House. Recognizing the threat to their power, the Lords immediately rejected the Bill, and made it clear that they were prepared to fight to the end. Prime Minister Asquith[1] called another election for December, 1910. Again the Liberals emerged with a minority government supported by the Labourites and Irish Nationalists. The Lords' insistence on continued rejection of the Bill in the face of hostile public opinion, forced Asquith to ask George V to agree to create enough peers favourable to the Parliament Bill, so that a favourable majority could be reached in the Upper House. It was 1832 all over again. Finally, rather than face defeat, the die-hard Lords or "ditchers" failed to appear when the vote was taken. In 1911 the Parliament Bill became law.

The Parliament Act provided that the Lords could never again amend money bills. In addition, *any* bill passed on three separate occasions by the Commons would automatically become law. Finally, the life of Parliament was reduced from seven to five years. The last vestige of aristocratic power had been removed.

The Politics of Violence

The constitutional crisis was only one of the problems facing the government in the first years of the 20th century. The death of Queen Victoria in 1901 marked the close of an era in which the atmosphere and mood were already changing. There was now an increasing willingness to use force and violence to attain ends, as opposed to the old reliance on persuasion and debate. The calm of Victorian England was giving way to the turbulence of the Edwardian era.

Three particular problems dominated the British political scene. The first was the question of women's voting rights. Determined not to be denied the same political rights as men, a number of militant "suffragettes", as they became known, began to force the government to acknowledge their demands. Organizations were formed, such as the Women's Social and Political Union, created in 1903 and led by Mrs. Emmeline Pankhurst. When their petitions and peaceful demonstrations failed to achieve their purpose, the suffragettes turned to violence. They broke into political meetings, defaced public buildings, organized hunger strikes, and chained themselves

---

[1] Successor to Campbell-Bannerman, who died in 1908.

Arrested suffragette being led away after an attack on Buckingham Palace, May, 1914.

to railings. Before they finally gained part of their demands in 1918, they had shocked the British public by their willingness to use force.

The second source of difficulty was the aggressive labour movement, which had been given new stimulus by the success of the recently formed Labour Party. The first decade of the century saw prices rising faster than wages. Labour, anxious to close the gap between the two, became more violent in its demands. In 1911-1912 an epidemic of strikes by transport workers, railway workers, and miners virtually paralysed the country. It was the first time in Britain that strikes had been nation-wide; at one point one and a half million men were on strike, requiring government action to keep order.

The third difficulty was that most vexatious of British problems, the Irish Home Rule question. After the 1910 elections, the Liberals no longer had a clear majority in the House of Commons, and were

A scene in Dublin during the "Easter Rising." April 24-August 1, 1916.

compelled to seek the support of the approximately eighty-six Irish Nationalist M.P.s in order to control the government. This support was bought at the price of passing a third Home Rule Bill,[1] which accordingly was introduced in 1912. The political problems presented by such a course, however, were formidable. So uncompromising were the Irish Nationalists in their demand for the Bill, and so adamant the English traditionalists and imperialists in their opposition, that any attempted solution was certain to be resented bitterly by one group or the other. A complicating factor was that within Ireland, one province, Ulster, was utterly opposed to Home Rule, and did not hesitate to exploit English suspicions and misgivings to keep opposition burning at a fever pitch. And as a further complication, within Ulster itself there were sharp divisions, with the anti-Home Rule Protestants outweighing the nationalist Catholics by only a small margin. It was a problem as complicated and confused—and as insoluble—as the racial dilemma in the Austro-Hungarian Empire. By the summer of 1914 both sides had their own uniformed armies that paraded belligerently, armed to the teeth. Had not the fires already sweeping across the Balkans sucked

---

[1] The first two Home Rule Bills had been submitted in 1886 and 1893 and were both defeated; see pp. 356-357.

On strike.

all of Europe into the World War, it is probable that civil war would have begun in Ireland.

The Home Rule Bill was passed in 1914, but with the outbreak of the First World War was suspended. The Easter Rebellion in Dublin in 1916 ensured that the atmosphere of non-compromise would not be relaxed. By 1920, open conflict between Irish and British forces (the "Black-and-Tans") was raging, marked by fierce reprisals and counter-reprisals by both sides, particularly the British. In 1921, the southern counties separated from Great Britain to form the Irish Free State. Finally, in 1949, Ireland severed her last ties with the Commonwealth and became the Republic of Eire. Ulster remained as an integral part of the United Kingdom. Even today, the problems that arose from the Home Rule issue still remain to vex both Britain and Ireland.

5. IMPERIALISM

Between 1815 and 1914, Great Britain was not involved in any major military conflict in Europe. The only wars, the Crimean (1854-56) and the Boer (1899-1902), were waged to protect or extend her imperial possessions. The major aim of British foreign policy was to preserve peace through an international balance of power. She was prepared to ally herself with any weak Power in Europe threatened by a hostile and aggressive neighbour whose intention was to dominate the Continent. This had been her policy at the height of Napoleon's power in Europe and so it remained until the beginning of the 20th century, when continued isolation from European affairs appeared to be dangerous. The second aim of her foreign policy was to protect the trade routes to her colonial possessions. It was for this reason that Britain became involved in the Crimean War, coming to the support of the Ottoman Turks against Russia. Russian control of Turkey, it was feared, could threaten India and the Mediterranean.

Britain's attitude towards colonial possessions went through several distinct phases. In the early stages of discovery and exploration, colonies were regarded almost as the hallmark of national prestige and power. Then, as Britain began establishing her enormous lead in manufacturing and export, and the principle of free trade became a general policy, colonies became less highly prized possessions. Among the many Britons who discussed the question of empire, even Lord Palmerston, champion of British international prestige, showed little interest in colonies. At a time when he had searched unsuccessfully for a Colonial Secretary to complete a new cabinet, he was forced to tell his aide: "I suppose I must take the thing myself. We will look at the maps and you shall show me where these places are." And Disraeli's famous statement that the colonies were a "millstone around the neck of England"—although it would later haunt him—did reflect popular opinion at mid-century. Colonies had to be defended at a cost to the taxpayer, and if, as with the Thirteen Colonies, they would eventually seek independence, why delay the inevitable? Moreover, the vast European markets opened to English manufacturers by free trade policies made colonial markets insignificant. The celebrated trade treaty with Napoleon III arranged by Cobden in 1860, allowing for reciprocal exchange of a specified list of commodities, was proof that former enemies provided more economic security than one's own kith and kin throughout the Empire. The argument against colonies was strong enough to allow the granting of responsible government to the British North American colonies in the 1840's, and to those in Australia and in New Zealand in the following decade.

The one major exception to this pattern was India. There, a severe revolt breaking out in 1857 among native Indian troops took two years to be quelled. The result of the Indian Mutiny was the end of the long reign over the great sub-continent by the East India Company, and the beginning of direct rule over India by the British government. Tradition, Indian cotton, and the huge Indian market which brought tightened British control, proved the exception rather than the rule in the movement to break up the Empire.

The severe business depression of the 1870's, and the consequent decline in British markets, produced a dramatic alteration in the attitude toward colonies. With tariff walls being raised by all European nations and the United States, the colonial markets again became a somewhat less appealing but more hopeful alternative. Competition with foreign manufacturers also meant that raw materials were no longer available in quantity. Soon uncharted areas of Africa and Asia were being claimed by Europeans, since raw materials such as rubber, copper, tin, and lumber, as well as additional markets, were to be found in new colonies. Finally, the possesa vital result of the new imperialism made more vibrant by the support of public opinion. "We don't want to fight, but, by Jingo, if we do, we've got the men, we've got the ships, we've got the money, too!" In 1898 General Herbert Kitchener marched into the Sudan and, with Khartoum as his base, followed the rebels and defeated them in the great Battle of Omdurman. "Kitchener of Khartoum" became a national hero overnight.

In South Africa, British interests had been established since 1806, when the Cape Colony was captured during the Napoleonic Wars. The Dutch inhabitants of the area, called Boers, were embittered by the Emancipation Act of 1833 abolishing slavery. Resenting the loss of their slaves and the inadequate compensation offered, many of them began the "Great Trek" northward in 1836, which ended in the formation of the Transvaal Republic and the Orange Free State. In 1877, the British annexed the Transvaal as part of a plan to strengthen the white communities against the threat of attack by Bantu tribes. Three years later the Boers retaliated, and, after defeating British troops at the Battle of Majuba Hill (1881), secured from the British the re-establishment of the Transvaal Republic.

Relations between Boers and British, although not smooth, remained peaceful until gold was discovered at Witwatersrand in the Transvaal in 1886. Thousands of fortune-seekers from the Cape Colony, both Dutch and English-speaking, rushed into the area and soon were more numerous than the Boers. Although they soon owned half the land and had come as permanent residents, the Transvaal government refused them citizenship. Relations became tense. Then, in 1895, Cecil Rhodes, at that time Prime Minister of Cape Colony and a fervent British imperialist with dreams of British control from the Cape to Cairo, planned an ill-timed scheme. A group of armed volunteers led by Dr. Starr Jameson invaded the Transvaal in an unsuccessful attempt to overthrow the government. The results were unfortunate for Rhodes, as the British were easily captured.[1] Although Jameson and his followers were returned, negotiations broke down, and Jameson's Raid of 1895 eventually became the spark that set off the Boer War.

[1] Jameson's Raid also had important implications for international affairs which are discussed below. See pp. 388-389.

The treatment of the Boers—the British view and the foreign view. LEFT: the Boer is ill-temperedly rejecting the olive branch of peace offered by the (presumably pro-British) angel of peace. RIGHT: a French cartoon of a British concentration camp entitled "The proverbial gallantry of the English soldier."

The Boer War brought almost universal condemnation of Britain. The sight of the great British Empire at war with a small nation of farmers won Britain no new friends. Finally, in 1902, peace was arranged.

The International Implications of Colonization

Britain's suddenly-revived search for colonies in the 1870s and 1880s was intensified not only by the presence in the race of the old rival, France, but by the entrance of new competitors including Germany, Italy, Belgium, and even the United States. The course was the globe itself. Africa, which attracted British explorers such as Mungo Park and David Livingstone, was soon claimed and charted. Then South America, Asia, and even the polar areas attracted the imperial Powers. Trade and often religion followed the flag as missionaries entered into the heart of central Africa and on to the shores of China. The desperate scramble for new lands brought Europeans much closer together in the distant corners of the globe. Soon colonial claims, commercial rivalry, the arms race, and the alliance system would lead to an inevitable confrontation.

While Great Britain began to acquire new colonies, the movement toward independence was growing among her older possessions. In 1867 four of the British North American colonies were federated into the Dominion of Canada. In 1901, another federation, the Commonwealth of Australia, came into existence. In 1910, showing as much political wisdom as both sides had shown lack of it eleven years earlier, the British government generously created from Cape Colony, Natal, and the former Boer states, the Union of South Africa along lines suggested by Dr. Starr Jameson in 1906.

At a series of Imperial Conferences beginning in 1887, a new spirit of co-operation was being evolved between Britain and her colonies. Extensive schemes for an Imperial Federation proposed by Joseph Chamberlain in 1897 were rejected by the colonies as a backward step in their development. In 1907, the word "Dominion" was substituted for "colonies" to describe the new status of the self-governing nations. The British Commonwealth of Nations had begun its development.

By the middle of the 19th century England was approaching the peak of her Industrial Revolution. The great transformation in the methods of production of manufactured goods had been credited to the economic philosophy of *laissez-faire*. Free trade and growing industry were the keys used by the middle class to open the doors to social and political status in Victorian England.

As the century progressed, English industrial supremacy began to vanish, as declining markets caused cutbacks in industrial production, which brought a new problem and a new word to England —unemployment. Gradually political leaders recognized that the demands for reform would have to be met and slowly the middle-class Parliament began to introduce legislation to help the lower classes.

The economic decline of England produced two significant results: the revival of imperialism and the emergence of socialism. These two movements and the recurrent problem of a dissatisfied Ireland greatly altered the policies and fortunes of English political, economic, and constitutional life. In the dozen years which preceded the outbreak of the First World War, the optimism, even the self-assurance, of Victorian England, was shattered by the political and economic problems that beset English society.

After the war, the scene was profoundly changed, as new political and economic problems faced the people. One result was the demise of the Liberal Party, which dropped to third place in the election of 1924. Victims of their adherence to free trade and other outdated policies, they have not since been an electoral threat. Liberal England and the Liberal Party were victims of the age of violence.

16 The Background to the First World War

"If we are going to probe far back into history, it is no good asking, 'What factors caused the outbreak of war?' The question is rather, 'Why did the factors that had long preserved the peace of Europe fail to do so in 1914?' "
—A. J. P. Taylor

Few circumstances in modern history have aroused such heated debate as those which led to the outbreak of the First World War. At the end of the war, the Allies, swayed by hatred and eager for revenge, sought to place upon Germany and her allies the entire legal and moral responsibility for the conflict. Having fixed the blame, they felt justified in extorting oppressive reparations. The Germans, on the other hand, angered by the "war guilt lie" and convinced of the injustice of reparations, argued that all nations had been helpless victims of blind historic forces.

Socialists blamed the war on capitalists who reaped fat profits from the manufacture of arms, although socialist parties in Germany and France supported the war policies of their countries. Pacifists pointed to the influence of newspaper articles and books which glorified war. Economists, on the other hand, explained the conflict in terms of industrial and trade rivalry. They quoted statistics to illustrate the deadly competition for world markets, raw materials, and new fields for investment. Some historians point to nationalism and the crises it created as a prime cause, or to the existing system of competing alliances.

There is an element of truth in all these views, but historians have never been able to agree on the exact balance of factors, psychological and material, which provoked the disaster. From a detached viewpoint, over half a century later, two things appear certain: that the First World War had no single decisive cause, and that in this conflict, as in most disputes of the past, right did not lie wholly on one side. In all countries, the climate of opinion in 1914 was dangerously receptive to violence; in the final resort, there was no nation which was not willing to utilize war as an instrument of national policy.

1. THE UNDERLYING CAUSES OF THE WAR

Economic Rivalry

Among the basic factors which contributed to the outbreak of the First World War, none seems to be of more significance than the economic rivalry between Great Britain and Germany. Following the establishment of the German Empire in 1871, the Germans had developed their industrial power at a stupendous rate. Within three decades Germany was transformed from a largely rural economy into the most advanced industrial nation in Europe. By 1900, her heavy industry was producing as much iron and steel as Britain and by 1914 more than Britain and France combined.

Reaping the rewards of a system of education which gave a high priority to science, Germany leaped into world leadership in two vital new fields, the electrical and chemical industries. Her optical goods and her surgical and scientific instruments were acknowledged as second to none.

Part of the reason for this was that German industry had become more efficient than British, so that German businessmen could repeatedly undersell their British counterparts. Not only were German products replacing British in continental European markets, where Germany's central geographic position gave her a natural predominance, but the aggressive Germans were forcing their way into areas long considered by the British as their own political and economic preserves. In Asia, Africa, and the Americas, British manufacturers felt the hot breath of intense German competition. The magnitude of the German economic challenge became unmistakable when German finances and technology combined to begin construction of the Berlin to Baghdad railway through the Ottoman Empire, a Power buttressed by Great Britain throughout the 19th century and regarded as a British sphere of influence. The resulting rivalry was almost a commercial war. Although Britain in 1914 still held a narrow lead in the total value of exports, Germany was rapidly catching up.

There were many other examples of economic friction in the

period before the First World War. The French, who had lost the rich coal fields of Lorraine to Germany in 1871, were reduced to importing coal, and were understandably bitter at seeing German coal production increase nearly fourfold within thirty years. In the Balkans, Russia feared the establishment of an Austro-German trading monopoly, while Austria was equally afraid that Serbia, Bulgaria, and Greece would be drawn into the Russian economic orbit.

While the clash of economic interests did heighten European tensions, this can easily be exaggerated as a direct cause of the First World War. Trade competition of itself need not have led to armed conflict between the powers any more than had the intense competition for colonies in Africa during the 19th century. Economic interests tend to be too complex to run neatly parallel with diplomatic ties. A firm in Sheffield, England, for instance, found it profitable to sell to the Krupp armament works in Essen, Germany, machine tools which shortly after were used to manufacture guns for use against Britain. Only six months before the outbreak of hostilities the Anglo-Persian Oil Company, the main supplier of oil for the Royal Navy's most modern oil-burning ships, reached a private agreement with German companies which aimed at excluding Russian and American competitors from the Persian Gulf. If, in fact, war had broken out between Britain and Russia in 1914, instead of between Britain and Germany, it might have been explained almost as convincingly in economic terms.

The Arms Race

Closely paralleling the Anglo-German economic rivalry was the burgeoning arms race between the same two countries. To a not-inconsiderable degree, the blame for this development lies personally with the German king, Kaiser Wilhelm (William) II. William succeeded to the throne in 1888, at the age of thirty-one. A grandson of Queen Victoria and a nephew of King Edward VII, he had many admirable qualities. He had a quick and imaginative mind, a capacious memory, a high sense of duty, and an immense capacity for hard work. His interests were broad and his curiosity insatiable. Yet with all these good qualities William II's character contained certain fatal flaws which made him quite unfitted for power or statesmanship. In many respects he was childishly vain

Three views of Kaiser Wilhelm II. TOP: to the Dutch caricaturist Raemaekers, he is Falstaff. BOTTOM: on an Italian playing card, he is the "Prince of Swords." LEFT: as he actually appeared, "charming, impulsive, erratic, the sort of ruler many Germans wanted."

and arrogant. He would accept the most blatant flattery at face value; he loved to be the centre of attention; he would posture in absurd, theatrical-looking uniforms and, if piqued, he would indulge an ungovernable temper. Though to his closest companions he was often charming and vivacious, he could also be despicably malevolent and vindictive. But the quality which made William least fitted to be a statesman was a nervous excitability which clouded his analysis of men and events and frequently provoked him to rash and impulsive acts. And with the dismissal of Bismarck in 1890,[1] William was left completely without the steadying influence of an experienced statesman to moderate his sometimes erratic leadership. The combination of near-absolute power—the result of the constitutional weakness of the German Parliament—and William's unpredictable personality, was in itself a contributing cause of the war.

One of William's greatest ambitions was to establish his nation as a leader among the world's powers—to forge for Germany "a place in the sun." It soon became apparent that by this he meant challenging Great Britain's position of world leadership, not only in economic power, but in naval strength. This desire for naval strength was intensified by the influence of the "Mahan thesis,"[2] which argued that in a protracted struggle, "a sea-power must always choke off and ruin a power operating on land." For William, such a prospect was unacceptable. Boldly asserting that "Imperial might means sea power," he appointed Admiral Alfred von Tirpitz to head the Imperial Naval Office. Tirpitz, the ennobled son of a civil servant, was not only a brilliant organizer but also an intense Anglophobe. In a memorandum of 1907 he wrote: "This constant danger of war with England . . . will cease and even change into England's desire to befriend us only when our fleet is further strengthened." Backed by the forceful propaganda techniques of the German Navy League, his own creation, whose members echoed the Kaiser's slogan that "Our future lies on the seas," Tirpitz skilfully piloted through the Reichstag two Naval Laws (1898 and 1900). By the first years of the 20th century, the German navy, virtually non-existent before the 1890's, was second in size only to Great Britain's. A naval race had begun to develop,

[1] See p. 337.
[2] Named after Admiral Mahan, an American naval theorist.

The Naval Race		
Dreadnoughts	Great Britain	Germany
1906	1	—
1907	3	—
1908	2	4
1909	2	3
1910	3	1
1911	5	3
1912	3	2
1913	7	3
1914	3	1
total:	29	17

H.M.S. *Dreadnought*, the first of the super-battleships that upset the naval balance of power. At left, the table shows how Britain and Germany competed for supremacy.

and when the suddenly-aroused British accepted the challenge by constructing the super-battleship, the *Dreadnought*, in 1906, the gauntlet had been laid down. The German reaction to this ship, which rendered all others obsolete, was to attempt to match British ship-builders dreadnought for dreadnought.

The British criticized the German naval program as provocative. Germans were quick to respond to these British accusations. Did not Great Britain have a large navy? Was this not necessary to protect the life-line of the extensive British Empire? Germany, despite her late entry into the colonial scramble in the 1880's, had far-flung imperial possessions in Africa and Asia. She too must defend her Empire. Therefore she, too, required a navy, that could in no way be inferior to the British. Neither Power was prepared to back down until the other moved first, but neither was willing to move first. The ensuing naval race greatly heightened the tension that was partly responsible for the First World War.

Nationalism

Foremost among the underlying causes of the war was that troublesome state of mind called nationalism. At its best, nationalism may be simply a healthy love of one's country, an emotion which satisfies also a deeply felt human need for security and protection. The term "nationalism" may also, as we have seen, be used to describe an intense desire for independence and self-rule felt by people sharing the same language, the same customs and traditions, and in some cases the same religion. Too often, however, in pre-war Europe nationalism amongst powerful people gave rise to a bullying or domineering outlook; men and women wished to see their own nation become so strong as to be able to go its own way with utter disregard for neighbours. Too often, also, amongst weaker, less well-organized people, nationalism became—then as now—"an outlet for aggression, anxiety or a sense of inferiority."

It was only in retrospect, after the war had broken out, that the depth and danger of these unsatisfied national feelings became apparent. For several decades before the outbreak of the First World War there appeared to be an encouraging growth of internationalism, that is, of friendly co-operation between nations for the common good. There was a rapid increase in travel and the exchange of ideas; scholars and musicians from many countries studied in Germany or Austria; Paris became a mecca for the world's painters, and there were more friendly international conferences and contests than ever before. Meetings took place between labour leaders, suffragettes, doctors, architects, engineers, and theologians. The first Olympic Games of modern times took place in Athens in 1896. In 1895 the first of three Hague Conferences was called, at the instigation of Czar Nicholas II of Russia, to promote world peace. But all these, and many other well-intentioned efforts to promote international goodwill, proved ineffectual in the face of deeply-rooted and conflicting feelings of nationalism.

French Nationalism

A constant source of bitterness for French nationalists was the border territory of Alsace-Lorraine, which had been seized by Germany at the close of the Franco-Prussian war despite the fact that more than half the inhabitants of the region were French. Germany made a determined effort to assimilate the two provinces, discouraging the teaching of French in schools and forbidding the use of the French language for any official purpose. These clumsy measures served only to inflame the hatred which French nationalists felt for the German occupation. So intense were these feelings that one eminent politician declared there was no purpose for his generation to go on living "except to recover the two lost provinces." In Paris itself, from 1871 until the provinces were recovered forty-seven years later, the statue symbolizing the city of Strasbourg remained continuously draped in black.

German Nationalism

Yet whatever the bitterness of Frenchmen, the exultant nationalists of Germany would have gone to any lengths rather than surrender Alsace-Lorraine. The retention of the territory was deeply satisfying to German national feeling. Alsace-Lorraine represented not only the first conquest made by a new, united Germany but also the recovery of territory seized long before from the Holy Roman Empire by the armies of Louis XIV. Moreover, the region had great strategic and economic value. Militarily it safeguarded the Rhine; economically, with its fertile agricultural plain, its great city of Strasbourg, and its rich deposits of iron and coal, it gave thrust to Germany's industrial development.

One offshoot of German nationalism was the "Pan-German League," founded in 1891, which dreamed of a *Mittel-Europa,* dominated by Germany and incorporating all the Teutonic peoples of the Continent—the Austrians, the Flemings, the Luxemburgers, the Dutch, the Swiss, and the Danes. It aimed "to awaken and foster the sense of racial and cultural kinship of all sections of the German people" and "to further German interests in the entire world." It pressed for a stronger navy, the acquisition of overseas colonies, and even scholarships to enable the sons of Germans living in foreign countries to attend "schools in the Fatherland." Although its membership was not large, the Pan-German League, like the

Pan-Slavonic movement in Russia, exerted an influence out of proportion to its size. Its adherents included university professors, Reichstag deputies, and highly placed businessmen and civil servants. Among its more humble converts was a feckless and unemployed youth named Adolf Hitler.

Underlying German nationalism was the almost mystic belief, held by many middle and upper class Germans, that theirs was a superior race whose mission it was to impose Teutonic culture upon inferior nations. The writings of Hegel, Heinrich von Treitschke, and other philosophers and historians impressed upon the minds of many such Germans a militant, narrow patriotism, a reverence for the great state, and a respect for power politics. War, according to Treitschke, was "a radical medicine for the ills of the state."

Many Germans, disappointed with their nation's lean share of overseas colonies, and eager for Germany to occupy a larger place on the world stage, urged a *Drang Nach Osten* or thrust to the east. Some advocated colonization of the lower Danube valley and even of fertile and thinly-populated areas of Asia Minor and Mesopotamia. They saw Turkey as a ripe field for economic exploitation. Financial and economic control of the Ottoman Empire would, in turn, give to Germany control of the southern Balkans and the eastern Mediterranean. As early as 1881, German officers were sent to train and advise the Turkish army and, in a bid to bolster German status in Asia Minor, William II declared in 1898, "The three hundred million Mohammedans who live scattered over the globe may be assured of this, that the German Empire will be their friend at all times."

The following year the ambitions of the German Empire became still more alarmingly apparent with the announcement that a German company had received a concession to build a railway running from the Bosporous to the Persian Gulf. Since a rail line already linked Constantinople with Berlin, the so-called "Berlin-Baghdad railway" promised to open the way for further German political and commercial domination of the faltering Ottoman Empire.

These German ambitions in Asia Minor, however, the outcome of a restless and assertive nationalism, could only be realized at the expense of Russia and Britain. For Russia was determined, in the event of any dissolution of the Ottoman Empire, to gain control of

Constantinople and the western outlet of the Black Sea, and Britain was concerned about the security of her communications to the Far East.

Nationalism in Austria-Hungary

No state was more threatened by racial and nationalist passions than the cumbersome Dual Monarchy of Austria-Hungary. Within its borders lived nearly a dozen different races—Germans, Hungarians, Czechs, Poles, Slovaks, Romanians, Ruthenians, Italians, Serbs, Slovenes, Croats, and others—speaking over a dozen different languages. For long the German-speaking people of Austria had dominated the other races but in 1867, following their defeat by Prussia, the Austrians were forced to surrender authority in the eastern half of the Empire to the Hungarians. Austria and Hungary became two virtually separate states, each with its own capital, its own Parliament and its own official language. They remained linked by a common allegiance to the Hapsburg monarch—the Austrian Emperor being crowned also King of Hungary—and by joint foreign and financial ministries and a common army and navy. Tension continued between the two dominant races of the Empire, however, as the Hungarians pressed for a still greater degree of independence, with fewer commercial ties, and an end to the joint armed services.

Still greater tensions existed between the two dominating races of the Empire and the large, restless minority groups. In the western Empire, twelve million German-speaking Austrians faced their greatest challenge from the Czechs and Slovaks, ambitious and hard-working peoples numbering eight and a half million. They also had to contend with the nationalist aspirations of several million fiercely patriotic Poles and with large Italian majorities in the two southern provinces of Trentino and the Tyrol.

In the eastern half of the Empire, the agitation for self-government grew stronger each year, for the proudly nationalistic Hungarians, forming barely fifty per cent of the population, ruled their subject races with much more severity than the Austrians. Their attitude was clearly summed up by the words of a Hungarian Premier to a German-speaking Chancellor of Austria: "You look after your barbarians and we will look after ours."

Ruthless steps were taken in Hungary to suppress the nationalist yearnings of millions of Romanians, Slovaks, Croats and Serbs. Voting was limited to those able to speak the Hungarian (Magyar) language, and the minority groups had far less than their rightful share of representatives in the national Parliament, or Diet. Such minority representatives as were elected reduced assemblies to "a racial pandemonium." There was every likelihood, in fact, that the Austro-Hungarian Empire would be torn apart by secessions.

The most immediate danger lay with some seven million Croats and Slovenes who inhabited the southernmost province of Austria-Hungary. These peoples were closely related in their language, customs, and traditions, both to each other and to the Serbs who lived just beyond the frontiers to the south. The Serbs, Croats, and Slovenes thought of themselves collectively as Southern Slavs—or Yugoslavs—and nurtured one other common bond—an intense hatred for the Hungarians. So long as the Serbians had been an oppressed minority within the Turkish Empire, the Croats and the Slovenes had remained devoted to the Hapsburg monarchy and, for generations, had fought bravely in the armies of Austria. In 1878, however, Turkey reluctantly gave full independence to Serbia, and almost overnight this rugged little kingdom became the champion of all the Slavonic peoples of the Balkans. It aspired to unite in one Yugoslav kingdom not only all the Croats and Slovenes within the Hapsburg Empire, but also those Slavs still under Turkish rule in the adjoining provinces of Bosnia and Herzegovina. These two provinces would also give to a greatly enlarged Serbia valuable access to the Adriatic Sea.

Thus, although relatively insignificant in area and population, the Kingdom of Serbia with its grandiose ambitions came to be regarded by Austria-Hungary as a deadly enemy. Serbia's very existence served to inflame the restless nationalism of millions of Slavs dwelling within the Hapsburg Empire. Yet Austria feared, with good reason, that if the Slavs were allowed to secede from the Empire to join Serbia, there would be no holding the nationalist passions of millions of their other subjects in the central and northern areas. The Austrian Empire, already divided, would probably break up.

In 1903 Austria's apprehensions were temporarily reduced when a group of Serbian army officers, members of a secret nationalist organization called the Black Hand, burst into the Royal Palace and murdered the Serbian king and queen. The dead monarch,

sion of an empire came to be a status symbol among modern industrial nations. Almost overnight, England found herself in the insane race for new territories, whose course was to lead eventually to war.

Probably the starting point in the revival of imperialism in Great Britain was Disraeli's brilliant purchase of shares in the Suez Canal Company in 1875. The Khedive of Egypt, always in debt, offered for sale his portion of ownership in the Company. Disraeli, without parliamentary approval, secured a loan of four million pounds from the great banking house of Rothschild and bought out the Khedive, whose shares amounted to forty-four per cent of control. Then he wrote to Queen Victoria: "It is just settled; you have it, Madam." Disraeli identified the Conservatives with being the foremost defenders of the Empire. In 1876 he proclaimed Victoria Empress of India. Two years later he went to the Congress of Berlin which followed the brief Russo-Turkish War (1877-78). In a pre-arranged deal with the Turks, he pledged renewed British support for the "sick man of Europe." Then he announced to the Congress that in return Great Britain had obtained the island of Cyprus from Turkey. Returning home in triumph, he announced that he had brought "peace with honour." Without a shot being fired, Great Britain had gained another strategic Mediterranean base on the route to India via the Suez Canal. This inexpensive brand of imperialism appealed to the business-oriented Englishmen.

British expansion overseas now began accelerating to a whirlwind pace. In Asia, British New Guinea, North Borneo, and Upper Burma were claimed. But the most attractive area was Africa, where Britain established interests in both the northern and the southern parts of the continent. In 1883, Egypt was made a British protectorate. British attention was next drawn to the Sudan, where a rebellion against Egyptian rule was in progress, led by the militant religious fanatic the *Mahdi*. General Gordon, a former governor-general of the Sudan in Egyptian service, was sent to withdraw the Egyptian garrison and civilian officials. He was trapped in Khartoum by the *Mahdi's* army, and when the city fell after a short siege, was murdered. The Liberal government in Britain felt the overpowering wrath of an almost hysterical public, who charged that Gladstone had failed to send British troops in time to rescue Gordon. This feeling of intense patriotism, called "jingoism," became

Alexander, was known to be conservative and pro-Russian. His successor, King Peter, a gentle and scholarly man, was thought to be, if not pro-Austrian, at least neutral, and Austria gave him prompt recognition. It soon became apparent, however, that the new king of Serbia was no more than a puppet in the control of the unprincipled Black Hand and of the fiercely nationalistic Radical Party. The Austrians knew, too, that the Black Hand was only one of a number of organizations of reckless fanatics who would stop at nothing to further the cause of Slavic unity.

Irritated by the results of a tariff dispute with Serbia, known as the "Pig War," and determined to thwart Serbia's nationalist ambitions and to block her expansion to the sea, Austria in 1908 annexed Bosnia and Herzegovina. Thereafter the hatred of the Serbian nationalists was directed exclusively against the Dual Monarchy. Austria, increasingly exasperated, longed to crush Serbia, and being a far more powerful state, could have done so at any time. Yet it was impossible for Austria to strike without grave danger of provoking a large-scale European war. For behind little Serbia stood a far more powerful Slavonic people—the Russians.

Nationalism in Russia

The Serbian nationalists were encouraged in their fierce ambitions by the Pan-Slavist movement which had as its political aim the uniting of all peoples of Slavic blood under the leadership of Russia, a somewhat vague, nationalist theory supported by some newspaper proprietors and members of the ruling class. The Pan-Slavists preached that it was the historic mission of Russia, as the "big brother" of the Slavonic family, to liberate all the Slavs of southeastern Europe from the tyranny of Austrian and Turkish rule.

Although Pan-Slavism was not openly or officially encouraged by the Russian government, it proved a useful tool of Russian foreign policy, for it weakened and held in check Austria, Russia's rival in the Balkans. By encouraging Serbia, the rulers of Russia hoped to gain a dominating position in the Balkans. This would benefit them in two ways. It would give to their country that control of the Straits leading from the Black Sea to the Mediterranean which she had long coveted. It would also win the Russian government popularity at home, and distract the minds of the great masses of the Russian people from domestic problems. For in Russia the government seemed to concern itself with the interests of only a tiny handful of wealthy landowners and nobles, and there was mounting agitation for a more democratic representative government.[1]

However, in condoning the Pan-Slavist agitation and seeking control of the Black Sea Straits, Russia was playing a dangerous game. For the ground swell of Pan-Slavist sentiment tended to draw Russia deeply into every dispute between the headstrong Serbs and the increasingly desperate Austrians, and an attempt by Russia to seize the Bosphorus or the Dardanelles would inevitably lead to a head-on clash with Austria.

2. THE SYSTEM OF ENTANGLING ALLIANCES

Any one of the treacherous currents of nationalism which swirled below the placid surface of prewar Europe might have been sufficient to draw two or even three nations into the vortex of war. There was the wounded pride of France, still raw forty years after her defeat in the Franco-Prussian war; there was the throbbing, feverish nationalism of suppressed minority groups in the Balkans, in Poland, and in Austria-Hungary; there were Russia's nationalistic ambitions (frustrated by the actions of Britain, France, and Turkey in the Crimean War of 1854-56) to expand towards Constantinople. There was the swaggering exuberant nationalism of the new German Empire, dynamic, restless, and set upon its drive to the east, and the determination of Great Britain to maintain her position of leadership in export manufacturing and as a naval Power. But there was another element which made it fatally certain that if any war broke out, however small, it would almost instantly turn into a conflict involving every major European Power. That element was a complex system of entangling alliances, bred of suspicion and mutual fear, by which the different European Powers were pledged to come to each other's defence should war break out.

The system of alliances originated with Bismarck, who had woven a network tying different countries with Germany, ostensibly for mutual interest, more accurately for Germany's advantage. By the *Dreikaiserbund*, Germany, Austria-Hungary, and Russia agreed to maintain a "benevolent neutrality" in case of

[1]Russia's internal political problems are discussed in Chapter 18.

an attack by a fourth Power on one of the members. This alliance proved short-lived, but was replaced by the Dual Alliance (with Austria) and the Reinsurance Treaty (with Russia) by which Germany continued to protect her interests. Of these, the Dual Alliance was ultimately to have by far the greatest significance. Its most important clause bound each nation to come to the help of the other in case of attack by Russia. To Bismarck the agreement meant exactly that and no more; he was not prepared to see Austria-Hungary destroyed as a major Power, but on the other hand he was determined not to back her in reckless adventures in the Balkans. The Austrians, however, assumed from the start that they could count on German backing should they come to blows with Russia, no matter *what* the circumstances. Thus there began "a diplomatic tug-of-war between Berlin and Vienna" which resulted ultimately in Austria's dragging Germany into war, in 1914, over a Balkan quarrel in which Germany had no direct interest. The Dual Alliance may therefore be seen in retrospect as an important precursor to the war.[1]

The Breakdown of Germany's Alliances

In 1890 Bismarck was abruptly dismissed from power by William II. Almost immediately his elaborate schemes for maintaining the isolation of France and the European *status quo* began to come apart.

The first Power to be estranged was Russia. William could never find any reason to admire Czar Alexander III, and while he wished to remain on good terms with Germany's eastern neighbour, he finally believed Austria-Hungary to be the more reliable ally. Accordingly, when Russia pressed for a renewal of the Reinsurance Treaty in 1890, William denied the request.

For the Russians this rejection was the second that she had received in a short space of time. When Russia had encountered financial difficulties in the late 1880's, Alexander III's ministers sought help in the Berlin money market and had been turned down. Now, financial instability and desire for security raised Russian sights westward, beyond Germany, to France.

[1]The Dual Alliance was later expanded into the Triple Alliance. Bismarck's alliances are discussed more fully on pp. 333-337.

The opportunity was quickly grasped by France. After two large Russian loans were easily floated in French financial circles, French munitions firms won contracts to supply arms to the Russian army. The next step was singularly awkward, and made possible only by the common belief of its awful necessity. The two countries regarded each other with repugnance; to Russia, France was the home of Jacobins and regicides; to France, Russia was the last haven of the decadent aristocracy of the *ancien régime*. Nevertheless, negotiations began in 1891 and culminated at last, in 1894, with the signing of the Franco-Russian Alliance, a mutual defence pact aimed against Germany. Now, dramatically, after twenty years, one of Bismarck's major achievements had been destroyed. France was no longer isolated. Of equal importance was the fact that through the loss of her former eastern ally, Germany now faced hostile Powers on either side.

One of the cornerstones of Bismarck's foreign policy had been to keep Britain as a friendly neutral. The next event of outstanding importance in the breakdown of Bismarck's system was the estrangement by Germany of Great Britain. Germany and Britain had habitually enjoyed good relations, having often been allies in their various struggles against France. The respective royal families of the two nations were related, and in an age of social Darwinism the racial affinity between the two peoples struck an appealing note to many. In 1890 Britain was even considering becoming a fourth partner in the Triple Alliance.

There were strains between Germany and Britain, however, and in the late 19th century these were rapidly becoming acute. The British resented the German tariff system, worried about the embryonic but rapidly growing German navy, feared the already formidable German competition for export markets, and disliked the strident personality of William II. The Germans, on the other hand, envied Britain's huge colonial empire, but otherwise tended to regard the age of British greatness as past—and to regard themselves as the inevitable successors.

The event that acted as a catalyst to reveal the widening gulf between the two countries was Jameson's Raid in 1895.[1] The German government at first wanted to send German troops through

---

[1] Jameson's Raid, as the prelude to the Boer War, is described on p. 370.

Mozambique to aid the Boers—whom they regarded as "racial cousins" and potential allies in Africa—against Jameson and his followers. Then, when President Paul Kruger of the Transvaal announced the capture of the British insurgents, the Kaiser sent him a flamboyant telegram of congratulations for having driven off the "disturbers of the peace" and "having safeguarded the independence of the country from outside attacks." British public opinion was so enraged that any government policy of friendship towards Germany was made much more difficult.

In spite of the unfavourable public attitude, however, Joseph Chamberlain, the British colonial secretary, made overtures in 1898 for an Anglo-German alliance—but he was turned down. The German Chancellor, Bernhard von Bulow, chortled over Chamberlain's "feverish attacks of friendship." As with Russia eight years before, William lacked the foresight to realize that England might seek the friendship of enemies, if she were rejected. This is precisely what happened!

German rejection of the proferred British alliance and the Kaiser's sabre-rattling in Africa jolted many Britons. Great Britain had not been involved in an alliance since she had left the Quintuple Alliance of the 1820's. British statesmen had indeed boasted of their "splendid isolation." They had just begun to recover from the shock created by the recent German coolness when they were confronted by the almost global opprobrium generated by their conduct of the Boer War (1899-1902). Not only an unpopular war among the British people, this African imperial venture was roundly attacked in Europe. Suddenly Britons realized how friendless they had become.

Yet where could the British turn? Russia, the ancient foe, was causing concern near the Afghanistan and Persian borders, posing a threat to India. France? Just before the outbreak of the Boer War a dangerous crisis developed with that country when both imperial Powers seemed headed on a collision course in central Africa. France was eager to create a solid west-east strip of territory from Dakar to the Gulf of Aden, while England wanted a similar south-north belt of land from the Cape to Cairo. Finally, in 1898, the inevitable occurred. A small French force of troops confronted a similar British force at Fashoda, on the upper Nile. Both governments spoke menacingly, but the French

Foreign Minister, Theophile Delcassé, perceived the situation as an opportunity for French diplomacy to make the most of a bad situation. France could not afford to antagonize Great Britain. Delcassé, therefore, backed down and made no territorial demands on the region.

The Emergence of the Anti-German Entente

The Fashoda incident and its successful resolution was the first step to an Anglo-French understanding. Three years later, Edward VII, a known Francophile, succeeded Queen Victoria to the British throne. By this time, British statesmen had begun to recognize more clearly the extent to which their nation had become isolated. Accordingly, in 1904, Edward VII went on a remarkably successful tour of France where he was warmly received. This was followed by the establishment of a colonial agreement by which France recognized Britain's interests in Egypt while Britain allowed France a free hand in Morocco. Although no military convention or alliance was formed, the creation of an *Entente Cordiale* was seen by all European Powers as a blow to Germany.

For France, already allied to Russia, the formation of the Anglo-French Entente was merely a prelude to the completion of her plans. If an Anglo-*Russian* rapprochement could be effected, Germany could not establish a *détente* with the British. Certainly the task would not be simple. Through fear of Russian designs in Asia, Great Britain had at last broken out of her isolation in 1902 to enter into a military alliance with Japan, who was Russia's enemy. By 1907, however, with Germany increasingly viewed by the British as her chief danger, they were more willing to forget old scores against Russia. In that year, British and Russian statesmen reached an imperial agreement in their respective spheres of interest in Asia. To German amazement and almost disbelief, a Triple Entente of Great Britain, France, and Russia had been created.[1]

By 1907, a precarious balance of power existed in Europe. So delicate was this balance that any crisis might catapult the two sides into war. Triple Alliance faced Triple Entente.

---

[1] By the terms of the Triple Entente, however, Britain did not assume binding contractual obligations similar to those of the Franco-Russian alliance.

3. THE CRISES LEADING TO WAR

And crises there were in the decade which led to the outbreak of the First World War. The first important threat to peace resulted from the German desire to test the *Entente Cordiale*. In 1905 Chancellor von Bulow chose Morocco as the testing ground. Although this small territory was nominally independent from her adjacent colony of Algeria, France exercised police powers and had been pumping in money, and therefore regarded it as her own sphere of influence. In a dramatic manner, Kaiser Wilhelm arrived in Tangier in late March, 1905, aboard a German warship. There he made a startling speech in which he recognized the independence of the Sultan of Morocco and demanded an open-door policy for all nations in Moroccan trade. The German venture was an overt attempt to break the Anglo-French connection. The immediate results were favourable to Germany. France, uncertain of British support, backed down, and Delcassé was even forced to resign. The exultant von Bulow, however, overplayed his hand, and demanded an international conference to underwrite German demands. By the time that the conference was called, in Algeciras, the French had recovered from their setback and won powerful British support. While the German case for equal economic privileges was supported by the Powers, only Austria backed the German insistence that France not be allowed to interfere in Moroccan affairs. When France was guaranteed the right to police Morocco, it was clear to all that the Anglo-French *Entente* had held and that Germany had been rebuffed.

Franco-German friction in North Africa continued. In 1911 France announced her intention to send troops to restore order in Morocco. This provoked an immediate German reaction. A German gunboat, the *Panther,* was dispatched to Agadir ostensibly to protect German residents in that Moroccan city. As a result of negotiations during which Germany demanded the whole of the French Congo, she finally obtained some trifling territorial concessions in that region. France, meanwhile, was granted the right to establish a protectorate over Morocco.

"The Mailed Fist." Kaiser Wilhelm intervenes at Agadir.

The Balkan Crises

Tension and crises were developing in the Balkans also. After Russia's disastrous war with Japan in 1905,[1] her policy was again focused on the Balkans and her ancient desire to gain access through the Straits of the Bosporus and the Dardanelles to the Mediterranean. At the same time, growing Serbian nationalism increased Austro-Hungarian concern for developments in this area.

Both Austria-Hungary and Russia, however, were deeply concerned by the possible results of a revolution carried out in Turkey in 1908, which had given that age-weakened country a new lease on life. Fearful of renewed Turkish strength in the Balkans, the Russian and Austro-Hungarian foreign ministers met secretly in the autumn of 1908 and agreed verbally to call an international conference. The gist of the agreement was Rus-

---

[1] The Russian-Japanese War, which had serious implications for Russian internal developments, is discussed more fully in Chapter 18.

Franz Josef of Austria removes Bosnia-Herzegovina from the Turkish Empire, and Prince Ferdinand of Bulgaria declares his country's independence. Sultan Abdul Hamid II of Turkey watches in helpless frustration.

sia's willingness to accept Austro-Hungarian occupation of Bosnia-Herzegovina, a former Turkish province administered since 1878 by Austria-Hungary and coveted by Serbia as part of the latter's proposed Yugoslav union. In return Russia would receive Austro-Hungarian support for the opening of the Straits to Russian ships.

Following the meeting, however, Austria-Hungary immediately proclaimed her annexation of the territories without calling for a conference as arranged. Russia was caught flat-footed. While Germany announced support for the Dual Monarchy, France and

Great Britain informed Russia that they were unwilling to support her in military action against Austria-Hungary. Russia, enraged and humiliated, was in an awkward position. As "protector" of the Slavic peoples in the Balkans she had failed to resist Austro-Hungarian acquisition of Slavic territory. Lacking support, she backed down.

For a few years life became more peaceful in the Balkans. Then, in 1912, a newly-formed Balkan League (Serbia, Bulgaria, and Greece), seeing an opportunity to profit from a war between Italy and Turkey, declared war on the unfortunate Turks. To the surprise of the European Powers, the Balkan League won a decisive victory. With the exception of Constantinople, Turkey had been driven out of Europe.

The situation that resulted was highly unstable. Serbia, seeking above all an outlet on the Adriatic, had overrun Albania. Austria-Hungary, however, was determined to prevent this, and accordingly sponsored Albania as an independent state under Austrian protection. Consequently, Serbia was compelled to relinquish her gains there. This meant, however, that the victorious Balkan League Powers had been rewarded very unevenly for their efforts. Thus the victors soon began to wrangle over the spoils, with the result that in 1913, war broke out again, this time *within* the Balkan League! Bulgaria attacked Serbia, with Greece and this time Romania entering to support Serbia. Even the Turks jumped in to regain lost ground. By the Treaty of Bucharest (July, 1913), Bulgaria lost all the land she had won. Serbia, annexing large parts of Macedonia, almost doubled her territory, but once again was blocked from expansion to Albania by the outright threat of Austrian force.

To the Serbs, the creation of Albania, in addition to the Austro-Hungarian annexation of Bosnia and Herzegovina, demonstrated the determination of the Dual Monarchy to box in the tiny Slavic republic. The "Piedmont of the Slavs," Serbia, too, realized she could not "go it alone." As Piedmont had turned to France against Austria, so Serbia would turn to Russia against Austria-Hungary. Thus Serbia became the trigger that would bring the major Powers, Austria-Hungary and Russia—and through them, their supporting alliances—into conflict. Russia had supported Serbia's claim to Albania at the Treaty of Bucharest and had lost. Neither Russia nor Serbia could afford another loss in the Balkans. On the other hand, the fact that Serbia had gained substantial territory by the so-called Balkan Wars represented a defeat to Austria-Hungary. The third confrontation of Serbia versus Austria-Hungary would be the last and it would lead to war, one that would involve all of Europe.

"The War to End All Wars"

> The Allied and Associated Governments affirm and Germany accepts the responsibility of Germany and her allies for causing all the loss and damage to which the Allied and Associated Governments and their nationals have been subjected as a consequence of the war imposed upon them by the aggression of Germany and her allies.
> —Article 231 of the Treaty of Versailles

At the turn of the 19th century, Emile Zola, the French novelist, wrote an article *On War*. The theme of Zola's thought was his refusal to believe that a general European war would again be possible:

And the further we go, the more impossible war seems to become, the more it appears to develop into a crime of high treason against humanity—an atrocity for which no nation would be responsible.

Other authors accepted Zola's line of reasoning and echoed his arguments. Modern nations possessed fantastically powerful weapons capable of destroying entire regiments. The nearly incredible costs of war made them impossible.

Yet while the general public was being reassured that all was well with the world, by the spring of 1914 the signs of war were becoming increasingly ominous. British shipyards continued to turn out dreadnoughts and German factories mass-produced long-range artillery. Russia had been almost openly promising help to the small Balkan nations to enlarge their territory at Austria's expense. Austria-Hungary's ultimatum to Serbia to surrender her claims in Albania was power politics at its most naked. France increased the strength of her army, and increased her agitation under the ardently nationalistic President, Raymond Poincaré, for the return of Alsace and Lorraine. With all these factors operating, by the summer of 1914, "peace was at the mercy of an accident."

1. THE MACHINERY OF WAR IS PUT IN MOTION

On June 28, the accident took place. On that day the Archduke Francis Ferdinand, heir to the thrones of Austria and Hungary, was assassinated, together with his wife, in the Bosnian town of Sarajevo. The assassin, Gavrilo Princip, was a Bosnian acting as an agent for the Serbian terrorist organization, the Black Hand.

The Serbian authorities may or may not have been aware of the plot to assassinate the Archduke—it has never been conclusively proved either way. Certainly there was no great grief in Vienna at his death, but nevertheless he had been the heir apparent, and his murder gave Austria the excuse needed for a final decisive blow at Serbia. World opinion, shocked by the outrage, appeared strongly sympathetic to Austria. Encouraged by the reaction, the Austrian government sought German backing prior to taking strong measures. The Kaiser, while satisfied with the Serbian reply, was anxious to retain Austria as an ally. Believing that Russia, as Serbia's supporter, was too unprepared to force an issue, he promised support and agreed that steps be taken while world opinion was still favourable.

On July 23 Austria took the next-to-final step. This was an ultimatum presented to Serbia, demanding crippling and humiliating concessions with a forty-eight-hour time limit for their acceptance. Heeding Russian advice to yield, Serbia accepted all but two of the Austrian demands. Austria, however, wanted nothing less than unconditional surrender.

This time Russia was determined not to abandon Serbia as she had done in the 1908 Bosnian crisis. The following day she warned Austria that Serbia must not be annexed; the day after that, France declared her support for Russia. Serbia, however, began mobilizing her army in preparation for the possibility of an Austrian attack. Seeing this, Austria began to mobilize *her* army, and on July 28 declared war on Serbia. Committed beyond retreat, Russia too prepared to mobilize for war.

What did Russia intend to do? This was the terribly critical question that the German government had to ask itself. Russia had two alternative mobilization plans. One was for partial mobilization, which would send armies into position against Austria-Hungary alone. The other was for *total* mobilization, which would send troops to the German border. Germany, however, was unaware of Russia's choice of two plans, and fully believed that partial mobilization was only a prelude to total mobilization, aimed at Germany herself. Therefore, on July 29, Germany warned Russia that *any* mobilization meant war.

Now what was Russia to do? If even partial mobilization meant war, then why not full mobilization, which would come anyway? And so, on July 30, the following day, the order for total mobilization was given. Russian troops began moving westward toward Germany.

Now what was *Germany* to do? Were the Russians trying to steal a march by attacking first? In the circumstances, could Germany dare take the chance of assuming otherwise? On July 31 a twenty-four-hour ultimatum was given to the Russians to withdraw, while at the same time Germany's own plans for mobilization were put into action. Russia did not reply to the ultimatum. On August 1, Germany declared war on Russia.

The critical question *now* was what would *France* do? There was no reason to doubt that France would fulfil her obligations to Russia and would therefore attack Germany. This meant that Germany would be faced by the military nightmare of a war on two fronts. Her strategy in such a situation was the so-called *Schlieffen Plan*, which called for a lightning blow to eliminate the western enemy, France, before the eastern enemy, Russia, could reach German soil.

Fatally, however, the Schlieffen Plan required that for the attack on France to be made with maximum effectiveness, the German army would have to advance through Belgium. This raised the question of British intervention.

Great Britain was not firmly committed to entering the war on the side of France, and it was still doubtful whether she would join in. The British government, however, with its traditional policy that no strong Continental power be allowed to control the Low Countries, had guaranteed the neutrality of Belgium. A warning was given that an invasion of Belgium would bring Britain into the war.

Thus Germany was faced with an impossible dilemma. To wage war effectively would bring in Great Britain as an enemy. To keep Britain neutral, German strategy against France would be crippled. To do *nothing* appeared to invite the risk of a full-scale onslaught from Russia—and the Russian trains were already rolling westwards. This was the deciding factor. On August 3, Kaiser Wilhelm passed the point of no return by declaring war on France and attacking through Belgium. On August 4, Great Britain declared war on Germany. That night, physically and mentally exhausted from the strain of the continuous diplomatic crisis of the past five weeks, the British Foreign Secretary, Earl Grey, made the prophetic remark: "The lamps are going out all over Europe. We shall not see them lit again in our lifetime." The Great War had begun.

2. THE WAR TO END ALL WARS

Strange as it seems to modern minds, the Europeans of 1914 welcomed the coming of war. Crowds cheered in the streets, and in Britain young men rushed to enlist, anxious not to miss the adventure because "the war would be over by Christmas." Nor was the idea that the war would be a short one held only by ignorant civilians. The German military authorities planned their campaign in the belief that complete victory was only months away.

The opposing forces, however, were too evenly matched and their movements too ponderous for such a quick decision to be possible. The Central Powers, Germany and Austria-Hungary, were later joined by Turkey and Bulgaria. The Entente Powers, or, as they were later called, the Allies, included France, Russia, Serbia, and Great Britain and her Dominions and colonies. Italy and Romania, able to free themselves from the Triple Alliance in 1914, the United States, Japan, China, and a number of South American nations, eventually came to the aid of the Allies. The Allied superiority in manpower was matched to some degree by the incomparable efficiency of the German army. The notorious inefficiency of the Russian army was almost offset by the weak Austro-Hungarian army, in which the numerous Slavic units had little heart for war. The French pinned their hopes to a simple plan—to attack with fury, with the *élan* that had carried the armies of the Revolution to victory over all odds. Britain had her navy. Germany had the Schlieffen Plan.

As the first blows were struck in that fatal August of 1914, it became apparent that several major miscalculations had been made. The first was that the swift French advance into Alsace and Lorraine was brought to a halt and then turned into a retreat by the superiority of German artillery. *Elan* was not enough. The second

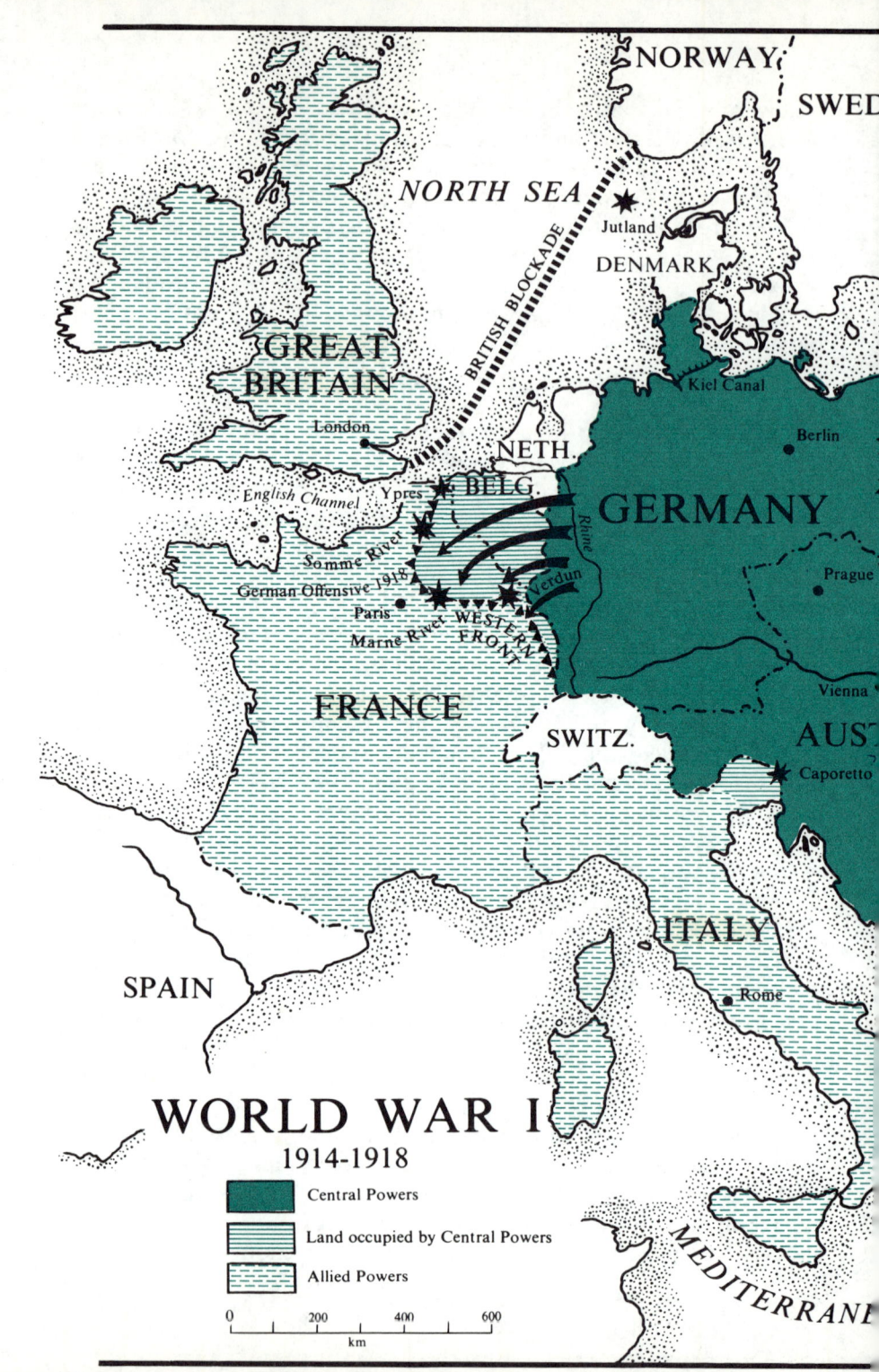

miscalculation was that on the Eastern Front the Russians, in spite of their inefficient railways and ponderous mobilization methods, had moved faster than the German and Austrian generals had thought possible. They were moving steadily westwards into East Prussia and steps had to be taken to stop them. Two corps were diverted from the attack on France to strengthen German forces facing the Russians. On August 28 the opposing armies met, at the Battle of Tannenburg. The result was a total victory for the Germans; the Russian army was so badly mauled that its effectiveness was substantially reduced for the remainder of the war. Even more important, however, was that the diversion of German troops from the Western Front was partly responsible for causing the third miscalculation—the fact that the Schlieffen Plan failed to work.

The Germans came within twenty-three kilometres of Paris and appeared to have victory within their grasp. Nevertheless, the advance through Belgium had been thrown off schedule because the Belgians resisted, instead of standing aside or surrendering, as anticipated by the Schlieffen Plan. By the time the leading German forces turned south into France, a small but capable British contingent—"an incomparable army"[1]—had come to the aid of the French. The German army might still have seized Paris and defeated France had not the generals made a critical tactical error. A gap was allowed to open between the left wing and the right wing of the attack, which enabled the French and British forces to mount an effective counter-attack on the German flank. Because they had diverted the two corps to the Russian Front, the Germans were particularly vulnerable to such a counter-thrust. With Parisian taxi drivers transporting thousands of French soldiers to the battlefield less than forty kilometres north of the capital, the battle raged along the Marne River from September 6 until September 9. By then, the Schleffen Plan had failed and the German armies were in an organized retreat northward.

The "Miracle of the Marne" was the turning point of the war. Victory by lightning thrust was no longer possible. Now, the outcome would be decided by attrition. The side which was exhausted last would win. What followed was four years of siege warfare. Troops, plagued by lice, rats, mud, and cold, lived in the trench lines from which they emerged from time to time to make costly

[1] The words were those of the German General von Kluck, who opposed them.

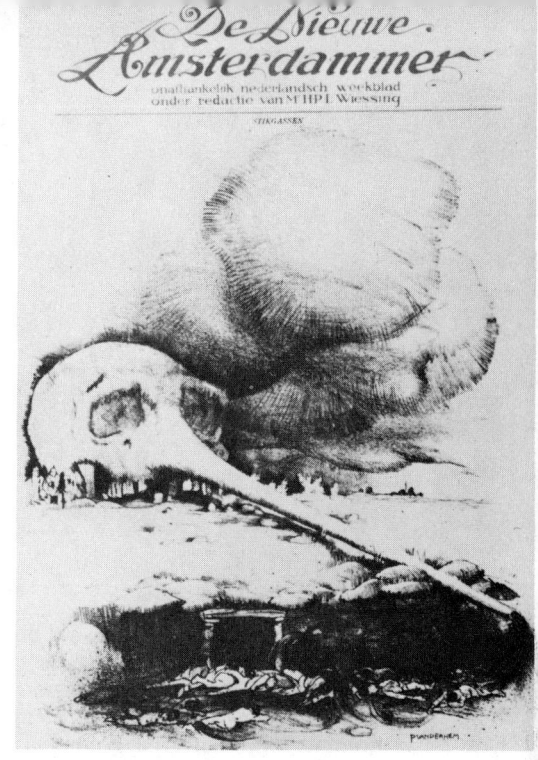

"The Propaganda War." TOP LEFT: a British poster, remarkable for its lack of subtlety. TOP RIGHT: a Dutch cartoon, "The New Death," representing the horror of gas warfare. BOTTOM: "War is an element in God's order of things," a remark made by General von Moltke; believe it or not, this is a package of cigarettes—so thoroughly had war-fever penetrated German thinking!

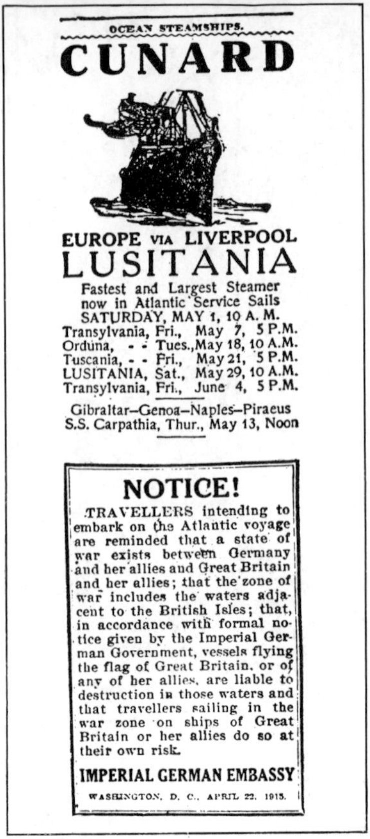

CUNARD

EUROPE VIA LIVERPOOL
LUSITANIA
Fastest and Largest Steamer
now in Atlantic Service Sails
SATURDAY, MAY 1, 10 A.M.
Transylvania, Fri., May 7, 5 P.M.
Orduna, - - Tues., May 18, 10 A.M.
Tuscania, - - Fri., May 21, 5 P.M.
LUSITANIA, Sat., May 29, 10 A.M.
Transylvania, Fri., June 4, 5 P.M.

Gibraltar—Genoa—Naples—Piraeus
S.S. Carpathia, Thur., May 13, Noon

NOTICE!
TRAVELLERS intending to embark on the Atlantic voyage are reminded that a state of war exists between Germany and her allies and Great Britain and her allies; that the zone of war includes the waters adjacent to the British Isles; that, in accordance with formal notice given by the Imperial German Government, vessels flying the flag of Great Britain, or of any of her allies, are liable to destruction in those waters and that travellers sailing in the war zone on ships of Great Britain or her allies do so at their own risk.

IMPERIAL GERMAN EMBASSY
WASHINGTON, D. C., APRIL 22, 1915.

"The War at Sea." TOP: an advertisement by the German Embassy, printed immediately beneath an advertisement by Cunard. BELOW: a German U-boat in action. RIGHT: a comment by the savagely anti-German caricaturist Raemaekers, "Looks like a neutral; let's sink him!"

"THE WAR TO END ALL WARS"

"The War on Land." TOP: Blinded victims of a gas attack. BOTTOM: "The Ravages of Battle"—a New Zealand soldier collects identification papers from a dead comrade.

TOP: The U.S. 23rd Infantry at Argonne, 1918.
BOTTOM: the "Ironclads of Cambrai"—British tanks in action.

TOP: "The Courage of the Early Morning" — Captain W. A. Bishop, V.C., standing beside his Nieuport Scout. CENTRE: A French Nieuport chasing a German Brandenburg C. BOTTOM: Rittmeister Manfred von Richthofen.

frontal attacks on the trench fortifications opposite, perhaps gaining a few metres, a fraction of a kilometre, by the expenditure of thousands killed or wounded.

The war of movement continued a little longer in the east. In 1915 the Russians beat the Austrians only to be themselves heavily defeated once more by the Germans. Then on this Front, too, the war became static along a line running from the Gulf of Riga to the Black Sea.

At sea the British Royal Navy was supreme, although it too suffered shock and defeat. Off Coronel (November 1, 1914) on the coast of Chile a British squadron under Admiral Craddock was beaten and his ships sunk or put to flight by a squadron of newer, more heavily armed and more efficient German ships. A month later, however, the situation was reversed and von Spee's ships, victorious at Coronel, were sunk by British battle cruisers at the Falkland Islands.

The most important naval battle of the war was fought near Jutland (May 31, 1916). Again the British suffered heavy losses of men and ships, but the German navy, hidden by fog and darkness, fled back to its bases and never again emerged to challenge the British for the remainder of the war. The Royal Navy's blockade of Germany and her allies continued as before.

Germany, if her surface ships were ineffective, had another weapon—the submarine. Driven to desperation the Germans began an unrestricted submarine warfare on shipping destined for Allied ports. While it did not succeed in starving the British into surrender as the German admiralty hoped, it did great damage and caused heavy losses of men, ships, and cargoes. But it had another unforeseen effect. One of the ships sunk was the Cunard liner *Lusitania*, and among the twelve hundred passengers who lost their lives were a hundred or more Americans. The American public, trained from childhood to look on the British with suspicion as the ancient enemy, because of the *Lusitania* now swung over to favour the Allied cause.

In 1917 the war entered a new phase, in which the whole world was involved in one way or another. Turkey and Bulgaria had joined Germany and Austria. Romania and Greece had joined the Allies. Italy, originally a member of the Triple Alliance with Germany and Austria, had entered the war against them after receiving promises from the Allies of major territorial gains after victory.

The British Dominions and India were heavily engaged. Japan snapped up the small parts of China which had been held by Germany. It was in this year that the United States entered the war against Germany and in which Russia, torn by revolution, dropped out.

The year 1917, too, saw the Canadian Corps capture Vimy Ridge, and the capture of Jerusalem by General Allenby and his British, Australian, and Arab forces. The last German force in Africa was broken by the brilliant South African soldier-philosopher Jan Smuts. In spite of these victories and successes not all the news was favourable for the Allies. France had been bled white by battles such as those at Verdun which lasted from February to November, 1916, and were repeated in August, 1917. Parts of the French army were ready to mutiny while France herself was exhausted and anxious for peace.

It was evident that the war could not last much longer. The naval blockade was bringing whole populations in Germany and Austria to the danger of starvation, while the use of closely guarded convoys not only brought food and military supplies to Britain and France, but by 1918 American troops as well. In March, 1918, Ludendorff launched what was to prove the last great German attacks of the war. One hit the thinly held British lines in the valley of the Somme, the other drove back the French to the Marne once more. Both attacks were at first successful but Germany simply did not have the strength left to push on to final victory.

After March, 1918, Germany was in retreat. British, French, and, by late summer, American armies began the steady advance that did not end until victory had been won.

Germany's allies were being defeated one by one. Bulgaria and Turkey dropped out of the war on September 30 and October 30 respectively. The whole Austro-Hungarian Empire was in a state of collapse. Czechoslovakia proclaimed itself a republic. The Slavic Croats and Slovenes declared their lands part of "the national and sovereign States of the Serbs, Croats and Slovenes" (Yugoslavia). On November 3, Austria-Hungary surrendered. Nine days later the Emperor Charles abdicated, and Hungary and Austria became independent republics. The Austro-Hungarian Empire had vanished and the once-proud imperial city of Vienna was now the capital of a small rather unimportant republic.

ARMIES MOBILIZED AND CASUALTIES IN WORLD WAR I*

Countries	Total mobilized forces	Killed and died	Wounded casualties	Prisoners and missing	Total casualties	Percentage of mobilized forces in casualties
Allies and Associated Powers:						
Russia	12 000 000	1 700 000	4 950 000	2 500 000	9 150 000	76.3
France	8 410 000	1 357 800	4 266 000	537 000	6 160 800	73.3
British Empire	8 904 467	908 371	2 090 212	191 652	3 190 235	35.8
Italy	5 615 000	650 000	947 000	600 000	2 197 000	39.1
United States	4 355 000	126 000	234 300	4 500	364 800	8.2
Japan	800 000	300	907	3	1 210	0.2
Romania	750 000	335 706	120 000	80 000	535 706	71.4
Serbia	707 343	45 000	133 148	152 958	331 106	46.8
Belgium	267 000	13 716	44 686	34 659	93 061	34.9
Greece	230 000	5 000	21 000	1 000	27 000	11.7
Portugal	100 000	7 222	13 751	12 318	33 291	33.3
Montenegro	50 000	3 000	10 000	7 000	20 000	40.0
Total	42 188 810	5 152 115	12 831 004	4 121 090	22 104 209	52.3
Central Powers:						
Germany	11 000 000	1 773 700	4 216 058	1 152 800	7 142 558	64.9
Austria-Hungary	7 800 000	1 200 000	3 620 000	2 200 000	7 020 000	90.0
Turkey	2 850 000	325 000	400 000	250 000	975 000	34.2
Bulgaria	1 200 000	87 500	152 390	27 029	266 919	22.2
Total	22 850 000	3 386 200	8 388 448	3 629 829	15 404 477	67.4
Grand total	65 038 810	8 538 315	21 219 452	7 750 919	37 508 686	57.6

* As reported by the United States War Department in February, 1924.

Germany was the only member of the Central Powers still fighting, but the end unmistakably was near. On November 7, the Kaiser abdicated and three days later fled to Holland. There was a mutiny of the sailors of the fleet, and *soviets*[1] on the Russian model were set up in several towns by workers and by soldiers back from the war. In Bavaria a short-lived republic was established. It was only with the help of the army that the new Socialist government, which succeeded that of William II, was able to put down these attempts of the Communist and other parties of the extreme Left to establish themselves as the rulers of Germany. The German Empire so carefully constructed by Bismarck was gone.

In the early morning of November 11, 1918, German delegates signed the papers of surrender in the railway car of Marshal Foch, the Commander-in-Chief of the Allied Armies. At precisely 11 a.m. that same morning, the guns stopped their firing, and all hostilities ceased. The war was over.

About eight million people had been killed in the fighting and probably three times that number had died of hardships created by the war. Malnutrition affected a whole generation in central Europe, so that in parts of Austria, for example, over ninety per cent of the children had rickets. Enfeebled by wartime conditions, millions more people died when, in 1918-19, the world was swept by a very virulent form of influenza, a great plague that was like the other dread plagues of history. Thus was the reckoning of the cost.

3. THE PEACE

In the cold winter of 1919, the victors of the Great War assembled to restore order to Europe and deal out justice to defeated Germany. Between January, 1919 and August, 1920, five separate treaties, each named after the town in which it was signed, were drawn up. Collectively these treaties, Versailles, St. Germain, Neuilly, Trianon, and Sèvres, were known as the Peace of Paris. The conference opened on January 18, 1919, amid the glitter and magnificence of the majestic Hall of Mirrors at Versailles. The timing and the setting were deliberate and set the tone for the proceedings—it was on the same day and in the same location that in 1871 Bismarck had proclaimed the formation of the German Empire.

Delegates from thirty-two nations came to Versailles, but the

[1]See p. 433.

truly important decisions remained in the hands of the Big Four: Woodrow Wilson of the United States, David Lloyd George of Great Britain, Georges Clemenceau of France, and Vittorio Orlando of Italy. Each man viewed the Treaty of Versailles from a different angle. Lloyd George, a captive of his own election promises to make Germany pay, and urged on by Tory nationalists and the Dominion Premiers, wanted to increase the extent of the British Empire. Clemenceau represented the almost fanatic French desire for protection against renewed German aggression. Orlando wanted land as promised by the Allies for Italy's intervention in the war. Set against these politically hardened and realistic bargainers was Wilson, who made no territorial or financial demands on the defeated Germans, but instead was anxious to have the world accept his famous *Fourteen Points*. This document, first enunciated a year earlier, was a general statement of humane and idealistic principles on which the peace settlement should be based.

The Wilsonian approach to peace was not enthusiastically accepted by the three Old World statesmen. Clemenceau is supposed to have sneered: "God gave us the Ten Commandments. Wilson has given us the Fourteen Points." Despite the Allies' criticism of his programme, however, Wilson had an important influence in guiding the peace settlements. The creation of the League of Nations, for example, was one of Wilson's favourite ideas. Similarly, from the *Fourteen Points* came the democratic aim to allow the various European nationalities to determine for themselves their own form of government, to secure "self-determination for all peoples, great and small."[1]

The Germans soon learned, however, that much of the Wilsonian liberal idealism was not to benefit them. The Treaty of Versailles returned Alsace and Lorraine to France, as well as the coal-rich Saar valley which France would occupy for fifteen years. Belgium and Denmark took small pieces of German territory. To allow the re-created state of Poland access to the Baltic Sea, East Prussia was severed by the formation of the Polish Corridor. At its head on the Baltic shore, the German city of Danzig was internationalized under the administration of the League of Nations. Germany lost all of

---

[1]It was on the basis of the Fourteeen Points that the Germans had surrendered. When the much harsher terms of the Treaty of Versailles were revealed, reaction in Germany was extremely bitter—a factor which contributed to the Germans' antipathy for their post-war democratic government.

her colonies, which were parcelled out chiefly among Japan, France, and Great Britain and her Dominions.[1]

To crush German militarism, it was decided that the German army would be limited to a hundred thousand men and the General Staff abolished. The navy was reduced to a skeleton fleet. No warplanes, submarines, or tanks could be built. A fifty-six kilometre wide belt on the right bank of the Rhine was to be demilitarized.

All of these terms hardened German hearts, but none so bitterly as Article 231. This was the so-called "guilt clause" by which Germany was forced to admit that she and her allies had caused the war and had thus committed a "crime against civilization." Subsequently many people, including Americans, Frenchmen, and Britons, would denounce the guilt clause. No one, certainly, would use it to his advantage more effectively than Adolf Hitler.

Because the Germans were considered guilty, it was agreed that territorial compensation was inadequate atonement for their sins. They would be required to pay for the loss of life and property in gold dollars. While a Reparations Commission was formed to determine the exact and final sum, Germany was ordered to surrender five billion dollars to the Allies. In 1921, the Commission presented the grand total to be taken from Germany—a staggering thirty-three billion dollars.

On June 28, 1919, the German delegates travelled to Versailles to sign the Treaty. They had not been allowed to negotiate themselves, but were ordered to accept the agreement unconditionally. In a cold ceremony, the German plenipotentiary deliberately revealed his contempt for the Treaty by sitting while addressing the Allied leaders. As the German delegates bitterly left the room, Clemenceau remarked: ". . . A great moment, but I fear a peace without victory, just as we had a victory without peace."

The other peace treaties were drawn up in the same mood. By the Treaty of *St. Germain,* Austria was reduced to the area inhabited by her German-speaking subjects. Her small population was forbidden ever to join Germany. All her surrounding land was divided among the several national groups which had made up the Austro-Hungarian Empire. Hungary, under the terms of the Treaty

---

[1]Theoretically, the ex-colonies were not to be treated as victors' spoils but as mandates from the League of Nations. The administering Power was obliged to prepare each colony for eventual nationhood, and was subject to League control.

of *Trianon*, lost territory to Romania and to the new nations of Czechoslovakia and the Kingdom of Serbs, Croats, and Slovenes (Yugoslavia). Confined to a small area inhabited by Magyars, Hungary was ordered, like Austria and Germany, to reduce her military forces to the point of being powerless. The Treaty of *Neuilly* forced Bulgaria to give up land to Greece, Romania, and Yugoslavia. The settlement with Turkey was complicated by internal political difficulties. The Treaty of *Sèvres*, which virtually liquidated the Ottoman Empire by limiting it almost entirely to Asia Minor, was signed by the weak government of Sultan Mohammed VI. Within Turkey, however, a nationalist movement bitterly resented the Sultan's submission to the Western Powers; this faction, led by the war hero Mustapha Kemal, established a rival government to the Sultan's. The Sèvres agreement was denounced, and war broke out between Greece and Turkey (1921-22). In 1923, under British pressure, Kemal agreed to the Treaty of Lausanne, which brought peace to the eastern end of the Mediterranean.

One of the major accomplishments of the Paris conference was the formation of the League of Nations. Led by President Wilson and Jan Smuts of South Africa, a committee was selected to draft a constitution, called the Covenant, which became an integral part of the Treaty of Versailles. The purpose of the League was to afford mutual protection for all its members by the guarantee of assistance in the event of aggression by a foreign Power. The members agreed to refrain from aggression themselves, and to submit all grievances to arbitration. An important secondary purpose of the League was to promote international co-operation for improvements in problems such as health, education, labour, and administration of the world's peoples.

The League finally came into existence in January, 1920. A permanent Secretariat was established at Geneva which took care of routine operations. An Assembly was created, in which every member state was represented and had one vote. The League's executive body was the Council, which consisted of representatives of the Great Powers who were permanent members, and four additional Powers who were elected by the Assembly.[1]

As originally planned, the five permanent members of the

---

[1] The number of "additional Powers" progressively increased in succeeding years.

Council were to be Great Britain, Italy, France, Japan, and the United States. In the United States, however, a strong tide of isolationist sentiment had developed after the First World War, and despite President Wilson's efforts in championing the creation of the League, his country rejected the idea of American participation in the new organization. The absence of the United States was a crippling blow which considerably undermined the League's value. As events were soon to prove, the League was incapable of effective action as an arbiter of world politics.

Almost from the beginning, the Peace of Paris was attacked from all sides. One of the most criticized aspects was the settlements made on the basis of the principle of self-determination. Several new nations were formed in East Central Europe mainly upon the basis of language. Czechoslovakia, Yugoslavia, Poland, Lithuania, Latvia, and Estonia were all granted statehood. Yet these divisions along linguistic lines were anything but flawless. More than six million Germans lived under Polish or Czechoslovakian rule. In Czechoslovakia, within the province of Bohemia alone were more than three million Sudeten Germans, as well as more than a million Magyars. Because Italy had been promised territory, German-speaking Austrians in the South Tyrol became Italian subjects. Another criticism of the principle of self-determination applied chiefly to the nations formed from the former Austro-Hungarian Empire. Although the Empire had been a hodge-podge of nationalities, it had at least maintained an economic unity. Now, with each state erecting tariff walls and using its own currency, it appeared that the economic unity of the Danube basin had been destroyed.

Nor were the problems caused by the search for self-determination the only difficulties resulting from the Peace of Paris. Despite the severe measures taken against German military strength, the French remained unsatisfied in their longing for security. Clemenceau had wanted the Rhineland to be made into an independent buffer state between France and Germany, but was opposed by Britain and the United States. To placate French forces, Wilson and Lloyd George agreed to sign a defence agreement with France against Germany. The American Congress, however, refused to ratify the treaty, which therefore rendered the American signature invalid. When this happened, the British too backed down. The result was that France, unwilling to rely upon the League of Nations and collective security, went on an endless search for alliances.

Other nations, too, were dissatisfied. Germany, of course, was bitterly unhappy with every aspect of the Peace of Paris. Italy resented the creation of a potential powerful Adriatic rival, Yugoslavia. Russia—not invited to the conference—was suspicious that the newly created states along its western border were intended as a blockade against communism. And so, in many ways, the Peace of Paris was unsatisfactory, leaving Europe weakened, angry, unstable, and vulnerable to the outbreak of another war. In the words of a modern historian, "About all that could be said in its favour is that it might have been worse."

18 The Russian Revolution

> ... it was with a sense of awe that [the Germans] turned upon Russia the most grisly of all weapons. They transported Lenin in a sealed train like a plague bacillus from Switzerland into Russia.
>
> —Winston Churchill, *The World Crisis*

A sudden incident occurs; a spark that sets off widespread anger leads to rioting. The rioters, jostling one another, excited, each learning, perhaps for the first time, that others share their grievances, gain confidence. Then, perhaps, there may be shooting and casualties. Anger explodes, and the rioters attack the police or government chambers. The police vacillate, and offer no resistance. The government leaders are pushed aside, sometimes by execution or imprisonment, and the reins of power fall into new, sometimes very different, hands.

This is the climax, the explosion point of *revolution,* the moment that history finally moves in one violent quantum leap in some new direction. But revolution as an historical process is seldom an abrupt event. There are long roots, deep causes. Why should the revolutionaries be so angry? Sometimes their anger may be traced back for decades, even centuries. How does the ruling class come to the point of losing control? Perhaps the causes lie in mistakes made generations before. Why were the police, the army, the officers, unsuccessful in protecting the government? Did the intellectuals play a key role in precipitating discontent and anger? All these questions must be examined before a revolution can be understood.

1. THE ROOTS OF REVOLUTION

The Growth of Discontent

As we have seen earlier, Russia had long been the most backward of the major European nations in terms of her political and social development. The Tartar invasion left her centuries behind the

"Gambling for 'Souls'." A caricature by Gustave Doré depicting Russian serfdom about mid-19th century. The landowners are gambling with "souls" (the Russian description of serfs). The serfs, to the aristocracy, were simply property.

other European countries in growth. Under Peter the Great and Catherine the Great, Russia finally emerged from her "dark ages" of isolation as a major international Power, but her internal development became, if anything, more retarded than ever. There was nothing resembling a representative body or Parliament (the *Duma* had been abolished by Peter); there was virtually no middle class, the usual motivators of social change; the nobles, the officers of the army, and the Church were all firmly entrenched in opposition to social progress, and the Czar controlled absolute political power. After the widespread but unsuccessful peasant revolt in 1773, the position of the peasantry deteriorated still further. The peasants had no rights at all; they could be arbitrarily punished, put to forced labour, or even sold—a peasant quite literally was regarded as *property*. Unquestionably Catherine accomplished worthwhile social improvements, but by the end of the 18th century, the gulf between the Czar and the ruling class who held all political power, and the peasantry, was wider than ever.[1]

For the first quarter of the 19th century, prospects for modernization seemed brighter. The Czar, Alexander I, was genuinely progressive in outlook. Moves were made towards the abolition of serfdom, but meaningful reforms were postponed for an endless succession of wars, culminating in the titanic struggle against Napoleon. By the end of his reign, Alexander had become more reactionary than progressive. Following his death in 1825, a group of rather unrealistic young army officers, intoxicated by their exposure to the heady ideals then prevalent in France, where they had served in the occupying forces, attempted to institute their progressive ideas by overturning the Czardom. This was the Decembrist Revolt; it was pathetically unsuccessful, being crushed in a day by the new Czar Nicholas I.

Nicholas was a firm believer in the strictest authoritarianism, and used the Revolt as a signal for applying tighter controls than ever. For the rest of his reign, until 1855, he opposed liberalism and social change with every means in his power, for which he received the title "the Iron Czar." To maintain his autocratic government, he created a force of secret police, whose task was to seek out and destroy plots against the state. In spite of all his efforts, however, the Russian administrative system continued to crumble. The significance of the thirty years of Nicholas' government was that during this period the gulf between the aspirations of the peasants and the wishes of the ruling class became unbridgeable. As Russia fell farther and farther behind the other major nations of Europe in political development, an ever-increasing number of persons began to realize how bad their system was. Whereas the peasant had once had no ambition or hope greater than to live in poverty with a minimum of misery and abuse, by the mid-19th century the demand for improvement was beginning to grow. During Nicholas' reign there were over five hundred peasant revolts. Had the Czar and the nobles been more far-sighted, they might have devised some policy by which their own needs, as well as those of the peasants, might have been satisfied. Instead they responded by increased repression. Punishments for crimes of all degrees were made stricter than ever—a not untypical penalty was for an accused to run a

[1] These aspects of Russian history were discussed in greater detail on pages 120-123.

gauntlet of one thousand men twelve times. Other offenders were exiled to Siberia. Thus by 1855 the political situation in Russia was approaching the stage that no course of action could be taken that would be acceptable both to the peasants and the ruling class.

Nicholas' successor, Alexander II, realized the need for substantial reforms. One of these was a first tentative introduction of liberalism. The universities were given a degree of freedom, foreign travel was permitted, censorship was relaxed, and even journals written by Russians in exile were allowed into the country.

The major reform, intended as the beginning of Russian modernization, was the abolition of serfdom in 1861. It was on this measure that Alexander had pinned his greatest hopes: "It is better to abolish serfdom from above than to wait until it begins to be abolished from below."

The peasants, their expectations wildly excited by prospects of free land to go with their personal freedom, anticipated a new Utopia. They were not given land, however, just the opportunity of sharing it as members of the village commune (*mir*). Approximately half the cultivated land remained with the lords, and the other half was given to the mir. The lord was compensated by the government for the land he lost, and the mir in turn was required to repay the government over a period of forty-nine years, at six per cent interest.

In many ways, the emancipation of the serfs was a revolutionary measure, comparable to the abolition of feudalism in the French Revolution or the freeing of the slaves in the British Empire (1833) and the United States (1863). Unfortunately it was not really a success. By 1861 the situation in Russia had deteriorated too far for anything less than truly radical measures. The reforms that were made, instead of satisfying the peasants, served only to aggravate their discontent. Expecting to receive *all* the land, the peasants saw large portions of it, land that had been worked by their fathers and their fathers in turn for generations, taken from them altogether. Expecting to get the land as their *own,* they received it only as joint proprietors in the communal ownership of the mir. Expecting to receive the land free, they were burdened with heavy payments lasting half a century. In some ways, the peasants were actually worse off than before. Utterly discouraged, many abandoned the land and drifted to the cities, to swell the ranks of an impoverished and exploited proletariat. It was here, in the poorest districts of St.

Petersburg and Moscow, that revolutionary agitators later found their most receptive audience.

Since the Emancipation Edict had ended the lords' jurisdiction over the peasants, new systems for both local government and local courts were needed. To provide a replacement, the second major reform of Alexander's reign was made, in 1864. A series of elected local councils were formed, called *zemstvos*, which gave the various districts a limited control over education, public health, and agricultural improvements. This was the first taste of representative government ever enjoyed by Russians. Even greater improvements were made in the administration of justice. Class distinctions in determining guilt (although not necessarily punishments) were ended, courts were made independent of state control, and judges, who were now paid respectable salaries and were properly trained, could not be removed from their positions by powerful nobles. Trials were made public, a proper sequence of higher and lower courts was established, the choice of lawyer was allowed the accused, and juries appointed after the English system were introduced. These changes were an unqualified improvement, making judicial reform the most successful of Alexander's measures.

With these reforms by Alexander II, there appeared some hope that general improvements might be made in Russia. In 1863, however, the Czar's attention was distracted from domestic matters by a serious uprising in Poland that was not subdued for over a year. With the Polish rebellion, Alexander's sympathies for liberal ideas suffered a drastic decline. For the next decade and a half, his reign was marked by a return to repression and reaction. Zemstvo powers were restricted, censorship was again tightened, and the secret police again began arrests of suspects. As a response to this move, however, numerous small, ultra-secret groups of conspirators began to appear, dedicated to terrorism and assassination. An endless spate of bombings resulted, culminating in 1881, when one such group, called the *People's Will*, assassinated the Czar.

Not surprisingly, the assassination ushered in another period of reaction under the new Czar, Alexander III, who reigned until 1894. Criticism of the government was silenced, agitators exiled, revolutionary groups stamped out, and a programme of forced "Russification" adopted against all national minority groups within the country. Under the leadership of the Russian Orthodox Church, liberalism and western culture were rejected as decadent.

The hanging of the conspirators of the *People's Will*.

Despite the anti-western attitude of the government, however, such influences as industrialism were beginning to appear. And although Russia still remained far behind the advanced western nations in this phase of her development, with industrialization came a familiar by product, the growth of a discontented proletariat. Workers were underpaid and forced to accept miserable conditions, and although unions and strikes were illegal, a series of widespread strikes in the 1890s served to indicate the extent of the workers' discontent.

In the countryside, unrest for a time was less pronounced. The mir appeared to be flourishing, providing a degree of communal security for the peasant farmers, who still comprised eighty per cent of Russia's population. Even though the peasants' "land-hunger" continued unabated, the peasantry for a time seemed to be becoming less receptive to revolution than before. In 1891-92, however, a severe famine caused widespread suffering. By the end of the century, peasant revolts against the landlord and the tax collector were

THE RUSSIAN REVOLUTION 425

again a fairly frequent occurrence. Thus the peasants, while not the "vanguard of revolution," were nevertheless reaching the point where revolution would receive their support.

The Role of the Intelligentsia

One group that remained constantly and unalterably opposed to the Czarist regime, was the intelligentsia. By themselves the intellectuals had no power, no leverage, no threat to pose against the massive weight of the autocracy. What they could do, however, was constantly to stimulate the mass of the people to a more acute awareness of their own grievances and to prod them into action to seek reform. By this means the intellectuals had an effect that incomparably exceeded their numbers. The most extreme among them became dedicated missionaries to the idea of revolution.

And missionaries they were. The reformers came from every social class, and despite the danger of the police, their penetrating criticism attacked every area of Russian life and thought. Intellectuals toured Russia, fanning the discontent of peasants dissatisfied with the land reform. Some, called "Westernizers," advocated the adoption of European ideas and institutions. Others, who believed that Russia should develop on her own, using her historic Slavic background as a guide, were called "Slavophiles." The two most important of the early groups, in terms of the influence of their ideas, were the Populists (*narodnici*) and the Anarchists.

The less influential of these groups, in terms of widespread appeal, were the Anarchists, most prominent of whom was Michael Bakunin. The Anarchists were quite literally professional revolutionaries, "devoured by one purpose, one thought, one passion—the revolution." The only policy of the Anarchists was terror, which was met with pitiless suppression by the police, and resentment from the people.

More constructive in their approach were the Populists. These were intellectuals who believed that the wealthy and educated had the obligation to raise the social and economic standards of the peasants. As much spontaneously as by organization, hundreds of young people fanned out through the Russian countryside to live with the peasants to provide them with a rudimentary education. Underlying the Populist movement was the idea that in the Russian mir, with its tradition of agrarian co-operative ownership reinforced by the Emancipation Edict, socialism might succeed where it had failed in the European *débâcle* of 1848.

Soon, however, it became apparent that the peasants were indifferent or even hostile to Populist socialism—their only interest was the *petit bourgeois* concern of acquiring more land. The Populists, too, were heading to a dead end.

Revolutionary philosophy was at a crossroads: it needed to take a new direction or die. The crucial figure at this point was George Plekhanov, the "father of Russian Marxism," who was the first to realize that the revolution would begin not with the peasants, but with the steadily growing Russian proletariat.

Plekhanov's writings—which were passed by the Russian censors in the hope that they would cause divisions among the socialists—were soon influencing an increasing number of Russian revolutionaries, including some of outstanding ability. Marxist groups began forming in all the major cities of Russia, where they provoked strikes and demonstrations and circulated their ideas by means of illegal printing presses. In 1898, a conference of all the Marxist organizations in Russia was held: this was the formal founding of the Russian Social Democratic Party, an organization that nineteen years later was to have decisive effect on the history of Russia and the world.

By the turn of the century, the Social Democrats were steadily growing in number and influence, even though most of their leaders were in exile. They had a newspaper, *Iskra* (the Spark), published in Germany, a system of couriers for making deliveries inside Russia, an intricate network of "cell" organizations that spread across much of the country, a system of finance (which depended substantially on outright robbery), and an "underground" for smuggling political refugees to neutral countries. By 1903, the Party had developed to a stage that a second conference was necessary to establish a programme of tactics and strategy.

As head of an organization that was both Marxist and Russian, Plekhanov was in a peculiar dilemma. The whole structure of Marxist theory was applicable only to an advanced, mature, industrial society—and Russia, despite the advent of industrialism, was anything but this. As Marxists, the Social Democrats should simply wait for industrialization to come. As Russians, however, they shared the tradition of revolutionary action, to which the thought of passive inactivity was intolerable.

The inevitable confrontation between the pure Marxist faction and the activists came at the 1903 Conference. The crucial question concerned the philosophy of Party organization. Were the Social Democrats to be an open democratic party in which everybody could participate in decision-making, or would it be in effect a dictatorship, organized secretly, and run by a central committee? The question was precisely parallel to that of classic Marxism versus immediate activism—those willing to await a *bourgeois* industrial society could afford to organize democratically, while those who demanded forceful revolutionary action needed a dictatorial organization to avoid the secret police. The leading spokesman of the first approach was Plekhanov. The leader of the second was the most brilliant and energetic of his disciples, V. I. Lenin.

Lenin, whose real name was Ulyanov, was born in 1870. While Lenin was still young, his older brother, Alexander, was executed for an unsuccessful attempt on the life of the Czar, Alexander III. This event was the turning point in Lenin's life, leaving him with a black hatred for the Czarist regime, and was partly responsible for his later dedication to revolution. Brilliant and intense, he was expelled from the University of Kazan, arrested for revolutionary activity, then admitted to the University of St. Petersburg, where he completed a four-year course in twelve months, and finished with the highest mark. Already a confirmed follower of Plekhanov, he formed a Marxist group in Russia and travelled throughout the country disseminating seditious literature. Arrested again, he was exiled to Siberia, where he spent three years, after which he went to Switzerland to work with Plekhanov and other Russian Marxists. Together they founded *Iskra*, which was soon virtually controlled by Lenin.

By the 1903 Conference, Lenin and Plekhanov had moved far apart. In a dispute between the two, Plekhanov had the advantage of his established position; Lenin, however, had total self-confidence and incomparable will and energy. Ruthlessly he split the Conference into two factions. Deliberately provoking one group of delegates to walk out, he gained a momentary advantage for his faction and forced through a vote on the critical issue of Party organization. By winning this crucial vote, he claimed for his group the title *Bolsheviks* (meaning "those in the majority") and disparaged the rival group as *Mensheviks* ("those in the minority").

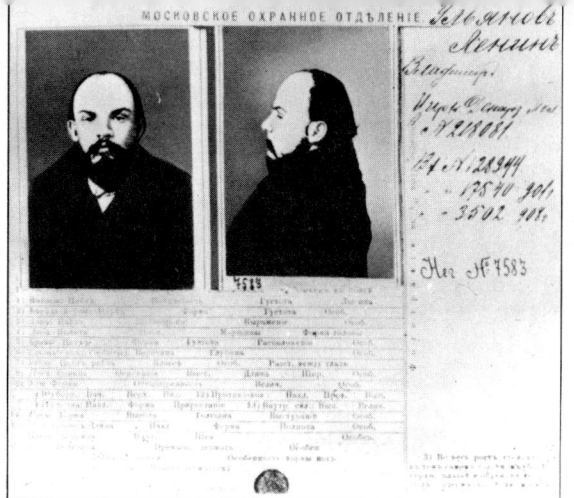

"Three Who Made a Revolution." TOP: Police "mug-shot" of Lenin. CENTRE: Trotsky, age 26. BOTTOM: Stalin, early 1900's.

Lenin's victory was artificial. Because of his tactics, the Party was hopelessly split, and for this Lenin received the greatest blame. Many of his friends and followers deserted him and sided with the Mensheviks. Foremost among these was Leon Trotsky, who was destined to play a role in the Russian Revolution second in importance only to Lenin himself. The two groups never reached a reconciliation, and although they co-operated to a certain extent, they later virtually separated. The Bolsheviks, with their emphasis on dictatorial organization, were regarded as the extremists, while the Mensheviks, more concerned with democratic methods, were the moderates, although certainly both groups were extremist enough.

The influence and effect of the Bolsheviks and Mensheviks were felt in several ways in Russia. First, the exiles, such as Lenin, worked tirelessly writing propaganda for the consumption of the Marxists and the interested workers in Russia. Second, their networks throughout the country served not only to give exiles' writings a far wider circulation than they would otherwise have received, but existed also as a nucleus of organization to perform guiding functions in the critical moments of revolution. Finally, and perhaps most important, they provided the key leaders—Lenin and Trotsky—whose roles at the crucial moments were to spell the difference between failure and success.

The Decline of the Czar

By the beginning of the 20th century, certain prerequisites for revolution—the discontent and resentment of a substantial proportion of the populace, and the ceaseless agitation of an intelligentsia dedicated in its enmity—were already in existence. Despite these factors, however, the balance of political power was still overwhelmingly in favour of the existing system. Foremost among the reasons for this was the almost mystic reverence in which the Czar was held by the Russian masses. The next step, therefore, in the path to revolution, was the destruction of the Czar's prestige and the erosion of his control of government.

In 1894, Alexander III was succeeded by his son Nicholas II. The new Czar was a man of refinement, charm, and intelligence, but also, unfortunately, of indecisiveness and weak-will. More unfortunate still, his wife, the German princess Alexandra, was completely unsuited for court life in Russia, and eventually became thoroughly hated by both the aristocracy and the masses. "Unbelievably gullible and superstitious," she contributed substantially to Nicholas' already considerable inability to make decisions.

The first major disaster for the Czar was the ill-fated Russian-Japanese War of 1904-05. Nicholas, intent on imperialistic expansion in the East, established effective Russian control of Manchuria and began preparations to extend his influence to Korea. This development, however, was considered unacceptable by Japan, who saw her own interests threatened. After a futile attempt at a negotiated solution, war began with an undeclared Japanese attack on Russian installations in China. In a short period Russia suffered an uninterrupted series of defeats, which were all the more humiliating for being at the hands of an "inferior yellow race." Nicholas' handling of the war had been incompetent in the extreme, and left him personally discredited in Russia. Reverence and respect were swept away by the resentment and humiliation of defeat.

Worse was still to come. Under the pressure of war, the already bad conditions in which many of the peasants and city workers lived deteriorated still further. Popular anger was growing. The Minister of the Interior, Viacheslav Plehve, was assassinated. Nicholas, lacking the determination of his father to pursue a firm course, was sufficiently frightened by this event to attempt a rather weak policy of conciliation. All this succeeded in doing was to enable the revolutionary movement to organize more efficiently.

Knowing the danger posed by the radical underground revolutionary movements in such circumstances, the police were willing to tolerate, even encourage, more moderate leaders of protest as a "safety valve" against excessive discontent. One such leader was an Orthodox priest, Father Georgi Gapon. Gapon, however, was considerably more radical than the police had realized. On January 22, 1905, he led an enormous demonstration of petitioners to the Czar's palace in St. Petersburg. The marchers were far from revolutionary in intent, asking for nothing more radical than an eight-hour day and no overtime. Many carried ikons of Nicholas and sang "God Save the Czar" as they marched. When the police realized the size of the demonstration, however—there were probably in excess of two hundred thousand marchers—they panicked and fired point-blank into the crowds. Several hundred persons were killed, and over one thousand wounded.

Dispersal of the petitioners by the police on "Bloody Sunday."

The event, known as "Bloody Sunday," was of crucial significance, for it was the abrupt, brutal end of the people's love for the Czar. Father Gapon, having fled to Finland, wrote Nicholas:

The innocent blood of workers, their wives and children, lies ever between thee, oh soul destroyer, and the Russian people.... Let all the blood that is to be shed, hangman, fall upon thee and thy kindred!

It was now irrevocably clear that the Czar was not the people's friend, but their enemy.

Another important factor in the crippling of Nicholas' ability to control the Russian situation, was the growing disaffection of the armed forces. Continuing disasters in the Russian-Japanese War seriously demoralized the troops. In January, 1905, the sailors on the battleship *Prince Potemkin* mutinied. Further mutinies threatened. And without complete control of the military, the usual Czarist methods of government by suppression and force were no longer workable—especially in the face of widespread opposition from the Russian masses. Thus another segment of the pattern was falling into place.

2. PRELUDE—1905

In September, 1905, the humiliating peace with Japan was signed. Shortly after, the soldiers, angry, disillusioned, and near the point of mutiny, began returning in numbers to Russia. It was a situation in which an uprising was almost inevitable.

The signal came with a strike in a Moscow printing factory. With amazing speed, the strike spread to other industries, until both Moscow and St. Petersburg were virtually paralysed. Russia was a hairsbreadth from revolution.

For the strikers, efficient organization and leadership were essential. In factories in St. Petersburg, workers quickly elected delegates to represent them in a central council, called a *soviet*, which functioned to control the strike. In Moscow a similar soviet was established. The tightly organized revolutionary networks, particularly those of the Social Democrats, were an essential part of the quick establishment of the soviet system. A number of the leaders in exile returned to participate, including Lenin, who helped lead the strike in Moscow. Above all, one brilliant leader emerged— Leon Trotsky.

Trotsky, at the time of the 1905 rising, was only twenty-six years old, but had already lived a remarkable life of revolutionary activity. Born Lev Bronstein, he was arrested before he was twenty, and exiled to Siberia. He escaped to become a leader in the underground organization, then smuggled himself to western Europe, where he participated in the 1903 Conference that saw the Bolshevik-Menshevik split. Originally a supporter of Lenin, he was disgusted with the Bolshevik leader's tactics, and became a rather uneasy member of the opposition. Soon he tired of the endless inter-factional disputes and went to Finland, where, at the Russian border just twenty miles from St. Petersburg, he was able to function as an effective leader of the underground. Then, in October, 1905, he entered St. Petersburg to assume control of the uprising.

For several weeks the strike continued to paralyse Russia. Most dangerous of all, it showed signs of spreading to the armed services. There was a naval mutiny at Kronstadt, and another at Sevastopol. Army garrisons as widely removed as Vladivostok and Kiev rose in rebellion. Although these risings generally were short lived, they did indicate that Nicholas could not use suppression to end the strike, but rather would have to offer concessions. Accordingly, late in October, a form of constitution was drawn up, the first in Russia's history, that included among its measures the establishment of an elected Parliament, or Duma. The October Manifesto, as it came to be known, fell far short of establishing complete democracy, but it did signify a decisive break with the principle of unqualified autocratic power.

Russia was not at this point ready for a genuine revolution. The grievances of the people were not so deep that they would support a condition of turmoil and upheaval indefinitely. The October Manifesto satisfied a number of the moderates who had supported the strike to obtain reform, but had no desire for a complete overthrow of the system. The extremists—that is the Social Democrats and the Social Revolutionaries[1]—could no longer attract enough support to sustain the uprising. Gradually the government began to reassert control. The St. Petersburg soviet was suppressed by mid-December, and Trotsky and other prominent leaders imprisoned. In Moscow, where Lenin was in charge, the strike lasted several months longer and saw some particularly bitter street battles between police and the revolutionaries before it was finally broken. By early 1906, the government was once again in control. The danger of revolution, temporarily at any rate, was over.

The Lessons of 1905

The 1905 revolution, while unsuccessful, was nevertheless a major event in the development of the ultimately successful revolution of November, 1917. Particularly, the emergence of the soviet as an organized body capable of providing leadership was an important source of experience for a similar body that appeared twelve years later.

The year 1905 also had its influence on the development of the revolutionary leadership. During the general strike, all parties of the far left—Menshevik, Bolshevik, Social Revolutionary—had worked reasonably well together, and it was hoped that even with the crisis over they might continue to co-operate. Before long, however, it was evident that their divisions were as sharp as ever. The Social Revolutionaries could not shake their addiction to terrorism, which the Social Democrats regarded as dangerous. Between the Bolsheviks and Mensheviks the split became even more funda-

---

[1] The descendants of the narodnici.

mental. The Mensheviks, who had dominated the soviet throughout the crisis, were deeply disturbed by the complexity of controlling political power. Accordingly they began to lay a growing emphasis on the orthodox Marxist approach that the revolution should wait until Russia became a mature industrial state with a liberal Parliament, in which the revolutionaries could gain more political experience. As a result, the Mensheviks increasingly tended to accept a more passive approach to revolution in the years following 1905. To the Bolsheviks this approach was intolerable; *they*, certainly, had no intention of waiting idly for history to catch up to them. The Menshevik strategy was perhaps more correct in Marxist terms, but ultimately it put them at a strong disadvantage against the ruthlessly determined followers of Lenin.

3. INTERLUDE

From the perspective of 1905, the most obvious accomplishment of the uprising was the concession by the Czar to establish a representative assembly, the Duma.

In the first years following 1905 there was every sign that the re-established control of the Czar might be successful and enduring. The creation of the Duma was received with reasonable satisfaction by the middle class liberals and progressives. Under the outstanding leadership of the Prime Minister, Peter Stolypin, an Agrarian Reform Act was implemented, which enabled the peasants to acquire land for themselves, thereby setting the stage for an impressive growth in agriculture. Partly as a result, Russia experienced a period of rapid growth and prosperity, with both agricultural and industrial output setting new records.

In the struggle between the forces of revolution and stability, the balance now definitely favoured the established government. The peasants were gratified by the land reforms, while industrial workers were generally satisfied with the benefits of growing prosperity—the marked decline in terrorist activities and strikes is reasonably clear evidence of this. The revolutionary movements were declining in strength, so much so that Lenin himself admitted that he had given up hope of seeing the revolution in his lifetime.

There was one factor that again began to tip the balance in favour of revolution, however. This was the remarkable decline in

"Now comes your reign of will and power—be the Emperor, be Peter the Great, Ivan the Terrible, the Emperor Paul—crush them all under you. Now don't you laugh, naughty one. . . . Send Lvov to Siberia, Miliukov, Guchkov and Polivanov to Siberia. . . ."—From a letter by Czarina Alexandra to Czar Nicholas II.

the leadership capacities of the Czar. Nicholas, by nature weak-willed, began increasingly to let his wife Alexandra influence his decisions on matters of state. The Czarina in turn was willing to accept advice from some of the most unlikely sources imaginable. Unique among these was Gregory Rasputin, an extraordinary monk with an apparently miraculous power to ease the sickness of the Czarina's only son, who suffered from haemophilia.

By 1910 Rasputin had become the deadly enemy of Stolypin, with the result that Nicholas, influenced by the Czarina, began to withdraw his support from his Prime Minister. Thus the one man who more than any other might have saved Russia from revolution found his programmes thwarted and undermined. In the following years, any official whom Rasputin disliked was in danger of

The dark man of God—Rasputin.

being dismissed. Worse still, the government was being filled with persons often of utter incompetence, who owed their positions entirely to Rasputin's favour. If Nicholas resisted Rasputin's requests —as he did when these were particularly preposterous—the Czarina persisted until he agreed. Logic and rationality almost disappeared from the decision-making process; in a figurative sense, the government was becoming insane. In the words of one historian:

> The fairly honourable and efficient group who formed the top of the bureaucratic pyramid degenerated into a rapidly changing succession of the appointees of Rasputin. It was an amazing, extravagant and pitiful spectacle, and one without parallel in the history of civilized nations.

In times of prosperity, such as the years of Stolypin's Prime Ministership, the decay of the government might have been tolerated. On August 1, 1914, however, the First World War began. Prosperity changed to crisis.

The immediate reaction to the declaration of war was an overwhelming emotional wave of patriotism and loyalty to the Czar. Churches filled, processions began, demonstrations and strikes

Russian soldiers surrendering at Tannenburg.

ended, volunteers flocked to join the army, crowds sang "God Save the Czar."

Despite the enthusiasm, the Russian army was poorly equipped, with outdated methods and little organization. Its commanders were of low calibre and in several cases grossly corrupt. All told, Russia was badly prepared for war. Within a month the Russians were slaughtered at the Battle of Tannenburg; within a year of their initial advance into Germany they had been driven back two hundred miles in a series of uninterrupted defeats, with casualties estimated at an incredible four million.

Now the mood of jubilation changed to one of black pessimism and rapidly growing anger. The incompetence of the command was unmistakable: soldiers were often sent into battle with neither arms nor ammunition—sometimes there would be a ratio of one rifle for ten men—and the wounded were simply left to die. Among the politicians, opposition to the conduct of the war was growing, and by late 1916 had reached such a level that every party from extreme

Left to extreme Right had united against the government. Among the ordinary people, bitterness was greater still; there was scarcely a family in Russia that had not suffered at least one death. Most dangerous of all, resentment within the army was reaching a point where discipline was threatened. Mutinies were constantly occurring and men were deserting literally by the thousands every day. And ominously for the future ability of the government to control armed opposition, a detachment of soldiers had refused orders to fire on striking workers in Petrograd.

The government had by now disintegrated almost completely. Under the combined influence of his wife and Rasputin, Nicholas dismissed a total of twenty-one ministers who were invariably replaced with incompetents. Examples were Boris Stürmer, for a short period the Prime Minister, who was totally corrupt and quite possibly in league with the Germans; or Alexander Protopopov, Rasputin's choice for Minister of the Interior, who was suspected of being insane. If Nicholas demurred at such nominations, the Czarina persisted, often hysterically, until he agreed. Even the Commander-in-Chief of the army was replaced on Rasputin's request.

On December 29, 1916, Rasputin was murdered by a small group of aristocrats, who hoped that with him gone, the government might somehow be salvaged. Nicholas was unable or unwilling to reassert control, however, and disintegration continued to disaster.

4. THE RUSSIAN REVOLUTION

In 1905, a revolution which did not succeed in a critically short period—a period of days—was certain to fail. The opposition to the regime was not so deep-seated among the people that it could be sustained indefinitely in the face of the danger and uncertainty of an uprising. This lack of total determination meant that the point would soon come that if the government did not fall, the people would waver in their opposition, compromise, and accept the old regime providing reasonable concessions were made. Particularly in 1905, the opposition itself had been divided in its own aims, and when a substantial proportion of those opposed to the government ceased their resistance in response to concessions (the October Manifesto), the balance returned in favour of the government.

In 1917, however, several critical conditions had changed. For one, the opposition of the great masses of the people was far deeper, far more bitter, more likely to persist for an extended period. For another, all parties, from extreme Left to moderate to extreme Right, were in unquestioning agreement that the Czar must go. This time, there could be no concession or compromise to dilute resistance. Moreover, the government, certainly no model of resolution in 1905, was now completely rotted with its coterie of sycophants chosen at the behest of Rasputin. Again, the revolutionary agitators had had twelve more years to infiltrate the ranks of the populace and amplify discontent. All these factors had an important effect. The most important development of all, however, was the change in attitude of the military. In 1905, there had been substantial discontent in the armed services, but in a crisis military discipline could be relied upon to keep the forces in control. *By 1917 this was no longer so.* Nowhere had the socialist agitators been more active than among the soldiers, where they were constantly spreading sedition and constantly arguing for disobedience. Nowhere was the depressing evidence of the rottenness of the system more inescapable than at the Front. Never before had there been such sympathy among the soldiers for the cause of revolution. For the first time, the armed forces could no longer be depended upon to protect the government.

The March Revolution

The Russian Revolution was really a culmination of two revolutions: in the first, power transferred from the old Czarist regime to the moderates; in the second, from the moderates to the extremists. The first stage occurred in March, 1917, the second in November of the same year.[1]

On March 3, a strike began in the Putilov steel works in Petrograd (the new name for St. Petersburg). The demonstration continued growing in size and momentum daily, until the police found they could no longer cope with the crowds. By March 9, three hundred thousand workers were marching in the streets.

The strike, now out of control, was on the point of becoming revolution. Bolshevik and Menshevik organizers were hard at

---

[1]The calendar used in Russia at this time was thirteen days behind the western calendar. Therefore, the "March revolution" is sometimes referred to as "February," and the November revolution as "October."

work, urging more workers to join the strike, harrying police counter-measures, and generally contributing to the rapidly growing paralysis. Nicholas, at the Front, regarded the emergency with detached complacency, issuing to his ministers the command: "I order that the disorders in the capital shall be stopped." The ministers, however, were quite incapable of handling the problem. The turning point came when the Cossacks refused to fire on the crowd, and in some cases began fraternizing with the demonstrators. In other instances the soldiers aimed their rifles at the sky rather than obey orders to fire into the ranks of workers. Mutinies began in a number of regiments, often resulting in officers being murdered. By March 12, more and more soldiers, far from merely failing to obey orders to fire on the strikers, were joining them in the attack on the government. Police stations and arsenals were stormed for arms. Under pressure the police, too, refused to obey orders. The government was without protection, and on March 15, Nicholas abdicated. The old regime was dead.

With all semblance of order gone, new *ad hoc* organizations of government were formed to reassert emergency control. The first of these was the Provisional Government, made up of moderates and progressives of the Duma. The leaders were Prince Lvov, a prominent aristocrat, who became Prime Minister, and Alexander Kerensky, a Social Revolutionary, who was made Foreign Minister. The second organization was the soviet, which had reappeared, patterned on the 1905 model and again led by the Mensheviks and Bolsheviks.

In the wild turmoil of the March Revolution, both the soviet and the Provisional Government performed different and essential functions; and each was useful, perhaps even necessary, for the other's survival. The Provisional Government was the more moderate of the two, and, being an outcropping of the Duma, was *legitimate*—that is, more than any other group, it was generally considered to be *entitled* to power. The generals and the officers of the army, the upper and middle classes, the moderates who could never have tolerated the soviet, were willing to accept the rulings of the Provisional Government. Because of this, the revolution could be kept alive until the soviet was powerful enough to seize control. The soviet, on the other hand, tended to receive the natural support of the rank-and-file soldiers and workers. Partly, the reason for this was the famous "Order Number One," by which the soviet announced its policy that soldiers of the ranks should keep their arms and were not obliged to obey their officers while not on duty. Another aspect of soviet policy that appealed strongly to the soldiers and the working class was that of withdrawing from the World War at the soonest possible moment, in contrast to the Provisional Government's intention of pursuing the war regardless of cost. As a consequence of these factors, the soviet eventually would acquire superior armed strength.

In the first weeks following the overthrow of the Czar, when the threat of a counter-revolution led by Nicholas was the greatest danger to both organizations, a thin, tentative co-operation could exist between the Provisional Government and the soviet. Beneath this, however, each clearly recognized the other as its mortal rival for control. Eventually a showdown would be inevitable.

It was within the soviet that the developments whose ultimate significance would be greatest, were taking place. Another soviet was formed in Moscow, and then in most other major cities as well, although in 1917, as in 1905, it was in Petrograd that the critical action was taking place, and this time also it was the Mensheviks rather than the Bolsheviks who were in charge. A major difference between the two occasions, however, was that one of the key figures would soon change parties. This was Trotsky, the foremost leader of the 1905 uprising, who was abandoning the Mensheviks and closing ranks with Lenin. The combination of these two men gave the Bolsheviks a formidable advantage over their rivals.

In March both Lenin and Trotsky were in exile, Lenin in Switzerland and Trotsky in New York. With the Revolution an evident success, they began to make preparations for returning to Russia to lead the soviet in the coming struggle against the Provisional Government. The story of their return is one of the most fascinating intrigues of history. Germany, faced with the entry of the United States into the World War, desperately needed to remove Russia from the fighting in order to concentrate her full forces on the Western Front. On the calculated risk that under Lenin the Bolsheviks would first overthrow the Provisional Government and then withdraw Russia from the war, the German government made arrangements for his transport through Germany from Switzerland to Russia. On April 16, he arrived in Petrograd, and immediately set about displacing the Mensheviks and bringing the soviet under Bolshevik control. A month later Trotsky appeared, after having spent a four-week detainment period in Halifax, Nova Scotia. Despite considerable opposition, the Bolsheviks were gradually emerging as the leading revolutionary party.

The July Days

In early July the war suddenly took a turn for the worse, with the collapse of a major Russian offensive. One of the results was a new crisis in Petrograd; a number of ministers resigned from the Provisional Government, and a feeling of violent anger began spreading rapidly among the people. On July 16, wild riots and demonstrations broke out. The role of the Bolsheviks in this event is still not entirely clear, but it seems likely that agitators had been acting among the workers, soldiers, and sailors to precipitate the uprising as a first step toward an attempted *coup d'état*. Several thousand armed sailors surged through the streets, and for two days the life of the government hung in the balance. Then, by July 19, the uprising began to peter out.

Now came the reaction. Despite the enthusiasm shown by some of the rioters, the majority of the populace had been badly frightened by the crisis. The Bolsheviks, who were held responsible, suddenly became the objects of mass anger. Particularly damaging, the rumour was circulated that Lenin was a German agent who was cynically manipulating the workers for Germany's advantage —a rumour which gained added credence from the circumstances of his return to Russia and from the timing of the riots to coincide with the collapse of the offensive. Trotsky and other Bolshevik leaders were arrested and Lenin narrowly escaped to Finland.

In the aftermath of the July Days, the Bolsheviks reached the low point of their fortunes. If the Provisional Government had been able to function effectively it might at this stage have drawn ahead of the soviet and become the sole government of Russia. The Provisional Government, however, made a number of fundamental mistakes. Primarily, it insisted on continuing the war, rather than accepting the fairly reasonable terms that Germany was at this point offering. Then, nothing was done to meet the peasants' angry demands for a solution to the land problem. Similarly, in the cities a severe food shortage that had existed for months showed no signs of improving.

Kerensky.

By late August, the reaction against the Bolsheviks had largely evaporated. The Bolsheviks were as strong as ever, and in some ways better organized. The Provisional Government was proving incapable of handling problems of the magnitude facing Russia. Kerensky—who had displaced Prince Lvov as Prime Minister—was distrusted and disliked. Now a new danger was looming—the threat of counter-revolutionary reaction from the Right.

The Kornilov Affair

With almost half a year passed since the abdication of the Czar and Russia still in seemingly hopeless turmoil, a number of moderates and conservatives were beginning to turn against the Provisional Government. Even a dictator, it seemed to them, would be preferable to a repetition of the July Days. Accordingly, a plan was begun for the Provisional Government to be overthrown by the Commander-in-Chief of the army, General Lavr Kornilov.

Kornilov, while himself a sincere supporter of the Revolution, found the political chaos prevailing in Russia intolerable. After splitting with Kerensky over the issue of army discipline and the treatment of mutineers, he prepared to take matters into his own hands, and in mid-September turned his army against the government. For the second time in two months, the Provisional Government was against the wall. Ironically, its only strong ally was its strongest enemy, the soviet. With the greatest of reluctance, Kerensy called upon the soviet for help, issued arms to its members and freed its leaders from prison. The soviet in turn, fully recognizing the fatal danger posed by Kornilov to its own existence, cooperated fully. Through the activities of its agitators, Kornilov's soldiers were induced to desert, and workers sabotaged railways that were necessary for his advance. In less than a week, the threat had vanished, and Kornilov himself was arrested.

Kornilov's attempted *coup*, being a failure, had no especially great significance in itself, but it did have several important consequences. The first was that the Bolsheviks were now fully armed, having received their share and more of the arms distributed during the crisis. The second was that the black mark of the July Days was erased: the "German agent" rumour was reversed, and it was the right-wing extremists who now appeared the enemies of the people. The effect was a reaction against the reaction, and a wave of sympathy and approval for the Bolsheviks. For the first time, the Bolsheviks displaced the Mensheviks as the leaders of the soviet, with Trotsky becoming President. The Bolsheviks now were clearly the most powerful political force in Russia. Then, on October 22, Lenin, "like some predator closing in on its quarry," again returned from Finland. The final Russian Revolution was at hand.

November

By the beginning of November, the Bolsheviks could rely on the support of approximately four hundred thousand members throughout Russia. Similarly they had the support of the army, particularly in Petrograd—it was calculated that of all the troops stationed in the capital only two regiments were opposed to them.

The Bolsheviks now began systematically finishing their preparations for takeover. Trotsky—on his own authority—signed an order for the supply of five thousand rifles, which were delivered to the Bolsheviks without question. Bolshevik "commissars" were imposed on regiments throughout Petrograd, instructing the soldiers to obey them rather than their commanders. The soldiers

"Give us an organization of revolutionists and we shall overturn the world."
—V. I. Lenin.

of the principal arsenal, the fortress of St. Peter and St. Paul, were won over by Trotsky and made available a further one hundred thousand small arms. The sailors of the cruiser *Aurora* were given "orders" to arm, in readiness to come to the Bolsheviks' assistance when required.

By November 7 they were ready. Early that morning the telephone exchanges, railway stations, the state bank, the bridges, and the electric plants were seized. *There was no resistance from the police.* By evening the Bolsheviks were in complete control of Petrograd. The Provisional Government helplessly awaited the final Bolshevik attack. Late the following night, November 8, the *Aurora* began shelling the Winter Palace. Kerensky had already left, the garrison melted away, and Bolshevik Red Guards overran the building virtually unopposed.

The same evening as the Bolsheviks were establishing military control of Petrograd, from which their control of all Russia could be extended, the Second All-Russian Congress of Soviets was meeting in the city. The Bolsheviks won an enormous majority; it was the first time in history that their name was legitimate. The Mensheviks had been outmanoeuvred completely: they were now, almost against their will, a party of opposition. Trotsky triumphantly rose, and in a jeering tone said "You are a mere handful, miserable, bankrupt; your role is finished, and you may go where you belong—to the dustbin of history."

The greatest ovation, of course, was reserved for Lenin. The long years, often bitter, often filled with frustration, even despair, were over. Unquestionably problems of the greatest magnitude remained, but to the Bolsheviks anything and everything seemed possible. At the end of his speech, Lenin said, simply, "We shall now proceed to construct the socialist order."

UNIT FOUR **WAR AND PEACE**

19 Society and Technology after the First World War

"I will build a motor car for the great multitude. It will be large enough for the family but small enough for the individual to run and care for. It will be constructed of the best materials by the best men to be hired after the simplest designs that modern engineering can devise. But it will be so low in price that no man making a good salary will be unable to own one and enjoy with his family the blessing of hours of pleasure in God's great open spaces."

—Henry Ford

SOCIETY AND TECHNOLOGY AFTER THE FIRST WORLD WAR

The pace of modern history is rapidly accelerating. In earlier periods of western civilization, many changes in the daily lives of ordinary men and women were characterized by what might be described as the "inevitability of gradualness." Even today, in certain parts of Asia and Africa, many people still live in much the same manner as did their ancestors in ancient times. However, we have seen how the Industrial Revolution quickly transformed the society of western Europe and the New World.

This process, a quickening of all aspects of human existence, attained a crescendo in the 20th century—more particularly following the First World War. To take but one example, the horse—still a common means of transportation during the first quarter of this century—has now disappeared from our streets. Even railways have been largely displaced, as a means of public transportation, by automobiles and aircraft. We shall now examine these developments in relation to social and technological, economic, and political forces.

1. THE TECHNOLOGICAL REVOLUTION

The First World War had profound effects on both sides of the Atlantic. In Europe the conflict had taken a terrible toll of lives and many more would carry their wounds to the grave. But war damage extended far beyond the lives of soldiers and civilians. Four long years of trench warfare had devastated northern France and much of Belgium. Farmlands had been churned up by millions of artillery shells; many areas had also been blighted by gas attacks. Mines had been flooded, villages destroyed, and industries ruined.

Nor were the effects of the war confined to the battlefields. Although German and Austrian soil had been spared the rigours of fighting, the Allied naval blockade had drastically reduced available stocks of food. Hunger stalked the streets of Berlin, Vienna, and other large centres. Lack of food and other necessities had reduced people's resistance to disease, and eastern Europe was ravaged by cholera, typhus, and influenza.

The first large-scale participation of Canadian and United States forces in a European war had less devastating but no less profound effects on the North American economy. Many homes were saddened by sacrifice (over sixty thousand Canadian and more than one hundred thousand American servicemen found their last resting place in Europe), and few aspects of normal life remained unaffected by the far-away struggle. On the other hand, both agriculture and industry expanded enormously to meet the demands of wartime. Spurred on by high profits, both farmers and manufacturers increased their production to the limit. Mechanization made rapid progress, with the appearance of automobiles and tractors. Too often, however, these factors created an artificial "boom" that could not be sustained when something like normal conditions returned with peace.

Transportation

In other aspects, the warring governments' lavish expenditures had beneficial and far-reaching effects. Science and technology made great progress, especially in the field of transportation. During the winter following the Armistice of 1918, the first regular air service was established between London and Paris; in the summer of 1919 two British pilots, John Alcock and Arthur Brown, made the first transatlantic flight.

However, the major stimulus to transportation in the post-war period came from the United States, where Henry Ford was the first manufacturer to make a cheap and efficient automobile. The gasoline engine had been invented by a German, N. A. Otto, as far back as 1876, but mechanical difficulties, bad roads, and prejudice against the innovation delayed its application to transportation. Speed limits were restricted to sixteen kilometres per hour in

"Free of the belt, he took off his flying gloves and, armed with an opened clasp knife, stepped out of the cockpit onto the lower wing. The vicious blast of freezing air nearly swept him into space, but he grimly hung on to a horizontal strut leading from the fuselage to the engine nacelle, and sidestepped outward to the engine. With one arm hooked around the strut Brown reached high up and began to chip at the ice that had formed around the intake. The big four-bladed wooden propeller flashed only inches from his freezing hand; the slightest slip, a glancing blow off the ice, and Brown faced a cruel death. He aimed his knife blade with deliberation, slowly chipping the ice away. Finally, the intake was clear and the port engine again picked up its song of power. Now Brown inched his way back toward the fuselage, each step on the icy wing accompanied by a silent prayer. He arrived safely at the cockpit, numb with cold, his eyes aching painfully from the blasts of air that had swept underneath his fur-rimmed goggles."—An incident on the first transatlantic flight by Alcock and Brown.—From *Bold Men, Far Horizons*, by H. M. Mason.

some cases, a journey of one hundred and sixty kilometres almost invariably involved a puncture and tire-change, and the cost of cars placed them beyond the reach of the ordinary citizen. By developing the technique of "mass production" (with pre-fabricated parts put together by specialized labour on assembly lines), Ford revolutionized the automotive industry. By 1927 he had sold no less than fifteen million of his famous Model T cars, the later models costing

Ford assembly line. So important was the concept of mass production pioneered by Henry Ford that Aldous Huxley, in his novel of the future, *Brave New World*, based his calendar system on Ford's life—dates were determined by the number of years "After Ford" (A.F.).

less than three hundred dollars each. Such large-scale production was not achieved without a high degree of standardization—as illustrated by Ford's declaration that the customer could have his car "any colour he wanted provided it was black."

The United States took an early lead in the automobile industry, with eight times the total European output in 1929. However, as British, French, German, and other Continental factories began to copy American methods, this ratio was reduced so that by 1937 total European production had risen to one-quarter of the American output.

The revolution in transportation had great influence on allied industries. Thus, there was a vastly increased demand for gasoline and lubricants. Between the outbreak of the First World War and 1938 world production of crude petroleum rose from about four hundred million to one and a half billion barrels. New oil fields were developed in Central and South America, the Dutch East Indies, Romania, Russia, and Asia Minor, as well as in the United States and Canada. Similarly, the manufacture of rubber tires for cars necessitated a great expansion of crude-rubber production, while the demand for better roads led to technical improvements and construction of intricate networks of communications.

The Rationalization of Production

Post-war developments connected with the automotive industry were merely part of a larger process known as the "rationalization of production." A combination of wartime experience and American innovations (especially the assembly line technique) made ever-greater efficiency the goal of every factory owner and business leader. "Rationalization" was distinguished, on one hand, by the shutting down of inefficient plants and, on the other, by the introduction of better machinery and more scientific management of companies. In many European countries, notably Russia after the Bolshevik Revolution, these efforts culminated in planned economies under governmental control.

Agriculture

The drive for greater efficiency was not restricted to industry. Both in western Europe and America a similar trend developed, at a slower pace, in agriculture. Due to war casualties and a general movement of people from farms to towns and cities (urbanization), a shortage of rural manpower appeared in Britain, France, and Germany. Consequently, mechanization invaded agriculture, with tractors replacing horses, and other machinery (such as harvesting "combines") eliminating much manual labour. But these improvements did not penetrate far into southern and eastern Europe where, because of extreme poverty, agricultural methods followed a pattern not greatly dissimilar to that of ancient times. Progress was even slower in most parts of Africa and Asia.

Regardless of the modernization of farming in many areas of the world, it was perhaps inevitable that, after the artificial demands of wartime, prices for agricultural products would suffer a sharp, protracted decline. By the end of the First World War, wheat-growing countries like Canada, the United States, Australia, and Argentina had greatly increased their production, and their abundant crops caused a rapid lowering of world prices. Thus the prices of farm products dropped from a world price index[1] of 226 in 1919 to only 134 in 1929—and the subsequent economic depression brought prices still lower, to an index of 61 in 1934. In only fifteen years prices of these commodities had sunk to less than thirty per cent of their former value! This deplorable situation resulted in what is sometimes described as the "open scissors" problem: the farmer was caught between an upper blade representing rising industrial prices (especially for farm machinery) and a lower blade representing declining agricultural prices.

Communications

In other fields of science and technology, the third and fourth decades of the 20th century witnessed great advances. Among the most significant developments in the field of electricity was the coming of the radio. As early as 1897 the Italian inventor, Guglielmo Marconi, had succeeded in sending a message by wireless telegraphy a distance of twenty-nine kilometres; only four years later signals were passing across the Atlantic.

During the First World War this new medium of communication was employed primarily for military and naval purposes; but thereafter radio was soon adapted to general use. The first broadcasting station with regular programs was established in the United States in 1920, and within a few years every nation had its own facilities. It would be difficult to overestimate the influence of this invention on the life of mankind. Henceforth no part of the globe could remain insulated from the knowledge of events in distant lands. Subject to linguistic difficulties and self-imposed censorship, there was no longer any barrier to rapid transmission of news and culture. Whether living on remote farms, on vessels at sea, or in crowded cities, the owner of a radio had only to flick a switch to learn what was happening in foreign capitals as well as on the

---

[1] A price index is a means of showing relative change in value, and in the purchasing power of money, over a period of time. The prices of selected commodities are weighted according to quantities purchased, and then aggregated. The resulting figure will give an approximately accurate comparison of the prices of commodities in different years.

Leading "personalities" of the new mass-media. ABOVE LEFT: Will Rogers, one of the top radio entertainers. TOP RIGHT: Charlie Chaplin, in *The Great Dictator*. BOTTOM LEFT: a "personality" in his own right, *King Kong*.

Mary Pickford, Canadian born Hollywood star and co-founder of United Artists.

SOCIETY AND TECHNOLOGY AFTER THE FIRST WORLD WAR

domestic scene. Market and weather reports became immediately available, aviation was assisted, and soon political campaigning took on new forms—as illustrated by President Franklin D. Roosevelt's famous "fireside chats" in the 1930's. Every aspect of individual and family life felt the impact of the new development.

Unfortunately, the cultural implications of radio broadcasting were not always desirable. In the United States the high cost of the new service was assumed mainly by sponsors who purchased advertising time on the air. Their principal concern was to break down sales resistance to the products they were trying to sell. Consequently, there was a strong tendency for the standard of broadcasting to be determined, not by its quality, but by the number of listeners who could be attracted. In Great Britain and some other countries, this tendency was resisted because radio was long controlled by an agency responsible ultimately to the public through parliamentary channels. But in the United States private enterprise —notably rival networks such as the National and Columbia Broadcasting companies—dominated the airwaves. Commentators vied with each other in dramatic interpretations of news events; sportscasters enlivened the existence of enthusiasts with play-by-play broadcasts of baseball and football games. Radio was particularly successful in overcoming technical difficulties such as presenting dramatic themes without visual aid—the reverse problem of the early "silent" motion pictures. This was a period when the celebrated comedy team of "Amos 'n Andy" could keep millions of listeners glued to their sets.

Apart from its commercial and cultural possibilities, radio opened the door to a sinister political development: the opportunity for dangerous demagogues to sway large populations. Particularly in Italy and Germany, under the dictators Mussolini and Hitler, respectively, radio was to offer a powerful means of establishing personal, arbitrary regimes with disastrous consequences for the entire world.

By the 1920's European and American physicists were experimenting with television; but, strangely enough, it did not become a commercial success until after the Second World War.

Along with the automobile and radio, the introduction of motion pictures greatly influenced the lives of the post-war generation. This form of entertainment soon caught the popular interest in Europe and America. Even countries with relatively lower standards of living, such as Italy and Spain, had thousands of cinemas with a total seating accommodation for millions of people. Almost from the beginning, the major centre of the film industry was located in Hollywood, California, where a combination of favourable climate, capital, and acting and producing talent achieved phenomenal success.

When talking pictures appeared in 1927, the industry revealed its versatility and amazing capacity to extend the limits of its medium. (Stars who could act, but not speak effectively, were discarded in the process.) Among the memorable performances of the early artists were those of Mary Pickford, a Canadian-born actress who personified girlish innocence, Douglas Fairbanks, the swashbuckling hero of many a colourful tale, Charlie Chaplin, who combined comedy and pathos in an unexcelled degree, and Rudolph Valentino, the romantic lover of the silent screen.

Under the influence of great promoters like Cecil B. de Mille, the Hollywood industry rapidly achieved a position where enormous sums were spent on elaborate productions, including salaries for performers far in excess of those paid to professional and administrative wage-earners for services of greater significance to the welfare of society. Another less desirable effect of the Hollywood productions was the presentation, for overseas viewers, of a frequently misleading image of life in the New World.

2. SCIENCE AND MEDICINE

Technological advances in industry and agriculture were accompanied by even more significant progress in natural science. Like other great intellectual achievements of the past, these new discoveries did not begin at any specified date or in any particular country. They were frequently the product of research carried out independently by many thinkers in many countries. However, the importance of their contribution was reflected in changing social concepts. Even before the end of the 19th century, a distinguished British statesman (Lord Balfour) remarked of scientists: "They are the people who are changing the world and they don't know it. Politicians are but the fly on the wheel—the men of science are the motive power." As men moved into the century of nuclear energy and exploration of outer space, they would find prospects of future development both fascinating and terrifying.

Apart from their accelerated rhythm, these scientific advances were distinguished from earlier scientific progress by their direct impact on vast populations. In the middle of the 16th century Copernicus had shown that the earth revolved about the sun and not vice versa; about a hundred years later Newton formulated his theory of gravitation, and little more than a century ago Darwin's *Origin of Species* radically revised accepted views of man's beginnings. But these great thinkers had little direct influence on the majority of their contemporaries—the significance of their contributions was appreciated by only a minority of intellectuals. By contrast, the progress of public education in the 20th century has meant that many more people have become aware of the extent to which their lives are affected by research in remote laboratories.

The popular imagination has been caught by the results of research into two major problems at the opposite poles of human understanding: the structure of the atom and the nature of the universe. On the one hand, human beings seemed close to a new understanding of the essence of all matter; on the other, they began to grasp the meaning of infinity.

The Universe

At the beginning of the 20th century, fairly accurate measurements of stellar distances were restricted to about twenty stars. Astronomers believed in a relatively simple model of the universe, which was essentially static and unchanging. Then, as greatly improved equipment became available, such as the giant reflector telescopes at Mount Wilson and Mount Palomar in California, the frontiers of outer space were steadily pushed back. New theories, supported by observation using the telescope at Mount Wilson, have suggested that the universe is in a process of overall expansion. The tremendously challenging questions of "What started the expansion?" and "Has the universe a beginning and an end?" still await satisfactory theoretical answers. One result of these new developments is a growing realization of a person's comparative insignificance in relation to former concepts of time and space.

The Atom

At the other extreme of research in physics, revolutionary theories were advanced to explain the atom and radioactivity. Most of this

The mechanism of the world's largest optical telescope, Mount Palomar. The observer is sitting in the "prime focus cage"; in front of him is the giant mirror, more than sixty centimetres thick and with a mass of more than fourteen tonnes, with light-gathering power six hundred thousand times greater than the human eye.

vital work was performed in European laboratories. New concepts were associated with three developments: the quantum theory, the principle of relativity, and the study of atomic structure and activity.

Max Planck, a German scientist, developed his quantum theory in 1901. He maintained that light energy was given off irregularly in small units called "quanta" and not in a steady stream, as believed by earlier physicists. Both Planck and Niels Bohr, who carried forward research on the quantum theory at the University

"The most beautiful thing we can experience is the mysterious."—Albert Einstein. The above photograph was taken in 1905, when Einstein was 26; he had just published papers on the production and transformation of light, which led eventually to his theories of relativity.

of Copenhagen, were awarded the Nobel Prize for their discoveries.

Meanwhile, a German Jew named Albert Einstein, Director of the Physics Institute at Berlin until 1931, formulated his famous theory of relativity. (After Hitler's rise to power in Germany, Einstein was forced by anti-Semitic policy to take refuge first in England and later in the United States.) He suggested that neither time nor space could be considered absolutes, because man had no fixed base from which to measure and no stationary points between which to calculate the lapse of an absolute period of time.

Einstein's great theory was expressed in the simple equation $E = mc^2$ in which E represents energy, m is the mass, and c is the speed of light. In essence, what this meant was that matter and energy, considered separate entities ever since the days of Newton, were now seen to be merely two aspects of the same idea. Time was to be regarded as a fourth dimension, in addition to length, breadth, and thickness.

The third major breakthrough in 20th century physics occurred in the field of atomic research. In 1911 Lord Rutherford, a native New Zealander, doing research at the University of Manchester, deduced a new theory about atoms from his studies of radioactivity and the spectra of light and X-rays. It was now believed that atoms of different elements were analogous to miniature solar systems, each composed of a positively-charged nucleus (or proton) surrounded by negatively-charged particles (electrons). The importance of Rutherford's theory was that it rejected the previous conception of a solid atom, dating back to classical times, and described matter as mostly empty space.

Further research with the mass spectroscope (invented in 1919) revealed the existence of more than two hundred stable isotopes, or variants of basic atoms. Moreover, physicists learned that the atom was more complicated than Rutherford had originally believed—that, in fact, its structure included neutral particles, such as neutrons, bearing no electrical charge, which could pass freely through atoms.

These developments revived possibilities of "transmutation"—or changing of elements—a process eagerly sought by ancient alchemists in their attempts to convert lead into gold or silver. But the scientist of the 20th century sought something of much greater significance than merely an expensive method of obtaining precious metals—his goal was the release of enormous energy through the splitting of the atom.

By 1931 British physicists at Cambridge University were using high voltages of electricity to facilitate the process of transmutation. Then a cyclotron (an enormously powerful device used to accelerate atomic particles in order to bombard the nucleus of the atom) was produced at the University of California. In 1936 Enrico Fermi demonstrated that many new radioactive elements could be obtained by bombarding various atoms with neutrons.

Further research carried out in Germany early in 1939 proved that splitting the nucleus of the atom (that is, atomic fission) was feasible. Perhaps tragically for mankind the coming of the Second World War meant that these wonderful discoveries were exploited solely for their militarily destructive potential.

Biology and Biochemistry

In other fields, notably biology and medicine, progress was made towards the understanding and improvement of human life. Modern research has confirmed Darwin's basic assumption—namely that life processes have been evolutionary. However the origin and nature of life have eluded explanation.

Biologists of this century, such as the American Thomas Morgan, have established the close connection between hereditary qualities and "chromosomes," those small, thread-like bodies within each cell-nucleus. (Interestingly enough, vital information on these bodies has been gathered from the humble fruit-fly and the garden pea.) Applying their conclusions to human development, scientists have proved that because the number of permutations and combinations within a single cell are so large, the variations possible within the human race are for all practical purposes infinite. Biologists also showed that older theories were incorrect in suggesting that *acquired* characteristics could be inherited. A contrary view, influenced by political considerations, persisted in the Soviet Union for some time, but eventually was abandoned.

Many other important aspects of biology and biochemistry were investigated. Study of the process by which plants use solar energy in the production of carbohydrates was important to a fuller understanding of the nature of the world's food reserves. Again, much attention was devoted to research on metabolism—the intricate reactions by which an internal balance is maintained in the lives of organisms. Vitamins, first discovered in 1912, became another subject of intensive study. If discovered only a few years earlier, they would have eliminated the dietary deficiency that caused the tragic end of Scott's South Polar Expedition (1910-12). For a long time not much was known about the chemistry of vitamins other than D; but with the break-down of Vitamin A in 1929, a new field of analysis and synthetic production opened up.

The War on Disease

The first half of the 20th century was also a period of notable progress in medicine. Before the First World War, the rural G.P. (general practitioner) in North America seldom saw his patients in a hospital. He made house calls, driving at all hours with his horse and buggy, or saw patients in his office, usually part of his residence. There were few hospitals outside the large cities, and even a major operation might be performed on a patient's kitchen table. With the coming of the automobile the range of the doctor's visits was extended; but there was still little thought of transferring rural emergency cases to civic centres.

In the United States, Johns Hopkins University took the initiative in making hospital facilities more widely available. At the turn of the century a group of brilliant young medical men at this institution (including a Canadian, Sir William Osler, later Regius Professor of Medicine at Oxford) provided the leadership for medical reform. Their efforts were supplemented and augmented by other organizations such as the Rockfeller Institute for Medical Research, the Children's Hospital at Boston, and the Mayo Clinic at Rochester, Minnesota.

Much progress was recorded in the unending war against disease. Vital statistics reflected the impressive contributions of medical science. Thus, during the first third of the 20th century, infant mortality rates in the United States fell by two-thirds, while life expectancy rose from forty-nine to fifty-nine years.[1] In most European countries the infant mortality rate was halved during the first half of the century, in spite of war losses and attending upheavals. Comparative rates per thousand for the United Kingdom and France were fifty-four and seventy-one, respectively, in the years immediately preceding the Second World War. By 1950 Sweden, with only twenty-one per thousand, held the record for the lowest rate in the world.

The discovery of antitoxins, beginning at the end of the 19th century, was a powerful factor in the virtual elimination of certain diseases. Victory over smallpox was followed by similar success against diphtheria, yellow fever, and tetanus. Other diseases attacked included malaria, pellagra, and hookworm. In the United States,

[1] The infant mortality rate is the number of deaths between birth and the age of one per one thousand of population.

Sir Alexander Fleming, discoverer of penicillin, photographed in 1944, the year he won the Nobel Prize for medicine.

during the first third of the century, the death rate for tuberculosis dropped from a hundred and eighty to forty-nine per hundred thousand; for typhoid from thirty-six to two, and for measles from twelve to one. Sulfa drugs and penicillin (discovered almost accidentally by Sir Alexander Fleming) banished much of the fear of pneumonia. British and American experience with sulphanilamide drugs proved that they could be successfully used against many infections such as meningitis, gonorrhea, and undulant fever.

In Canada, Frederick Banting and Charles Best earned the gratitude of all sufferers from diabetes when, in 1922, they discovered insulin.

Yet in spite of these great advances, much remained to be done. Although, as we have seen, the ravages of tuberculosis were much reduced, no completely satisfactory answer had been found. Heart disease and mental illness, although more readily recognized than before, became increasingly common sources of human suffering. Still casting its sinister shadow over mankind, cancer continued to take a heavy toll.

3. POST-WAR SOCIETY

The early decades of the 20th century witnessed a rapid rise in the standard of living of most western peoples. In general, there was a notable improvement in physical health and longevity; a shortening of the working day and week; a raising of the school-leaving age, and great progress in the material well-being of large populations.

Within most countries the trend towards the realization of democratic ideals was accompanied by a perceptible "levelling off" of incomes. Just as the medieval merchant had risen to challenge the feudal lord, the successful businessman of the early 20th century rapidly displaced the older landowning aristrocrat. (In many cases the latter quickly adjusted his fortunes to new circumstances by making marriage alliances with the new capitalists.) The rise in average incomes was reflected in heavier expenditures on items formerly classified as luxuries, including such articles as cars, radios, recreational equipment, and a wide range of entertainment.

Urbanization

Another dominant characteristic of life in the western world was the increasing trend towards urbanization—or movement of people from the countryside to towns and cities. This movement was due to a variety of reasons, the most important of which were the expansion of large-scale industry in urban areas and the diminished requirement for farm labour as a result of the mechanization of agriculture. Even France, sometimes described as the most agrarian of advanced nations, illustrated the trend. Before the First World War nearly half the French working population was engaged in agriculture; by 1931 this proportion had dropped to only slightly more than a third.

Paradoxically, increasing urbanization did not mean a sharper division between farmers and city folk. Due to radio and easier means of transportation, the rural dwellers were much less isolated than formerly. They could maintain close contact with current ideas and fashions in the larger centres. On the other hand, inhabitants of towns and cities found new interest in the countryside. The introduction of annual holidays with pay, availability of cheaper transportation by road and rail (and the popularity of cycling clubs in Britain, France, and many European countries), the Boy Scout movement, and post-war restlessness of young people—all combined to break down barriers between cities and rural areas. But there were still large regions, for example in southern and eastern Europe, where the tempo of life was slower, and where social differences persisted for longer periods.

"A World Safe for Democracy"

Social life between the World Wars was more relaxed than in earlier decades. The blurring of class distinctions was merely one aspect of the rapid growth of political democracy immediately following the end of hostilities in 1918. President Woodrow Wilson had proclaimed that the war had been fought "to make the world safe for democracy." For a time it seemed that this high goal might be attained. Apart from Russia, which exchanged the tyranny of the Czars for the more efficient dictatorship of Communism, all Great Powers, and most of the lesser ones, adopted or extended democratic forms of government. Three of the oldest European ruling dynasties—the German Hohenzollerns, Austrian Hapsburgs, and Russian Romanovs—had been swept into the dustbin of history. Of the larger Powers, only Great Britain, Italy, and Japan retained crowned heads—and of these the first two were properly constitutional monarchies, subject to the popular will. Republics arose, not only in the new states of Europe (such as Poland, Czechoslovakia, Finland, Lithuania, Latvia, and Estonia), but also in Turkey, Latin America, and, briefly, in China. In most countries much greater emphasis was laid on individual liberty, representative popular government, with free elections and secret ballots, and ministerial responsibility, making the executive (often a cabinet) answerable to a popular chamber, which might be called a Parliament, Reichstag, or Diet.

The Emancipation of Women

A feature of the transformation of social life in the modern world has been the emancipation of women. Their social and political independence has grown out of economic conditions. From its beginning in the middle of the 18th century, the Industrial Revolution revealed that many types of factory work could be done by women as well, if not better, than men. For a long period women's working conditions were deplorable; but employment in industry offered an increasingly bright prospect of financial independence. Moreover, with the appearance of new household appliances such as washing machines and vacuum cleaners, women escaped much of the drudgery formerly connected with household management. Their world of fashion expanded through the medium of the new popular press and, in rural areas, the commercial catalogues. (In many Canadian farmhouses the familiar "Eaton's catalogue" occupied a position of importance beside the family Bible.)

Politically, the new status of women was reflected in slow and painful progress towards equality of voting rights with men. There was much agitation and some disorder before women won their rights. On a memorable occasion English suffragettes chained themselves to the gates of Buckingham Palace! It is interesting to note that the earliest successes in the feminist movement were scored in far-off New Zealand, where women were granted full voting privileges before the end of the 19th century.[1]

Before 1914 Norway and Finland were the only European states extending the franchise to women. However, their increasingly important role, especially during the emergencies of the First World War, meant that wider recognition could not be long denied. In 1918 women over thirty got the vote in Great Britain; in the following year all those over twenty were enfranchised in the new German republic. A decade passed before the British Parliament gave women voting privileges at the same age as men. Meanwhile, an amendment to the American Constitution achieved the same result in 1920. In most countries women also improved their legal status —although, even after the First World War, the French civil code preserved a man's rights over the female members of his family.

We have seen that, between the World Wars, the western world underwent profound social and technological changes. Other parts of the globe were also stirring with events of great significance. As yet, there was little sign of developing nationalism in Africa, where

---

[1] In certain parts of French Canada women voted occasionally during the early part of the 19th century; but women in Quebec were not formally enfranchised until 1940. Canadian women had voted in western provincial elections in 1916; but full rights in Dominion elections were withheld until 1918.

The father of modern Turkey — Ataturk.

the colonial powers continued to exploit rich natural resources with varying degrees of concern for the natives' welfare. Latin America, having won its freedom from the Old World in the 19th century, had split into numerous independent states, and material progress was slow by comparison with European and North American standards.

4. THE NON-WESTERN WORLD

However, new forces were evident in the Near and Far East. Turkey, long a crumbling empire, revived rapidly after the First World War under the enlightened leadership of Mustapha Kemal, better known as Ataturk. Considerable progress was made in reducing the Turkish illiteracy rate from ninety-five to sixty-five per cent in the fifteen years commencing in 1920. Transportation, hydro-electric development, irrigation, and reclamation projects received close attention.

In the Far East the most progressive social organizations were to be found in Japan and India, the latter still under British administration. The "westernization" of Japan, one of the most interesting phenomena of modern history, was evident in that Empire's industry, intellectual life, and society. Throughout the 1920's the steady growth of liberal democratic ideas augured well for Japan. Unfortunately, as we shall see, a nationalistic and militaristic reaction in the succeeding decade led to disaster.

India, under British rule, had seen much material progress since the great Mutiny of the mid-19th century; her civil service was a model for the Asiatic world. But Indian nationalists under the spiritual leadership of Mahatma ("Great Soul") Gandhi were becoming impatient to assume control of their own destiny. How this could be accomplished peacefully in so complex a civilization, divided deeply by racial and religious antagonisms, was by no means clear.

In the Soviet Union a great mass of humanity, severely regimented, was working out its own distinctive solution to social and technological problems. Under this system, unlike that of the western democracies, the individual person had no rights as against the State. What to western minds would have seemed intolerable oppression was easily accepted by the Russian people as a mere continuation of traditional methods. With their minds directed to specific goals—the construction of huge power stations and the cultivation of enormous collective farms—the Russians responded enthusiastically to the possibility of achieving a socialist Utopia on earth.[1]

Could the diametrically opposed concepts of capitalism and communism exist side by side, without friction, in the modern world? Would a world-wide economic depression bring down the social and economic bases of western civilization? Was the survival of selfish nationalism an impassable barrier to the realization of higher living standards on a basis of world co-operation? These were some of the questions remaining unsolved when the world turned its back hopefully on the catastrophe of the First World War.

---

[1] However, the collectivization of land (eliminating private ownership) was not achieved without ruthless suppression of the *kulaks,* or more prosperous peasants, who bitterly resisted confiscation of their property. See Chapter 21.

20 Economic Forces

Once I built a railroad and made it run,
I made it run against time.
Once I built a railroad and made it run,
Buddy—can you spare a dime?
—Depression song

In terms of world history a period of twenty years is not a very long time. Yet the two decades between the end of the First World War and the outbreak of the Second witnessed two economic developments of far-reaching significance: the displacement of Europe, mainly by the United States, as the centre of the world economy, and the general collapse of business which we identify as the "Great Depression." The eclipse of European economic supremacy was already becoming apparent at the end of the 1914-18 war; but the Depression followed a period of notable recovery and expansion lasting right to the end of the 1920's.

1. THE REALIGNMENT OF THE WORLD ECONOMY

As late as 1914 Europe was still the most powerful continental region on earth. We have seen that she had achieved her dominant position through her overseas discoveries and conquests, and her prior experience with the Industrial Revolution. London was the financial capital of the world: British overseas investments had played an important part in the development of North and South America, Africa, Australia, and the Far East, especially India and such focal ports as Singapore and Hong Kong. Similarly, Berlin and Paris represented European centres of industrial and financial control. The overall pattern of pre-war world trade, while increasingly complex, could be explained as primarily an exchange of manufactured European goods or services like shipping, banking, and insurance, for the raw materials and foodstuffs of less developed regions.

However, during the last quarter of the 19th century the United States had already advanced from a position in which she exchanged staples such as wheat and cotton for finished manufacturers, to one in which her exports of finished products exceeded her imports. Between 1900 and the beginning of the First World War, the volume of American industrial production nearly doubled. The further expansion that occurred during the great conflict merely confirmed a trend already clearly established.

The Dislocations of Trade

The revolution in international trade was clearly illustrated in the foreign investments of the leading nations. In 1914 the United Kingdom had the equivalent of eighteen billion dollars invested abroad; French and German investments totalled 8.7 and 5.6 billion, respectively, while the United States had a net *debit* of about three billion dollars in her foreign trade. But during the war many European nations (including Britain) were compelled to sell their securities to the United States and obtain American loans. Consequently, by the end of the war, British foreign investments had declined to three-quarters, and French investments to a half of pre-war values. Defeated Germany had lost virtually all her foreign credits. Meanwhile, the United States had become a creditor nation, exporting large sums of capital assistance to ravaged Europe—a portent of even larger credits to be made available to the Continent after the Second World War.

Apart from this significant shift in regional economic strengths, the great conflict of 1914-18 fractured the earlier structures of national economies. Wartime exigencies demanded that industries concentrate on goods and services related directly to the war effort —in particular, production of iron and steel, coal and textiles, munitions and transportation—rather than on luxuries and non-essentials. Inevitably, this meant that production of certain items expanded far beyond the requirements of peacetime. In the post-war period many industrialists on both sides of the Atlantic faced the same problem of converting their machinery and output to the changed conditions—and this, in turn, had correspondingly grave effects upon the labour supply.

Another obvious dislocation resulting from the First World War concerned the international exchange of goods and services. We have already seen that when western European agricultural production sagged and whatever eastern European crops there were could not find an outlet through the blocked Dardanelles, farmers in North America, Australia, and elsewhere were encouraged to increase their cultivated areas beyond the demands of normal conditions. Again, the Allied wartime blockade of Germany restricted that nation's imports of vital commodities such as oil and nitrates. Although German scientists discovered other methods of producing these items, for example extracting oil from coal, these processes could not always compete with the restoration of less expensive sources of supply in peacetime. On the other hand, the diversion of shipping to suit the purposes of belligerents meant that some nations, notably the United States and Japan, constructed their own merchant fleets. These additions to the world's merchant marine naturally had a serious competitive effect upon the normal carrying trade of countries such as the United Kingdom.

International Finance

There were equally significant developments in the field of international finance. For several decades before the First World War, the "gold standard" had regulated payments among most countries of the world. In essence, this system worked on the principle that each nation's currency bore a fixed ratio to gold. Thus a British pound sterling had a value equal to that of 113 grains of gold. Since other nations' units of exchange could also be expressed in terms of gold, it was possible to establish a direct ratio between the currencies—for example, a British pound was worth $4.87 in New York, 25.22 francs in Paris, 20.43 marks in Berlin, and so forth.

Moreover, the gold standard had simplified the otherwise complicated transactions by which a nation paid for its imports and, in turn, received payment for its exports. With London acting as the great international clearing house before 1914, any nation's debits and credits could be cancelled out, and the movement of relatively small amounts of gold among world capitals kept the system in balance.

However, the enormous financial burdens of the First World War (it is estimated that the total monetary cost to European belligerents was about 170 billion dollars) imposed an intolerable strain on this delicately adjusted system. In order to pay the rising costs of war, every European belligerent was forced to borrow heavily, with the inevitable result that national debts reached unprecedented levels. During the war the British debt multiplied twelve times, the French and German debts seven and twenty times, respectively.

One expedient adopted by the warring governments was to increase the amount of paper currency in circulation. Since, however, no European government had sufficient gold reserves to back up its expanded commitments in paper money, the pre-war system broke down. Payments in gold were suspended during the war, and although about thirty nations tried to resume the former pattern in the 1920's, the world financial situation lacked stability. So long as American capital was available to support the post-war European economy, the "gold standard" survived. But when, as we shall see, the effects of the great economic Depression were added to the burdens of the war, the system of international payments broke down completely.

The Migration of Populations

Another major factor in the world's economic development during the post-war period was the movement of populations, especially from Europe to the New World. These migrations did not, of course, represent a new phenomenon in world history. Throughout the middle and latter part of the 19th century, immigration had played a substantial role in the growth of the United States and British dominions such as Canada and Australia. But the early decades of the 20th century witnessed large-scale movements in other regions. For example, even before 1914, many Poles migrated to Germany, France, and Russia; nearly four million people moved from European to Asiatic Russia, and there were similar large-scale migrations in the Far East, from India to Burma, Malaya and East Africa, and from China to Manchuria and South-East Asia.

Of greater significance in relation to commercial and industrial development was the inter-continental movement from Europe to North and South America. The number of European emigrants to the New World rose sharply in the early years of the 20th century. Between 1911 and 1914 the average annual number of Europeans crossing the Atlantic was 1 650 000. Even allowing for the fact that a substantial number, possibly a third, eventually returned to their homelands, it is evident that the movement was of major significance.

The booming economy of the United States attracted many immigrants from Europe—not only because of brighter economic prospects, but also because of a desire to escape the more rigid social conditions and recurring political disturbances in the "Old Land." During the first decade of the 20th century, the United States absorbed nearly nine million settlers from Europe. An interesting aspect of this migration, tending to emphasize the urbanization of the American scene, was the pronounced shift in favour of immigrants from southern and eastern Europe by comparison with earlier "waves" from northern countries such as Great Britain and Ireland, Germany, and Scandinavia. Alarmed by the influx of cheap labour, the American Congress introduced a quota system in 1924, drastically reducing the number of immigrants from southern and eastern Europe.

Central and South America offered alternative homes to the crowded populations of Italy, Spain, and Portugal. These people were prepared to work hard in their adopted lands, further stimulating the economies of the newer nations. Men and women, frequently entire family units, established small businesses or became salaried workers in industry. Since they often sent back regular remittances to impoverished members of their families remaining in Europe, the immigrants in America helped to sustain the economies of their homelands. Others, more easily discouraged, became disillusioned and returned to a precarious livelihood in Europe. Throughout this period Canada and Australia continued to draw their main stream of immigrants from the British Isles.

Within Europe, the First World War had the effect of uprooting and displacing large populations—millions of refugees were driven from their homes by revolutions and hunger. Perhaps the Bolshevik Revolution in Russia produced the most striking illustration of these migrations. It has been estimated that, by the end of the Civil War in that country (1920), one and three-quarter million Russians had left their native land, scattering themselves over other parts of Europe, with a notable concentration in Paris.

Generally speaking, a nation's capacity to absorb displaced populations varies directly with its degree of industrialization. Newcomers can more easily be added to the payrolls of large factories than they can, for example, be provided with farm land. Even with its territory shrunk by the Treaty of Versailles, Germany was able to take in nearly three-quarters of a million people from the lands restored to Poland (and more than a hundred thousand sympathizers from Alsace-Lorraine) because of the more advanced state of the German economy. On the other hand, predominantly agrarian Hungary experienced great difficulty with an influx of several hundred thousand refugees from its border-lands.

France was one of the few European countries that welcomed immigrants—partly because of her great loss of manpower in the First World War, and partly because of her declining birth rate. In the 1920's a million and a half Italian, Polish, Swiss, and Belgian workers poured into France. Without these arrivals the French population in 1939, at the outbreak of the Second World War, would actually have been less than it was in 1914.

Apart from France and, to some extent, Germany, the gradual growth of European population, reaching 534 million in 1928, was uneconomically distributed: the countries with the fastest growing populations, more particularly the agrarian areas of southern and eastern Europe, were least able to support additional people. Lacking raw resources for industrial expansion and, after 1924, unable to migrate in large numbers to the United States, the unfortunate inhabitants of these regions were confronted by ever-increasing pressure on the available soil. Rural wages declined and the agricultural crisis had a depressing effect on all other branches of the economy.

A Period of Recovery

In spite of the material losses and industrial dislocation resulting from the First World War, the lack of stability in international finance, and difficulties associated with the growth and movement of populations, the period of the 1920's was generally one of steady economic recovery. Between 1924 and 1929 the world's production of food and raw materials increased by eleven per cent and manufactured goods by twenty-six per cent. Aided by construction of additional shipping, commerce regained much of its pre-war multilateral character.

In 1914, the value of world imports had been about twenty billion dollars; fifteen years later this figure had risen to thirty-six billion dollars. Perhaps only one-third of the increase was "real"—because much of the difference was due to higher prices of commodities—but there still remained evidence of substantial improvement. As already suggested, the key factor in this recovery was the dominant role assumed by the United States in foreign investment. There were few countries that did not become beneficiaries, directly or indirectly, of American loans. Even Soviet Russia profited by aid from the leading exponent of capitalistic enterprise.

2. THE ECONOMIC CRISIS IN GERMANY

Perhaps nowhere was the effect of American finance more apparent than in defeated Germany. In order to understand the influence of American policy, it is necessary to look at the situation which developed in Germany after the war.

Reparation and Inflation

Condemned by the Allies to pay the unrealistic sum of thirty-three billion dollars in reparations, Germany was unable to meet her obligations. With the advantage of hindsight we can see that there were only three methods by which Germany could have paid reasonable reparations: by shipments of gold, of which she had little; by borrowing from private sources, little inclined to regard post-war Germany as a good financial risk; or, finally, by achieving a surplus of exports over imports in her foreign trade with her creditor nations, which was politically impossible in the harsh climate of Allied post-war opinion.

Germany's economic policy complicated the problem still further. The vast expenses not only of reparations but of internal rebuilding were met by floating loans and issuing paper money, not by taxation. Taxes, indeed, were actually reduced, being identified in the popular mind with reparations; it became a "patriotic act" to refuse to pay, and politically dangerous to wish otherwise. The result was an ever-widening gap between revenue and expenditure that led to spiralling inflation.

Then, in 1923, Germany defaulted on her reparations. France and Belgium reacted by occupying Germany's industrial heartland, the Ruhr, in an effort to force resumption of payments. The Germans in turn, encouraged by the government, responded by passive

Inflation in Germany. For even the smallest transaction, literally baskets full of banknotes were necessary. The value of currency dropped from day to day, even from hour to hour.

resistance and general strikes. The government attempted to remunerate the "patriotic idleness" of the people by wages which increased the supply of paper money by fantastic amounts. Inflation, already at a dangerous level, went completely beyond control. Germany was left bankrupt, her currency practically worthless.

As the value of the mark sank lower and lower, a whole suitcase of paper money was needed to settle a small transaction. Eventually, marks with a paper value of millions were being bailed as waste paper in Berlin junk shops. The purchasing power of German money declined so steadily that, in 1923, postage stamps issued at the astonishing face value of a hundred million marks soon had to be surcharged, that is marked up, to ten *billion* marks. Financial chaos enveloped Germany. Long-range industrial planning became impossible, many people's life savings were wiped out, and a primitive form of barter became the normal means of exchange. Strangely enough, the larger industrialists profited from this disastrous situation: they retained tangible assets, such as factories and real estate, and were able to buy out their weaker competitors when the latter were unable to withstand financial pressure. Thus the I.G. Farben combine, with three hundred thousand employees, became the largest trust in the world.

At the end of 1923 the German government finally succeeded in stabilizing the value of the mark—but only at the fantastic ratio of one *trillion* old units of currency to the new mark. This terrible ordeal was to have an important influence on later political developments in Germany leading to the rise of the Nazi party under Adolf Hitler.

American Aid

American aid to Germany began in 1924 with the so-called "Dawes Plan,"[1] facilitating the payment of reparations to the Allies. An international loan, with more than half the money coming from American investors, was floated to support the German economy, and all foreign troops were withdrawn from the Ruhr. Five years later the "Young Plan," identified with the Wall Street financier, Owen D. Young, scaled down the total of German obligations to nine billion dollars, to be paid within sixty years.

Largely due to these arrangements, Germany was able to make regular reparation payments between 1924 and 1931. Fundamentally, however, her recovery depended on the confidence of foreign investors, mainly American, whose loans made it possible for Germany to balance her budget. These loans were not restricted to federal, state, and municipal governments, but also included a wide range of banks, public utilities, and private businesses. The total amount of American financial assistance to post-war Germany was not less than 2.6 billion dollars. Internally, the defeated power experienced rapid recovery and expansion; her industrial output rose above pre-war figures, partly due to modernization of equipment.

Unfortunately for Germany, and for the world, the whole basis of post-war recovery rested on the shoulders of the United States. So long as the latter continued to prosper—and the 1920's were "boom years" in the history of North America—there was no lack of funds for foreign investment. But any development affecting the

---

[1] Charles G. Dawes was a Chicago financier (later Vice-President under Calvin Coolidge).

American economy adversely was bound to have world-wide effect, because of the dominant position of American finance.

The extent to which nations other than Germany were bound to the wheels of the American chariot is clearly illustrated by the sequel to the story of the Dawes and Young Plans. In effect, what happened under these arrangements was that the United States loaned money to Germany which was then used to pay reparations to Britain, France, and other Allies. They, in turn, applied these payments against their own wartime indebtedness to the United States. Consequently the sums collected by the American government from European debtor nations really originated in loans made by Americans. They were really financing the purchase of their own goods and services abroad, the full implications of the system being hidden by the apparent prosperity of the United States.

By 1931, when the world-wide economic depression ended Germany's attempts to meet her obligations, she had paid four and a half billion dollars in reparations. More than half of this sum represented American loans. The United States also obtained repayment of over two and half billion dollars from her wartime Allies; but three-quarters of the Allied debts were ultimately written off. The history of reparations is an instructive commentary on the unreality of certain aspects of international finance.

3. CHINA AND JAPAN

Up to this point we have focused our attention on economic developments in the West. In the Soviet Union also, economic developments of the highest importance were taking place. These were more closely linked with the particular political problems of that country, however, and were largely independent of the economic problems of the capitalist world; for this reason they can better be discussed in connection with Soviet political development.[1]

Attention must now be given to trends in the Far East. Although it is not easy to obtain reliable data for this region, we know that on the eve of the First World War the entire Far East could claim only about three per cent of the world's manufacturing production. Over the succeeding quarter of a century this figure rose slowly, so that in the years immediately preceding the Second World War, Far

[1] See Chapter 21.

Eastern production was still under six per cent of the world's total. In the late 1930's the output of coal and steel in the orient was only about one-fifth and one-seventh, respectively, of European production.

Rates of economic growth varied widely among the eastern countries. In general, progress depended upon the degree of oriental willingness to accept western ideas. Behind China's relatively slow acceptance of modern technological methods were the vast cultural differences between East and West—differences multiplied and intensified by numerous racial and religious factors. On the other hand, Japan was an outstanding exception to the slow acceleration of economic developments in the Far East. Her rapid advance in the last half of the 19th and the opening decades of the 20th centuries rivalled that of Germany—and, in many respects, was more spectacular.

Before being exposed to western influence, Japan lacked power-driven machines. Traditionally, however, she had achieved a high standard of craftmanship in the manufacture of silk and cotton textiles, metal goods, and pottery. Older techniques were soon displaced by modern methods after American ships, commanded by Commodore Matthew Perry, made their dramatic appearance in Tokyo Bay in the middle of the 19th century.

Realizing that they must modernize their economy or fall under foreign control after the manner of China, Japanese leaders took effective steps to revolutionize their industries. Cotton-spinning and woollen mills, engineering and chemical factories, were soon equipped with western machinery; foreign technicians were brought into the country, while native Japanese were sent abroad for special instruction. Mining, transportation, and banking were all modernized. By the beginning of the First World War, Japan was already well ahead of other Asian countries in industrialization, but she was still far behind the advanced countries of the West.

During the 1914-18 conflict, Japan profited by western preoccupation with the European struggle to expand both her markets and her industrial capacity. Her output of manufactured goods nearly doubled, giving her a favourable balance of trade with other nations. In spite of great destruction caused by a devastating earthquake (1923), and serious deficiencies in such vital materials as iron ore, the Empire of the Rising Sun was becoming increasingly self-sufficient by the end of the 1920's. Unfortunately, like other leading industrial states, she then passed under the dark cloud of the economic depression.

Only ten years after the signing of the Treaty of Versailles, the world economy appeared to be riding a wave of continuing prosperity. The post-war output of food and raw materials had increased much faster than population, seemingly providing a sound basis for the future. There was a general feeling of confidence in the continuation of good times. The optimism which generated the "Spirit of Locarno"[1] in international affairs also found expression in great industrial expansion and rising graphs of stock market transactions. In the western world it was the era of "Big Business," with the United States in the forefront.

4. "BIG BUSINESS" IN THE UNITED STATES

One of the significant features of American economic development in the inter-war period was the concentration of financial power in the hands of relatively few corporations. This trend was particularly noticeable in relation to public utilities. In this important field there were only twenty-two mergers in 1919; but seven years later the number had risen to more than a thousand.

The usual method of consolidation was to form what was called a "holding company," not concerned directly with trading or producing operations, but with providing an instrument for an individual or group of businessmen to control other enterprises. These men did not necessarily require large assets. Frequently a promoter would organize a holding company and secure control by obtaining a majority of the company's common stock. By selling bonds and manipulating securities of this parent corporation, the promoter would then gain control of utilities engaged in actual operations. The process could be continued through several successive stages —a technique known as "pyramiding"—thus extending the interests of the holding companies over a wide range of enterprises.

A leading figure in the development of American public utilities was Samuel Insull. The son of a poor English preacher, Insull went to work in London at an early age and learned stenography. Eventually he attracted the attention of the great American inventor,

[1] See p. 536.

Thomas A. Edison, through reports prepared for the latter's British representatives. In 1881 Edison brought Insull to America, making him his private secretary. The young assistant profited by his new opportunities to such an extent that he soon became head of Edison's flourishing interests in Chicago. Insull was particularly successful at combining smaller utilities into larger and more efficient units.

By 1930 the process of consolidation had reached a point where it was estimated that one-half of all the electric power generated by the larger utilities in the United States was controlled by three large holding groups. Actually, ninety per cent of this production of electrical energy was in the hands of only fifteen groups. Insull's combined assets totalled two and a half billion dollars, and his utilities produced one-eighth of American electrical power.

The growth of big business was not, of course, limited to the realm of public utilities. Communications, banking, and the manufacture and distribution of packaged goods were all strongly influenced by consolidation, as were retail businesses such as drug stores, groceries, and tobacco outlets. By the 1920's "chain stores" were rapidly displacing small proprietors, who could not compete with the bulk-buying, advertising campaigns, and other facilities of their larger competitors.

One result of this consolidation was popular apprehension over the influence of the so-called "power trust"—the marked tendency for wealth to concentrate in few hands, and to mould public opinion at the possible expense of the consumer. Although various American authorities (mainly the governments of the states) endeavoured to curb the practices of Insull and others, the reformers were not very successful. On the eve of the Second World War ten American companies controlled about eighty-eight per cent of steel production; three corporations turned out ninety per cent of the automobiles; four meat-packing businesses controlled seventy per cent of that industry; four rubber companies produced eighty per cent of automobile tires, and four tobacco companies manufactured eighty-five per cent of the cigarettes. It is, however, interesting to observe that these consolidations did not necessarily mean a lessening of competition. On the contrary, a decline in the number of manufacturers in any field was usually accompanied by an intensification of competition among the survivors.

While the activities of giant corporations suggested a pressing need for tighter governmental regulation, the industrial expansion and apparent prosperity of the late 1920's gave no hint of interrupted progress. A particularly buoyant spirit prevailed in banking, finance generally, and investment. Between 1919 and 1929 the total banking resources in the United States grew from less than forty-eight billion dollars to more than seventy-two billion. During the same period, life insurance income and policies increased nearly three hundred per cent. Great financial firms, such as the House of Morgan, founded by J. Pierpont Morgan, exercised considerable influence on governmental policy, apart from their important activities on Wall Street, the heart of the country's business and financial life. Nevertheless, a shrewd observer, gifted with unusual insight, might have viewed with some alarm the tendency of American banks to become more and more involved in stock speculations at the expense of more conservative methods of banking.

5. THE GREAT DEPRESSION

The beginning of the Great Depression, that shattered the illusion of uninterrupted prosperity, is usually dated from "Black Thursday," October 24, 1929. This was the day when a sudden panic developed among speculators on the New York Stock Exchange. During previous days there had been a steady drop in the prices of stocks but nothing had occurred that prepared bankers and investors for the sudden sale of nearly thirteen million shares on the 24th. As the avalanche gathered momentum, more and more people tried to dispose of their dwindling paper assets, and the total volume of sales rose steeply, ticker tapes being unable to keep up with the transactions on the market. The resulting uncertainty contributed to the panic, forcing prices down and ruining those least able to face the crisis.

Leading financiers attempted to stem the flood. A hurried meeting of bankers held at noon on the same day at the Wall Street offices of J. P. Morgan & Co. agreed to pool their resources and support the market. By moving in and buying large blocks of shares, especially in steel, the bankers hoped to stabilize the situation. In fact, the senior partner of Morgan's tried to reassure newspapermen by describing the tidal wave of sales as merely "a little distress selling on the Stock Exchange."

But in reality this was only the beginning of the crash—the greatest business recession in modern times. The present generation, raised in what has come to be known as the "affluent society," can scarcely hope to understand fully the consequences of the crash on society.

At the end of 1929 American business had recorded a loss of forty billion dollars in stock values. The crash caught all types of investors—those who had a genuine interest in production as well as those who merely indulged their gambling instinct. Among the latter, those who had traded heavily "on margin" (that is, without full payment for stocks at the time of purchase) could not meet their brokers' demands for more funds as prices sank; on the other hand, more conservative speculators, who ventured into the market to pick up anticipated "bargains," expecting them to regain their former strength in due course, were soon sadly disillusioned.

But the effects of the crash spread far beyond the precincts of Wall Street and those of other great exchanges in the United States. The economic basis of American prosperity had been the smooth functioning of many complex factors such as international trade, investment in capital equipment and plants, construction generally, and the production of manufactured goods, especially automobiles. When public confidence in this vast complex was shattered, the resulting *débâcle* had ramifications not only in every urban and rural district of the United States, but throughout the world.

Summarizing the economic impact of the Depression on the United States, we find that in the four years following the crash the national income fell from nearly eighty-eight billion dollars to little more than forty billion; per capita income shrank from $681 to $495; dividends on securities declined by about fifty-seven per cent, and wages in manufacturing industries dropped sixty per cent. On the other hand, those individuals and corporations saddled with long-term debts could expect no comparable decrease in their interest payments.

This, then, was a period of extreme *deflation*—that is of greater value of money—in sharp contrast to the *inflation* that had occurred in Germany after the First World War. Because there was less money in circulation in the United States after 1929, a dollar was worth much more in 1933 than before the crash.

The Causes of the Depression

The causes of this economic catastrophe have been the subject of intensive study. In this brief analysis we can suggest only a few of the factors involved. One of these was the long depression in agriculture which followed the First World War. We have seen that wartime conditions encouraged American farmers to over-extend themselves, while other producers in Canada, the Argentine, Australia, and elsewhere became serious competitors. Declining exports meant that farm prices fell precipitately while the cost of machinery remained high during the industrial boom of the 1920's. By the latter part of 1921 the price of wheat had already dropped to about forty per cent of its maximum price in the previous year. The depression in agriculture had a pervasive effect throughout the entire American economy, restricting purchasing power and leading to the failure of thousands of country banks.

Another factor in the Depression was the unequal distribution of income in the United States. There is evidence to show that only five per cent of the total population received more than a quarter of the total national income. Inevitably, this situation gave distorted emphasis to investment (more frequently speculation in stocks) and expenditures on luxuries.

We have already seen that business practices, especially the creation of holding companies and the "pyramiding" of enterprises on unsound foundations, exposed the entire system of investment to grave abuses. When the Insull empire collapsed in 1932—the largest failure in American business history—trusting investors lost a billion dollars. Closely associated with the bad corporate structure of American business was a defective banking system, favouring a multiplication of small banks with inadequate resources to meet a sudden emergency. When these failed individually they had what might be described as a "falling domino" effect upon other financial institutions.

Another cause of the Depression, as already suggested, was the inherently unstable nature of international trade due to the dominant position of the United States in world trade. As long as the United States was able to pour money and credits into post-war Europe, the latter was able to recover a large measure of her former economic stability. But when the crisis in America terminated all possibility of continued assistance, the Old World plunged into its own economic morass.

Finally, in attempting to explain the origin of the Depression, the human factor must not be overlooked—the wave of over-confidence which carried speculation in stocks far beyond reasonable limits long before "Black Thursday." Generally speaking, investors were obsessed with visions of quick wealth. The fact that a certain enterprise might be economically unsound was of little consequence if the speculator was convinced that he could "earn" a quick profit. Perhaps the reason for this human factor is the hardest to understand. Fundamentally, it reflected the social attitudes of the time—in particular, the misplaced optimism of a generation that believed in continuous economic progress no less than in the myth of "the war to end wars." But public confidence is a fragile thing, easily punctured; when it finally struck the jagged edges of economic reality, in October, 1929, the bubble broke and widespread disaster was inevitable.

The Spread of the Depression

From the United States the crippling effects of the Depression spread rapidly throughout the world. Prices and production fell everywhere while, simultaneously, figures for unemployment rose alarmingly. Little more than three years after the Wall Street crash there were fourteen million unemployed persons in the United States. The impact of unemployment hit the industrialized countries, such as Britain and Germany, hardest; but even areas dependent mainly on agriculture found their markets shrinking, with resulting dislocation of their economies. By 1932 the manufacturing production of the world (apart from the Soviet Union) was only about two-thirds, by volume, of what it had been in 1929. But although the industrialized countries bore the brunt of the Depression, their problems were alleviated to some extent by the fact that the prices of raw materials and food also tumbled. Consequently, while a British worker received less pay in 1932 than in 1929, he also paid less for many of the necessities of life.

The Depression destroyed the delicate balance of international finance. Creditor nations, notably the United States, not only found themselves unable to make new loans abroad, but were compelled to

Impact of the Depression. TOP: Shacktown in West Virginia. CENTRE: Bayonets versus strikers. BOTTOM: Unemployed Parisians hoping for assistance from a student volunteer organization—but even this is closed for lack of contributions.

recall funds previously invested in foreign lands. Consequently, debtor nations could not balance their budgets and meet their external obligations. Germany was unable to continue paying reparations to the European Allies who, therefore, were unable to pay their debts to the United States. The vicious circle was complete, with sinister ramifications on the internal politics of certain nations. Moreover, the Depression gave a strong stimulus to economic nationalism, resulting in the erection of tariff barriers, and further restriction on international trade.

The Human Costs

But the real casualties of the Great Depression were not to be found in the coldly abstract statistics of disorganized international finance, reduced imports and exports, and declining production. It was in its corrosive effect upon human values that the Depression took its heaviest toll. Unemployment cast a dark shadow over millions of homes, where breadwinners found themselves unable to support their families. Through no fault of their own men and women were compelled to "go on relief"—that is, accept meagre financial assistance from governmental sources—or, worse, line up at communal soup kitchens for a minimum of subsistence. "Panhandlers" roamed the streets of cities with outstretched hands and the constant plea of "Buddy, can you spare a dime?"

Social discipline broke down; families disintegrated as the more active members sought improved fortunes in other areas. Many transients "rode the rods," stealing rides on freight trains. Many jobless slept on park benches or in doorways. Impoverished farming families abandoned their holdings, piling a few articles on their old cars and setting out for new locations—usually in already congested urban centres. Others tended to concentrate in "jungles"—collections of improvised shacks constructed of loose lumber, packing cases, and corrugated iron.

The Depression struck at all classes: even moderately well-to-do citizens lost their homes when they were unable to keep up mortgage payments. On the other hand, loan companies were burdened with the repossession of unwanted real estate and other property for which there was no prospect of sale. Professional and administrative classes suffered salary reductions. Many intelligent, deserving students were unable to pursue their education at universities

San Francisco Bread Line, 1933.

because of lack of funds; most of the fortunate few who did reach university had part-time jobs or worked hard in their summer "vacations" for the privilege of continuing their studies. Even for the top students, bursaries and scholarships were few in number and restricted in benefits.

Roosevelt and the New Deal

Gradually it was realized that an economic *débâcle* on the worldwide scale of the Depression was a unique phenomenon, presenting problems incapable of solution by traditional, more conservative methods. Above all, leaders like Franklin D. Roosevelt, who took office as President of the United States at the beginning of 1933, realized that government must take a much more direct hand in business, must spend public money lavishly to "prime the pump" of industry and, above all, must restore public morale.

The recovery of the world economy in the late 1930's was a slow and painful process. Just as the catastrophe had originated in the United States, the gradual revival of commerce depended largely upon American developments. The role of Roosevelt and his New Deal in the economic recovery has been a subject of much controversy. To some more affluent Americans, he was a dangerous harbinger of socialism; to many more less fortunate citizens, he was the saviour of his country in its darkest hour. Near the beginning of his first term in office (he was re-elected in 1936, 1940, and 1944), a brash reporter accosted him with the inquiry: "Mr. President, are you a Communist?" Roosevelt replied that he was not. "Are you a Fascist then?" Again the reply was negative. "What, then, are you, Mr. President?" After a pause, in which he appeared both puzzled and amused, Roosevelt said: "Why, I'm a Christian—and a Democrat."

Whatever reservations his critics may have had about the effects of his policies, they could not deny the immediate, positive impact of the new President's personality. Although of patrician origins, he had a deep instinctive sympathy for underprivileged sections of society, a feeling enhanced by his own courageous struggle against the crippling effect of an attack of polio. Roosevelt was able to implement many of his policies of economic recovery because he was a skilled politician, able to manipulate factions and achieve compromise solutions. He also greatly expanded the President's

"I pledge you, I pledge myself, to a new deal for the American people."
—Franklin Delano Roosevelt

legislative functions. He took the initiative, constantly sending drafts of bills to Congress and using devices like the party caucus and direct influence with Congressmen to ensure enactment of desired legislation. Inevitably, he became the symbol of revived American determination to find a way out of the chaos of the Depression.

Roosevelt was no academic theorist, like Woodrow Wilson, and it is difficult to establish any direct connection between the New Deal and the contemporary writings of the noted British economist, John Maynard Keynes. The latter, author of the devastating attack on the economic consequences of the Treaty of Versailles, formulated the "New Economics" to cope with the Depression. The answer to the crisis, according to Keynes, was not for governments to try to balance their budgets by traditional methods of reducing expenditures, but actually to *over*-spend (that is, adopt deficit financing) in order to stimulate the recovery of private enterprise.

Although some of Roosevelt's advisers may have been influenced by Keynesian thinking, the President was never prepared to go as far as Keynes advocated in making massive expenditures to "prime the pump" of the economy. Nevertheless, it has been suggested that while Keynes's "complex arguments" had little direct influence on the New Deal, "his general prescription eventually prevailed."

At his inauguration in March, 1933, Roosevelt sounded a challenging note: "This great nation *will* endure as it has endured, *will* revive and *will* prosper. . . . Let me assert my firm belief that the only thing we have to fear is *fear itself*." He made it clear that, if Congress failed to provide adequate remedies, he would ask for "broad executive power." The mood of the country was such that, at this time, Roosevelt probably possessed a power unprecedented in American peacetime history.

Effective measures poured swiftly from the presidential desk. Only five days after his inauguration, Roosevelt signed the Emergency Banking Act, which strengthened private ownership and management in the financial field. Two days later an Economy Act reduced federal expenditures. Then the President made use of the new medium of radio, in the first of a series of "fireside chats," to explain his policies and solicit popular support. The effect on the national economy was electric. By the first week in April, 1933, over a billion dollars in currency had flowed back to the banks, and hoarders were returning gold to the Federal Reserve banks. Then the Treasury began a double-barreled policy of strengthening weak banks and eliminating over twenty-three hundred unsound ones.

Roosevelt was particularly active in attacking the big holding companies, whose unsound practices had contributed to the Depression. The President sought to bring these huge corporations under rigorous federal control. A protracted battle over the issue was fought in Congress during 1935, the corporations spending large sums in a lobbying campaign. Eventually a form of compromise resulted: a government commission was given complete supervisory control over the operations of the holding companies, with the object of breaking up the larger utilities within five years, while the smaller corporations were permitted to survive.

Other reforms of the New Deal included assistance to homeowners to refinance and adjust their debts, and stimulation of the construction of private homes through federal support of the mortgage market. A particularly interesting aspect of the recovery pro-

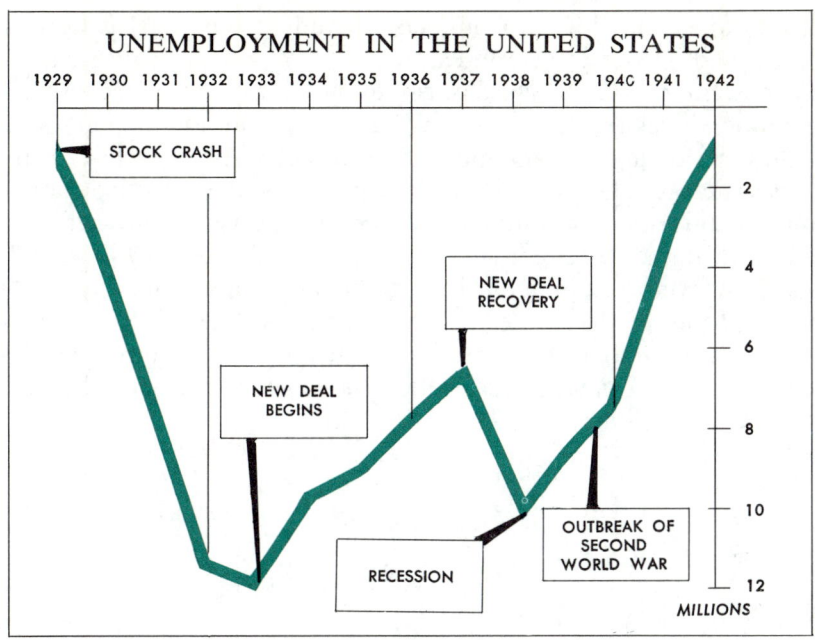

gramme was the creation of the Civilian Conservation Corps (C.C.C.) to cope with the problems of millions of youthful unemployed. Roosevelt had the imagination to see that this waste manpower could be utilized for the conservation of natural resources and similar public works. (The objects of the C.C.C. may be contrasted with the militaristic aims of the Hitler Youth organization.)[1] Over two and half million American youths passed through the C.C.C. camps, performing a wide variety of tasks: planting trees, building dams, reservoirs, and bridges, restoring battlefields, clearing camping grounds, and improving parks. In the words of one historian: "They did more than reclaim and develop natural resources. They reclaimed and developed themselves."

The New Deal was not an unqualified success. The National Industrial Recovery Act (N.I.R.A.), aiming at ending cut-throat competition in industry, was declared unconstitutional by the Supreme Court in 1935. But other notable measures, such as the Works Progress Administration (W.P.A.) and the Social Security Act, were implemented. In six years the W.P.A. spent over eleven

[1] See Chapter 21.

billion dollars on 250,000 projects, including the construction of airports and university campuses.

The significance of what is sometimes termed the "Roosevelt Revolution" was that there was in fact *no* "revolution" comparable to those occurring in contemporary European states such as Italy and Germany. The New Deal was basically conservative rather than socialist in conception—and the old party system survived without recourse to "direct action," purges, and executions. Indeed, nothing was more significant than the decline of communism as a political force in the United States during the late 1930's. Unfortunately, subsequent recovery was linked to the sombre requirements of rearmament to meet the challenge of transatlantic and transpacific totalitarianism.

21 The Rise of Totalitarianism

"Someone must have been telling lies about Joseph K., for one fine morning without having done anything wrong he was arrested."

—Franz Kafka, *The Trial*

One of the few safe generalizations to be deduced from world history is that wars seldom solve political differences. The conquests of the victor nearly always contain irreconcilable elements, leading in due course to internal dissension, strife, and disintegration. From ancient times, through the medieval period and into the modern era, experience generally points to the same conclusion. Far from being a means of achieving political conclusions, wars seldom bring more than a postponement of political problems and often added complications in their wake. Cynically-minded historians know countless incidents of bloody conflict ending in stalemate, of high principle sacrificed to selfish interest, even of belligerents changing sides in the course of the struggle. But in modern times technological advances, increased pressure of populations, and intensified nationalism have heightened the drama and pathos of war as a political instrument.

We have seen that social and economic forces after the First World War reflected an accelerated tempo of life and, in many respects, a more progressive attitude towards the world's problems. Mass production in industry, expansion of world trade, advances in medicine and sanitation, and the emancipation of women seemed to offer prospects of better living standards for larger numbers of the world's growing population.

Despite these improvements, however, the economic foundation of the post-war world was unsound, leading to the great economic Depression and much human misery. Economic retrogression accompanied, and to some extent stimulated, ominous political developments. Revolutionary forces were appearing in the world.

Generated partly by discontent with the peace settlement following the First World War, these forces gathered momentum during the great economic Depression and, together with the failure of world disarmament,[1] posed a new, more sinister threat to international security. The new menace was absolutism reborn, a more thorough, more *total*, form of authoritarian government, than had been seen before.

Internal political convulsions accompanying the First World War had virtually eliminated autocracy as a form of government in the major European Powers. Gone were the Romanovs from St. Petersburg, the Hohenzollerns from Berlin, and the Hapsburgs from Vienna. In place of these ruling dynasties there appeared new popular movements, generally responsible to the will of the people, although it could be argued that the Communist Party in Russia was an exception to this pattern. There, and in two major Powers of western Europe—first in Italy, and later in Germany—the new forces ultimately facilitated the establishment of tyrannies much worse than those of the pre-war regimes. Spain, a nation of secondary importance, passed through a similar cycle.

Any explanation of these developments must begin by noting that the countries in which these tragic events occurred lacked the long traditions of democratic liberty which distinguished the politics of Great Britain, France, and smaller nations such as Switzerland, the Low Countries, and the Scandinavian democracies.

1. FASCISM IN ITALY

Italy at the end of the First World War was a nation facing dangerous problems. Although she had been represented among the victors at Versailles, her territorial ambitions in Dalmatia and Fiume, at the head of the Adriatic, clashed with those of the newly-created nation of Yugoslavia, and Italian claims were only partly recognized by the major Powers. Dissatisfaction with the treatment of the "Adriatic problem" caused the Italian delegates to walk out of the Conference, although they later returned. The acute frustration felt by Italy contributed to a disillusionment not only with the western democracies that had thwarted her ambitions, but also to a certain contempt for the Italian government that had failed to present the nation's case more effectively.

---

[1] Disarmament is discussed below, pp. 535-537.

Internally, Italy was badly affected by economic and political problems. The burden of wartime debt, severe depression, unemployment, and strikes in transportation and heavy industry, all combined to intensify general discontent. In 1920, for instance, there were over two hundred strikes involving nearly two million workers. The strikes particularly indicated the irreconcilable split between different elements of Italian society. The working classes, whose importance had grown during the industrial expansion of the war, were inclined to look approvingly on the post-war Russian experiment. At the beginning of 1919, when Filippo Terrati, a leading Italian socialist, told a meeting that Italy must work for the *"gradual transformation of society,"* he was interrupted by impatient cries of "Russia, Russia, long live Lenin!"

Revolutionary sentiments such as these, and the organization of workers' councils, alarmed Italian landowners and businessmen who feared that a socialist revolution would lead to the expropriation of their property. Their opposition to the radical movement was supported by war veterans, whose patriotism was offended by the workers' open criticism of Italian participation in the First World War and of post-war foreign policy. Violence between armed bands of left-wing and right-wing extremists became commonplace.

Contributing to the disorder and unrest was the weakness of the parliamentary government. Before the war, the prestige of Parliament had been low; after the war, following the Italian failure at Versailles, it sank to the abyss. The weak, shifting coalition ministries, led by "purposeless men with little or no plan for rescuing Italy from her economic dilemma," were regarded with contempt by everyone. Most dangerous of all, however, was the government's toleration of political violence, which it made little effort to stamp out. The right-wing extremists were even tacitly encouraged, in the hope that they would defeat the left-wing agitators. It was a policy fatal for Italian democracy.

Mussolini

Out of this troubled background emerged a bombastic, and, as events proved, a tragic leader of Italian destiny. Born in 1883 in the Romagna, a region well known for its radical tradition, Benito Mussolini led a stormy and erratic life during his early years. As

"If I go forward, follow me! If I go back, kill me! If I die, avenge me!"—Benito Mussolini. The illustration is a poster depicting Fascist Black Shirts cast in the image of *Il Duce*.

a young man, he fled to Switzerland to avoid military service, where he earned an uncertain livelihood, sometimes by manual labour. He mixed with other malcontents and revolutionaries and was finally expelled from the country. Returning to Italy he became editor of a leading Socialist newspaper, *Avanti*. When Italy entered the First World War, he found himself in the army, where he attained the rank of corporal.

In 1919, Mussolini organized a small group of discharged soldiers into a military-political movement called the *Fascio di Combattimento*, so-named for the Latin *fasces*, the bundle of rods bound to an axe which had been a symbol of authority for the ancient Romans. At first, the Fascists expressed Mussolini's enmity against capitalism and "big business," and demanded a high tax on profits, and other socialist measures. But Mussolini, more than a supporter of any particular ideology, was essentially a political opportunist, an ambitious demagogue, always looking for a political current to carry him upwards. A convinced adherent of Machiavelli, he was always willing to sacrifice principle if there was gain to be made: as he himself remarked, "I am reactionary and revolutionary according to the circumstances." Accordingly, when it was to his advantage to abandon his support of the working class and turn instead to other segments of society, he felt no qualms about forsaking his old socialist ideals, and pledged his Fascists to support the aims of the propertied interests—"to hold law and order, national honour, and property." With this policy, the Fascists soon attracted support and funds from numerous landholders and financial concerns who held an exaggerated fear of the danger of a socialist takeover.

At first, the Fascists were not a political party in the conventional sense. Mussolini described the movement as "born of a need for action, and it itself was action." But those Italians who flocked to hear his fiery speeches or read his violent articles in his own newspaper, *Popolo d'Italia*, were perhaps less interested in what fascism stood *for* than what it was *against*. In some curious way, the movement seemed to offer an antidote to all the frustration and discontent in Italy. From Milan, where it originated, fascism spread into other towns and cities as well as rural areas, and by 1921 could claim a quarter of a million supporters in Italy.

Mussolini's contempt for democracy ("Fascism denies that numbers, as such, can be the determining factors in human society") was soon obvious. Squads of armed Fascists attacked and broke up the organizations of the Communists, Socialists and Republicans. The infamous "castor oil squads" forcibly administered large doses of castor oil to their victims, which would cause excruciating pain without leaving any trace or mark that could be used as evidence against them. Despite their attitude towards democracy, the Fascists were quite willing to use Parliament as a stepping-stone in their drive for power. In the 1921 election they won 35 out of 535 seats. Simultaneously, however, the campaign of violence against political enemies was intensified. Socialists and Communists were murdered, and Socialist local administrations eliminated: in the first four months of 1921, for instance, there were 207 killed and 819 wounded from Fascist attacks. And all the time the government watched impassively, not merely tolerating Fascist illegality, but abetting it—the Fascists would freely be given the use of army trucks and firearms, while the police would be made available to defend them against Socialist counter-attacks.

In 1922 came the climax. The Fascists demanded a new election or else the inclusion of their members in the cabinet. The government refused. The Fascists decided to force the issue: while Mussolini waited discreetly in Milan, fifty thousand armed Fascist Black Shirts converged on Rome. Too late, the government realized the danger; an ineffective effort was made to declare martial law, which the king, Victor Emmanuel III, refused to approve. The cabinet resigned, and the king appointed Mussolini his Prime Minister, and invited him to form a government. Mussolini then came to the capital by train, appearing in borrowed formal clothes to receive his appointment.

Fascism in Power

Soon the façade of constitutional change was dropped. Fascists took over key positions in the country's administration; a Fascist Grand Council was established as a link between the government and the Party, and Mussolini gradually assumed dictatorial power as *Il Duce* (the Leader).

Now began the emergence of *totalitarianism*, a form of absolutism so *total* in its control as to render resistance to the government virtually impossible. The first step towards this end was the elimination of all political opponents. The leader of the Socialist Party, Matteotti, was murdered, and other prominent political opponents were forced into retirement or exile. By 1926 all political parties other than the Fascists were banned. Elections were still held, but these were a farce—only Fascist candidates were allowed to run for office.

The next stage was to eliminate criticism of the government. This was largely accomplished by the rigid control of the press and the banning of all opposition and independent newspapers. Any criticism that might have remained was prevented by the use of the secret police, who would not hesitate to employ violence to silence anyone expressing opposition to Fascism. A network of spies and informers was begun, and any comment by anyone that remotely implied criticism of authority was likely to be reported. It became a not uncommon occurrence for the midnight visit from the police to take an "offender" to prison. Together with Fascist control of information and the police went control of the judiciary. Fascist magistrates were placed in the law courts, so that opponents of the regime could be disposed of by due "legal" process. There was no provision for a statement of charges in open court, for a properly conducted trial with the benefit of defence counsel, or for a judgment rendered by an impartial tribunal.

Fascist regulation also extended to all important aspects of the economy. While economic organizations were generally left in the hands of private owners (as long as these were sympathetic to the Fascist cause), the placement of Fascists in key positions within the firms ensured that they functioned compatibly with Fascist policy. Workers were organized into *syndicates*, which were completely controlled by the government. All major officials of the syndicates had to be Fascists themselves or approved by the Fascists, and workers belonging to nearly every industry were required to pay dues to the syndicate. Strikes were made illegal, and for all intents and purposes wages and working conditions were regulated by the government without meaningful consultation with the workers. With this control of the economy, Mussolini could embark on virtually any economic policy he wished—the construction of great highways and ocean liners, the "hardening" of Italy's currency and the restoration of her international credit, and—ultimately—the growth of militarism. Economic control also meant a further degree of political dominance—minor opponents or critics of the regime ran the risk of finding themselves without the means of livelihood. This discrimination extended into cultural activities, limiting the free expression of literary and artistic ability.

As a result of all these measures, organized resistance to the Fascist government was practically eliminated. Beyond this, however, the totalitarian state sought to make even *passive* resistance by the individual citizen impossible. Through control of the press and all other means of information, the government could determine the thinking of its citizens with considerable, if not complete, effectiveness. Education was controlled, in order to indoctrinate young people with Fascist ideals:

the government . . . requires that the whole school, in all its levels and all its teaching, shall educate Italian youth to understand Fascism, to ennoble itself in Fascism and to live in the historical climate created by the Fascist revolution.

Indoctrination was carried a step further by means of youth organizations, by which boys as young as six became "sons of the wolf," and were imbued with militaristic discipline; the motto of the youth groups typified the Fascist concept of authority and the individual: "Believe, Obey, Fight."

The only autonomous source of ideals and thought which might potentially have opposed the Fascists was the Church. In 1929, with the Lateran Accord, Mussolini moved to assure, if not the Church's blessing, then at least its non-opposition. The Church was granted a small area in Rome (the Vatican) which would have complete sovereign independence from Italy, and a large payment in gold and Italian bonds. Mussolini also undertook to recognize Roman Catholicism as the official religion of Italy. In exchange for these concessions, Pope Pius XI directed all Italian ecclesiastics to support the Fascist government. A lay organization, Catholic Action, which had criticized Mussolini's labour policy, was restructured and brought under the control of bishops to prevent further conflict. By these measures, much of the potential opposition between the Roman Catholic Church and the Fascist State disappeared.

Fascist Italy was now a genuinely totalitarian state; only an ideology was needed to make the system complete. The ideology was *corporatism,* an ideal that combined aspects of Plato's theory of the harmonious just state, Rousseau's "General Will," Hegel's "Divine State," Sorel's idealization of violence, and various other

Italian priests giving the Fascist salute.

philosophies. The essence of corporatism was that all members of the state should have a complete identity of purpose and interest. An illusion of popular control was retained through the syndicates, which, theoretically, spoke for the various working interests they represented. The syndicate, therefore, took the place of territorial units of representation (that is, the "constituencies" of the British system); in terms of the corporatist ideology, they served to eliminate the opposition of interest between employer and employee: they would "relegate the class struggle to the textbooks of subversives." The individual alone was considered worthless; only as a member of the state, as a personal embodiment of the Fascist ideal, could the citizen live a meaningful life:

> The Fascist conception of life stresses the importance of the state and accepts the individual only in so far as his interests coincide with those of the state. . . . Fascism reasserts the rights of the state as expressing the real essence of the individual . . .

It went without saying that the "interests of the state" were decided, not by general consent, but by the wishes and the intuition of *Il Duce*, Mussolini.

Despite its oppressive qualities, it would be inaccurate to suggest that the Fascist state was unpopular. Millions of Italians accepted a tyranny greater than that of the Caesars because of lack of confidence in democratic parties, fear of communism, and a feeling of frustration over their country's post-war ventures in foreign affairs. Fascism can also be credited with some useful reforms and more efficient administration of certain aspects of the internal economy. For example, large marshy areas were drained and malaria eliminated; many public buildings, reflecting the grandiose ambitions of *Il Duce*, were erected, and agriculture, especially the growing of wheat, was stimulated. Mussolini himself delighted to take his turn at harvesting crops in the presence of admiring photographers. Also, while Italian workers lacked the freedom enjoyed by unions in democratic countries, they were the beneficiaries of social legislation covering such matters as health insurance and compensation for disability.

These successes in the early years of Mussolini's regime, bolstering the popular impression that positive action was being taken to improve Italy's situation, won many admirers at home and abroad for totalitarian methods. But as time passed the repressive aspect of Fascism, its brutal attitude toward human liberty, appeared to be a heavy price to pay for whatever efficiency was attained. As we shall see, the downfall of Mussolini's elaborate structure began when he turned his attention to imperialistic designs outside Italy.

2. MILITARISM IN JAPAN

While Italy became the spearhead of the movement towards totalitarianism in post-war Europe, Japan was assuming an aggressive and militaristic role in the Far East. From the time this eastern empire had embarked upon a plan of rapid modernization, its government had become increasingly sensitive to western influences. After the First World War, in which Japan made important contributions to Allied victory, there had been a definite strengthening of liberal, democratic feeling in the island kingdom. In 1925, for example, universal male suffrage had been instituted.

But Japan's satisfaction at being recognized by the other Great

Powers at Versailles was coupled with resentment at lingering traces of racial discrimination, especially in the immigration laws of the United States and "white" Dominions, such as Australia and Canada, and dissatisfaction with certain aspects of the peace treaties. Gradually the more progressive elements in Japanese society were submerged by a rising tide of nationalism and militarism. Centuries of authoritarian rule had conditioned the people to political subservience. This tradition, reinforced by the effects of Shintoism—the state religion that venerated the Emperor—the centralizing power of government modelled on western lines, the inherent conservatism of wealthy industrialists and service officers, a tendency towards extremism in politics, including assassination of prominent public figures, and economic distress resulting from the world-wide Depression—all gave reactionary forces a new lease on life during the 1930's.

Then, in 1931, came the "Manchurian Incident," by which Japan successfully occupied this strategically important area on the neighbouring mainland. In undertaking this operation, the army commanders had acted on their own initiative, in defiance of the conciliatory policy of the civil government in Tokyo. This was possible, since the service chiefs were not responsible to that government, as in more democratic nations, but directly to the Emperor. In practice, military and naval commanders took the initiative in determining external policy, thereby forcing the hand of the civilian government. As the rapid conquest of Manchuria stimulated popular enthusiasm in Japan for more aggressive action, the dominance of the military became greater than ever.

The Manchurian crisis had a double significance. In terms of internal development, it marked a further stage in the post-war trend away from democratic institutions and towards more despotic and arbitrary government. A terrible blow had been struck at the aspirations of those who had hoped to bring Japanese internal politics in line with the practices of the most progressive nations of the West. Under reactionary leadership, Japan was henceforth committed to a policy of aggression that would end tragically. And secondly, it provided a clear indication of the inability of the League of Nations to deal effectively with an aggressive action committed by a Great Power.[1]

[1]The international implications of the Manchurian Incident are discussed on pp. 534-535.

3. RUSSIA: REVOLUTION AND REACTION

In its ultimate influence on world history, the Russian Revolution overshadowed all other authoritarian movements of the 20th century. Fascism and Nazism did not survive the Second World War, but Communist participation in Allied victory expanded Soviet control over eastern Europe beyond the wildest dreams of the Czars. Not only Europe, but Asia, Africa, and Latin America—indeed, all parts of the world—were to be profoundly affected by the dramatic events in the streets of Petrograd (now Leningrad) in the days of 1917.

The Bolshevik Consolidation

On the morning of November 7[1] the citizens of Petrograd awoke to read a new proclamation: "The Provisional Government has been overthrown. Governmental authority has passed into the hands of the Revolutionary Military Committee which leads the proletariat and the garrison of Petrograd. . . ." The proclamation ended: "Long live the revolution of soldiers, workers and peasants!"

A Council of People's Commissars was formed headed by Lenin, with Trotsky as Commissar for Foreign Relations. The new regime at once approved two decrees of great significance: a Decree on Peace, calling on all belligerents to begin negotiations for a just, democratic peace without annexations, and a Decree on Land, stating simply that "landlord property is abolished forthwith without compensation."

Together with measures to consolidate its newly-won power, the Bolshevik government was most anxious to end Russian participation in the war. Lenin in particular realized the need for a "breathing-space" in which to prepare for the coming internal struggle with counter-revolutionary forces. For these reasons, the Bolsheviks accepted the harsh terms imposed by the Central Powers at Brest-Litovsk on March 3, 1918. Russia renounced her sovereignty over Finland, the Baltic provinces and Poland, and recognized Ukrainian independence. She also made territorial concessions to Turkey, an ally of the Central Powers.

The difficult negotiations at Brest-Litovsk were merely the prelude to civil war in Russia between "Red" Bolsheviks and "White"

[1] October 24 by the old calendar.

counter-revolutionaries led by former generals of the imperial army. In the initial stages of this bitter struggle, Czar Nicholas II and his family were executed without a trial, but with the subsequent approval of Soviet officials in Moscow.

It was not until after the Armistice on the Western Front (November 11, 1918), that the civil war in Russia entered its most critical phase. The reason for this was an armed intervention on Russian territory by the Allied Powers, originally on the grounds that the Bolsheviks had conspired with Germany at Brest-Litovsk, and that counter-revolutionary elements offered the only real prospect of continuing the war on the Eastern Front. Later Allied policy was dominated by distrust of the new regime and the ill-founded belief that it would soon collapse. Allied forces landed in north Russia, in the vicinity of Murmansk and Archangel; in the south, in the Caspian region, and in the east, through the port of Vladivostok.

Under the dynamic leadership of Trotsky, as Commissar for War, the Bolsheviks fought back desperately. They were favoured by a unified command and by the fact that they operated within interior lines—that is, with shortened lines of communication to exposed fronts. The turning-point of the struggle came in 1919 by which time the Red Army comprised three million men organized in sixteen armies. Gradually Allied forces were withdrawn from Russia, and before the end of 1922 Soviet authority had been established over all the former imperial domains. Two years later a federal constitution was adopted, forming the Union of Soviet Socialist Republics (U.S.S.R.).

Power Struggle—the Emergence of Stalin

Although the revolution had succeeded, there remained the problem of the succession to Lenin, who died on January 21, 1924. Certainly, one of the strongest candidates to succeed the founder of the Bolshevik government was Leon Trotsky. Another was the iron-willed General Secretary of the Communist Party,[1] Joseph Stalin. Unlike Trotsky, Stalin was neither an intellectual nor a polished orator, and consequently tended to be underestimated by the other leading Party members. His position gave him tremendous

[1] In 1918 the Bolshevik Party became officially the Russian Communist Party.

Procession at the funeral of Lenin, in Red Square, Moscow.

influence, however, and he showed remarkable skill in playing off his rivals against each other. Lenin, before his death, prepared his last will and testament, in which he criticized both Trotsky and Stalin. One of the most dramatic events in the history of the Party was the reading of the will, four months after Lenin's death, before a full meeting of the powerful Central Committee. On this occasion an eye-witness observed that Stalin "looked small and miserable." However, the future dictator of Russia was saved by a favourable combination of elements within the Party, which decided against publication of the document.

For a short time a triumvirate (including Stalin, but excluding Trotsky) ruled Russia—but Stalin was determined to attain sole control. Wide differences existed between him and Trotsky over future policy—notably on the issue of whether Communism should actively pursue the goal of world revolution, as Trotsky desired, or whether, as Stalin wished, the government should concentrate on "socialism in one country" (the U.S.S.R.). Meanwhile, Stalin exploited the supposed threat of "capitalist encirclement" of **Russia** and consolidated his position within the Party. By the end of 1927 he was strong enough to expel Trotsky from the country. After fomenting anti-Stalinist activities in various parts of Europe, Trotsky settled in Mexico, where he was assassinated by a Stalinist agent in 1940.

Having ensured his complete political control—the few rivals who remained were virtually powerless—Stalin began a series of Five Year Plans in which great emphasis was laid on industrialization and collectivization of agriculture. These ambitious programmes, ruthlessly implemented, had important political repercussions. In proportion as Stalin's authority grew, he became increasingly apprehensive of threats to his position. Ironically, the successor to the Romanovs was to share their "occupational hazard."

The Purges

In December, 1934, in Leningrad, a young Communist murdered a Party official named Sergei Kirov. The assassin was one of a small group embittered by the oppressive atmosphere of the dictatorship; the victim was closely identified with the inner circle of Stalin's advisers; the event triggered one of the greatest political purges in history. It is doubtful whether the true facts behind this assassination will ever be known. Stalin, however, used the occasion to eliminate all remaining opposition to his authority. A series of secret trials began. The accused included all surviving members of the revolutionary Old Guard, and Trotsky *in absentia*. N. I. Yezhov, head of the dreaded secret police (N.K.V.D.) prepared the indictments, charging the accused with attempts to assassinate Stalin, to restore capitalism, and to sabotage the country's military and economic efforts. Although these allegations were unsupported by direct evidence, they were "substantiated" by fabricated testimony and "confessions." The latter were obtained, not by physical brutality, but by the use of psychological pressure—especially by the technique of endless interrogations to break the victim's will to resist. In some cases the accused may have been induced to believe that his "confession" was the last service he could render to the cause of Communism—and the only means of avoiding death.

Joseph Stalin—". . . a man of steel, ruling a people of stone, and trying to shape them: a painful process for both sides."—A. J. P. Taylor.

Those who did not acknowledge their guilt were disposed of without public trials. The victims were not restricted to Party leaders. Persecution was extended to the families, friends, and even acquaintances of the accused. Wives were often given the alternative of divorce or separation from their husbands.

A feature of the "Great Terror" of the 1930s was the purge of the Red Army. It has been estimated that there were as many as thirty-five thousand military victims, including top-ranking generals and about one-half of the officer corps. Senior officers were accused of treasonable dealings with the Nazis and of plotting against Stalin. There may have been some justification for the latter charge, but no real evidence was produced to prove their complicity with the Nazis. An important result of the military purge was that foreign observers were inclined to deprecate the fighting efficiency of the Red Army, a factor which further weakened Anglo-French diplomatic opposition to Hitler before the outbreak of war in 1939.

The significance of the "Great Terror" has been the subject of much controversy. Some historians believe Stalin's ruthless tactics reflected his genuine fear of espionage and foreign intervention in Russia. It has been pointed out that the protracted purge coincided with Hitler's reoccupation of the Rhineland and the weakening of the British and French positions. Stalin might well have thought that the western policy of appeasement was designed to involve the Nazi and Communist states in a mutually destructive conflict.[1] Other authorities suggest that the Russian dictator needed scapegoats to explain the hardships of the Five Year Plans.

In any case, the ultimate result of the Terror was the elimination of all remaining resistance to Stalin within Russia. Henceforth the "Stalinist cult" flourished unchecked, virtually deifying the sole survivor of the original revolutionary leaders. He, alone of the principal authoritarian rulers, would survive the Second World War, with greater power than any other individual on earth.

Soviet Economic Policy

"WAR COMMUNISM"

In the turmoil immediately following the First World War there was no opportunity to apply Marxist doctrine. The grim practical necessities of trying to equip the Red Army and avoid widespread starvation took precedence over theory. This was the period of what was termed "war communism," when urban workers were organized in labour battalions and food was forcibly requisitioned from the peasantry.

By 1920 Russia was in a desperate state. Three years of civil

---

[1] This suspicion by the Russians was extremely significant for Soviet policy immediately prior to the Second World War. See below, p. 562 and p. 605.

"Help!" A Russian poster desperately requesting aid for victims of the famine.

war, following the earlier struggle with the Central Powers, had devastated large regions of the country. Communications were disrupted, thereby multiplying the problems of distributing food and other vital commodities, and industrial production had fallen to only sixteen per cent of the level in 1912. People tended to desert the larger centres, hoping to find subsistence in the countryside, but actually increasing the pressure on the already heavily-taxed resources of farmers. Many thousands of disbanded soldiers roamed the land, adding to the disorder. Finally, conditions approached a catastrophe with the occurrence of persisting droughts in the Volga Basin. The resulting famine caused the deaths of three million people.

THE "NEW ECONOMIC POLICY"

Lenin recognized the necessity of adopting temporary expedients in order to restore the agricultural foundation of Russia. "Only an agreement with the peasantry," he told a Party Congress, "can save the socialist revolution in Russia."

Accordingly, the "New Economic Policy" (N.E.P.), launched early in 1921, was an attempt to conciliate the farming population by abolishing requisitions and offering inducements to stimulate production. In many respects the new policy represented a compromise between socialism and capitalism. Peasants were permitted to dispose of surplus crops for their own profit, and many of their rights to the land were confirmed. Moreover, the New Economic Policy was extended to small-scale industries, and commerce showed a strong tendency to revert to a basis of private enterprise. Even in the realm of state finance, capitalistic principles were reintroduced into Russia: the *rouble* currency was restored on a basis of gold, as in the western countries, and ruinous inflation was ended.

The New Economic Policy did much to aid the Russian post-war recovery. By 1927 the area of land brought back under cultivation was equal to that of the pre-revolutionary period. Industrial expansion was most evident in the production of such important commodities as coal, oil, and cotton material. However, there was no real justification for the belief, held in certain quarters outside Russia, that the Soviets were renouncing communism and returning to capitalism. On the contrary, N.E.P. was no more than a temporary retreat, an attempt to gain a breathing-space before completion of the socialization of the entire economy. Even during the period the Policy was in effect, the Communist government retained strict control over certain "commanding heights" of the economic development, such as foreign trade, transportation, and heavy industry.

THE FIVE YEAR PLANS

Later economic development in the Soviet Union, representing the apex of state control over its economy, was identified with the Five Year Plans. Since Russia could not obtain abroad the immense amount of capital needed to finance her long-range projects, she turned to a rigorous policy of accumulating the necessary funds within her own frontiers. A feature of this policy was the sacrifice of what we call "consumer goods," that is articles intended primarily for individual use, such as clothing for "producer goods," or heavy industry. In other words, cars, radios, and household appliances were sacrificed for tractors, locomotives, and hydro-electric installations.

The First Five Year Plan, covering the period from 1928 to 1933, was designed to double Soviet production. Basic industry was to expand by three hundred per cent, electrification by five hundred per cent. At first, enthusiastic Russian workers appeared likely to exceed their quotas; later, however, shortages and bottlenecks developed and a rise in prices upset the original basis of calculations. Nevertheless, the main goals were attained. The Second and Third Plans were inaugurated in 1933 and 1937, the Third being modified by the coming of the Second World War.

The Soviet record, although regarded sceptically by western capitalists, was impressive. Reversing the earlier trend of the New Economic Policy, the Five Year Plans virtually eliminated private enterprise. It is true that this form of state control imposed great hardships on the people; but they were conditioned by centuries of Czarist rule to accept conditions which would not have been tolerated in the more advanced countries of western Europe. According to reliable estimates (taken from statistics prepared for the League of Nations), the output of Russian industry rose from an index of 100 in 1929 to 477 in 1938. By comparison, the world's industrial production (excluding the Soviet Union) rose only 8.7 points between 1925 and 1938. Dramatic evidence of the material progress in the new Russia was to be found in great dams on rivers such as the Dnieper, factories at Stalingrad and Rostov-on-Don, steel mills at Magnitogorsk in the Urals, and an oil pipeline from Grozny, in the Caucasus, to the Black Sea.

COLLECTIVIZATION

Unfortunately, there was a sinister aspect to the Soviet achievement. It might be argued that the application of socialism in Russia has been least successful in agriculture. In this respect communism has had a hard battle with the inherent conservatism of tillers of the soil.

Determined to sweep away existing inefficient agricultural methods while simultaneously reinforcing its control over the peasantry, the government embarked upon a policy of forced collectivization. Instead of small farming units, dispersed and uncoordinated, the new Russian system unified small holdings into huge farms, organized on a collective instead of individual or village basis.

While the poorer peasants stood to gain by the new policy, the more prosperous farmers (known as *kulaks*) naturally resisted official efforts to deprive them of their holdings. It is important to realize that these *kulaks* were by no means "prosperous" in the western European or North American sense. In many cases, they were distinguished from their poorer neighbours merely by possession of a few animals or implements. But they were determined to keep what few articles they had. Consequently, the Soviet authorities (under Stalin's leadership) waged a ruthless campaign of extermination against the *kulaks* who, with their families, numbered about eight million. Whole villages were eliminated by soldiers with machine-guns, while many of the persecuted class were deported to the inhospitable regions of Siberia. In retaliation, the *kulaks* slaughtered their own animals, burned their crops, and destroyed their buildings, rather than comply with the government's orders.

It is difficult to assess the ultimate effects of collectivization. We know that the resulting disorder, aggravated by crop failures, probably cost Russia five million lives. In addition, the country lost over half its livestock. On the other hand, by the outbreak of the Second World War, about ninety-five per cent of Russian farms had been collectivized. Undoubtedly, more effective governmental control had been established in rural areas, with increased productivity. By 1933 there were two hundred thousand tractors and twenty-five thousand combines in use. A more efficient system of distribution brought food from the collective farms to the cities, while increased mechanization of agriculture furthered the movement of surplus labour to industrial centres. Yet the passive resistance of a suspicious peasantry, reflecting the traditional attitude of farmers everywhere towards bureaucracy, remained one of the principal problems of the Soviet regime.

4. NAZISM IN GERMANY

Meanwhile, the foundations of another post-war dictatorship were being laid, in Germany. In that country, as in contemporary Japan, the years following the end of the First World War seemed to offer

Anti-Bolshevik propaganda poster.

encouraging prospects for a new democratic tradition, but circumstances conspired against this.

At the end of the war, the political scene in Germany was chaotic. The Rhineland was occupied by the soldiers of the victorious nations, agitators from Russia were inciting revolution, and a "soviet" was temporarily established in Bavaria.

Revolutionary governments, influenced by current developments in Russia, appeared in many German states. In Berlin, radical extremists known as the "Spartacists" had control of the capital for a week in January, 1919. This movement was bloodily suppressed, with the murder of its leaders, Karl Liebknecht and Rosa Luxemburg, by counter-revolutionary organizations financed by the industrialists and landowners. The failure of the "Spartacists" had an important influence on subsequent political developments, for it meant that the Bolshevik model was not adopted in Germany.

The Weimar Republic

In the face of these conditions, a constitution for a new democratic government was drawn up. The resulting *Weimar Republic*, so named for the town in which the constitution was formulated, was designed with the specific purpose of guaranteeing the maximum possible degree of democracy in Germany.

If careful design could guarantee success, the Weimar Republic should have been outstanding. In the words of a British historian, it enjoyed the "most mechanically perfect of all democratic constitutions, full of admirable devices—parliamentary sovereignty, the referendum, the most elaborate and perfect system of proportional representation ever conceived—a textbook constitution for the Professor of Political Science." Tragically, it was doomed to fail, because the Republic was disliked, even detested, by the majority of the German people. Fairly or unfairly, Weimar was the scapegoat for defeat, an attitude kept alive by the different political parties, all of which—with the exception of the tiny Democratic Party—opposed the Republic with varying degrees of bitterness.

It was with these negative attitudes that the German people regarded the democracy which governed them. If the Republic had performed impressively, it might have eventually acquired sufficient prestige and respect to win acceptance. Unfortunately, this was not the case. In the years following the war, Germany was ravaged by devastating economic crises, first inflation, then depression, for which the government was to a considerable degree blameable.[1]

The country's mood became increasingly disillusioned and desperate. In times of such uncertainty, there is a tendency for people to seek a strong authority, capable of restoring order and direction to national affairs—even at the expense of political and civil liberties. In Germany this tendency was strengthened by the lack of strong democratic traditions comparable to those of Great Britain, France, and the Scandinavian countries. By contrast, earlier German history suggested that periods of national achievement coincided with the rule of strong men such as Frederick the Great and Bismarck.

Ironically, one of the gravest weaknesses of the Weimar Republic was the highly vaunted constitution itself. The constitution was designed to make the government so democratic—to reflect the feelings and wishes of the people so accurately—that it was actually unworkable. The use of proportional representation, for example, was intended to ensure that the strength of different parties in the Reichstag, or Parliament, would be proportionate to their popularity with the electorate. What this produced, however, was a proliferation of splinter parties, whose inability to co-operate in coalition paralysed the government. Not once in its history was the Weimar Republic governed by a single majority party. The ceaseless

[1]See pp. 476-479.

scheming between the different party leaders, as each sought power at the expense of the others, or followed some strange and uncompromising and ideological path, completely undermined the ability of the Reichstag to function with any sense of purpose. The government was terribly vulnerable to anyone ruthlessly dedicated to the destruction of the system. The Weimar Republic could not cope with Adolf Hitler and his Nazi Party.

Another significant feature of the constitution was the extraordinary power given the President. Article 48 provided that, "if the public safety and order be seriously disturbed or threatened," the President was authorized to set aside certain rights under the constitution and govern by decree. In practice, the President decided what constituted a threat to public safety. Use of this provision facilitated the process whereby Hitler ultimately came to power.

Hitler

The new leader to whom Germans turned in the 1930's did not come from a distinguished dynasty. Indeed, he was not even a German, in a technical sense—for Adolf Hitler was born in the Austrian town of Braunau in 1889. However, like the great Corsican, Napoleon, Hitler rose above his remote origins to become master of the most powerful state on the European continent.

It is ironical that the man who later fashioned the most disciplined tyranny of modern history was, himself, a natural rebel from youth. Hitler rejected both parental and scholastic authority at an early age, moving to Vienna where he earned a precarious living as an odd-job man and commercial artist. He was a moody, introspective youth, fond of those aspects of opera and mythology that glorified the Teutonic past. Refused entrance to the Viennese academies of art and architecture, Hitler developed a neurotic hatred for society—the moderately successful bourgeoisie, or middle class, and especially the Jews. The frustrations of his early life aggravated a keen sense of social inferiority, driving him to adopt extreme views. Soon he was to be heard in obscure corners of Vienna arguing vehemently for radical changes in society and the creation of a new, racially pure German state.

Hitler had a minor but honourable role in the First World War. He was a dispatch runner in a Bavarian regiment on the Western Front, where he was wounded twice, awarded the Iron Cross for

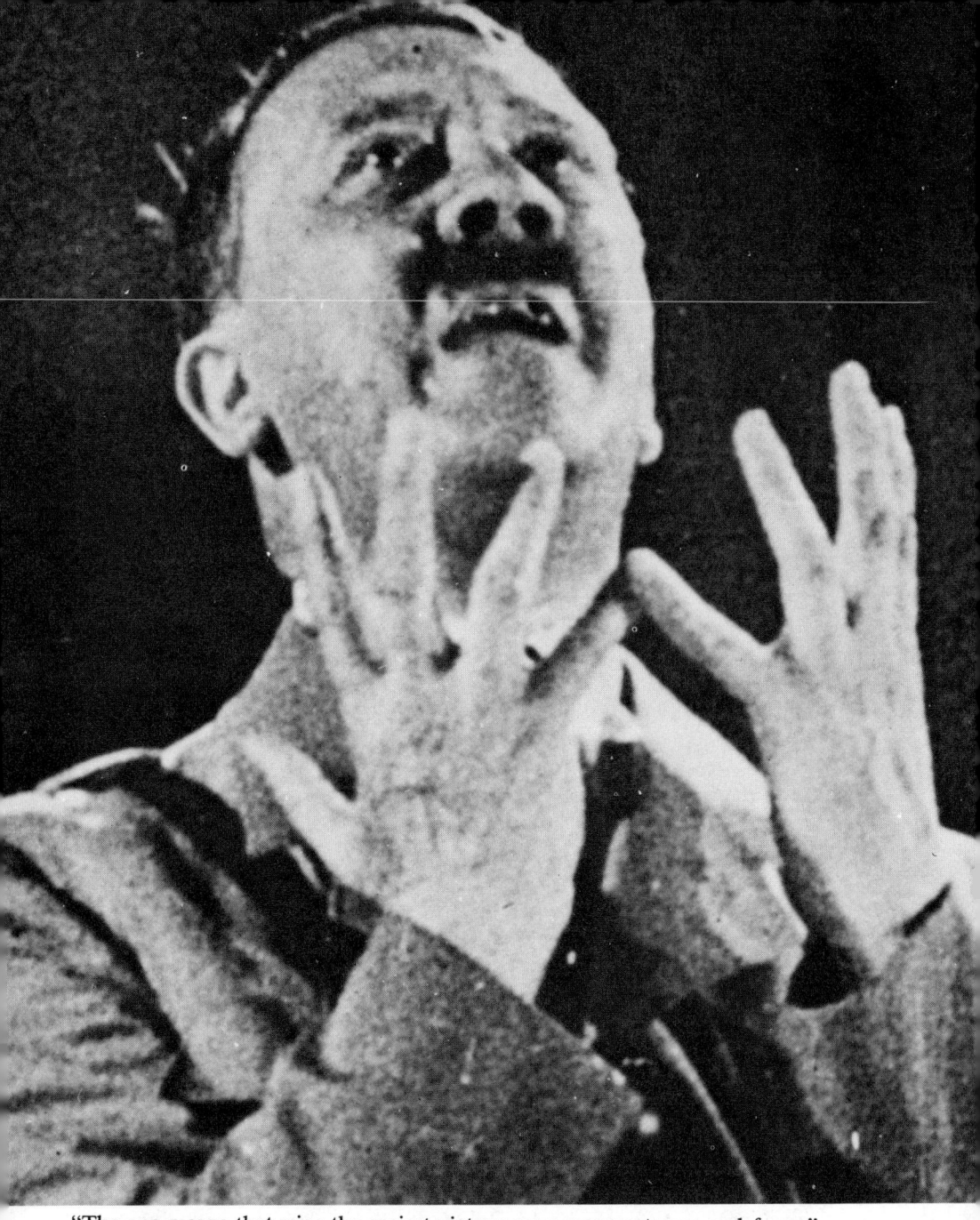

"The one means that wins the easiest victory over reason: terror and force."
—Adolf Hitler

bravery, and promoted to the rank of corporal. Unlike other soldiers, whose thoughts frequently turned to their homes and families, Hitler was absorbed by military life, revelling in its comradeship in conditions of adversity.

Germany's defeat gave Hitler a new vocation. "On November 9, 1918," he later declared, "I resolved to become a politician." He joined the National Socialist German Workers' Party, or Nazi Party, which blossomed in the post-war period of uncertainty, disillusionment, and depression. The political significance of the Nazi movement was not due to its pursuit of a positive programme of constructive objectives—but rather to its bitter criticism of the Versailles Treaty, of Jewish influence and, to a lesser degree, of abuses connected with capitalism, such as excessive interest rates.

Gradually, the new party attracted supporters from many walks of life who were dissatisfied with conditions in Germany. Among these men were some who later became Hitler's chief lieutenants: Hermann Goering, the corpulent aviator and war hero; Dr. Josef Goebbels, an intellectual with a flair for propaganda; Heinrich Himmler, a poultry farmer who later became head of the *Gestapo,* (the Nazi secret police) and others. The Nazis also attracted the support of high-ranking army officers, such as General Ludendorff, and important industrialists who heartily endorsed the party's implacable opposition to communism. The swastika became the symbol of the party, *"Heil"* became the obligatory greeting of members, and the brown-shirted S.A. (*Sturm Abteilung,* or "Storm Troops"), became the Nazi instrument of oppression, terrorizing all opposition.

While the Nazi strength was steadily growing, conditions in Germany were getting worse. The main factor in this decline was the world-wide economic depression. In three years (1929-32) the number of unemployed rose from a little over two million to six million persons. The middle class, disillusioned first by the great inflation and then by the depression, lost all faith in the economic system and its future; fearful of a drift to communism, they were attracted to the Nazis as the only seemingly effective alternative. Nazi criticism of the Versailles Treaty struck a sympathetic note in depression-stricken Germany. Many Germans chose to believe that the problems faced by their country were caused by the post-war treatment they had received from the Allies—the reduction of their territory, the loss of their colonies, markets, shipping, and foreign investments, the huge reparations imposed upon them, and the occupation of the Ruhr. Even an attempt to achieve an Austro-German customs union was blocked by France for political reasons. Is there any wonder that the Germans were bewildered and resentful?

Despite the conditions favourable to Nazism, however, Hitler's rise to power would almost certainly have been impossible had it not been for the fatal divisions among those who opposed him. Particularly on the Left, the numerous parties in the Reichstag were utterly incapable of co-operating. The Communist Party, which had never recovered from the earlier failure of the "Spartacists," was so preoccupied with discrediting the moderate-left Social Democrats that it was ineffective in opposing the Nazis. As a result, both left-wing parties were exposed as easy prey and destroyed. Part of the blame for this belongs to the amazingly inept foreign policy of the Soviet Union, who continually advised the German Communists that the Social Democrats—"the Social Fascists," as they called them—were a more dangerous enemy than the Nazis!

It was not just the left-wing parties, however, that were unable to resist the Nazis. In 1930 Heinrich Brüning of the Centre Party became Chancellor of the Reichstag (a position approximately equivalent to that of Prime Minister in our system) in coalition with other moderate right-wing parties. The coalition failed, however; receiving no co-operation from the other parties, Brüning was unable to maintain a majority in the Reichstag. He had only two choices: to resign, or to govern by *decrees*, which were issued independently of the Reichstag by the President. It was a highly unstable situation, that could endure only as long as the President was willing to co-operate with the Chancellor.

Unfortunately, the President, the war hero Paul von Hindenburg, was very old, possibly senile, and almost certainly malleable in the hands of the Army Officers' Corps and the *Junkers*, who loathed both the Weimar Republic and Brüning. At their persuasion, Hindenburg withdrew support of the Chancellor, who had no choice but to resign (May, 1932).

The new Chancellor, Franz von Papen, was no more successful than Brüning in obtaining a majority in the Reichstag. Two elec-

Nazi election poster —"Our Last Hope: Hitler."

tions were held in five months, in the hope that party strengths would be favourably altered, but the situation only deteriorated.

By this point the Nazis were the largest party in the Reichstag, and even though they were in Opposition, no other party could govern without their co-operation. But from the Nazis came not co-operation but conspiracy. A series of intrigues between Hitler and the leaders of other parties brought the dismissal of von Papen in November, 1932, and the dismissal of von Papen's successor, Kurt von Schleicher, only two months later. The stage was set. On January 30, 1933, Hindenburg took the fatal step of inviting the former corporal to become Chancellor, an offer which was quickly accepted by Hitler.

Within a month the true nature of the new regime was apparent. First, Hitler made a key move by installing his deputy, Wilhelm Frick, as Minister of the Interior, to give the Nazis control of the police. Then he called a new election, the third within a year. Using his extraordinary powers as an orator to the fullest advantage, Hitler exploited ruthlessly the prejudices and longings current in the German people. Despite these efforts, however, it was apparent that the Nazis would not receive a majority. Then, a week before the election, the Reichstag building was burned almost to the ground. It is probable, although not certain, that the Reichstag fire was a deliberate act of arson perpetrated by the Nazis themselves, but in the hysteria that followed, Hitler was able to persuade Hindenburg that it had been a Communist plot that presaged a Bolshevik-style revolution. Using his power under Article 48 of the Weimar Constitution, Hindenburg issued emergency decrees suspending guarantees of free speech and the free press, thereby crippling the Nazis' opponents in the election. Newspapers favourable not only to the Communists and Social Democrats, but even to the Centre Party, were closed down. The Nazi Storm Troopers openly intimidated opponents and broke up their meetings. The victims were unable to secure protection from the police because these too were under the direction of the Nazis.

The election gave the Nazis 43.9 per cent of the vote, more than any other party. In combination with their allies, the Nationalists, they had a clear majority in the Reichstag, and could therefore form an effective government. Immediately they excluded or arrested all the Communist deputies and a number of the Social Democrats; by this act, they gained a clear majority on their own. Then, by a combination of force and intrigue, Hitler gained the support of the Centre Party, which gave him the necessary two-thirds majority to suspend the Weimar Constitution and assume dictatorial powers.

By observing the form rather than the spirit of constitutional practice, Hitler achieved a dominant position in Germany eleven years after Mussolini's dramatic "March on Rome." While it might be argued that, unlike his Italian predecessor, Hitler came to power through democratic processes as leader of the largest political party in the Reichstag, the fact remains that the use of threats and brutal force behind the scenes was an important factor in his success. The suppression of all opposition by outright acts of terrorism meant that "elections" had little meaning as true indicators of popular opinion. Nevertheless, it cannot be denied that a large number, probably the majority, of Germans accepted Hitler's dictatorship as preferable to the continuation of uncertainty and disorder.

The Nazi Regime

As the Fascists had done a decade earlier, the Nazis immediately set about establishing a totalitarian state. All other parties were banned or dissolved, including the Nationalists. The private armies of the other parties of course were also eliminated. These measures gave the Nazis a complete monopoly of political power; effective opposition was rendered impossible.

The next step was the refashioning of Germany from a federal nation to a unitary one. The constitution was changed, abolishing the sovereignty of the states, and giving all power to the central government. By this means, the danger of a state government becoming a nucleus of organized resistance was effectively prevented.

Other changes consolidated the Nazi grip on political power still further. First, the civil service was re-made into a servant of Nazi policy. Then, the judiciary was reduced from a position of independence to little more than a rubber stamp for the government. The welfare of the regime—as interpreted by the Nazis—was made the principal standard for determining "guilt" or "innocence." A "People's Court" was established to try cases of "treason," which was defined to cover a very wide range of situations. Proceedings were held in secret, appeals could be made only to Hitler himself, and the usual sentence was summary execution. Worst of all, numerous concentration camps were set up, in which opponents of the regime could be imprisoned without trial.

Within six months of becoming Chancellor, Hitler had achieved near-total control of Germany. There were only three potential sources of opposition left for him to worry about. The first was Hindenburg; if the old general should suddenly see through the veil of legitimacy with which the Nazis had thinly disguised the nature of the regime, he would certainly use the army to throw them out. The second source was the army itself—would the generals allow Hitler to acquire absolute power? The third source—and potentially the most dangerous—was the Nazi Party itself. Could Hitler safely trust his own followers?

In the summer of 1934 Hindenburg conveniently died. Promptly Hitler combined the offices of President and Chancellor, filling both positions himself. His action was ratified by the overwhelming vote of a thoroughly-cowed electorate. Henceforth he was *Der Führer*; he was also one step closer to absolute power.

A Stormtrooper arresting Communist "enemies."

The second question, the behaviour of the army, was a source of continual concern to Hitler. (Later, during the Second World War, the dissatisfaction of Army leaders culminated in an unsuccessful attempt to assassinate the *Führer*.) However, the generals, while often contemptuous of Hitler's lower class manner, were basically in agreement with his aims, especially the restoration of German military strength, and were therefore open to persuasion. To make certain, however, Hitler afterwards established his supremacy over the regular forces by organizing the *Oberkommando der Wehrmacht* (O.K.W.), or High Command of the Armed Forces, with himself as Commander-in-Chief.

Totalitarian control was now almost complete, but there remained one final question. An essential element in the Nazis' violent journey to power had been the Storm Troopers, whose brutal tactics had been so useful in intimidating opponents of the government. But what would happen, now that the Nazis themselves were the government, if the S.A. should turn against *them*?

It was not just an academic question. Many of the Storm Troopers were genuine revolutionaries, and were showing signs of rebelling against Hitler's authority. But what force could be used to intimidate the S.A.? The answer was the even more intimidating, black-shirted S.S.—the dreaded *Schutzstaffeln*, or security formation—a hand-picked elite guard sworn to serve Hitler personally. On the night of June 30, 1934, occurred the "Blood Purge," in which several hundred Storm Troopers, including the leader, Ernst Roehm, were murdered by the S.S. The S.A. was not disbanded, but as a potential opposition to Hitler it had been rendered impotent.

Having thus established absolute political domination, Hitler, like Mussolini, began implementing measures to dominate even the non-political aspects of society. As in Italy it was necessary to integrate the economy, religion, and education within state authority.

The first priority in the Nazi control of the economy was the abolition of the trade unions. Despite their tradition of militancy, the unions succumbed almost without resistance. Workers were forbidden to organize or to strike, and had no hand in determining wages or working conditions. As compared with Italy, however—or indeed, with that dictatorship of the proletariat, the Soviet Union—the worker in Germany was fairly well off. Genuinely worthwhile benefits were available, such as free vacations at state expense, and workers' recreation clubs. Prices and interest rates were kept low. Important also was the fact that Nazi Germany made a surprising recovery under the guidance of a brilliant, unconventional economist, Dr. Hjalmar Schacht. Prosperity increased, unemployment disappeared. Most Germans were prepared to accept the loss of economic freedom as a not unreasonable price for economic recovery.

As with the Fascists, it was essential for the Nazis to neutralize opposition to their regime from the Church. But whereas the Fascists sought to accomplish this through compromise (the Lateran Accord), the Nazis first tried to distort the Church's purpose and function for their own ends, and then attacked openly in an attempt to compel its submission. The first phase was marked by an attemped re-interpretation of Christian doctrine. The Old Testament was thrown out entirely, along with numerous "unsuitable" parts of the New Testament. Jesus was depicted as a warrior-hero who had saved the world from Jewish domination—a striking

Poster advertising an anti-Jewish film, "The Eternal Jew."

parallel with the *Führer* who thus became symbolically a second Christ. The second phase began roughly with Hitler's attempt to put the Lutheran Church under direct Nazi control, with his nominee as *Reichsbishop*. The Church reacted with such defiance that Hitler retreated. Many Lutheran bishops also refused the loyalty oath, choosing the concentration camp rather than submit. The Roman Catholic Church also resisted Nazi attempts to prohibit Catholic education of youth groups, the publication of Catholic literature, and other activities. Nor would they stop celebrating Mass, despite Nazi threats. One unexpected result of the struggle between the Nazi regime and the Church was the rebirth of German interest in religion. Attendance at church was the only means of expressing defiance of the government. Thus, if only in a spiritual context, the Church remained the one centre of resistance to German totalitarianism. In practice, however, this meant that the Church had little influence on the actual course of events in Germany.

More successful was the Nazi indoctrination of youth. With far greater seriousness and determination than had been shown in Italy, German children were marshalled in Spartan youth groups, such as the *Hitler Jugend*, where they were imbued from early childhood with a love for the glory of Germany, for Hitler, and for war; for them, Nazism was made a religion. Above all, the children were taught to obey. These were the ultimate totalitarian citizens; had the Nazi regime not been destroyed by military defeat before they reached maturity, German totalitarianism might have reached extremes almost unimaginable today.

The development that really distinguished Nazi Germany as unique even among totalitarian states was its utterly ruthless persecution of the Jews. At first the Nazis restricted their harsh treatment of Jews to financial extortion and discrimination, compelling them to wear distinguishing badges and forbidding marriage between Jews and supposedly racially pure "Aryans." (There was, of course, no foundation in fact for the belief that there was a "pure" race, Aryan or otherwise.)

But later Hitler turned to what he described as the "Final Solution" of the Jewish problem—a satanic policy of wholesale extermination. When the enormity of this policy was finally revealed to a horrified world at the end of the Second World War, a new word "genocide" (from the Greek *genos* meaning "race", and the Latin *caedere*, meaning "to kill") had to be invented to describe this relapse into barbarism. It is believed that some six million Jews perished at the hands of Hitler's executioners. Many victims welcomed death as an end to unspeakable torture. The same policy of genocide was waged against certain other races also considered inferior, for example Slavs and Gypsies.

Summarizing, we can distinguish certain essential features of the totalitarianism that flourished between the two World Wars. Italian Fascism, Japanese militarism, Russian Communism, and German Nazism were all based on rejection of democracy and reversion to despotic methods of government. But advances in technology, particularly in the field of mass media of communications, and more centralized administration enabled the dictators of the 1930's to enforce a social, economic, and political discipline unattainable in previous centuries.

Louis XIV may have said: *"L'Etat, c'est moi."* But in his period, and even later under Napoleon, there were definite limits to the impact of authority on the individual. In a much more literal sense, both Hitler and Stalin were the personifications of their regimes, with demonstrated ability to overcome all internal opposition.

None of these dictatorships could expose itself to a spirit of free criticism and evaluation. "In a totalitarian country," as one historian remarks, "the very notion of a loyal opposition is a contradiction; any opposition to the regime or to official dogma is by definition disloyal." The totalitarian philosophy, like that of the earlier believers in the "divine right" of monarchs, permitted no challenge to its fundamental assumptions. In numberless instances a terrible price was paid by those who rebelled against the internal implications of dictatorial systems. But the ultimate tragedy of the totalitarian regimes was the misery they forced on *all* mankind by their insatiable demands outside their own frontiers.

22 The Twenty Years' Crisis

"Any war or threat of war, whether immediately affecting any of the Members of the League or not, is hereby declared a matter of concern to the whole League, and the League shall take any action that may be deemed wise and effectual to safeguard the peace of nations."—Article 11 of the Covenant of the League of Nations.

In the previous chapter we discussed the nature of totalitarian governments in terms of their own internal development and characteristics. What would happen when these regimes turned their attention beyond their own borders to the realm of international relations? Such a development was inevitable. The militarist government of Japan was avowedly expansionist, determined to carve an empire in the East. Nazi Germany was dedicated to the revocation of the Treaty of Versailles, a restoration of military parity, and the acquisition of *lebensraum,* or living space, which quite simply meant territorial expansion at the expense of her neighbours. The Soviet Union, while far more concerned with consolidation of the new regime, had by no means forgotten the Marxist-Leninist ideal of promoting communist revolution in other countries; nor had the Czarist quest for extended borders and warm-water ports diminished under the Bolsheviks. The Fascists in Italy wished to exalt "national honour" by warfare and conquest. And the democracies? Crippled by depression, politically isolated and indecisive, these seemed almost to invite aggression by their weakness. The totalitarian states saw a chance for easy gain, and reacted accordingly. This was the decisive issue of the 1930's, leading inexorably to the Second World War.

1. THE LEAGUE OF NATIONS

International politics of the two decades separating the First and Second World Wars were dominated by the fortunes of the League of Nations.[1] The tragic fate which overtook this instrument of conciliation in the 1930's has obscured the idealism and achievements

[1] The organization of the League was discussed on p. 415 and p. 418.

of its early years. It is also important to remember that the League's purpose was never purely *political*, in the sense of preventing war. A second, and most important aspect of its work, was to promote international co-operation in the general sphere of social and economic welfare. The two functions were not unrelated, since most responsible opinion recognized that social and economic discontent within a nation might easily lead it into external aggression against its neighbours. The prospects for international peace seemed brighter as more and more of the world's population could benefit from rising standards of living.

A decision of paramount importance, taken at the beginning of the League's history, sought to reinforce the moral authority of the new body. In the eyes of the world, the concept of the League, however admirable, was clearly associated with the peace settlement imposed on the Central Powers by the Allies at Versailles. Therefore, there was a real danger that the League might be considered merely a continuation, in disguised form, of the victors' wartime alliance. Provision was made in the Covenant for an increase in the permanent membership of the Council to include Germany and Russia. Thus, it was hoped, the League would become more truly representative of world opinion, and at the same time recognize the special interests and responsibilities of the larger nations.[1]

The Admission of Russia and Germany

As was only to be expected, the question of German and Russian participation in the League aroused intense feeling among their traditional enemies. Poland, for example, feared a revival of German power and put forward her own claim to a permanent seat on the Council, as did Spain and Brazil. After much difficult negotiation among the nations principally concerned, Germany was finally admitted to the League, with "permanent" representation on the Council, in September, 1926. But the circumstances attending their country's entry left many Germans with the conviction that they were still not really accepted back into the world community.

The admission of Soviet Russia was even more difficult because the Allied Powers had unwisely intervened against the Bolshevik Revolution.[2] It is not too surprising that post-war Russian leaders

---
[1] The United States, although a champion of the League's formation, was not a member. See above, p. 418.
[2] See p. 507.

remained suspicious of a world organization created, in their view, by the old "imperialist" nations.¹ Moreover, as we have seen, Communism in Russia had to overcome great internal problems of collectivization of agriculture and industrialization, and had less interest in developments outside her frontiers. Consequently, it was not until 1934, when the German threat to world peace was becoming unmistakably clear, that the Soviet Union finally entered the League and took her place as a permanent member of the Council.

Attempts to Keep the Peace

Although the League fulfilled more than one role, its principal business was the prevention of war by the peaceful settlement of disputes. When reviewing its achievement in this field, we must not overlook the fact that the League did not enjoy the advantage of universal jurisdiction. Quite apart from the American refusal to participate and the temporary absence of Germany and Russia, it was recognized that the League's authority did not extend into certain regions. For example, it was acknowledged that the United States had the paramount interest in Central America, that Great Britain had a peculiar status in relation to Egypt, and that foreigners, Japanese as well as occidental, had special interests in China.

Nevertheless, during the early years of its existence, the League proved to be a flexible and efficient instrument of conciliation. Its success can be illustrated by solutions found to three international disputes in historically "sensitive" regions. The first of these arose out of trouble over the frontier between Turkey and Iraq, then a British mandate. Late in 1924 this issue was complicated by a revolt of the Kurds—a hardy, nomadic people living in and near the disputed area of Mosul—against their Turkish governors. The matter was referred successively to the Council of the League and the Permanent Court of International Justice, which was associated with the League. Eventually, reluctant Turkey was persuaded to accept a decision that transferred most of the troubled area to Iraq.

The Balkans, long the powder keg of south-eastern Europe, were

---

[1] In turn, the "imperialist" nations were highly suspicious of the Soviet Union. It was not until 1924 that a Great Power (Britain) was willing to grant diplomatic recognition to the U.S.S.R.

"The process of civilization has always been towards the League of Nations." — Jan Smuts. In the above illustration, the British representative, A. J. Balfour, is addressing the first meeting of the Council of the League, on February 11, 1920.

the scene of the next disturbance. For many years Greeks and Bulgarians had clashed over control of Macedonia. Following a border incident in 1925, a Greek Army marched into Bulgaria and the latter at once appealed to the League. In the end, Greece withdrew her forces and reluctantly agreed to pay compensation to Bulgaria for the violation of her territory. Greek reluctance to accept the League's verdict was accentuated by recollections that in an earlier incident, when Greece had been the victim of Italian aggression on the island of Corfu, the major Powers had forced a decision in favour of Italy.

The third dispute settled by the League arose in north-eastern Europe, where Lithuania, one of the republics created after the First World War, refused to recognize Polish occupation of the town of Vilna. In 1927, Lithuania brought her grievance to the League. The latter was unable to reconcile the differences between the parties; but it was credited with a relaxation of tension between the two countries which otherwise might have resorted to open war.

In other respects the League showed a useful capacity to resolve disputes not affecting the vital interests of the larger Powers. A satisfactory settlement was arranged between Finland and Sweden regarding the Aaland Islands in the Baltic; the Memel Statute (1924) granted autonomy to Germans living in an area acquired by Lithuania; the boundaries of Upper Silesia, an important industrial region, were defined, as were those of other territorial units in central Europe. The League also assisted the financial rehabilitation of Austria and Hungary and dealt with the difficult economic and racial problems of the Saar Basin and the "free city" of Danzig.[1]

These constructive achievements during the first decade of its existence augured well for the future of the League of Nations. But the question remained: if the interests of two or more *major* Powers came into direct conflict, could they be settled by the procedures used in less critical issues?

The Manchurian Incident

The first such test came in late 1931; this was the Manchurian Incident, already discussed above in terms of its effect upon the internal policies of Japan.[2] For many decades Japan had been engaged with China and Russia in a three-cornered contest for this strategically important area. Not only did it represent a potential barrier to Russian advance and a valuable source of natural resources—in addition, Manchuria was the indispensable springboard for Japanese expansion into Mongolia.

After the Russian-Japanese War Japan had obtained the right to keep troops in Manchuria for the protection of her interests in the South Manchurian Railway. In September, 1931, Japanese soldiers at Mukden claimed that they had intercepted a Chinese attempt to demolish the main line. On the basis of this allegation, which was never satisfactorily proven, the Japanese military authorities occupied the whole of Manchuria. The speed with which the operation was conducted strongly suggested that the army commanders had

---

[1] The reconstituted Polish State, established by the Treaty of Versailles, had been granted access to the Baltic by the so-called "Polish Corridor," which separated East Prussia from the remainder of Germany. The special problem of the German-speaking seaport of Danzig, at the northern end of the Corridor, was recognized by making it a "free city" under the League's supervision.

[2] See p. 505.

seized a pretext to carry out a deliberate design well prepared in advance.

China appealed to the League of Nations under Article 11 of the Covenant, which read in part: "Any war or threat of war, whether immediately affecting any of the Members of the League or not, is hereby declared a matter of concern to the whole League, and the League shall take any action that may be deemed wise and effectual to safeguard the peace of nations." The League's Council grappled with the problem, endeavouring unsuccessfully to persuade Japan to withdraw her troops to their original positions in Manchuria. However, far from relinquishing his hold on Manchuria, the aggressor set up a puppet state, known as Manchukuo, to control the region, and attacked Shanghai when the Chinese began a boycott of Japanese goods.

In the end, all efforts to solve the Manchurian crisis proved unavailing, and Japan remained firmly in possession of her conquest. The Lytton Commission, composed of British, American, French, German, and Italian representatives, made a lengthy on-site investigation of the situation. Although reporting that there was no basis for the Japanese action, the Commission carefully avoided any opinion that would have exposed Japan to the threat of sanctions under the Covenant. When this report was adopted by an overwhelming vote of the League's Assembly, early in 1933, Japan formally withdrew from membership in the League.

Apart from its significance for internal politics in Japan, the Manchurian crisis constituted clear evidence of the inability of the League of Nations to deal effectively with an aggressive action committed by a Great Power. It was an inauspicious beginning for a series of events in the 1930's in which the interests of larger nations clashed with the ideals of the League as expressed in its Covenant.

Disarmament

Another critical problem was that of world disarmament. After the First World War, most statesmen agreed that a solution to this crucial issue was indispensable to the preservation of world peace. If nations remained armed to the teeth with the devastating weapons of modern war, there was a strong probability that, inflamed by underlying nationalistic passions, some irresponsible government would precipitate another disastrous conflict.

For a time, in the late 1920's, there appeared to be some prospect of achieving disarmament through better international relations. By the Locarno Treaties, negotiated in 1925, France and Germany sought to end their age-old strife over their common frontier. Moreover, Great Britain and Italy agreed to guarantee both the Franco-German frontier and the frontier between Germany and Belgium. This was a far cry from the traditional detachment with which British governments had usually regarded commitments on the Continent. The "Spirit of Locarno" generated an optimistic feeling throughout the world. Unfortunately, the Pact did not specifically bind Germany to refrain from aggression to change her southern and eastern frontiers; consequently, these were soon to become major sources of tension.

By recognizing Germany's right to negotiate with other Great Powers, the Locarno Pact made the disarmament issue much more pressing. Obviously, the former Allies could not treat their defeated enemy as a diplomatic equal, and, while adhering to the Covenant of the League, preserve a manifestly unequal proportion of armed strength in their favour. At the same time, Locarno established an atmosphere of trust and confidence, in which it was much easier for a sensitive issue such as disarmament to be discussed.

At the end of 1925, the League set up a preparatory commission for a disarmament conference to be held in the following year. Very soon, however, wide differences of outlook on basic questions were evident among the nations' representatives. Even on the fundamental problem of defining "armaments" there was no general agreement. Modern war has so many ramifications—impinging on virtually all aspects of human existence—that it is extremely difficult to decide what is properly included in the definition. Is an automotive industry to be considered part of a nation's war potential because it can produce tanks and army vehicles? Are textile factories within the definition because they can easily produce uniforms? What of industries producing agricultural implements (spades are indispensable for digging trenches); canning factories (tinned rations are needed to support large armies in the field) and oil refineries (aviation fuel and gasoline are basic requirements for mobile warfare)? The same difficulty of definition appeared in all branches of national defence. For example, some nations wanted a limitation of the overall tonnage of war shipping; others wanted specific limitations on each category of ship.

Some progress was made in the direction of limiting naval strengths; but it was not until 1932 that a full meeting of the Disarmament Conference assembled at Geneva. Representatives of sixty-one states, including the United States and the Soviet Union, grappled with intractable issues. The record of the Conference during the next two years is a sad commentary on the nations' inability to place the true interests of humanity above their own selfish goals.

Early in the proceedings, the French delegation produced a novel plan for the creation of a League of Nations police force including, among other weapons, a monopoly of bombing aircraft. This proposal was not acceptable to either Great Britain or the United States. Then there were endless arguments over what distinguished "offensive" from "defensive" weapons; whether trained reserves should be included in computations of military manpower and what principle should govern financial expenditures on armaments. In the background was the irreconcilable conflict between French demands for security, based on bitter memories of German invasions in 1870 and 1914, and German insistence on equality of armaments with the other Great Powers. In October, 1933, Germany effectively wrecked hopes for disarmament by walking out of both the Conference and the League of Nations. Finally, in the summer of 1934, renewed efforts to reach an accommodation were ruined by the unyielding attitude of France, and the Disarmament Conference adjourned in a spirit of frustration and disillusionment. After more than two years of fruitless negotiation at Geneva, the effort to find a rational solution to an irrational situation had failed. Then, in March, 1935, Hitler took the decisive step in destroying the restrictions imposed on Germany by formally denouncing the disarmament clauses of the Treaty of Versailles. Actually, senior officers had been secretly preparing the ground for a restoration of German military might long before Hitler came to power. But Hitler's pronouncement, besides stimulating the vast war potential of Germany, extinguished any lingering hopes of relieving international tension, and precipitated another arms race among the Great Powers similar to that which had occurred before 1914.

2. THE PRELUDE TO WAR

The Manchurian crisis, the failure of the World Disarmament Conference, and German rearmament were devastating blows at post-First World War attempts to attain collective security. Hopes of achieving amicable settlements of disputes between major Powers received their next serious check in the Ethiopian crisis of 1935-1936.

Italy and Ethiopia

It will be remembered that Italy's reaction to decisions taken at Versailles with respect to her frontiers was an important factor in Mussolini's takeover in 1922. But Italian aspirations went beyond the Alps and the Adriatic. Previously unable to obtain substantial colonies in Africa, apart from arid, unproductive strips in Libya and East Africa, Italy still retained grandiose ambitions of carving out a new empire in the "Dark Continent." Moreover, she felt strongly impelled to avenge the defeat she had suffered at Adowa (1896) when she had failed in an earlier attempt to conquer Ethiopia (Abyssinia). As the only surviving example of a native African community which had successfully resisted European imperialism, Ethiopia offered a particularly attractive target for Mussolini's plans.

The trouble between Italy and Ethiopia began, as in the Manchurian crisis, in an obscure skirmish. At the end of 1934 a force from Italian Somaliland clashed with Ethiopian troops in what appears to have been Ethiopian territory, although the frontier in this region had never been clearly defined. Because a few of his soldiers lost their lives, Mussolini immediately demanded an apology and a large indemnity from Ethiopia—but these were mere pretexts for a policy of outright aggression. Although Italy made a show of accepting the League's authority in settling the dispute, the Fascist dictator had no intention of cancelling carefully made plans for the subjugation of Ethiopia. While Mussolini's delegates were assuring the League of their country's willingness to accept arbitration on the issue, reinforcements and arms were being poured into Italian Somaliland and nearby Eritria.

In October, 1935, the Italian war machine, complete with tanks and aircraft, began the invasion of Ethiopia without the formality of a declaration of war. For a time it seemed that Mussolini might have bitten off more than he could chew. Not only did the victims of his aggression put up a stout defence under the indomitable leadership of their Emperor, Haile Selassie, but world opinion was strongly critical of the Italian policy, and the League reacted quickly in the emergency. The Council declared Italy an aggressor, while the Assembly, by an overwhelming vote, approved the application of economic sanctions. This meant that members of the League could restrict or eliminate all trade between their countries and Italy, refuse financial assistance, and generally impose an economic "quarantine" on the offender. Outside the League, the United States co-operated to the extent of implementing its neutrality by refusing to trade with either Italy or Ethiopia.

But powerful forces were at work to neutralize effective action against Mussolini's infamous design. Although the western democratic nations, especially Britain, seemed prepared to face the ultimate test of war with Italy if necessary to maintain the ideals of the Covenant, their resolution was undermined by intrigue and fear of the repercussions on Germany.

Pierre Laval, the shifty French Prime Minister (later executed for treason), persuaded the British Foreign Secretary, Sir Samuel Hoare, to make a joint proposal for a partition of Ethiopia that would have reduced that unhappy country to one-third of its former size. Although these suggestions were immediately repudiated by British and French public opinion (Hoare was forced to resign), their publication weakened resistance to Mussolini. Moreover, there was no agreement among the members of the League as to the necessity of including oil in the list of articles to be covered by sanctions.[1] Obviously mechanized units of Mussolini's army would have been hard hit by restrictions on the supply of oil; on the other hand, Italian reaction to such a move might well have led to a war in which Britain and France, because of naval commitments, would have been heavily engaged without the prospect of effective assistance from other members of the League. British and French leaders were understandably reluctant to assume the entire burden of dealing with the dictator. They also feared that any increase in pressure on Italy might lead to a close alliance between that nation and

---

[1] The Canadian delegate to the League, Dr. W. A. Riddell, advocated that oil should be included on the list. In a startling move that has continued to be controversial, Prime Minister King publicly repudiated him.

resurgent Germany. These feelings were intensified, early in 1936, when Hitler sent his troops into the demilitarized Rhineland. It was significant that the later Rome-Berlin Axis originated in Italo-German co-operation over Ethiopia and the Rhineland.

While his diplomatic opponents wasted their time in futile discussion, Mussolini took advantage of seasonable weather to complete his conquest of Ethiopia. Utterly unscrupulous, and oblivious to world opinion, *Il Duce* did not hesitate to use flame-throwers and mustard gas against his ill-equipped foes. Gradually the advantages of modern equipment wore down the resistance of Haile Selassie's gallant forces. Early in May, 1936, the capital, Addis Ababa, fell to the invaders, the king of Italy, a mere figure-head in the Fascist regime, was proclaimed Emperor of Ethiopia, and the entire country was annexed to Italy.

Haile Selassie fled to exile in England little knowing that only five years later he would be returned to his ancient throne, having had the satisfaction of seeing British forces drive out the usurpers. But in the dark days of May, 1936, the Emperor paused at Geneva to address the Assembly. To a shamefaced audience he pointed out that "it is international morality that is at stake . . . God and history will remember your judgment." In a sense, the Emperor stood before the world as the conscience of humanity.

The Beginning of German Aggression

German actions in withdrawing from the Disarmanent Convention and the League of Nations in 1933, and in denouncing the Versailles Treaty in 1935, had served as a clear indication of the revival of militarism under the Nazis. Hitler's next move, coming in June, 1935, was to drive a wedge between France and Britain by making a private naval agreement regarding submarine strength with Britain only. Then, in March, 1936, came Hitler's greatest triumph to that point—the reoccupation of the Rhineland. The act was in blatant defiance of both the Treaties of Versailles and Locarno, and an open courtship of war.

It was an extraordinary chance that Hitler took; his leading advisers had all urged him desperately not to risk a war which Germany would certainly lose. But Hitler had prepared his ground thoroughly, with a remarkably shrewd understanding of the minds of his opponents. Italy, he knew, was preoccupied with Ethiopia;

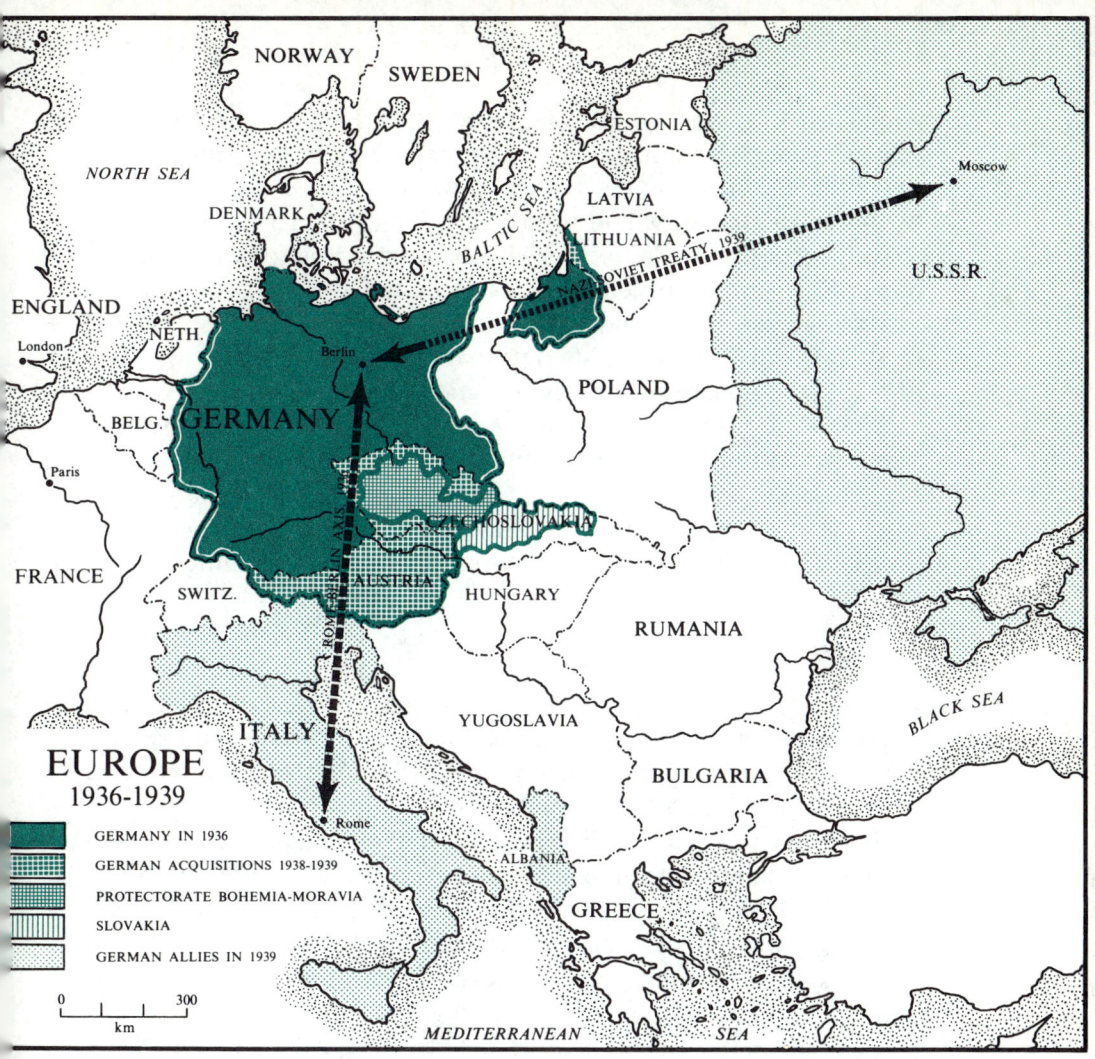

Hitler had taken pains to win Mussolini's gratitude by remaining neutral on the question of League sanctions against Italy. Britain, Hitler calculated, was satisfied with the naval agreement, and would do nothing. Russia was no worry unless France moved. And here was the biggest question—would France, whose interests were not directly threatened, retaliate in the face of German provocation?

France vacillated. Neither the General Staff nor the government would decide on a firm course to follow. With the danger of involvement in Ethiopia still pressing, could she afford also to become embroiled in a war against Germany? The biggest worry was the cost of general mobilization, which the French government was unwilling to incur unless Britain too would take action. France would act if Britain would follow suit, but Britain was determined to wait for a French initiative. And so, after nothing more formidable than strongly-worded protests from the democracies, Hitler's march into the Rhineland went unchallenged. It is known that the German army had orders to retire if opposed by force. By such narrow margins are the affairs of nations determined!

The results were entirely unfortunate. The League of Nations was dealt yet another grievous blow. The credibility of Britain and France as the guarantors of democracy was badly weakened. And worst of all, the reputation of Hitler, the *Führer* inspired and invincible, rose almost beyond the point of challenge within his own country.

The Democracies in Decline

How was it possible for Hitler to take such drastic actions without interference from the peace-loving nations? There is no simple answer. Economic problems, political instability, and the mood of the people, all had an important effect.

The two nations who might have played the greatest role in resisting totalitarian encroachment, Britain and France, were both beset by political and economic problems. In Britain, severe unemployment, the worst in her history, preoccupied the attention of the government. In France, the depression contributed to a growing political instability. Constantly shifting coalitions allied right-wing parties with left-wing, and divided left-wing parties among themselves. Between 1918 and 1939, there were fifteen ministries, ranging from the right-wing Poincaré to the Socialist-Communist "Popular Front" coalition headed by Léon Blum. In such circumstances, a coherent foreign policy was difficult, if not impossible.

Another important factor was that popular attitudes in both countries strongly opposed war. Britain had suffered 908 000, and France, 1 358 000 dead from the First World War; in both countries there was intense revulsion at the thought that such a disaster might be repeated. Many people began to feel that the Great War had gained nothing, and that allegations of German "war guilt" were not supported. Wars were fought for the profits of the armsmakers, it was argued; all else was propaganda. In England, students at Oxford and other universities began a pacifist movement in which they vowed never to bear arms for any reason. In a situation such as this, any policy that suggested a move to war could have been politically fatal. Stanley Baldwin, British Prime Minister from 1935 to 1937, commented: "Supposing I had gone to the country and said that Germany was rearming and that we must rearm, does anybody think that this pacific democracy would have rallied to that cry at that moment? I cannot think of anything that would have made the loss of the election from my point of view more certain." This and similar remarks are revealing indications of why the democratic leaders failed to take action in the face of the totalitarian threat.

Similarly, the attitude existed that Fascism and Nazism were desirable forces that should be cultivated as a *cordon sanitaire* against the much worse threat (so it was felt) of Bolshevism. In both France and Britain influential persons and groups expressed openly their admiration of *Il Duce* and *Der Führer*. As a result of all these factors, it became the policy of both British and French governments to appease the dictators at almost any cost. The Anglo-French attitude was also conditioned by the knowledge that the strength of American isolationism precluded effective participation by the United States in resistance to Nazi and Fascist aggression.

A further weakening factor was the military strategy adopted by the democracies. Britain had voluntarily limited the tonnage of her capital ships and had done little to develop a modern air force—even though it was believed that Germany was spending an estimated two and a half billion dollars per year on arms.[1] Only Winston Churchill and Anthony Eden seemed aware of the grave danger of German military superiority, but their warnings were scarcely heard. Eden resigned as Foreign Secretary in protest against the weak policy of the government, but was not heeded. In France, a large portion of the military budget was spent on massive fixed fortifications such as the Maginot Line, which were expected to provide an impregnable defence against any invader. At the same time, however, the French army was unprepared to

---

[1]There is evidence to show, however, that even on the eve of the Second World War, the percentage of the German gross national product spent on armaments was actually little or no greater than the British equivalent.

Il Duce and *Der Führer*: ". . . a very nasty and ridiculous pair. The worst part of the story is that millions of people believed in them and applauded their every action." — A. J. P. Taylor.

take any meaningful military initiative short of full-scale mobilization—and this the government refused to do for any provocation short of war. The army might have been able to occupy Luxemburg, one French general remarked, but little more.

The dictators seemed now in ascendancy, the democracies in decline. It was apparent that the interests of Fascist Italy and Nazi Germany were largely similar, not least in respect of their common opposition to the democratic governments. Their co-operation in

Ethiopia and the Rhineland suggested that a more formal alliance might be mutually advantageous. Accordingly, in October, 1936, Germany and Italy reached a diplomatic agreement, the so-called Rome-Berlin Axis, "a diplomatic axle around which the world might turn." A month later Germany negotiated an extension of the agreement to Japan, and a year after that, Italy too concluded arrangements with Japan. Thus the three "right-wing" totalitarian governments linked themselves together in a military pact in opposition to the democracies. Ostensibly, the Rome-Berlin-Tokyo Axis existed to prevent the spread of Communism; in reality, its outlook was primarily aggressive. In the words of one of its principal architects, Count Ciano,[1] the Axis was ". . . . the most formidable political and military combination which had ever existed." Although events were to prove that the Axis was more impressive on paper than in operation, its creation and development was only a further indication of how the balance of power was shifting away from the favour of the democracies.

Repeated blows at the moral authority of the League of Nations—first in Manchuria, then in Ethiopia and the Rhineland—seriously jeopardized any remaining hopes of preserving collective security. The final scenes in this grim inter-war tragedy were played out, with alarming rapidity, in the three years following the Italian victory in Africa. The focal centres of later developments were to be found in such widely dispersed regions as Spain, China, and Central Europe.

The Spanish Civil War

Spain had fallen from the position of pre-eminence she had enjoyed in the 16th century to a position of secondary importance. Her problems were partly economic—her industrialization lagged far behind that of other western European communities—and partly political and social, in the widening divisions between parties and classes. At the end of the 19th century she had suffered a humiliating defeat in the Spanish-American War, losing nearly all of her colonies, including Cuba and the Philippines. Yet her worst trials did not come until the late 1930's.

[1]Ciano, the Foreign Minister of Fascist Italy and Mussolini's son-in-law, recorded his impressions in his *Diary*, which is an interesting source of information for many of these events.

After the First World War the government of Spain moved from monarchical to dictatorial and republican extremes, with increasing bitterness between political groups supported by Communists and Fascists. Assassinations and terrorism became more and more common in a country where the art of deliberation and compromise proved unusually difficult. A constant problem was that of reconciling a strong central government with the desire for local autonomy. In few modern countries is there such fierce pride in local customs and traditions.

Finally, in the summer of 1936, the long-feared explosion occurred and Spain was plunged into one of the bloodiest civil wars of modern history. General Francisco Franco, a small man whose impassive face masked ruthless determination, led the Nationalist revolt against the Republican government, which had been proclaimed only five years before. Essentially, the war was a struggle between the more reactionary elements of Spanish society, the large landowners, the Church, and the military leaders who fought against the government; and the radicals, including Socialists, Communists, and Anarchists, who supported the government but were often divided among themselves. Following the tradition of many civil wars, the conflict in Spain was fought with extreme severity: many atrocities were committed by both sides, with civilians as well as soldiers bearing the full impact of summary executions and reprisals. An American novelist, Ernest Hemingway, caught something of the desperate spirit of the struggle in his celebrated book, *For Whom the Bell Tolls,* while the Spanish artist, Pablo Picasso, depicted the brutality of aerial bombardment in his famous allegorical painting, *Guernica,* a reproduction of which is on the cover of this book.

The importance of the Civil War was by no means limited to Spain. It was regarded as a testing-ground for the rival fascist and communist ideologies arising in Europe. For this reason both Italy and Germany sent large forces of "volunteers" and equipment to aid Franco, while Soviet Russia gave material assistance to the Republican government. The Western Powers, Britain and France, made honest but ineffective attempts to prevent the spread of the conflagration by limiting foreign intervention. Their efforts failed principally because Mussolini delayed the withdrawal of his legions from Spain until the issue had been decided in Franco's favour.

The Civil War dragged to an end in the spring of 1939, having probably cost Spain the lives of one million people by death or exile. Her already backward economy was further retarded by widespread devastation. From the international point of view the significance of this bloody struggle was that it witnessed the setting up of yet another Fascist regime, with Franco as *Caudillo*, or Chief of State; and a further break-down of the machinery to preserve collective security. Indeed, the war may justly be considered a prelude to the greater catastrophe of the Second World War.

Sino-Japanese War

While war raged in Spain, there was a further deterioration in the Far Eastern situation. Not content with her earlier success in Manchuria, Japan persisted in a policy of deliberate encroachment in China. This pressure culminated in open warfare between the two nations in the summer of 1937.

China had been split internally by the bitter antagonism of Communists and Nationalists, the latter under the leadership of Chiang Kai-shek, a wily general who was closely identified with conservative interests. The two factions joined forces against the common foe; but throughout the long war that followed Communists and Nationalists watched each other almost as closely as they did the enemy. It was clear that, if China survived the war as an independent nation, further internal convulsions could be expected. Meanwhile, Peking, Shanghai, and Nanking, the capital, fell before the methodical Japanese onslaught, which was accompanied by merciless bombardment of helpless civilians. In spite of the defenders' dogged resistance, the Japanese extended their control over all of the major Chinese seaports and occupied a wide belt of the hinterland in 1938. The League of Nations could do no more than formally condemn Japanese aggression. Although the Chinese received aid from Soviet Russia and British sources in Burma, the increasingly critical trend of affairs in Europe precluded effective intervention by the Western Powers.

Nazi Encroachments in Central Europe

During 1938 momentous events occurred in Central Europe, marking a further stage towards the inevitable show-down between the Fascist-Nazi Axis and the democracies. As a native-born Austrian

Japanese soldiers quartered in a Shansi shrine—an act which, to the Chinese, constituted deliberate sacrilege.

with a not unnatural desire to unite German-speaking people in a Greater Germany, Hitler was determined to bring about an *Anschluss,* or union, of Austria and Germany. It was not so much his object, which was viewed sympathetically by many Austrians, as his method which was at fault. The impatient dictator could not await a favourable situation in which the Austrians might voluntarily join their great neighbour—in his eyes the application of force was the only solution. Summoning the Austrian Chancellor, Schuschnigg, to his mountain retreat at Berchtesgaden, Hitler unleashed a torrent of invective and threats. Then, when Austria showed signs of wishing to retain her independence, the dictator dropped all pretences, ordered his troops into Austria, and forcibly annexed the country. The only Power which might have intervened to save Austria was Italy—but Mussolini remained loyal to the Rome-Berlin Axis, thereby earning Hitler's enduring gratitude.

Hitler was now in the position of a bold and successful gambler, constantly raising and winning higher stakes in the game of international poker. With each success, his reputation for infallibility seemed more firmly established, while his democratic opponents appeared correspondingly weak and ineffective.

The final, brutal demonstration of totalitarian superiority occurred shortly after the *Anschluss.* Within a month of devouring Austria, Hitler was casting greedy eyes on small but strategically important Czechoslovakia, which contained some three million "Sudeten" Germans. The crucial questions for Hitler were whether France would give military support to Czechoslovakia, with whom she had a defensive alliance, if Nazi forces menaced that country, and whether Britain would join in its defence. As Hitler pressed his demands, the answer to this question was painfully apparent at three dramatic conferences held in September, between the British Prime Minister, Neville Chamberlain, and Hitler.

In the first conference, at Berchtesgaden, Hitler openly stated his readiness to risk war in order to annex Sudeten Czechoslovakia. Chamberlain returned to London to confer with the French Premier, Daladier; together they advised the Czechs—whom they had not consulted—to concede to German demands. Otherwise, they threatened, French guarantees of military support would be withdrawn.

Reluctantly, the Czechs agreed to the German ultimatum. But when Chamberlain returned to Germany for his second visit a week

"The Sudetenland is the last territorial claim I have to make in Europe."
—Adolf Hitler, September 26, 1938.

"For the second time in our history, a British Prime Minister has returned from Germany bringing peace with honour. I believe it is peace in our time." — Neville Chamberlain, September 30, 1938 (above photo).

"The German dictator, instead of snatching the victuals from the table, has been content to have them served to him course by course." — Winston Churchill, October 5, 1938.

later, he found that Hitler had raised his requirements. What he wanted now was the virtual dismantling of Czechoslovakia. To support his threat, the German war machine was mobilized and poised on the Czechoslovakian border.

There seemed no alternative. The British fleet mobilized, as did the French army. The Great Powers were on collision course for war. If Czech resolution had not weakened under this terrible pressure, war might have resulted immediately. The Czech army of thirty-five divisions was well equipped and held strong defensive positions. The Czech air force comprised twelve hundred machines. No one can say with certainty what the ultimate result of a conflict at this time would have been—certainly the German military leaders were gravely concerned about the risk Hitler was taking.

Almost at the eleventh hour, Hitler postponed his deadline for invasion, and invited Chamberlain and Daladier to a third conference, to be held at Munich. Mussolini also attended, ostensibly in the role of a mediator, but actually as an Axis collaborator; no Czech representative was invited. This time, Britain and France conceded most of the German demands, with only one or two German concessions being allowed for the democracies to save face. Czechoslovakia, a "far-away country," as Chamberlain described it, was dismembered by Germany; small leftovers were afterwards seized by Hungary and Poland.

Chamberlain returned to London from Munich with the proud declaration that he brought "peace in our time." A great sigh of relief went up from the peace-loving peoples of the western democracies—including those of the New World. Hitler had publicly stated that, with the termination of the dispute over Czechoslovakia, he had "no more territorial claims in Europe." Yet relief was mixed with apprehension. Could his solemn declaration be accepted as sincere—or was it merely the prelude to some irretrievable act which would still plunge the world into the horror of another war?

After Munich, Britain and France realized that their own programmes of rearmament, so long neglected, must be accelerated. Although the democracies had lost a series of diplomatic battles, obviously there must be a limit even to their "appeasement." They had gained time at the expense of Czechoslovakia, but they were beginning to realize that, in the end, they might soon be compelled to stand up to the Nazi-Fascist dictators. Any further aggressive act by Hitler or Mussolini would demonstrate the futility of reason, argument, and conciliation as means of dealing with them. A large-scale war, which the League had sought desperately to avoid, would then become inevitable. By the beginning of 1939 the world once more found itself perched on the edge of a terrifying abyss.

23 Global Warfare

"Hitler knows that he will have to break us in this island or lose the war. If we can stand up to him, all Europe may be free and the life of the world may move forward into broad, sunlit uplands. But if we fail, then the whole world, including the United States, including all that we have known and cared for, will sink into the abyss of a new Dark Age made more sinister, and perhaps more protracted, by the lights of perverted science."—Winston Churchill, from speech delivered in House of Commons, June 18, 1940.

A world war might have been averted in 1914; twenty-five years later the catastrophe was inevitable. Whereas restraint, persuasion, and flexible negotiation might have found a peaceful solution to the crisis that precipitated the First World War, the international situation in early 1939 rapidly deteriorated to a point where further discussion between the conflicting Powers was fruitless.

Inexorably, a chasm widened between the mutually conflicting views of the Berlin-Rome-Tokyo Axis and the western democratic nations. The Manchurian and Ethiopian crises had demonstrated the inability of the League of Nations to curb the ambitions of powerful states. Encouraged by these devastating blows to the prestige of the League, and the resulting collapse of the system of collective security, Hitler had seized the initiative—remilitarizing the Rhineland, contrary to the Treaty of Versailles, and annexing both Austria and Czechoslovakia by a show of force.

In these circumstances it is debatable whether, even if Hitler and Mussolini had abandoned further aggressive policies, peace could have been preserved in 1939. There had been too much provocation on the part of the dictators, and too much weakness on the part of the democracies, for any hope of a lasting settlement between the two ideologies. Nazism and Fascism depended upon dynamic, aggressive policies that could not be reconciled with the more pacific intentions of their war-weary opponents. National attitudes hardened until ordinary citizens in most countries, including many in the strongly isolationist United States, came reluctantly to the conclusion that future issues could be settled only by resort to arms. Patience had ceased to be a virtue.

1. RESORT TO ARMS

The immediate cause of the Second World War was Hitler's determination to expand German control over eastern Europe. Unhappy Poland, long the victim of her larger, rapacious neighbours, was his first target. But Poland was only an intermediate objective, because Hitler's eyes were focused on the rich agricultural lands of the Ukraine in western Russia. It is possible that he dreamed of an empire greater than Napoleon's, extending from the Urals to the Atlantic.

Poland Invaded

In his preliminary, diplomatic offensive against Poland, the German dictator once more blew loudly on the trumpet of racial minorities. The Free City of Danzig and the Polish Corridor contained the last large groups of Germans living outside the Third Reich—it was essential, Hitler maintained, that these people be united with their homeland. It should be noted that, in his treatment of the Polish question, as in his dealings with Austria and Czechoslovakia, Hitler never considered a *voluntary* migration of Germans as a solution. In all three cases the existence of racial minorities was used as an excuse for the annexation of disputed territory.

Two dramatic developments distinguished the new crisis from the earlier pattern of events. On one hand, the western democracies, mainly Britain and France, finally reached a common determination to oppose Hitler, if need be, with force. On the other, Soviet Russia —previously a strong supporter of the forces opposed to Nazism and Fascism—suddenly concluded a non-aggression pact with Germany. The reasons for this reversal of Russian policy are still a subject of debate. However, it seems likely that Stalin had lost faith in the capacity of Britain and France to resist Hitler, and even suspected the Western Allies of favouring a mutually destructive war between Germany and Russia. Stalin may also have concluded that he needed time to prepare for a later struggle with Germany. A secret protocol to the pact made provision for the future partition of Poland between Germany and Russia. The latter was also to have a free hand in the Baltic area (that is Estonia, Latvia, and Finland), while Germany exercised similar "rights" in Lithuania.

At the same time, the Soviet Union reaffirmed its traditional "interest" in Romania's Bessarabia. After German forces invaded Poland on September 1, 1939, Stalin's Red Army quickly occupied the eastern half of the country.

The Nazi invasion of Poland at once committed Britain and France to war, as they had guaranteed the frontiers of their distant ally. Tragically, however, they were quite unable to give effective assistance to Poland, which was subdued by co-ordinated German and Russian attacks before the end of September.

Blitzkrieg

The Second World War, which now began, was very different in its military techniques from the First. With a few notable exceptions, one of whom was Charles de Gaulle, later President of France, the political and military leaders of democratic nations were still thinking of static warfare, of long lines of trenches, of massed infantry, or protracted artillery bombardments, and limited objectives. Aircraft, especially long-range bombers, were regarded suspiciously. On the other hand there was, as events proved, an unnecessary fear of gas warfare. Yet the blueprint of a new military technique known as the *Blitzkrieg* (or "lightning war") was clearly revealed in the opening phases of the German invasion of Poland. Mechanization had revolutionized warfare, no less than agriculture and industry, during the period between the two wars. As in ancient times, infantry still marched long distances on their feet, but they were now supported by mechanical transport, and the foot soldier often rode in trucks or other types of carriers. The horse was virtually replaced by efficient tanks and armoured cars. Moreover, the utility of aircraft, recognized in the First World War, but dependent on technological developments, could now be exploited to the full.

The essence of *Blitzkrieg,* as demonstrated by Hitler's legions, was an all-out, co-ordinated attack, delivered with overwhelming power and lightning speed to disable the enemy's defences and morale before he had time to organize resistance. Using this system, the aggressor first concentrated his attention on his adversary's air defences (the Polish air force was eliminated in a matter of hours), forcing fighters into unequal air battles, bombing airfields,

Stuka divebombers, one of the principal weapons of the Blitzkrieg.

and disrupting communications. Then large *panzer* (tank) formations rolled forward into the invaded territory, by-passing pockets of resistance and securing key points, such as bridges over rivers and canals. A feature of these tactics was close co-operation between tanks and aircraft, especially the demoralizing dive-bombers, which could be quickly called up to deal with difficult targets. Panic-stricken civilians, fleeing the bombers, clogged the roads and highways, blocking the defending troops moving to the Front. The Polish campaign proved conclusively that former military concepts, such as reliance on static defences, cavalry, and slow-moving infantry, were obsolete, but most Allied leaders remained complacent, still unaware of the implications of the new technique.

Allied lethargy in preparing for the next German attack was partly due to the misleading calm that descended over Europe after the conquest of Poland. Unable to intervene effectively in that campaign, Britain and France thereafter contented themselves with sporadic bombing raids against Germany, and a leisurely concentration behind the fixed defences on the north-eastern French frontier known as the Maginot Line. Construction of this elaborate system of heavily fortified positions, complete with underground living quarters, revolving turrets, and anti-tank obstacles, was a good illustration of the extent to which defensive considerations dominated Allied thinking before, and even after, the outbreak of the Second World War. The result was that throughout the first winter of the war the armies of the Western Allies remained in static roles, enjoying a false sense of security from their supposedly impregnable defences.

This "Phony War," or *Sitzkrieg* as it was sometimes called, ended abruptly in the spring of 1940 when, in rapid succession, Hitler invaded and overwhelmed Denmark, Norway, the Low Countries, and France. Seldom in world history has there been a series of large-scale operations so carefully planned and executed. In each instance the technique of the *Blitzkrieg,* already tested in the Polish campaign, was repeated with devastating success.

Beginning before dawn on April 9, German armoured formations and airborne troops entered and occupied a stunned Denmark with virtually no resistance. Norway, better protected by geography, fought bravely but was overrun in less than a month. Then, allowing the Allies no respite, Hitler's forces struck the neutral Netherlands, Belgium, and Luxemburg on May 10. As part of their deliberate policy of demoralizing civilian populations, the Germans unleashed a terrifying air bombardment of Rotterdam, demolishing the entire centre of the city and killing many people. Only four days later the Dutch army was compelled to capitulate. For a short time Belgium was able to hold out with the help of British and French troops—but her strategic position had been undermined by an earlier decision to return to a policy of neutrality after Hitler remilitarized the Rhineland. Belgian neutrality meant that the western flank of the Maginot Line remained undefended, and there was no proper co-ordination of Belgian and French plans in advance of hostilities.

The Fall of France

The shortcomings of Allied preparations during the "Phony War" were rudely exposed when it became apparent that Hitler was directing his main attack in an unanticipated sector—through the difficult country of the Ardennes, which the French had optimistically believed to be impassable. Soon the *panzer* divisions were cutting through the Allied armies, separating the Belgians, British, and remnants of French forces in the north from the main body of the French army in the south. On May 27 the Belgian king was forced to accept defeat, and his soldiers laid down their arms.

A supreme crisis now faced the British and French leaders. The remnants of the British Expeditionary Force and some French troops retreated hastily to the French port of Dunkirk, where it seemed that nothing but a miracle could save them from the onslaught of German tanks and aircraft. Yet, during the first week of June, the British were able to evacuate 366 000 men, one-third of whom were French, to England.

Nevertheless, a high price was paid, for those who returned had lost all their equipment. Guns, transport vehicles, and all the vast stores needed to support the force had necessarily been abandoned to the enemy.

Meanwhile, France was entering her final agony. The French failure to stop the invaders can be accounted for by the incompetence of the High Command, which had never understood the real significance of the *Blitzkrieg*. Civilian morale was adversely affected, leading to charges of treason in high offices. The French also resented the British government's refusal to sacrifice its reserves of fighter aircraft for the defence of France—although, not without reason, Britain was deeply concerned with her own security. On June 22, by which time the enemy occupied more than half of France, resistance ended. In 1940 Hitler could not resist the temptation of receiving the French surrender in the same railroad car in which the German representatives had accepted Allied terms in 1918.

The Axis Powers were now the masters of all western Europe except neutral Sweden and Switzerland, and the Iberian Peninsula, where Franco's dictatorship seemed to offer prospects of future co-operation. Continued British resistance seemed almost hopeless. The French generals, having underestimated their enemy, confidently predicted the quick collapse of their recent ally: "England," they said, "will have her neck wrung like a chicken."

2. BRITAIN ALONE

The British position was indeed desperate—but by no means hopeless. As in the days of Napoleon the insular kingdom could rely on her navy and her geographical location for a large measure of protection—the English Channel was the widest anti-tank ditch in Europe. Moreover, the very rapidity of the German penetration of western Scandinavia and conquest of the Low Countries and France meant that Hitler's staffs were unprepared to launch an immediate assault against the British Isles. They lacked the assault shipping which was essential to such an enterprise. In any case, Hitler assumed that he could deal with the British at his leisure, negotiating from the overpowering position he had achieved on the Continent. His estimate of future British action contained a fatal flaw — like the French generals, he grossly miscalculated the strength of British morale and determination.

Churchill Becomes Prime Minister

In their hour of need the British turned to the incomparable leadership of Winston Churchill. A descendant of the great Duke of Marlborough, Churchill was a man of wide experience as army officer, war correspondent, historian (he wrote detailed, penetrating accounts of both World Wars), painter, and politician. Thoroughly patrician by origins and inclination, he nevertheless had a deep understanding of the fears, hopes, and aspirations of the ordinary Briton. For years before the outbreak of war, he and Anthony Eden, the brilliant young expert on foreign affairs, had stood almost alone in resisting Neville Chamberlain's policy of appeasing the dictators. Hostilities had vindicated their warnings. Shortly after Hitler launched his spring offensive in western Europe, Churchill succeeded Chamberlain as Prime Minister with the grim promise of nothing but "blood, toil, tears and sweat." For the next five years his bulky figure, determined chin, "V for Victory" signal, and inevitable cigar epitomized the courage and determination not only of Britain and the Commonwealth, but of all freedom-loving peoples in the world.

Under such a leader there could be no serious doubts about continued British resistance to the dictators. As the tide of German conquest ran against France, Churchill announced his government's policy in ringing words that will be remembered as long as English is spoken: ". . . We shall fight on the seas and oceans, we shall fight with growing confidence and growing strength in the air, we shall defend our island, whatever the cost may be, we shall fight on the beaches, we shall fight on the landing grounds, we shall fight in the fields and in the streets, we shall fight in the hills; *we shall never surrender!"*

The Battle of Britain

British determination was soon tested. Unprepared for the hazards of a waterborne assault across the Channel, Hitler turned to his air arm for the massive bombardment which, Goering assured him, would crack British morale. Wave after wave of German aircraft attacked British airfields as a preliminary to the now well-tested technique of the *Blitzkrieg*. But Royal Air Force Fighter Command, flying the famous Spitfires and Hurricanes, was more than equal to the task. Throughout the Battle of Britain, which lasted through the summer and well into October of 1940, the R.A.F. took a heavy toll of the invaders, destroying 1 733 German aircraft for a loss of 915 British fighters.

Apart from the excellence of their machines and the high morale of their pilots, the defenders enjoyed two significant advantages over their opponents. First, R.A.F. pilots forced to bail out over the Channel or their own territory were often saved, and could return to battle. Second, the existence of a radar chain covering the eastern approaches to the British Isles made the task of interception easier for the numerically smaller R.A.F.[1] Although the enemy switched his attacks to huge raids on London, Coventry, and other centres, starting huge fires, demolishing ancient landmarks and killing thousands of civilians, he was unable to either gain control over British skies or seriously damage British morale.

Hitler made belated and half-hearted plans for a seaborne invasion of Britain, but the failure of the German air offensive really robbed all preparations of reality. Almost incredibly, Britain had proved too tough a nut to crack—and, after the summer of 1940, Hitler turned his attention to other projects. However, an intensive German naval offensive, with the ubiquitous submarine as the main weapon, continued to cause the British government grave anxiety during most of the remainder of the war.

The consequences of the Battle of Britain were of the highest significance. From this time onward, the British Isles represented a

---

[1]Credit for the military application of radar (using "radio reflection," or the echo of radio beams from an object against which they are projected) belongs to the British scientist, Sir Robert A. Watson-Watt.

"... we would rather see London laid in ruins and ashes than that it should be tamely and abjectly enslaved." — Winston Churchill, July 14, 1940.

springboard for future assaults on Axis-dominated Europe and northern Africa. When Hitler later invaded Russia, he never could be certain that a second, or even third, Front would not open behind him. Also, the moral effect of the successful defence of Britain was very great. Throughout the Commonwealth and the free world, those who believed in democracy and freedom were given renewed hope and courage. For a full year after the fall of France, the Commonwealth stood virtually alone against the totalitarian forces of conquest and aggression. The British people were making good Churchill's reply to the French generals: "Some chicken! Some neck!"

American Sympathy

Fortunately for the Commonwealth and the remaining democracies there were other incalculable forces operating in their favour. One of these was the deep, pro-British sympathy of the American President, Franklin D. Roosevelt. It was perhaps Roosevelt's greatest contribution to Allied victory in the Second World War that he was able to lead public opinion in his country away from the isolationism of earlier years to a realization that the United States must sustain the only other remaining democratic Power in the world.

In the fateful summer of 1940, Roosevelt inaugurated the famous "lend-lease" arrangements whereby Britain exchanged the use of certain overseas bases to the United States for fifty over-age destroyers which were urgently needed to combat the growing menace of German submarines. These and other measures gradually brought the United States closer to actual participation in the war. Another significant step was taken in September, 1941, when Roosevelt and Churchill held a conference on their warships off the coast of Newfoundland and issued a statement of common aims known as the Atlantic Charter. This document, later used as a model for the United Nations Charter, formulated the principles for a future peace.

3. THE INVASION OF RUSSIA

Meanwhile, Hitler had taken a decision that was to prove a major factor in his downfall. The Nazi-Soviet Pact of August, 1939, had never really hidden the continued mutual suspicion of Teuton and Slav, whose quarrels had long disturbed the history of eastern Europe. After his victories in the west, Hitler proposed a division of future spheres of influence whereby Russia might expand south in the direction of the Indian Ocean. Such a move would also have the useful effect of increasing the pressure on British commitments in the Far East.

But one of the Soviets' principal objectives, inherited from the Czars, was to achieve a strong position in the Balkans, especially in relation to the Dardanelles and the exit from the Black Sea to the Mediterranean. Tension beween the two Powers became much more acute after Germany came to the aid of Italy (who had unwisely attacked Greece) and overran the Balkans. For his part, Hitler had never regarded his pact with Stalin as more than a convenient guarantee against a war with Russia while he was dealing with the western European democracies. As we have seen, the *Führer* coveted the rich grainlands of the Ukraine—and beyond these lay the invaluable oil wells of the Caucasus, essential for the maintenance of German industry.

As early as December, 1940, Hitler had already taken the fatal decision to invade Russia; but his timetable was set back some weeks by the Balkan enterprise. Although Stalin was repeatedly warned by both his own and Allied intelligence of German intentions, he gave no apparent heed, continuing to fulfil commercial obligations with Berlin and avoiding any defensive acts that might be considered provocative. Russia's lack of preparation for the attack, which began on June 22, 1941, remains something of a puzzle.

In the first months of operation "Barbarossa," the German code name for the invasion, it appeared that nothing could save the Soviet Union from the fate that had overtaken most of western Europe. Three huge army groups penetrated Russia on a wide front that eventually extended three thousand kilometres. Powerful *panzer* divisions, well-equipped and superbly led, cut through the Soviets' inadequately prepared formations. Perhaps the easy success in these first battles aggravated later German difficulties by encouraging a false sense of confidence in an early conclusion of the campaign. Hitler and his generals failed to consider that the *Blitzkrieg* technique, so successful over relatively short distances in Poland and western Europe, might not be effective in the vast space of Russia.

The essence of "Barbarossa" was an all-out German effort to bring victory before the end of 1941. Like Napoleon in 1812, Hitler counted on the devastating strength of his forces to overwhelm his slower-moving adversary and compel a decision before winter set in. Already heavily engaged in the North Africa campaign to take Egypt and the vital Suez Canal zone, the German dictator had no wish to become involved in a protracted, wasting struggle of uncertain duration in Russia.

What Hitler most feared became a reality mainly because of two factors: the time lost by German participation in the Balkan war, and the skill and determination of the Soviet leaders. Regardless of the importance given to the more powerful Allies' contribution to final victory over Germany, it must be remembered that it was the heroic defence of the Yugoslavs and Greeks which originally dislocated Hitler's timetable. Any account of these momentous campaigns on the Eastern Front must also stress the competence

In the town of Kertsch, the German invaders committed their first deliberate large-scale killing of Russian civilians. When the soldiers left, the survivors returned to search for relatives among the dead.

and determination of the Soviet leaders, ably supported by their courageous countrymen.

Another important factor, too, was the arrogant treatment by the Germans of the Slav peoples whose lands they had won. Many of these, particularly the Ukrainians, had little love for their Communist government, and would willingly have supported the invaders. The Germans, however, behaved with such barbarity that they were soon resisted with a courage and determination born of despair.

How close Hitler came to achieving the object of "Barbarossa" may be judged from the fact that, before the winter set in, his armies encircled the great centre of Leningrad in the north, reached the outskirts of Moscow in the centre, and overran most of southern Russia. It was at this crucial stage of the war that the weeks lost in the Balkans probably proved decisive. The capture of Moscow would not necessarily have meant the end of the war on the Eastern Front, for Stalin was quite prepared to continue the struggle from behind the Urals. But possession of the capital would have represented a great strategic and psychological victory for Germany, with incalculable results elsewhere in the world.

In the west Hitler had been denied complete success by the English Channel and British determination; in the east his hopes were dashed by the severity of the climate and the equally uncompromising resistance of the Russian people. The German armies were untrained and poorly equipped for the winter which now enveloped them. Lacking warm clothing; struggling to cope with unfamiliar problems of mechanized transport in low temperatures, and constantly harassed by a population, both civilian and military, which gave a terrible meaning to "total war," Hitler's proud legions were forced back onto the defensive. On December 8, even the German dictator recognized the inevitable, ordering a temporary suspension of operations. Almost simultaneously, a sudden development in the far-off Pacific precipitated a new crisis.

4. TURN OF THE TIDE

Throughout the early phases of the war, Japan had been taking advantage of the major Powers' preoccupation with Europe to expand and consolidate her position in the Far East. After the fall of France, the militaristic government at Tokyo had German support for what became a virtual Japanese protectorate over former French Indochina. The Soviets, anxious to avoid any extra commitments on their eastern frontiers, also proved accommodating to Japanese ambitions, signing a treaty of neutrality with Japan only two months before the German invasion of Russia. Still Japan's appetite was unsatiated—she dreamed of establishing a "New Order" in the Far East, in which she would occupy a dominating position. There was, however, one major obstacle—the United States, which was rapidly becoming concerned about Japanese policy in the Pacific.

Pearl Harbor

President Roosevelt was in a difficult position. Fully aware of the danger to the United States of a world in which the Axis Powers

"Yesterday, December 7, 1941—a date which will live in infamy—the United States of America was suddenly and deliberately attacked by naval and air forces of the Empire of Japan." — F. D. Roosevelt, War Message to Congress.

might overcome Russia and the British Commonwealth, he could still not intervene in the conflict without the support of American public opinion. Many American citizens, still isolationist in sentiment, refused to believe that their country's vital interests were affected by far-off battles; other Americans did not look favourably upon the prospect of an alliance with Soviet Communism. However, there was a growing realization that drastic action might be needed to restrain Japan from further aggression.

The Japanese resolved all Americans doubts, and plunged the United States into the Second World War on the side of Britain and Russia, when their carrier-based bombers suddenly attacked Pearl Harbor in the early hours of December 7, 1941.

Right up to the time of the attack, Japanese diplomats had been negotiating at Washington, supposedly for a settlement of issues between the two nations. Consequently, the violent reaction of the American people to their heavy naval losses was aggravated by a sense of outrage at the enemy's treachery and deceit. While the operation at Pearl Harbor had been planned and executed with great skill, achieving maximum surprise, it had not been taken without much heart-searching in Tokyo.[1] Indeed, the Emperor had urged caution and restraint on his government; but the latter, dominated by the warlike General Tojo (executed by the Allies as a war criminal after the war), had insisted upon the desperate gamble. Significantly, the Japanese militarists launched their campaign of conquest in the Pacific without co-ordinating their plans with their Axis partners. The sole object of Japanese strategy was to establish control over a huge area of South-East Asia in such strength that the Japanese position would be recognized as impregnable. Therefore, the aggressors also attacked British outposts at Hong Kong and in Malaya, including the great naval base at Singapore, heavily armed to meet a naval assault but hopelessly vulnerable to a landward approach.

Successive victories carried the Japanese southwards and eastwards—American resistance in the Philippines was eliminated in May, 1942—menacing both Australia and India. Within six months of the opening attack, the Emperor's dedicated warriors had won almost eight million square kilometres of territory, establishing effective control over ninety-five per cent of the world's natural rubber, seventy per cent of its tin, and important sources of oil.

In retrospect, it is apparent that the Axis Powers scored their greatest triumphs in their initial campaigns. Both in Europe and Asia the advanced techniques of "lightning war" earned quick results, overwhelming outdated defensive concepts, such as the Maginot Line and the Singapore fortifications, demoralizing civilian populations and governments, and leading to quick surrenders of entire nations. Yet these impressive conquests were more apparent than real: in Europe, Germany was deprived of *total* victory by the unexpected survival of Britain and the failure to achieve a decision in Russia; in Asia, Japan's rapid expansion was mainly influenced by the situation in Europe. Viewed in another way, Hitler's plans were only indirectly affected by Japanese operations, although he counted on these to distract the attention of the United States from Europe; on the other hand, Japanese retention of early

---

[1] Although the Japanese inflicted great damage at Pearl Harbor, they failed to destroy fuel depots and, more significantly, missed four American aircraft carriers then absent from the base.

conquests would largely depend upon the outcome in Europe. It was, therefore, vital for the Allies to establish a priority of targets, as between the Nazi-Fascist combination and the Japanese, in order to win what had become a global war.

The Strategy of the "Grand Alliance"

The efficient instrument which co-ordinated Anglo-American strategy throughout the remainder of the war was known as the Combined Chiefs of Staff. This organization consisted of Prime Minister Churchill and President Roosevelt together with their senior naval, army, and air advisers. They met first in Washington, immediately following the attack at Pearl Harbor, and took decisions of fundamental importance to the course of future operations.

It was agreed that, in spite of the Japanese threat to the United States and the Commonwealth in the Pacific, Germany remained the principal enemy, and that only minimum force would be diverted from the main effort against Hitler's *Fortress Europa* to restrain Japan. The "Grand Alliance" (Churchill's phrase) of the Commonwealth and the United States also took steps to secure close co-operation with other Allies. On New Year's Day, 1942, a pact was signed at Washington by the British and American leaders, and the Soviet and Chinese representatives. They bound their nations to accept the principles of the Atlantic Charter and issued a "United Nations Declaration," pledging their military and economic resources to the struggle against the Axis Powers. Eventually twenty-two other nations, including five members of the British Commonwealth and eight nations whose governments functioned in exile in England, added their signatures to the document. This wartime association was the beginning of the United Nations organization, which was established in the last months of the global struggle.

The entry of the United States into the war and the recovery of Russia transformed the character of the Second World War. Henceforth a mighty coalition of manpower and industry confronted the Axis dictators. However, the Allies required time to mobilize their full resources: starting with relatively few weapons, they had to manufacture thousands of tanks and aircraft, launch entire fleets of warships and merchant vessels, and train, organize, and equip millions of men for combat on the ground, in the air, and on and beneath the sea. For this reason 1942 was a crucial year during which the Axis Powers sought desperately to achieve victory on widespread Fronts, while the Allies hung on grimly, confident that time was on their side. By the end of the year the pendulum was already swinging in favour of the Allies.

South-western Russia, North Africa, and the South Pacific were the key regions in this phase of the great conflict. Thwarted by implacable Russian resistance and winter warfare, Hitler gathered new forces for a renewal of the assault on Russia in the summer of 1942. German efforts concentrated against the southern Front, in the hope of capturing the important industrial centre of Stalingrad on the Volga, and reaching the Caspian Sea. Always the Caucasus beckoned—offering the invader the double advantage of depriving the Russians of their principal source of oil and satisfying the insatiable thirst of the German war machine.

Again the German armies rolled irresistibly eastward. Soon they were deep into the Crimea, capturing the great port of Sevastopol after a bitterly contested siege. By the late summer of 1942 they had crossed the Don River and their patrols stood on the shores of the Caspian. Although the main Caucasian oil fields at Grozny and Baku were still just beyond Hitler's reach, he now held in his grasp about one-third of Russia's population, one-third of its chemical industries, and about half of its coal and electric power.

Stalingrad and El Alamein

Meanwhile, at Stalingrad, one of the decisive battles of the war was being fought for higher stakes than control of the valley of the Volga. A German victory at this point would have cut Soviet Russia in half, ending communications between the central and southern regions. Some historians see the struggle at Stalingrad as the greatest battle in history. Both sides were prepared to commit huge resources of men and machines to the cauldron. In a preliminary bombardment the Germans levelled three-quarters of the city, but the Russians fought desperately for the rubble. Then Stalin gave the order for a huge pincer movement by Marshal Zhukov to encircle the enemy at Stalingrad. As the battle raged on into the autumn it became apparent to everyone other than Hitler that, if he wanted to save the remnants of his forces, he must withdraw them quickly from their exposed position. But Hitler stubbornly

Stalingrad—the transfer-point of initiative.

forbade any retreat, thereby sealing the fate of his doomed legions. Hopelessly surrounded, reduced by hunger, cold, and disease, the remnants held out until the end of January, 1943. Hitler's refusal to face realities cost him a well-equipped army of 300 000 veterans; Stalin claimed that the bodies of 146 700 Germans were burned on the battlefield.

The Russian victory at Stalingrad marked a dramatic change in the strategic situation on the Eastern Front. Thereafter, the German armies never recovered the initiative they had held in the opening phases of the invasion. After Stalingrad the Soviet leaders no longer thought defensively—their goal became the capture of Berlin.

Hitler's defeat in Russia nearly coincided with another serious German check in North Africa. There the British Commonwealth had been engaged in a protracted war of fluctuating fortunes with Italo-German armies under the capable command of General Rommel, the "Desert Fox," a leading German exponent of mechanized combat. In the summer of 1942 Rommel appeared to be on the point of breaking through the British positions at El Alamein, the last defences on the road to Alexandria and control of the vital Suez Canal. In this emergency Churchill despatched an experienced, energetic, and outspoken leader, General Montgomery, to restore the situation. Capable of inspiring great confidence in his troops by his unorthodox approach, jaunty manner, and obvious efficiency, Montgomery completely reorganized the British Eighth Army at El Alamein. Then, late in October, he launched a devastating offensive against Rommel, driving the latter back along the North African coast towards Tunisia. Almost simultaneously with El Alamein, a combined Anglo-American force under the American General, Dwight D. Eisenhower, landed in French North Africa and moved eastward to menace the rear of the German position. Montgomery's army advanced steadily from El Alamein, winning new battles, and Rommel's formations surrendered to the Allies in May, 1943. A feature of the final phase of the campaign was the emergence of "Free French" forces under De Gaulle, who now symbolized his country's hopes for the future.

In the summer of 1943 British, American, and Canadian troops invaded Sicily and rapidly drove the Axis defenders out of the island. The Italians had long since lost any incentive to continue the war. Popular revulsion in the country culminated in the fall of Mussolini and, early in September, a new government concluded

British soldiers in North Africa.

an armistice with the Allies. The Germans fought a series of skilful delaying actions, however, and it was not until June, 1944, that the Allies reached Rome. By then, further operations in this theatre were eclipsed by developments in France.

The Tide Turns in the Pacific

In the Pacific the tide also turned against the Japanese. Although they had overrun Malaya, Indonesia, and Burma, establishing their military authority over all of South-East Asia and the south-western waters of the Pacific, the Japanese eventually reached the limit of their power. They could not undertake the further tasks of attempting invasions of India and Australia. While American naval power in the Pacific had been virtually eliminated at Pearl Harbor, and the Royal Navy had suffered the grievous loss of two great warships, the *Prince of Wales* and *Repulse* in the China Sea, the United States needed only time to recuperate and strike back with new fleets on the sea and in the air. Recovery of Allied initiative in the Pacific was, however, a lengthy and painful process.

In the Coral Sea, off the north-eastern coast of Australia, American naval and air forces launched a heavy attack (May, 1942) on a Japanese fleet, sinking over a hundred thousand tonnes of enemy shipping. This success was closely followed by another victory in a great naval battle near Midway Island, on the western fringe of the Hawaiian Islands. Nevertheless, there was fierce fighting in the Solomon Islands before the Japanese were evicted, releasing the pressure on Allied communications with Australia. During 1943 the Allies adopted a strategy of "island hopping" to regain possession of carefully selected outposts in the Pacific. However, faithful to the original Anglo-American decision, the Allies restricted their efforts against Japan in favour of a decisive offensive against Germany.

5. LIBERATION OF EUROPE

With the Red Army rolling back the German invaders in the direction of their homeland, the stage was set for the final, decisive assault on Hitler's *Fortress Europa*. Since the Allied forces participating in the opening of a new Front in north-west Europe would eventually contain a majority of American soldiers, the Allied leaders agreed that the overall command must be given to an American general. The officer selected for this high post was Eisenhower, who had displayed great skill in achieving Allied co-operation in the Mediterranean.

D-Day

The preparations for "Overlord," the code name for the Allied invasion of north-west Europe, took many months—in certain aspects, years—of research, calculation, and experimentation. Valuable experience had already been gained by an earlier assault at Dieppe on August 19, 1942, in which a largely Canadian force had suffered many casualties in an unsuccessful reconnaissance in force on the mainland.

The selection of the target area and the timing of the attack were not easy matters. While in theory a very long stretch of the western European coast, from the North Sea to the Bay of Biscay, was exposed to invasion, in practice only certain sectors offered any prospect of success after the initial landings. For example, the fuel

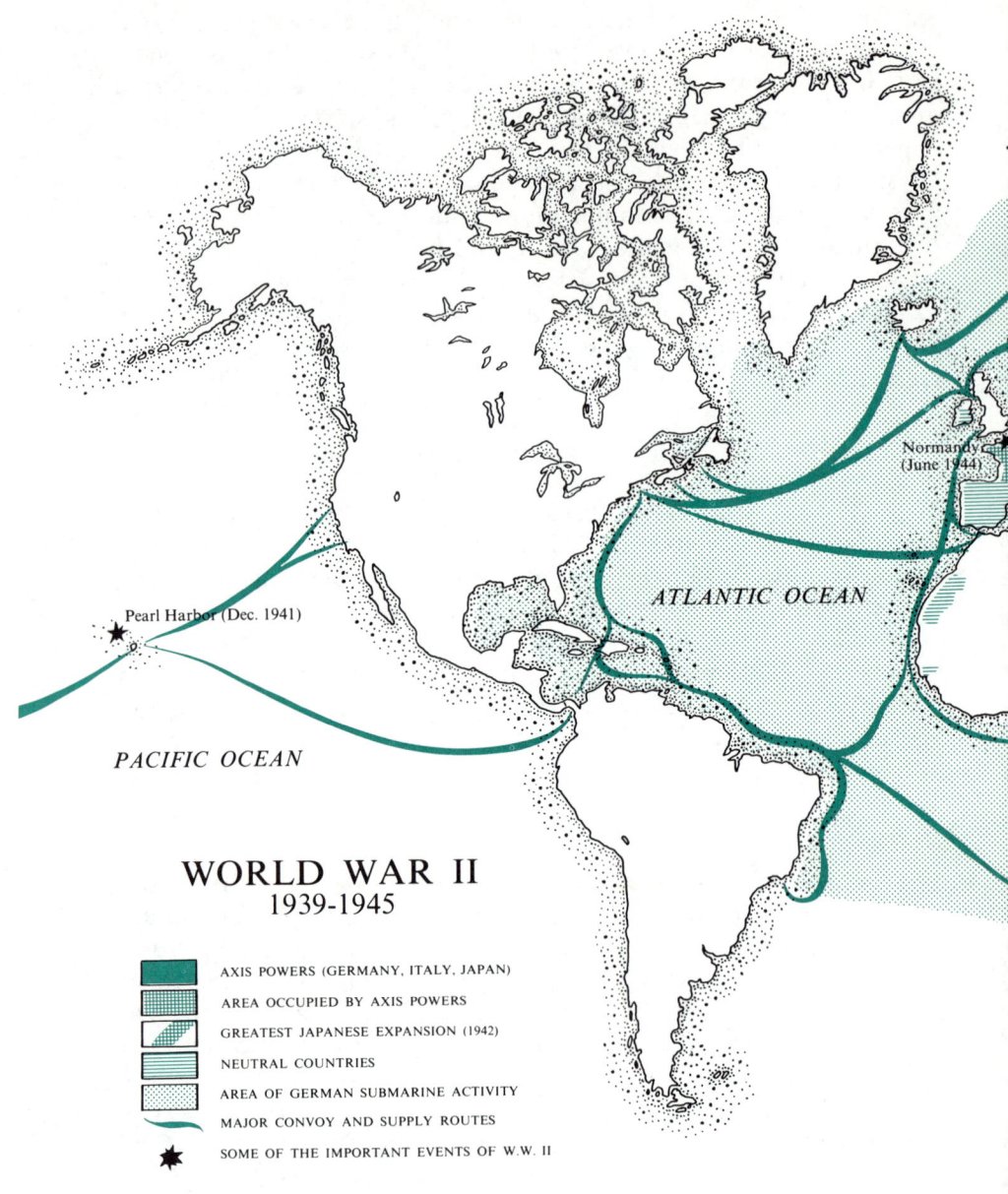

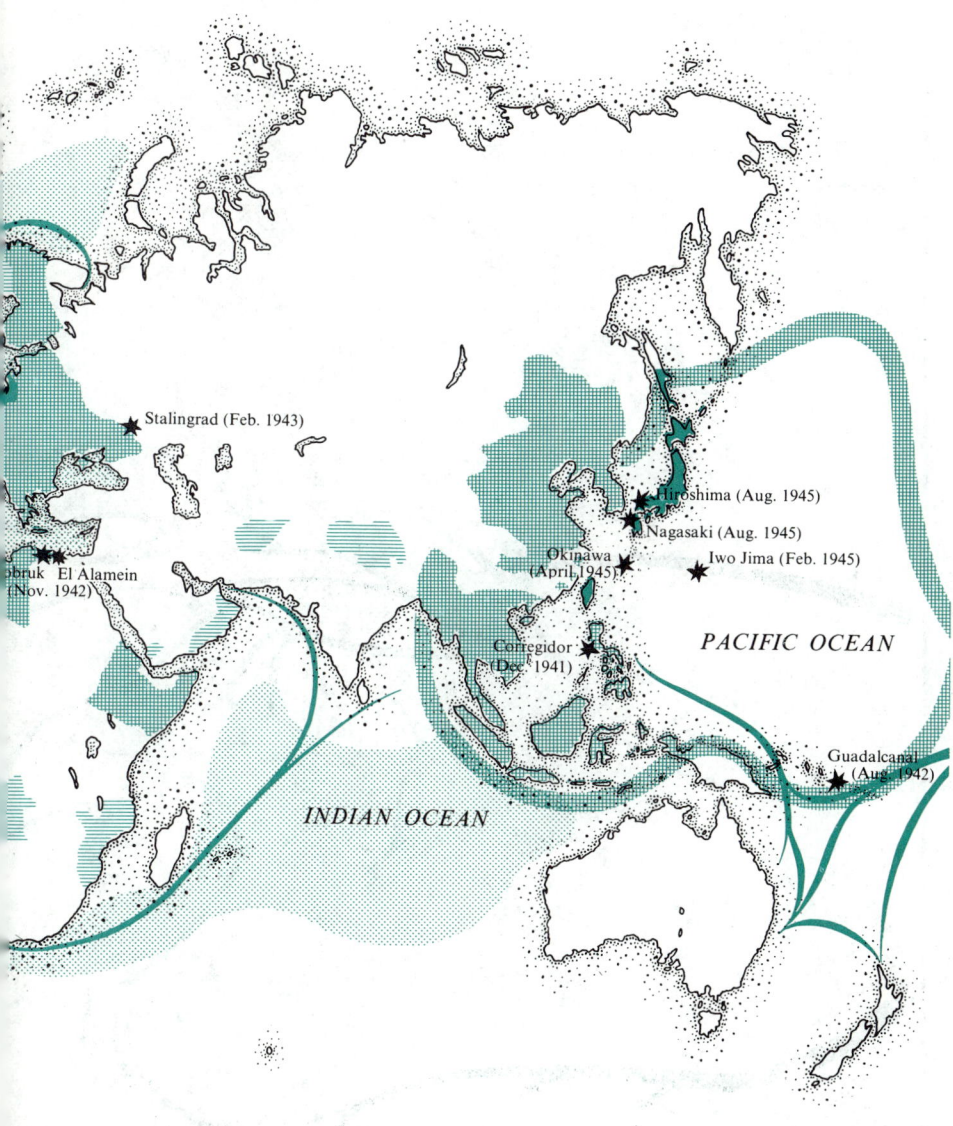

GLOBAL WARFARE 575

range of available fighter aircraft restricted the choice of target areas to the northern latitudes.

After the most careful consideration, Allied planners selected the Caen sector of the Normandy coast as most suitable for the landing of a large invasion force. Here, in the Bay of the Seine, the beaches had a high capacity for unloading men and stores; they were partially sheltered from the prevailing winds; German defences were lighter than elsewhere, and nearby ports (such as Cherbourg) offered the prospect of accelerating the build-up of Allied armies. Similarly, considerations of tide and moonlight, important for airborne troops, narrowed acceptable timing to a period of only a few days in each month.

Gradually, a huge force of Commonwealth and American soldiers and equipment was assembled. More than seven thousand vessels of various types were needed to convey, protect, and maintain the huge invading force and all its equipment.

The naval contribution included specialized landing craft with shallow draught and ramps that facilitated rapid disembarkation. Unfortunately, production of these essential craft could not meet the competing demands of the European and Pacific theatres. Consequently it became necessary to set back the planned date of the assault (D-Day) a full month in order to obtain adequate numbers for operation "Overlord."

The long-awaited invasion of German-occupied France began on June 6, 1944. Although the Germans resisted strenuously in certain sectors, their defence was hampered by divisions of opinion in their High Command over the best means of meeting the Allied onslaught. Important factors in the Allies' favour were their supremacy in the air, which impeded German movements on the ground, and a highly successful deception plan, which kept many German formations in the vicinity of Calais in expectation of an assault across the Strait of Dover.

The Battle of Normandy, lasting until the end of August, cost Hitler a total of four hundred thousand men, of whom about half were taken prisoners of war. Allied losses were roughly half those of their foes. Although the war dragged on in the west for another eight months, German losses in this bitterly contested struggle were

American soldiers eliminating pockets of German resistance.

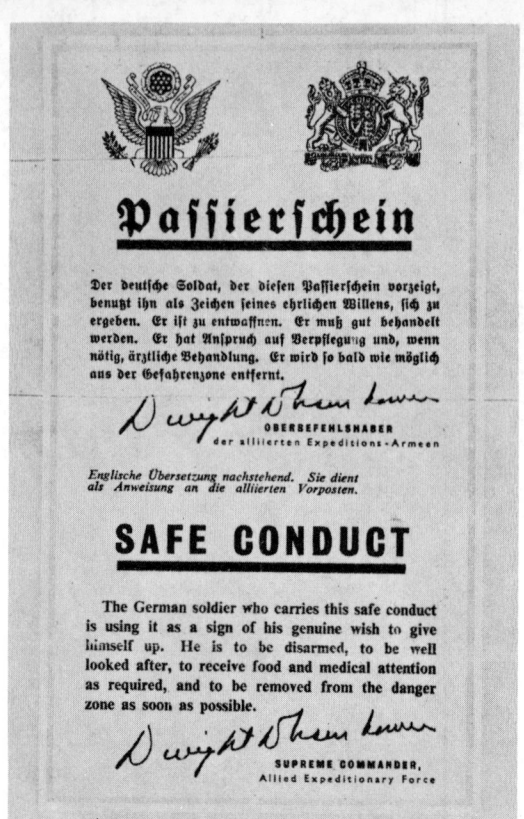

irreplaceable. Except for a brief period in the following December, when Hitler launched a formidable but futile counter-offensive in the Ardennes, his badly-mauled armies never recovered the initiative. Nevertheless, we must view the Western Allies' victories in Normandy in perspective. At the height of the battle, in mid-July, Hitler had committed forty-five divisions to the Western Front. Many of these were his best trained and equipped formations; but, by comparison, there was a total of 168 German and Axis divisions still engaged in the titanic struggle with Russia.

After their great victory in Normandy, the Allied commanders disagreed over future strategy. Montgomery wished to preserve his tight control over all Allied ground forces, but Eisenhower was determined to take over this function in addition to his duties as Supreme Allied Commander. Of even greater significance was the argument between the two over the pattern of future operations. Sensing the possibility of a quick victory on the Western Front, with far-reaching repercussions on the post-war political settlement in Europe, Montgomery urged Eisenhower to concentrate his forces for a single, overwhelming drive into Germany's vital Ruhr region. However, Eisenhower preferred a more cautious "broad front" strategy by which *all* Allied formations advanced more or less simultaneously at roughly the same rate, preserving an unbroken front. We shall never know which of these opinions was correct— but, as the campaign developed, Eisenhower's views (supported by his American superiors) generally prevailed. Historians have recognized that the controversy had great significance in relation to the extent of later Soviet advances in central Europe.

Towards Victory

During the autumn of 1944 the Allies drove the Germans back towards the naturally strong defensive line of the Rhine. Montgomery attempted an ambitious airborne operation to secure crossings over this and other difficult waterways in the Netherlands, but was only partially successful, failing in an epic battle at Arnhem.

Germany's only hope at this stage lay with her revolutionary "V weapons," with which she hoped even yet to force Britain into submission. On June 13, 1944, the first V-1, or "buzz-bomb," was launched against London. Throughout the following months, as many as two hundred of the missiles rained down upon England each day. Fortunately, radar and anti-aircraft guns, as well as fighter aircraft, were sufficiently developed to destroy many of them, thereby reducing the threat to manageable proportions. Constant bombing of the V-1 launch sites and factories also reduced the danger. More fearful, however, was the V-2 rocket, whose tremendous speed, about 5 500 km/h, made all defence impossible. Highest priority was given to destruction of the V-2 factories by bombing. After the Normandy invasion, also, the factories and launching-sites were systematically captured or destroyed. Thus the V-weapons did not prove the decisive blow Hitler had hoped for, but they did provide the first vision of a terrifying new dimension of warfare.

In the spring of 1945 Eisenhower's forces, mainly American and British, but including substantial Canadian, Free French, Polish, and other national contingents, cleared the Rhineland and drove

A remarkable photograph taken only seconds after the explosion of a V-2 in London, March 8, 1945. One hundred and ten persons were killed.

deep into Germany. Again, supported by his government, Eisenhower chose to continue the advance on a wide front, rather than accept British advice to make a quick, concentrated effort to seize Berlin.

So far as is known, no such arguments over strategy divided Russian commanders on the Eastern Front. Thoroughly confident of their own ability to defeat the aggressor on his own soil, they advanced steadily westward in the direction of his capital. In the spring of 1944 the Red Army liberated the Crimea and the Ukraine. Soon Stalin's soldiers were in Poland and on the Danube, and large areas of eastern Europe were under his control.

Nazi Germany was caught in a gigantic trap—the simultaneous large-scale war on two Fronts, which had always been the nightmare of her strategists—and defeat was apparent to all but Hitler. He remained in his Berlin bunker, alternately issuing orders to nonexistent divisions and berating the German people for having failed him. Then on April 30, as Russian tanks and artillery closed in on the *Führer's* lair, he shot himself and his body was burned. The Russians claimed that they were able to identify his remains from dental records. His bombastic Axis partner, Mussolini, had already

Victory.

been executed by his outraged countrymen. On May 7, 1945, Hitler's successors surrendered unconditionally to the western Allies and the Soviet Union.

6. VICTORY IN THE PACIFIC

The war in Europe was over—but there remained the problem of Japan. In 1944 Allied forces (principally American) continued their strategy of "island hopping" in the Pacific, leading to the liberation of the Philippines early in the following year. Simultaneously troops of the British Commonwealth were regaining control of Burma. Although the Japanese conducted a successful

U.S. Marines in Saipan, 1944.

offensive on the Chinese mainland against Chiang Kai-shek's armies, superior American naval and air strength remorselessly tightened the noose around the island Empire. By the spring of 1945 the Americans had captured Iwo Jima and Okinawa, suffering heavy losses but bringing the Allies within range of the final assault on the enemy's homeland.

Victory was near in the Pacific—yet Allied leaders feared the cost of the final thrust. As their forces closed in on Japan, they encountered increasing resistance from fanatical Japanese troops, including *kamikaze* pilots who sacrificed their lives in order to crash their explosive-laden planes against American warships. Many hundreds of thousands of Allied casualties might be anticipated in an amphibious assault on the enemy's inner fortress.

The Atom Bomb

The Allies' answer to this terrible question cost them no casualties, but opened the door to even more frightening questions in the future. We have already seen that, even before the Second World War, scientists realized that a weapon of unprecedented power might soon be available through the release of nuclear energy.[1] Concerted efforts of many western scientists eventually produced an atomic device that was secretly exploded in the United States during the summer of 1945. It was at once apparent that all earlier concepts of warfare were rendered obsolete by the new development which, in its significance, could be compared only with the invention of gunpowder.

On August 6 the first atomic bomb was dropped on Hiroshima, a large city in southern Japan, killing perhaps seventy thousand people. (We may note that, by comparison, the entire German aerial bombardment of Britain had killed only sixty thousand civilians over a period of *five years*.) Three days later a similar bomb completely destroyed an area of some fifteen square kilometres at Nagasaki. Bowing to the inevitable, the Japanese government surrendered unconditionally on August 14, 1945, only eight days after the first atomic attack.

After six long years, peace once more reigned in a broken and apprehensive world. The first, spontaneous demonstrations of joy and relief were not followed by any lingering jubilation. Too many lives had been sacrificed, too much misery and devastation endured, too much uncertainty clouded the future. In both Europe and Asia the Allies had barely scraped through the early, critical years— when both the British Commonwealth and Russia looked defeat squarely in the face. In the end, it was the almost limitless resources

[1] See above, pp. 461-462.

Street scene in Hiroshima two hours after the explosion. This point was three kilometres from "ground zero." The photographer who took the picture subsequently died of injuries. The film was partly fogged by radiation. INSET: The U-235 bomb dropped on Hiroshima.

of the United States and the reserves of Russian manpower that carried the Allies through long and arduous campaigns to victories over hard, ruthless foes. Yet this was no unmixed triumph. As often before in history, a victorious coalition of nations found the problems of peace more complicated, more intractable, than those of war.

At the end of the greatest war in the records of mankind the world faced three interlocking problems of vital significance. First and foremost, could past hatreds, distrust, and suspicion be forgotten; in particular, could the widely differing ideologies of Soviet communism and western democracy co-operate harmoniously? Secondly, could a new international organization be established to succeed the discredited League of Nations, profiting by its failures? Finally, what effect would the first use of atomic weapons have on global politics in the future?

Like the character in the ancient tale who released the evil genie from the bottle, the Western Powers realized that the mushroom-shaped clouds of destruction over Japan carried a threat to all mankind.

UNIT FIVE | # THE WORLD IN TRANSITION

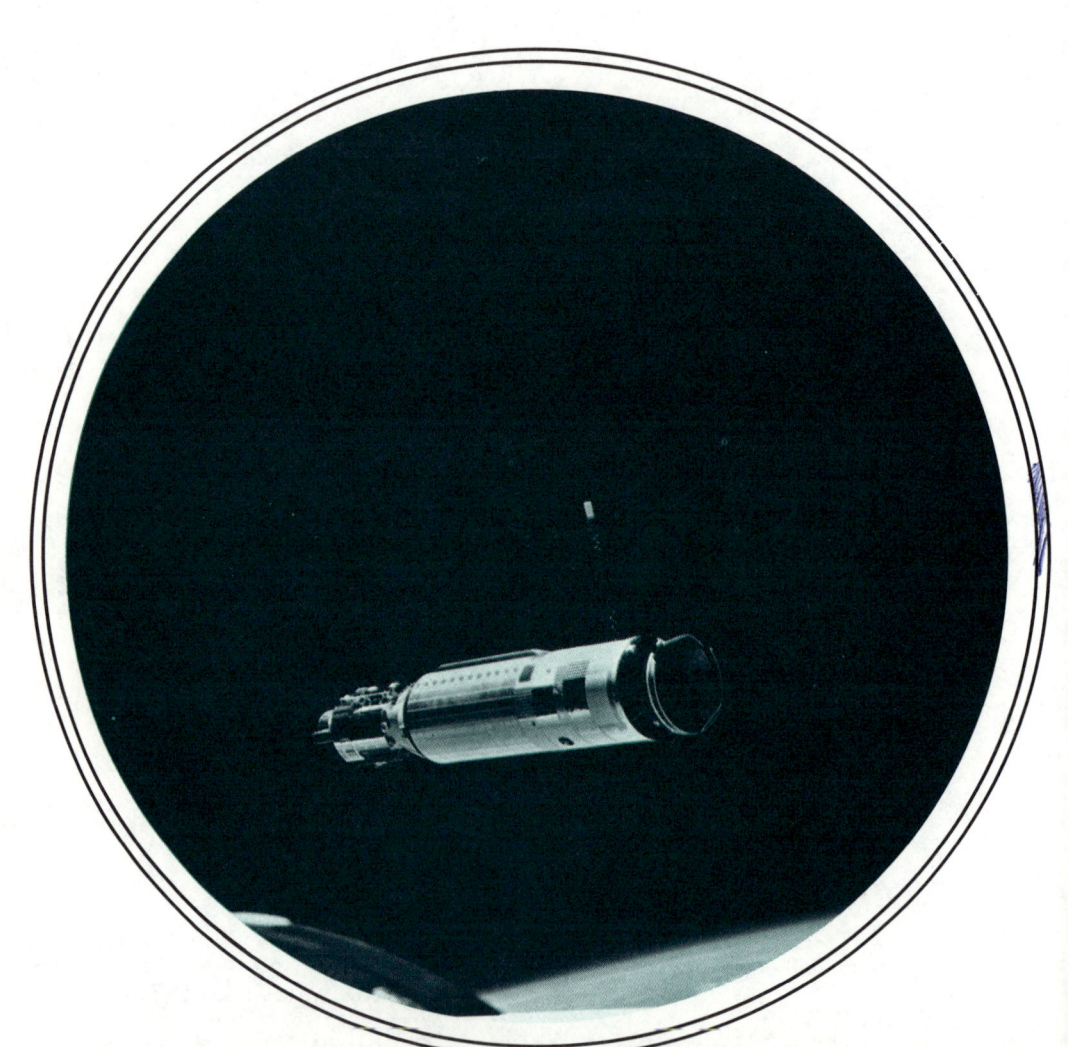

24 Cold War and Coexistence

Either we move forward, boldly, confidently and imaginatively, to the creation of a new relationship with that country [U.S.S.R.] in the military field, or we deliver up ourselves and the rest of the civilized world to the appalling dangers of a nuclear weapons race totally out of control—a development devoid of any visible hopeful end, devoid of any imaginable end at all other than a wholly disastrous and apocalyptic one.—George F. Kennan

The Second World War represented another catastrophic setback for all mankind. It will never be possible to reach an accurate figure for the total number of casualties. In Europe alone, there were probably seventeen million killed and over thirty million wounded just in the armed services. By reason of aerial bombardments and the ghastly toll taken by Nazi concentration camps, civilian populations suffered unprecedented losses. Moreover, the use of the atomic bomb to end the Japanese war carried its own grim commentary on the threat of future warfare: more Japanese civilians were killed at Hiroshima than were killed in Britain by aerial bombing throughout the entire war. The devastation of industries, the difficulties of re-establishing normal patterns of peacetime existence, and the uncertainties of the future all combined with wartime casualties to darken the sombre glow of victory in the summer of 1945.

The political consequences of the war were similarly far-reaching. Many of the nations that emerged from occupation by foreign armies were affected by radical changes in their internal balance of power. Parties of the Right were largely discredited by the *débâcle* of the Fascist-Nazi collapse, whereas left-wing parties, which generally had acquitted themselves very well as leaders of the opposition to both the Nazis and the Fascists, gained in prestige and strength. Similarly, right-wing ideologies were more or less purged from the western democracies. In the East, the end of the war saw not only the liberation of the countries that had been overrun by the Japanese, but also the drastic weakening of the pre-war pattern of colonialism. Internationally, the balance of power had been totally upset. The most important change was that Europe was no longer the political centre of the world. Russia, with her enormous army

> ## THE COST OF MODERN WAR
>
> THE TOTAL COST OF WORLD WAR II, ESTIMATED AT $1 384 900 000 000, WOULD HAVE BEEN SUFFICIENT TO PAY FOR ALL OF THE FOLLOWING:
>
> A $60 000 house for every family in the United States, Belgium, and Portugal.
>
> A $10 000 000 library for every city of 200 000 inhabitants and over in the United States, Great Britain, and the U.S.S.R.
>
> A $50 000 000 university for each of these cities.
>
> A $6 000 automobile for half the families in the United States.
>
> The salaries of 15 000 teachers and an equal number of nurses at $20 000 a year for 100 years.
>
> A free college or vocational education (at an estimated cost of $9 000) for every school graduate in the United States from 17 to 21 years of age.

poised throughout eastern Europe, and the United States, with its incomparable superiority in industrial production combined with a transitory monopoly of atomic weapons, dominated international politics completely.

1. THE WORLD AFTER 1945

Britain

In Britain the most striking political result of the long conflict was the rejection of Churchill's leadership in the general elections of 1945. This surprising event was not so much due to loss of confidence in the great wartime leader (he returned to power, for the last time, in 1951) as to a national determination to "wipe the slate clean," and give the Labour Party, under Clement R. Attlee, an opportunity to govern.

The new administration lost no time in implementing a programme of nationalization (or socialism), including removal of railways and coal mines from private ownership, and erection of an elaborate and expensive system of social services. Much attention was also devoted to the improvement of educational facilities and housing projects. Unfortunately, the high cost of these reforms imposed an ever-increasing burden on taxpayers, and this, together with the inevitable dislocation of post-war trade, meant that Britain was soon in the grip of a severe financial crisis. Initially, the Marshall Plan helped to bolster the British economy, but by 1949 the situation was so serious it was necessary to devalue the pound sterling from $4.03 to $2.80. Subsequently, Britain sought an answer to her economic problems by entry into the European Common Market, her efforts being temporarily frustrated by the delaying tactics of President de Gaulle's government in France.

France

France had emerged from the Second World War with mixed feelings of joy and bitterness—profound relief at escape from Nazi domination, but internal dissension and recrimination over the causes of her defeat in 1940. To bewildered foreign observers, the French government often seemed to be a rather deceptive game of musical chairs, in which, however, frequent changes of ministries did not necessarily imply fundamental changes in policy. The main contenders for power in the immediate post-war period were the Communists, the Socialists, and the MRP (*Mouvement Républicain Populaire*), the latter being a Catholic party identified with the Resistance fighters of the war. General Charles de Gaulle, the provisional President of France, insisted that the powers of the chief executive should be strengthened so that he could cope with his country's problems. However, when his views were rejected by the new National Assembly which drew up the Constitution of the Fourth Republic, De Gaulle retired into a lengthy, self-imposed political exile.

France, like Britain, faced crushing problems of internal reorganization and rehabilitation. In addition, serious trouble broke out in Indo-China and, most dangerously, in Algeria, where the *colons* (Algerians of European origin) were determined to resist movements towards independence.[1] In the national emergency, France turned again to De Gaulle—the only man with sufficient prestige to convince his country that she must allow Algeria to go its own

[1] See p. 700.

Leaders in the post-war world. TOP LEFT: Clement Attlee, Labour Party Prime Minister of Britain, 1945-51. TOP RIGHT: Harry S Truman, the Democrat President of the United States. BELOW LEFT: General Charles de Gaulle, both a symbol and an agent of France's post-war recovery. BELOW CENTRE: Konrad Adenauer, the shrewd Chancellor of West Germany. BELOW RIGHT: Nikita Khrushchev, whose cunning and mercurial personality brought him to the leadership of the Soviet Union following Stalin's death.

way. The soldier-statesman returned to power in 1958, as President of the reconstituted Fifth Republic, with extensive powers to aid the recovery of France.

Germany

Across the Rhine, the Third Reich had disintegrated in the spring of 1945. Out of the carnage of war emerged two Germanies—the Federal German Republic, comprising the American, British, and French zones of occupation and, in the east, the German Democratic Republic, controlled by the Soviet Union. The development of the "Cold War" between East and West was nowhere more clearly illustrated than in the difficult relations between these artificially-created states. Berlin presented a particularly difficult problem because it was entirely surrounded by the Soviet occupation zone. The solution was to divide the former capital into western and eastern sections, under western democratic and Russian control, respectively, with separate municipal governments.

With painful recollections of the failure of the earlier Weimar Republic, the new Federal German Republic set to work, under the capable leadership of Konrad Adenauer, to reconstruct its shattered economy. In their capital of Bonn, Adenauer and his associates established a thoroughly democratic form of government with guarantees of the fundamental liberties of the individual. Largely due to its own efforts and American financial assistance, West Germany achieved a rapid recovery and was soon on its way to re-establishing German influence in the political and economic life of western Europe. A particularly encouraging development was the important role played by the Federal Republic in the evolution of the European Common Market.

East Germany, under the iron rule of the Communists, followed a very different path. Its political and economic structures were closely integrated with those of the U.S.S.R. and the other Soviet-dominated states in eastern Europe. While considerable progress was made in the rehabilitation of the German Democratic Republic, standards of living were appreciably lower than those in West Germany.

In the background of the post-war German problem remains the question of the future reunification of the two Germanies. Could a continuous process of indoctrination by opposing ideologies keep

Rejected! Great Britain (Prime Minister Harold MacMillan) refused entry to the Common Market. However, Britain eventually entered the E.E.C. in 1973.

the western democratic and eastern communist states apart? A permanent schism seems unlikely. Upon succeeding Adenauer as Chancellor in 1963, Dr. Ludwig Erhard said: "We are told that the division of our country is a 'reality' that has to be accepted: of course it is a reality, but it is an unbearable one . . . and we shall have to do all possible to remove it."

The European Common Market

No aspect of post-war developments in Western Europe has been more significant than the movement towards closer economic integration. Great advantages were anticipated for plans of economic co-operation which would restore confidence in war-torn countries, speed the rehabilitation of western Europe as a whole, and reduce dependence on American aid. Moreover, there was the inspiring prospect of a *political* federation which might be built upon the co-ordinated efforts of industries operating on an international, rather than national, basis.

The first step in the new direction was taken by Belgium, the Netherlands, and Luxemburg in January 1948, when they announced the formation of Benelux. This was a customs union which established a common tariff against other nations and eliminated many of the customs barriers separating the three participants. One important result of the Benelux agreements was removal of all restrictions on the free movement of workers between the member states.

The success of the Benelux experiment soon led to a more imaginative and expanded conception. A major factor in the rehabilitation of western Europe was the marked improvement in relations between France and Germany. In the spring of 1949 a brilliant French planner, Jean Monnet, put forward proposals for a vast industrial complex to integrate the resources of France, Germany, and neighbouring states. This idea found formal expression in the Schuman Plan, named after Robert Schuman, Foreign Minister in eight consecutive French cabinets from 1948 to 1953. He pointed out that "by pooling basic production and by instituting a new higher authority, whose decisions will bind France, Germany and other member countries, these proposals will lay the first concrete foundation of a European federation which is indispensable to the preservation of peace." It may be noted that French arguments for the Plan were strongly influenced by realization that it offered an effective means of controlling the reconstruction of German industry.

On behalf of the German Federal Republic, Chancellor Adenauer welcomed these proposals for closer co-operation with the Republic's western neighbours. Adenauer was keenly aware of the need to improve relations with France—even though the prospect of closer ties with the West might mean postponement of the reunification of the two Germanies.

Out of this background emerged the European Coal and Steel Community (E.C.S.C.), inaugurated by a draft treaty signed at Paris in April, 1951. The signatories were France, West Germany, Italy, Belgium, the Netherlands, and Luxemburg. By the terms of this agreement, the E.C.S.C. passed through a five-year transitional stage, at the end of which all tariff and quota restrictions on coal and steel were eliminated within its jurisdiction. Elaborate machinery was set up to co-ordinate the economic activities of the "Six": a High

Authority with headquarters in Luxemburg, a Common Assembly of delegates from the participating parliaments, a Consultative Committee of producers, workers and consumers, a Council of Ministers, and a special Court of Justice. Thus, the E.C.S.C. has been described as "Europe's first genuinely supranational authority."

Efforts directed towards closer economic co-operation did not end with the creation of the E.C.S.C. In March, 1957 the Six signed the Treaty of Rome, which established the European Economic Community (E.E.C.) or "Common Market." This ambitious enterprise was intended to bring some one hundred and seventy-five million people within a completely free-trade area over a period of fifteen years. Ultimately, within this huge bloc, there would be a standardized system of social security and an equalized scale of wages. Provision was made for a common external tariff, guaranteed minimum prices for agriculture, and financial assistance for under-developed and colonial areas.

At the same time the Six set up the E.E.C. they also established the European Atomic Energy Community, or Euratom, to promote the growth of nuclear industry. In this field close co-operation was required with the United States and Canada,[1] since these countries controlled the uranium and fissionable materials needed by the Six. These developments held great significance for the future, because it was calculated that nuclear energy would compete with oil and coal by the mid-1970's. Consequently, members of the Common Market could anticipate decreased dependence on imports of coal and oil shipments from the Middle East.

One particular difficulty, with political overtones, concerned the relationship of Britain to the Common Market. Originally, British opinion was divided over the advisability of seeking to enter the E.E.C. Concern for traditional patterns of Commonwealth trade, and the effects of participation on their agriculture, led some British critics to oppose their country's entry into the Common Market. This opposition gradually receded as the British government came to recognize that the nation's economic future necessitated closer identification with Europe.

At this point a major stumbling block appeared in the person of President de Gaulle who was deeply suspicious of the "Anglo-Saxon" influence represented by the close ties between Britain and

[1]Canada was the only country exporting uranium in appreciable quantity.

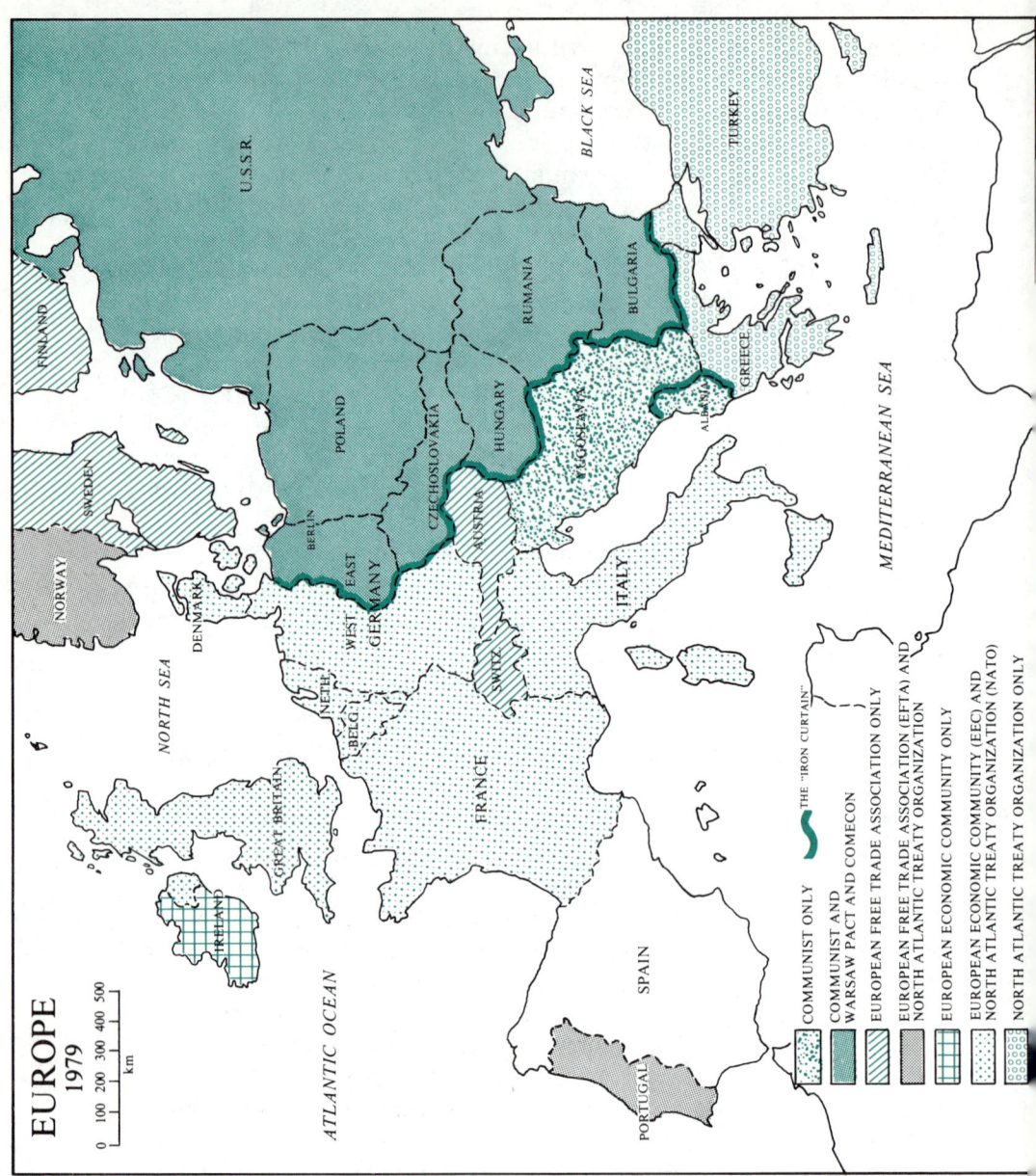

France remains in the NATO Alliance, but does not participate in its integrated military forces.

the United States. More specifically, the French leader feared that British participation in the Common Market would threaten his nation's dominant role in that organization. Therefore, in spite of the fact that other members of the E.E.C. warmly welcomed the prospect of including Britain, De Gaulle brusquely vetoed the British application. "England is . . . insular, maritime," he declared, "linked through its trade, markets, and food supply to very diverse and often very different countries. . . . The nature, structure, and economic context of England differ profoundly from those of states on the Continent." Although much criticized, both inside and outside the E.E.C. for his action, the French President refused to relent, and the whole question of the British entry into the "Common Market" was virtually shelved for the time being. Eventually, hard economic factors prevailed over these political manoeuvres. In 1972 Britain signed a treaty by which she was formally admitted to the E.E.C. in the following year. (Ireland and Denmark also joined the Common Market at this time.) Then, internal British politics led to the election of a government pledged to renegotiate the treaty. The issue was finally settled in 1974 when, by a large majority in a referendum, the British people endorsed their country's entry into the E.E.C.

The U.S.S.R.

Apart from Nazi Germany, no country had suffered worse devastation during the war than the Soviet Union. In all probability the total of military and civilian dead due to enemy action approached fifteen million; great regions of European Russia had been subjected to "scorched earth" tactics during the early Russian retreats, and had suffered systematic destruction at the hands of Nazi invaders. Perhaps twenty-five million people were homeless in 1945—many were driven to caves for shelter. A British correspondent in Moscow reported: "The country stripped itself to the very bone and everything they gave was consumed in the furnaces of war. When victory came the Soviet Union was virtually without any of the essential means by which to set about repairing the damage it had sustained."

Yet, like her German adversary, the U.S.S.R. displayed amazing recuperative powers after 1945. Five Year Plans, continuing the pre-war pattern of nationalized industry and agriculture, renewed and surpassed earlier levels of achievement. Beyond the immediate demands of rehabilitation, the supreme Soviet objective was attainment of nuclear power to match the western advantage. By 1949 Soviet scientists were able to make their first nuclear test and, four years later, they had successfully developed thermonuclear weapons.

Russia paid a heavy price for these advances. By the end of the Second World War, Stalin, the dictator of Russia, was the most powerful man on earth. His authority, originally established by a tyranny comparable to that of Hitler, had been reinforced by the great victories of the Red Army. "Stalinism" became a cult, attributing all progress to his wisdom and all failures to the errors of his opponents. "We had long forgotten," wrote Ilya Ehrenburg, "that Stalin was a mortal. He had changed into an omnipotent and mysterious deity." The political atmosphere in the U.S.S.R. became stifling. Fear and suspicion penetrated all ranks of Soviet society until Stalin's death on March 5, 1953.

After an uneasy interval, while the Kremlin witnessed a grim, behind-the-scenes struggle for power, a new leader emerged to take effective control of the Communist Empire. This was Nikita S. Khrushchev, whose record illustrates the tortuous course of politics under the hammer and sickle.

Although he obviously owed his early political success to his support of Stalin, Khrushchev did not hesitate to denounce the dictator's tyranny after his death. In a famous speech at the Twentieth Congress of the Communist Party of the U.S.S.R. (1956), Khrushchev gave a detailed review of the crimes of the Stalinist regime. Thus he cleverly identified himself with the silent convictions of the great Russian masses, who desired to see an end to secret trials, prison camps, executions, and other sinister aspects of the recent dictatorship. Publicity organs which for years had been devoting all their efforts to the virtual deification of Stalin now worked assiduously in reverse, endeavouring to erase his memory from his former subjects. Portraits of Stalin disappeared from public buildings; even Stalin's body was removed from its place of honour beside Lenin in Red Square. More significantly for the Russian people, many of the repressive aspects of the government were eased. Meanwhile, Khrushchev disposed of his rivals for the succession, and in 1957 he assumed supreme power in the Soviet Union. He was to hold this position until October, 1964, when he was suddenly deposed in another palace revolution headed by Alexei Kosygin and Leonid Brezhnev.

The deposition of Khrushchev meant that the new Soviet leaders relaxed, to some degree, the policy of "de-Stalinization." In 1970, as evidence of the new official attitude, a monument and bust of Stalin were placed near his grave in the Kremlin wall. Many of Khrushchev's over-optimistic plans, including his pledge to surpass American per capita production and attain "the final stage of a Communist society by 1980," were quietly discarded. At the same time, there was little relaxation of the repressive features of Soviet society. The powers of the secret police, restricted during the period of "de-Stalinization," were revived and harsh censorship was imposed on literary and cultural activities. The Party Presidium was renamed the Politburo and Brezhnev assumed the title of General Secretary, previously held only by Stalin.

In the 1970's the U.S.S.R. made notable advances in economic expansion (including the export of cars and tractors to North America) and in the exploration of outer space. However, the vast Soviet expenditure on defence (estimated at twelve per cent of the gross national product) has operated as a brake on economic development in a country where productivity and per capita income are still low by western standards.

Japan

Military defeat had particularly severe repercussions on Japan. Not only was an aggressive, authoritarian regime overthrown, as in Nazi Germany and Fascist Italy, but the whole basis of the Shinto state religion of Japan was undermined. A proud empire which had never known invasion in modern times was suddenly subjected to a western military occupation. As a result, Japan was redirected on a new course, diverging widely from old imperial goals.

Nevertheless, the American occupation did not represent a complete break with the past. For a brief period during the 1920's, liberal democratic trends had permeated Japanese life—before the nationalistic, imperialistic reaction set in during the following decade. Consequently, there was a pre-war foundation for such reforms as universal suffrage, the emancipation of women, and relaxed control of the press. Moreover, the Allied Occupation authorities (under General Douglas MacArthur) displayed considerable skill in their handling of Japanese problems. In particular, wherever possible the Occupation employed native Japanese, rather than western personnel, to carry out its programme. For example, at the highest level, the Emperor was left on the throne, although he became largely a figurehead, divested of most of his former authority. (On New Year's Day, 1946, the Emperor renounced all former pretensions of imperial divinity.) The result of this wise policy was the transformation of Japan into a thoroughly modern democratic state—without, however, undue displacement of traditional institutions. In large measure, the Occupation was assisted by the co-operative attitude of the Japanese, who unanimously rejected the authoritarian leadership which had resulted in their disastrous defeat.

As in Germany, the post-war rebuilding of Japan posed formidable problems. Important cities had been devastated by aerial bombardment (including the atomic attacks at Hiroshima and Nagasaki). Foreign markets were gone, as was the merchant marine on which Japanese trade depended. Large numbers of people were homeless and dispirited.

In form, the Occupation was international, but in fact it was almost exclusively American in direction and policy. During the initial period of reform, lasting from the surrender until 1948, the Occupation revised and democratized the Japanese constitution, and sought to eradicate lingering elements of the former regime. The armed services were eliminated, political prisoners were released, and laws were introduced to protect individuals from arbitrary interference. A system of party government, such as had existed in the 1920's, was revived, and the principle of cabinet responsibility to the Diet (Parliament) was firmly established.

By the latter part of 1948, much of the reform phase of the Occupation had been completed, and the Occupation then passed into a period of retrenchment. This change in tempo was strongly influenced by external factors. As the Cold War widened the gap between East and West, Japan became increasingly important as a base of American influence in the Far East. In this new phase of post-war evolution greater emphasis was given to economic recovery. Any earlier thoughts of removing Japanese industrial plants, as reparations for wartime aggression, were abandoned. Renewed efforts were directed towards a revival of Japan's export trade—the keystone of her eventual recovery.

Meanwhile, American preoccupation with other global responsibilities, and the gradual recovery of Japanese confidence, meant that the time was fast approaching when the Occupation would end and Japanese autonomy could be restored. This transition was accelerated by the outbreak of the Korean War in 1950,[1] which magnified the importance of Japanese co-operation. Negotiations for the conclusion of a Peace Treaty with Japan were pressed forward, and on September 8, 1951, formal signatures were added to the final text at San Francisco. Thus, little more than six years after atomic bombs fell on Hiroshima and Nagasaki, Japan regained control of her own affairs, while still remaining clearly within the American orbit of influence. In the words of her then Prime Minister, Shigeru Yoshida, "the peace conference gave to Japan the foundation for making a fresh start on the international scene."

The post-war recovery of Japan, like that of West Germany, has been remarkable. Although almost totally dependent on imports of fuel, feed and food (other than rice), as well as virtually all industrial raw materials, she has achieved a unique position in international trade. Japanese exports of automobiles, transistors and textiles have been a major factor in making the *yen* one of the strongest currencies on international exchanges. At the same time, Japan has had to cope with alarming internal problems of transportation and pollution. Yet, in the words of a western observer: "The Japanese cult of industry, their strong sense of community, their patience and adaptability to crowded conditions have given them a marvelous cushion against modern technological and cultural shock."

The U.S.A.

If Europe and East Asia emerged shattered, disillusioned, and uncertain from the second great conflict of the 20th century, the United States, by contrast, had achieved an unprecedented position of material power and political leadership. Although the United States had played a decisive role in the final phase of the First World War, she had thereafter retreated into an isolationism which persisted well into the early years of the struggle with the Axis Powers. Not until Japanese bombs fell on Pearl Harbor was American opinion prepared to accept the challenge of outright participation in the war.

[1] See pp. 625-626.

However, in 1945—unlike 1919—the United States realized the extent of her global responsibilities and the impossibility of returning to isolationist policies. Therefore, she took steps—participating in the organization of the United Nations, extending material assistance to foreign countries, and fashioning the NATO Alliance—to assume a share of world commitments commensurate with her new stature. Some years were to pass before it became painfully evident, in Vietnam, that a high price might be exacted for the new American sense of mission.[1]

Internally, the post-war period brought new problems. Harry S Truman, the pugnacious Vice-President who had succeeded Roosevelt when the latter died (April 12, 1945), soon dispelled any impression that he was a "stop-gap" figure by assuming firm direction of affairs in the face of a hostile Republican Congress. In the elections of 1948 he scored a resounding victory over his opponents, appealing to those who feared that Republican attacks on the New Deal programme could bring a renewal of the Great Depression. In his inaugural speech in January, 1949, Truman announced his determination to continue and extend his predecessor's reforms as part of a "Fair Deal." Henceforth, increased emphasis would be given to civil rights legislation, a national health programme, education, and financial support for low-income housing.

Soon, however, American opinion was distracted by internal divisions resulting from the Cold War between East and West. Between 1949 and 1954 the nation was gripped by what has been described as the "Great Fear." A belief spread, mainly fostered by a Republican senator, Joseph McCarthy, that Communists had infiltrated sensitive departments of the government at Washington. While there was little doubt that the Soviets had active sympathizers in influential circles (several Americans were tried and convicted of espionage, some being executed), McCarthy was never able to substantiate his wholesale indictment of government agencies and, in particular, the State Department. Eventually, his smear tactics brought discredit on himself in the eyes of the public and condemnation from his colleagues in the Senate. The improvement of relations between the United States and Russia, resulting from the decline of Stalinism and the proposal for "peaceful coexistence," ended a period in which hysteria and demagoguery threatened to

[1] See below, pp. 688-697.

upset traditional guarantees of individual freedom in America.

The post-war success of African countries in gaining independence from European colonizers stimulated a vigorous movement by American blacks to improve their status. They became increasingly impatient with obstacles to their legitimate aspirations, this resentment culminating in the "Black Power" movement of the 1950's and 60's aimed at increased participation in the political process. This agitation resulted in the passage of such federal legislation as the Civil Rights Act of 1964 and the Voting Rights Act of 1965 with the object of increasing black participation in all aspects of government. The social and cultural aspects of the liberation movement were represented by the slogan "Black Is Beautiful," by desegregation of white and black children in schools and by improved opportunities for blacks in business and the professions. While discrimination on the basis of colour was not easily eradicated, the United States was moving towards a society in which black men and women could confidently anticipate a degree of political, social and economic equality with whites hitherto unknown.

2. THE COLD WAR

Allied victory in the Second World War rescued the world from unprecedented tyranny, and with the end of hostilities men everywhere hopefully anticipated a new age of prosperity and rising standards of living. Simultaneously, the organization of the United Nations offered new prospects of preserving peace throughout the world.[1] Bitterly disillusioned by its experience following the 1914-18 conflict, mankind desperately desired a cessation of struggle and international tension. The great advances of science—even the awesome release of nuclear energy — could confer incalculable benefits if human activity could be concentrated on constructive rather than destructive goals.

For a brief period the world recaptured some of its earlier enthusiasm and faith in the future. Veterans and refugees were reunited with long-separated relatives—although, in millions of homes, there were poignant gaps in the family circle. In most of the western countries, certainly in the United States, Canada, and Britain, rapid demobilization was the only acceptable policy. No democratic government which might have sought to delay this extremely diffi-

[1]See Chapter 25.

cult transformation could long have retained power over its electorate.

Unfortunately, this overwhelming sentiment among the western nations was not matched by a corresponding policy in the Soviet Union. There, too, there was a great feeling of war weariness—but the people were not free to express their opinions. The soldier in the Red Army was doubtless no less eager than his British, American, or Canadian counterpart to return to his homeland and readjust his life to peacetime pursuits. But the ruler of the Kremlin—not subject, like the British Prime Minister or the American President, to the verdict of the people—had no intention of relinquishing any of his wartime conquests, or speedily converting Russia to a peacetime basis. Old pre-war anti-capitalistic suspicions persisted in Stalin's mind, and the tremendous victories of the Red Army in eastern and central Europe offered expanded theatres of influence beyond the wildest expectations of the Czars. Consequently, the Second World War was almost immediately succeeded by a "Cold War" between Russia and the Western Allies, lasting until Stalin's death in 1953.

The Origins of the Cold War

The origins of the Cold War might be traced back to the early days of Communism in Russia and the ill-feeling generated by Allied intervention in the Civil War.[1] Although the Soviet Union had co-operated fully with the League of Nations in subsequent attempts to restrain Japanese, Italian, and German aggression, she was always conscious of the ideological differences between herself and the western democracies. This mistrust was intensified by the roles played, on the one hand, by Russia in the Spanish Civil War, and, on the other, by Britain and France in the Munich crisis. Thus, as we have seen, Stalin was not conscious of any "betrayal" in making the purely opportunistic Nazi-Soviet Pact on the eve of the Second World War—although this agreement was bitterly denounced in London and Paris. Thereafter, Hitler's ill-judged invasion of Russia (1941) at once created a wartime alliance between the Soviet Union and the Western Powers. But not even the terrible emergencies of the global struggle could entirely eliminate sources of friction among the Allies. Britain and the United States poured

[1] See below, p. 507.

huge shipments of military supplies into Russia (these included large numbers of Canadian-built vehicles), at a heavy cost in casualties to convoys. Yet the Russians always felt that in the hour of their greatest peril—with the Nazi war machine at the gates of Moscow—they had been compelled to fight their own battle for survival, because of the delay in launching the so-called "Second Front" in the west. Actually, beginning in 1940, first the British Commonwealth and later the Allies were already heavily engaged in a second theatre, in North Africa. Also, operations against Nazi-dominated Europe were long delayed by difficulties over the provision of special amphibious equipment, and, after the Japanese attack at Pearl Harbor, by the competing demands of the Pacific War. Neither of these problems was fully understood or conceded, however, by the Russian leader. Soviet suspicions of western indifference towards relieving the pressure on the Eastern Front continued or even grew during the grinding middle years of the war, with the result that Russia's attitude towards the Western Allies remained relatively cold. Then, after Russia captured the strategic initiative in the Battle of Stalingrad—and began an irresistible western advance into the heart of the Third Reich—there was a corresponding upsurge of Russian confidence, contributing to the belief that the Soviet Union could finish the war without western assistance.

The Widening Gulf—Yalta and Potsdam

An ominous indication of the coming separation between Russia and the Western Powers was evident at the great conference of Allied leaders held at Yalta in February, 1945. Although primarily concerned with attempts to co-ordinate strategy in the final phase of the German war, Churchill, Roosevelt, and Stalin also had to discuss the future status of eastern European nations then being liberated from Nazi oppression. Inevitably, the form of government to be adopted in the liberated regions was a delicate subject at this meeting of democratic and totalitarian leaders.

At Yalta, President Roosevelt was most anxious to obtain Russian co-operation in defeating Japan (at that time the success of the atomic bomb was still in doubt, and the final campaign against Japan, it was feared, would be bloody and long); accordingly, he made several concessions to Stalin in eastern Europe and the Far East. More realistic than Woodrow Wilson had been, Roosevelt adopted a detached view of the fate of Europeans far removed from the vital orbit of American interests. Nevertheless, the President entertained strong hopes that Russian wartime co-operation would extend into the post-war period to allow a form of "self-determination" for the liberated countries.

Such hopes were soon to be shattered. Russian policy was dominated by powerful strategic, economic, and ideological factors. Reflecting on her experiences in the Napoleonic and World Wars, Russia was determined to achieve a wide buffer of satellite states on her western frontiers to bar the historic invasion routes to her heartland. Moreover, by controlling the economies of the eastern European countries, Russia could expect more easily to repair the war damage suffered by her own industries and eventually build up a closely integrated economic system extending from the Baltic to the Mediterranean. Finally, subjection of this vast area to Soviet influence would give greater impetus to the spread of Communism throughout the world.

The crux of the debate at Yalta on these significant issues centred on the fate of Poland. When that unhappy country had fallen before the concerted attacks of Germany and Russia at the beginning of the Second World War, a number of the Polish leaders had gone into exile in London. Naturally, these authorities were closely identified with the policies of the Western Powers during the later stages of the war, and were hostile to Russian influence because of earlier events in their tragic history. However, a rival Polish authority emerged under Russian auspices as the tide turned on the Eastern Front to bring the Red Army into Poland. In effect, a puppet government, dedicated to the goals of Soviet Communism, was ready to assume control of Polish affairs when the Germans were driven out of Poland.

Although the three Allied leaders all agreed on the necessity of a "democratic" solution to the Polish problem, Stalin's interpretation of this principle was very different from that of Churchill and Roosevelt. Baldly stated, since the Red Armies were in effective occupation of most of the country, the Soviet leader had no real intention of sharing its administration with the representatives of western-oriented groups.

Although a form of compromise was reached at Yalta, providing for a provisional Polish government to include both Communists and "western democratic" sympathizers, the latter were never able to function. From the beginning of the new regime, Polish Communists, supported by the Red Army, took over the government at Warsaw. No attempt was ever made to put into effect the formula, also accepted at Yalta, that "free and unfettered elections on the basis of universal suffrage and secret ballot" would be held in Poland.

During the spring and summer of 1945, as it became increasingly apparent that the Soviets intended to extend and maintain their direct political control of post-war governments in central and eastern Europe—without regard for normal democratic institutions as understood by the Western Powers—a profound sense of disillusionment and indignation crept over British and American relations with Russia. There was also a strong conviction in certain circles in the West that the ailing Roosevelt (who died only two months after the Yalta meeting) had been duped by Stalin into making vital concessions for what proved to be meaningless co-operation in larger issues. However, those who criticized Anglo-American policy at Yalta for these shortcomings were unable to supply a satisfactory alternative which would have *guaranteed* truly democratic institutions in Poland. Although Roosevelt and Churchill were strongly opposed to Russian policy in post-war Poland (ostensibly, Britain had gone to war in 1939 to preserve the integrity of Polish frontiers), they were certainly not going to precipitate a new crisis with the Soviets when the future of the United Nations was at stake. Thus, not for the first time in modern history, Polish interests were sacrificed for the supposedly higher considerations of international co-operation. As Churchill afterwards observed, "Poland had indeed been the most urgent reason for the Yalta Conference and was to prove the first of the causes which led to the breakdown of the Grand Alliance."

The British Prime Minister had early appreciated the political necessity of preparing to counter post-war Soviet aspirations. He had pressed for a rapid eastern advance of the Anglo-American forces to occupy, if possible, the main centres of Berlin, Vienna, and Prague before the Russians "liberated" them. But General Eisenhower, the Supreme Allied Commander, with the support of his American superiors, insisted on a conventional strategy to eliminate systematically the remaining German forces in the field,

The final major Allied conference following the war was held at Potsdam in Germany. Truman, who had been U.S. President barely three months, is seen with Churchill on his right, and Stalin. Before the conference was concluded, Churchill was replaced by the new British Prime Minister, Clement Attlee.

rather than secure political objectives.[1] Moreover, there was an unfortunate interval after Roosevelt's death before the incoming President, Harry S Truman, was able to take firm control of American policy. As a result the Red Army overran the major capitals of eastern and central Europe, including Berlin. On some fronts, Anglo-American forces even withdrew to accommodate Soviet wishes.

A final top-level conference was held at Potsdam, near devastated Berlin, in July, 1945. It was attended by Truman, Stalin, and Churchill—the latter being displaced during the proceedings by Clement Attlee, whose Labour Party had won the general election in Britain. Thus, within a matter of three months, the most experienced leaders of the West had been removed from the

[1] See above, pp. 580-581.

scene, while Stalin continued to give unquestioned direction to Russian policy. These factors undoubtedly favoured the Soviets in subsequent negotiations.

At Potsdam the Western Allies were compelled to accept the *fait accompli* in eastern Europe. Accordingly, they gave grudging approval to the Soviets' territorial changes in Poland, provisionally accepting the Oder-Neisse boundary, by which a large German population was incorporated in the Polish state. British and American approval of these arrangements was conditional, pending a final settlement at a regular peace conference. Since, however, such a gathering (similar to the Versailles Conference at the end of the First World War) was not possible during the ensuing Cold War, the Polish frontiers and the Polish government remained as arranged by the Soviets.

Similarly, the division of Germany into zones occupied by Russian, British, American, and French forces became a set pattern for the post-war period. The division of Berlin particularly was the source of continuing friction between Russia and the West, and within a short time became a focal point of the highest significance in the Cold War.

The Polarization of World Power

Despite the formal organization of the United Nations which was taking place at the time, that body had no part in the post-war European arrangements. After the Second World War, as after the First, the major Powers were determined to impose their own policies, however mutually inconsistent, without reference to the wishes of smaller states.

Following the Potsdam Conference, a Council of Foreign Ministers, restricted to Soviet, American, British, and ultimately French, representatives, endeavoured to work out details of the peace treaties with Italy and the wartime satellites of the Axis Powers. While the foreign ministers failed to reach agreement on the German settlement, treaties eventually were made with Italy, Bulgaria, Hungary, Romania, and Finland. The Soviet Union retained her territorial gains made during the war: Bessarabia, at the expense of Romania, and the Karelian Isthmus and the Arctic seaport of Petsamo, taken from Finland. Much trouble was experienced in dealing with Trieste, which was claimed by Yugoslavia (supported by Russia), although the bulk of the port's population was Italian. Protracted, bitter disputes resulted from an attempt to create a Free Territory of Trieste, until in 1954, the Western Powers permitted Italy to annex the city, while giving the adjacent rural district to Yugoslavia. However, long before the imposition of this solution, the Cold War had fundamentally altered the status of the countries involved.

By the spring of 1946 differences between East and West had resulted in a polarization of international affairs: the Soviet Union with its newly-acquired satellites confronted the western democratic Powers, led by the United States and Britain. In a famous speech at Fulton, Missouri, the great British wartime leader, Churchill, stated: "From Stettin in the Baltic to Trieste in the Adriatic an iron curtain has descended across the Continent."[1]

This ominous development was dramatically illustrated by a new crisis in one of the traditional sources of European tension—the Balkans. During the Second World War, Greece had fought a gallant but hopeless struggle against the overwhelming forces of the Axis. When peace was restored the pre-war royal government returned to Athens, where it encountered difficulties with the Communist wing of the Greek resistance movement, which had conducted guerrilla warfare against the Nazi and Fascist invaders. British troops assisted the royal government in suppressing the rebels, but in the autumn of 1946 the Greek Communists began to receive considerable help from the nearby Communist states of Yugoslavia, Bulgaria, and Albania.

The Balkan crisis was not without a precedent. As we have seen, the rulers of imperial Russia had constantly pursued a policy of trying to gain control of the vital Straits region—that is, the narrow channels of the Bosporus and the Dardanelles connecting the Mediterranean and Black Seas. The strategic and commercial advantages of achieving a dominating position in relation to this warm-water exit from Russia were obvious. Although sometimes close to attaining this much-prized goal, Russia had always been blocked by the opposition of Britain, supported by Austria and France. Now, in the confused period following the Second World

---

[1] The "iron curtain" metaphor had been used by others before Churchill, who himself had employed it in an earlier message to Truman. But the public pronouncement at Fulton (March 5, 1946) gave the phrase immediate, widespread application to the contemporary scene.

War, the new rulers of Russia doubtless saw an opportunity to gain what had eluded their predecessors, and extend their political influence throughout the Mediterranean area. Accordingly, Communist pressure against both Greece and Turkey increased perceptibly.

The threat to the Greek government, itself not free from charges of corruption and undemocratic practices, became serious in the opening months of 1947 because of British inability to continue assistance. Faced with its own financial problems, the British Government notified the United States that it could no longer bolster the Greek and Turkish authorities against open Communist attacks.

At this point, President Truman took the courageous decision of assuming the burden previously borne by Britain in the eastern Mediterranean. In a special message to Congress, during March, he announced that in future the United States would "support free peoples who are resisting attempted subjugation by armed minorities or by outside pressure." In response to his appeal, Congress at once allocated five hundred million dollars for military and economic aid to Greece and Turkey. Under this "Truman Doctrine," effective American aid gradually enabled the Greek government to re-establish its authority over mountainous regions under Communist domination. American assistance was not restricted to the preservation of Greek political security: large sums of money were also poured into Greece to support its precarious economy, and by 1962, when this form of aid terminated, the United States had contributed more than three billion dollars toward Greek development.

While the Truman Doctrine had been devised to deal with a specific emergency in the Balkans, a larger, more ambitious scheme of economic assistance to Europe soon followed.

After the war a notable programme of the United Nations Relief and Rehabilitation Administration (U.N.R.R.A.) had sent food, medical supplies, and other necessaries to the war-torn countries of Europe. But this great humanitarian project, partly financed by American capital, was scheduled to end in June, 1947. George C. Marshall, the American Secretary of State, therefore proposed that his country should offer large-scale economic aid to European nations through a co-ordinated programme of recovery.

It cannot be maintained that this "Marshall Plan" was entirely altruistic—the American government was well aware that unstable economic conditions fostered the growth of Communism in some European states, such as France and Italy. Nevertheless, the offer of assistance was made to *all* European countries, regardless of the ideologies of their governments, provided that they would co-ordinate their efforts in an efficient manner. A large number of European states, including Britain, France, and Italy, responded quickly to the American offer. However, fearing the political implications, the Soviet Union refused to allow any of its satellites to participate. Molotov, the Russian Foreign Minister, denounced the Plan as "dollar imperialism" and as an attempt to interfere in the internal affairs of independent nations. In view of the latter assertion, it was ironic that the Soviets quickly stifled Polish and Czech indications of co-operating with the American programme. Inevitably, therefore, the Marshall Plan became another important factor in the split between East and West.

Meanwhile, what has been described as the "Stalinization" of Eastern Europe continued unabated. The technique of the Communist takeover was skilfully adapted to the circumstances of each country. Where a wartime resistance movement had contained a strong Communist nucleus, efforts were made to identify the Party with the national, patriotic interest. This method was employed in the Balkans. In other regions "parliamentary infiltration" proved more useful: Communists, operating behind Soviet tanks, dominated anti-Axis parties—merely waiting for suitable opportunities to overthrow existing authorities and establish their own governments, as occurred in Hungary (September, 1947) and Czechoslovakia (February, 1948).

Finally, as we have seen in Poland, another method served the Communist purpose: a "baggage-train government," following the victorious Red Army, seized control of the administration when the Nazis were driven out. Similar techniques were used in East Germany and Romania.

Throughout this period of consolidation the Soviets exploited national antagonisms (as, for example, between Czechs and Slovaks) until, in the final stage of "Stalinization," Moscow ordered all parties to submerge their differences in a new doctrine of "proletarian internationalism."

As the chasm widened between the Soviet Empire and the Western Powers, the United States and its Allies had to consider what defensive policy should be adopted. The Truman Doctrine and the

Marshall Plan had provided temporary solutions to the economic problems of western Europe; but these could not be treated independently of political and military factors. The obvious danger of adopting too rigid a policy of confrontation would be the risk of an early war between the recent Allies. On the other hand, unless some coherent programme of defence was produced, there seemed to be a real danger of Soviet encroachment on western Europe. President Roosevelt's revelation, at the earlier Yalta Conference, of his government's intention to withdraw American troops from the Continent shortly after the end of the war, had been noted with interest by Stalin. It was clear that any political "vacuum" in Europe, or elsewhere, would be speedily filled by the Soviets.

Containment

In July, 1947, a thoughtful and imaginative article entitled "The Sources of Soviet Conduct" appeared in the influential American periodical, *Foreign Affairs*. The article was signed merely "X," but the author was afterwards identified as George F. Kennan, an American expert on Russia, then head of the State Department's Policy Planning Staff at Washington.[1] In his view it was essential to recognize the continuing incompatibility of Communism and western democracy, as well as to recognize the Communist belief in the infallibility of the Kremlin.

The answer, in Kennan's opinion, was for the West to develop an elastic policy of *containment*. He suggested that "the main element of any United States policy towards the Soviet Union must be that of a long-term, patient but firm and vigilant containment of Russian expansive tendencies." In other words, the correct line of policy would be one not of direct confrontation—such as had led eventually to the recent struggle with the Axis Powers—but flexible strength, anticipating and countering Soviet moves without an actual clash of arms. This concept of containment became the intellectual foundation for the western defence against Soviet advances—although its author disagreed with the rigid application afterwards given to his doctrine by the American government.

---

[1] Subsequently, Kennan was American Ambassador to Russia and, later, to Yugoslavia. Because of a disagreement with official American policy, he retired from the diplomatic service in 1950 at the early age of 46.

It should be noted, however, that the containment theory has not gone unchallenged by a later generation of historians. These "revisionists" argue that, during the period following the Second World War, Soviet Russia was not implacably dedicated to a programme of expansion such as Kennan and other western leaders believed. The "revisionists" maintain that the Soviet Union was actually anxious to reach an understanding with the United States during the former's temporary period of atomic weakness, and that it was really American policy that caused the Cold War. In support of this thesis, it is sometimes pointed out that Washington abruptly ended "lend-lease" arrangements with Russia in 1945, and prevented her from securing reparations from West Germany. However, we may note that the decision not to extend American aid under the Marshall Plan to countries under Soviet domination was taken in Moscow, not Washington. Perhaps future historians, further removed from these controversial issues, will find the seeds of the Cold War in mistakes made by both Stalin and western leaders.

In any case, the containment policy was soon matched by parallel activity in the Communist states. Two months after Kennan's article had appeared, the Third International[1] was revived under the new designation of "Cominform." Delegates from nine Communist countries reaffirmed their faith in Soviet leadership and declared that Communist Parties throughout the world were "to place themselves in the vanguard of the opposition against the imperialistic plans of expansion. . . ." Consequently, the formation of the Cominform may be seen as a direct challenge to the western policy of containment.

Within a short time the results of the Cominform declaration were clearly apparent. In both France and Italy, Communist-inspired general strikes affected millions of workers. Such actions were openly revolutionary in character.

Yugoslavia—First Crack in the Monolith

Nevertheless, there was not complete, monolithic regimentation of opinion among the Soviet satellites. In Yugoslavia a fiercely independent spirit, fostered by wartime guerrilla achievements against

---

[1] The Third International, while ostensibly the successor to the First and Second International Workingman's Associations discussed in Chapter 12, was organized under the auspices of the Russian government, and was in actuality little more than an agent of Soviet foreign policy. It was formed in 1919, and disbanded during the Second World War.

"The Communist Heretic" — President Tito of Yugoslavia, who has succeeded in maintaining his independence from the Kremlin, in contrast to most other East European leaders. Behind him is a painting of the peasants' rebellion in 16th century Croatia, where Tito was born.

the Axis Powers, was identified with the leadership of Marshal Tito. The son of a Croat locksmith, Tito had been captured by the Russians in the First World War. He afterwards joined the Red Army and returned to the newly-created state of Yugoslavia as a dedicated Communist, in 1923. He acquired considerable military experience through his efforts to organize the International Brigades which had supported the Republican government against Franco in the Spanish Civil War. In Yugoslavia during the Second World War, Tito established his reputation as leader of the famous *Partizans* who harassed the Axis invaders. Rewarding himself with the rank of Marshal, he became head of the post-war Communist government in Yugoslavia.

The very success of Tito's wartime activities made him suspect in the eyes of Stalin, because the Yugoslavs achieved their liberation mainly as the result of their own efforts, aided more by Britain and the United States than by the Soviet Union. Moreover, Tito had a post-war plan for a Balkan federation, to include Albania and Bulgaria, which was angrily rejected by Moscow. On the other hand, Russian efforts to control the economy and internal security of their country also antagonized the Yugoslavs, who rallied around Tito to resist Soviet demands. For these reasons it was evident that the process of "Stalinization," successfully applied to other European satellites of Russia, could not be enforced in this sturdy Balkan nation.

Matters came to a head in June, 1948, when the recently organized Cominform expelled the Yugoslav Communists from its membership. But this drastic action served only to strengthen Tito's hold on his people, for his countrymen were resolved to maintain their independence, in spite of their Communist ideology. Thus, Yugoslavia came to occupy an ambiguous position in international affairs—for while Tito insisted on the Marxist-Leninist purity of his doctrine, he reopened contacts with the West.

"Titoism," as it was called, represented a dangerous heresy to orthodox leaders of Communism.[1] It was the first significant breach in their post-war front, and from the beginning was recognized as potentially even more damaging as a precedent for independent action by other satellite countries. Much of later Hungarian, Polish, Romanian, and Czech resistance to Russian domination was due to the Yugoslav example.

Confrontation—The Berlin Blockade

Almost simultaneously with the Yugoslav defection came a dramatic threat of open hostilities between East and West over Berlin. Not surprisingly, the division of Berlin into four occupational zones, the rigid demarcation between the East and West German governments, and the fact that the former capital was an "island" within the Soviet zone, all greatly complicated the administration of the city.

Meanwhile, the Western Powers accelerated efforts to revive democratic traditions in West Germany, now centred in Bonn. The United States also provided economic assistance, under the Marshall Plan, towards the rapid recovery of the devastated country. These developments, watched jealously by the Kremlin, led to Soviet counter-measures, which took the form of restricting land communications between Berlin and the West. Reacting to further western efforts to reform the German currency, the Soviets tight-

---

[1] From the Western point of view, one favourable result of Tito's breach with the Cominform was the cessation of Communist assistance to rebels in Greece.

ened their control of access to Berlin—and in June, 1948, imposed a total blockade on land routes to the West.

The western democratic Powers, principally the United States and Britain, were determined not to accept the blockade. If they had accepted the situation, the Soviets would have won a resounding victory in the Cold War, with far-reaching effects outside Germany. On the other hand, American and British leaders realized that any attempt to break through the blockade with military force would, in all probability, precipitate a large-scale war with Russia. Accordingly the West found an ingenious solution—instead of attempting to break through the land barrier, they would employ their great resources in the air to fly over it.

The Berlin airlift had no precedent in peacetime. However, it benefited from experience in the late stages of the Second World War when the civilian population of the western Netherlands had been saved from starvation by massive air support. Each day the citizens of West Berlin required a minimum of four thousand tons of supplies to survive. Yet so great an effort was made by the British and American air forces that this figure was soon doubled, and even tripled. Throughout the summer and autumn of 1948 the tremendous flow of airborne supplies continued. With the approach of winter, the Soviets counted on a new "ally" in this crucial phase of the Cold War: how would the Western Allies be able to convey adequate quantities of coal to satisfy the needs of two million people? The British and American answer was simply to increase the number of aircraft in service and add coal to the other necessities brought to the besieged city.

Life was hard in Berlin during the blockade. Naturally, nothing but bare essentials could be brought into the city. West Berliners' diet featured such items as dehydrated vegetables; citizens also had to contend with shortages of fuel and electricity. Nevertheless, civilian morale proved equal to the challenge. Eventually, in the spring of 1949, the Soviet government accepted the hard fact that its attempt to strangle West Berlin had failed, and Communist prestige was suffering. Negotiations were begun at the United Nations to prepare the way for a reversal of Russian policy. On May 12 the blockade was lifted, and trucks from the West again began rolling into the city. During the course of the entire operation, the United States Air Force and the Royal Air Force had delivered over two million tonnes of supplies in nearly three hundred thousand flights. It was a tremendous achievement—whether viewed as a technological or a political solution to a grave, intractable problem. More important even than the physical survival of West Berlin was the proof that the Western Powers would not capitulate to Soviet threats. The Cold War had successfully passed through one of its most dangerous phases.

NATO

Even before the Berlin blockade was lifted, the western democracies had reached the fateful decision that their security required the resurrection of a defensive military alliance. This was not a sudden development, but rather the climactic stage in a series of negotiations extending over a period of two years.

The first step in the direction of a revived western coalition had been taken in March, 1947, when Britain and France made a military alliance to last for fifty years. At that time, however, the common enemy was still considered to be Germany, not the Soviet Union. A year later, the intensification of the Cold War between East and West gave a new impetus and direction to defensive planning. By the Treaty of Brussels, the Anglo-French alliance was extended to include the Benelux states, and the new pact was clearly oriented against Soviet expansion. Nevertheless, lacking the formal support of the United States, the new organization could not be considered a very formidable barrier to suspected Russian ambitions. There could be no balance of power in Europe while the U.S.S.R. maintained an enormous military force (estimated at not less than two hundred divisions) against the much inferior strength of the western European democracies.

The only hope of restoring the balance in Europe was through effective American participation. Washington had already shown that it would not relapse into an isolationist policy such as had exerted an adverse effect on world affairs after the First World War. The Truman Doctrine, the Marshall Plan, and the important American contribution to the Berlin airlift all reflected an increased sense of responsibility for European affairs. Yet the question remained whether the United States was prepared to reverse the demobilization of her forces and again send troops to the Continent, even if only in a precautionary role. Although President Truman and his advisers might appreciate the necessity of such action, could they overcome the precedent of Wilsonian failure in 1919-20 and rally public opinion behind a policy of military intervention in Europe?

In reality, the answer to this crucial question—perhaps the most significant issue of the Cold War—had been found as early as June, 1948. At that time the American Senate, a traditional fortress of isolationism, had authorized the United States government to associate itself with mutual defence agreements which contributed to the security of the nation. Thereafter, Washington opened negotiations with the five partners of the Brussels Treaty, and discussions were expanded to include Canada, Italy, Iceland, Denmark, Norway, and Portugal. (Sweden and Eire, like Switzerland, preserved their neutrality, while Spain under Franco pursued an independent course, and Finland was too much within the Soviet orbit to participate.) These twelve nations signed the North Atlantic Treaty in Washington on April 4, 1949. Subsequently they were joined by Greece and Turkey (1952), and the Federal German Republic (1955).

Western statesmen were most anxious to ensure that the new organization would conform to the letter and spirit of the Charter of the United Nations. This was affirmed in the preamble to the NATO Treaty, the signatories declaring their determination "to safeguard the freedom, common heritage and civilization of their people, founded on the principles of democracy, individual liberty and the rule of law." Accordingly, the participants agreed to consult together whenever the territory, independence, or security of any one of them was threatened. More specifically, Article Five of the Treaty stated that "an armed attack against one or more of them in Europe or North America shall be considered an attack against them all. . . ." The implications of this commitment, in relation to the menacing Soviet attitude in Europe, were obvious.

It was agreed that NATO affairs would be directed by a Council composed of the Foreign Ministers of member countries. The Council would meet regularly in ordinary sessions, but could be convened at any time to deal with an emergency.[1] An inevitable weakness of the new organization was the requirement that all decisions be unanimous.

---

[1] Dean Acheson, American Secretary of State, became the first chairman of the Council. Beginning in 1957 this designation was changed to that of President of the North Atlantic Council.

Under the Council an elaborate structure was erected to carry out the roles of NATO. Basically, a division was made between civilian and military functions. On the civilian side, following the U.N. example, there was a Secretary-General to supervise administration and control activities of various divisions dealing with political affairs, economics and finance, production, logistics, and scientific matters. The military organization of NATO, headed by a committee composed of senior service advisers from each participating country,[1] controlled the forces placed at its disposal in strategic commands covering most of western Europe, the Mediterranean, and the North Atlantic. Thus, for example, in 1951, General Dwight D. Eisenhower assumed the appointment of Supreme Allied Commander Europe, with his headquarters near Paris.

Because of her huge industrial potential and large resources of manpower, the United States naturally made the largest overall contribution to the setting up and maintenance of NATO. A primary feature of the American commitment was the deployment of air and land forces in defence of West Germany. While such forces (originally planned to include a total of fifty Allied divisions and four thousand aircraft by the end of 1952) could not be expected to stop an all-out Soviet offensive in the West, they could be considered an effective brake on Russian expansion.

It is probably correct to state that the NATO Alliance expressed a feeling of solidarity, never hitherto attained in peacetime, among the countries bordering the North Atlantic. The significance of the new organization was not, therefore, entirely negative—in the sense of merely opposing the Soviet Union. Together with the earlier Marshall Plan, NATO had the positive purpose of encouraging western European democracies to achieve closer co-ordination of their own political and economic affairs. Indeed, there were many, including President Truman and Dean Acheson, who hoped to see western Europe revive and emerge as a "Third Force," resisting both Communist and neo-Fascist influences.

The Balance of Terror

In spite of these impressive objectives, backed up by the resources of the "free" world, the organization of NATO did not lead to

---

[1] Iceland, having no military forces, was represented by a civilian.

any immediate lessening of tension between East and West. In September, 1949, the Soviet Union detonated its first atomic bomb, revealing that the western monopoly of nuclear weapons had ended. A terrible arms race ensued, with the United States regaining temporary superiority with the production of the hydrogen bomb late in 1952. By the following summer, however, Russia had duplicated the American feat.

It is difficult for the civilian (and perhaps even the military) to realize the full implications of these developments. Within only a few years of the end of the Second World War, military concepts had altered more drastically than at any time since the invention of gunpowder. Some idea of what this meant may be gained from a comparison of the destructive power of weapons. A "blockbuster" of the type used by Allied bombers in the Second World War contained about one tonne of the high explosive, T.N.T. The atomic bomb dropped at Hiroshima had the equivalent force of twenty thousand tonnes of T.N.T. But a single hydrogen bomb, of the kind perfected in 1952, had a power equal to twenty *megatons*—that is, twenty *million* tonnes of T.N.T. Or, expressed in another way, man's capacity to destroy had multiplied twenty million times in only seven years!

But the significance of these terrifying inventions did not end with the exploitation of nuclear energy. Systems of delivering atomic warheads were also advancing and becoming increasingly sophisticated. As we know, Hitler had employed ballistic missiles (the "V" weapons) in a futile effort to avert defeat in the late stages of the Second World War. Now, in the post-war world, research on and development of rockets and long-range guided missiles kept pace with nuclear advances. As with the latter, mankind had the choice of utilizing these inventions for either peaceful or warlike purposes. Tragically, the tensions built up during the Cold War meant that the prospect of achieving international co-operation in the production and use of these great technological advances was lost.

In these circumstances, the disaster of a nuclear war was avoided mainly by two factors: first, the very limited number of nations (initially only the United States, the Soviet Union, and Britain) possessing the facilities to produce such weapons and delivery systems; and second, the caution and good sense displayed by the leaders of these states, who were well aware that a nuclear conflict,

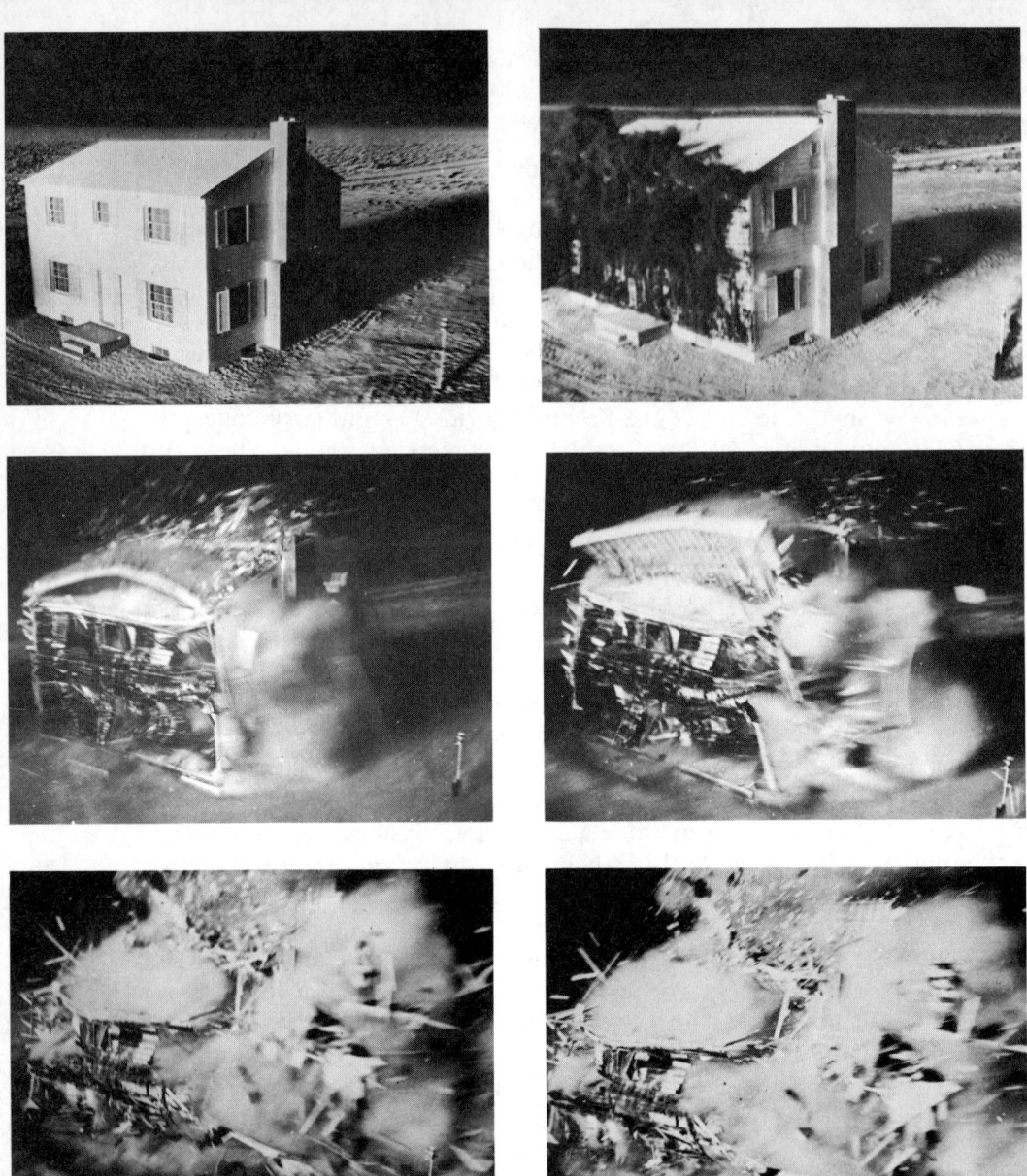

These six photograph are frames from a film made during an atomic test blast at Yucca Flat in the United States, on March 17, 1953. The house was one thousand metres from ground zero. The elapsed time between the first frame (upper left) and the last (lower right) was two and a third seconds.

once begun, might well end civilization. In short, the so-called "balance of power" had been replaced by a "balance of terror"—the awesome threat of retaliation proving the best guarantee that such weapons would not be employed.

Korea—The Critical Test

Almost simultaneously with the creation of the "balance of terror," however, the sense of responsibility and restraint of the "Nuclear Powers" was put to its severest test. This was the Korean War, in which the Western Powers and the Communist world came into the closest possible military confrontation short of an outright declaration of war on each other.

At the end of the Second World War, Korea, a warn-torn country long the object of conflicting national ambitions, was evenly split by the 38th parallel between North and South Korea, occupied by Russian and American forces, respectively. Attempts to establish an independent, united, and democratic state broke down. The United Nations recommended that supervised elections be held in the disputed land, but the Soviet authorities rejected this suggestion for North Korea. In due course elections were held in South Korea, a government headed by President Syngman Rhee was recognized, and the United States withdrew its troops from the area.

Suddenly on June 25, 1950, North Korean formations invaded South Korea, precipitating an immediate international crisis.

Under the leadership of the United States, the U.N. declared the North Korean invasion to be a breach of the peace, called for cessation of the fighting, and requested all member-nations to assist in carrying out the resolution.[1] President Truman promptly ordered American forces to support the South Koreans, and a unified U.N. command was speedily organized under the American general, Douglas MacArthur, with contingents from numerous other states, including Britain, France, and Canada. Other Powers contributed non-military aid to the U.N. Force, which, however, remained predominantly American in composition.

Before the U.N. Force could intervene effectively in Korea, the aggressors occupied most of the peninsula. The U.N. counter-attacked so strongly, however, that the North Koreans were driven

---

[1] The Korean War had important implications for the organization and functioning of the U.N.; these are discussed on pp. 647-648.

back to the Chinese border. The war entered a more threatening phase when, late in 1950, "volunteers" from Communist China joined the North Koreans, but despite this development the danger of the war exploding into global conflict was averted. Although the Soviet Union did not actually participate in the war, it supplied the North Koreans and Chinese with much of their armament. General MacArthur wished to strike at Chinese bases north of the Yalu River, that is within Manchuria, but this idea alarmed both President Truman and his Western Allies, who foresaw the possibility of the war expanding out of control if Chinese territory were attacked. MacArthur was dismissed from his command, and eventually the struggle entered a static phase of trench warfare in the vicinity of the 38th parallel. It became apparent that neither side could dislodge the other without making a greater effort than was considered feasible in the circumstances. Finally, after long months of negotiation, an armistice agreement was signed at Panmunjon, very near the 38th parallel, on July 27, 1953. In the absence of any peace settlement, the armistice remained in effect during succeeding years.

Korea represented a turning point in the Cold War. The major Powers had fought each other (albeit indirectly) for three years in a "hot war" that had followed a conventional pattern without the introduction of nuclear weapons. With the armistice of Panmunjon, it appeared that East and West might be approaching a more stable relationship. In particular, the United States government modified its rigid application of the Containment policy in favour of a more flexible diplomacy. The new approach was to avoid a static defence of the *status quo*, while "negotiating from strength" with the Communist bloc. As expressed in Dean Acheson's metaphor: "You can't argue with a river, it is going to flow; you can dam it up, you can put it to useful purposes, you can deflect it, but you can't argue with it."

The shift in American policy was accompanied by an even more significant change in Soviet leadership, which came with the death of Stalin, on March 5, 1953. A Russian proverb observes that "even the greatest of Czars must be put to bed with a spade"—and the death of the man who had controlled the destiny of the Russian Revolution for a full generation naturally had immense effect upon both internal and external policies.

3. "COEXISTENCE"

Following Stalin's death, the leading figure in the Kremlin emerged as Nikita Khrushchev. As described above, Khrushchev instituted a policy of "de-Stalinization" in domestic affairs, by which the almost intolerable oppression and tyranny of the government was relaxed. In international affairs the real significance of Khrushchev's tenure of power was his presentation of a theory of "coexistence" to replace the Cold War between East and West.

The changed Russian attitude was evident in Khrushchev's speeches, especially his pronouncements on Communist objectives—and, above all, in the highly successful visit he paid to the United States in 1959. On this occasion the Soviet leader displayed keen interest in the American economy; he toured farms and supermarkets and held amicable meetings with President Eisenhower.

Khrushchev's proposal for "peaceful coexistence" was elaborated in an article which appeared under his signature in *Foreign Affairs* (October, 1959). The Russian leader observed: "You may like your neighbour or dislike him. You are not obliged to be friends with him or visit him. But you live side by side, and what can you do if neither you nor he has any desire to quit the old home and move to another town?" International difficulties, he maintained, could be settled only by a suicidal nuclear war or by "peaceful coexistence." The essence of the latter was the unequivocal repudiation of war as a means of solving controversial issues. The Soviet Premier offered the western democracies a powerful inducement to accept his formula when he renounced one of the traditional goals of communism—world revolution through subversive activities within states.

"Coexistence" implied the substitution of economic competition for political and military rivalry. "Ultimately," declared the Soviet leader, "that system will be victorious on the globe which will offer the nations greater opportunities for improving their material and spiritual life." In other words, the future battlefields of contending nations would be the factories, research laboratories, and farmlands.

Not surprisingly, many western observers regarded the coexistence policy with some scepticism, which the Soviet record even in the six years that had elapsed since the death of Stalin seemed to

"Gulliver among the Lilliputians"—a statue of Stalin pulled down by the people of Budapest during the first day of the Hungarian revolt, October 23, 1956.

suggest was warranted. A major setback in the relaxation of international tension had come in 1955 with the signing of the Warsaw Pact, a military alliance between the Soviet Union and its satellites as a counter-measure to NATO. With this alliance, the dangers of an East-West war in Europe seemed to be increased.

A further source of suspicion and bitterness between the Soviet Union and the West was the brutal Russian suppression of an attempt by one of its satellites, Hungary, to obtain her independence (1956). Almost simultaneously with the unsuccessful Hungarian Revolution came the Suez Crisis, in which Russia's provocative policy made a settlement considerably more difficult to attain.[1]

With these events in the background, cynical western reactions to Khrushchev's coexistence proposal are perhaps understandable.

[1] The Suez Crisis, in which the United Nations played an important role, is discussed in greater detail on pp. 648-650.

The Cuban Missile Crisis

By far the most dangerous confrontation in the post-war period, indeed in human history, given the nature of the weapons involved, came in 1962 with the Cuban Missile Crisis. The background to the crisis was the Cuban Revolution of 1959, which brought the government of Fidel Castro to power. Castro, an idealist and accomplished mass-orator, began as a social and political reformer, without Communist leanings. However, a strong wave of anti-American sentiment in the island, directed against American "dollar imperialism," eventually carried Castro and his enthusiastic followers into the Communist camp. Regrettably, in 1961, the United States government fostered a small-scale attempt to invade Cuba (the Bay of Pigs fiasco), which embittered relations between Washington and Havana, driving Castro still further in the direction of close collaboration with the U.S.S.R.

The Cuban situation became much more critical in 1962, when the United States learned that the Soviet Union was building military bases on the island. In Washington it seemed highly probable that these installations were of a defensive nature, intended to prevent any repetition of the Bay of Pigs episode. But aerial reconnaissance soon revealed that missile sites were being constructed for weapons with an estimated range of 3 500 km. In effect, it now appeared that Russia was seeking to leapfrog the elaborate NATO defence system, exposing the eastern coast of the United States, including Washington and New York, to nuclear attacks. John F. Kennedy, recently elected President, reacted quickly and courageously to the threat. In an historic address, delivered over television on October 22, he declared "a quarantine on all offensive equipment to Cuba." He demanded that the weapons already in the island be removed, and warned the Kremlin that any missile attack on the United States would be answered by an overwhelming retaliatory assault on the Soviet Union.[1]

Evidence is still lacking on the Soviet motivation in provoking the Cuban Crisis. Many observers believed that Khrushchev was simply testing American reaction on a matter vital to the security of the United States. On the other hand, the almost ostentatious attempt to establish missile bases on the island seemed unnecessary

---

[1] Apart from intermediate and medium-range ballistic missiles and conventional bombers, the United States claimed that it had 144 Polaris, 103 Atlas, 105 Thor and Jupiter, and 54 Titan missiles available to attack the Soviet Union.

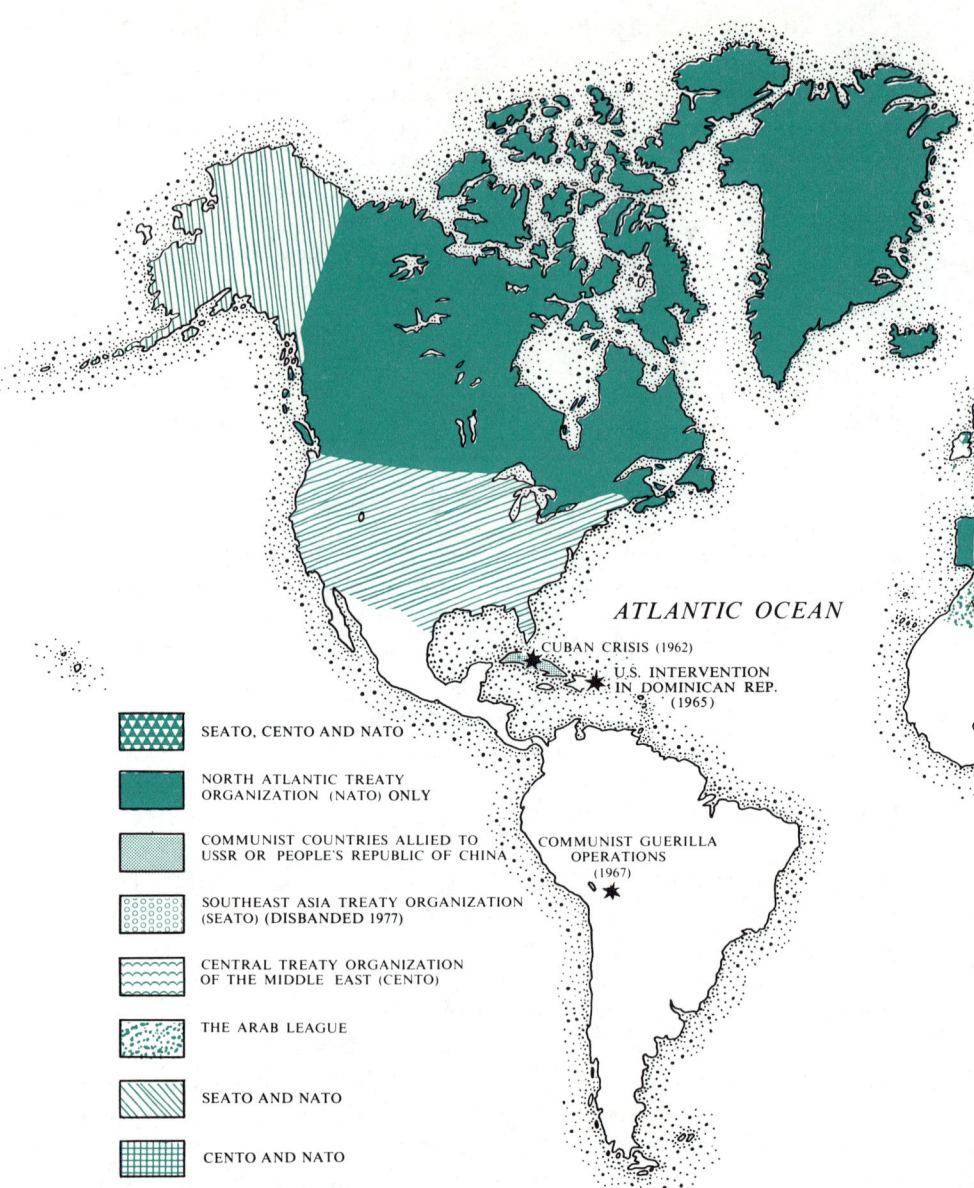

THE COLD WAR
AND OTHER WARS AND CONFLICTS
(1945-1979)

"The Dance of Death"—the Cuban Missile Crisis, November, 1962. The world watched with dread as leaders of East and West manoeuvred with agonizing slowness towards a settlement. Above, the Soviet freighter *Anesov* leaves Cuba with a presumed cargo of missiles under the surveillance of a United States naval plane and the destroyer U.S.S. *Barry*.

in view of the supposed availability of Russian intercontinental rockets. Moreover, such aggressive action did not seem consistent with Khrushchev's doctrine of "peaceful coexistence." A possible explanation of Soviet intentions was the necessity of bolstering the Cuban outpost of Communism against further efforts by the United States government to topple Castro.

For thirty-six hours following Kennedy's warning, an apprehensive world awaited the outcome of the latest and most dramatic confrontation between East and West. Eighteen Soviet cargo ships were heading for Cuba, their routes barred by American naval patrols. Then, at dawn on October 24, these ships either altered course or turned around. The Kremlin had backed down. But this was not the end of the crisis—there remained the acute problem of the missile sites already constructed in Cuba. Fortunately both sides remained open to consultation and compromise, and an exchange of notes between Kennedy and Khrushchev (October 26-28) led to a solution: Russia agreed to withdraw the missiles and dismantle the bases already in Cuba, while the United States promised to lift the naval quarantine and not invade the island.

The risk of a nuclear war between the super-Powers had perhaps been exaggerated. But the Cuban Crisis had the useful effect of clearing the atmosphere by defining the limits to Soviet encroachment in a sphere of vital American interest. Indicative of the changed atmosphere was the treaty signed at Moscow, in the following summer, by the representatives of the Soviet Union, the United States, and Britain. This treaty, which banned the testing of nuclear devices in the air, outer space, and under water,[1] represented a significant step in the ability of the Great Powers to coexist peacefully.

Unfortunately, new and ever more sinister inventions in military technology have given even greater urgency to the need for disarmament. Such weapons include anti-ballistic missiles, MIRVs (multiple warheads each capable of being aimed at separate targets) and, most recently, the American neutron bomb. The latter carries twice the deadly radiation of a conventional nuclear bomb and is capable of killing people without damage to buildings.

In 1969 the American and Soviet governments held Strategic Arms Limitation Talks (SALT) in a joint effort to limit the nuclear arms race. President Richard Nixon and Premier Kosygin discussed the problem at their meeting in Moscow in 1973. Further conversations followed, in succeeding years, without much positive result. Lack of agreement was mainly due to technical difficulties concerning limitations on missiles and the types and sizes of weapons. In the summer of 1978 the General Assembly of the U.N. held a Special Session on Disarmament. The Session succeeded in drawing up a Declaration which stated that the ultimate objective was general and complete disarmament under effective international control. As priorities, the Declaration listed effective measures of nuclear disarmament and the prevention of nuclear war; prohibition of other weapons of mass destruction, and balanced reductions of armed forces and conventional armaments. It was hoped that this convincing demonstration of world opinion would be reflected in the progress of further SALT negotiations.

---

[1] It did not, however, prohibit underground testing.

4. SHIFTING POWER BLOCS

Despite such moments of urgency as Hungary, Suez, or Cuba, when the enmity between the two major Powers seemed particularly bitter, the relations between the United States and the Soviet Union had slowly, but certainly, changed in their fundamental nature. There were several reasons for this. One was the advancing level of weapons technology. Another was the changing nature of Soviet society, which increasingly demanded improvements in the standard of living—which meant that resources previously channeled towards fighting the Cold War would have to be diverted to domestic consumption.

One of the most important developments of all was that within both blocs diverging national policies had imposed severe strains, threatening to disrupt the uneasy balance of power. In the West, considerable uncertainty and dislocation resulted from the independent stand taken by France under De Gaulle. In the Communist world the great schism between the Soviets and the Red Chinese[1] was succeeded by a growing restlessness among the Soviet satellite states of eastern Europe. Both situations, proceeding concurrently, have obscured the probable trend of future developments in international affairs.

Divisions in the Western Bloc

Alliances have traditionally been plagued by the conflicting interests of their various members and the western bloc has been no exception. Within NATO one of the most difficult dilemmas has been the dispute between Turkey and Greece over Cyprus, which on various occasions has threatened to erupt into open war.[1]

The next serious threat to the solidarity of NATO and the West came from France. In the 20th century, French prestige has oscillated widely between triumph and disaster. Victorious over her traditional German foe in the First World War, France succumbed to internal dissension and intrigue in the early stages of the Second. By the end of the conflict she was no longer considered a major Power; subsequently, her colonial problems in Algeria and Indo-China seemed to confirm the impression of weakness.

---

[1]The origins and causes of the Sino-Soviet dispute, which can best be seen in relation to the development of communism in China, are discussed separately in Chapter 26.

"'See below, pp. 653-655.

Yet France had one incomparable, unpredictable asset in the person of General Charles de Gaulle, a man long accustomed to adversity. Extremely proud and devout, a man whose patriotism was tinged with mysticism (in the Second World War he adopted as his symbol the Cross of Lorraine, traditionally identified with Joan of Arc), De Gaulle lacked no confidence in either his country or himself. His tall, soldierly figure and prominent nose, a favourite subject for caricaturists (see below) conveyed a definite impression of vigour, dignity, and determination. Returning to power in 1958, he set about energetically to extricate the Republic from the Algerian *débâcle*, to restore economic conditions in France and, above all, to regain a major role in world affairs for his country.

In foreign affairs De Gaulle proved to be a stormy figure. Deeply distrustful of the "Anglo-Saxon" domination of the western world, he was determined to adopt an independent line—seeking to create a "Third Force" between the Communist and Western blocs. This "Force," in the President's view, should be a revived Europe under French leadership.

"The Iceberg"

The new direction taken by French foreign policy caused Britain and the United States great difficulty and embarrassment in two respects. First, De Gaulle repeatedly vetoed the British application for membership in the European Common Market. In De Gaulle's view, Britain was not yet sufficiently "European" in her outlook to justify admission to the Common Market. Second, the President reacted strongly to American domination of the NATO Alliance. He refused to be committed unreservedly to either of the major power Blocs centred at Washington and Moscow.

"Since," he said, "the division of the world between the two great powers, and therefore into two camps, obviously does not further liberty, equality and fraternity of peoples, a different order, a different balance is necessary for peace." He lost no time in illustrating his intentions. By visiting the Soviet Union and making a commercial treaty with Romania (1964) he indicated his willingness to negotiate with Communist states. By the same token, he withdrew French troops from NATO in 1966 and inaugurated an independent programme for the development of nuclear weapons. Furthermore he compelled the Western Powers to withdraw all their forces from French soil and move the NATO command from Paris to Brussels. It is possible that much of this dislocation might have been avoided if the British and American governments had shown more disposition to share strategic decisions with the sensitive Head of State at Paris.

It was inevitable that French diplomacy would take a new direction after De Gaulle's death in 1970. This was particularly true of French relations with both Britain and West Germany. Under President Valéry Giscard d'Estaing and Chancellor Helmut Schmidt a realistic effort was made to promote a Franco-German entente within the E.E.C. (In 1974 the combined gross national products of France and West Germany equalled more than half of the European Community's G.N.P.) Similarly, French acceptance of Britain's admission to the Common Market removed the previous obstacle to better Anglo-French relations. In the words of the French statesman, Michel Debré, the object of French foreign policy was to "reconcile the demands of sovereignty and the need for concerted action with other states to advance world peace."

Problems in the Soviet Bloc

In recent decades the Communist world has suffered more serious blows from internal strife and ideological divisions than its western counterpart. Foremost among their problems has been the development of a seemingly irreparable split between the two titans of the Communist world, the Soviet Union and Communist China. The reversal of Soviet policy inherent in Khrushchev's doctrine of peaceful coexistence with the West was bitterly denounced by the Chinese. Soon the Russians and Chinese were competing with each other, as well as with the democracies, for influence in Asia, Africa, and elsewhere. So intense did mutual recriminations become that it often appeared that the two Communist leaders regarded each other with more suspicion and distrust than they did the capitalist West!

Scarcely less vexing for the Soviet Union was the distracting influence of "Titoism," which continued to complicate relations between Russia and her satellites in eastern and central Europe. Divisions within the Soviet system reached an almost unbearable intensity in the late 1960's, as the satellite states showed more and more signs of following the independent line already charted by the Yugoslav President. Certain members of the Warsaw Pact, notably Romania and Czechoslovakia, reopened contacts with western nations and began to relax their internal restrictions on the free expression of opinions. The rulers of the Kremlin regarded these developments with rising concern. Not only did they fear the disintegration of the Warsaw Pact, erected to oppose NATO, but they chose to regard defections from their policy as encouraging the prospect of a revived and revengeful Germany.

Matters came to a head in the summer of 1968 when the Communist government of Czechoslovakia, under the leadership of Alexander Dubček, began to implement a programme of "liberalization," restoring many former freedoms. Moscow reacted strongly —first with threats, and then with a military occupation of the small state. In Prague, as in Budapest in 1956, Soviet tanks rolled through the streets in a brutal display of overpowering force. Although Soviet claims that they had intervened merely at the "request" of the Czech authorities were bitterly refuted by the Czech Foreign Minister at the United Nations, the Czechs were sufficiently realistic to realize that military resistance was futile. As in the case of Hungary in 1956, the Western Powers were not prepared to risk a world war by intervening forcibly on behalf of Czechoslovakia. In 1938 the small republic had been sacrificed to appease Hitler; thirty years later there were those who wondered whether the Russian suppression of Czech independence would be merely another step along the gloomy road to an even greater tragedy. Certainly the Soviet action had dealt a serious blow to prospects for improved "peaceful coexistence" with the West.

By the end of the 1960's, the relations between the world's two most powerful nations seemed more confused and uncertain than ever. On the one hand, the deteriorating solidarity of both the eastern and western blocs seemed to blur and diminish the once unmistakable hostility with which they regarded one another. On the other hand, the Czechoslovakian crisis seemed to reaffirm all the old suspicions concerning the fundamental opposition between the two camps. Meanwhile, all nations were vitally concerned with the ramifications of a terrible struggle that was being waged in far-off Vietnam.[1]

A perceptible improvement in the Soviet Union's relations with both its satellite states and the Western Powers occurred in the 1970's. Antagonisms aroused by the Soviet action in Czechoslovakia and American involvement in the Vietnamese War diminished as recollections of these tragic events were overtaken by new developments. Tensions in eastern Europe were reduced by West German Chancellor Willy Brandt's *Ostpolitik*—a policy of closer co-operation with the U.S.S.R. and its satellites. In 1972 the American President, Richard Nixon, visited Moscow and in the following year the Soviet leader Brezhnev came to the United States. A number of bilateral agreements were signed by the two super-Powers. In all of these negotiations a notable contribution was made by the distinguished American Secretary of State, Henry Kissinger, who brought renewed courage, imagination and realism to the direction of American policy. Nevertheless, the threat of new crises in Africa, the Middle and Far East meant that the future of Soviet-American relations was uncertain. As the experienced George Kennan observed, at the end of 1977, the peace of the world might well depend "on the ability of the American and Soviet governments to remain in close communication, to give each other reasonable reassurance as to their intentions, and to co-ordinate their actions with a view to preventing local conflicts from growing to global dimensions."

---

[1] The Vietnam War, which began essentially as an anti-colonial struggle, is discussed in Chapter 26 in the context of the emergence of the "new nations" of Asia.

25 The Evolution of the United Nations

> The grim fact is that we prepare for war like precocious giants and for peace like pygmies.
> —Lester B. Pearson, on receiving Nobel Prize, 1957.

As mankind moves forward into the later decades of the 20th century, the problem of world government becomes more and more acute. For most of his history, man has sought the attainment of stability and security by means of this ideal. The essential issue is easily stated—but, so far, defies easy solution: how to erect a world organization with unrestricted power to preserve peace and collective security, while also satisfying national demands for autonomy and free development.

For many centuries nations were free to indulge in war without the penalty of universal destruction. By the end of the Second World War however, the situation had radically changed. Nuclear power as an offensive weapon—with the attending dangers of radioactive fallout—rendered all earlier concepts of war obsolete. Unless a solution could be found to the political problem of international co-operation, the human race would be faced with the prospect of annihilation.

1. EVOLUTION AND EARLY HISTORY

"This time we shall not make the mistake of waiting until the end of the war to set up the machinery of peace. This time, as we fight together to get the war over quickly, we work together to keep it from happening again." This declaration by President Roosevelt, early in 1945, echoed the Allies' firm intention to reconstruct an international organization out of the debris of the League of Nations to carry forward the highest hopes of mankind in the most critical stage of recorded history.

United Nations headquarters in New York. The complex of buildings is composed of the tall, slab-like Secretariat, the Dag Hammarskjöld Library in the foreground, the domed General Assembly, and the Council building behind the Secretariat.

A set of principles, suitable as a preliminary basis for such an organization, had already been drawn up by Churchill and Roosevelt at their first wartime meeting and publicly revealed in the Atlantic Charter.[1] At that time (August, 1941) pressure on the British Commonwealth had been relieved by Hitler's invasion of Russia, but the United States was still a spectator, not a participant, in the struggle. Consequently, the two great leaders of the English-speaking world had not endeavoured to go beyond the expression of very broad principles for post-war co-operation. These included

[1] See pp. 562, 568.

renunciation of any territorial changes without the consent of the peoples concerned; recognition of all peoples' rights to choose their own form of government; and acceptance of close co-operation in the economic field, with equal access of "victor or vanquished" to world trade and raw materials. President and Prime Minister also looked forward, perhaps not too optimistically, to an enduring peace secured by universal disarmament and abandonment of the use of force.

These necessarily vague principles were reaffirmed and endorsed by twenty-six Allied governments on the first day of 1942, in the Washington Declaration of the "United Nations." The name, suggested by Roosevelt, emphasized the continuing preoccupation with the immediate need for unity in war. Apart from giving a more formal character to the wartime coalition against the Axis Powers, the formation of the United Nations offered the only practicable method of approaching post-war problems in a realistic manner.

Since the United Nations organization was initiated at a time when the League of Nations was still technically in existence, the question might properly be raised: why was the League not continued as the instrument of post-war co-operation? Apart from the League's loss of prestige for failing to solve the crises leading to the Second World War, there were two main reasons why Allied statesmen turned their backs on the earlier experiment in world government. Early in the war, when the Soviet Union had committed unprovoked aggression against Finland, the League had taken the unprecedented step of expelling Russia from its membership.[1] Consequently any revival of the older organization would have offended one of the major Powers in the post-war period. A second reason for eliminating the League was the unfortunate history of the American refusal to join that body after the First World War. It was generally felt that, rather than risk the revival of old issues in the United States, an effort should be made to create an entirely new instrument of collective action. This decision was reinforced by the obvious difficulty of reintroducing the defeated Axis Powers, in the future, to the organization they had done so much to destroy.

Throughout the later stages of the Second World War the major

---

[1] The Soviets invaded Finland in the winter of 1939-40 in order to seize a belt of Finnish territory covering the western approaches to Leningrad. The Finns resisted strenuously (their ski troops demoralized the enemy), but eventually they were forced to capitulate.

Allied Powers continued to plan the post-war form of the world organization. In their Moscow Declaration of October 30, 1943, Britain, China, the United States, and the Soviet Union acknowledged the necessity of creating as soon as possible "a general international organization, based on the principle of the sovereign equality of *all peace-loving states*, and open to membership by all such states, large or small, for the maintenance of international peace and security."

The next important step was taken late in the summer of 1944 in exploratory conversations held at Dumbarton Oaks, a comfortable estate in Washington, D.C. A cordial, co-operative spirit prevailed, and agreement was soon reached on certain fundamental issues of organization and structure. But there were other delicate matters, of particular significance to the major Allies, which could not be settled so easily. For example, what was to be done with colonial territories held under trusteeship, such as the "mandates" of the old League system? Because of her interest in the disposition of Japanese colonies, the United States was as deeply concerned in this question as was Britain with her global commitments. Again, how were voting arrangements to be conducted in the proposed executive body, the Security Council? At an early stage of the discussions, the Soviets emphasized the importance they attached to retention of the veto by the Great Powers. In other words, they insisted upon a procedure which would guarantee that collective action by the Security Council would depend upon unanimous agreement of *all* members, not merely majority rule. Finally, there was the difficulty of determining what constituted "peace-loving states." In the Russian view this definition might properly be extended to include all sixteen republics of the U.S.S.R. The Soviet representatives supported their contention by reference to the diplomatic practice of granting separate recognition to each of the Dominions of the British Commonwealth.

Even though the conversations at Dumbarton Oaks achieved much, Allied statesmen realized that many questions remained to be settled before the U.N. could assume its great post-war responsibilities.

The next stage came with the Yalta meeting of Churchill, Roosevelt, and Stalin in February, 1945. This conference was concerned primarily with the co-ordination of Allied strategy in the final phase of the Second World War. Consequently, agreements on matters pertaining to the U.N. did not always receive the full and deliberate attention they deserved. For example, a plan was accepted for voting procedures in the future Security Council which later became the subject of heated controversy. The British and American leaders also promised Stalin that they would support the principle of separate memberships in the U.N. for the Byelorussian and Ukrainian Soviet Socialist Republics. In return Stalin was prepared to grant the United States two additional votes; but the American government never took advantage of the offer. It was also agreed at Yalta that a special conference would meet at San Francisco to prepare a formal Charter for the new organization.

The sudden, tragic death of President Roosevelt in mid-April, and already-mounting indications of disagreement between the Western Powers and the Soviet Union over the future of Poland, cast shadows over the meeting of national representatives at San Francisco on April 25, 1945. In other respects, the proceedings lacked the drama of the peace conference which had gathered at Versailles at the end of the First World War. The very fact that the Versailles conference attempted simultaneously to hammer out a peace settlement and establish a new world organization had lent a note of urgency to the deliberations which was absent at San Francisco. Again, in 1919, the leaders of the victorious Allies had attended in person, while in 1945 Churchill, Stalin, and Truman remained in their capitals, exercising their influence through their representatives in San Francisco. It has also been suggested that a world still reeling under the impact of the League's failure approached the U.N. experiment with understandable reserve and caution.

The most critical issue debated at the founding conference concerned the use of the veto in the proposed Security Council. From the beginning of discussions, the major Allies (Britain, the United States, China, and Russia) had agreed that in the new organization they must retain the principal responsibility for the maintenance of world peace. Although undemocratic in the sense that the Great Powers were unwilling to share their heavy burden equally with the smaller nations, this principle actually reflected a realistic approach to the problem. Indeed, lacking such a guarantee, the Powers would have been disinclined to join the U.N., which certainly could not have functioned successfully in their absence.

Voting arrangements within the Security Council were not easily settled, however. Apart from the five *permanent* seats on the Council (France having been invited to join the "Big Four"), there were to be six additional members elected by the General Assembly for two-year terms.[1] Each member would have one vote. But what rules were to regulate the veto powers of the permanent members? This issue threatened to disrupt the conference. At one stage discussions were virtually stalled for an entire week before agreement was reached. Eventually the method of voting decided at Yalta was written into the Charter. On all but "procedural" matters, of relatively minor concern, each of the Great Powers had the right to veto any action of which it disapproved. In the years that followed, the Soviet Union frequently exercised this right. Inevitably, arguments also developed over the definition of "procedural" matters. On the other hand, the rules permitted a major Power to abstain from voting without defeating a particular measure.

On June 26, 1945, the Charter of the U.N. was signed by the representatives of the fifty nations meeting at San Francisco. More than two hundred delegates took a full eight hours to inscribe their names on the documents. Over 2 600 correspondents, writing in many languages, described the event to readers throughout the world. Before the end of the following month, President Truman obtained the American Senate's approval of the Charter and, by October 24, the remaining Great Powers together with the majority of other signatory states added the necessary ratifications to bring the Charter into effect.

2. ORGANIZATION OF THE U.N.

The purposes of the U.N. are set forth in the first Article of Chapter I of the Charter:

1. To maintain international peace and security, and to that end: to take effective collective measures for the prevention and removal of threats to the peace, and for the suppression of acts of aggression or other breaches of the peace, and to bring about by peaceful means, and in conformity with the principles of justice and international law, adjustment or settlement of international disputes or situations which might lead to a breach of the peace;

[1]The number of elected members to the Council was increased to ten in 1965. Canada was elected a member in 1948, 1958, 1966, 1968 and 1978.

2. To develop friendly relations among nations based on respect for the principle of equal rights and self-determination of peoples, and to take other appropriate measures to strengthen universal peace;

3. To achieve international co-operation in solving international problems of an economic, social, cultural, or humanitarian character and in promoting and encouraging respect for human rights and for fundamental freedoms for all without distinction as to race, sex, language, or religion; and

4. To be a centre for harmonizing the actions of nations in the attainment of these common ends.

The principal organs of the United Nations are the General Assembly, the Security Council, and the Secretariat, all of which perform vital tasks in the general functions of the organization.

The relationship between the General Assembly and the Security Council has been affected considerably by the changing forces of international politics. One of the most significant developments has been the emergence of the "Afro-Asian Group," colonies in Africa and the Far East that have achieved independence since the Second World War. Twenty years after its founding the U.N. numbered 114 members,[1] over half of them former African and Asian colonies. Since every member in the General Assembly has an equal vote—in theory a small nation like Sierra Leone has the same voice as the United States—the control of the Assembly has virtually passed into the hands of these new countries, who have shown considerable independence in relation to the Security Council. Although the non-permanent membership of the Council has also been increased to take into account the changing composition of the Assembly, the existence of the Great Powers' veto means there is always the possibility of the two bodies pursuing divergent policies.

Paradoxically, however, frequent use of the veto in the Council, notably by the U.S.S.R., has given greater significance to the deliberations of the Assembly. On occasions when action has been paralysed in the Council, the world's attention has tended to focus on recommendations made by the larger body. The U.N. Assembly has been able to take the initiative because, unlike its counterpart in the League, the former does not require unanimity—a two-thirds majority is sufficient to settle any issue. Thus the majority

---

[1] By 1979 there were 151 member states in the U.N.

A view of the United Nations General Assembly in session. Nikita Khrushchev is at the speaker's rostrum. The Canadian delegation can be seen in the lower left corner.

opinion in the Assembly has become identified with the neutralist, or "non-aligned" policies of those smaller states who have no wish to be crushed by struggles between the major Powers.

The position of the Assembly was greatly strengthened in November, 1950, by adoption of what is known as the "Uniting for Peace" resolution.[1] Henceforth, when the Council was unable to act because of the veto, an emergency session of the Assembly could be called by the Secretary-General on only twenty-four hours' notice. This is the present situation: provided that a two-thirds vote can be mustered in support of appropriate action, the Assembly is authorized to make recommendations for "collective measures, including, in the case of a breach of the peace or an act of aggression, the use of armed force." Consequently, the "Uniting for Peace" resolution can be used to break a deadlock resulting from limitations on the activities of the Council.

The Secretariat

In any organization the Secretariat performs a vital role—preserving records, assuring continuity of direction, and assisting and carrying out the wishes of its executive. This role is emphasized in the organization of the U.N. by the duties of the Secretary-

[1]The circumstances under which the "Uniting for Peace" resolution was passed are discussed below on pp. 649-650.

General and his numerous staff, who must, of course, cope with intricate multilingual problems in addition to the normal tasks of administration. The first Secretary-General chosen by the U.N. was Trygve Lie, previously Foreign Minister of Norway; in 1953 he was succeeded by the Director-General of the Swedish Foreign Ministry, Dag Hammarskjöld, who served until his death (1961) in a plane crash while on duty. U Thant, previously chief delegate of Burma to the U.N., then took over these heavy responsibilities. In 1972 he was succeeded by Kurt Waldheim, the Austrian Federal Minister for Foreign Affairs, who earlier in his career had been his country's ambassador to Canada.

The Charter states specifically that members of the Secretariat are to consider themselves *international* officials responsible only to the U.N. The Secretariat combines a high standard of efficiency with due regard for the widest possible geographical representation in its staff. In one important respect, the Secretary-General enjoys a much more significant role than his predecessor in the League. If in his opinion any matter threatens the maintenance of international peace and security, he is empowered to bring the matter directly to the attention of the Security Council. In other words, he is given a status for this purpose equivalent to that of a member state. He is, in fact, recognized as "a kind of conscience for the world."

Other Principal Organs of the U.N.

Apart from the General Assembly, the Security Council, and the Secretariat, the principal organs of the U.N. are the International Court of Justice, the Trusteeship Council, and the Economic and Social Council.

The International Court of Justice, although a new body created by the U.N. Charter, really perpetuates the old Permanent Court of International Justice established in conjunction with the League of Nations. The Court consists of fifteen judges elected for nine-year terms, one-third retiring every three years. Care has been taken to ensure that no more than one judge from any one country sits on the bench at any one time; also that the principal legal systems of the world are always represented in the Court. However, the founding nations at San Francisco, as at Versailles, refused to make recourse to the Court obligatory. Consequently each member state determines for itself the extent, if any, to which it is prepared to accept the Court's jurisdiction. Political differences between the western and the Communist blocs have prevented the Court from assuming a more important function.

One of the most important organs of the U.N., reflecting the growing concern of world opinion for international justice and equality of opportunity, is the Trusteeship Council. Its main purpose is to administer territories whose inhabitants have not yet achieved their independence. The League of Nations had instituted a system of mandates by which the major Powers, especially Britain, France, and Japan, assumed special obligations for the government and welfare of former German colonies and other areas such as Syria, Palestine, and Mesopotamia. This enlightened concept was adopted and extended by the U.N. The Trusteeship Council, operating under the authority of the General Assembly, considers reports and petitions submitted with respect to trust territories, and arranges periodic visits of inspection. The primary concern of the Council is the political, economic, social, and educational advancement of the inhabitants.

Perhaps the most difficult problem of international trusteeships has arisen in connection with South West Africa, originally a German colony and later a mandate, under the League Covenant, of the Union of South Africa. The latter has steadily refused to recognize the jurisdiction of the U.N. in this matter, although other African states have repeatedly attempted to bring the problem before the world organization. Much of the bitterness generated by this issue is due to the South African government's extension of its policy of *apartheid* (rigorous separation of white and black races, and racial discrimination against "non-whites") to the former colony. Ethiopia and Liberia brought the jurisdictional problem before the International Court of Justice in 1960 and again in 1966. However the Court's opinion was inconclusive on the vital questions of whether the mandate was still in existence, and whether, of its *own* accord, South Africa could alter the terms of its original obligation to South West Africa. Meanwhile, the resentment of new African states is mounting against what appears to be a policy inconsistent with the objectives of the U.N. Charter.

As far back as the formation of the League of Nations, statesmen realized that the causes of war could be economic, social, and cultural no less than political. Appreciation of the importance of non-political factors (intensified by the impact of the Depression) had led, in 1934, to the convening of a World Economic Conference under the auspices of the League. Although this gathering achieved little because of the complexity of the problem, leaders in the post-war world did not lose sight of the overall significance of these factors in the preservation of future peace and stability.

As provided in the U.N. Charter, the Economic and Social Council is to investigate "international economic, social, cultural, educational, health, and related matters" and make recommendations to the General Assembly. In particular, the Council is charged with responsibility for "promoting respect for, and observance of, human rights and fundamental freedoms for all." Originally composed of eighteen members—later increased to twenty-seven—elected by the Assembly, the Council works on a basis of voluntary co-operation through a wide range of subordinate commissions. These are concerned with such important matters as transportation and communications, human rights, the status of women, technical assistance, and narcotic drugs. There are also regional commissions to deal with the special problems of Europe, Latin America, Asia, and the Far East.

Many other specialized agencies carry forward the important non-political tasks of the U.N. These include the International Labour Organization (a survival of the old League framework) dealing with labour problems throughout the world; the World Health Organization, a new agency waging war on disease; the International Monetary Fund, assisting member states with financial problems; the International Atomic Energy Commission, promoting peaceful uses of nuclear power, and the United Nations Children's Fund, furthering child welfare.

3. THE UNITED NATIONS IN ACTION

A review of the U.N.'s record as a peace-keeping organization reveals both strengths and weaknesses. In a number of severe crises, which threatened to erupt into large-scale wars, the U.N. has taken positive action to stabilize situations—even though it could not provide "final" solutions.

Korea

The first major test of the new organization came in 1950, in Korea. When the war began the Soviet Union was not attending the Security

Council, in protest against that body's recognition of the Nationalist Chinese instead of the newly-formed Communist Chinese Republic. Accordingly the Council was able to take immediate action that certainly would have been vetoed if the Soviet representative had been present. The United States at once brought the issue before the Security Council, which took prompt and resolute steps to counter the aggression. The Soviet Union quickly returned to the Security Council and, thereafter, the Russian representative repeatedly vetoed further action to support the U.N. Force. It was at this time that the Assembly adopted the "Uniting for Peace" resolution to break the deadlock in the Council.

The U.N. was not able to achieve its object of a unified, democratic, and independent Korea. On the other hand, by taking immediate positive action, the organization showed in its first major test that it would not succumb to the weak example of the League of Nations when confronted with open aggression, such as had occurred in Manchuria and Ethiopia. The U.N. also demonstrated that it would not permit a stalemate in the Security Council, resulting from the use of a Great Power's veto, to neutralize action by the General Assembly. (The Assembly assumed responsibility for the later phases of the war and arranged the truce at Panmunjon.) Nevertheless, it was also clear that the Assembly could only *recommend* action to member states. Moreover, the preponderance of American troops and equipment on the Korean battlefield gave the operations more of an American than a U.N. character, causing deep concern to supporters of the world organization who feared that it might lose control of operations.

The Suez Crisis

Only three years after the war ended in Korea, a new crisis confronted the U.N., this time at the Suez Canal. After the Second World War, the Western Powers, notably the United States, had offered Egypt financial assistance in building the huge Aswan Dam across the Nile River. This undertaking was vital to the economy of Upper Egypt, offering the prospect of harnessing the flood waters of the world's longest river for a vast irrigation project, and providing a great hydro-electrical potential.

What might have been an outstanding example of international co-operation was jeopardized when Colonel Nasser, the determined and resourceful President of Egypt, began to exhibit strongly pro-Soviet feelings. This attitude so antagonized the Western Powers that, led by the United States, they withdrew their offer of financial aid. Nasser's answer was to seize and nationalize the Suez Canal, in violation of the International Convention governing its operation. Meanwhile trouble was brewing in another quarter. Israel, which had been in open or concealed conflict with its Arab neighbours ever since the inauguration of the Jewish state in 1948, believed that Egyptian control of the Canal would mean the interruption of shipping bound for her ports. Israeli intelligence had also uncovered evidence of an Arab intention to mount a "holy war" against their country in the near future. Accordingly the Israelis determined to seize the initiative with a "preventive war," and on October 29, 1956, they launched a carefully-planned attack against larger Egyptian formations in the Sinai Desert. Smashing through the enemy's defences, the Israelis headed for the Suez Canal, while Nasser appealed to the U.N.

At this critical stage Britain and France intervened in the conflict. Smarting under the impact of Nasser's seizure of the Canal, and apprehensive of the growth of extremist nationalism in the Arab world, they agreed to join forces in an attack on Egypt. It is doubtful whether the Anglo-French operation was planned in conjunction with the Israeli attack, but both Britain and France knew of preparations for the latter, and their action against Egyptian defences in the Canal Zone began only two days after the Israeli invasion. Within the following week British and French parachute troops dropped on the northern end of the Canal and advanced on Cairo. Confronted by three powerful adversaries, Egypt seemed on the verge of imminent defeat.

But world opinion quickly consolidated against what many observers regarded as a revival of old-fashioned European imperialism. Both the United States and the Soviet Union announced their opposition to the intervention in Egyptian affairs, the U.S.S.R. going so far as to issue an ultimatum calling on the aggressors to desist from further attacks or face the possibility of rocket attacks.

Due to British and French exercise of the veto, there was no opportunity to introduce restraining measures in the Security Council. Thus, the Assembly again took action under the "Uniting for Peace" resolution. By an overwhelming vote on November 2, 1956, the Assembly adopted an American resolution urging an immediate ceasefire and the withdrawal of invading forces. At a late session of the exhausted Assembly, Lester Pearson, head of the Canadian delegation, suggested the formation of a United Nations Emergency Force (U.N.E.F.) to restore peace in the troubled area. In short order the Assembly approved detailed proposals for the Force, Britain and France agreed to withdraw their troops, and on November 15 the first contingent of the U.N.E.F. landed in Egypt. Much of the credit for the success of the difficult negotiations leading to this solution was due to Pearson, who, largely for his efforts in the emergency, was later awarded the Nobel Prize for Peace; and to the Secretary-General, Dag Hammarskjöld. All British and French troops were evacuated from Egypt before the end of 1956, and Israel withdrew her forces early in the following year.

U.N.E.F. was built up to a strength of about five thousand men from ten member states of the U.N. Excluded from the composition of this international police force were contingents from the permanent members of the Security Council and Near Eastern countries located in the vicinity of the disputed area. From its arrival in 1956, U.N.E.F. continued to patrol the frontier separating the Gaza Strip from Israel and the Sinai border between Egypt and Israel until withdrawn in 1967 at the demand of Nasser.

The Congo Crisis

U.N.E.F. served as a model for a similar organization in 1960 when the U.N. was called upon to take direct action in the former Belgian Congo. The difficulties which arose in this area are a good illustration of the dangers inherent in too swift a transition from colonial status to independence. Before 1960 the Congo had been ruled by a paternalistic Belgian administration, and the native population was far from being prepared to assume the heavy responsibilities of self-government. Only a small proportion of the people had received adequate education for such a role, and tribal rivalries cut across nationalist sentiment. Nevertheless, during the post-war wave of anti-colonialism which swept Africa and Asia, many other African colonies achieved independence. Their example, together with rising hostility to white residents in Leopoldville and elsewhere, convinced the Belgian government that independence must be conceded without delay. Consequently, a proclamation by King Baudouin on June 30, 1960, transformed the Belgian Congo into the independent Republic of the Congo.

There was a tragic sequel. Even while Belgians were leaving the country, the native Congolese army mutinied, and the new government proved unable to maintain order. In the resulting chaos a separatist movement, encouraged by Belgian business interests, gathered momentum in the rich mining province of Katanga. Worse still, the Soviet Union showed definite signs of interfering in the affairs of the new Republic.

Realizing the serious implications of the Congolese situation, Secretary-General Hammarskjöld for the first time exercised the special authority given him by Article 99 of the Charter to bring the matter directly before the Security Council. Arrangements were quickly made for a U.N. Force, originally composed exclusively of troops from African states, to enter the Congo while Belgian soldiers were evacuating the country. Unfortunately the Belgian withdrawal was delayed, giving the U.S.S.R. another opportunity to threaten intervention. Belgian compliance with the wishes of the U.N. was assured only after the Secretary-General warned the Security Council that "peace or war—and not only in the Congo" was the only alternative.

The international force in the Congo, eventually including Swedish, Irish, and Canadian, as well as African components, reached a peak strength of nearly twenty thousand men. It performed an exceedingly difficult task: restoring order among warring factions, supervising the distribution of food, and safeguarding the public health. A major problem was the necessity of bringing the rebellious province of Katanga back under the control of the central government. It was while visiting the Congo in this connection that the tireless Hammarskjöld was killed in an airplane crash. His efforts had not been in vain—the Republic of the Congo gradually regained a measure of stability, and by the end of 1963 the U.N. was able to reduce its military commitment to little more than five thousand men. With increased Belgian co-operation, the Republic seems destined for a more hopeful future.

Cyprus

Another area of international tension where a U.N. Peace-Keeping Force has played a major role has been Cyprus. An important naval base acquired by Britain in 1878, the island occupies a strategic position at the eastern end of the Mediterranean, facing exits from the Dardanelles and the Suez Canal. Its problems stem from two contradictory factors: the composition of the population, and the island's location in relation to neighbouring states. About eighty per cent of the population is Greek, the remainder being almost entirely Turkish. On the other hand, Cyprus is only sixty-four kilometres from the Turkish mainland, but over nine hundred kilometres from Greece.

Smouldering tension between Greeks and Turks, who have traditionally been the bitterest of enemies, burst into flames after the Second World War. British policy combined stern measures such as the imposition of martial law with attempts to reach a lasting solution agreeable to both factions, but terrorism in the form of riots, bombings, and assassinations hampered the progress of negotiations. In 1960, a compromise was achieved whereby an independent Republic of Cyprus was created, backed by a joint guarantee of Britain, Greece, and Turkey. The constitution included provision for a Greek President, a Turkish Vice-President (with a veto on major policies) and a ratio of seven Greeks to three Turks in the assembly and public services.

Unfortunately, racial animosities wrecked this attempted solution. The Greek population never fully relinquished its desire for *enosis* (union) with Greece; Greeks also resented the disproportionate representation accorded to Turkish inhabitants. The latter, for their part, remained suspicious of Greek sincerity.

When renewed civil strife occurred in Cyprus on a large scale, the U.N. realized it had to intervene. Over and above the internal problems of the island loomed the ominous danger of direct intervention by both Greece and Turkey, with incalculable international consequences.[1] Therefore early in 1964, the U.N. despatched a Peace-Keeping Force, which once again included Canadian troops, to Cyprus to maintain order. This precautionary action was unable to prevent a further outbreak of hostilities in 1974. After an attempted *coup d'état* by Greek elements, the Turkish Army intervened and occupied a large area of the island. Eventually, the U.N. Peace-Keeping Force was able to re-establish a measure of order. But the future of Cyprus remains a critical problem. Together with

---

[1] An added complication for the Western Powers was the fact that both Greece and Turkey were members of the North Atlantic Treaty Organization.

disputes over territorial limits on the mainland and oil-drilling rights in the Aegean, the Cypriot issue is likely to be a serious barrier to better Greek-Turkish relations in the future.

4. THE U.N.: A TENTATIVE EVALUATION

Has the U.N. been an efficient instrument of world co-operation? Has it achieved the objectives stated in its Charter? Can it look forward with confidence to its future role in the nuclear age? No clear-cut answers can be provided to these questions. However, on the basis of its past record, the U.N. has revealed certain strengths and weaknesses.

Critics of the U.N. emphasize flaws in the organization—for example, the paralysing veto exercised by the Great Powers in the Security Council (although without this provision the U.N. could never have been created).

For many years the absence of any Chinese representation was another source of weakness. No "world" organization that officially ignored one-quarter of the globe's population could claim to be truly representative. This glaring omission was not rectified until 1971, when China was finally admitted to the U.N. and took her seat on the Security Council. Nevertheless, Chinese representatives made no secret of their determination eventually to restore Chinese rule over Taiwan (formerly Formosa).

The Assembly and the Secretary-General have shown commendable courage and initiative in dealing with crises that have arisen through the inability of the Security Council to function. Yet it must be clearly recognized that the powers of the Assembly and the Secretary-General are closely limited and defined. Moreover, the Assembly must be seen as a purely *voluntary* organization; it is in no sense a "World Parliament of Man" with executive authority, except in very precisely-defined circumstances. For example, the Charter forbids members to interfere in the internal affairs of sovereign states. In practice this has meant that the U.N. was excluded from dealing with the Algerian war for independence from France, the conflict of Egypt and Saudi Arabia in the Yemen, and the upheavals in South-East Asia.

The weakness of the U.N. was strikingly demonstrated by the Soviet Union's brutal repression of the Hungarian Revolution in 1956. The U.N. could only look on helplessly while Soviet tanks and bombers crushed the Hungarian hopes for freedom. Again,

Secretaries-General of the United Nations

Trygve Lie (1946-1953)

Dag Hammarskjold (1953-1961)

U. Thant (1961-1971)

Kurt Waldheim
(1971-   )

This waterpump was installed by UNICEF as part of its program to bring safe drinking water to rural Bangladesh.

during the Cuban crisis six years later, the U.N. was forced into the role of an apprehensive spectator while the American President, John F. Kennedy, warned the Soviet Union to withdraw its missiles or face retaliatory action. Eventually Russia complied—but the solution to a grave issue which might have exploded into a global nuclear war had been found, not in action taken by the U.N., but in a direct exchange of messages between the White House and the Kremlin. The U.N. was also unable to prevent the Hungarian tragedy from being re-enacted in Czechoslovakia in 1968. Similarly, the American government had taken matters into its own hands, by forcibly intervening in the Dominican Republic in 1965 to overthrow a government which it feared was showing signs of being "unfriendly."

Almost certainly the most serious failures of the U.N. have been its inability to prevent the outbreak of hostilities on a large scale in the Middle and Far East. The Sino-Soviet conflict of interests in South-east Asia and elsewhere has magnified the dangers of the international situation. While some form of stalemate may serve as a temporary answer to these grave problems, the risk of a world conflict through the "escalation" of rival forces remains a terrible possibility.

Nevertheless, while conceding that there are many flaws in the U.N. organization, most impartial observers would agree that it has become a much more flexible and efficient instrument of collective action than its predecessor at Geneva. In a number of serious crises—notably in Korea, Egypt, the Congo, and Cyprus—the U.N. diverted aggressive nations and restored order. Moreover, the great social and humanitarian tasks performed by the U.N. would in themselves be sufficient justification for its existence. Medicine, engineering, and finance may finally open the door to an improved political prospect.

Perhaps most important, the U.N. has achieved a life of its own, independent of the policies of member states. The organization gives visible and continuing expression to certain rules of behaviour which members solemnly support in theory, if not always in practice. Erected on a purely voluntary basis, the U.N. is equipped to mediate, to advise, to encourage—on occasion even to warn and to act decisively. Further progress in the direction of maintaining international peace and security will depend on the willingness of member states to use the magnificent facilities at their disposal.

26 New Nations in Old Continents

"A hungry man is not a free man."

—Adlai Stevenson, 1952

By the middle of the 20th century a political transformation of great potential significance was sweeping Asia and Africa. For centuries these vast continents had remained generally under western (that is, European) domination: political control and economic exploitation were two sides of the same coin. In practice it mattered little whether "trade followed the flag" or vice versa. Yet it was inevitable that the disruptive force of nationalism, which had exerted decisive influence on European and American history, would eventually reach and transform the destinies of other continents.

There was a sombre background to these developments. Oriental cultures of great antiquity had paid a heavy price for their attempt to ignore the scientific and technological advances of western "barbarians." As we have seen, Japan was the only country in the Far East able to embark upon modernization without loss of independence. In Africa only Ethiopia and Liberia retained their autonomy. Elsewhere, huge native populations were either under the direct rule of colonial Powers or were within their "spheres of influence." Even the vast mass of loosely-organized China was effectively dominated by European interests.

It could be argued, with some justification, that western influence had brought material and spiritual progress to many primitive communities where tribal wars and savage rituals had been suppressed and sanitation and education introduced. Too often, however, these benefits had been conferred by imperial authorities in the expectation that alien rule would thereby prove more acceptable to the natives. The ultimate source of authority in the Asiatic and African colonies was the superior military force of the occupying Power—and, since such garrisons are always expensive, the subject populations laboured to supply the wealth which partly maintained the machinery of colonial rule. Meanwhile, in far-off capitals such as London, Paris, and Brussels, and in other great commercial centres, western business and industry developed a lucrative two-way traffic: importing raw materials from and exporting finished products to the colonies.

Signs of Asian and African restlessness under the European yoke had appeared in the 19th century, indicating a smouldering anti-foreign spirit, shared by peoples as widely separated as Egyptians and Burmese. This trend was sharply accentuated after the turn of the present century. Two World Wars strengthened Asiatic and African movements for independence by weakening European controls and stimulating the political consciousness of native populations.

1. ANTI-COLONIALISM IN INDIA AND PAKISTAN

In no country was this development more pronounced than in India, long the brightest jewel in the British imperial crown. This was partly due to deliberate British policy, which followed a far-sighted programme of gradually conceding an increasing measure of self-government to India, while retaining firm control over vital matters such as defence and foreign policy. Tragically, the Indian problem was rendered almost insoluble by racial and religious complications. Of these by far the most significant was the fatal division between Hindus and Moslems. The latter had invaded India from the north at the beginning of the modern era and established a Mogul Empire which, in turn, was succeeded by British rule in the 18th century. Thus a former ruling class, a Moslem minority, found itself threatened by the great Hindu majority as India moved from colonial status towards autonomy and democracy.

Major figures in the movement towards independence were the great Hindu leader, Mahatma Gandhi, and his successor, Jawaharlal Nehru. Over a period of almost three decades, from the end of the First World War to the gaining of independence (1947), Gandhi was the key figure on the Indian scene. Born in 1869, he had studied law in England before practising his profession, principally in defence of his countrymen, in South Africa. During this formative

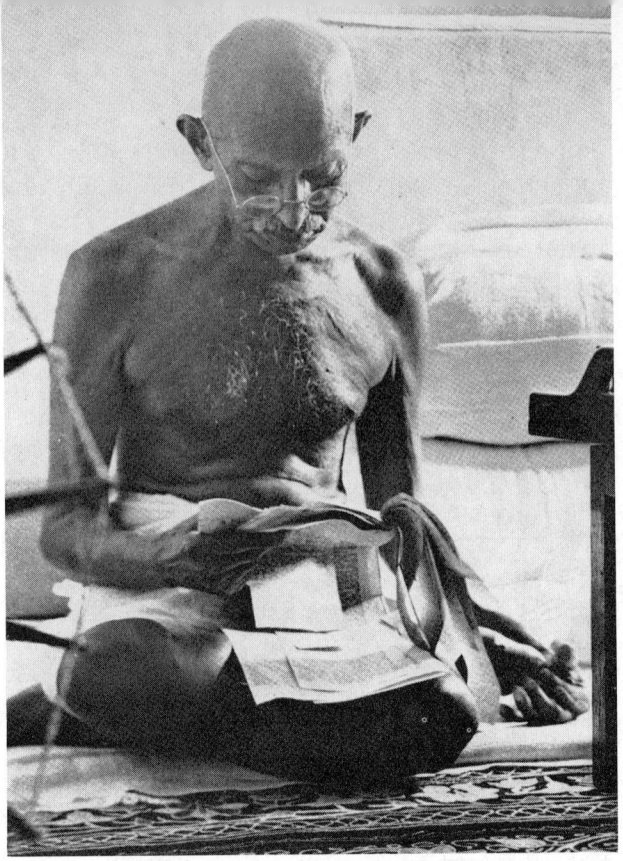

"People describe me as a saint trying to be a politician, but the truth is the other way around." — Mahatma Gandhi

period of his life he developed his unique philosophy of *satyagraha*, sometimes described as "passive resistance," which sought victory not through force, but by the conversion of an opponent by one's own suffering. In other words, moral pressure became an effective substitute for direct action.

Gandhi's great contribution was to adapt this "non-violent" approach to the alleviation of his country's problems. However it is only fair to point out that the success of this principle in India (as, to some extent, in later civil demonstrations of Negroes in the United States) was at least partly due to the government's reluctance to adopt a policy of coercion. Less humane methods adopted by other colonial Powers led to tragic developments in Indo-China, Indonesia, and Africa.

Gandhi's influence on his countrymen—and, indeed, on sympathizers in other lands—is difficult to define. Like a few other notable figures in history, he was a deceptively humble man, a mixture of mysticism and realism. Nehru has given a graphic description of his hypnotic voice: "It was quiet and low, and yet it could be heard above the shouting of the multitude; it was soft and gentle, and yet there seemed to be steel hidden away somewhere in it; it was courteous and full of appeal, and yet there was something grim and frightening in it; every word used was full of meaning and seemed to carry a deadly earnestness."

Recognizing India's valuable contribution to the Allied cause in the First World War, the British government promised her ultimate self-government. However, a full generation passed before the promise was fulfilled. During this troubled period, Gandhi frequently collided with the British authorities. His protests against official policy took the form of organized campaigns of civil disobedience, in which he continually repudiated violent action. So strict was he in the observance of this principle that when, at the height of one of his demonstrations, a single act of violence occurred in a remote village, he immediately called off his campaign. With his simplicity of dress, his spinning-wheel and goat's milk, he became a living symbol of the aspirations of millions of Indians.

Gandhi's tactics were well illustrated by the famous Salt March of 1930. Protesting the government's salt monopoly, he set out with seventy-eight disciples on a long walk to the sea. The march gained world-wide attention as movie cameras recorded its progress from village to village. Finally, at the end of the twenty-four-day journey, the *Mahatma* (Great Soul) reached the coast and ceremonially disobeyed the government by picking up salt lying on the shore. This simple act caused an explosion of anti-British feeling in India. Before the end of the year ninety thousand persons had been arrested, a boycott of foreign goods was in effect, and trouble had broken out on the north-west frontier. This widespread activity has been described as "the first truly mass political movement in Indian nationalism."

Following a series of Round Table Conferences in London, the British government responded to the demand for reform by passing the Government of India Act in 1935. This virtually conferred responsible government on the provinces of British India and provided a basis for an all-India Federation of the provinces and the

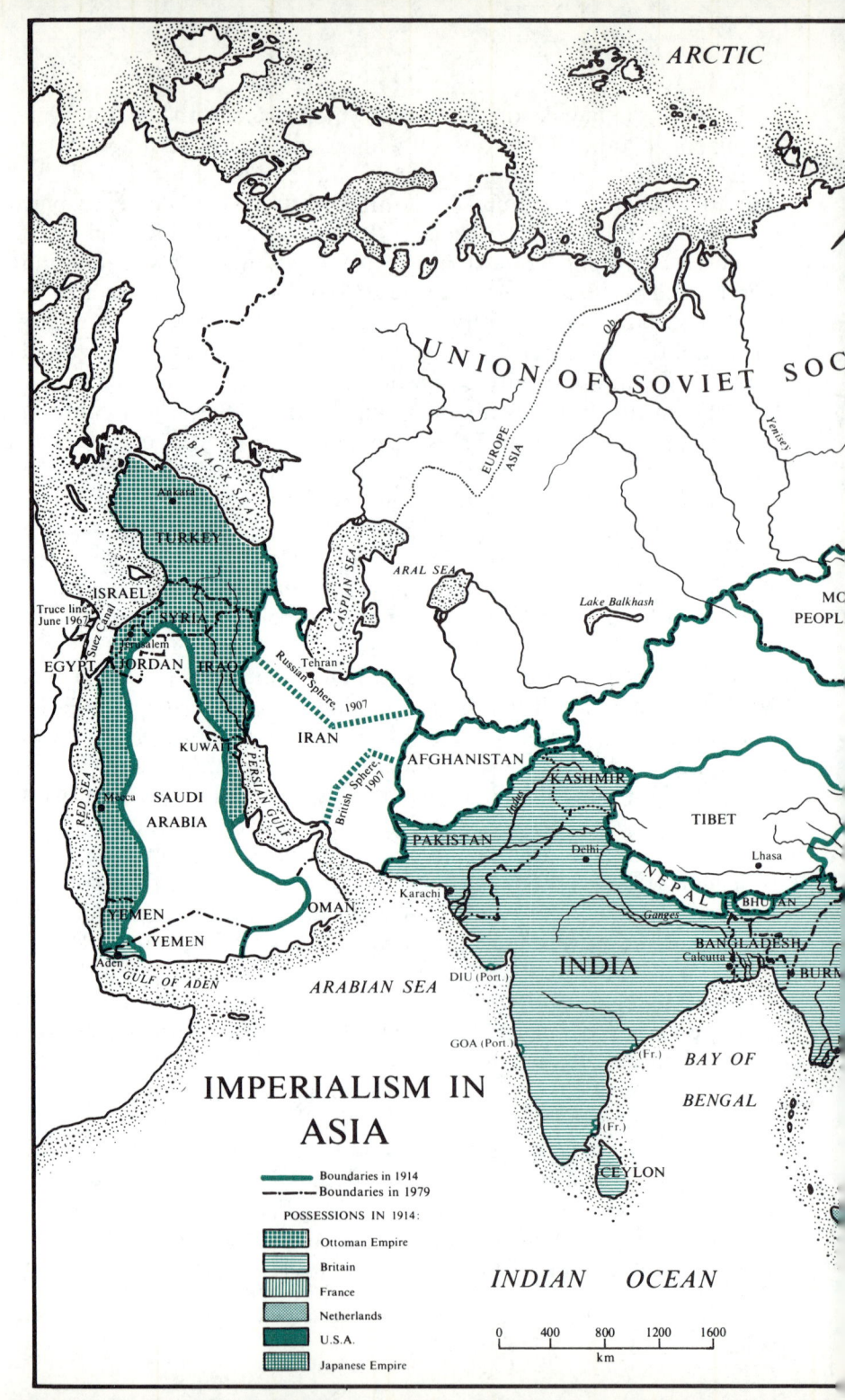

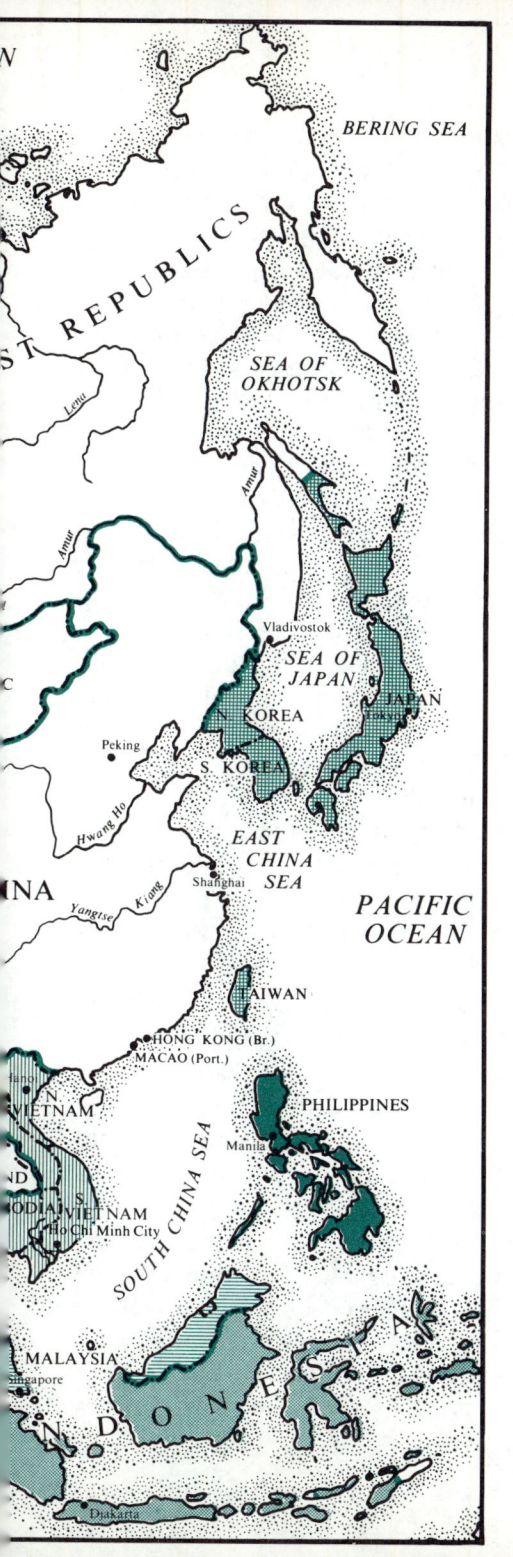

six hundred princely states, which had retained separate treaties with the British Crown. Concessions to the principle of self-government included provisions for provincial legislatures elected by a larger proportion of the population than in the past.

Nevertheless, the British government was still not prepared to go the entire distance and grant full independence. Over ninety articles in the Act reserved "discretionary powers" for the Viceroy, who also retained control over defence, external affairs, ecclesiastical matters, and sensitive frontier areas. Yet the Government of India Act was, in general, so well drafted that it became the basis of the Indian constitution after the achievement of independence.

The Second World War hastened the trend towards the realization of Indian aims. In 1942, with the Japanese in Burma, the British government realized the necessity of conciliating Indian nationalists. A special mission was sent from London offering Dominion status after the war, with the right of secession from the Commonwealth. Although Indian leaders rejected this offer—insisting upon a British policy of "Quit India"—the real difficulty was not so much British reluctance to give up India as mounting tension between Hindus and Moslems within the country.

Eventually it proved impossible to reconcile the aims of Hindus and Moslems. The former insisted upon a united India, after independence, while the latter were equally determined upon Partition. When negotiations broke down after the war there were terrible scenes in India—especially the "Great Calcutta Killing" of 1946, when four thousand people were killed and thousands injured. As the crisis worsened, there began huge migrations—perhaps the largest in history. Moslems fled in the direction of Pakistan, to the north-west, while Hindus and Sikhs concentrated in India proper. In the course of these movements a large-scale war of outright extermination was narrowly avoided; it is estimated that these disorders cost the lives of half a million people, a tragic outcome to Gandhi's campaigns of non-violence.

Soon after his arrival in India as what proved to be the last Viceroy, Lord Louis Mountbatten decided that Partition was the only solution. Under his tactful direction, procedures were worked out to ascertain the wishes of populations in sensitive provinces, such as Bengal and Punjab. An Act was then quickly passed by the British Parliament, and on August 15, 1947, two new states appeared—India and Pakistan. Although completely independent, both retained loose links with the Commonwealth—a striking tribute to British policy. Tragically, Gandhi, who had done so much to further a peaceful solution of his country's problems, was assassinated a few months later by a Hindu fanatic.

The new Prime Minister of India was Nehru, a man of great charm and a forceful personality, with a clear-cut vision of the future of India. He regarded national independence as merely the first step in the modernization of the new state along socialistic lines. However, he was no doctrinaire socialist, preferring in many matters to follow traditionally liberal and humanistic traditions.

Grave problems of policy, both in external and internal affairs, confronted Nehru. It has been said that the main features of the Indian economy in 1947 were "poverty, malnutrition, subsistence agriculture, and relatively little industry." Two-thirds of the huge population, nearing four hundred millions, were illiterate, and seventy per cent depended entirely on agriculture for their living. The gulf between Indian and western living standards was startling: the average income of an Indian was estimated to be about one-thirty-second of that of an American. In rural areas there was only one doctor to twenty-five thousand people and one hospital to fifty thousand.

Would India adopt a capitalist or communist approach to the solution of these problems—or would she find her own road to an improved standard of living for her millions? It might have been assumed that, reacting to centuries of western domination, the new state would adopt the opposing philosophy of communism. On the other hand, racial and religious factors separated India from the Soviet bloc no less than from the West. Moreover, at the time India gained independence, Russia still remained under the ruthless dictatorship of Stalin—and a regime backed by the grim apparatus of a "police state" could not be reconciled with India's newly acquired freedom.

The Indian solution represented a compromise between the alternatives, and its economy is called "mixed" because it represents a combination of capitalist and socialist principles.

In 1951, under Nehru's direction, a series of Five Year Plans were launched to stimulate industrialization and raise living standards. These goals were inconsistent, from a short-range point of view, because the government had to restrain popular consumption and services to the people in order to accumulate savings for steel plants, hydro-electric installations, and factories. Unfortunately these restrictions on public spending were still not enough to provide sufficient funds, and India has been dependent to a large extent on foreign aid for the capitalization of her industrial programme. On the other hand, she has had no difficulty in arranging loans, for the Western Powers (notably the United States) have given generous assistance in the not altogether altruistic hope of diverting India from closer association with the Communist blocs.

The primary cause of the dislocation of the Indian economy has always been the intolerable pressure of a huge population on available agriculture. It is difficult to believe that any scheme of industrialization, however vast and comprehensive, could absorb this population and substantially raise its living standards. The only other alternative appears to be a voluntary limitation of the population, and the Indian Government is taking far-sighted steps to explore this possibility.

In foreign affairs, India soon discovered that independence placed her in a difficult, but at the same time advantageous, position in relation to the competing western and Communist blocs in the Cold War. The danger of a nuclear war between the super-Powers held terrible implications for crowded India. On the other hand, Nehru and his successors have been fully aware of their strong bargaining position by pursuing a policy of neutralism or "non-alignment"—that is, refusing formally to commit India to either side. This attitude is reinforced by Hindu belief that no political system, or philosophy, has a monopoly of virtue, and that ultimately all systems of government represent only means to a common end. But Indian foreign policy has not been merely passive, content to assume the role of an observer—it has consistently sought to promote world peace and nuclear disarmament by co-operation and conciliation. Nehru himself endorsed the maxim that "a wise general is a person who wins battles without fighting." In practice, however, this object has not always been attainable, and since the achievement of independence India has had armed clashes with both her Pakistan and Chinese neighbours.

Not surprisingly, Pakistan pursued a very different foreign policy from that of India. From the beginning of its existence, Pakistan

Jawaharlal Nehru—"the lonely eagle in a flock of birds." "After Gandhi's, his is the one name that stands for India—is India."

threw in its lot with the West, and concluded a military alliance with the United States. However, the main bone of contention between Pakistan and India has not been due to ideological issues of world politics, but to acute differences over the future of Kashmir, a princely state at the northern apex of the frontier between Pakistan and India. When Partition occurred, the majority of the population of Kashmir were Moslems, but it was ruled by a Hindu Maharajah, who brought his state into India.

The passions inflamed by India's efforts to retain Kashmir against Pakistan's claims for possession can be compared with those aroused by Danzig and Trieste in modern European history. For Nehru, the dispute was much more than a territorial matter, as he had always rejected the "two-nations" concept of Moslem and Hindus as separate national identities. Fighting broke out when Pakistan forces occupied a portion of Kashmir, India citing its opponent's action as a reason for refusing to settle the dispute by a plebiscite. A cease-fire was eventually arranged by the United Nations; but there has been little relaxation of tension over the issue, which continues to absorb a disproportionate amount of the defence expenditures of both sides.[1]

India's relations with Communist China have also passed through a critical stage. These large states exercise great influence on their smaller neighbours in South-East Asia, and some degree of competition, political, economic, and cultural, is inevitable. Also, the fact that India has preserved her neutral attitude towards the Cold War, while Communist China has violently criticized both the Soviet and western blocs, has tended to prevent a closer association of the two Asiatic states. Nevertheless, in the period following achievement of independence, India went to some lengths to cultivate good relations with her northern neighbour. Apart from a long tradition of friendly understanding between Asia's oldest civilizations, an Indian conviction that China was preoccupied with internal problems, and a common hatred of European imperialism, India lacked military strength to become involved in a protracted conflict with China.

There was no trouble until 1950, when China occupied Tibet, historically within the Chinese imperial orbit. This action brought Peking and New Delhi face to face along the Himalayan "Roof of the World"—a frontier extending four thousand kilometres from Sinkiang to northern Burma. Four years later, India signed a non-aggression pact with China, formally recognizing Tibet as part of the new Communist state. But a revolt of the Tibetans, followed by the flight of many refugees (including their religious and political leader, the Dalai Lama), who sought asylum in India, caused a break-down in Sino-Indian relations. In 1962 war broke out over this issue, and Chinese forces quickly occupied frontier areas, appearing poised for an invasion of India. Then the Communists abruptly terminated hostilities and withdrew to a line that left them in control of the disputed territory. An uneasy truce followed, leaving the course of future Sino-Indian relations in doubt.

In 1966 Indira Gandhi, Nehru's daughter, became Prime Minister of India, holding power for more than a decade. She instituted a system of "executive democracy" in which her secretariat displaced the Cabinet as the principal source of policy formulation and co-ordination. Her regime coincided with a rapid growth of military and police establishments. Eventually, Gandhi placed India under

[1] After a bloody struggle in 1972 a new state of Bangladesh was formed out of what had formerly been East Pakistan.

Indira Gandhi with Pierre Trudeau

emergency rule, muzzling the press and detaining political opponents. Many of her attempted reforms, particularly those aimed at slum clearance and birth control, aroused popular resentment. She lost the electoral support of Muslims and "Untouchables," who collectively represented over one-quarter of India's 620 000 000 inhabitants. Charges of nepotism and corrupt electoral practices were levelled at the Prime Minister and, in 1977, she was decisively defeated by a loose coalition of her opponents headed by Morarji Desai.

In spite of these grave problems in her internal and external affairs, India has made the difficult transition from colonial to independent status and has dispelled fears about the stability of her government. It must be remembered that, in point of population, she is the world's largest democracy. At a time when underdeveloped countries in other parts of the world are struggling to maintain their autonomy, the Indian example is of great significance.

2. REVOLUTION IN CHINA

We turn now to consider the most dramatic political development of the mid-century—the rise of Communist China to a position among the leading Powers of the world. For centuries this ancient land seemed oblivious of the implications of the Industrial Revolution and western imperialism. Her contacts with Europeans in the 19th century—the infamous "Opium Wars," the coolie trade, and her partial division into western "spheres of influence"—were bitter reminders of her impotence. This feeling of frustration was a factor in the anti-foreign movement that resulted in the Boxer Revolt (1899-1900) and which later (1911) led to the collapse of the inefficient Manchu Dynasty.

The Kuomintang

Out of the resulting turmoil appeared two types of leaders: the "warlords," or military leaders, chiefly interested in furthering their own ambitions, and the young liberal intellectuals, such as Dr. Sun Yat-sen, who became the first President of the Chinese Republic. Born near Canton in 1866, Sun enjoyed the advantage of a western education, first at a British missionary school in Hawaii (where he became a Christian) and later in a medical school at Hong Kong. Early in his career he became convinced that the overthrow of the Manchu government was essential to Chinese progress. He organized a secret revolutionary group, but when its activities within China were suppressed he was forced to flee abroad, spending many years in Japan, the United States, and Europe. Some of his adventures read like pages from a spy thriller.

Even in exile, Sun's dedication to his political task stimulated the growth of underground resistance to the Manchu authority. He was very successful in obtaining financial contributions from Chinese living abroad—whether they were laundrymen in America or millionaires in Singapore. Consequently, when the Manchu Dynasty was finally overthrown, he was the logical leader of the new China.

Dr. Sun founded the Nationalist Party (the *Kuomintang*) to carry out his three principles: national unification, popular government, and social reform. But China was torn by civil war, as the selfish warlords struggled with each other for regional supremacy. The First World War, in which China joined the Allies, resulted in further frustration, for the Versailles Conference gave in to

LEFT: Sun Yat-sen, founder of the Kuomintang, or Nationalist Party. RIGHT: Chiang Kai-shek, who assumed leadership after Sun's death in 1925. Soldier and politician, revolutionary and traditionalist, Christian and Confucian, anti-Communist with a Leninist bias, Chiang embodies the crosscurrents and confusion that have frequently marked the last half century of Chinese history.

Japanese demands for compensation, partly at the expense of China.

Disillusioned by his early failures, Dr. Sun turned to the new Soviet government for assistance in 1923. While the Chinese leader did not agree that the Russian revolutionary system would work in his country, he was glad to receive Soviet help in reorganizing his political party. (From the Russian point of view, the advantages of expanding Communist influence in a suspicious and watchful world were obvious.) The Kuomintang was thoroughly remodelled along the lines of the Russian Communist Party. Simultaneously, Dr. Sun entrusted one of his younger followers, Chiang Kai-shek, with the task of building up a revolutionary army that would be capable of eliminating the warlords and supporting a progressive national government.

After Dr. Sun's death in 1925, Chiang assumed the mantle of leadership. Born in 1887, he came from a family of modest means. He had received military training in Japan, where he had joined Sun's revolutionary organization. At an early stage of their acquaintanceship Sun was impressed with the young officer's strong personality and sense of dedication. This impression was vindicated by Chiang's subsequent career. Three years after taking over the leadership of the Kuomintang, Chiang had suppressed the warlords and established a new Republic with its capital in the south, at Nanking.

The new Republic faced two grave perils: one from outside and the other from within. We have already seen that in the post-First World War period, reactionary forces seized control of the Japanese government, setting it on an imperialistic course.[1] The Manchurian Incident (1931) was the first indication of Japan's new designs on the Chinese mainland—an aggressive, predatory policy which ended fourteen years later with Allied atomic attacks on Hiroshima and Nagasaki.

The Communist Party

A more formidable threat to Chiang Kai-shek's Nationalist government grew up within China. This was the Communist Party, founded by twelve delegates at Shanghai on July 1, 1921. Soviet influence on the new organization was early apparent in its emphasis on iron discipline among members, compulsory subscriptions, obligatory attendance at party meetings, and the curious practice of self-criticism.

Included in the twelve founding delegates was a young man of twenty-seven from Hunan province named Mao Tse-tung—later to become one of the most powerful and influential figures of the 20th century. The son of a moderately prosperous farmer, Mao gave evidence of his independent spirit at an early age in encounters with his father. Pursuing his education against his father's wishes, Mao soon impressed his teachers with his literary knowledge and his grasp of history, geography, and the natural sciences. Later in life he displayed considerable poetic ability, as the following extract from a poem entitled "Loushan Pass" suggests:

> *Cold blows the west wind,*
> *Far off in the frosty air*
> *the wild geese call*
> *in the morning moonlight.*

[1]See above, pp. 504-505.

"... the enemy advances, we retreat; the enemy halts and encamps, we harass him; the enemy seeks to avoid battle, we attack; the enemy retreats, we pursue."—Mao Tse-tung. The illustration shows Mao addressing the students of the Anti-Japanese Military and Political University in Yenan, 1937.

> *In the morning moonlight*
> *Horses' hoofs ring out sharply*
> *And the bugle's note*
> *is muted.*[1]

In his early years Mao led a spartan life. He had a cold bath every day, and never lost his fondness for swimming and mountaineering. (It was reported that, even in old age, he could still swim across the Yangtze River.) His constitution was further toughened by long tramps in the countryside, during which he lived mainly on beans and water. Occasionally he profited by his scholastic talent, writing scrolls for farmers in exchange for food or money. At the time of the formation of the Chinese Communist Party, Mao was working as an assistant in the library of Peking University, where he became absorbed in Marxist literature.

The early Soviet attitude towards the Party is particularly instructive. Initially, Moscow encouraged the Chinese Communists to co-operate with the more conservative Kuomintang on the principle that it offered the best prospect of furthering the revolution. In Stalin's view the Kuomintang was a dictatorship of all classes, which could be converted to Communism at a later date. But Chiang Kai-shek was closely identified with wealthy business interests in the cities (his wife belonged to the influential Soong family, prominent in Chinese financial circles), and he had no intention of becoming a puppet of Moscow. In 1927 he moved swiftly and decisively against the Communist leaders, executing many and forcing others to flee. One of those who escaped was Chou En-lai, afterwards Premier of Communist China. Mao was arrested by the militia, but was able to conceal his identity and eventually regain freedom.

For a time events seemed to favour Chiang Kai-shek's Nationalist government. The Communists were driven back into rural areas and their Russian advisers were expelled from the country. The last of the troublesome warlords retreated into Manchuria, and Peking was occupied by Nationalist troops. Some progress was also made in dealing with China's formidable economic problems: the Finance Minister, T. V. Soong, succeeded in balancing the nation's budget, communications were improved, and, in conjunction with

---

[1] The Pass is south of Chungking, in Kweichow Province. Mao wrote the poem in 1935.

the Secretariat of the League of Nations, exploratory work was carried out in education and public health. Externally, Chiang conducted negotiations with the western Powers to end their extraterritorial rights and other encroachments on Chinese sovereignty.

Nevertheless, the Nationalist government could not simultaneously cope with internal economic and social problems, the growing threat of Japanese aggression, and persistent opposition from the Communist movement within China.

Curiously enough, both the Soviets and the Chinese Nationalists fell victims of the same mistake—exaggerating the significance of urban over rural developments in the future destiny of China. Basing their expectations on the orthodox Marxist theme that social revolution must proceed from the basis of an industrial proletariat, Stalin and his advisers failed to grasp the greater potential of the huge Chinese agrarian population. Similarly, Chiang's government was too sensitive to urban commercial interests to focus attention on the more pressing problem of land reform.

In the early 1930's Chiang adopted a policy of "internal pacification before resistance to external [that is, Japanese] attack." But he could not entirely suppress the Communists, who continued to control elements of the army. Moreover, Mao Tse-tung was actively converting his party to a realization of the importance of the peasantry in the struggle for power. He eloquently described the success of the Hunan peasants in seizing land and sweeping away the privileges of inefficient and corrupt landlords. He predicted: "Within a short time, hundreds of millions of peasants will rise in Central, South, and North China, with the fury of a hurricane; no power, however strong, can restrain them. They will break all the shackles that bind them, and rush towards the road of liberation."

For the time being, however, the Nationalists mobilized sufficient strength to keep the Communists on the defensive. In 1934 Chiang's pressure on the hard core of Communist resistance in south-eastern China forced the Red Army to begin its almost legendary "Long March"—a ninety-six hundred kilometre trek to the far western region of Sinkiang. This march lasted more than a year, during which the original force of over ninety thousand men dwindled to about twenty thousand survivors. Perhaps half the expedition perished in crossing eighteen high mountainous regions, some of which were never free from snow; others fell in numerous major

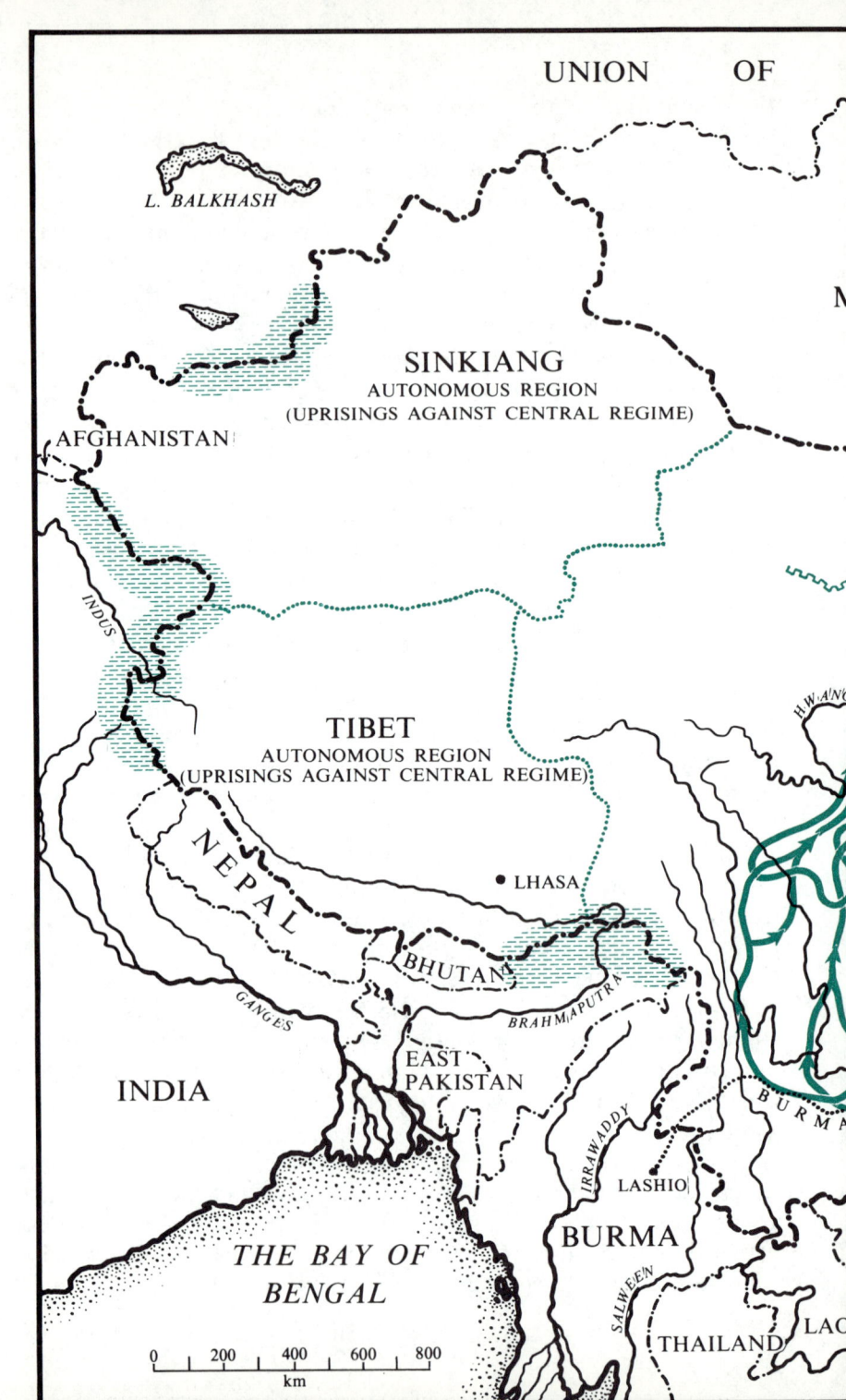

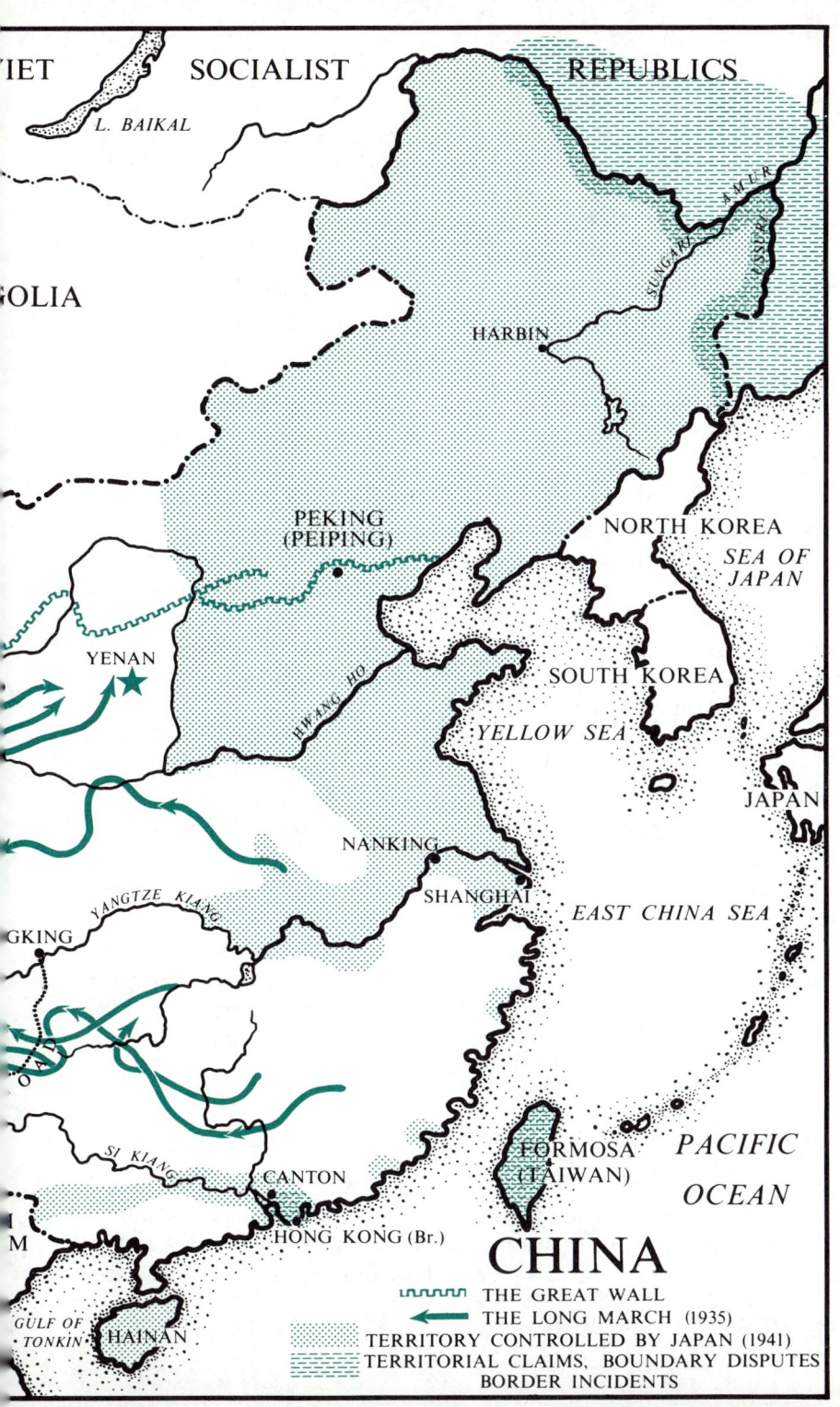

battles fought with the pursuing Nationalists. The remnants endured and eventually reached a remote area, adjacent to the Mongolian steppe, where they could recuperate and launch later counter-offensives to expand their influence. In the course of this ordeal Mao Tse-tung became the undisputed leader of the movement.

Communist propaganda now adopted a new line. Why were Chinese fighting each other instead of resisting Japanese aggression? This question was directed at the Nationalist forces with telling effect; soon the pace of operations against the Red Armies slackened, and dissatisfaction with Chiang's leadership appeared in government ranks. The result was the strange "Sian incident" at the end of 1936, when Chiang was "kidnapped" by his own subordinates and advised to accept Communist proposals for a united front against Japan. Chou En-lai, the Red representative, reinforced these arguments in private conversations with Chiang. The latter refused to give any commitment during his brief period of detention—he was held for thirteen days—but a basis had been established for subsequent negotiations. These led to active cooperation of Communist and Nationalist armies against the Japanese in the war which broke out in 1937 and continued until the Allied defeat of Japan in 1945.

The Sino-Japanese conflict developed into a war of attrition in which Chinese strategy—like that of Russia against Napoleon and Hitler—used space to counter the enemy's technical superiority. Some Allied assistance reached the Chinese from the U.S.S.R. and the Western Powers, notably along the celebrated "Burma Road." In the main, however, China fought the war with her own resources, principally her manpower. The Japanese overran a wide area of the eastern mainland including Peking and all the important ports on the Pacific, but the invaders failed to achieve their ultimate political objective, destruction of the Nationalist government, and Allied victory in Europe meant the inevitable collapse of the Japanese war effort in China as elsewhere.

The Communist Triumph

Even before the end of the war, old antagonisms between Communists and Nationalists resulted in a renewed struggle, behind the scenes, for the future control of the country. So rapid was the accelerated tempo of developments that, only four years after the end of the Sino-Japanese conflict, the Communists had displaced the Nationalists as the dominant political authority in mainland China. The reasons for this convulsion, with far-reaching effects on international affairs, are still the subject of keen controversy among historians. However, it is possible to distinguish certain factors that played an important part in the Communist victory.

It can easily be seen that the long war with Japan favoured the followers of Mao Tse-tung in two significant respects. First, Japanese occupation of the main urban centres in eastern China deprived Chiang Kai-shek of the support of commercial interests with which he had always been identified. Second, the nature of the war, in which guerrilla activity assumed great importance, suited Communist tactics much better than those of the Nationalists. Utilizing their previous experience in organizing the rural peasantry, the Communists were able to gain dominating influence in the regions they took over.

Many other factors contributed to the Nationalist downfall. Driven inland, away from its principal sources of economic strength, Chiang Kai-shek's government had to improvise new means of sustaining the war effort in western China. Unfortunately many of these enterprises were run by officials who acquired undesirable personal interests in the industries under their direction. The government was thereby exposed to charges of inefficiency and corruption.

Moreover, the loss of former commercial revenues compelled the Nationalists to levy unpopular salt and land taxes that bore heavily on the rural population. Being dependent largely on the co-operation of the landlords, Chiang Kai-shek also failed to grapple with the essential problem of land reform, although this was vital to the existence of eighty per cent of the population. Meanwhile, by contrast, the Communist programme of expropriation and dispossession of the landlords exerted an irresistible appeal on the impoverished peasantry. The Kuomintang also alienated its supporters in intellectual circles by its harsh and arbitrary policies. In their desperate efforts to combat the spread of Communism, the authorities exercised an increasingly severe censorship of all attitudes considered critical of the administration. The heavy hand of the authoritarian government was evident in the suppression of free speech, sudden and secret arrests, the disappearance of suspects, and even assassinations. Consequently, large numbers of intellectuals lost their fear of Communism and turned against the government. Chiang Kai-shek himself multiplied the confusion when he tried to centralize all authority, political, military, and economic, in his own hands. In the end he had made himself a symbol of the intolerable situation in China.

The final phase of the long struggle between the Communists and Nationalists began in 1947. Although Chiang Kai-shek enjoyed many advantages at the outset, including American support in the form of military supplies, his strategic errors ruined his chances of victory.[1] Obsessed with the necessity of securing Manchuria and occupying urban centres of Nationalist influence, he adopted a defensive strategy, splitting his numerically superior forces into garrisons and trying to hold as many cities as possible, instead of seeking out and destroying his foes. The Communists, on the other hand, were able to exploit their flexible military organization, consolidating their hold on rural areas, while maintaining an active strategy of cutting supply lines and harassing the Nationalist garrisons. The Communists also profited from the Soviet decision to turn over to them Japanese equipment captured in Manchuria at the end of the Second World War.

In these circumstances the end of the struggle was a foregone conclusion. During the summer of 1949 the Red Armies completed their conquest of southern China. Chiang Kai-shek and his remaining followers fled to Taiwan, where they have remained ever since. The Nationalists have never abandoned their claim to represent the legal government of *all* China; but actual power on the mainland is firmly in the hands of the Communists.

The People's Government of the People's Republic of China was proclaimed on October 1, 1949. In the words of Mao Tse-tung, the new state was to be a "people's democratic dictatorship" in which there would be "democracy for the people and dictatorship for the reactionaries." He defined the latter as the landlords, "bureaucratic capitalists," and elements of the Kuomintang. In practice the Chinese Communist Party (C.C.P.) has been the highly centralized instrument of government, headed by a Council

---

[1] Another important factor was that the United States, mindful of its losses in the Second World War and uncertain about the future of the Cold War, was not prepared to commit ground forces to the struggle.

of fifty-six members originally under the chairmanship of Mao Tse-tung.

The new regime had clear-cut objectives: to industrialize China in the shortest time, to raise the standard of living to that of other modern states, and to deal with the overshadowing problem of land reform. China did not lack the resources needed for industrial development, and in 1953 she inaugurated the first of a series of Five Year Plans. Although the original goals were not attained (an experience comparable to that of the first Soviet Plans), the results were impressive, particularly as viewed by other Asiatic peoples. In 1958 occurred the controversial "Great Leap Forward," when attempts were made to stimulate iron and steel production by building vast numbers of small plants all over the country. Soon, the Communists claimed, fifty million people were engaged in the huge project. (In one Manchurian city, it was stated, 2,855 furnaces were built in two days.) Great public works were also undertaken—such as the construction of dikes, canals, and irrigation schemes—and labour was driven to the point of exhaustion. Yet the results of these titanic efforts, although impressive, disappointed the government, and production quotas cut back to more realistic targets.

Another distinctive feature of life in Red China has been the redistribution of land and the establishment of People's Communes. The Communes are comprised of large groups of people, organized in teams along military lines, to work in agriculture and industry. A Commune may vary in size between tens of thousands and one hundred thousand men and women. They live together in barracks, using common kitchens, with their children cared for in nurseries and schools. There is no private property, the people being supplied with food, clothing, and medical supplies by the government. The workers rise at 06:00 and march to and from their tasks. Husbands and wives frequently work on separate assignments. Evenings are devoted to communal recreation and political indoctrination.

Until his death in 1976, Mao exerted firm control over all aspects of Chinese development. Under the "Great Helmsman" China was virtually isolated from foreign influence while, internally, directed towards self-sufficiency. In order to counter lingering counter-revolutionary influences, and to maintain the momentum of the ideological movement, the Communist Youth League was converted to a "Red Guard" corps in the 1960's. These "Guards" were permitted to harass factory manufacturers, university officials and even high-ranking members of the government. Victims were hauled before kangaroo courts, paraded in streets and subjected to both verbal and physical abuse. The resulting disruption of higher education aggravated China's shortage of trained engineers and scientists.

Events took a very different turn after Mao's death. Under the new leader, Hua Kuo-feng, quick action was taken to suppress the so-called "Gang of Four," an extreme leftist group led by Mao's widow, Chiang Ching. There was a very perceptible movement away from the hitherto slavish attitude towards Maoist ideology. People were no longer compelled to read and memorize *Mao's Thoughts* in the famous little "red books." The main emphasis of the new regime, in which Vice-Premier Teng Hsiao-ping played a very important role, was on relaxation of the regimentation of life and expansion of Chinese diplomatic and commercial contacts abroad. The new leaders of China were primarily concerned with realistic, pragmatic policies which would accelerate China's economic and social development.

In the summer of 1978, Chairman Hua made an unprecedented visit to Europe and the Middle East, exploring the possibilities of closer relations with countries such as Britain, Yugoslavia and Iran. These efforts were supplemented by Teng's negotiations with Japan, Thailand and Malaysia. Most notable was a complete reversal of Chinese hostility towards the United States, culminating in the signing of a treaty on January 1, 1979, by which each state accorded formal recognition to the other.[1]

The Sino-Soviet Dispute

After the Second World War, China emerged as a threat to *both* the Soviet and western blocs. Anti-western sentiment, regularly and violently expressed, is directed mainly against the United States for its continued support of Chiang Kai-shek's regime on Taiwan. For this reason Communist China sent large armies of "volunteers" to fight in the Korean War. More surprising to the western mind, however, was the deep abyss which widened between the Red Chinese and the Soviets. Superficially, both were originally united by Marxist-Leninist doctrines. Yet accumulated tensions of many

---

[1] The treaty was a heavy blow to Taiwan, previously recognized by the United States as the legitimate government of China.

centuries could not be dissipated. Russia and China have a long history of frontier disputes, particularly in such sensitive areas as Outer Mongolia and Manchuria. Also, as we have seen, Stalin was inclined to underestimate the potential strength of Chinese Communism in its early stages. Later, the Kremlin contributed both financial and technical assistance to the development of the new Republic, but this did little to narrow the growing ideological gap between the two countries.

A crisis in Sino-Soviet affairs occurred after the death of Stalin, when Khrushchev and his successors adopted the policy of peaceful coexistence in their contacts with the West. Peking was entirely opposed to what it considered a softening of the "hard line" which hitherto had characterized Communist dealings with the western world. For a time, mutual criticism between the two countries was disguised by the pretext of attacking the other's ideological ally. Thus, China would criticize Yugoslavia rather than the Soviet Union, and the U.S.S.R. would attack Albania when it meant China. Eventually the pretext was dropped, and as the attacks became stronger the opponent was named directly. Chinese criticism of Soviet policy became more and more virulent, until virtually all intercourse between the two states ceased. Finally, the Soviet leaders were denounced as "revisionists," who had betrayed fundamental principles of communism and were collaborating with the United States.

The significance of the bitter dispute between Peking and Moscow is that the former division of the world into Soviet, Western, and neutralist blocs has been modified by the addition of a Red Chinese sphere of influence. In 1967 China detonated her first hydrogen bomb. Four years later she was finally admitted to the U.N. In his first speech before the world assembly, the Chinese representative reaffirmed his nation's claim to Taiwan as an integral part of China.

The radical change in Chinese attitudes, following Mao's death, meant that diplomatic relations with western states, especially the United States, became increasingly more cordial. China could never forget that, at all times, the U.S.S.R. maintained large forces on their common frontier. Therefore, apart from wanting western technology to develop her resources, China urgently required modern military equipment to strengthen her defences. The inauguration of better relations with western Powers and the United

States, already mentioned, gave China greater confidence in her difficult position vis-à-vis the U.S.S.R. Cynics might well wonder what reality was left in the original Sino-Soviet dispute over peaceful coexistence when China was prepared to remove its barriers to a better understanding with the western world.

3. DEVELOPMENTS IN SOUTH-EAST ASIA

The aftermath of the Second World War virtually completed the process of decolonization in the Far East. During the war the Japanese authorities had stimulated local nationalism among Asiatic peoples as part of the campaign against western colonial Powers; later, many of the countries overrun by Japanese forces developed strong organizations of national resistance to their "liberators." Thus, movements towards self-determination, already well-defined before 1939, attained their climax after 1945.

We have already seen that Britain's major political responsibility in the Far East ended in 1947, when the independent states of India and Pakistan were created. Similarly, American control of the Philippines ceased, with the United States granting large sums of money towards the restoration of war-damaged areas in the islands. These transfers of power were accomplished with relatively little friction between the native peoples and their former rulers; but in Indo-China the ultimate solution was fiercely contested, leaving a bitter legacy for the future.[1]

Indonesia was the scene of much trouble during the last phase of its struggle for independence. Exploited by Dutch colonial authorities for more than three centuries, Indonesians profited by the disturbed situation following the Japanese surrender, to proclaim their independence on August 17, 1945. The leader of this movement was Achmed Sukarno, who had been agitating for self-rule since the 1920's. His oratory, political skill, and ability to sway the masses of the population made him the natural architect of a new state to be established on the "Five Principles" of nationalism, internationalism, representative government, social justice, and belief in one God.[2]

However, in 1945 the Netherlands had no intention of relinquishing control over its immensely wealthy Empire in the East Indies.

[1]See pp. 688-697.
[2]Islam has been the main religious and cultural force in Indonesia.

"Police actions" were launched against the newly-proclaimed Republic, resulting in bitter guerrilla fighting, destruction of property, and heavy casualties. Inevitably, there was a strong reaction to Dutch policy among western and Asiatic leaders of democratic opinion and within the United Nations. This pressure compelled the Dutch to negotiate a settlement with the nationalists, leading to recognition of the Republic of the United States of Indonesia at the end of 1949. There was some lingering difficulty over the status of Dutch New Guinea (or West Irian), where the Dutch claimed that the inhabitants were not ethnically related to the Indonesians. But this area was also transferred to the Republic in 1963.

Independence did not bring stability to Indonesian affairs. Sukarno, elected President in 1949, adopted a dictatorial policy, setting aside the new constitution and exercising unrestricted powers. He tried to indoctrinate the people with the idea that his judgment was infallible, that his teachings incorporated absolute and undeniable truth. As time passed, however, the President came to lean more and more on Communist support, thereby arousing growing opposition from masses of the population led by students and other political groups. These developments culminated in an abortive Communist coup in September, 1966, and the displacement of Sukarno by General Suharto. The new administration sought to restore democracy in the country and regain the confidence of Indonesia's neighbours, which had been jeopardized by Sukarno's policies in the past.

In spite of Indonesia's fluctuating relationships with her neighbours, she has played a leading role in the international affairs of South-East Asia. In April, 1955, she was the host nation for the Bandung Conference of Afro-Asian states—the most impressive gathering of non-western nations in the present century. Delegates came from twenty-three Asian and six African countries—including two Communist states (China and North Vietnam) and 15 anti-Communist states (Ceylon, Gold Coast, Iran, Iraq, Japan, Jordan, Lebanon, Liberia, Libya, Pakistan, the Philippines, Sudan, Thailand, Turkey, and South Vietnam.) Other participants in the Conference generally followed "non-aligned," or neutralist, policies —that is, they were most concerned to keep out of the Cold War between East and West. (These views were reflected, at the United Nations, in the growing strength of the Afro-Asian bloc which accompanied the post-war process of decolonization and admission of new states to the world organization.) Thus, referring to NATO at Bandung, Prime Minister Nehru declared that it was "an intolerable humiliation" for any Asiatic or African nation to become "a camp follower of one or the other power blocs."

Apart from differences over the Cold War, the representatives at Bandung were united in condemnation of colonialism and all policies and practices of racial segregation and discrimination. Yet, in spite of this apparent unanimity on basic issues, the subsequent relations of the nations represented at Bandung have shown deep divisions—such as the Sino-Indian conflict in the Himalayas, the clash of Indian and Pakistani interests in Kashmir, and tensions induced by the war in Vietnam.

The economic problems of South-East Asia, one of the major underdeveloped regions of the world, cannot be divorced from political factors—in particular, the triangle of competing forces represented by China, the U.S.S.R. and the United States. On the other hand, a certain identity of aims can be detected in the foreign policies of the new nations, otherwise divided by old traditions, ethnic, cultural, and religious differences. As Adam Malik, the Indonesian Foreign Minister, has observed: "No Asian country can detach itself from anything that happens in Asia. Although Asia is composed of many nations, with varieties of culture and political ideological outlook, every part feels the pulse of every other part."

4. THE VIETNAMESE MORASS

Few of the developments since the end of the Second World War have been more complex than the war in Vietnam, nor have any of the nations emerging from colonialism faced problems more vexing than that country. What are the origins of this long and frustrating conflict? To what extent does it reflect continuing tensions of the Cold War? What have been the obstacles to a peaceful settlement? These are some of the questions that inevitably arise in any discussion of Vietnam.

French imperialism in the South China Sea could be traced back to the end of the 18th century.[1] During the following century French influence spread over the adjacent mainland, gradually bringing Vietnam, Cambodia, Laos, and eastern Siam under the

[1] France acquired the island of Pulo Condore, off the coast of Indo-China, in 1787.

tricolour. There was no serious challenge to this colonial authority until the Second World War, when French capitulation to Hitler opened the door to Japanese penetration in Indo-China. While the fiction of French rule was retained, effective power in this region passed temporarily to the Japanese, who encouraged Indo-Chinese nationalism, which was already reacting to the earlier French policy of assimilation. However, Vietnamese nationalists waged underground resistance to both Japanese and French domination. Thus, when Japan was defeated by the Allies in August, 1945, a Republic of Vietnam was promptly set up by the "Viet Minh," or Vietnam Independence League, organized by Ho Chi Minh.

Ho Chi Minh (a pseudonym meaning "he who shines") had formed a Marxist group among Indo-Chinese students in Paris during the First World War. After a decade of political activity in South-East Asia, he organized the Communist Party of Indo-China at Hong Kong in 1930. Fifteen years later he was recognized as one of the ablest Asiatic Communists and, like Mao Tse-tung, was a master of guerrilla warfare.

In spite of the evidence of nationalist reaction to her rule, France sought to restore her authority in Indo-China when the global war ended in 1945. She was soon engaged in a deadly struggle with the Viet Minh, who were determined to end their colonial status. All efforts to arrange a compromise failed, and the Communist victory in China (1949) provided a great stimulus to renewed efforts by the Viet Minh in Vietnam. Meanwhile, France endeavoured to placate local feelings in this theatre by recognizing the independence of two neighbouring states, Cambodia and Laos, within the French Union. A puppet government was also established by the French in Saigon. On the other hand, Ho Chi Minh claimed to represent the only sovereign government of Vietnam, receiving formal recognition from Peking and the Soviet bloc. The stage was therefore set for a tug-of-war between the principal opponents of the Cold War over the devastated country of the Vietnamese.

The military conflict between French forces and the Viet Minh had some of the characteristics of the civil war in China between Nationalists and Communists. At the beginning Ho Chi Minh operated from bases in the difficult hill country of the Vietnamese hinterland, launching harassing attacks against French troops bot-

The late Ho Chi Minh blended Communist ideology with nationalism. Which predominated? What might have been Ho's position if, in his early days, there had been a genuine Nationalist Party in Vietnam and if the Communist Party had not been the only one in France to advocate self-government in France's South-East Asian colonies?

tled up in coastal towns and cities. These tactics kept the technically superior French on the defensive, unable to engage their elusive foe in a decisive contest. Then, following the defeat of Chiang Kai-shek in 1949, the Communists organized training centres in South China for the benefit of the Viet Minh. The latter also began to receive modern Russian weapons, such as antiaircraft guns, and Chinese technicians appeared in Vietnam to assist Ho Chi Minh's army. With these resources the Viet Minh adopted a more menacing role, shifting from purely guerrilla warfare to large-scale campaigns in the field.

Before long, French public opinion, alarmed by mounting casualties in the French army, compelled the government to seek other solutions. One was to recruit, equip, and train Vietnamese formations which could be substituted for French forces. Unfortunately for the French, the stabilization of the Korean conflict enabled the Chinese Communists to step up their assistance to the Viet Minh. By 1953 Ho Chi Minh had an army of between three and four hundred thousand men opposing a roughly equivalent French commitment, thus ending any possibility of relieving the latter by substituting Vietnamese troops. The climax came in May, 1954, when the Viet Minh captured the strategic fortress of Dien Bien Phu, in the mountainous region west of Hanoi. News of this disaster caused the downfall of the French government, and the new Premier, Pierre Mendès-France, advocated a peaceful solution by negotiation.

Simultaneously with the deterioration of the French position in Vietnam, an international conference was gathering at Geneva to deal with the Korean problem. At this meeting, attended by delegations from Russia, Communist China, the Viet Minh, Cambodia, Laos, Britain, the United States, and France, the French insisted that the question of the armistice in Vietnam be placed on the agenda. The resulting Agreements of July, 1954, marked the end of French rule in Indo-China. Unhappy Vietnam was "temporarily" divided at approximately the 17th parallel: the northern portion, including Hanoi, coming under the Communist regime of Ho Chi Minh, while the remainder continued under the control of the French-supported South Vietnam government. Communist guerrillas were to be withdrawn from Laos and Cambodia, which were neutralized and recognized as sovereign states.[1]

Apart from arranging a temporary solution to the military problem, the Geneva Agreements tried to lay the foundation for a unified Vietnam in the future. It was agreed that within two years a general election would be held throughout the land, under the

---

[1] Laos and Cambodia were Buddhist countries, traditionally within the cultural orbit of India, while Vietnam was historically identified with Confucian China.

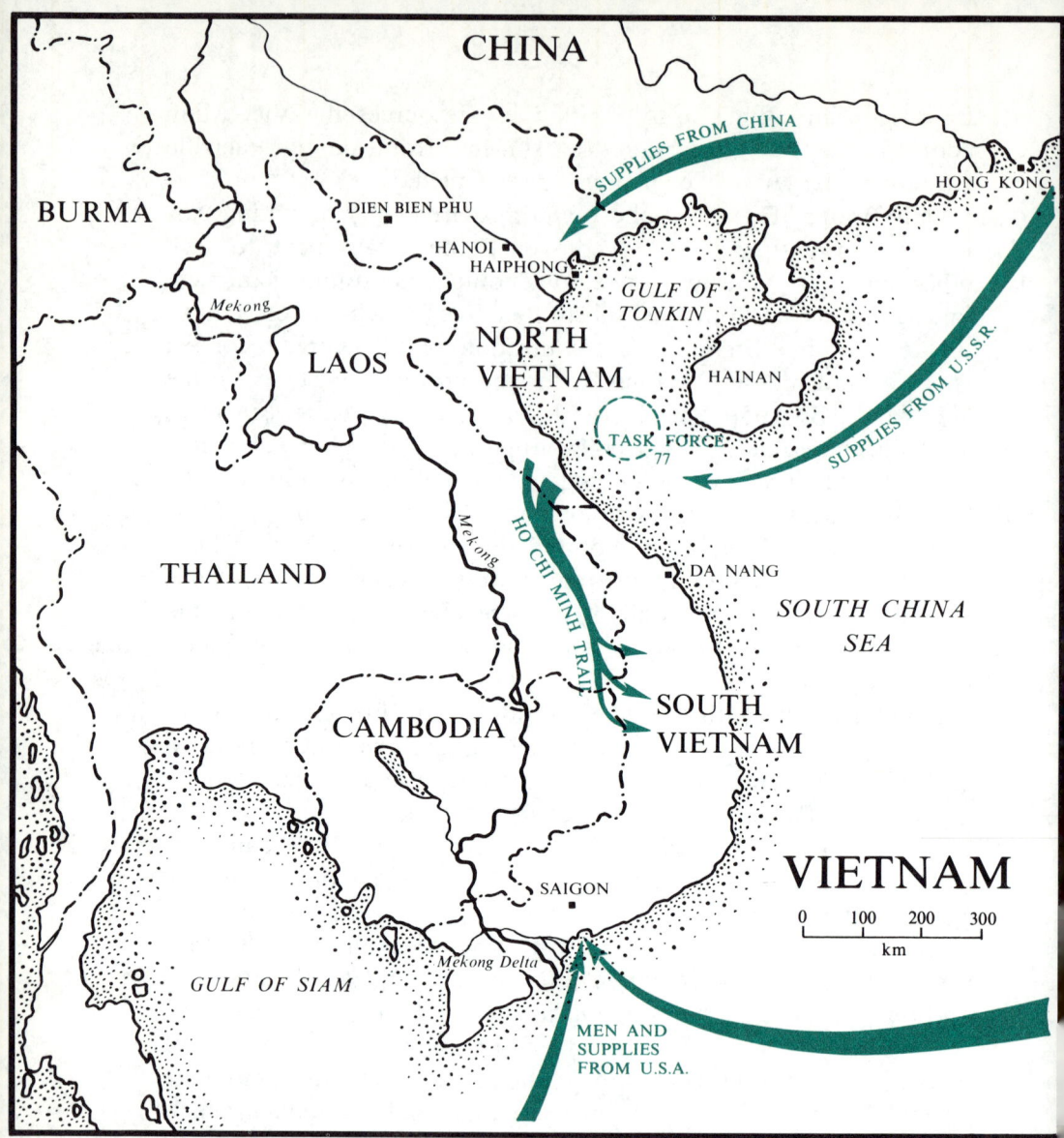

supervision of a neutral committee composed of representatives from Canada, India, and Poland. However, since each member had a veto on decisions, the work of the committee was severely restricted from the beginning.

There seems little doubt that, in the long run, the Agreements strengthened the Communist position in South-East Asia. Although

Communist guerrillas were withdrawn from Laos and Cambodia, the suspension of hostilities left the Viet Minh (and its Red Chinese supporters) well placed to continue the struggle by the usual methods of propaganda, infiltration, and subversion. At this critical point in the Cold War, which was at its most intense stage, future developments obviously depended on the attitude of the American government.

The United States had remained wary of making military commitments in Vietnam during earlier phases of the Franco-Communist duel. There were doubts about French intentions in the area (American opinion was traditionally hostile to colonial authorities), and in any case Washington's attention between 1950 and 1953 was focused on the Korean War. Yet, in response to a French plea for aid because of "the international character of the conflict begun by the Viet Minh, which threatens the future of South-East Asia," President Truman had already authorized large expenditures in material and money to support the French. Over a four-year period, beginning in 1950, this contribution exceeded four billion dollars. Also, in September, 1954, following the Geneva Conference, the United States called another meeting at Manila to form another defensive alliance—the South-East Asia Treaty Organization (SEATO). Although India, Burma, Ceylon, and Indonesia declined to participate, five "western" states (the United States, Britain, Australia, New Zealand, and France) and three Asian countries (Thailand, the Philippines, and Pakistan) agreed to coordinate their defences in this theatre against external aggression and subversion from within.[1]

Because of the way the local situation developed, the United States found itself dragged deeper and deeper into the Vietnamese morass. In April, 1954, even before the fall of Dien Bien Phu, President Eisenhower had publicly declared: "The loss of Indo-China will cause the fall of South-East Asia like a set of dominoes." This image of the "falling dominoes" later became a major justification for the American involvement against Communist ambitions in Vietnam. The major difficulty was the impossibility of holding really "free" elections in North Vietnam. Here the familiar

---

[1]SEATO was dissolved in 1977. In the meantime, an Association of South-east Asian Nations (ASEAN) had been formed in 1967. This was a loose economic alliance of the non-Communist states of Malaysia, Singapore, Thailand, the Philippines and Indonesia.

pattern of Communist takeovers in eastern Europe, China, and North Korea reasserted itself. Ho Chi Minh's Communist Party established a monolithic, authoritarian government, making political opposition virtually impossible in North Vietnam while preserving the right to compete with relative freedom in the affairs of South Vietnam. Since the latter was distracted by internal divisions, its Prime Minister, Ngo Dinh Diem, was understandably reluctant to expose his country to the perils of a simultaneous election in both states. The problem was aggravated by a mass exodus of refugees, eventually numbering over a million people from North to South Vietnam.

Meanwhile, the Communist underground movement in South Vietnam was gathering momentum. This was the Viet Cong, the southern equivalent to the Viet Minh. In the rich agricultural delta of the Mekong River, Ho Chi Minh's followers established secret depots and recruited groups to carry out a plan of widespread terror, assassination, and sabotage. The object was to gain control of the rural population of South Vietnam and gradually infiltrate into its urban districts.

In 1957 the Viet Cong began a campaign of systematically assassinating local leaders and the chief men in villages. Within three years the annual total of these killings had risen to four thousand. Major clashes were occurring between Communist guerrillas and regular troops of South Vietnam. Also, the Canadian and Indian members of the International Control Commission set up under the Geneva Agreements reported that the Communists were by-passing the northern frontier and entering South Vietnam through Laos, assisted by pro-Communist elements in that state. The long, narrow corridor of the southern democracy, squeezed between Laos and Cambodia, in the west, and the South China Sea, was particularly vulnerable to these tactics.

The United States now found itself taking over the former French role of forcibly opposing the spread of Communism in Vietnam. (It has been suggested that France gave up its rich colony with relief.) American economic assistance to the Diem government was soon followed by military aid. In June, 1961, Washington sent a group of experts in guerrilla warfare to assist the South Vietnamese and, in October, General Maxwell Taylor, later American Ambassador at Saigon, visited the scene to survey the situation. Before long, American service men, planes, and equipment were flowing

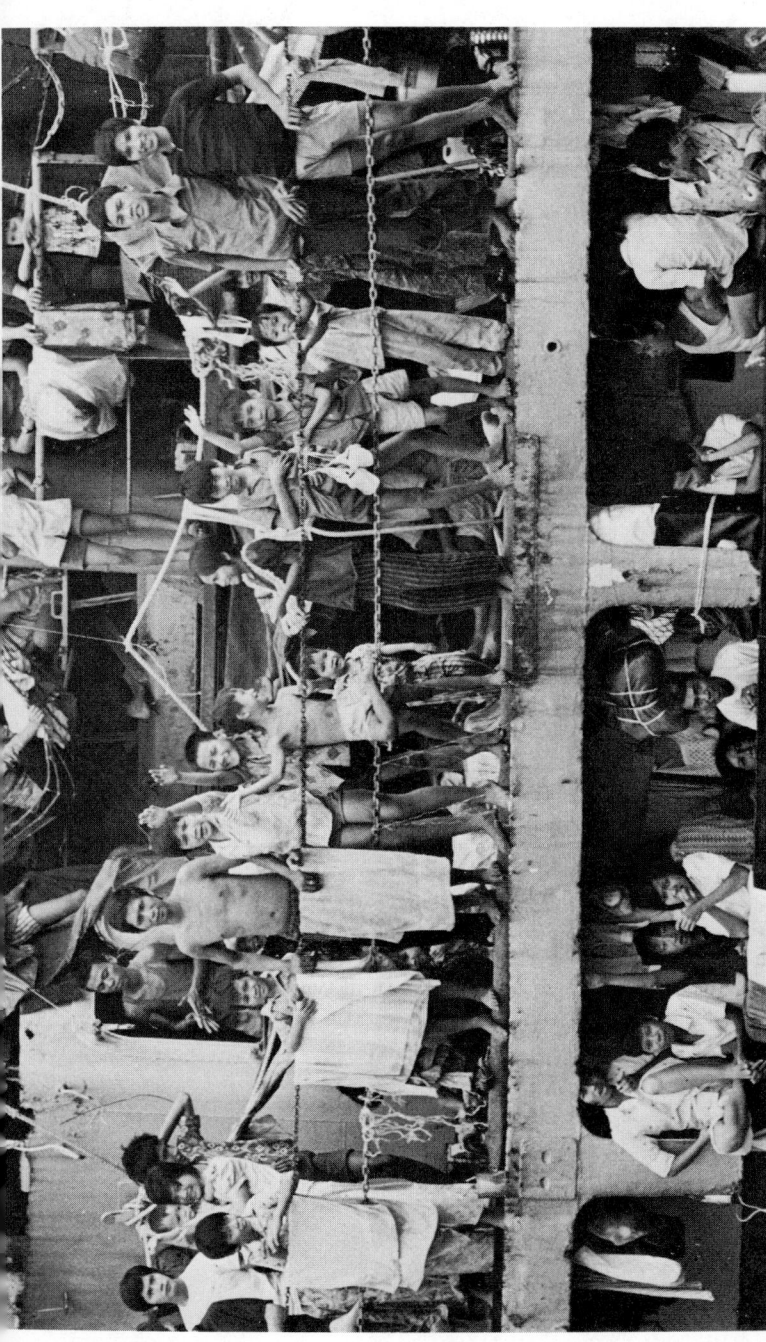

In the late 1970s the government of Vietnam expelled hundreds of thousands of people, the majority of them ethnic Chinese. Many others fled the repressive regime. They became known as "Boat People" as they sailed from port to port in the South China Sea, seeking a new home. Several poor and densely populated countries in the area refused to let the boat people land. Countries around the world were asked to accept these victims of the seemingly endless war in South East Asia as refugees.

across the Pacific, although American forces were not officially recognized as participating in the war. It was inevitable that this fine distinction was purely transitory in the face of growing Communist pressure.

President Kennedy, who succeeded Eisenhower at the beginning of 1961, viewed the struggle as one of defence against systematic aggression, and recognized that a large-scale effort would be required to defeat the Viet Cong. In this respect his views differed little from those of President Truman, who had stated (1947) that "it must be the policy of the United States to support free peoples who are resisting attempted subjugation by armed minorities or by outside pressures." Accordingly, during 1962 the number of American service men in South Vietnam rose steeply from three thousand to over ten thousand.

Over succeeding years the United States was compelled to commit more and more men and resources to the struggle. By 1965 there were nearly two hundred thousand American troops in Vietnam, and two years later the figure was rapidly approaching half a million. Accompanying this expanded commitment was a significant enlargement of the theatre of operations. In 1964, President Lyndon B. Johnson, who succeeded Kennedy when the latter was assassinated in 1963, took a critical decision. In retaliation for North Vietnamese attacks on the Seventh Fleet in the Gulf of Tonkin, he ordered the United States Air Force to bomb naval bases in North Vietnam. Before long, inland areas were also being subjected to daily bombing attacks.

The use of military force to achieve a political decision can only be justified, if at all, by success. In spite of an enormous diversion of American manpower and resources, the United States failed to subdue the Viet Cong. With the exception of Australia, New Zealand and South Korea, none of her allies showed any enthusiasm for participation in the war. At home, the American Congress became increasingly reluctant to authorize the huge sums required to finance the war during the early 1970's. A vociferous "protest" movement reflected growing public opposition to the government's policy, and thousands of draftees for the services evaded compulsory service in Vietnam.

The war lasted for nearly a decade, ending only in 1973, by which time 56 000 American troops and over a million Vietnamese had died in the struggle. The result was that Communist authority was firmly established throughout Vietnam. Five years later Vietnamese forces, supported by the U.S.S.R., overran neighbouring Cambodia. Then, early in 1979, reacting to the Soviet intervention, China mounted a punitive invasion of Vietnam. These events suggest that, in an era of continuing Sino-Soviet tension, no South-east Asia state can exist in a political vacuum.

5. THE NEW NATIONS OF AFRICA

While the achievement of Indian independence, the rise of Communist China, and the Vietnamese War have been the most dynamic events in the Far East since the end of the Second World War, equally dramatic and significant developments have occurred during the same period in Africa.

Long the "Dark Continent" because of delayed exploration, Africa was suddenly partitioned and exploited in an outburst of European imperialism during the 19th century. The African scene has been infinitely complicated by widely differing racial, linguistic, sociological, and economic considerations. Basically, the northern half of the continent is Arabic-speaking with a vast grouping of Bantu languages south of the equator. However, some indication of the perils of oversimplification may be gathered from the fact that, even within the Bantu area, there may be as many as one thousand separate languages and dialects. (Five million people on Madagascar speak a distinct language of Asiatic origin.) On top of this welter of races, religions, and customs, the conquering Europeans superimposed their own artificial systems of boundaries, attempting to reconcile their own selfish ambitions without regard for native cultures. Consequently when African states later emerged as independent entities, they were frequently saddled with frontiers that bore no relation to ethnic and racial backgrounds.

The colonial Powers governed their African possessions along widely varying lines, with very different consequences. Both France and Belgium adopted heavily paternalistic policies, being more concerned with efficient production and the health and social welfare of their native peoples than their political advancement. For example, Belgian colonial administrators were fond of remarking: "The African has no vote, but he does have a shirt and shoes." French policy, on the other hand, was designed to share the dominant civilization with the Africans, believing that ultimately they

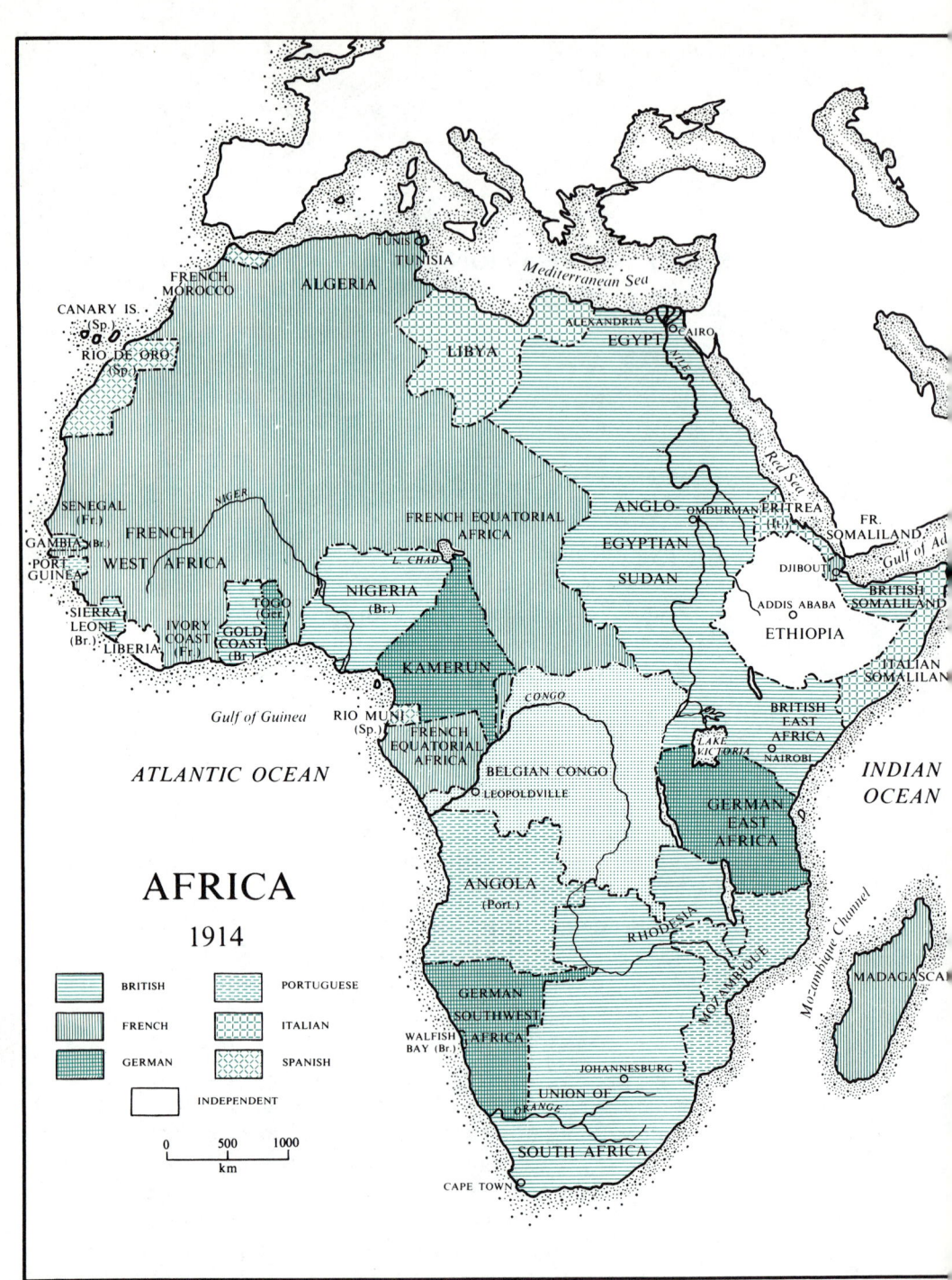

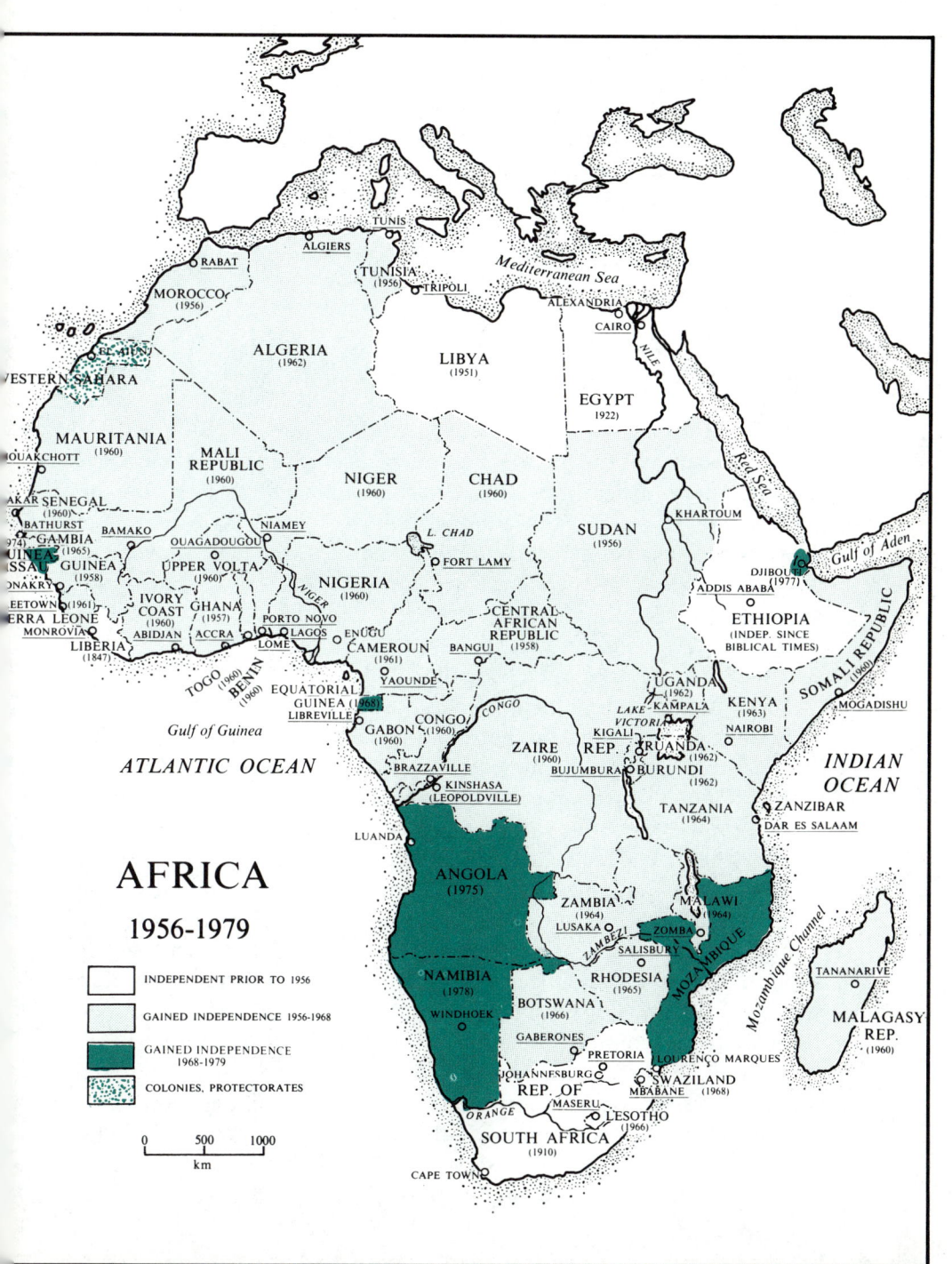

would become "French" themselves. The government of the African colonies was centralized in Paris. There was no colour bar, some Africans attaining posts of high responsibility. Nevertheless, the French colonial authorities found there was no substitute for liberty in the minds of a politically-aroused people, and in Africa, as elsewhere in the mid-20th century, the winds of change blew strongly.

French Africa

After her defeat in Indo-China, France decided to try a more conciliatory approach to nationalist feelings in her African colonies. As a result both Morocco and Tunisia became fully independent in 1956. But the problem of Algeria could not be solved so easily: about one-tenth of the population was of French origin—these were the *colons*, or settlers, many of whom had become wealthy on the fertile lands between the Mediterranean and the Atlas Mountains. These people were naturally determined to resist any movement towards Algerian independence which threatened their political and economic privileges.

In 1945 Algerian nationalism exploded in rebellion, and within two years twenty thousand guerrillas, with assistance from Tunisia and Egypt, were tying down four hundred thousand French troops. So serious did the situation become that it produced a major political crisis in France, leading to the downfall of the Fourth Republic and De Gaulle's assumption of power in 1958. De Gaulle favoured a compromise solution, permitting the Algerian people a choice of complete independence, closer identification with France, or a looser form of federal organization. In spite of an attempted revolt by the *colons*, led by some of the most distinguished French generals, public opinion, both in France and Algeria, revealed strong support for the principle of self-determination. Thus, Algerian independence was proclaimed on July 3, 1962, and all French troops left the country during the next two years. The long bitter struggle had cost France thousands of lives as well as annual expenditures of one billion dollars. Now that independence is assured, it may be anticipated that joint Franco-Algerian exploitation of rich Saharan oil reserves will facilitate better relations between France and her former colony.

British Africa

From the beginning, British colonial policy in Africa (as in India and elsewhere), followed a course very different from that of other European Powers. Instead of trying to make Britons out of Africans, British officials sought to teach the Africans how to run their own affairs. Natives were trained for future self-government, under the principle of "indirect rule," by which chiefs were given a large measure of control over local affairs. The main idea was that British power would operate discreetly and unobtrusively in the background. Gradually this principle was extended so that natives became familiar with voting procedures and some of the mechanisms of government.[1] Therefore, when the post-war wave of nationalism struck her African colonies, Britain was already in a position to effect a generally peaceful transfer of authority to the native peoples under her rule.[2]

The most difficult British problems arose in East Africa. In Kenya the Mau Mau, a secret tribal society dedicated to the elimination of western influence, embarked on a campaign of terror in 1952. The resulting strife cost the lives of three thousand people during the following two years, Britain being compelled to deploy fifteen thousand troops to restore order. Thereafter rapid progress was made towards self-government and, at the end of 1963, Kenya became an independent member of the Commonwealth of Nations. Jomo Kenyatta, who had been imprisoned for seven years on suspicion of complicity in Mau Mau activities, became the first Prime Minister of the new state.

Other former British colonies in East Africa have followed an easier path to self-determination. Uganda achieved its independence in 1962, coming under the turbulent and brutal leadership of Idi Amin, whose reign of terror ended when he was overthrown in 1979. In 1964 the United Republic of Tanzania was formed out of the earlier mandate of Tanganyika and the protectorate of Zanzibar. The new government of Tanzania has resisted Communist influence in favour of a larger African unity.

In West Africa the focal point of nationalism was the Gold

[1] Despite these preparations, the growth of political "sophistication" has been slow; in Kenya, for instance, due to the persistence of illiteracy, in the first national election parties were identified on ballots by symbols such as roosters and palm trees.

[2] In September, 1968, the last remnant of Britain's African Empire, the land-locked colony of Swaziland, was granted independence.

Coast, where Kwame Nkrumah took over the leadership of a radical extremist party. As in the case of Kenyatta, Nkrumah's clashes with British authority led to imprisonment; also like the Kenya leader, he became his country's first Prime Minister when Ghana was granted full independence in 1957.

But Nkrumah became an increasingly controversial figure in African politics. At the United Nations he was a consistent supporter of the Soviet position. He had a vision of a continental federation in which he would play the chief role; but his grandiose project came to nothing. Internally, his extravagance and corruption impoverished the country, soon raising its debt to a staggering total of one billion dollars. Free speech was suppressed and political opponents were thrown into prison. Eventually a military group took advantage of Nkrumah's temporary absence from the country to expose and overthrow him, and Ghana set about the difficult task of restoring its financial position.

Rhodesia and South Africa

No part of the former "Dark Continent" has produced problems of greater potential danger to future relations between white and coloured races than Rhodesia and the Republic of South Africa. In these relatively efficient and prosperous states the clash between dominant white minorities and subject coloured majorities is clearcut and seemingly insoluble. It is important to realize that this is not a problem of "decolonization," or removal of imperial authority, in the sense understood elsewhere in Africa. The reason is that the white inhabitants of Rhodesia—and more particularly South Africa—do not consider themselves primarily representatives of an external, European Power. In some cases their families have lived continuously in Africa for over three hundred years, and their concept of their own acquired identity is comparable to that of the descendants of the original white settlers in North America.

For these people, especially the South Africans of Dutch origin, there is no possibility of returning "home" to Europe—as, for example, occurred in connection with British and French officials in India and Algeria—because South Africa and Rhodesia are their adopted homelands. Furthermore, not without considerable justification, these white populations are keenly aware of their overwhelming contribution to the exploration, development, and technological advancement of their regions. It is the great disparity in numbers of white and coloured populations, with corresponding differences in standards of living, that has intensified the racial crisis in southern Africa. There are little more than two hundred thousand people of European origin in the total Rhodesian population of over four million; only one person in six is of European ancestry in the Republic of South Africa.

Unlike the old imperial Powers, most of whom came to realize the necessity of relinquishing their colonies to the original inhabitants, Rhodesia and the South African Republic were determined to retain the white man's dominant status in their lands. The most extreme manifestation of this determination is the South African policy of *apartheid*, an *Afrikaans* word meaning "separateness." This term has a religious significance, for the *Afrikaners* (that is, the descendants of the original Dutch colonists at the Cape) seek to justify their theories by a fundamentalist interpretation of the Bible. As practised in the Republic, *apartheid* means the rigid segregation of white and coloured populations. In this respect it is quite unlike the social pattern which prevailed in the Old South of the United States, where inter-racial marriage was not uncommon. The Afrikaner is convinced that the Bantu are an inferior people, that they must be kept under political and economic domination, and must never be permitted to use their much greater numerical strength in direct competition with white men.

Two aspects of *apartheid* illustrate its operation—the "reserves" and the "pass system." The South African government has set up a number of separate territorial units, called "Bantustans," to be occupied exclusively by natives. The intention is that the Bantus will elect a spokesman and an assembly to manage their own local affairs, while the white authorities at Cape Town continue to direct defence, foreign affairs, and justice. Critics of the scheme have suggested that it is designed to reinforce white domination by crowding the coloured population into less desirable rural areas.

Under the "pass system" each native must carry an identification card at all times, severely restricting his movements. Difficulties of enforcement are suggested by the fact that, in a single year, nearly a million arrests were made for infringements of the regulations. Although the government has taken some steps to improve deplorable housing conditions in the Bantu reserves, and has introduced

On March 21, 1960, a large crowd of Africans in the South African town of Sharpeville demonstrated against the country's *apartheid* policy of complete racial segregation. Police fired into the crowd, killing and wounding many of the demonstrators.

better educational and medical facilities, it is clear that *apartheid* will perpetuate a festering sore in the life of the country. Moreover, the South African doctrine has aroused the moral indignation not only of black African states but of other nations as well. In 1962 the General Assembly of the United Nations adopted a resolution calling on its members to end all relations with South Africa.

The *apartheid* issue was aggravated by disputes over the Republic's legal status in South-West Africa (now known as Namibia), the region taken over from Germany as a mandated territory after the First World War. In 1966 the Mandate System instituted by the League of Nations came to an end and, by a resolution of the General Assembly, the former South-West Africa became a direct responsibility of the U.N. Nevertheless the Republic of South Africa refused to withdraw from the territory and proceeded to implement its own plans for the administration of the former mandate. The Security Council then declared South Africa's continued presence in Namibia "illegal and contrary to the principles of the [U.N.] Charter." The situation was aggravated by clashes between the South African authorities and guerrilla movements based in nearby

Angola. By the end of 1978, negotiations were proceeding between South Africa and the U.N. for elections to be held in Namibia in 1979, under U.N. supervision, to determine its future.

Racial issues in Rhodesia were complicated by constitutional links between the former colony and London. Following dissolution of the Federation of Rhodesia and Nyasaland in 1963, Southern Rhodesia reverted to its status as a self-governing colony.[1] Both white settlers and natives desired full independence, but the natives were split by internal divisions, while the white population had no intention of surrendering its political and economic privileges. Because Rhodesia was still nominally under the Crown, the British government found itself in the unenviable position of intervening to protect the interests of the natives against the wishes of the white minority, most of whom were of British descent.

London advised Rhodesia that British approval of her independence would be conditional upon the granting of basic constitutional rights to the natives—looking forward to universal suffrage for all races in the colony. A unilateral declaration of independence, Britain warned, would be an act of treason. Nevertheless this drastic step was taken in November, 1965, when Prime Minister Ian Smith's government at Salisbury severed all formal links with the mother country.

Shaken by violent criticism in the United Nations, Britain condemned the Rhodesian move and initiated economic sanctions against the rebellious colony. It was soon evident, however, that any attempt to use military force against the white Rhodesians would create a major political crisis in Britain. On the other hand, while existing sanctions severely hurt the Rhodesian economy, the rebels have had the tacit support of the South African Republic to bolster their cause.

Initially, the new black states of Africa were too weak and disunited to do more than protest loudly against these developments. World opinion was hostile to Rhodesia, but was not prepared to intervene with effective force to change the situation. As time passed, however, a small-scale war broke out between Rhodesia and guerrillas mounting raids from neighbouring black countries. Considerable casualties and much damage accompanied this conflict. There was a steady exodus of white Rhodesians, who feared their

---

[1] The former protectorates of Nyasaland and Northern Rhodesia became the independent states of Malawi and Zambia, respectively, in 1964.

future under eventual black domination. Meanwhile, Ian Smith made desperate efforts to achieve a compromise under which authority could be transferred to the black majority with adequate safeguards for white Rhodesians. There were bitter exchanges between Smith and the British and American governments over details of this compromise. While the ultimate transfer of power to blacks in Rhodesia seems assured, there is little possibility of this being accomplished without further disorders and loss of life. The future of a black-dominated Rhodesia in a continent where the expulsion of European imperialisms has not brought peace to its inhabitants remains very uncertain.

Angola

The complexity of African developments has nowhere been better illustrated than in Angola. By the early 1970's it was obvious that Portugal was losing its grip on her colony. The Portuguese problem was complicated by political developments at Lisbon, where the armed forces took over the government in 1974. Within Angola three competing insurgent movements emerged, reflecting different ethnic backgrounds. When Portuguese authority in the colony collapsed in 1975, the internal divisions of the country were an irresistible invitation to outside intervention. American policy was sensitive to pressure from Portugal, as a NATO ally, and because the United States had strategic air and naval facilities in the Azores. But American public opinion was very much against a large-scale commitment in Angola. On the other hand, both China and the U.S.S.R. were determined to exploit the situation for their conflicting purposes. Soon Chinese arms and instructors were pouring into Angola, to be matched and eventually exceeded by large shipments of Soviet rifles, machine guns, bazookas and rockets. Furthermore, the U.S.S.R. prevailed upon its ally, Cuba, to send thousands of combat troops to Angola. This massive intervention proved to be the determining factor in the erection of a "Peoples Republic of Angola" late in 1975.

We have seen that movements towards national independence have gathered great momentum in Asia and Africa. Both India and China have thrown off the last vestige of foreign control—although in the case of India there is a continuing need for outside assistance, both financial and technological. Also, with the notable exceptions of South Africa and Rhodesia, most of Africa has returned to the control of her native peoples.

The removal of external restraints on national aspirations has undoubtedly meant much for the native populations concerned. To a considerable degree they now direct their own political destinies, no longer suffering under imperialist exploitation, and are free to express their points of view in world organizations. On the other hand, internal progress towards democratic government has been much more difficult. Under Chinese Communism the individual still counts for little as against the arbitrary demands of the State. In India, largely due to the example and advice of retiring British authority, the democratic process has worked reasonably well. However, even in India difficulty has been experienced in attempts to introduce a common language, Hindi, since very large elements of the population speak other tongues and English remains the common language of educated Indians.

It is in Africa that the democratic form of government has been subjected to the severest strains and convulsions. One reason for these difficulties is inherent in the process whereby these states attained their independence. In the normal operation of a western parliamentary system, the party in power at any time is confronted by an opposition whose function is to scrutinize and criticize the measures taken by the government. As political parties were formed in the emerging African states, however, their principal object was national independence—to which, in the native populations, there could be little or no opposition. Consequently, differences between parties arose over the means to the end, rather than the primary goal. In practice this meant that very frequently there was no effective opposition to the party which assumed the task of self-government. The result has been a marked tendency for Indian and African governments to perpetuate their existence and discourage all political dissent. In a number of instances, as in Ghana and the Congo, dictatorial methods have caused sudden upheavals inconsistent with the democratic tradition.

In brief, the peoples of Asia and Africa have found that it is perhaps easier to break the chains of colonialism than to govern themselves. These issues are of the greatest significance in a world constantly exposed to the competing ideologies of capitalism and communism. It can only be hoped that with patience, restraint, and tactful assistance from more technologically advanced nations the new states will ultimately find appropriate and enduring solutions to their unique problems.[1]

6. LATIN AMERICA IN THE MODERN ERA

Although not an area of newly-emerging nations, Latin America, like Asia and Africa, has become one of the major regions of political and economic disturbances in the post-war world. In this vast area, including Mexico, Central America, and Cuba, as well as South America, the familiar problems of large populations, extreme poverty, malnutrition, and revolutionary discontent present a continual challenge to the interests of the wealthier nations, especially the United States.

American relations with Latin American countries have fluctuated considerably during the 20th century. During the first three decades, repeated manifestations of American imperialism—evident in periodic occupations of the Dominican Republic, Haiti, and Nicaragua, and heavy-handed use of political and economic pressures—caused bitter resentment among the Latin Americans. A refreshing change in this deplorable situation occurred in 1933, when Franklin D. Roosevelt became the American President. In his inaugural address he said: "I would dedicate this nation to the policy of the good neighbour—the neighbour who resolutely respects himself, and because he does so, respects the rights of others—the neighbour who respects his obligations and respects the sanctity of agreements in and with a world of neighbours." Thereafter the United States adopted a more generous attitude in its relations with the Latin American states, so that many of their grievances were eliminated. These favourable developments acquired greater significance in 1941, when the United States entered the war. The Central American republics (Panama, Haiti, the Dominican Republic, and Cuba) immediately declared war on the Axis Powers and, after some uncertainty on the part of Chile and Argentina, the remaining Latin American states broke off relations with the Allies' enemies.

[1]One recent example of Big Power involvement in Africa is the savage war which broke out between Ethiopia, supported by the U.S.S.R., and Somalia in 1978. Control of this area has great strategic significance for the Powers interested in the Indian Ocean.

From the early part of the 19th century a movement towards closer collaboration of the Latin American countries had steadily gathered momentum, resulting in the creation of a Pan-American Union in 1910. But the tendency of the United States to adopt a dominating role in the Union's affairs caused much dissatisfaction, and in 1948 it was reorganized, giving Latin Americans a greater voice in making decisions, under the name of the Organization of American States.[1]

In the post-war period Latin American problems reflected many deficiencies characteristic of the developing countries. Some states suffered from excessively narrow bases of production—an example being Cuba's dependence on the sugar market. Nearly all sought stabilization of prices for raw materials, more financial assistance for industrial and agricultural developments, and technical co-operation. American willingness to provide aid was combined with an attempt to secure Latin American adherence to a policy of combatting the spread of Communism. This policy was widely regarded by the Latin Americans, however, as unjustified intervention in the internal affairs of other nations, and thus revived many of the old suspicions of American motivation. Relations between Latin America and its northern neighbour were also severely strained by American efforts to influence the government of Guatemala (1954), by supplying arms and speedy recognition to rebels who overthrew that government. Above all, anger resulted from American participation in the "Bay of Pigs" fiasco (1961), when the United States took unilateral action against Cuba. Another major cause of resentment was the fact that the United States granted relatively small loans to Latin America, compared to the billions of dollars poured into western Europe and the Far East. Between the end of the Second World War and 1958, for instance, 175 million Latin Americans received $625 million from American public funds, while during the same period only twenty million Yugoslavs obtained nearly $800 million.

In 1961 President Kennedy inaugurated a bold and imaginative "Alliance for Progress" to assist Latin America. The new plan forecast an investment during the 1960's of at least one hundred billion dollars, of which twenty per cent would come from external sources

[1]It has been frequently suggested that Canada should join the O.A.S.; but the Canadian government has never welcomed a move which, in its opinion, might lead to embarrassing commitments in Latin American affairs.

"One, two, many Vietnams."—Fidel Castro, dedicated enemy of the United States, and foremost protagonist of revolution in Latin America.

—that is, U.S. public funds and private capital, west European and Japanese sources, the World Bank, and other international agencies. On the other hand, foreign investment in Latin America has had to contend with corrupt governments, absentee landlords, and military dictatorships, with marked tendencies to misappropriate funds made available for the betterment of their countries.[1] The continuing trend towards authoritarian governments has led to a situation in which three out of every four Latin Americans live under military rule. Moreover, a grossly disproportionate amount of wealth is squandered on military expenditures. In 1965 Latin American military spending reached a total of a billion and a half dollars, fifty per cent in excess of current American appropriations for economic aid. States such as Argentina and Brazil each maintain fleets of more than a hundred warships and submarines.

Latin American problems in the 1970's continue to be mainly

[1] See below, pp. 722-725.

political and economic. In 1973 the radical Chilean government of Salvador Allende was overthrown by a military coup. Three years later the armed forces of Argentina forcibly took over the administration of that country. Similar developments had taken place, earlier, in Brazil and Peru. In most cases the reasons for these upheavals were political corruption and economic distress. Some authoritarian regimes, as in Brazil (by far the biggest state in Latin America), have maintained that their object was to rebuild the economy and gradually restore democratic forms of government. But the efforts of most governments have been hampered by bitter internal dissension and strong suspicions of American imperialism. A Guatemalan writer once compared the twenty Latin American states to "sardines trying to escape from the voracious North American shark." This feeling was closely related to allegations that the American government had a clandestine responsibility for such events as the overthrow of democratically-elected Allende in Chile. While Washington officially repudiated these charges, there is little doubt that important American business interests have not hesitated in the past to use their powerful financial resources in attempts to influence the direction of Latin American politics.[1]

On the credit side of the ledger, it is refreshing to note that not all aid to Latin America has developed as official or private commercial enterprise. Organizations such as the Peace Corps (American) and Canadian University Service Overseas, employing the dedicated talents of many young men and women from more affluent societies, have made an impact on Latin American life out of all proportion to the modest expenditures involved. Living in slums and rural villages on subsistence wages, these young Canadians and Americans have helped to build schools and houses, dig wells, install sewers, promote hygiene, and generally care for the welfare of their adopted charges.

In the long run the Latin Americans, like the Asians and the Africans, will have to find their own solutions to grave problems such as the proper relationship of populations to available resources. Meanwhile, fully alive to the competing attractions of Communism, the "rich nations" of the West will be compelled to supply massive assistance, both financially and technologically, with a minimum of political interference in the internal affairs of Latin American states.

[1] The United States has recently renegotiated its treaty with Panama to define American interest in the Canal to 2000.

7. THE MIDDLE EAST

As we have seen, the Middle East exploded in the Suez Crisis of 1956.[1] Little more than a decade later a new war broke out between Arabs and Israelis in this highly inflammable region. The circumstances were different, the war was short (six days) and the Israeli triumph was complete.

In a certain sense, the period between 1956 and 1967 was little more than an armistice in the relations of the new Jewish state and its neighbours. Acutely aware of the tragic deaths of six million of her people in Europe during the Second World War, Israel faced a constant threat from fifty million hostile Arabs. They, for their part, regarded the Jews as usurpers of Arab lands, with a million Palestine refugees as constant reminders of an intolerable existence. The situation worsened when the "Palestine Liberation Army" began mounting raids into Israel from bases in Syria and Jordan. In October 1966 the Syrian Prime Minister declared: "We are not sentinels over Israel's security and are not the leash that restrains the revolution of the displaced and persecuted Palestinian people." Shortly thereafter Syria and Egypt concluded a "defense agreement" aimed at co-ordinating and integrating the military commands of the two countries.[2]

When Israel retaliated against raids, inflicting casualties on Jordanian soldiers and citizens, the U.N. Security Council censured Israel, declaring that "actions of military reprisal cannot be tolerated and that if they are repeated, the Security Council will have to consider further and more effective steps . . . to ensure against the repetition of such acts." However, it was soon apparent that the Arab states were not united and that Jordan, in particular, was dissatisfied with the "unified Arab Command" in Cairo. Throughout succeeding years, this disunity in the Arab world was a major factor in Israel's survival.

In April 1967 a severe border clash between Syrian and Israeli forces precipitated a more dangerous phase of the conflict. Israeli Prime Minister Eshkol stated publicly that his government was determined to meet aggression with powerful retaliation. Issues were intensified when the Soviet Union, pursuing a pro-Arab policy, gave warnings that Israel intended to invade Syria. Soviet concern for

---
[1] See, above, pp. 650-52.
[2] In 1958 the "United Arab Republic" had formally united Egypt and Syria. In 1971 this union was dissolved and Egypt became the United Arab Republic of Egypt.

Syria was undoubtedly linked to expectations of extending Soviet influence in the Middle East.

Reacting to these developments on 16 May the Egyptian government requested and obtained the withdrawal of the U.N. Emergency Force which had occupied the Sinai since the 1956 crisis.[1] Egypt did this in order to move in her own forces. President Nasser followed up this action by reimposing a blockade against Israel in the Strait of Tiran, at the north-eastern extremity of the Red Sea. (It was this Strait which had enabled Israel to by-pass the Suez Canal after that waterway was closed in 1956.) Israel immediately proclaimed Nasser's action "a flagrant violation of international law" and "an act of aggression against Israel." In an unusual demonstration of Arab solidarity, armed forces of Egypt, Jordan and Syria were concentrated on Israel's frontiers.

The Israeli government decided that it could no longer refrain from offensive action, on a large scale, against its enemies. In a campaign reminiscent of the German *Blitzkriegs* of 1939-40, the Jewish forces attacked in all vital sectors on June 5. By the end of the first day the opposing air forces had been destroyed and Israeli armoured forces had achieved deep penetrations. In only six days Israel advanced across the Sinai to the Suez Canal (described as the best "tank ditch" in the Middle East) and occupied the strategic Gaza Strip, Jerusalem, the West Bank of the Jordan River and the Golan Heights. Before the campaign, Tel Aviv had been only twelve minutes' flying time from Egyptian bases in the Sinai; at the cease-fire on June 11, with radars in the Sinai, Israel could rely on thirty minutes' warning of an Egyptian air strike. The total land area under Israeli control had quadrupled and, in general, her new frontiers were based on natural features.

Although the Israeli triumph in the Six Day War seemed decisive, it merely ushered in a further period of acute tension with the Arab states. Between 1967 and 1972 Israel's defense spending more than doubled (reaching $1.375 billion) and, by mid-1973, her full-time forces numbered 115 000. On the other hand, the Arab states were rapidly re-building their strength, aided by sophisticated surface to air and anti-tank missiles and other armament from the U.S.S.R.

On October 6, 1973, the Arabs attacked Israeli forces along the Suez Canal and on the Golan Heights. (This conflict is known as the Yom Kippur War because it broke out on the Jewish Day of

---

[1] See above, p. 652.

Atonement.) Although Israel had been aware of the Arab build-up, Defence Minister Moshe Dayan afterwards claimed that Israel had decided against a pre-emptive strike in order to retain the political and moral advantage in the renewed conflict. There is, however, the distinct possibility that Israeli intelligence had failed to evaluate correctly information on the enemy's preparations. This deficiency could have been related to over-confidence resulting from Israel's dramatic success in the Six Day War.

By seizing the initiative in 1973 the Arabs were able to dictate battle conditions that favoured them. In particular, they were able to impose a deliberate pattern of operations, where numerical superiority of manpower and equipment was most significant, while their opponents preferred a war of rapid movement and encirclement. Initially, Egyptian troops and tanks poured into the Sinai and Syrian forces pushed the Israelis back in the Golan Heights. Soviet tanks and aircraft supported the Arab offensives; some of this equipment was airlifted by giant cargo carriers, other supplies were brought by ships through the Dardanelles. On the other hand, the United States supplied Israel with arms on a massive scale, using stocks on hand in Europe and some NATO facilities. The danger of an open conflict between the superpowers could not be discounted.

Eventually the Israelis recovered from their initial reverses, using their armour and air force effectively to retake ground lost in the Golan Heights and penetrate Syrian territory. Moshe Dayan reminded the Syrians that "the same road that leads to Tel Aviv also leads to Damascus." By October 15 Israeli forces had crossed to the west bank of the Suez Canal and it was reported that each side had more than 1 000 tanks committed to the battle. In the ensuing struggle an entire corps of the Egyptian Army was trapped on the east bank of the Canal.

On October 22 the U.N. Security Council called on the belligerents "to cease all firing and terminate all military activity." But two more strongly-worded resolutions by the Council were required before even a start could be made in halting hostilities. In the meantime, alarmed by reports that Soviet airborne troops were headed for Egypt, the United States put its military forces at home and abroad on a "precautionary alert." The Soviet leader, Leonid I. Brezhnev, then accused the United States of an "artificial drumming up" of a crisis to justify its global alert. The United States ended this alert on October 31, although its 6th Fleet remained in a state of advanced readiness in the Mediterranean.

By the end of October the belligerents had accepted the U.N. resolutions for a ceasefire. Each side then held substantial bridge heads across the Suez Canal and into territories previously held by the other. Israeli Prime Minister Golda Meir stated that peace must be achieved by direct negotiations between Israel and the Arabs and that the demarcation of frontiers would have to be determined by the parties concerned. On the other hand, the Arab states were reluctant to accept bilateral negotiations, with their implied recognition of Israel's existence. The United Nations Emergency Force (U.N.E.F.) was then reinstated to prevent a renewal of hostilities. At the request of Secretary-General Kurt Waldheim, Canada agreed to provide logistic support for this Force.

It is important to realize that the later stages of the 1973 war were profoundly influenced by economic factors outside the immediate theatre of operations. Thus, the Arabs were able to use their "oil weapon" to considerable advantage.[1] Even before the war began, Arab leaders had warned the western nations and Japan that oil supplies upon which their industries largely depended might be curtailed if they maintained pro-Israel policies. This threat was put into effect in October 1973 when the Organization of Arab Petroleum Exporting Countries agreed to cut exports to the United States. Arab spokesmen stated that the cutback was not intended to "harm the Arabs' friends," although it was conceded that some Europeans would experience hardships which, it was hoped, would bring additional pressure on the United States to change its pro-Israel policy. Before the end of October the Arabs had imposed a total ban on oil exports to the United States. The American Secretary of State, Henry A. Kissinger, denounced the embargo as "a form of blackmail" detrimental to American efforts to restore peace in the Middle East. The embargo was not lifted until the spring of 1974, by which time the Arabs recognized a shift away from Israel in American policy.

During succeeding years the United States made repeated attempts to secure a lasting solution to the Arab-Israeli conflict. In September 1978 the American President, Jimmy Carter, invited Prime Minister Menachem Begin of Israel and President Anwar el-Sadat of Egypt to a peacemaking conference at Camp David. Although the Egyptian and Israeli leaders signed a "Framework for Peace in the Middle East" it was soon apparent that the parties were

[1] See page 730.

Israeli army armoured cars with machine-guns, patrolling on the West Bank of the Jordan River.

Egyptian President Anwar Sadat, U.S. President Jimmy Carter and Israeli Prime Minister Menachem Begin clasp hands after signing the 1979 peace treaty between Egypt and Israel.

still far from agreement on vital issues. Israel was prepared to withdraw all its armed forces and civilians from the Sinai and, together with Egypt, recognized the "permanent boundary" between the two states as that which had existed between Egypt and the former mandated territory of Palestine, "without prejudice (reference) to the issue of the status of the Gaza Strip." However, there was no immediate agreement over a proposed timetable for Palestinian autonomy. Feverish negotiations carried out under constant American pressure eventually led to the signing of a treaty by the Egyptian, Israeli and American leaders in March 1979. However, no solution had been found to sensitive matters such as the future status of the Palestinian Arabs. Moreover, the treaty intensified divisions within the Arab world because states like Saudi Arabia believed Egypt had made too many concessions to Israel. The Middle East remained a potential threat to international peace in the future.

27 Towards the Twenty-first Century

Fear, desire, hope draw us towards that which is to come and remove us from that which is.

Modern civilization has reached the most critical phase of life in history. In the past, cataclysmic destruction through wars, floods, and plagues was a recurring, if irregular, pattern of human existence. But even though millions of lives might be lost, as in the two World Wars, there was never a total threat to *all* human life on the globe. Today, this situation has drastically changed: through the development of nuclear weapons and intercontinental ballistic missiles, man has released an evil genie capable of ending all life on the planet. Humanity is faced with the desperate need to find enduring political solutions to many grave problems before irresponsible action makes all such efforts futile.

In an earlier chapter we saw how, following the Second World War, the Cold War divided Russia and her satellites from the western democratic nations, and how in turn this tension was relaxed in a period of "peaceful coexistence." Even in sudden emergencies, such as the Suez Crisis, the Soviet suppression of the Hungarian revolt, and the later Cuban Crisis, Russia and the United States exercised sufficient restraint to prevent a Third World War and a nuclear holocaust.

However, the acrimonious Sino-Soviet dispute, and continuing internal strains within both the Soviet bloc and the NATO Alliance, have all combined to perpetuate an atmosphere of uncertainty and confusion in international affairs. Like the old League of Nations, the United Nations organization has revealed a limited capacity to deal effectively with small-scale conflicts—as in the Congo, Cyprus, and Kashmir—but it is still true that, partly due to use of the veto in the Security Council, the U.N. provides no guarantee of collective security. The organization frequently functions as a forum for otherwise small and powerless nations. However, we still live in an era of "power politics," with crucial decisions affecting millions being taken by a few men and women in Washington, Moscow, and Peking.

1. "RICH" AND "POOR" NATIONS

Effects of the "Population Explosion"

While conflicting ideologies battle it out on the world's stage, and diplomats debate dramatically in the Security Council, a large portion of the human race still struggles for the very basics of existence: shelter over their heads, and enough to eat. Due to modern medical techniques that have reduced the infant mortality rate and prolonged life expectancy everywhere, the population of the world has increased at an alarming rate. According to available statistics, the world's population multiplied five-fold in the three centuries after 1650. In 1800 the world had a population of about a billion. In 1960 a U.N. survey estimated a world population of almost three billion, with an annual increase of forty-eight million. It is predicted that if present trends continue the world's population will reach seven billion by the year 2000; and five-sixths of this total will be in Asia, Africa, and Latin America.

Highly industrialized societies have the technical and scientific resources to cope with their growing populations. Although poverty and malnutrition have not been completely eliminated, western countries are able to increase their productive capacities in order to feed, clothe, and house their people, and in the process provide most of them with jobs. It is apparent, however, that underdeveloped countries in the non-western world have little hope of bridging the terrifying gap between their slow economic growth and rapidly expanding populations. Famine is still a grim possibility in many densely populated parts of the earth. Millions in India survive on an individual intake of 7 000 j per day, compared to an average of 13 000 j in the United States and western Europe.

The gulf between the living standards of the so-called "rich" and "poor" nations is actually *increasing*. The more affluent nations add to their wealth at a much faster rate than the less-developed countries, so while the rich nations have been getting richer, the poor nations, relatively, are getting poorer.

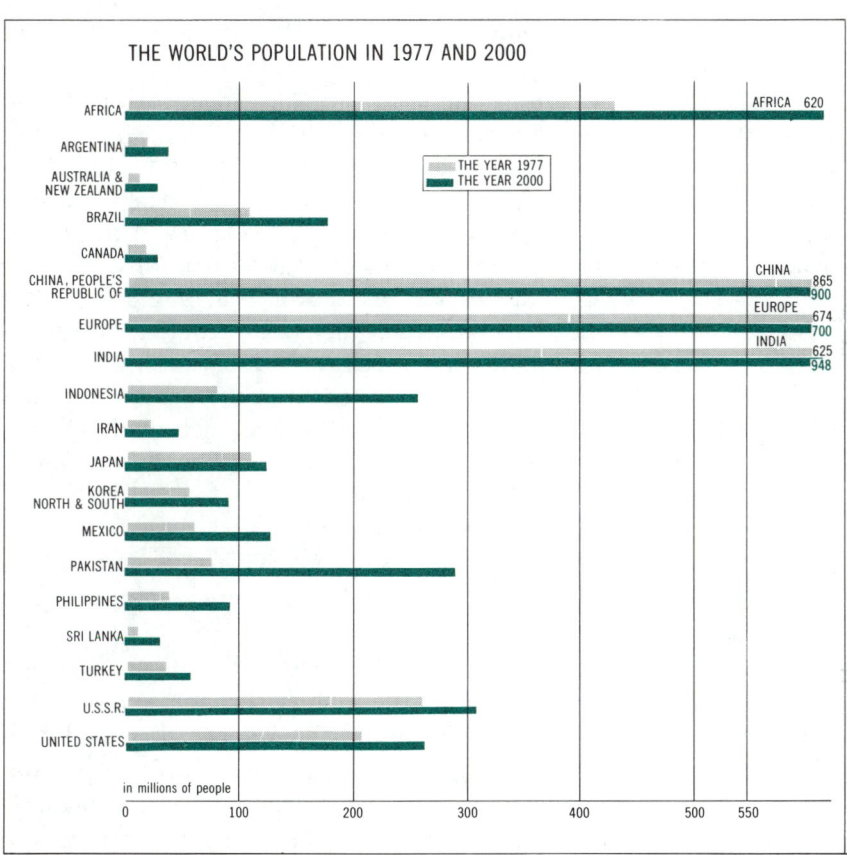

Foreign Aid

The wealthy nations of the western world dare not stand idly by while masses of humanity grow bitterly discontented with their economic conditions and cast envious eyes at their more prosperous contemporaries. A war between the "haves" and "have-nots" would be disastrous for mankind. Selfish considerations of national survival, therefore, no less than humanitarian ideals, dictate the necessity of extending assistance to the teeming multitudes of the "third world." Thus a three-way competition—western influence versus Soviet versus Chinese Communism—exists for the good will of the underdeveloped countries.

Whatever the motivation, the most difficult aspect of foreign aid is to determine the form it should take. Simply making large sums of money available, as loans or as outright gifts, is not a satisfactory answer, because many of the "poor" nations are so backward and illiterate that they do not know how best to utilize such resources. There is also the danger that foreign capital will be diverted into the pockets of unscrupulous officials, never reaching those who need it most. When that happens, the well-meaning efforts of wealthier nations can be identified with the preservation of corrupt and inefficient governments. The United States, in particular, has learned that it is not easy to play the role of a "rich uncle" in the world—and that gratitude is not to be expected for well-intentioned but misdirected schemes of assistance.

What steps can be taken by the underdeveloped countries, themselves, to improve their economic position? This is acknowledged as preferable to receiving foreign aid, but here again, difficult obstacles are encountered.

A distinguished British economist, Barbara Ward, has devoted much study to the problems of the rich and poor nations. She points out that "saving and science are the keys to the revolution of economic growth." But it is not easy for a large population, living near the subsistence level, to accumulate the financial resources needed to transform archaic systems into modern economies. What has happened is that the rate of increase in population (two per cent annually in India, three in parts of Latin America) forces up levels of consumption, absorbing all available savings.[1] Communist nations, such as Russia and China, solve this problem by the rigid discipline of forced savings. Since the state controls

---

[1] Economists calculate that, merely to keep pace with a three per cent increase in population, a nation has to invest approximately nine per cent of its national revenue each year.

the distribution of all profits from industry, it can arbitrarily apply them wherever it wishes. On the other hand, new democracies, such as India, cannot ignore public opinion when considering how far they should go in the direction of compulsory savings. An electoral defeat could ruin the most comprehensive programme of economic reform.

The one positive step the "poor" nations can take themselves to raise their standard of living is to limit the natural increase of their populations. Consequently, in recent decades Asian governments have tended to put much emphasis on methods of birth-control. India and Japan have taken the lead in exploring this solution, which is not repugnant to their dominant religions. However, intensified campaigns of education and propaganda are necessary to change the customs and prejudices of centuries.

Granting all these difficulties, there remains the crucial question of how the wealthier nations can best assist the underdeveloped countries. Neither the Western Powers nor Russia has been blind to the need for action. In 1950 the Colombo Plan for co-operative economic development in South and South-East Asia was inaugurated. Besides the Asian nations directly concerned, the participants included the United States, Britain, Australia, Canada, New Zealand, and Japan. Much of the aid provided under this Plan has taken the form of technical assistance. Similarly, the U.S.S.R. has made numerous contributions to the improvement of underdeveloped economies of Asia and Africa.

Great strides have been taken, with the assistance of the more advanced nations, towards the reduction of disease and the improvement of public health generally in the underdeveloped lands. Much of this great humanitarian work has been carried out by the World Health Organization in co-operation with the U.N. Technical Assistance programme. Spectacular progress has been made in certain regions—for example, the near-elimination of malaria in India and Ceylon, and reduction of the incidence of tuberculosis in Asia, Africa, and Latin America. Similarly, much thought has gone into programmes designed to increase available stocks of food in the poor nations. Fertilizers, insecticides, and machinery have been introduced to make agriculture more efficient; reforestation has been used to stop soil erosion, one of the most persistent problems in dry lands; in the Middle East the Soviet

Union has co-operated with western nations in the use of aircraft to control locusts. Japanese techniques have doubled the Indian production of rice. American capital has built refrigeration plants in Venezuela for the storage of perishable foods such as fish, and Canadian assistance has produced similar plants in India (the "Mysore Project" being one example). The list of improvements and innovations is endless—but the pressure of expanding populations on available resources continually mounts.

J. K. Galbraith, the Canadian-born economist with a distinguished record of service in the United States, has suggested the need for more flexible policies, appropriate to the needs of widely differing regions. He divides the "poor" nations into three "models," or categories. In the first, identified broadly with Africa south of the Sahara, the primary problem is the shortage of trained and educated people, and the lack of training facilities. Here, what is needed is not huge expenditures of money, but the provision of teachers to raise standards of literacy and thus create efficient administrations. Much valuable work towards this objective has been performed by organizations such as the Peace Corps and the Canadian University Service Overseas.

"Model II countries" exist in Latin America, where there is a lack of neither teachers, engineers, and administrators, nor of natural resources. In the most depressed areas of Latin America the greatest obstacle to economic advance is the social structure— that is, the control exercised by selfish, reactionary elements of society, usually military leaders and wealthy landlords, who resist reforms that would endanger their private interests. Galbraith exposes the fallacy of suporting these groups as supposed bulwarks against Communism. Western aid for these countries must, he thinks, be directed towards the evolution of more progressive governments.

The final group ("Model III countries") are those like India, Bangladesh, and Egypt, where as we have seen the main problem is that of too many people with insufficient land and capital. Education is important, but illiteracy is not the principal barrier to progress. Nor is government divorced from sincere efforts to improve social and economic conditions, as in some parts of South America. Therefore western aid can take the more obvious forms of direct financial assistance, especially for the expansion of industrial and agricultural capacity and encouragement for schemes to limit the growth of population. As Galbraith points out, the provision of food from abroad is justified only if it "enlarges consumption for an *existing* population"—otherwise such aid merely aggravates problems by inducing an increase in numbers.

It is apparent that the future destinies of the rich nations cannot be isolated from those of the poor nations. Also it is clear that the latters' problems are extremely varied and complex, necessitating separate solutions for each category. Yet such solutions must be found if a future catastrophe of global proportions is to be avoided.

Planning—Problems and Potential

But the rich nations, too, have their problems, many of them reflecting the need for long-term *planning*.

As agricultural techniques become more highly scientific and efficient, more and more workers are released from the land and gravitate to the cities. In the United States, in 1900, eighteen out of every twenty Americans still earned their living with their hands, ten of these eighteen on the land. By 1979 this ratio had been reduced to four out of twenty, with only one of the four on farms. In Canada, in 1945, about twenty-eight per cent of the population was working in agriculture. By 1979 this number had dropped to five per cent. It is estimated that in 1980 more than ninety per cent of Canadians will live in less than one per cent of the area of the country, with one in three concentrated in the three major cities: Montreal, Toronto, and Vancouver. This trend is apparent in every industrialized country.

The effect on planning is apparent. Rural areas, having large open spaces with few people, require special consideration in being supplied with services like schools and roads. Urban centres, on the other hand, will require more and more services, and these too must be provided by the government.

Cities must have adequate means of transportation. Provision must be made for recreation and amusement, for parks and open spaces. Moreover, large urban concentrations usually include many people who do not have the skills considered useful and important to a healthy technological society. As a result there is a real danger that urban ghettoes will develop, where the unemployed and the unemployable live in sub-standard housing, requiring health and welfare services from the government. The excessive increase in urban populations and continuing industrial expansion also create the danger of pollution of air, water, and land resources.

Increasingly, then, the governments of western Europe and North America will have to accept the responsibility for planning economic and social developments. In many cases, this has involved a substantial modification of the *laissez-faire* principles upon which western society has traditionally been based. At the same time, however, those countries which traditionally have stressed central planning and control, have also had to adjust their approach to economic and social questions. Russian Communism, for example, had developed a strongly centralized economy, whereby all decisions were made in one place, and the local factories were told what to produce and when. Unfortunately, centralized decisions were not always responsive to local needs and situations, and more recently there has been a move to decentralize the decision-making process.

Since the Russian Revolution, the two systems of free enterprise and communism faced each other as combating theories or ideologies. The sharp contrast between the two points of view provided an additional emphasis to the political character of the Cold War. Economic and social influences, however, have forced both sides to moderate the way in which they put their theories into practice. Although in both capitalist and communist societies the "pure theory" is still propounded, the day-to-day decisions are made on a more practical basis.

In both societies also, the concentration of population and the need for centralized planning have produced large bodies of civil servants who implement and research government policy, a development which has caused problems of its own. Large bureaucracies tend to be cumbersome and inflexible; when a large number of people are involved in any organization, they often resist any changes that would upset their routine system of operation. This inherent "conservatism," or inertia, of bureaucracies is complicated by the rapidly-expanding use of such complex and expensive techniques as control by computers. An organization that has spent a great deal of money on expensive computer equipment often finds it easier to make the people serve the equipment rather than vice versa. Policy decisions, therefore, are often in terms of what is most suitable to the technology of the institution.

2. THE TECHNOLOGICAL REVOLUTION

Since 1945 the acquisition of scientific knowledge has progressed at a phenomenal rate. Over ninety per cent of all the scientists in history were living in the late 1970's! And of all the books ever published, more than seventy-five per cent have appeared in the past ten years. The extent and importance of this development can hardly be over-estimated.

In each field, the amount of knowledge available is expanding in geometric proportions. A person living in the 18th century could hope to master several disciplines. By the 19th, a person might hope to become an expert in one field, like physics or biology. In the late 20th century, it is as much as a scientist can do to keep abreast of developments within his or her own small section of a specific field. The high degree of specialization required has in fact produced its own problems, in the need for those who can intelligently synthesize apparently unrelated discoveries.

This increase in knowledge has had a direct influence on the way we live. What the scientist has discovered, the engineer has applied. Our style of life has been revolutionized in literally thousands of ways. In 1945, for instance, television was still experimental; there were no home freezers; refrigerators were not common; automatic washing machines did not exist; heating was usually done with coal; there was little indoor plumbing in country areas; even automobiles were much less common. Compare that with the situation of today!

Automation

The near-endless changes that have so radically affected everyday life are merely a small part of the Technological Revolution. The once rudimentary machines that made possible the Industrial Revolution, have now become so complex and self-regulating that it is common practice to manufacture articles without their being touched by human hands. The factory worker's task is no longer to run the machine, but merely to supervise an automatic production line and to watch for faults. This, briefly, is the meaning of "automation"— the substitution of machines for manual labour in carefully integrated systems of production. In agriculture, too, its influence is growing: cows are milked, fields are ploughed, crops are harvested, all by machines, and often by remote control.

While traditions of fine craftsmanship may suffer in the process, it is undeniable that automation has released millions of men and women from menial tasks, simultaneously raising their standards of living to unprecedented levels.

One of the keys to this more economical use of human resources has been the availability of wider educational opportunities for more than a privileged few. At no time in history, indeed, has so great a premium been placed on the value of education, for knowledge and its skilled application is essential to the continued growth of a technological society.

Computers

One of the principal reasons for our great progress in science, and an essential ingredient in many automated systems, has been the development since 1945 of "thinking machines."

Computers are not modern in conception. The abacus, an elementary manual computer using a frame with sliding markers, can be traced back to the first millenium B.C. The ancient Greeks had a form of odometer, an ingenious arrangement of gears, to compute distances covered by carriages.

The modern electronic computer, however, with bulky radio tubes long-since replaced by compact transistors, can do the most involved calculations in a fraction of a second, solving complicated mathematical equations that would previously have taken years, if not lifetimes, to accomplish.

Computers do not, of course, "think" in the human sense; that is they cannot evaluate emotional tension, nor are they capable of creative thought. They must be programmed in advance, and so are dependent on the minds of their human creators; but their capacity to store, analyse, and reproduce information in an instant, means they have virtually limitless applications—from simplifying routine commercial transactions and correlating masses of statistical data, to performing the incredible calculations necessary to land a space-ship on the moon; from aiding in city planning and crime control to making possible advanced medical research.

Communications

Electronic advances have also revolutionized communications. The use of microwaves has made it possible to send telephone messages and television programmes across whole continents without the expensive installation of cables. Communications satellites, like *Echo* and *Telstar*, have made it possible not only to beam live television programmes to the other side of the world, but also to receive instantaneous televised reports from astronauts. LASERs (light amplification by stimulated emission of radiation) promise immense information-carrying capacity for the future. Millions of television programs or a billion telephone calls might be transmitted on a single light beam.

In the field of radio-astronomy, equipment of such sensitivity has been developed that radio communication with life on other planets—if such there be!—is by no means inconceivable.

3. THE ENERGY CRISIS

The enormous productive capacity of modern industry is threatened by a growing energy crisis. In the period from 1968 through 1972 energy consumption in the non-Communist world increased at a rate of 5.6% per year. More significantly, the consumption of oil increased 7.5% per year. While substantial amounts of energy can be obtained from coal, gas, hydroelectric power and nuclear fission, it is oil that remains the primary source of power. There are large global resources of oil, mainly in the Middle East, but these will dwindle during the foreseeable future. This factor, together with the accelerated demands of industry, have meant a rapid escalation in the cost of oil. In 1972 the cost of foreign oil supplies for all importing countries was $20 billion; only two years later the equivalent cost was over $100 billion. These figures continued to increase at an alarming rate, disrupting normal patterns of world trade and raising political and strategic problems of great significance.

While the main reason for the energy crisis has been the accelerated demands of industry, principally in Europe, North America and Japan, the oil producing states have profited by the situation to make unprecedented financial gains. In order to understand their motivation it must be realized that, until about 1969, the international oil companies (with head offices in western capitals) determined levels of production, exports and prices. Consequently, Iran and the Arab states principally concerned, such as Saudi Arabia, Kuwait, and Iraq, maintained that their interests had suffered by the imposition of too low a level of prices, favouring the developed countries at the producers' expense. From 1969 onwards the Arabs were in the fortunate position of possessing huge resources of a commodity indispensable to the continued growth of western and Japanese industry. Realizing that this great asset would be exhausted, perhaps by the end of the present century, the Arabian states were determined to use their temporary advantage to strengthen their own economies and raise the standard of living of their peoples. The producing countries also argued that, by raising their prices, they were indirectly encouraging oil conservation and restricting non-essential consumption.

Unfortunately, the economic problem could not be separated from political considerations. We have already seen that, in 1973, during the renewed conflict between Israel and the Arab states, the latter employed their "oil weapon" to influence western policies.[1] In the United States, against whom the oil embargo was mainly directed, informed opinion was aghast at the consequences. The distinguished American diplomat and scholar, George F. Kennan, has observed: "Never, since the days when coal was the lifeline of all industrialized societies, and possibly not even then, has a great nation had a more vitally sensitive economic artery, and one by the damage of which it could more easily be paralyzed, than has the United States of 1977 in the flow of oil as a source of energy for a great portion of its economy." Yet, since the 1973 crisis, the American authorities have permitted their dependence on Arab producers to increase from 11 to 18%. In 1979 gas rationing was introduced in certain parts of the United States.

It is, however, in terms of high finance that the true dimensions of the energy crisis are most clearly seen. Briefly stated, by rapidly escalating oil prices over a relatively short period, the producing states have severely dislocated the world's monetary system. They have accumulated vast sums of money, far greater than the requirements of their own economies, which they can project at will into foreign investments or other enterprises. These huge transactions have an almost incalculable influence on international trade balances and rates of exchange of currencies. Indirectly, they stimulate an ever-rising inflationary trend (that is, higher cost of goods and services) from which virtually no nation is exempt. In the words of the West German statesman, Helmut Schmidt, "Oil has shaken the very foundations of the present world economic system."

The oil income of the Middle East producing countries increased from $4 billion in 1970 to $9 billion in 1972 and to $60 billion in

---

[1] See, above, Section 7 of Chapter 26.

1974. By that time the oil revenues of all participants in the Organization of Petroleum Exporting Countries (OPEC) reached nearly $100 billion. (By comparison the total national revenues of the Canadian Government in the fiscal year 1974-75 were $30 billion.) There is reason to believe that by 1985 American, European and Japanese oil imports will cost some $200 billion, or $150 billion more than in 1973.

What have the Arab states done with this enormous wealth? Some has been diverted for the strengthening of their internal economies, construction of public works, purchase of armaments, and improvement of social welfare and educational facilities. However, these expenditures, however lavish, are merely a drop in the bucket by comparison with the disposable surplus of funds available. The result has been that the OPEC countries have been able to make huge investments in the industrialized states which have been responsible for the surplus. This has raised the question of whether the international monetary system can sustain transfers of wealth of such unprecedented dimensions without serious disruption, or possibly even collapse. On the one hand, consuming countries have had to contend with almost intolerable strains due to rapidly rising prices and balance-of-payments problems. On the other, the oil producing countries have acquired increasing control over foreign industries through their investments. It might seem obvious that one solution would have been for the importing countries to make drastic cutbacks in oil imports and consumption. However, it was realized that such policies, resulting in an immediate reduction of total energy, would inevitably lead to a decline in production, employment and trade at a time when political leaders of the non-Communist world were desperately seeking means of stimulating these factors.

Nevertheless there have been some limitations on the Arab states' ability to exploit the energy crisis. While prepared to exact the maximum profit from a situation so favourable to their interests, they have at the same time shown an obvious disinclination to kill "the goose that lays the golden eggs." Any crisis resulting in a collapse of the industrial nations' economies would certainly not be beneficial to the OPEC countries. Indeed, it might mean that they would be in a much weaker position in relation to the Soviet Union, itself largely self-sufficient in oil. Since the Second World War the U.S.S.R. has exercised considerable influence in Iraq and Syria. The spectre of the hammer and sickle looming over their oil fields has been sufficient to keep the eyes of Middle Eastern potentates riveted on their lucrative markets in North America, Western Europe and Japan.

Moreover, the Arab states have not always agreed among themselves on economic and political issues. Although they achieved an impressive unity with their "oil weapon" during the 1973 war with Israel, they have been divided by internal disputes. Thus, Iran's consistent attempt to establish herself as the major strategic power in the Persian Gulf[1] and the Indian Ocean has led to bitter relations with Iraq and possibly Saudi Arabia. There are also disputes between Iraq and Kuwait and between Saudi Arabia and Abu Dhabi, at the entrance to the Persian Gulf.

One of the most interesting aspects of the energy crisis has been the attitude of the oil producing states to the needs of developing countries. It might be thought that, having so recently escaped from the economic feudalism of the international oil companies, these states would be particularly sensitive to the urgent needs of the developing countries. In some instances, as in the case of Iran, large credits have been extended to less fortunate states. In general, however, the oil magnates have exhibited extreme caution in such ventures. They have carefully assessed the creditworthiness of developing states and have preferred the more advanced and economically reliable countries for the investment of their oil revenues.

No one can say whether satisfactory solutions will be found to the energy crisis. It seems imperative that the oil consuming states must achieve a closer organization to provide a united front to the demands of OPEC. It also seems essential that the two groups must work together to attain a rational and equitable answer to their conflicting interests. Meanwhile, during the remaining decades of this century, and on into the next, the industrialized nations will redouble their efforts to exploit their own resources and other sources of energy. By 1980 Britain will be close to the self-sufficiency in oil already enjoyed by Norway. Apart from the working of unused oil reserves, including those in sands and shales, the consumer countries will concentrate research on the utilization of natural gas, coal and both hydroelectric and nuclear power. It is even possible that, at some distant date, the final solution to this difficult problem will be found in solar energy.

---

[1]The Iranian situation was complicated by an Islamic revolution leading to the deposition of the Shah in 1979.

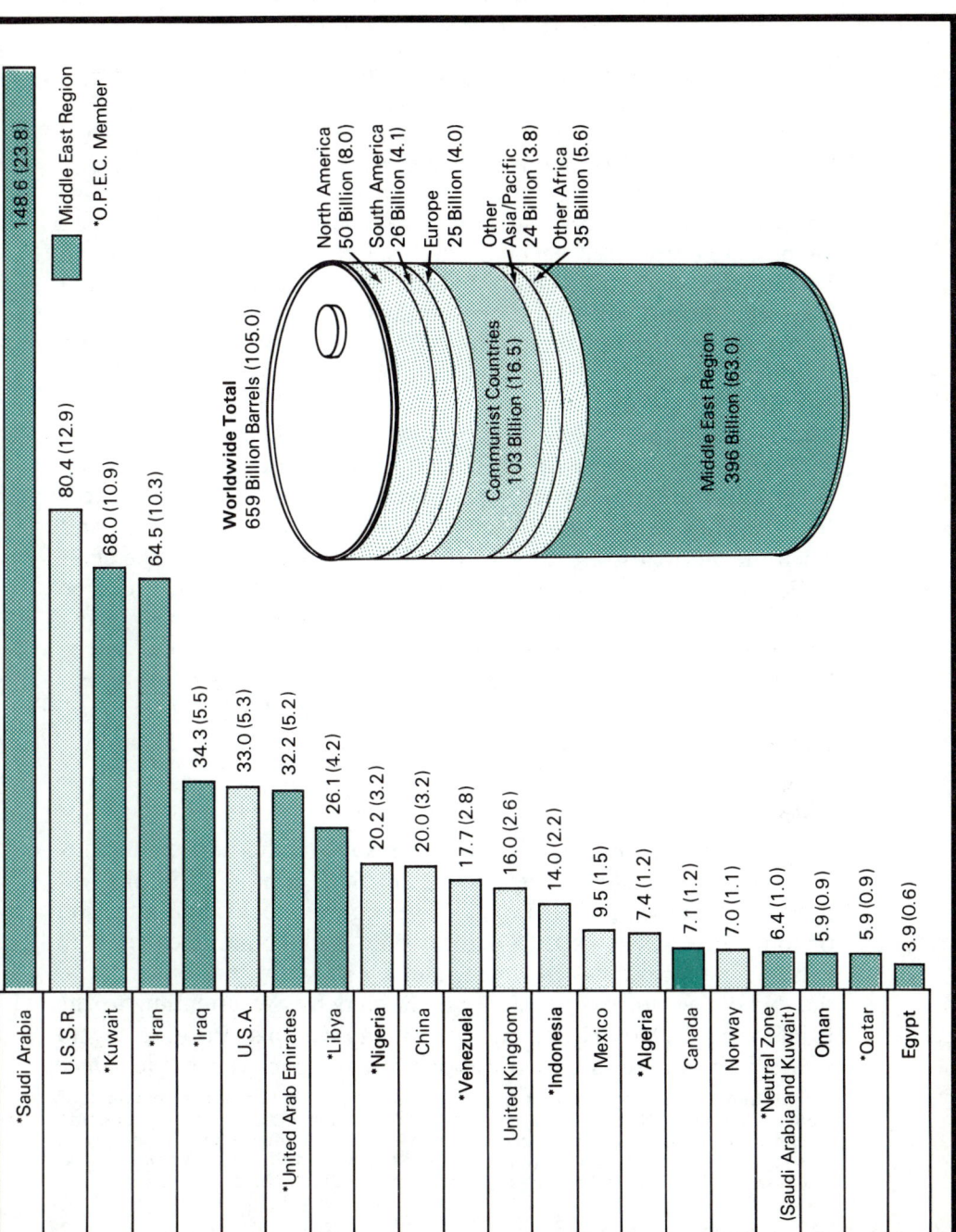

This chart illustrates the oil reserves of principal oil-producing nations and the worldwide total in 1976 in billions

4. THE IMPACT OF TECHNOLOGY ON MODERN THOUGHT

The Technological Revolution has invoked a number of moral and philosophical problems involving our very nature and our functions. Previously, we discovered our identity in our ability to work. Now, however, work is done more efficiently by machines, and our usefulness is often determined by the way in which we subordinate our actions to the effective use of the computer and the automated factory. Control has become impersonal rather than personal. People often seem in danger of becoming mere tools to be used, and may lose sight of themselves in the pursuit of what is called "progress." In the light of these new conditions created by technology, the dilemma of what it means to be human has become critical.

Four answers are suggested herein to this dilemma. The electronic age can be seen as *good* in promoting human values. It can be seen as *bad*, but inevitable, so that the only option the individual has is to retreat into himself to discover moments of unconditioned, free decision. It can be seen as bad, but *not* inevitable, if and when the all-inclusive character of this technological world be challenged and destroyed so that a new option can appear. Or it can be seen as *neutral*, presenting good and bad possibilities, and placing the responsibility on man to construct a more humane world on the foundation supplied by automation and technology. These alternatives are presented by four intellectual theorists: Marshall McLuhan, Jean-Paul Sartre, Herbert Marcuse, and John Kenneth Galbraith.[1]

Marshall McLuhan—Technology as Good

Marshall McLuhan suggests that the results of the new technology have been favourable. When the mechanical printing of books was introduced in the 15th century, people began to focus their attention on only one sense—sight. Before, they had communicated with each other by sounds, by touch, and by personal messenger. Now the "wholeness of experience" was limited by the attention to the printed word. This had a number of implications. Printing meant that the reader stood at a distance from the one who wrote. Since

---

[1] These four provide by no means a complete insight into modern thinking, of course, but they were selected here for their sharply differing approaches and backgrounds—Galbraith is an economist, Marcuse a philosopher and historian, Sartre a philosopher and novelist, while McLuhan defies categorization—and because they have all made a notable impact on public thinking.

he or she was not in direct contact, he or she was able to observe from outside, without becoming involved in what was said or what was described.

Modern electronic technology has changed that situation, argues McLuhan. Radio, television, and the telephone have reintroduced communication by sound. The person receiving information hears it at the same time that it is given, and he or she is able to feel more directly involved in what is happening. This sense of direct involvement has spread so that it affects much of contempory life, particularly among the young. They see directly, by television, the violence of wars at the other end of the world. They are immediately made aware of crises, wherever they occur. The electronic speed of communication through sound and sight overcomes the distance which the printed page had created. In this way the whole world has become a "global village," where each member of the human race feels a part of everything that is going on.

McLuhan suggests, then, that modern technology has opened up possibilities of rediscovering human values which were lost with the advent of the printed page. He is aware of the dangers which might be involved, but argues that if people understand what is going on, they can seize the new opportunities in such a way that their potential as human beings is increased rather than diminished.

Jean-Paul Sartre—Technology as Neutral

A quite different approach to the problem has been taken by the French thinker, Jean-Paul Sartre. Following the Second World War, Sartre attracted a great deal of attention by developing in books and plays the philosophy of *existentialism*. The roots of this philosophy go back into the 19th century, but Sartre sought to apply it to the critical situation in post-war Europe.

Sartre emphasized the danger that man would give up his humanity to impersonal forces. Anyone who acted on the authority of someone else, or simply allowed circumstances to determine what he did, was in danger of losing the essential qualities which made him really a man.

Man's responsibility, argued Sartre, lay in accepting that he had to "make himself." Every decision he took was an act by which he created his own nature. Therefore every decision was important. In the most critical decisions there is no reason to choose one way over the other, but the individual must face up to the fact that the decision is his alone, and once he has decided, he must accept full responsibility for what he has done. In this way he constructs his character.

Sartre illustrated this type of decision by telling the story of a young man who came to him for advice during the Second World War. His father had been a collaborator with the Germans, and was separated from his mother. His brother had been killed in the German offensive of 1940. The young man passionately wanted to revenge his brother, but at the same time he was the only support and centre of interest for his mother. Should he go to England and join the Free French, leaving his mother alone in despair, or should he remain with his mother in Nazi-occupied France? "I had but one reply to make," says Sartre. "You are free, therefore choose—that is to say, invent. No rule of general morality can show you what you ought to do."

The answer Sartre would give to the problem posed by technology, then, is clear: man is not a victim of circumstance, forced to comply with the restraints of society. Man is free to choose continually in the process of becoming himself. The future is a multitude of *potential* possibilities which only become *actual* by man himself making a choice. At every moment of decision man is free to determine what he will become. He need only accept his freedom and decide. In this way he will become master of his fate rather than be controlled by it, and technology, in these terms, becomes merely another tool man may use as he will.

Herbert Marcuse—Technology as Bad

Herbert Marcuse moves beyond this analysis. Instead of leaving the decision to the individual, he suggests that what is necessary is a challenge to the total structure of society. Marcuse was born in Germany and experienced the rise of Hitler. But he has more recently been working in the United States, and his thought has influenced many of those who are challenging the basic assumptions of western society.

Marcuse suggests that we are no longer free. Once we allow ourselves to become members of the society created by western technology and capitalism we can only become an expression, a reflection, of that society. Our thought is determined by radio, television, and newspapers to accept the values of our society. The decisions of what we must do to live, and how we are to spend our time, are already made for us: the need to use mechanical and electronic machines economically decides what people are needed to do what particular jobs. In other words, the demand dominating all of western society—to make as much money as possible in as efficient a manner as possible—has decreed that all people must fit into the order of society like cogs into a wheel. When anyone tries to think for him or herself, or question the values, their own sanity is questioned, and efforts are made to overcome the obstruction.

The modern technical, capitalistic world, argues Marcuse, is totalitarian. This does not mean that it uses tools of terror like Hitler or Stalin did. Rather, the total organization of life is accomplished with much more subtlety, through advertising and other media which permeate all of society with values determined by the machine. No one consciously decides that society is to be this way; indeed, even the persons at the top of the decision-making process are shaped by the values inherent in the system.

The only way that we can achieve a genuine system of values in which we can decide our own future, is by challenging the whole social structure. Only by saying "no" is one able to transcend the value system in which one lives. But when a single individual says "no," the prevailing consensus overwhelms him or her and incorporates him or her as an oddity into its total life. Organized groups are necessary, then, many people who together say "no," in order to overthrow the contemporary social structure and enable us to become our own masters again.

John Kenneth Galbraith—Technology as Potentially Good

The despair concerning current society and the call for revolution which mark Marcuse's thought are rejected by John Kenneth Galbraith. Galbraith, whose proposals for foreign aid to help the underdeveloped countries of the world were examined earlier in this chapter, wrote *The Affluent Society* and other books which have had an important impact on modern thinking.

Like Marcuse, Galbraith is aware of the tendency within the technological society of the machine to dominate people. He is also aware that the concern for maximum profits results in serious inequalities. But he does not feel that such implications as Marcuse draws from these trends are inevitable. Capitalism and technology ultimately are instruments which we can use to improve and enrich our lives. Society is free either to allow its whole life to be dominated by the goals of the industrial system, or to recognize that the industrial system "is only a part, and relatively a diminishing part, of life."

Therefore human values can be encouraged and developed within the patterns of contemporary society. But this possibility requires that there be those who are aware of what is happening, who understand the nature of the processes which influence the post-war world, and then are prepared to act. The action involved is political, for the political structures are the only ones which have sufficient power to direct and control the economic system. For it is in the political sphere that decisions can be taken which will determine the character of life. These decisions may be solely in response to the pressures of the industrial system and technology. Or they may seek to control this system so that the full range of human values in art, science, philosophy, religion, and culture can be extended and maintained. To accomplish this, however, it is necessary to have an educated and aware electorate, and to elect competent politicians to positions of responsibility.

5. THE CHANGING ROLE OF WOMEN IN THE MODERN AGE

Over 200 years ago Rousseau wrote: "Man is born free, and everywhere he is in chains."[1] Until comparatively recently, his statement might have been more applicable to woman. The emancipation of women has been a long and painful process; many would argue that it is still far from complete. Although history has recorded many instances of women attaining positions of great responsibility and exercising considerable influence on events, the vast majority have remained very much in the background. Not until this century did women achieve political rights equal to those of men.[2] Socially and economically their activities have been largely circumscribed by the nursery, kitchen and other demanding aspects of human existence.

It is ironical that much of the progress towards women's emancipation can be connected with their wartime efforts during the two global conflicts of this century. By replacing men in industry and undertaking a multitude of wartime tasks (including service in the

---
[1] See, above, p. 115.
[2] See, above, pp. 363-4.

armed services) women obtained increasing measures of economic independence and social recognition. In countries under Socialist or Communist domination this development has been assisted by what has been described as "the egalitarian ethic"—that is, the removal of class distinctions and the general levelling of social orders. However, in many parts of the world, particularly in Africa, Eastern Europe, Latin America, the Middle and Far East, women are still compelled to perform menial tasks. In these vast areas women still have very few of the fundamental rights taken for granted in the western world.

The feminist movement has made notable gains in the generation since the Second World War. In all walks of life women have shown greater confidence and determination to achieve actual, as well as theoretical equality of status with men. In politics this has meant representation in the highest legislative bodies; in the professions it has meant prominence in law, medicine and education; in business it has meant assumption of executive positions; in the arts it has meant increasing contribution to and influence on cultural standards.

The International Women's Year Conference held in Mexico City during the summer of 1975 testified to both the solidarity and diversity of women's ambitions. Here were gathered distinguished women from all parts of the globe, representing all colours, religions and political systems. It was, therefore, not surprising that the discussions reflected sharp disagreements between black and white, Arab and Israeli and rich and poor points of view. In the words of an American commentator, these conflicts "signified that the event was taking place in the real world, not as an academic exercise or an oversized coffee-klatch."

Soviet women at the conference saw essential issues in political terms — that is, the continuing struggle between capitalist and developing countries and the problems of the developing world. At a press conference the popular cosmonaut, Valentina Tereshkova, insisted that the majority of delegates were primarily concerned with imperialism, apartheid, racism and colonialism. The orthodox Soviet view was that the 1917 Revolution had liberated women, as part of the working masses, from all forms of oppression. In support of this contention the Soviets could point out that, in the U.S.S.R., over seventy per cent of the doctors were women, as were over forty per cent of all administrators and specialists in industry and over a third of the engineers. Russian women had attained numerical equality with men in professional employment. Moreover, Communist authorities in the U.S.S.R. and Eastern Europe had provided maternity benefits and social services on a generous scale for working mothers. In addition to five months' maternity leave, a Hungarian mother was entitled to three full years off with a government allowance. At the end of that time she could have her job back if she so desired. On the other hand, the Soviets could not deny that very few women in Russia had attained high positions of authority. Only six per cent of the heads of industry were women; only four per cent had attained the Communist Party's Central Committee and only one woman had become a member of the Presidium, the supreme governing authority in the U.S.S.R. Much of the menial work, including street cleaning, is still done by older women.

At Mexico City women from poorer countries of the Third World voiced a strongly anti-colonial point of view. Their resentment was directed particularly against the United States because it was the leading capitalist power, recently engaged in war against North Vietnam. The representatives of the developing countries were also more concerned with rural than urban problems. As expressed by the female Prime Minister Sirimave Bandaranaike of Sri Lanka (formerly Ceylon): "It is in the rural areas that the problems of poverty and underdevelopment are most acute. It is in these areas that the bulk of the population in the developing nations have to find a meaning or fulfilment in life." African and Asian women voiced discontent with western aid programmes which too often emphasized training for men at the expense of labour-saving devices for women. "They described the workday of the rural women, many of whom must walk miles fetching water and gathering firewood, as well as spending hours grinding millet or pounding cassava—after working a full day in the fields."

Nearly one-sixth of the world's women live in India, where Indira Gandhi was Prime Minister for eleven years. But it is only a small, educated elite (perhaps in a ratio of one to three hundred) that has had the opportunity to hold positions of influence. It must, however, be conceded that men's opportunities for advancement are similarly limited. An official report issued by the Indian Government in 1974 stated that "the great mass of Indian women are still abysmally backward and this, indeed, is the main reason why India moves so slowly in the total process of modernizing herself." More than four-fifths of Indian women are illiterate and forty per cent of the remainder are considered semi-literate. Despite exposure to western ideas, many still observe traditional values of Indian family life, including acquiescence to the husband's authority and acceptance of ties imposed by a high birth rate. Occasional cases of *sati* (burning a widow on her husband's funeral pyre) still occur. It is clear that the Indian woman's progress to true emancipation will be long and difficult.

Elsewhere, Latin American women have had many grievances arising out of a tradition of male domination. In Moslem countries severe codes of conduct regulate all aspects of feminine activity. Japanese labour laws discriminate against women in pay, hours of work and promotion prospects, and widows receive only one-third of their husband's estate, the remainder going to the children.

In the western world women have fared much better, although old customs making women subordinate to men have not died easily. As Lady Birk, the British Undersecretary of State for the Environment, stated: "Parliament can change laws, but it cannot change minds." Even today one college at Oxford University still bars women as undergraduate students. However, a great advance was recorded in the British elections of 1979 when the Conservative leader, Margaret Thatcher, became the first woman prime minister in British and European history.

Members of the European Economic Community have agreed in principle to abolish sex discrimination in jobs and promotions, and to enforce equal pay for equal work. In 1978 Sweden had six women cabinet ministers. British legislation has permitted women to enter into legal contracts in their own right, guaranteed them equal pay and safeguarded the jobs of pregnant women. The French constitution guarantees equal rights for women. In practice, however, many west European women still work as clerks and typists, earning on the average thirty per cent less than men in similar employment.

North American women have made considerable progress towards true equality with men in social, economic and political matters. However, there are lingering injustices in some fields and relatively few women have attained positions of high authority in national, state or provincial arenas. It must be noted that restricted and expensive facilities for child care are a factor; but, to some extent, the reason for this retarded development may be due more to lack of motivation on the part of the majority of women than to repressive legislation.

In the United States the problems of black women have been the

Several outstanding women of the 20th century

Left: Gold Meir, Prime Minister of Israel 1969-1974

Lower right: Katherine Graham, publisher of The Washington Post

Lower left: Margaret Thatcher, Prime Minister of Great Britain 1979 -

Left:
Valentina Tereshkova, first woman to fly in outer space (1963)

Lower left:
Simone de Beauvoir, philosopher, novelist, playwright

Lower right:
Dr. Margaret Mead, anthropologist, author, lecturer, social critic

subject of intensive study. The movement towards "black liberation" in the 1960's did not work entirely in the women's interests. As one investigator concluded: "The black man grapples to achieve social justice and parity with the white male—essentially to attain white male power, privilege and status—while black women are shoved to the back of the bus." However, black feminists have shown a capacity to combine and fight for their rights, partly by the formation in 1973 of the Black Women's Organization for Action (B.W.O.A.) and the National Black Feminist Organization (N.B.F.O.). Nevertheless United States census statistics have consistently revealed that black women have a long way to go, since they are the poorest paid in the occupational structure.

While exceptional figures like Indira Gandhi and the late Golda Meir have exerted great influence on the world during recent decades, women have not yet exerted their full potential in international affairs. There is a great need for their participation in the formulation of world policies at the U.N. and elsewhere, especially policies dealing with food, housing, population control, community planning and standards of living. As Margaret Mead, the noted American anthropologist, has stated: "When there are no women's voices heard in the international councils related to food or population control, the debate is one-sided, limited to the traditionally or recently preempted activities of men. The people of the world therefore suffer."

6. RELIGION IN THE TECHNOLOGICAL AGE

Religious bodies have also responded to the changed demands of the post-war period. This can be seen most dramatically in the Roman Catholic Church. Over the four centuries since the Reformation, the Roman Church had become hardened into a position which affirmed as absolute the values and practices of the late Middle Ages. Latin was still used in worship. All decisions were made in Rome, even though they were often only of local interest. Strict care was taken lest, by co-operating with other Christian Churches, the faith as it had been affirmed would be diluted.

In the fall of 1962, however, a council of all the Roman Catholic bishops in the world convened at the Vatican in Rome. Previous councils had met to assert the Church's position against dangerous beliefs and heresies; this one was called by Pope John XXIII to renew the vitality of the Church. The bishops, aware of the dramatic new forces operating in the technological society, and conscious that representatives of other Christian denominations were observing them, instituted many reforms over the four years of the Ecumenical Council.

One of the most important of these changes was the recognition that the Roman Catholic Church should not be a centralized bureaucracy. The bishops in each country were given some freedom to determine the character of the Church in their own land, and in this way they have been able to adapt worship and Church organization to the particular concerns of their area.

A second important change was the recognition of the Christian values to be found in other denominations. As a result, co-operation between Roman Catholics, Protestants, and Orthodox Christians has developed in study and action for social change. To a limited extent Roman Catholics have begun to worship together with other Christians. This interest in dialogue and discussion has gone beyond the limits of Christendom, and contact has been made with Jews, Moslems, and Marxists.

The new openness of 20th century society led many Roman Catholics to question aspects of the way in which their faith had been understood and practised. Theologians began to rethink their belief. Others questioned the traditional stand against using artificial contraceptives as a means of birth control. While some pushed for change, others were afraid that by changing too much, too hastily, the Church would lose the deposit of faith it had acquired by strict adherence to traditional dogma. Tension developed between the progressives and the conservatives. As a result, Pope Paul VI, John XXIII's successor, attempted to steer a middle course. In some ways he had been willing to break with precedent. He was the first Pope, for instance, ever to go to Israel, India, South America, and to the United Nations. On the other hand, he checked some of those who argued for change, particularly in his encyclical which reaffirmed the traditional stand against artificial methods of birth control. In 1978 the Vatican suffered a double loss when Paul VI died and his successor, John Paul I, died shortly afterwards. The new Pope, John Paul II, was the first Polish bishop to hold this high office. A vigorous personality with wide interests (he has written a play, *The Jeweller's Shop,* and is an ardent skier) the Pope has taken positive positions against materialism and for Christian unity.

World Council of Churches

This tension between those who argue that the Church should keep pace with changing society, and those who argue that the Church has a basic obligation to an unchanging faith has also affected Protestants.

One of the most significant moves made in the post-war world was the establishment of the World Council of Churches in 1948. Many of the main denominations agreed to co-operate in a common body. The purposes of this body were two-fold. On the one hand they would discuss their faith so that they might clarify their differences, and then see if it were possible for denominations to unite. In the second place, they would co-operate in areas of social action and social need. Later the World Council undertook also to regulate and encourage the extension of the Christian faith and values in areas where there was no strong local Church.

Initially the World Council included, among others, Anglicans, Methodists, Presbyterians, Congregationalists, some Baptists, and some Lutherans. Gradually the membership increased, until in 1961 many Orthodox Churches, including the Russian Orthodox and a couple of Pentecostal Churches in Chile, had joined the organization. More recently the World Council has co-operated with the Roman Catholic Church, although the latter has not become a member of the Council.

While there have been discussions over differences in doctrine, there has not been much evidence that the various denominations are willing to unite. Although the United Church of Canada was formed in 1925 from the Methodists, the Congregationalists, and some of the Presbyterians in Canada, Church union negotiations in most countries have generally broken down or been delayed. Only the Church of South India has achieved notable success in uniting different traditions.

However, the World Council has been effective in the area of social concern. It has held regular conferences which have discussed the relationship between Church and society. And it has established a central agency for relief and aid, so that funds and other resources can be focused quickly in emergencies. In many areas, Church relief, undertaken by the World Council or national Church groups, has proven more effective than that undertaken by other bodies, particularly in refugee relief work, and the emergency supply of provisions to disaster areas.

"Religionless" Christianity

But it is not only in these official ways that the Protestant Churches have attempted to relate to the world since 1945. Their theologians have also struggled to express the significance of the faith in a rapidly changing society. The keynote to this process of rethinking was sounded in some letters written from a Nazi concentration camp during the Second World War by Dietrich Bonhoeffer, a German who had taken part in the plot to assassinate Hitler. While he was in prison, he noticed that his fellow prisoners did not react to the uncertainty of their position in a religious way. When air attacks came they did not pray, and they did not rely on a belief in God to explain what was happening to them. Bonhoeffer asked himself if modern society was moving beyond the age of religion, and he suggested that Christianity needed to be rethought in non-religious terms.

The idea of a "religionless Christianity" intrigued other Protestant thinkers after the war, although not all followed the same direction as Bonhoeffer. Bonhoeffer interpreted Christianity as a means by which men would share the suffering of the world as a way of expressing their faith. Some interpretations have tried to spell out the nature of Christianity without using the idea of God. Others have suggested that all theories and ideas about God should be dropped, and that Christians should work out the meaning of their faith in the social and political arena. Thus, in the United States particularly, many of the leaders of the Civil Rights movement and anti-war protests have been clergymen.

Another major effort to reinterpret Christian thought was made by Paul Tillich, a German theologian who settled in the United States during the 1930's. Tillich suggested that by analysing human nature and character, one could become aware of the basic questions which dominate one's life: Why is there "something" rather than "nothing?" What does it mean to be a human being? What type of life should I live? Having clarified the questions, Tillich then suggested that the Christian understanding of God, of Jesus, and the Spirit could be reinterpreted to provide ultimately satisfying answers. Thus he called God "the ground of being," and he considered Jesus to be a man who was "transparent," so that this ground of being could become visible in the world.

A contrary school of thought centred around the writings of Karl Barth, a Swiss theologian who also had been forced out of Germany by the Nazis. Barth claimed that people on their own could not even ask the right questions. Only when God reveals himself can people begin to know what God and life are all about. Since God revealed himself only in Jesus, it was the task of the theologian to spell out the significance of Jesus' life, death, and resurrection. However, Barth and his followers recognized the necessity for critically examining the Bible as an historical document.

Evangelism

There are many Christians who still claim that the Bible is the Word of God, given in such a way that whatever it says can be taken as literally true. These Christians may be loosely called "conservative evangelicals," although there is much disagreement among themselves and they are continually dividing into different groupings. The Christians who belong to this group have refused to become involved in the World Council of Churches. Since many of the Churches which belong to the World Council are willing to submit the Bible to the critical examination of historical scholarship, the conservative evangelicals argue that the former have abandoned the basic Christian belief. In addition, they claim that the concern of the World Council for social and political matters represents a turning away from the religious faith which is concerned with *personal* salvation.

In an age when change occurs so quickly, the conservative evangelicals affirm that only one focal point provides security and a firm footing: the writings contained in the Bible. The best-known proponent of this approach to Christianity is Billy Graham. Graham believes firmly in the literal authority of the Bible, and he uses its writings as the foundation for comments on the changing patterns of society. He claims that human beings are basically sinners and can overcome their sin only by believing in Jesus. Using modern media techniques, Graham confronts people with the need to make a "decision for Christ." While he is willing to co-operate with other Christians, he is still critical of those who are not prepared to commit themselves to the search for personal salvation. Billy Graham and other high-powered evangelists, on the other hand, have been criticized for "selling" religion as if it were a commodity.

Judaism

For Judaism the most significant post-war development has been the establishment of the State of Israel. The almost-successful policy of genocide undertaken by the Nazis during the Second World War united all Jews throughout the world, and those who escaped the Nazi-dominated lands fled to Palestine. In 1948, the United Nations decreed that a part of Palestine would become a separate Jewish State.

This decree has had serious political repercussions, since the Arabs of the Middle East have never accepted that the land was legitimately taken away from them. But its importance to Jews cannot be overestimated, for Israel has become the one nation in the world where there is no possibility of anti-Semitic persecution. The fact that the land of Palestine, according to their tradition, is the land promised to them by God, gives it added religious significance.

Other religions, too, have begun to be more aware of their own traditions and culture. Buddhism in the Far East, Hinduism in India, and Islam in the Near East, have attempted to spell out more clearly the specific nature of their particular faith.

Religious Strife

For all the co-operation and interaction represented by the World Council of Churches and the latest Vatican Council, many of the conflicts of the post-war era have had religious aspects. India, on gaining her independence, was torn apart by strife between Hindus and Moslems. Moslems and Christians fought over the future of Cyprus. Moslems and Jews still threaten each other in the Middle East. Northern Ireland has been the scene of continuing tension and outbursts of violence between the Protestant majority and the Catholic minority. In Nigeria, a civil war divided Christian Biafra and the predominantly non-Christian remainders of the country from 1967 to 1970.

Wars of religion are not yet over, for religions claim to make an ultimate affirmation about the nature of life; and when two conflicting ultimates confront each other, they must be willing to compromise or there will be an explosion. It is a confrontation similar to the conflict between the capitalist West and the Communist East. The greatest need of the latter part of the 20th century is to find a way by which ultimate claims of allegiance can learn to live side by side.

7. TOWARDS THE TWENTY-FIRST CENTURY

In 1800 a person's speed was limited on land by that of a horse, on water by the speed of a sailing ship. One could travel from one place to another hardly faster, in fact, than one could make the same journey two thousand years previously. Only a century ago it took days to cross France, and it was many weeks' arduous journey by stagecoach to cross America. Today a person can eat breakfast in London, lunch in Montreal, and dinner in Vancouver. Within living memory the French novelist, Jules Verne, entertained a sceptical public with his vivid account of a fictional submarine, the *Nautilus*, twenty thousand leagues under the sea. Today a whole family of atomic-powered submarines can perform all that Verne visualized and more. And in outer space, where people have travelled millions of kilometres at speeds many times that of sound, the last physical frontier is yielding its secrets to exploration by manned rockets.

A single generation has indeed seen science fiction become fact. Today there would appear to be no limit to our potential material progress. The question becomes only in what field of endeavour we should concentrate our resources.

Radar and Jet Propulsion

It is one of the ironies of history that money which cannot be found for research projects in peacetime is readily available when national security is at stake. Two examples of this are radar—short for "radio detection and ranging"—and jet propulsion.

Before the Second World War a brilliant British scientist, Sir Robert Watson-Watt, had been experimenting with the use of radio echoes in meteorological research. He discovered that short radio waves were reflected by solid objects at a constant speed, thus making it possible to measure the distance between the transmitter and a given target. As we have seen, application of this principle to the air defence of the United Kingdom was a major factor in the success of the R.A.F. against the *Luftwaffe* in the Battle of Britain.[1] After the war, radar became an indispensable aid to air and marine navigation, giving pilots reliable information at night and in conditions of poor visibility.

Similarly, the principle of jet propulsion first found practical

[1] See above, p. 560.

"The Faces of Famine."

ABOVE: astronaut David Scott emerging from the Apollo-9 Lunar Module.
BELOW: the surface of Mars, photographed by Mariner 4 spacecraft.

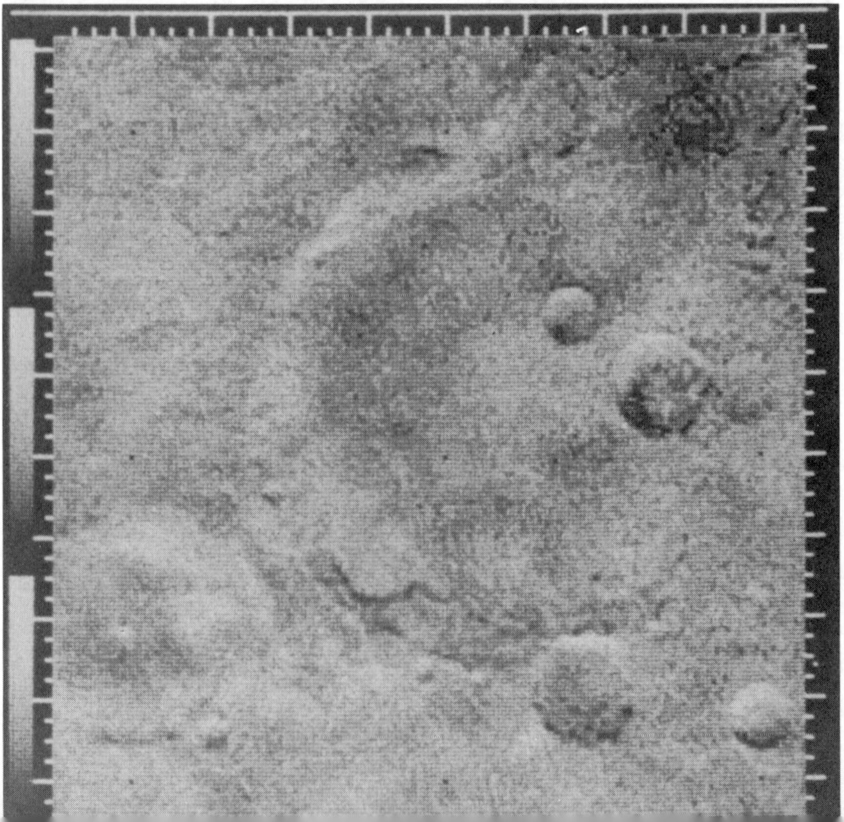

ABOVE: ". . . to explore the nature of the smallest thing."—the world's largest proton synchroton, under construction near Moscow. RIGHT: Having read over 700 pages of *Modern Perspectives*, you should certainly recognize this place!

application in military aircraft. In England and Germany the pioneers in this field were Frank Whittle and Hans von Ohain, respectively. Technical problems and the heavy costs of production delayed the appearance of jet aircraft in civilian transportation, but the turbojet-powered transports were brought into use during the 1950's. Commercial airlines were not slow to realize the advantages of planes that combined faster, smoother speeds with lower maintenance costs. The first supersonic airliner, the Soviet Tu-144, flew in 1969. At the end of 1977 the *Concorde,* a joint Anglo-French production, introduced a new phase in transatlantic travel, reducing the time taken to three and a half hours.

Rockets and Space Travel

Much of the impetus for space research, too, has come as an almost incidental consequence of military competition. To develop atomic and hydrogen bombs, sophisticated scientific research was required into the fundamental nature of matter. To deliver such bombs without using manned aircraft, I.C.B.M.'s (inter-continental ballistic missiles) were produced. It was this missile research that led to the technology necessary for the exploration of space.

The first use of heavy rockets was by Germany against Britain in the Second World War. The liquid-fuel (V-2) rocket became the basis for great advances in peacetime by the United States and the Soviet Union, who alone had the financial and industrial resources, and technological knowledge, to profit immediately from German experience. Spurred on by the desire to achieve missile superiority over each other, these Powers were soon engaged in a so-called "space race" that captured the world's imagination.

October 4, 1957, was the date of an electrifying event in the history of science. On that date the U.S.S.R. projected its first *sputnik* (meaning, literally, travelling companion) into an orbit circling the earth at a speed of about thirty thousand kilometres per hour. This satellite had a mass of a mere ninety kilograms and reached an altitude of only eight hundred kilometres. A month later the Russians scored again, sending the half-tonne *Sputnik II* about seventeen hundred kilometres into space. Two-and-a-half years later, in April, 1961, the Russian Major Yuri Gagarin became the first man to orbit the globe, remaining aloft for eighty-nine minutes.

American progress in the exploration of outer space was initially delayed by organization problems. It was decided that the satellite programme (Project "Vanguard") would be carried out under civilian direction and would not be permitted to interfere with the higher priority granted military programmes for ballistic missiles. Consequently, those entrusted with "Vanguard" had to design, develop, and test their own three-stage rockets, and it was not until January, 1958, that the first American satellite, Explorer I, was launched. Four years passed before the United States had its first manned capsule in orbit around the earth.

In the meantime, rockets were launched in orbit around the sun, and probes photographed from close range the surfaces of Mars and Venus. At Christmas, 1968, the American Apollo 8 spacecraft circled the moon carrying three astronauts. For the first time in history human beings were temporarily unable to see the planet Earth—the moon was in their way. Then came what surely must be one of the most extraordinary events of all time—a human being, Neil Armstrong, took the first steps on a non-terrestrial body and, most incredible of all, the whole world was watching. July 20, 1969, the date men reached the moon, will always be marked as the day a new age began.

The great achievements of the 1960's have been continued in the succeeding decade. Both the United States and the U.S.S.R. have launched probes to study the characteristics of solar wind, cosmic rays, ultraviolet and X-ray radiation and gamma rays in outer space. Scientists of both countries have paid particular attention to the exploration of Venus, earth's inhospitable neighbour. The Soviets were successful in landing their "Venera 7" probe on Venus in 1970. At the end of 1978, the American "Orbiter" spacecraft completed a 480 million kilometre, seven-month journey to circle Venus. This vehicle used radar to map a large area of the planet while continuing measurements of the upper atmosphere. Another American spacecraft, "Voyager I", launched in 1977 passed near Jupiter in 1979, and was scheduled to reach Saturn in 1980. Scientists believe that information gained from these explorations may cast new light on the mysteries of the solar system.

With modern advances in technology, are we not nearer a Utopian society—a life in which the drudgery of the past will be replaced by leisure and opportunities for self-fulfilment? The question is not easily answered. Certainly through the ages human beings have painfully raised their standard of living to a high level in certain regions of the earth. But, as we have seen, this notable advance has not been universal, and a large part of the world's

"... but what shall be the birthright of man?"

population still remains close to the subsistence level. The ghastly threat of nuclear warfare, or even more sinister weapons of destruction such as the neutron bomb, is always present.

It is also becoming more and more apparent that new conveniences create new problems. A common example is the automobile, designed to give us more mobility. The very factor (mass production) which placed this vehicle within the reach of ordinary people has also created terrible problems of traffic congestion, highway accidents, and even air pollution. Indeed, pollution not just of the air, but also of land and water, casts a dark shadow over many modern achievements. For decades scientists and technologists have been sounding the alarm about the terrible effects of pollution, mainly due to industrial waste. In all probability drastic remedies will be required to control the injurious aspects of certain technological advances.

Beyond these difficulties lies an even greater problem. As our working hours are shortened, as all our normal requirements are satisfied, what will we do with our leisure?

Will we find complete satisfaction in intellectual, cultural and athletic activities? Will we, for the first time in the history of ordinary people, be satisfied with a life without struggle for essentials? Will we become more humanitarian, in the sense of helping less-favoured inhabitants of the globe, or will we become intoxicated with a new surge of aggressive power? Will we be content with an earthly existence when the mystery of outer space beckons? On the answers to these, and similar questions, will depend the future happiness—perhaps even the existence—of humanity.

Source Readings

I ABSOLUTISM

It can be a very illuminating study of the nature of absolutism to observe some of its proponents in action. The following readings provide revealing glimpses of two great monarchs: Louis XIV of France, and Frederick William of Prussia.

1. LOUIS DE RONVRAY, Duc de Saint-Simon (1675-1755) *was a soldier, diplomat, and gossip. He recorded the doings of the court at Versailles in great detail, and his description of Louis XIV is the most vivid that has come down to us. These passages are drawn from his* Memoirs, *which he began to write in 1740 at the age of sixty-five.*

The King Arises

At eight o'clock the chief *valet de chambre* on duty, who alone had slept in the royal chamber, and who had dressed himself, awoke the King. The chief physician, the chief surgeon, and the nurse (as long as she lived) entered at the same time. . . . At quarter past the hour the grand chamberlain was called and all those who had what was called the *grandes entrées*. The chamberlain drew back the curtains which had been closed again, and presented the holy water from the vase, at the head of the bed. These gentlemen stayed but a moment, and that was the time to speak to the King, if anyone had anything to ask of him; in which case the rest stood aside. When, contrary to custom, nobody had aught to say, they were there but for a few moments. He who had opened the curtains and presented the holy water, presented also a prayerbook.

Then all passed into the cabinet of the council. A very short religious service being over, the King called, and they re-entered. The same officer gave him his dressing-gown; immediately after, other privileged courtiers entered, and then everybody, in time to find the King putting on his shoes and stockings, for he did almost everything himself and with address and grace. Every other day we saw him shave himself; and he had a little short wig in which he always appeared, even in bed. . . . No toilet table was near him; he had simply a mirror held before him.

As soon as he was dressed, he prayed to God, at the side of his bed, where all the clergy knelt, the cardinals without cushions, all the laity remaining standing; and the captain of the guards came to the balustrade during the prayer, after which the King passed into his cabinet. He found there a very numerous company, for it included everybody in any office. He gave orders to each for the day; thus within less than ten minutes it was known what he meant to do; and then all this crowd left directly. . . .

All the court meantime waited for the King in the gallery, the captain of the guard being alone in the chamber, seated at the door of the cabinet. . . . During this pause the King gave audiences, when he wished to accord any, and gave secret interviews to foreign ministers. They were called "secret" simply to distinguish them from the uncommon ones by the bedsides.

The King Dines

The dinner was always *au petit couvert,* that is, the King ate by himself in his chamber upon a square table in front of the middle window. It was more or less abundant, for he ordered in the morning whether it was to be "a little," or "very little" service. But even at this last, there were always many dishes, and three courses without counting the fruit. The dinner being ready, the principal courtiers entered; then all who were known; and the first gentlemen of the chamber on duty, informed the King. . . .

The King Retires

At ten o'clock his supper was served. The captain of the guard announced this to him. . . . This supper was always on a grand scale, the royal household at table, and a large number of courtiers and ladies present, sitting or standing. . . .

After supper the King stood some moments, his back to the balustrade of the foot of his bed, encircled by all his court; then, with bows to the ladies, passed into his cabinet, where on arriving, he gave his orders. He passed a little less than an hour there, seated in an armchair. . . .

The King, wishing to retire, went and fed his dogs; then said good night, passed into his chamber, where he said his prayers, as in the morning, and undressed. He said good night with an inclination of the head, and while everybody was leaving the room stood at the corner of the mantelpiece, where he gave the order to the colonel of the guards alone. Then commenced what was called the *petit coucher,* at which only specially privileged persons remained. They did not leave until he got into bed.

T. C. Mendenhall, B. D. Henning, and A. S. Foord,
Ideas and Institutions in European History, 800-1715
(Henry Holt, 1948), pp. 303-304.

2. *Another ruler who took great pains to see that his son was properly versed in the role of the absolute monarch was* FREDERICK WILLIAM I *of Prussia (1713-40). Here is a condensed version of his practical instructions for the upbringing of the future Frederick the Great.*

. . . Above all else, it is important that his character—and it is character which governs all human action—should be, from earliest youth, so formed that he will love and delight in virtue and feel horror and disgust for vice. . . .

For other men are guided toward virtue and away from evil by the rewards and punishments dealt out by those who are set above them, but the prince must rely on the fear of God alone, since he is subject to no human law, punishment, or reward.

My son and all his attendants shall say their prayers on their knees both morning and evening, and after prayers shall read a chapter from the Bible.

He shall be kept away from operas, comedies, and other worldly amusements and, as far as possible, be given a distaste for them. He must be taught to pay proper respect and submission to his parents, but without slavishness.

His tutors must use every means they can devise to restrain him from puffed-up pride and insolence and to train him in good management, economy, and modesty. And since nothing is so harmful as flattery, all those who are about the person of my son are forbidden to indulge in it on pain of my extreme displeasure. . . .

As for the Latin language, he is not to learn it, and I desire that no one shall even speak to me on this subject; but his tutors shall see to it that he acquires a terse and elegant style in writing French as well as German. Arithmetic, mathematics, artillery, and agriculture he must be taught thoroughly, ancient history only superficially, but that of our own time and of the last one hundred and fifty years as accurately as possible. He must have a thorough knowledge of law, of international law, of geography, and of what is most remarkable in each country; and, above all, my son must be carefully taught the history of his own House.

His tutors must take the greatest pains to imbue my son with a sincere love for the soldier's profession and to impress upon him that nothing else in the world can confer upon a prince such fame and honor as the sword, and that he will be despised by all the world if he does not only love it but seek in it his only glory; and his chief tutor shall provide for his being taught the practice of arms as play in his recreation hours. . . .

The instructions seemed to have been in vain. Here is what the crown prince, at sixteen, timidly wrote to his father:

WUSTERHAUSEN, September 11, 1728

I have not ventured for a long time to present myself before my dear papa, partly because I was advised against it, but chiefly because I anticipated an even worse reception than usual and feared to vex my dear papa still further by the favor I have now to ask; so I have preferred to put it in writing.

I beg my dear papa that he will be kindly disposed toward me. I do assure him that after long examination of my conscience I do not find the slightest thing with which to reproach myself; but if, against my wish and will, I have vexed my dear papa, I hereby beg most humbly for forgiveness, and hope that my dear papa will give over the fearful hate which has appeared so plainly in his whole behavior and to which I cannot accustom myself. I have always thought hitherto that I had a kind father, but now I see the contrary. However, I will take courage and hope that my dear papa will think this all over and take me again into his favor. Meantime I assure him that I will never, my life long, willingly fail him, and in spite of his disfavor I am still, with most dutiful and childlike respect, my dear papa's

Most obedient and faithful servant and son,

FREDERICK

And Frederick William harshly replied:

A bad, obstinate boy, who does not love his father; for when one does one's best, and especially when one loves one's father, one does what he wishes not only when he is standing by but when he is not there to see. Moreover you know very well that I cannot stand an effeminate fellow who has no manly tastes, who cannot ride or shoot (to his shame be it said!), is untidy about his person, and wears his hair curled like a fool's instead of cutting it; and that I have condemned all these things a thousand times, and yet there is no sign of improvement. For the rest, haughty, oafish as a country lout, conversing with none but a favored few instead of being affable and popular, grimacing like a fool, and never following my wishes out of love for me but only when forced into it, caring for nothing but to have his own way, and thinking nothing else is of any importance. This is my answer.

FREDERICK WILLIAM

J. H. Robinson and C. A. Beard, *Readings in Modern European History* (Ginn, 1935), I, 65-67.

II DUEL FOR EMPIRE

With the discovery that new lands lay overseas, nations saw that in the future the source of wealth and power would lie in foreign holdings. How did kingdoms and empires gird themselves for the competition? The following selections illustrate some of the ways in which France and Prussia prepared themselves for the duel for empire.

1. COLBERT (1619-83) *was keenly ambitious to promote French trade and industry. The memoranda printed below show how carefully he watched for weak spots in France's economic structure, and how ruthlessly he accepted any means to eliminate competition.*

A Memorandum, 1666

It is necessary to observe carefully, on all purchases, that they must always be made in France rather than in foreign countries, even if the goods should be a little inferior in quality and a little more expensive, because when money does not go out of the kingdom the advantage to the state is double, in that since the money stays in it, it does not grow poor, and the subjects of the king earn their living and use their energy.

For example, the three thousand musket barrels, 3½ feet long and of the calibre of 16 to the pound, ordered in Biscaye, could easily be ordered either in Forez or Nivervais; and it would be a fine thing to begin to establish the manufacture of them in Angoumois, or in Guienne, or in Brittany.

A Memorandum, 1670

Your Majesty has undertaken a war of money against all the states of Europe. Your Majesty has already conquered Spain, Italy, Germany, England, and some others, in which he has caused great misery and want, and by despoiling them he has enriched himself. Only Holland is left, and it fights with great resources: its commerce with the North, which brings it so many advantages and such a great reputation for its sea forces and its navigation; that of the East Indies, which brings it every year 12 000 000 in cash; its commerce with Cadiz and that with Guinea and an infinity of others in which its strength consists and resides. Your Majesty has formed companies which, like armies, attack them everywhere. . . .

Many other new establishments that your Majesty is making are so many reserve corps that your Majesty creates and brings out of nothingness to perform their duty in this war, in which your Majesty sees clearly that he is winning every year some considerable advantage of such a sort that even the vanquished cannot conceal their losses and make them known by the continual complaints that they utter, through the mouths of their merchants, as to the decrease of their commerce.

This war, which consists only in wit and energy, and of which the spoil is the most powerful republic since that of the Romans must be the prize of victory, cannot soon be finished. Or to put it better, it should be one of the chief objects of the application of your Majesty during his whole life.

A Memorandum, 1672

If the King conquers all the provinces subject to and forming part of the States of the United Provinces of the Netherlands, their commerce becoming commerce of the subjects of the King, there would be nothing more to desire; and if afterwards His Majesty, examining what would be most advantageous to do for the commerce of his old and new subjects, thought it for the good of his service to divide the advantages of this commerce by cutting down a part of that of the Dutch so as to transfer it into the hands of the French, it would be easy to find the necessary expedients to which the new subjects would be obliged to submit.

T. C. Mendenhall, B. D. Henning, and A. S. Foord,
Ideas and Institutions in European History, 800-1715
(Henry Holt, 1948), pp. 320-321.

2. *In 1738, two years before his accession to the throne,* FREDERICK THE GREAT (1740-86) *wrote a youthful essay entitled* Considerations on the Present State of the Body-Politic in Europe. *In it he analyses the European political scene and gives his master plan for building up a first-class power.*

. . . The prince is to the nation he governs what the head is to the man; it is his duty to see, think, and act for the whole community, that he may procure it every advantage of which it is capable. . . . Here follow my ideas concerning his duties.

He ought to procure exact and circumstantial information of the strength and weakness of his country, as well relative to pecuniary resources as to population, finance, trade, laws, and the genius of the nation whom he is appointed to govern. . . .

As every person who does not proceed on principle is inconsistent in his conduct, it is still more necessary that the magistrate who watches over the public good should act from a determinate system of politics, war, finance, commerce, and law. Thus, for example, a people of mild manners ought not to have severe laws, but such as are adapted to their character. The basis of such systems ought always to be correspondent to the greatest good society can receive. Their principles ought to be conformable to the situation of the country, to its ancient customs, if they are good, and to the genius of the nation.

As an instance, it is a known truth, in politics, that the most natural allies, and consequently the best, are those whose interests concur, and who are not such near neighbours as to be engaged in any contest respecting frontiers. It sometimes happens that strange accidents give place to extraordinary alliances. We have seen, in the present times, nations that had always been rivals, and even enemies, united under the same banners. But these are events that rarely take birth, and which never can serve as examples. Such connections can be no more than momentary; whereas the other kind, which are contracted from a unity of interests, are alone capable of exertion. In the present situation of Europe, when all her princes are armed, and among whom preponderating powers rise up capable of crushing the feeble, prudence requires alliances should be formed with other powers, as well to secure aid, in case of attack, as to repress the dangerous projects of enemies, and to sustain all just pretensions, by the succour of such allies, in opposition to those by whom they are controverted.

Nor is this sufficient. It is necessary to have among our neighbours, especially among our enemies, eyes and ears which shall be open to receive, and report with fidelity, what they have seen and heard. . . . European politics are so fallacious that the most sage may become dupes, if they are not always alert, and on their guard.

The military system ought, in like manner, to rest on good principles, which from experience are known to be certain. . . . The warlike customs of the Greeks and Romans are interdicted, in these ages. The discovery of gunpower has entirely changed the mode of making war. A superiority of fire at present decides the day. Discipline, rules, and tactics have all been changed, in order that they may conform to this new custom. . . .

There are states which, from their situation and constitution, must be maritime powers: such are England, Holland, France, Spain, and Denmark. They are surrounded by the sea, and the distant colonies which they possess oblige them to keep a marine, to maintain communication and trade between the mother country and these detached members. There are other states, such as Austria, Poland, Prussia, and even Russia, some of which may well do without shipping; and others that would commit an unpardonable fault, in politics, were they to divide their forces by employing a part of their troops at sea, of the services of which they indispensably stand in need by land.

The number of troops which a state maintains ought to be in proportion to the troops maintained by its enemies. Their force should be equal, or the weakest is in danger of being oppressed. It perhaps may be objected that a king ought to depend on the aid of his allies. The reasoning would be good were allies what they ought to be; but their zeal is only lukewarm; and he who shall depend upon another as upon himself will most certainly be deceived. . . .

But neither politics nor the army can prosper if the finances are not kept in the greatest order, and if the prince himself be not a prudent economist.

. . . The economy of the sovereign is the more useful to the public good, because if he have not sufficient funds in reserve, either to supply the expenses of war, without loading his people with extraordinary taxes, or to succour citizens in times of public calamity, all these burthens will fall on the subjects, who will be without the resources, in such unhappy times, of which they will then stand in the most need.

No government can exist without taxation, which is equally necessary to the republic and to the monarchy. . . . This money must all be necessarily levied on the people; and the grand art consists in levying so as not to oppress. That taxes may be equally and not arbitrarily laid on, surveys and registers should be made, by which, if the people are properly classed, the money will be proportionate to the income of the persons paying. . . .

Excise is another species of taxes, levied on cities, and this must be managed by able persons; otherwise, those provisions which are most necessary to life, such as bread, small beer, meat, &c, will be overloaded; and the weight will fall on the soldier, the labourer, and the artizan. The result will be, unhappily to the people, that the price of labour will be raised; consequently merchandise will become so dear as not to be saleable in foreign markets. . . . To obviate such inconveniences, the sovereign ought frequently to remember the condition of the poor, to imagine himself in the place of the peasant or the manufacturer, and then to say, "Were I born one among the class of citizens whose labours constitute the wealth of the state, what should I require from the king?" The answer which, on such a supposition, good sense would suggest it is his duty to put in practice.

In most of the kingdoms of Europe there are provinces in which the peasants are attached to the glebe, or are serfs to their lords. This, of all conditions, is the most unhappy, and that at which humanity most revolts. No man certainly was born to be the slave of his equal. We reasonably detest such an abuse; and it is supposed that nothing more than will is wanting to abolish so barbarous a custom. But this is not true; it is held on ancient tenures, and contracts made between the landholders and the colonists. Tillage is regulated according to the service performed by the peasantry;

and whoever should suddenly desire to abolish this abominable administration would entirely overthrow the mode of managing estates, and must be obliged, in part, to indemnify the nobility for the losses which their rents must suffer.

Introduction to Contemporary Civilization in the West: A Source Book
(Columbia University Press, 2nd edition, 1954), I, 1115-1119.

III THE SCIENTIFIC REVOLUTION

The development of the modern scientific method required both the philosophical justification of a thinker such as Descartes, and the practical observations and experiments of a scientist such as Galileo. The following extracts illustrate how, in the space of less than a century, the foundations of the Scientific Revolution were securely laid.

1.   *When* RENE DESCARTES (1596-1650) *stated the logic of mathematical reasoning in his* Discourse on Method, *a short selection from which appears below, he exerted a tremendous influence on the scholars of his day. It has been said, in fact, that he may have given a greater impetus to the development of modern science than even Newton himself.*

Good sense is of all things in the world the most equally distributed, for everybody thinks himself so abundantly provided with it, that even those most difficult to please in all other matters do not commonly desire more of it than they already possess. . . . For myself I have never ventured to presume that my mind was in any way more perfect that that of the ordinary man; I have even longed to possess thought as quick, or an imagination as accurate and distinct, or a memory as comprehensive or ready, as some others. . . .

But I shall not hesitate to say that I have had great good fortune from my youth up, in lighting upon and pursuing certain paths which have conducted me to considerations and maxims from which I have formed a Method, by whose assistance it appears to me I have the means of gradually increasing my knowledge and of little by little raising it to the highest possible point which the mediocrity of my talents and the brief duration of my life can permit me to reach. . . .

But like one who walks alone and in the twilight I resolved to go so slowly, and to use so much circumspection in all things, that if my advance was but very small, at least I guarded myself well from falling. . . .

Among the different branches of philosophy, I had in my younger days to a certain extent studied logic . . . [but] instead of the great number of precepts of which logic is composed, I believed that I should find the four which I shall state quite sufficient, provided that I adhered to a firm and constant resolve never on any single occasion to fail in their observance.

The first of these was to accept nothing as true which I did not clearly recognize to be so: that is to say, carefully to avoid precipitation and prejudice in judgments, and to accept in them nothing more than what was presented to my mind so clearly and distinctly that I could have no occasion to doubt it.

The second was to divide up each of the difficulties which I examined into as many parts as possible, and as seemed requisite in order that it might be resolved in the best manner possible.

The third was to carry on my reflections in due order, commencing with objects that were the most simple and easy to understand, in order to rise little by little, or by degrees, to knowledge of the most complex, assuming an order, even if a fictitious one, among those which do not follow a natural sequence relatively to one another.

The last was in all cases to make enumerations so complete and reviews so general that I should be certain of having omitted nothing. . . .

J. H. Hexter and others, editors, *The Traditions of the Western World* (Rand McNally, 1967), pp. 440-441.

2. GALILEO GALILEI (1564-1642) *was one of the pioneers in the exploration of space. It was he who first examined the heavens through a telescope, and in* The Sidereal Messenger *(1610) he describes some of his discoveries.*

Let me first speak of the surface of the moon, which is turned toward us. For the sake of being understood more easily I distinguish two parts in it, which I call respectively the brighter and the darker. The brighter part seems to surround and pervade the whole hemisphere; but the darker part, like a sort of cloud, discolours the moon's surface and makes it appear covered with spots. Now these spots, as they are somewhat dark and of considerable size, are plain to everyone, and every age has seen them, wherefore I shall call them *great* or *ancient* spots, to distinguish them from other spots, smaller in size, but so thickly scattered that they sprinkle the whole surface of the moon, but especially the brighter portion of it. These spots have never been observed by anyone before me; and from my observations of them, often repeated, I have been led to that opinion which I have expressed, namely, that I feel sure that the surface of the moon is not perfectly smooth, free from inequalities, and exactly spherical, as a large school of philosophers considers with regard to the moon and the other heavenly bodies, but that, on the contrary, it is full of inequalities, uneven, full of hollows and protuberances, just like the surface of the earth itself, which is varied everywhere by lofty mountains and deep valleys. . . .

The difference between the appearance of the planets and the fixed stars seems also deserving of notice. The planets present their disks perfectly round, just as if described with a pair of compasses, and appear as so many little moons, completely illuminated and of a globular shape; but the fixed stars do not look to the naked eye bounded by a circular circumference, but rather like blazes of light, shooting out beams on all sides and very sparkling, and with a telescope they appear of the same shape as when they are viewed by simply looking at them, but so much larger that a star of the fifth or sixth magnitude seems to equal Sirius, the largest of all the fixed stars.

But beyond the stars of the sixth magnitude you will behold through the telescope a host of other stars, which escape the unassisted sight, so numerous as to be almost beyond belief. . . .

C. W. Hollister, ed., *Landmarks of the Western Heritage*
(Wiley, 1967), I, 554-555.

IV THE ENLIGHTENMENT

The Enlightenment in France was a family of *philosophes*, but it was also a cultural climate, a world in which the *philosophes* acted, from which they noisily rebelled and quietly drew many of their ideas, and on which they attempted to impose their programme for reform. While the underlying tenor of the Age was a feeling of optimism and a belief in the supremacy of reason, it must be remembered that there was no compact body of thought they all adhered to. Voltaire and Rousseau, for instance, were both eminently representative of their period, and both were later to be hailed as "fathers" of the French Revolution, yet the work and ideas of the one have little in common with those of the other.

1.   VOLTAIRE (1694-1778) *was a prolific writer against what he called* l'infâme *(infamy). His reputation rests on the enthusiasm and witty indignation with which he attacked superstition (in which he included Christianity), oppression, and injustice, and exposed the manners and morals of his contemporary society. He believed in the dignity of the individual, but did not accept the idea of social equality. He advocated legal and moral reforms, but desired neither unrestrained political liberty nor the overthrow of the monarchy. His ideal would have been a "philosopher king," worthy of absolute power. The following passages are from his* Philosophical Dictionary.

On Equality:

It is clear that men, in the enjoyment of their natural faculties, are equal: they are equal when they perform animal functions, and when they exercise their understanding. . . . If this world were what it seems it should be, if man could find everywhere in it an easy subsistence, and a climate suitable to his nature, it is clear that it would be impossible for one man to enslave another. . . . All men then would be necessarily equal, if they were without needs. It is the poverty connected with our species which subordinates one man to another. It is not the inequality which is the real misfortune, it is the dependence. . . .

In our unhappy world it is impossible for men living in society not to be divided into two classes, the one the rich who command, the other the poor who serve; and these two classes are subdivided into a thousand, and these thousand still have different gradations. . . .

All men are born with a sufficiently violent liking for domination, wealth, and pleasure, and with a strong taste for idleness; consequently, all men covet the money, the wives, or the daughters of other men; they wish to be their master, to subject them to all their caprices, and to do nothing, or at least to do only very agreeable things. You see clearly that with these fine inclinations it is as impossible for men to be equal as it is impossible for two preachers . . . not to be jealous of each other.

On Democracy:

As a rule there is no comparison between the crimes of great men, who are always ambitious, and the crimes of the people, who always want, and can only want, liberty and equality. These two sentiments, Liberty and Equality, do not lead straight to calumny, rapine, assassination, poisoning, etc. But ambitious might and the mania for power plunge men into all these crimes, whatever the time, whatever the place.

Popular government is in itself, therefore, less iniquitous, less abominable than despotic power.

The great vice of democracy is certainly not tyranny and cruelty. There have been mountain-dwelling republics who were savage and ferocious; but it was not the republican spirit that made them so, it was nature.

The real vice of a civilized republic is expressed in the Turkish fable of the dragon with many heads and the dragon with many tails. The many heads injured one another, and the many tails obeyed a single head which sought to devour everything. . . .

Which is better—runs the endless question—a republic or a monarchy? The dispute always resolves itself into an agreement that it is a very difficult business to govern men. . . .

B. R. Redman, ed., *The Portable Voltaire* (Viking Press, 1956), pp. 102-3, 112-15.

2. JEAN-JACQUES ROUSSEAU (1712-1778) *maintained a consistent belief in three things: the inalienable human right to liberty, the natural goodness of man, and the necessity of basing political institutions on democratic sovereignty as the means of expression of the General Will. Unlike Voltaire and most other Enlightenment thinkers, Rousseau saw material progress and civilization as the cause of man's moral decline. Because he exalted the "noble savage" and "natural man," Rousseau has been called the first of the Romantics.*

From The Social Contract:

Man is born free; and everywhere he is in chains. One thinks himself the master of others, and still remains a greater slave than they. How did this change come about? I do not know. What can make it legitimate? That question I think I can answer.

. . . I suppose men to have reached the point at which the obstacles in the way of their preservation in the state of nature show their power of resistance to be greater than the resources at the disposal of each individual for his maintenance in that state. That primitive condition can then subsist no longer; and the human race would perish unless it changed its manner of existence.

But, as men cannot engender new forces, but only unite and direct existing ones, they have no other means of preserving themselves than the formation, by aggregation, of a sum of forces great enough to overcome the resistance. . . .

This sum of forces can arise only where several persons come together: but, as the force and liberty of each man are the chief instruments of his self-preservation, how can he pledge them without harming his own interests, and neglecting the care he owes to himself? This difficulty, in its bearing on the present subject, may be stated in the following terms:

'The problem is to find a form of association which will defend and protect with the whole common force the person and goods of each associate, and in which each, while uniting himself with all, may still obey himself alone, and remain as free as before.' This is the fundamental problem of which the *Social Contract* provides the solution.

The clauses of this contract are so determined by the nature of the act that the slightest modification would make them vain and ineffective; so that, although they have perhaps never been formally set forth, they are everywhere the same and everywhere tacitly admitted and recognized, until, on the violation of the social compact, each regains his original rights and resumes his natural liberty, while losing the conventional liberty in favour of which he renounced it.

. . . If then we discard from the social compact what is not of its essence, we shall find that it reduces itself to the following terms:

'Each of us puts his person and all his power in common under the supreme direction of the general will, and, in our corporate capacity, we receive each member as an indivisible part of the whole.'

At once, in place of the individual personality of each contracting party, this act of association creates a moral and collective body . . . [called] *Republic* or *body politic*; it is called by its members *State* when passive, *Sovereign* when active. . . .

In order then that the social compact may not be an empty formula, it tacitly includes the undertaking, which alone can give force to the rest, that whoever refuses to obey the general will shall be compelled to do so by the whole body. This means nothing less than that he will be forced to be free; for this is the condition which, by giving each citizen to his country, secures him against all personal dependence. In this lies the key to the working of the political machine; this alone legitimizes civil undertakings, which, without it, would be absurd, tyrannical and liable to the most frightful abuses.

G. D. H. Cole, ed., *The Social Contract and Discourses* (Dent, 1968), pp. 121-5, 160, 192, 199, 220-1, 3, 11-13, 15.

V THE BACKGROUND OF THE FRENCH REVOLUTION

What were the causes of the French Revolution? To what degree was the misery of the populace responsible for triggering the overthrow of the government? Indeed, did the people really suffer such oppression that revolution was inevitable? The two following readings give opposing interpretations of the questions in point.

1. JULES MICHELET, *a prominent 19th century French historian, argued that the suffering of the peasantry was not only intolerable; it was constantly growing worse.*

Read the foreign travellers of the last two centuries; you behold them stupefied, when travelling through our plains, at their wretched appearance, at the sadness, the solitude, the miserable poverty, the dismal, naked, empty cottages, and the starving, ragged population. There they learn what man is able to endure without dying; what nobody, neither the English, the Dutch, nor the Germans, would have supported.

... The evil consists in this, that the nation, from the highest to the lowest, is organized so as to go on producing less and less, and paying more and more. She will go on declining, wasting away, giving, after her blood, her marrow; and there will be no end to it, till having reached the last gasp, and just expiring, the convulsion of the death-struggle arouses her once more and raises that pale feeble body on its legs—Feeble?—grown strong perhaps by fury!

Let us minutely examine, if you will, these words *producing less and less*. They are exact to the letter.

As early as under Louis XIV the excise *(aides)* already weighed so heavily, that at Mantes, Etampes, and elsewhere, all the vines were plucked up.

The peasant having no goods to seize, the exchequer can lay hold of nothing but the cattle; it is gradually exterminated. No more manure. The cultivation of corn, though extended in the seventeenth century, by immense clearings of waste land, decreases in the eighteenth. The earth can no longer repair her generative strength; she fasts, and becomes exhausted, as the cattle may become extinct, so also the land now appears dead.

Not only does the land produce less, but it is less cultivated. In many places, it is not worth while to cultivate it. Large proprietors, tired of advancing to their peasants sums that never return, neglect the land which would require expensive improvements. The portion cultivated grows less, and the desert expands. People talk of agriculture, write books on it, make expensive experiments, paradoxical schemes of cultivation; and agriculture, devoid of succour, of cattle, grows wild. Men, women, and children yoke themselves to the plough. They would dig the ground with their nails if our ancient laws did not, at least, defend the ploughshare—the last poor implement that furrows the earth. How can we be surprised that the crops should fail with such half-starved husbandmen, or that the land should suffer and refuse to yield? The yearly produce no longer suffices for the year. As we approach 1789, Nature yields less and less. Like a beast over-fatigued, unwilling to move one step further, and preferring to lie down and die, she waits, and produces no more. Liberty is not only the life of man, but also that of nature.

Histoire de la Révolution Française, by Jules Michelet (Paris, 1879) translated by C. Cocks in *Historical View of the French Revolution* (London, 1908)

2. ALEXIS DE TOCQUEVILLE, *perhaps the most celebrated of all French historians, presented the case that in France more than anywhere else in Europe, feudalism was declining, that the peasants throughout the country were becoming small landlords in their own right, and that the feudal impositions by the lords were less onerous than often believed, and were diminishing in scope and severity.*

. . . In France the peasants could move about, buy and sell, work, and enter into contracts as they liked. Only in one or two eastern provinces, recent annexations, some last vestiges of serfdom lingered on; everywhere else it had wholly disappeared. Indeed, the abolition of serfdom had taken place in times so remote that its very date had been forgotten. However, as a result of recent research work it is now known that as early as the thirteenth century serfdom had ceased to exist in Normandy.

Meanwhile another revolution, of a different order, had done much to improve the status of the French peasant; he had not merely ceased to be a serf, he had also become a landowner.

. . . Until quite recently it was taken for granted that the splitting up of the landed estates in France was the work of the Revolution, and the Revolution alone; actually there is much evidence in support of the contrary view. Twenty years or more before the Revolution we find complaints being made that land was being subdivided to an unconscionable extent. "The practice of partitioning inheritances," said Turgot, writing at about this time, "has gone so far that a piece of land which just sufficed for a single family is now parceled out between five or six sons. The result is that the heirs and their families soon find that they cannot depend on the land for their livelihood and have to look elsewhere." And some years later Necker declared that there was "an inordinate number" of small country estates in France.

In a confidential report made to an Intendant shortly before the Revolution I find the following observations: "Inheritances are being subdivided nowadays to an alarming extent. Everybody insists on having his share of the land, with the result that estates are broken up into innumerable fragments, and this process of fragmentation is going on all the time." One might well imagine these words to have been written by one of our contemporaries.

... In certain villages ... the number of landowners was as high as half, often two thirds, of the present number.[1] These figures are impressive, and all the more so when we remember that the population of France has risen by over twenty-five per cent since that time.

... When Arthur Young visited France for the first time, among a multitude of new experiences, none impressed him more than the extent to which ownership of the soil was vested in innumerable peasant proprietors; half the cultivable land was owned by them. "I had no idea," he often says, "that such a state of affairs existed anywhere"—and in fact none such existed outside France.

There had once been many peasant proprietors in England, but by now their number had greatly dwindled. ... In Germany ... this type of ownership was always exceptional, there never were many of these small landed proprietors. ... as in no other part of Europe, our agriculturists had been emancipated from the control of their lords—a revolution no less momentous than that which had made them peasant proprietors. ... the rights of the lords to exploit the peasants still functioning in 1789 fell into a relatively small number of categories; others survived, no doubt, but they were operative only in exceptional cases.

Of the old seigneurial *corvée*, or statutory labour obligation, traces remained everywhere, but half obliterated. Most of the toll charges on the roads had been reduced or done away with, though there were few provinces in which some had not survived.

The point ... on which I would lay stress is that exactly the same feudal rights were in force in every European land and that in most other countries of the continent they pressed far more heavily on the population than in France. Take, for example, the lord's right to forced labour, the *corvée*. It was rarely exercised and little oppressive in France, whereas in Germany it was stringent and everywhere enforced.

Moreover, when we turn to the feudal rights which so much outraged our fathers and which they regarded as opposed not merely to all ideas of justice but to the spirit of civilization itself (I am thinking of the tithe, irredeemable ground rents, perpetual charges, *lods et ventes*, and so forth, all that in the somewhat grandiloquent language of the eighteenth century was styled "the servitude of the land"), we find that all these practices obtained to

[1] i.e., in 1856.

some extent in England and, indeed, are still found there today. Yet they do not prevent English husbandry from being the best organized and most productive in the modern world; and, what is perhaps still more remarkable, the English nation seems hardly aware of their existence.

Why then did these selfsame feudal rights arouse such bitter hatred in the heart of the French people that it has persisted even after its object has long since ceased to exist? One of the reasons is that the French peasant had become a landowner, and another that he had been completely emancipated from the control of his lord.

The Old Regime and the French Revolution,
by Alexis de Tocqueville. Translated by
Stuart Gilbert (Doubleday, 1955).

VI DARWIN AND DARWINISM

One of the chief pillars of "tradition" was the concept of social order expressed in the Bible, especially as interpreted by most churches. When the scientific research undertaken by Charles Darwin appeared to challenge the most fundamental premises of this intepretation, the resulting ferment in European and North American society was extraordinarily great.

1.   *Darwin's conclusions were contained primarily in two books,* The Origin of Species, *and* The Descent of Man. *Below is Darwin's summary of his views of evolution and man's origins, from the last chapter of* The Descent of Man.

The first chapter of this book is a summary of the evidence for the view that man is descended from the brutes. We have pointed out his bodily similarity to the lower animals, the striking analogies in his embryonic development, and the overwhelming evidence of his rudimentary or vestigial organs. The second chapter takes up various important aspects of the evolutionary process, and considers the general topic of natural selection. In the third chapter we discuss man's mental faculties, and compare them with those of the lower anmials, showing that the differences between them are differences of degree, not of kind.

The fourth chapter deals with the so-called moral sense, or conscience, and defends the idea that this faculty is only a development of the social instincts, which are common to many of the lower animals. In the fifth chapter we follow the intellectual growth of the various races of men, from the ape-like beings of the prehistoric period to the civilized men of modern Europe. In chapter six there is a brief discussion of man's proper zoological classification, and some speculations about his antiquity and his probable birthplace. The seventh chapter offers a general introduction to the subject of sexual selection, and a discussion of the rôle which this force has played in the evolution of the human race.

The main conclusion of the whole work is simply that *man is descended body and mind from the lower animals*. I regret to think that this conclusion will be highly distasteful to many people, who will regard it as inimical to both morality and religion. But we scientists are not concerned with hopes or fears—only with the truth as far as we are able to discover it. Having considered the evidence, it seems to me that we must acknowledge that man still bears indelible and unmistakable traces of his lowly origin. His body is still the body of an animal, and the mark of the beast is still clearly discernible in all his mental and moral faculties.

Charles Darwin, *The Descent of Man*
(Appleton, New York, 1876).

2.   *Adherents of various and contrasting ideologies hailed Darwin's discoveries as validation for their own theories. Among these was* KARL MARX, *who claimed that Darwin had given support to his theory that the powerful and rich were inescapably locked in a struggle to the death with the workers and other "productive members" of society. Here in a very brief condensation of the famous* Communist Manifesto *is the germ of 19th century socialist thought.*

The history of all hitherto existing society is the history of class struggles.

Freeman and slave, patrician and plebeian, lord and serf, guildmaster and journeyman, in a word, oppressor and oppressed stood in constant opposition to one another, carried on an uninterrupted, now hidden, now open fight, a fight that each time ended, either in a revolutionary reconstitution of society at large, or in the common ruin of the contending classes.

In the earlier epochs of history, we find almost everywhere a complicated arrangement of society into various orders, a manifold gradation of social rank. In ancient Rome we have patricians, knights, plebeians, slaves; in the Middle Ages, feudal lords, vassals, guildmasters, journeymen, apprentices, serfs; in almost all of these classes, again, subordinate gradations.

The modern bourgeois society that has sprouted from the ruins of feudal society has not done away with class antagonisms. It has but established new classes, new conditions of oppression, new forms of struggle in place of the old ones.

Our epoch, the epoch of the bourgeoisie, possesses, however, this distinctive feature: It has simplified the class antagonisms. Society as a whole is more and more splitting up into two great hostile camps, into two great classes directly facing each other—bourgeoisie and proletariat.

* * * * *

The Communists turn their attention chiefly to Germany, because that country is on the eve of a bourgeois revolution[1] that is bound to be carried out under more advanced conditions of European civilization and with a much more developed proletariat than that of England was in the 17th, and of France in the 18th century, and because the bourgeois revolution in Germany will be but the prelude to an immediately following proletarian revolution.

In short, the Communists everywhere support every revolutionary movement against the existing social and political order of things.

In all these movements they bring to the front, as the leading question in each, the property question, no matter what its degree of development at the time.

Finally, they labour everywhere for the union and agreement of the democratic parties of all countries.

The Communists disdain to conceal their views and aims. They openly declare that their ends can be attained only by the forcible overthrow of all existing social conditions. Let the ruling classes tremble at the communist revolution. The proletarians have nothing to lose but their chains. They have a world to win.

Workingmen of all countries, unite!

Selected Works of Karl Marx and Friedrich Engels
(Marx-Engels-Lenin Institute, Moscow, 1942).

[1] Written in December, 1847.

3.   *Another thinker who was affected by Darwin was the German philosopher* FRIEDRICH NIETZSCHE (1844-1900). *Nietzsche abhorred Christianity, and also democracy and socialism, whose origins (he asserted) lay in Christianity. Greatly influenced by Darwin's theories, he saw evolution as a means for man to develop "beyond good and evil." If man were willing to apply his will and exercise his strength, he could create a race of "supermen" (a word coined by Nietzsche). The following selection is from his* The Will to Power.

Man has one terrible and fundamental wish; he desires power, and this impulse, which is called freedom, must be the longest restrained. Hence ethics has instinctively aimed at such an education as shall restrain the desire for power; thus our morality slanders the would-be tyrant, and glorifies charity, patriotism, and the ambition of the herd. . . .

There is a universal need to exercise some kind of power, or to create for one's self the appearance of some power, if only temporarily in the form of intoxication.

There are men who desire power simply for the sake of the happiness it will bring; these belong chiefly to political parties. Other men have the same yearning, even when power means visible disadvantages, the sacrifice of their happiness, and well-being; they are the ambitious. Other men, again, are only like dogs in a manger and will have power only to prevent it falling into the hands of others on whom they would then be dependent.

The will to power.—How must those men be constituted who would undertake this transvaluation. The order of rank as the order of power: war and danger are the prerequisites which allow of a rank maintaining its conditions. The prodigious example: man in Nature—the weakest and shrewdest creature making himself master, and putting a yoke upon all less intelligent forces.

I distinguish between the type which represents ascending life and that which represents decay, decomposition and weakness. Ought one to suppose that the question of rank between these five types can be at all doubtful? . . .

The modicum of power which you represent decides your rank; all the rest is cowardice.

The advantages of standing detached from our age.—Detached from the two movements, that of individualism and that of collectivist morality; for even the first does not recognize the order of rank, and would give one individual the same freedom as another. My thoughts are not concerned with the degree of freedom which should be granted to the one or to the other or to all, but with the degree of power which the one or the other should exercise over his neighbour or over all; and more especially with the question to what extent a sacrifice of freedom, or even enslavement, may afford the basis for the cultivation of a *superior* type. In plain words: How *could one sacrifice the development of mankind* in order to assist a higher species than man to come into being. . . .

It is necessary for *higher* men to declare war upon the masses! In all directions mediocre people are joining hands in order to make themselves masters. Everything that pampers, that softens, and that brings the "people" or "woman" to the front, operates in favour of universal suffrage—that is to say, the dominion of *inferior* men. But we must make reprisals, and draw the whole state of affairs (which commenced in Europe with Christianity) to the light of day and to judgment.

A teaching is needed which is strong enough to work in a *disciplinary* manner; it should operate in such a way as to strengthen the strong and to paralyse and smash up the world-weary.

The Complete Works of Friedrich Nietzsche
(T. N. Foulis, London, 1910).

4. *Many opponents of Darwinism feared its effects on organized Christianity, which the theory of evolution seemed to challenge. Most churches were being attacked by liberals who demanded more latitude in theological interpretation and less adherence to dogma. In the midst of this age of controversy,* POPE PIUS IX *introduced the strongest and most forthright attack against the new ideas, including Darwinism; this was the* Doctrine of Papal Infallibility.

That which the Prince of Shepherds and great Shepherd of the sheep, Jesus Christ our Lord, established in the person of the Blessed Apostle Peter, to secure the perpetual welfare and lasting good of the Church, must, by the same institution, necessarily remain unceasingly in the Church; which, being founded upon the Rock, will stand firm to the end of the world. For none can doubt, and it is known to all ages, that the holy and Blessed Peter, the Prince and Chief of the Apostles, the pillar of the Catholic Church, received the keys of the kingdom from our Lord Jesus Christ, the Saviour and Redeemer of mankind, and lives, presides, and judges, to this day and always, in his successors the Bishops of the Holy See of Rome, which was founded by him, and consecrated by his blood. Whence, whosoever succeeds to Peter in this See does by the institution of Christ Himself obtain the Primacy of Peter over the whole Church. The disposition made by Incarnate Truth therefore remains, and Blessed Peter, abiding in the rock strength which he received, has not abandoned the direction of the Church. Wherefore it has at all times been necessary that every particular Church —that is to say, the faithful throughout the world—should come to the Church of Rome, on account of the greater princedom it has received; so that in this See, whence the rights of venerable communion spread to all, they might, as members joined together in their head, grow closely into one body.

If, then, any shall say that it is not by the institution of Christ the Lord, or by divine right, that Blessed Peter has a perpetual line of successors in the Primacy over the universal Church; or that the Roman Pontiff is not the successor of Blessed Peter in this primacy; let him be anathema.

. . . Faithfully adhering to the tradition received from the beginning of the Christian faith, for the glory of God our Saviour, the exaltation of the Catholic Religion, and the salvation of Christian people, with the approval of the Sacred Council, we teach and define that it is a dogma divinely revealed: That the Roman Pontiff, when he speaks *ex cathedra*, that is, when in discharge of the office of Pastor and Teacher of all Christians, by virtue of this supreme Apostolic authority, he defines a doctrine regarding faith or morals to be held by the universal Church, is, by the divine assistance promised to him in Blessed Peter, possessed of that infallibility with which the divine Redeemer willed that His Church should be endowed in defining doctrine regarding faith or morals; and that therefore such definitions of the Roman Pontiff are of themselves, and not from the consent of the Church, irreformable.

Sheffe and Fisher, A Sourcebook for Modern History
(McGraw-Hill, Toronto, 1966)

VII THE DEPRESSION

In spite of notable advances in technology and social reform, the western world had not mastered economic forces. The first public indication of the great economic Depression was the Wall Street stock market crash of 1929.

1.   JOHN KENNETH GALBRAITH, *a Canadian-born economist, who has held posts of high responsibility in the United States, describes the initial stages of the panic in the business world.*

Thursday, October 24, is the first of the days which history—such as it is on the subject—identifies with the panic of 1929. Measured by disorder, fright, and confusion, it deserves to be so regarded. That day 12 894 650 shares changed hands, many of them at prices which shattered the dreams and the hopes of those who had owned them. Of all the mysteries of the stock exchange there is none so impenetrable as why there should be a buyer for everyone who seeks to sell. October 24, 1929, showed that what is mysterious is not inevitable. Often there were no buyers, and only after wide vertical declines could anyone be induced to bid.

The panic did not last all day. It was a phenomenon of the morning hours. The market opening itself was unspectacular, and for a while prices were firm. Volume, however, was very large, and soon prices began to sag. Once again the ticker dropped behind. Prices fell farther and faster, and the ticker lagged more and more. By eleven o'clock the market had degenerated into a wild, mad scramble to sell. In the crowded boardrooms across the country the ticker told of a frightful collapse. But the selected quotations coming in over the bond ticker also showed that current values were far below the ancient history of the tape. The uncertainty led more and more people to try to sell. Others, no longer able to respond to margin calls, were sold out. By eleven-thirty the market had surrendered to blind, relentless fear. This, indeed, was panic.

Outside the Exchange in Broad Street a weird roar could be heard. A crowd gathered. Police Commissioner Grover Whalen became aware that something was happening and dispatched a special police detail to Wall Street to insure the peace. More people came and waited, though apparently no one knew for what. A workman appeared atop one of the high buildings to accomplish some repairs, and the multitude assumed he was a would-be suicide and waited impatiently for him to jump. Crowds also formed around the branch offices of brokerage firms throughout the city and, indeed, throughout the country. Word of what was happening, or what was thought to be happening, was passed out by those who were within sight of the board or the Trans-Lux. An observer thought that people's expressions showed "not so much suffering as a sort of horrified incredulity." Rumor after rumor swept Wall Street and these outlying wakes. Stocks were now selling for nothing. The Chicago and Buffalo Exchanges had closed. A suicide wave was in progress, and eleven well-known speculators had already killed themselves.

J. K. Galbraith, The Great Crash: 1929
(Houghton Mifflin, 1961), pp. 103-105.

2. *As the Depression cast lengthening shadows across North American life, the numbers of the unemployed grew alarmingly. Jobless men were forced to adopt desperate expedients to avoid starvation. The following extract is taken from the pages of* The New York Times *of June 5, 1932.*

Once the average New Yorker got his shine in an established bootblack "parlor" paying 10 cents, with a nickel tip. But now, in the Times Square and Grand Central zones, the sidewalks are lined with neophyte "shine boys," drawn from almost all walks of life. They charge a nickel, and although a nickel tip is welcomed it is not expected.

In one block, on West Forty-third Street, a recent count showed nineteen shoe-shiners. They ranged in age from a 16-year-old, who should have been in school, to a man of more than 70, who said he had been employed in a fruit store until six months ago. Some sit quietly on their little wooden boxes and wait patiently for the infrequent customers. Others show true initiative and ballyhoo their trade, pointing accusingly at every pair of unshined shoes that passes. . . .

Shining shoes, said one, is more profitable than selling apples—and he's tried them both.

"You see, when you get a shine kit it's a permanent investment," he said, "and it doesn't cost as much as a box of apples anyway. . . ."

According to the Police Department, there are approximately 7 000 of these "shine boys" making a living on New York streets at present. Three years ago they were so rare as to be almost non-existent, and were almost entirely boys under 17.

David A. Shannon, *The Great Depression* (Prentice-Hall, 1964), pp. 10-11.

VIII NAZISM AND FASCISM

Frustrated by political and economic problems of the period following the First World War, the people of Italy and Germany turned to extremists for solutions. An Italian Socialist, Angelo Tasca, observed: "Fascism is like a completely successful operation, the patient dies and all his illusions are removed." The following extracts from statements made by the leaders of the Fascist and Nazi movements throw light on their motivation.

1. *In 1929* MUSSOLINI *declared:*

For us Fascists, the State is not merely a guardian, preoccupied solely with the duty of assuring the personal safety of the citizens; nor is it an organization with purely material aims, such as to guarantee a certain level of well-being and peaceful conditions of life; for a mere council of administration would be sufficient to realize such objects. Nor is it a purely political creation, divorced from all contact with the complex material reality which makes up the life of the individual and the life of the people as a whole. The State, as conceived of and as created by Fascism, is a spiritual and moral fact in itself, since its political, juridical, and economic organization of the nation is a concrete thing: and such an organization must be in its origins and development a manifestation of the spirit. The State is the guarantor of security both internal and external, but it is also the custodian and transmitter of the spirit of the people, as it has grown up through the centuries in language, in customs, and in faith. And the State is not only a living reality of the present, it is also linked with the past and above all with the future, and thus transcending the brief limits of individual life, it represents the immanent spirit of the nation. The forms in which States express themselves may change, but the necessity for such forms is eternal. It is the State which educates its citizens in civic virtue, gives them a consciousness of their mission and welds them into unity, harmonizing their various interests through justice, and transmitting to future generations the mental conquests of science, of art, of law and the solidarity of humanity. It leads men from primitive tribal life to that highest expression of human power which is Empire: it links up through the centuries the names of those of its members who have died for its existence and in obedience to its laws, it holds up the memory of the leaders who have increased its territory and the geniuses who have illumined it with glory as an example to be followed by future generations. When the conception of the State declines, and disunifying and centrifugal tendencies prevail, whether of individuals or of particular groups, the nations where such phenomena appear are in their decline.

Nathanael Greene, ed., Fascism: An Anthology
(Crowell, 1968), pp. 43-44.

2. *In 1923-24* HITLER *was imprisoned for a year, following the failure of the Munich* Putsch *(or revolt) against the German government. While in prison he wrote* Mein Kampf *(My Struggle), which became the Bible of the Nazi movement. In the following passage from this book he describes the origin of his anti-Semitism, which was to have catastrophic effects for millions of the Jewish race.*

I gradually became aware that the Social Democratic press was directed predominantly by Jews; yet I did not attribute any special significance to this circumstance, since conditions were exactly the same in the other papers. Yet one fact seemed conspicuous: there was not one paper with Jews working on it which could have been regarded as truly national, according to my education and way of thinking.

I swallowed my disgust and tried to read this type of Marxist press production, but my revulsion became so unlimited in so doing that I endeavoured to become more closely acquainted with the men who manufactured these compendiums of knavery.

From the publisher down, they were all Jews.

I took all the Social Democratic pamphlets I could lay hands on and sought the names of their authors: Jews. I noted the names of the leaders; by far the greatest part were likewise members of the "chosen people," whether they were representatives in the Reichsrat [upper chamber in the government] or trade-union secretaries, the heads of organizations or street agitators. It was always the same gruesome picture. The names of the Austerlitzes, Davids, Adlers, Ellenbogens, etc., will remain forever graven in my memory. One thing had grown clear to me: the party with whose petty representatives I had been carrying on the most violent struggle for months was, as to leadership, almost exclusively in the hands of a foreign people; for, to my deep and joyful satisfaction, I had at last come to the conclusion that the Jew was no German.

Only now did I become thoroughly acquainted with the seducer of our people.

From this conclusion, Hitler went on to propound certain principles supposedly of universal application:

The Jewish doctrine of Marxism rejects the aristocratic principle of Nature and replaces the eternal privilege of power and strength by the mass of numbers and their dead weight. Thus it denies the value of personality in man, contests the significance of nationality and race, and thereby withdraws from humanity the premise of its existence and its culture. As a foundation of the universe, this doctrine would bring about the end of any order intellectually conceivable to man. And as, in this greatest of all recognizable organisms, the result of an application of such a law could only be chaos, on earth it could only be destruction for the inhabitants of this planet.

Adolf Hitler, *Mein Kampf* [translated by Ralph Manheim]
(Houghton Mifflin, 1943), pp. 61-65.

IX CZECHOSLOVAKIA (1968)

After the death of Stalin (1953) there was a gradual relaxation of tension between East and West. Much of this was due to the policy of "peaceful coexistence" advocated by Nikita Khrushchev, who directed Soviet affairs from 1955 until his enforced retirement in 1964. Nevertheless, successive crises in Hungary and at Suez (1956), in Cuba (1962) and Czechoslovakia (1968) revived suspicion and distrust between the Soviet and Western blocs. The following extracts illustrate British, West German, and Russian reactions to the Soviet occupation of Czechoslovakia in the summer of 1968.

1.   *A British commentary* (The Financial Times):

The Soviet invasion of Czechoslovakia was carried out to the background of a deafening silence from most Western Governments, particularly from Washington. The reason for this was the fear—shared in London—that in a situation as explosive as this it was essential to avoid any move that the Russians could construe as provocation. Troop movements, NATO alerts, even "tough" statements were avoided because they could be interpreted as evidence of some sort of identity of interest between the Czechs and the NATO Alliance—the fiction chosen by the Russians as justification of their action.

The trouble with this tactic, of course, was that it left the Western leaders vulnerable to criticism for doing nothing and to accusations of cynicism and indifference. It also risked giving the Russians the impression that no one in the West would do anything to obstruct the same fate for, say, Romania, and it probably also contributed to an impression that has been gaining ground in some circles that the NATO members were caught napping by the Soviet move.

2.   *A West German commentary* (Die Zeit):

The German Federal Republic—more than any other NATO country—should draw the following conclusions from this: Firstly: The Soviet invasion represented an offensive action within the Warsaw Pact which was, however, of a defensive nature vis-à-vis the West. Any vacuum in the West—such as a Federal Republic which has been isolated from the solidarity of NATO—would increase the temptation of the Soviets to add to the Eastern European security area another zone which would be subject to the massive political pressure of Moscow. The active Eastern policy which is being pursued by the Federal Government required the protection of Germany by the Western alliance, co-ordination of foreign policy and military security.

Secondly: The hardening and freezing of the Eastern power bloc requires an equivalent, but not an identical, counterweight. A regeneration of NATO which would lead to isolation would make no sense. It is particularly the German Federal Republic which Moscow has in mind in trying to stop any attempt at improving relations with Eastern Europe. . . .

3. *A Soviet commentary (reproduced in the French newspaper,* Le Monde, *from an article by a former Paris correspondent of the Soviet press agency* Novosti):

Since at first sight the facts testify against us, let us attempt to analyse the underlying events more thoroughly. First of all, the question of the "armed occupation" of Czechoslovakia and "interference" in her domestic affairs. At the root of any occupation can as a general rule be found either the intention of making an attempt on the territorial integrity of the State in question or plans to abolish or modify its system of government. Can the "occupation" of Czechoslovakia by allied [Communist] armies be regarded in this light? It is quite clear that the aim of this military and political action consists, on the contrary, of preserving the territorial integrity of Czechoslovakia and consolidating her system of government, that is to say the existing Socialist system.

The entry of allied troops into Czechoslovakia did in fact take place without any formal request from that country's government in the sense that no official instrument invited the troops of the five Socialist countries on to Czechoslovak territory. All they had was a call for help from a group of State and Party personalities, the legality of which is contested by Western propaganda. But even without this document, the situation which had developed gave the countries allied to Czechoslovakia in the framework of the Warsaw Pact the moral right to intervene.

Relations between Socialist countries are based on the common principles of equality, respect for sovereignty, and non-interference in domestic affairs, just as are relations between countries with other social systems. But such relations are not and cannot be restricted by the application of these common international principles. One cannot treat problems concerning the sovereignty and independence of Socialist countries outside the context of proletarian internationalism, the guiding principle which defines relations between Communist parties and Marxist workers, nor outside the context of the pitiless struggle at present engaged on an international scale between Socialism and imperialism, nor, finally, outside the context of the political struggle of the Communist parties and workers. In all Socialist countries they are fighting to defend what has been attained by the workers in each Socialist country in face of attempts to restore the capitalist system.

NATO Letter (October, 1968) Vol. 16, No. 10, published by the NATO Information Service, Brussels, pp. 3, 6, 26.

X THE CHANGING ROLE OF WOMEN IN THE MODERN AGE

The role of women in the family, the community and the work force has undergone a significant change in the second half of the twentieth century. "Women's liberation" became a rallying cry for women seeking equal opportunities with men. The degree of their success has varied widely from country to country, but a fundamental shift in society's values and attitudes, one which can be agonizing and slow, has begun.

1. During International Women's Year in 1975, the United Nations sponsored a conference in Mexico City attended by thousands of women from around the world. The conference dealt with a broad range of issues of vital concern to women.

Outside the communist world, women's feelings about their situation are expressed more openly, and these vary according to the religious, familial, legal and material structures which demarcate their lives. The Westerners are of course the angriest. They always have been. They have led the way. Their thesis, posed against the antithesis of male power, resulted in the first part of the twentieth century in "Emancipation"—which was then passed along to Asian women and to Africans at their independence. Western women's anger seems directly related to their inability to exploit this emancipation further. It is striking—and was strikingly evident at the conference—that despite their years of education, economic security and relatively unfettered lives, Western women have come no closer to a real sharing in public power and participation than many of their less advantaged sisters. Ms. Marcos' description of the Philippine delegation, "headed by a woman member of the cabinet," and including "a woman who is a justice of the Supreme Court, an ambassador and a distinguished writer," might give Americans pause.

The institutions and attitudes which have held Western women back are, as everywhere, complex: Roman law, Christian sexual guilt and the ideal of woman as a pure and passive procreator, as well as the idea of the family as the sole source of succor. In addition, technological specialization consigns women to the kitchen and the nursery—and the only alternative often is trading places with her husband on the assembly line. The close relationship between money and status in our society has made the acquisition of wealth a masculine priority; women's exclusion from the realm of business and finance is a corollary. Moreover, the West's wealth and property has decreased social flexibility—empires must be guarded.

Looking at the developing world, one can begin to understand more clearly the role which wealth and property play at different stages. In India, for example, Hinduism resulted in a tightly fettered and secluded life for upper-class women, a life within the strict confines of the home, and of motherhood. The poor, however, could not afford these restrictions, for women had to help with subsistence farming and petty trading, as well as feeding their families. This situation certainly prevails today in most of Africa and among the Indians of Latin America. The poor cannot afford the dubious luxury of a feminine mystique.

In Asia, the Buddhist societies of Burma, Thailand, Laos and Cambodia have offered women a relatively greater measure of economic autonomy and power. According to Buddhism, man's spiritual supremacy is established, but beyond that, an ideal of harmony—and some equality—prevails in the secular realm. Indeed, women in these societies have long been active and successful even at the upper levels of business and land ownership. This power has rarely extended into politics, however, and it seems likely that man's spiritual precedence translates easily into preeminence in the transcendent sphere of secular life.

The religion which has notoriously curbed women, especially in the Middle East, is of course Islam. The religion of Mohammed, with its male domination and restrictive protection for women, is especially resistant to change in general and changing the position of women in particular. Like Christianity it sets forth an all-embracing theocratic ideal which involves close monitoring of the details of secular life, and has a history of violent persecution of heretics and unbelievers. While oil may smooth the way for women's emergence from purdah, the obstacles embodied in these theocratic states still appear formidable. In at least one area, however, the Muslim woman is freer than women in Christian cultures. There is no societally induced mystique of sentimental love binding the wife in service to the husband. The self-interest on the part of both partners is overt.

As for mystiques, African women seem, on the surface at any rate, to be least hampered by ideals of femininity, perhaps because their religions, like their economic structures, remained least stratified and elaborated with ideologies about the relationship of men and women. The Latin American women, on the other hand, are probably the most encumbered in this respect, combining a repressive Christianity with a history of violence; in their world, male honor and aggression and female chastity and passivity were cast as two sides of a coin. The message to the conference of Joaquin Balaguer, President of the Dominican Republic, seemed intended to express strong support for women's equality, but its language conveys the flavor of the society: "the influence of the delicate nature of the feminine soul on all aspects of man's public and private life must of necessity initiate a new stage on the history of mankind."

Extracted from "Women of the World: Report from Mexico City",
by Jennifer Seymour Whitaker in Foreign Affairs
(October 1975), Vol. 54, No. 1, pp. 180-181

2. The late DR. MARGARET MEAD, a world famous American anthropologist, made a major contribution to our knowledge about the interrelationship between personality and culture. Dr. Mead championed the cause of liberation from the debilitating effects of sex role stereotyping.

One of the salient characteristics of today's rapidly changing world is that it is no longer possible to wait until changes in one part of the system filter down or well-up elsewhere before action is taken. In a more slowly changing era the education of princes and prelates could, in later generations, become the possession of the unlettered poor, just as the evening dress of men in Anglo-American circles became the appropriate dress for waiters in a later generation. Conversely, where once poor women labored in factories and offices to support themselves and their children, supplementing the inadequate wages of their men, now sheltered daughters of the affluent demand the right to work outside the home. Where mass media has made it possible for a rapid diffusion of ideas, changes in one part of the system are reflected, in time, elsewhere. For example, women's suffrage, granted in Europe and America, became the unquestioned birthright of the tribal women of Papua, New Guinea, a right which many of them put on with the first blouse that covered their hitherto uncovered bosoms.

There are many good arguments against slow change. Many innovations are distorted because they occur in an unharmonious context and require, in turn, discrepant adjustments—the invention of "adaptive culture" which itself becomes dysfunctional"—like the present day welfare system, the American system of financing suburban developments, or the practice, recently stigmatized by the Federal Trade Commission, of installment buying which has spawned the socially dysfunctional practice of selling accounts so that disappointed consumers have no redress.

Part of our present predicament derives from the combination of very rapid change in one part of a system—an industry, a country, or the world—with the persistence of older practices in another part. To accommodate extremely rapid change today it is necessary to make as many simultaneous changes as possible, a task made easier by a revolutionary environment. The modern world cannot wait until the children are educated in some new practice or attitude. By that time the problems themselves will have changed. When we rely on education and slow change for the solutions of our problems, we build Maginot Lines against almost inevitable disaster.

So, in the arrangements that must be made for the involvement of women in international affairs, all the precursors of change must go on at once: the appointment of women to the highest posts and the reorganization of the demands on those positions so that they do not handicap women who hold them; the insistence on proportional representation of women in all international teams, delegations, etc.; the creation of professional institutions in which both boys and girls are first taught to respect all fields of human activities and then given access to professional participation in any of them—for women: agriculture, irrigation, town planning, architecture and the conduct of military affairs and for men: nutrition, child care, para-medical services, domestic services, architecture and planning. Attention must be given to upgrading the position of today's women who work without recognition or protection in subsistence agriculture, in home-based commercial agriculture, and in household maintenance. By relying on such a set of simultaneous initiatives at both the highest and the lowest levels of social hierarchies, we may hope to bring women into the decision making process in international affairs, in time taking full advantage of the experience derived from their historic roles in the evolution of human society.

Extracted from "Women in the International World", by Margaret Mead, in *Journal of International Affairs,* Vol. 30, No. 2, 1976-1977, pp. 159-160

BIBLIOGRAPHY
UNIT ONE

1. GENERAL
ANDERSON, M.S., *Eighteenth-Century Europe, 1713-1789* (Oxford, 1966)
ANDREWS, S., *Eighteenth-Century Europe: The 1680s to 1815* (Longmans, 1965)
ASHLEY, M., *The Golden Century: Europe, 1598-1715* (Weidenfeld and Nicolson, 1969)
ASHLEY, M., *A History of Europe, 1648-1815* (Prentice-Hall, 1973)
ASTON, T., editor, *Crisis in Europe, 1561-1660* (Routledge and Kegan Paul, 1965)
BLITZER, C., *Age of Kings* (Time-Life, 1967)
BLUM, J., CAMERON, R., and BARNES, T.G., *The Emergence of the European World* (Little Brown, 1966)
CLARK, G.N., *The Seventeenth Century* (Oxford, 1960)
DURANT, W., and DURANT, A., *The Age of Reason Begins* (Simon and Schuster, 1961)
GAY, P. and WEBB, R.K., *Modern Europe to 1815* (Harper and Row, 1973)
GILBERT, F., editor, *The Norton History of Modern Europe* (Norton, 1970)
GREEN, V.H.H., *Renaissance and Reformation: A Survey of European History between 1450 and 1660* (Arnold, 1964)
KNAPTON, E.J. *Europe: 1450-1815* (Scribners, 1958)
LANGER, W.L., editor, *Western Civilization*, 2 volumes (Harper and Row, 1968)
MAJOR, J.R., *The Western World: Renaissance to the Present* (Lippincott, 1966)
MALAND, D. *Europe in the Seventeenth Century* (St. Martin's, 1966)
OGG, D., *Europe in the Seventeenth Century* (Collier, 1962)
OWEN, J.B., *The Eighteenth Century, 1714-1815* (Nelson, 1974)
PALMER, R.R. and COLTON, J., *A History of the Modern World to 1815* (Knopf, 5th ed. 1978)
ROBERTS, J.M., *The Hutchinson History of the World* (Hutchinson, 1976)
RUDÉ, G., *Europe in the Eighteenth Century* (Weidenfeld and Nicolson, 1972)
WHITE, J.L., *The Origins of Modern Europe* (Washington Square, 1966)
WHITE, R.J. *Europe in the Eighteenth Century* (Macmillan, 1965)
WILLIAMS, E.N., *The Ancien Regime in Europe: Government and Society in the Major States, 1648-1789* (Bodley Head, 1970)
WOLF, J.B., *The Emergence of European Civilization from the Middle Ages to the Opening of the Nineteenth Century* (Harper, 1962)

2. SPAIN
DAVIES, R.T., *The Golden Century of Spain, 1501-1621* (Torchbook, 1965)
ELLIOTT, J.H., *Imperial Spain, 1469-1716* (Mentor, 1966)
KAMEN, H., *A Concise History of Spain* (Thames and Hudson, 1973)
LYNCH, J., *Spain under the Hapsburgs*, Vol. I, *Empire and Absolutism, 1516-1598* (Blackwell, 1964)
PETRIE, E., *Philip II of Spain* (Eyre and Spottiswoode, 1963)
WERNHAM, R.B., editor, *The New Cambridge Modern History*, Vol III, *The Counter-Reformation and Price Revolution, 1559-1610* (Cambridge, 1968)

3. FRANCE
ASHLEY, M., *Louis XIV and the Greatness of France* (Free Press, 1965)
BOULENGER, J., *The Seventeenth Century in France* (Capricorn, 1963)
BURCKHARDT, C.J., *Richelieu: His Rise to Power* (Vintage, 1964)
CARR, J.L., *Life in France under Louis XIV* (Batsford, 1966)
CARSTEN, F.L. *The New Cambridge Modern History*, Vol. 5, *The Ascendancy of France, 1648-88* (Cambridge, 1961)
DENIEUL-CORMIER, A., *A Time of Glory: The Renaissance in France, 1488-1559* (Doubleday, 1968)
DURANT, W., and DURANT, A., *The Age of Louis XIV* (Simon and Schuster, 1963)
GOUBERT, P., *Louis XIV and Twenty Million Frenchmen* (Random House, 1970)

LEWIS, W.H., *The Splendid Century: Life in the France of Louis XIV* (Doubleday, 1957)
MITFORD, N., *The Sun King*, (Hamilton, 1966)
OGG, D., *Louis XIV* (Oxford, 1967)
TREASURE, G.R.R., *Seventeenth Century France* (Rivingtons, 1966)
TREASURE, G.R.R., *Cardinal Richelieu and the Development of Absolutism* (Black, 1972)
WEDGWOOD, C.V., *Richelieu and the French Monarchy* (Collier, 1962)
WOLF, J.B., *Louis XIV* (Norton, 1968)

4. AUSTRIA, PRUSSIA, RUSSIA

BARRACLOUGH, G., *The Origins of Modern Germany* (Capricorn, 1963)
BELOFF, M., *The Age of Absolutism, 1660-1815* (Torchbook, 1962)
CARSTEN, F.L., *The Origins of Prussia* (Oxford, 1954)
FAY, S.B., and EPSTEIN, K., *The Rise of Brandenburg-Prussia to 1786* (Holt, Rinehart and Winston, 1964)
FITZGIBBON, C., *A Concise History of Germany* (Thames and Hudson, 1972)
FLORINSKY, M.T., *Russia: A Short History* (Macmillan, 1969)
HARRIS, R.W., *Absolutism and Enlightenment, 1660-1789* (Blandford, 1967)
HEER, F., *The Holy Roman Empire* (Weidenfeld and Nicolson, 1967)
HOLBORN, H., *A History of Modern Germany: The Reformation* (Knopf, 1959)
HOLBORN, H., *A History of Modern Germany: 1648-1840* (Knopf, 1964)
LINDSAY, J.O., editor, *The New Cambridge Modern History*, Vol. VII, *The Old Regime, 1713-63* (Cambridge, 1957)
OGG, D., *Europe of the Ancien Regime, 1715-1783* (Fontana, 1965)
PALMER, A., *Frederick the Great* (Weidenfeld and Nicolson, 1974)
PIPES, R., *Russia under the Old Regime* (Weidenfeld and Nicolson, 1974)
RIASANOVSKY, N.V., *A History of Russia* (Oxford, 3rd ed., 1977)
STEINBERG, S.H., *The Thirty Years' War and the Conflict for European Hegemony, 1600-1660* (Norton, 1966)
SUMNER, B.H., *Peter the Great and the Emergence of Russia* (Collier, 1962)
WALLACE, R., *Rise of Russia* (Time-Life, 1967)
WALSH, W.B., *Russia and the Soviet Union: A Modern History* (Michigan, 1958)
WEDGWOOD, C.V., *The Thirty Years' War* (Doubleday, 1961)

5. ENGLAND

ASHLEY, M., *England in the Seventeenth Century* (Penguin, 1961)
ASHLEY, M., *The Glorious Revolution of 1688* (Hodder and Stoughton, 1966)
ASHLEY, M., *Oliver Cromwell and His World* (Thames and Hudson, 1972)
AYLMER, G.E., *The Struggle for the Constitution: England in the Seventeenth Century* (Blandford, 1963)
BINDOFF, S.T., *Tudor England* (Penguin, 1950)
FARMER, D.L., *Britain and the Stuarts* (Bell, 1965)
HILL, C., *The Century of Revolution, 1603-1714* (Nelson, 1961)
HILLARY, A.A., *Oliver Cromwell and the Challenge to the Monarchy* (Pergamon, 1969)
JONES, J.R., *The Revolution of 1688 in England* (Norton, 1972)
KENYON, J.P., *The Stuarts* (Fontana, 1966)
LOCKYER, R., *Tudor and Stuart Britain, 1471-1714* (Longmans, 1964)
MANNING, B., *The English People and the English Revolution, 1640-1649* (Heinemann, 1976)
PRALL, S.E., *The Bloodless Revolution: England, 1688* (Doubleday, 1972)
REESE, M.M., *The Tudors and Stuarts* (Arnold, 1959)
WEBB, R.K., *Modern England: From the Eighteenth Century to the Present* (Dodd, Mead, 1968)
WERNHAM, R.B., *Before the Armada: The Emergence of the English Nation, 1485-1588* (Harcourt, Brace and World, 1966)
WESTERN, J.R., *Monarchy and Revolution: The English State in the 1680s* (Blandford, 1972)

6. EMPIRES AND WARS

BOWLE, J., *The Imperial Achievement: The Rise and Transformation of the British Empire* (Secker and Warburg, 1974)
BUSH, M.L., *Renaissance, Reformation and the Outer World* (Blandford, 1967)
CIPOLLA, M., *Guns and Sails in the Early Phase of European Expansion, 1400-1700* (Collins, 1965)
DORN, W.L., *Competition for Empire, 1740-1763* (Torchbook, 1963)
HALE, J.R., *Age of Exploration* (Time-Life, 1966)
NOWELL, C.E., *The Great Discoveries and the First Colonial Empires* (Cornell, 1965)
PARRY, J.H., *The Establishment of the European Hegemony, 1415-1715* (Torchbook, 1966)
PARRY, J.H., *The Age of Reconnaissance* (Mentor, 1964)
PENROSE, B., *Travel and Discovery in the Renaissance, 1420-1620* (Antheneum, 1962)
REYNOLDS, R.L., *Europe Emerges: Transition Toward An Industrial World-Wide Society, 600-1750* (Wisconsin, 1967)
ROBERTS, P., *The Quest for Security, 1715-1740* (Torchbook, 1963)
SEARS, S.W., ed., *The Horizon History of the British Empire* (McGraw-Hill, 1973)
WILLIAMS, G., *The Expansion of Europe in the Eighteenth Century* (Blandford, 1966)
WOLF, J.B., *The Emergence of the Great Powers, 1685-1715* (Torchbook, 1962)

7. THE SCIENTIFIC REVOLUTION

BOAS, M., *The Scientific Renaissance, 1450-1630* (Torchbook, 1966)
BROWNOWSKI, J. and MAZLISH, B., *The Western Intellectual Tradition from Leonardo to Hegel* (Torchbook, 1962)
BUTTERFIELD, H., *The Origins of Modern Science, 1300-1800* (Free Press, 1957)
BUTTERFIELD, H., and others, *A Short History of Science: Origins and Results of the Scientific Revolution* (Doubleday, 1951)
CROMBIE, A.C., *Medieval and Early Modern Science*, 2 vols. (Doubleday, 1959)
DAMPIER, W.C., *A Shorter History of Science* (Meridian, 1957)
FERMI, L. and BERNARDINI, G., *Galileo and the Scientific Revolution* (Premier, 1965)
FRIEDRICK, C.J., *The Age of the Baroque, 1610-1660* (Torchbook, 1962)
GILMORE, M.P., *The World of Humanism, 1453-1517* (Torchbook, 1962)
HALL, A.R., *The Scientific Revolution, 1500-1800* (Beacon, 1962)
KEARNEY, H.F., *Origins of the Scientific Revolution* (Longmans, 1964)
KEARNEY, H., *Science and Change, 1500-1700* (McGraw-Hill, 1971)
MIDDLETON, W.E.K., *The Scientific Revolution* (Canadian Broadcasting Corporation, 1963)
NUSSBAUM, F.L., *The Triumph of Science and Reason, 1660-1685* (Torchbook, 1962)
RANDALL, J.H., *The Making of the Modern Mind* (Houghton Mifflin, 1940)
SINGER, C., *A Short History of Scientific Ideas to 1900* (Oxford, 1962)
THIEL, R., *And There Was Light: The Discovery of the Universe* (Mentor, 1960)

UNIT TWO

1. THE ANCIEN REGIME, THE FRENCH REVOLUTION, AND NAPOLEON

BRINTON, C., *A Decade of Revolution, 1789-1799* (Harper and Row, 1963)
——— *The Jacobins* (Russel and Russel, 1957)
BRUUN, G., *Europe and the French Imperium 1799-1844* (Harper and Row, 1963)
BURKE, E., *Reflections on the Revolution in France* (Oxford University Press, 1958)
COBBAN, A., *A History of Modern France*, Vol. I (Penguin, 1963)
DE TOCQUEVILLE, A., *The Old Regime and the Revolution* (Oxford University Press, 1958)
FISHER, H.A.L., *Napoleon* (Home University Library, 1945)
GERSHAY, L., *From Despotism to Revolution, 1763-1789* (Harper and Row, 1946)
——— *The French Revolution, 1789-1799* (Harper and Row)
——— *The Era of the French Revolution 1789-1799* (Anvil, 1957)
GEYL, P., *Napoleon, For and Against* (Jonathan Cape, 1964)
GREENLAW, R.W., *The Economic Origins of the French Revolution* (Heath, 1958)
HAVENS, G.R., *The Age of Ideas: From Reaction to Revolution in Eighteenth Century France* (Holt, Rinehart, Winston, 1955)

HUNTER, T.M., *Napoleon in Victory and Defeat* (Queen's Printer, 1964)
LEFEBVRE, G., *The Coming of the French Revolution* (Random House, 1961)
MARKHAM, F.M.H., *Napoleon and the Awakening of Europe* (English Universities Press, 1954)
SCHAPIRO, J.S., *Condorcet and the Rise of Liberalism* (Octagon Books, 1963)
SEE, H., *Economic and Social Conditions in France During the Eighteenth Century* (Cooper Square, 1968)
STEWART, J.H., *A Documentary Survey of the French Revolution* (Macmillan, 1963)
THOMPSON, J.M., *Robespierre and the French Revolution* (English Universities Press, 1962)
_____ *Leaders of the French Revolution* (Harper and Row, 1967)
_____ *The French Revolution* (Oxford, 1959)
WENDEL, H., *Danton* (Yale University Press, 1935)

2. EUROPE 1815-48

ALBRECHT-CARRIE, R., *Italy from Napoleon to Mussolini* (Columbia University Press, 1950)
ARTZ, F.B., *Reaction and Revolution (1814-32)* (Harper and Row, 1961)
CIPOLLA, C.M. *The Emergence of Industrial Societies* 2 vols. (Franklin Watts Inc., 1973)
FLENLEY, RALPH, *Modern German History* (Dent, 1964)
FLORINSKY, M.T., *Russia, a History and Interpretation,* 2 vols. (Macmillan, 1954)
KARPOVICH, M., *Imperial Russia* (Holt, Rinehart and Winston)
KOHN, H., *Basic History of Modern Russia* (Anvil, 1957)
_____ *Nationalism, Its Meaning and Its History* (Anvil, 1953)
LANGER, W.L., *Political and Social Upheaval 1832-1852* (Harper & Row 1969)
MAUROIS, A., *History of France* (Minerva, 1956)
MAY, A.J., *Age of Metternich, 1814-48* (Holt, Rinehart and Winston)
MACARTNEY, C.A., *The Hapsburg Empire, 1790-1918* (Macmillan, 1969)
MORAZE, C., *The Triumph of the Middle Classes* (Peter Smith, 1966)
NICOLSON, H., *Congress of Vienna* (Methuen, 1961)
SCHAPIRO, J.S., *Liberalism: Its Meaning and History* (Anvil, 1958)
SEAMAN, L.C.B., *From Vienna to Versailles* (Methuen, 1964)
SNYDER, L.L., *Basic History of Modern Germany* (Anvil, 1957)
TAYLOR, A.J.P., *Course of German History* (University Paperbacks, 1961)
WRIGHT, G., *France in Modern Times: 1760 to the Present* (Rand McNally, 1974)

3. EUROPE — REVOLUTION OF 1848

BRUUN, G. *Revolution and Reaction, 1848 to 1852* (Anvile, 1958)
FASEL, G. *Europe in Upheaval: The Revolutions of 1848* (Rand McNally, 1970)
NAMIER, L.B. *Eighteen Forty-Eight: The Revolution of the Intellectuals* (Doubleday, 1964)
ROBERTSON, P., *Revolutions of 1848: A Social History* (Harper and Row, 1952)
STEARNS, P.N. *1848: The Revolutionary Tide in Europe* (W.W. Norton & Co., 1974)

UNIT THREE

1. ENGLAND 1815-48

ASHTON, T.S., *The Industrial Revolution, 1760-1830* (Oxford University Press, 1962)
BIRNIE, A., *An Economic History of the British Isles* (University Paperbacks, 1961)
COLE, G.D.H., and POSTGATE, R., *The Common People* (Methuen, 1964)
GREGG, P., *Modern Britain: a Social and Economic History Since 1760* (Pegasus, 1967)
JENNINGS, I., *The British Constitution* (Cambridge University Press, 1964)
THOMPSON, E.P., *The Making of the English Working Class* (Random House, 1964)
THOMSON, D., *England in the Nineteenth Century* (Penguin, 1950)
TREVELYAN, G.M., *British History in the Nineteenth Century and After (1782-1919)* (Penguin, 1966)
WOODWARD, E.L., *Age of Reform 1815-50* (Oxford, 1938)

2. SCIENCE AND SOCIALISM

BARZUN, J., *Darwin, Marx, Wagner* (Doubleday, 1958)
BERLIN, I., *Karl Marx* (Home University Library, 1948)

CARR, E.H., *Studies in Revolution* (Methuen, 1964)
CROWTHER, J.B., *Men of Science* (Cresset Press, 1960)
CURIE, E., *Madame Curie: A Bibliography* (Doubleday, 1938)
HOOK, S., *Marx and the Marxists* (Anvil, 1955)
IRVINE, W., *Apes, Angels and Victorians* (World Publishing Co., 1962)
JACKSON, J.H., *Marx, Proudhon, and European Socialism* (English University Press, 1957)
JOLL, J., *The Second International* (Harper & Row, 1974)
McLELLAN, D., *Karl Marx: His Life and Thought* (Harper & Row, 1973)
PELLING, H., *Origins of the Labour Party* (Clarendon Press, 1966)
WAGAR, W.W., *Good Tidings: The Belief in Progress from Darwin to Marcuse* (Indiana University Press, 1972)
WIGHTMAN, W.P.D., *The Growth of Scientific Ideas* (Greenwood Press, 1951)
WILSON, E., *To the Finland Station* (Doubleday, 1953)

3. EUROPE 1850-71

BEALES, D., *The Risorgimento and the Unification of Italy* (George Allen & Unwin, 1971)
BINKLEY, R.C., *Realism and Nationalism 1852-71* (Harper, 1941)
BURY, J.P.T., *Napoleon III and the Second Empire* (English University Press, 1964)
EYCK, E., *Bismarck and the German Empire* (Norton, 1964)
GUERARD, A., *Napoleon III, a Great Life in Brief* (Knopf, 1955)
HAYES, C.J.H., *Essays on Nationalism* (Macmillan, 1926)
PIPES, R., *Russia under the Old Regime* (Charles Scribner, 1975)
RICH, N., *The Age of Nationalism and Reform, 1850-1890* (W.W. Norton, 1970)
SETON-WATSON, H., *The Decline of Imperial Russia 1855-1914* (Praeger, 1962)
TAYLOR, A.J.P., *Bismarck, the Man and the Statesman* (Hamish Hamilton, 1965)
THOMPSON, J.M., *Louis Napoleon and the Second Empire* (Oxford, 1965)

4. EUROPE 1871-1914

BRUUN, G., *Clemenceau* (Anchor Books, 1963)
CHAPMAN, G., *The Dreyfus Case: A Reassessment* (Hart Davis, 1955)
GOLLWITZER, H., *Europe in the Age of Imperialism (1880-1914)* (Harcourt, Brace, 1969)
HALE, O.J., *The Great Illusion 1900-14* (Harper & Row, 1971)
HAYES, C.J.H., *A Generation of Materialism, 1871-1900* (Harper, 1963)
JACKSON, J.H., *Clemenceau and the Third Republic* (Oxford, 1965)
MUNHOLLAND, J.K., *Origins of Contemporary Europe, 1890-1914* (Harcourt, Brace, 1970)
TUCHMAN, B., *The Proud Tower* (Macmillan, 1966)

5. ENGLAND 1850-1914

AUSUBEL, H., *The Late Victorians* (Princeton, 1955)
DANGERFIELD, G., *The Strange Death of Liberal England* (Putnam & Sons, 1935)
ENSOR, R.C.K., *England, 1870-1914* (Oxford, 1936)
FREMANTLE, A., *This Little Band of Prophets* (Allen & Unwin, 1960)
HAMMOND, J.L., and FOOT, M.R.D., *Gladstone and Liberalism* (English University Press 1952)
HOBSON, J.A., *Imperialism: A Study* (J. Pott, 1902)
JONES, J.T., *Lloyd George* (Harvard, 1951)
MAGNUS, P., *Gladstone* (J. Murray, 1954)
MAUROIS, A., *Disraeli* (D. Appleton, 1928)

6. WORLD WAR ONE

CONGDON, D. *Combat: World War One* (Dell, 1964)
CRUTTWELL, C.R.M., *A History of the Great War, 1914-1918* (Oxford, 1934)
FALLS, C., *The Great War* (Longmans, 1961)
FAY, S.B., *The Origins of the War* (Free Press, 1966)
LEE, E.E., (ed.), *Outbreak of the First World War. Who Was Responsible?* (Health, 1958)
NOCOLSON, H., *Peacemaking* (Constable, 1945)
TUCHMAN, B., *The Guns of August* (Macmillan, 1962)

UNIT FOUR

1. TECHNOLOGY AND ECONOMICS
COCHRAN, T.C., *The Great Depression and World War II, 1929-1945* (Scott, Foresman, 1968)
GALBRAITH, J.K., *The Great Crash 1929* (Houghton Mifflin, 1961)
KRANZBERG, M., and PURSELL, C.W., *Technology and Russian Civilization: Vol. II* (Oxford, 1967)
LEUCHTENBURG, W.E., *Franklin D. Roosevelt and the New Deal 1932-1940* (Harper & Row, 1963)
NEVINS, ALLEN, *Ford: The Times, the Man, the Company* (Scribner's, 1954)
SHANNON, D.A., *Between the Wars: America, 1919-1941* (Houghton Mifflin, 1965)
WECTOR, D., *The Age of the Great Depression, 1929-1941* (Macmillan, 1956)

2. TOTALITARIANISM
BENEDICT, R., *The Chrysanthemum and the Sword: Patterns of Japanese Culture* (Routledge and K. Paul, 1967)
BLACK, C.E. and HELMREICH, E.C., *Twentieth Century Europe* (Knopf, 1966)
BULLOCK, ALAN, *Hitler: A Study in Tyranny* (Harper & Row, 1964)
DZIEWANOWSKI, K.M., *A History of Soviet Russia* (Prentice-Hall, 1979)
FISCHER, L., *The Life of Lenin* (Harper & Row, 1964)
GREENE, N. ed., *Fascism: An Anthology* (Crowell, 1968)
GRUNBERGER, R., *Germany 1918-1945* (Harper & Row, 1966)
HITLER, ADOLPH, *Mein Kampf*, trans. by R. Manheim (Houghton Mifflin, 1943)
HUGHES, H.S., *Contemporary Europe: A History* (Prentice-Hall, 1963)
MACKENZIE, DAVID and MICHAEL W. CURRAN, *A History of Russia and the USSR* (Dorsey Press, 1977)
MACGREGOR-HASTIE, R., *The Day of the Lion* (Macdonald, 1963)
REISCHAUER, E.O., *Japan: The Story of a Nation* (Knopf, 1974)
SETON-WATSON, H., *From Lenin to Khrushchev: The History of World Communism* (Praeger, 1960)
SHIRER, W.L., *The Rise and Fall of the Third Reich: A History of Nazi Germany* (Simon & Schuster, 1960)

3. INTERNATIONAL RELATIONS
CARR, E.H., *International Relations between the Two World Wars (1919-1939)* (Macmillan, 1963)
CLUBB, O.E., *20th Century China* (Columbia University Press, 1964)
HUGHES, H.S., *Comtemporary Europe: A History* (Prentice-Hall, 1963)
THOMAS, H., *The Spanish Civil War* (Eyre and Spottiswoode, 1961)
WHEELER-BENNETT, SIR JOHN, *Munich: Prologue to Tragedy* (Macmillan, 1963)
ZIMMERN, SIR ALFRED E., *The League of Nations and the Rule of Law, 1918-1935* (Macmillan, 1939)

4. THE SECOND WORLD WAR
CALVOCORESSI, PETER and GUY WINT, *Total War: Causes and Courses of the Second World War* (Penguin, 1974)
CHURCHILL, WINSTON, *The Second World War: The Gathering Storm* (Houghton Mifflin; Thomas Allen 1948); *Their Finest Hour* (1949); *The Grand Alliance* (1950); *The Hinge of Fate* (1950); *Closing the Ring* (1951); *Triumph and Tragedy* (1953)
COCHRAN, T.C., *The Great Depression and World War II, 1929-1945* (Scott, Foresman, 1968)
FEIS, H., *The Atomic Bomb and the End of World War II* (Princeton University Press, 1966)

UNIT FIVE

1. THE COLD WAR AND THE UNITED NATIONS
BLACK, C.E. and THORNTON, T.P., *Communism and Revolution: The Strategic Uses of Political Violence* (Princeton University Press, 1964)
DEUTSCHER, I., *Stalin: A Political Biography* (Oxford University Press, 1967)

———*The Unfinished Revolution: Russia 1917-1967* (Oxford University Press, 1967)
FISCHER-GALATI, S. ed., *Twentieth Century Europe: A Documentary History* (Lippincott, 1967)
GATZKE, H.W., *The Present in Perspective: A Look at the World Since 1945,* 3rd ed., (Rand, McNally, 1968)
HENDERSON, J.L. ed., *Since 1945: Aspects of Contemporary World History* (Methuen, 1966)
KENNAN, G.F., *Realities of American Foreign Policy* (Norton, 1966)
LUKACS, J., *A New History of the Cold War* (Doubleday: Anchor Books, 1966)
MAY, A.J., *Europe Since 1939* (Holt, Rinehart and Winston, 1966)
NETTL, J.P., *The Soviet Achievement* (Thames & Hudson, 1967)
NICHOLAS, H.G., *The United Nations as a Political Institution,* 2nd ed., (Oxford University Press, 1963)
REES, D., *The Age of Containment: The Cold War 1945-1965* (Macmillan, 1967)
REYNOLDS, E.E. and BRASHER, N.H., *Britain in the Twentieth Century 1900-1964* (Cambridge University Press, 1966)
SCHLESINGER, A.M., *A Thousand Days: John F. Kennedy in the White House* (Houghton Mifflin, 1965)
SHULMAN, M.D., *Beyond the Cold War* (Yale University Press, 1966)
WILLIS, F.R., *Europe in the Global Age: 1939 to the Present* (Dodd, Mead, 1968)
———*European Problem Studies: DeGaulle: Anachronism, Realist, or Prophet?* (Holt, Rinehart & Winston, 1967)

2. THE NEW NATIONS

BLACK, C.E. and THORNTON, T.P., *Communism and Revolution: The Strategic Uses of Political Violence* (Princeton University Press, 1964)
BRECHER, MICHAEL, *The New States of Asia: A Political Analysis* (Oxford University Press, 1963)
CH'EN, JEROME, *Mao and the Chinese Revolution* (Oxford University Press, 1967)
CLUBB, O. EDMUND, *China & Russia: The "Great Game"* (Columbia University Press, 1971)
FITZGERALD, C.P., *The Birth of Communist China* (Praeger, 1966)
GEERTZ, C. ed., *Old Societies and New States: The Quest for Modernity in Asia and Africa* (Free Press of Glencoe, 1963)
GUNGWU, WUNG, *China and the World since 1949* (Macmillan, 1977)
JANSEN, MARIUS, B., *Japan & China: from War to Peace, 1894-1972* (Rand McNally, 1975)
WARD, BARBARA, *The Rich Nations and the Poor Nations* (Norton, 1962)

INDEX

Absolutism, 2-47, 62, 135, 337, 421, 496, 500, 760-764
Abu Dhabi, 732
Acadia, 72, 82
Acheson, Dean, 621-2, 626
Acre, Battle of, 176
Adenauer, Konrad, 594-6
Adler, Alfred, 289
Adriatic problem, 496
Africa, 336, 345, 368-72, 375-6, 389-91, 453, 467-8, 470, 473, 538-40, 569, 571-2, 650-3, 662, 697-708, 720, 723-4
Afro-Asian Group, 645, 687
Agrarian Reform Act (Russia), 435
Agriculture, 105-6, 118, 210, 235, 251-3, 257, 284, 295, 349, 435, 450, 453-4, 465, 485, 509, 513-15, 667, 723, 725, 727
Aides (sales tax), 16, 134, 776
Aix-la-Chapelle, Congress of, 227; Treaty of, 35
Albania, 394-6, 612, 617
Alcock, John, 450
d'Alembert, Jean (1717-83), 108
Alexander I, of Russia (1777-1825), 194, 200-2, 225, 228-30, 422
Alexander II, of Russia (1818-81), 423-4
Alexander III, of Russia (1845-94), 387, 424, 428, 430
Alexander, of Serbia, 384-5
Alexandra, of Russia, 430-1, 436, 439
Alexandria, 175
Algeciras Conference, 391
Algeria, 391, 591, 634, 655, 700
Allenby, General, 410
Allende, Salvador, 711
Alliance for Progress, 709
Alsace, 336, 338, 345, 381, 396, 399, 413, 475
Amalgamated Society of Engineers, 358
American Revolution, 80, 110, 117, 140-1
Amiens, Treaty of, 181, 183, 187
Anarchists, 298, 339, 359, 426, 546
Anatomy, 94-8
Anglican Church, 49, 52, 57, 61, 266-7, 269
Angola, 706
Anglo-Persian Oil Company, 376
Anschluss, 549
Anti-Corn Law League, 276
Anti-Semitism, 342-4, 460, 518, 520, 528, 788-9
Antitoxins, 463-4
Apartheid, 648, 703, 704, 739
Appeasement, 511, 551, 559
Arabs, 649, 651, 712, 749
Ardennes, battles of, 557, 580
Argentina, 454, 485, 708, 710-1
Aristarchus of Samos, 85
Aristocracy, *see* Nobility
Aristotle (384-322 B.C.), 83, 98, 101; concept of universe, 83, 85, 89-91

Arkwright, Richard, 256, 258
Arms race, 371, 376-80, 537
Armstrong, Neil, 755
Arnhem, Battle of, 581
Artois, Count of, 148, 205
Asquith, Lord, 363
Assembly of Notables (France), 142
Association of South-East Asian Nations (ASEAN), 693
Astronomy, 83-94, 101-2, 458-9
Aswan Dam, 650
Ataturk (1880-1938), 415, 468
Atheism, 106, 151
Atlantic Charter, 562, 568, 640
Atomic power, 458-62, 585-7, 590, 597, 599-600, 605, 623, 633, 649, 685, 754; test ban treaty, 633
Attlee, Clement R. (1883-1967), 590, 610
Auerstadt, Battle of, 189
Augsburg, Peace of, 22
Ausgleich, 324
Austerlitz, Battle of, 189-90, 204, 209
Australia, 368, 372, 454, 470, 472-4, 485, 505, 567, 572, 693, 696, 723
Austria (*see also* Dual Monarchy), 17, 34-40, 80-2, 119-20, 123-4, 162, 168, 172-4, 176, 181, 187-90, 200, 204, 220-34, 237, 240-5, 249, 304, 307, 312-26, 383-7, 397-412, 414, 534, 549, 553-4, 612
Austrian Succession, War of, 34, 80-1
Automation, 727-9
Aztecs, 69

Bach, J.S. (1685-1750), 105
Bacon, Francis (1561-1626), 87, 98-101
Baden, 189, 323
Bakewell, Robert, 253
Bakunin, Michael, 426
Baldwin, Stanley (1867-1947), 543
Balfour, Arthur (1848-1930), 357, 457
Balkans, 230, 281, 292, 324, 333, 336, 376, 382, 384-7, 392-7, 532-3, 562-3, 612-18; Balkan League, 394-5; Balkan Wars, 394-5
Ballot Act (England), 355-6
Baltic States, 42, 44, 506
Baltimore, Lord, 75
Banalités (taxes), 133
Bandaranaike, Sirimave, 740
Bandung Conference, 687
Bangladesh (formerly East Pakistan), 670
Banking, 258-9, 295, 470, 480, 482-5, 492
Banting, Frederick, 464
Bantu, 703
Bararet, Jean-Joseph, 296
Barras, Paul, 169-70, 177
Barth, Karl, 747
Bastille, fall of, 146-8, 220
Batavian Republic, 168
Battle of Britain, 560-1, 750
Bavaria, 189, 204, 323, 327, 412, 516
Bay of Pig's fiasco, 629, 709
Baylen, Battle of, 198-9
Beauharnais, Eugène de, 195

805

Beethoven, Ludwig van (1770-1827), 216
Begin, Menachem (1913-   ), 716
Belgium, 34, 120, 163, 172-4, 181, 187, 224, 232-4, 292, 305, 371, 398-9, 413, 449, 476, 536, 557, 596
Bell, Alexander Graham, 281
Benedetti, 325
Benelux, 596, 620
Bentham, Jeremy, 267
Berlin blockade, 618-20
Berlin Decree (Napoleon), 193
Berlin-Baghdad Railway, 280, 375, 382
Bernstein, Eduard (1850-1932), 302
Berthelot, Marcelin, 280
Bessarabia, 611
Bessemer, Henry, 280, 347
Best, Charles, 464
Biafra, 749
Bill of exchange, 63
Bill of Rights (England), 61-2
Birth control, 745
Bismarck, Otto von, (1815-98), 304, 317-38, 378, 386-8, 412, 517
Black Hand society, 384-5, 397
"Black liberation", 742
"Black Power" Movement, 605
Black Women's Organization for Action, 742
Blanc, Louis (1811-82), 238, 298
Blanqui, Auguste (1805-81), 237, 298
Bleriot, Louis, 281
Blitzkrieg, 555-8, 560, 563, 567, 714
Bloody Sunday (Russia), 431-2
Blücher, General, 206
Blum, Léon, 542
Boer War, 370-1, 389
Boers, 70, 367, 370-1, 389
Bohemia, 34, 240-3, 418
Bohr, Niels, 459
Bologna, 174
Bolsheviks, 266, 428-30, 433-5, 440-7, 506-7, 516, 523, 530, 543
Bonaparte, Louis Napoleon, *see* Napoleon III
Bonaparte, Napoleon, *see* Napoleon Bonaparte
Bonhoeffer, Dietrich, 747
Booth, William, 294
Borelli, Alfonso, 87, 98
Borneo, 369
Borodino, Battle of, 201
Bosnia, 384-5, 393, 395, 397
Bossuet, Bishop (1627-1704), 25-6
Boulanger Affair, 342
Boulton, Matthew, 259
Bourbons, 11, 127, 185, 189, 198, 204-6, 219, 223, 229, 231-2, 234-5, 341
Bourgeoisie, see Middle class
Boxer Revolt (China), 672
Brahe, Tycho (1546-1601), 86-7
Brandenburg (Prussia), 36
Brandt, Willy, 638
Brazil, 68, 71, 76, 315, 531, 710-11
Brest-Litovsk, Treaty of, 506-7

Brezhnev, Leonid (1906-   ), 601, 638
Bright, John (1811-89), 267, 276, 352, 355
Brittany, 9, 182
Brown, Arthur, 450
Brumaire, 182
Brüning, Heinrich, 521
Brussels, Treaty of, 620-1
Bucharest, Treaty of, 395
Budapest, 241, 247
Buddhism, 619, 749
Bulgaria, 376, 394-5, 399, 409-10, 533, 611-2, 617
Bulow, Bernhard von (1849-1929), 389, 391
Bundesrat, 323, 327-8
Burgundy, 4, 9
Burke, Edmund (1729-97), 220
Burma, 369, 473, 547, 572, 583
Burschenschaft, 227-8, 318
Byron, Lord George Gordon (1788-1824), 213, 230

Cabot, John, 73-4
Cabral, Pedro Alvares, 68
Cadoudal, Georges, 185
Calonne, Charles Alexander de (1734-1802), 141-2
Calvinists, 9, 22, 49
Cambodia, 689, 691, 694, 697
Campbell-Bannerman, Sir Henry, (1836-1908), 357, 361, 363
Camp David, 716
Campo Formio, Treaty of, 174
Canada, 281, 368, 372, 410, 450, 453-4, 464, 467, 473, 485, 505, 571, 573, 581, 597, 621, 625, 644, 647, 652-4, 692, 694, 709, 711, 723-5, 731, 746; colonization of, 72-5, 473
Canadian Pacific Railway, 281
Canadian University Service Overseas (CUSO), 711, 724
Cannizzaro, Stanislao, 280
Cape Colony, 370, 372
Capitalism, 257-9, 300-3, 374, 469, 481-3, 490-5, 509, 513-14, 520, 667, 707, 726, 736-7
Capitation (tax), 134
Carbonari, 229, 237, 247, 306, 311
Carnot, Lazare Nicholas (1753-1823), 166, 219, 309
Cartels, 292
Carter, Jimmy (1924-   ), 716
Cartesian philosophy, 101
Cartier, Jacques (1491-1557), 72
Cartwright, Edmund, 256
Castro, Fidel (1927-   ), 629, 632
Cathay, 73-4
Catherine II (the Great), of Russsia (1729-96), 44-6, 120-3, 421
Catherine de' Medici, of France (1519-89), 10
Caucasus, 563
Cavaliers, 53, 57
Cavour, Count Camillo Benso di (1810-61), 304, 307, 312-18

Cayley, Sir George, 281
Censorship, 89, 108, 129, 138, 228, 305, 423-4, 501-2, 637, 681, 702
Centre Party (Germany), 330, 332, 521, 523
Ceylon, 224, 723
Chamberlain, Joseph (1856-1914), 357, 372, 389
Chamberlain, Neville (1869-1940), 549-51, 559
Champlain, Samuel de (1567-1635), 72
Champollion, 175
Charbonarie, 237
Charlemagne, (742-814), 4, 16
Charles I, of England (1600-49), 50-5, 61
Charles II, of England (1630-85), 56-8, 75
Charles IV, of Spain (1748-1819), 198
Charles V, of Spain (1500-58), 4
Charles VI, of Austria (1685-1740), 34
Charles IX, of France (1560-74), 10
Charles X, of France (1757-1836), 232, 235
Charles Albert, of Piedmont (1798-1849), 245, 312
Charles Stuart, *see* Charles II, of England
Charter Constitution (France), 232
Chartered companies, 65
Chartists, 275-6, 358
Chateaubriand, François René (1768-1848), 220
Chiang Kai-shek (1887-1975), 547, 584, 673-82, 690
Chile, 708, 711
China, 40, 371, 399, 410, 431, 466, 473, 479-80, 532, 534-5, 547, 672-680, 706; Communist, 547, 626, 634, 637-50, 655, 668, 672-87, 689, 697, 706-7, 722; Nationalist, 547, 584, 643, 649-50, 672-77, 680-2
Chopin, Frederick François (1810-49), 216
Chou En-lai (1898-1976), 676, 680
Christian Socialism (Kingsley), 294
Chrisitianity, 40-1, 108, 113, 225, 294, 526, 744-8, 782-4
Church and State, 2, 5, 22, 184; separation of, 343-4
Churchill, Sir Winston (1874-1965), 81, 543, 559-62, 568, 590, 607-10, 612, 640, 642-3
Ciano, Count Galeazzo, 545
Circulation of the blood, 96-8
Cisalpine Republic, 174, 189, 208
Civil Code, French, *see* Code Napoléon
Civil Constitution of the Clergy (France), 151
Civil Rights Act (1964), 605
Civil Wars: England, 53, 61; France, 339; Russia, 474, 506-7, 511-12, 606; Spain, 545-7, 606, 617
Civilian Conservation Corps, 493
Clemenceau, Georges (1841-1929), 413-14, 418
Coal Mines Act (England), 269
Coalition Wars: First, 162-3, 172; Second, 176, 181; Third, 187-200

Cobbett, William (1763-1835), 267
Cobden Richard (1804-65), 276, 352, 368
Code Napoléon, 184-5, 195, 200, 208, 232
Colbert, Jean-Baptiste (1619-83), 28-32, 72, 764
Cold War, 594, 634, 668, 688, 693, 726
Coligny, Admiral de, 10-11
Collective bargaining, 294-5
Collective farms: China, 683; Russia, 514-15, 532
Colonialism, 4-8, 68-82, 224, 337, 345, 367-72, 379, 381-2, 388, 414, 468, 589, 642, 648, 660-71, 688-9, 698, 700-3, 705-7, 739, 764-9
Columbus, Bartholemew, 73
Columbus, Christopher, (1446-1506), 69, 73
Combination Acts (England), 273-4
Combined Chiefs of Staff, 568
Cominform, 616, 618
Commercial Revolution, 63-8
Committee of Public Safety (French Revolution), 163-8
Common Market (E.E.C.), 591, 594-9, 636
Commonwealth, British, 372, 559, 561, 566, 568, 571, 578, 583, 585, 607, 640, 642, 666-7, 701
Commune, Chinese, 683; of Paris (1871), *see* Paris Commune
Communications, 281, 284, 454-7, 482, 528, 638, 728-9
Communism (*see also* Bolsheviks, Communist Parties, Marxism), 298-303, 330, 340, 466, 494, 504, 506-15, 520, 528, 530, 532, 545-7, 564, 566, 586, 601, 604-6, 608, 612-8, 622, 627-32, 634-6, 667-8, 687, 696, 707, 709, 711, 722, 724, 726, 791-2
Communist Manifesto (Marx), 301, 780-1
Communist Parties: China (*see also* China, Communist), 674-683; France, 542, 591; Germany, 412, 521, 523; Indo-China, 688-93; Italy, 499-500; Russia (*see also* Bolsheviks), 507-9, 513; Spain, 546
Company of New France, 72
Company of the West, 72
Computers, 718
Concert of Europe, *see* Congress System
Concord, aircraft, 754
Concordat, 183, 343
Confédération Général du Travail (France), 296
Confederation, North German, 323-4, 327
Confederation of the Rhine, 189, 208, 223
Congo Crisis, 652-3, 659, 707
Congress System, 211, 219-20, 224-31
Conservatism, 153-5, 211, 218-20, 227-34, 245-9, 265, 494, 505, 514, 726
Conservative Party (England), 351-8, 369
Constable, John, 213
Constantine, of Russia, 230
Constantinople, 40, 175, 383-4, 386, 394
Constituent Assembly, Austro-Hungary, 241-3; France, 238

INDEX 807

Constitutions: Cyprus, 654; France, (1795) 168-9, (1799) 180, (1814) 232, (1875) 341, (Fourth Republic) 591; Imperial Germany, 327-8; Japan, 602; Nazi Germany, 524; North German Confederation, 323; Weimar Republic, 516-18, 523; Russia, (1905) 434, (1924) 507
Containment Policy (U.S.A.), 615-16, 626
Continental System (Napoleon), 193-4, 198, 200-1, 209
Co-operative movement, 294-5, 297-8, 426
Copernicus, Nicholas (1473-1543), 83-91, 94, 102, 458
Corday, Charlotte, 163-4
Cordelier Club, 153, 158, 161, 163
Corfu, 533
Corn Laws, 275-7, 349, 352
Coronel, Battle of, 409
Corporatism, 502-3
Cort, Henry, 255
Cortes, Hernando, 69
Corvée (labour tax), 133
Cottage industries, 253, 256-7, 259
Council of Elders (France), 168
Council of Five Hundred (France), 168, 178-80
Council of People's Commissars (Russia), 506
Counter-Reformation, 5
Craddock, Admiral, 409
Crimean War, 306-7, 322, 325, 367, 386
Croats, 240, 243, 383-4, 410
Crompton, Samuel, 256
Cromwell, Oliver (1599-1658), 53-6
Crop rotation methods, 251-3
Cuba, 545, 706, 708-9
Cuban Missile Crisis, 629-33, 659
Cunard steamship line, 281
Curies, Pierre and Marie, 288
Cyprus, 369, 634, 653-5, 659, 749
Czechoslovakia, 242, 244, 249, 410, 415, 418, 466, 549, 551-4, 614, 618, 637-8
Czechoslovakian Crisis (1968), 637-8, 659, 789-92

Da Gama, Vasco, 68
Daladier, Edouard (1884-   ), 549, 551
Dalmatians, 240, 496
Danish War, 322
Danton, George (1759-94), 158-63, 166, 168
Danzig, 413, 534, 554
Darby, Abraham, 254-5
Darwin, Charles (1809-82), 284, 299, 458, 462
Darwinism, 284, 286, 293, 388, 779-84
David, Jacques, 181, 186
Dawes Plan, 478-9
Dayan, Moshe, 715-6
D-Day, 573, 578
Debré, Michel, 636
Decembrist Revolt (Russia), 230, 422
Declaration of Independence (U.S.A.), 117, 141, 368
Declaration fo Pillnitz, 155

Declaration of Rights of Man (France), 149-50, 244
Declaration of Rights of the German People, 244
Deflation, 484
De Gaulle, Charles (1890-1970), 555, 571, 591-4, 597, 599, 634-6, 700
Deists, 106-7
Delcassé, Theophile (1852-1923), 390-1
Democratic Party (Germany), 517
Denmark, 17, 42, 224, 295, 322, 413, 557, 599, 621
Départements (France), 135, 150, 182
Depression (1930's), *see* Great Depression
Derby, Lord, 355
Desai, Morarji, 671
Descartes, René (1596-1650), 87, 100-1, 769-70
"de-Stalinization", 601
Dialectic, 300-1
Dialogues (Galileo), 89
Diaz, Bartholomew, 68
Diderot, Denis (1713-84), 108, 121
Diem, Ngo Dinh, 694
Dien Bien Phu, Battle of, 691, 693
Directory (France), 168, 177-80
Disarmament, 496, 633, 641, 668; Geneva Conference, 538, 540
Discourse on Method (Descartes), 100-1
Disraeli, Benjamin (1804-81), 293, 352-6, 359, 368-9
Divine right of kings, 25-6, 46-8, 51, 56, 61, 127, 529, 601
Divine state (Hegel), 218, 502
Dominican Republic, 659, 708
Donne, John, 101-2
Double-entry bookkeeping, 65
Draft, 63, 65
Drang Nach Osten, 382
Dreadnoughts, 379, 396
Dreikaiserbund, 333, 336, 386
Dreyfus Affair, 343
Dual Alliance, 333, 336, 387
Dual Monarchy (Austria-Hungary), 324, 333, 383-7, 392-7, 410, 414, 418
Dubĉek, Alexander, 637
Ducos, Roger, 178, 180
Dukhobors, 121
Duma, 44, 421, 434-5, 441
Dumbarton Oaks Conference, 642
Dumouriez, Charles François, 161, 163
Dunkirk, Evacuation of, 558

East Germany, 594-5, 614
East India Companies; Dutch, 30, 70; English, 30, 76, 257, 259, 368; French, 30
East Indies, 68, 70
Easter Rebellion (Ireland), 367
Economic and Social Council (U.N.) 647, 649
Economics, 257-9, 289, 470-94, 513, 720-6, 738
Eden, Anthony (1897-   ), 543, 559
Edison, Thomas Alva, (1847-1931), 482

Education, 119, 129, 195, 208, 219, 265, 269, 273, 292-5, 341, 349, 351, 375, 424, 426, 458, 488, 490, 502, 526, 648, 677, 724, 728, 740
Education Acts (England), 351
Edward VII, of England (1841-1910), 376, 390
Egypt, 174-7, 184, 187, 369, 390, 532, 563, 650-2, 659, 712, 714-8
Einstein, Albert (1879-1955), 460-1
Eire, Republic of, 367, 620
Eisenhower, Dwight D. (1890-1969), 571, 573, 580-2, 609, 622, 629, 693, 696
El Alamein, 571
Eleven Years' Tyranny (Charles I), 51-2, 55
Elizabeth I, of England (1533-1603), 7, 47-9, 52, 76
Emancipation: of serfs, 243, 424, 427; of slaves, 370; of women, (see Women's Roles) 466-7, 495, 601
Ems dispatch, 325
Enclosure movement, 252-3, 259, 266
L'Encyclopédie, 108-10, 121, 123
Encyclopedists, 110, 138
Energy Crisis, 729
England, 7-9, 29-30, 34, 46-62, 65, 72-82, 107, 110-11, 140, 162, 168, 172, 174-6, 181, 183, 187-94
Enlightened depotism, 46, 113, 118-24
Enlightenment, 46, 105-24, 138, 213, 218, 771-5
Enosis, 654
Entente Cordiale, 390-1
Erhard, Dr. Ludwig, 595
Escorial, 1-2, 8
Eshkol, 712
Estates-General (France), 14, 127-8, 142, 144-5
Estonia, 418, 466, 554
Ethiopian crisis, 538-41, 545, 553, 650, 708
European Coal and Steel Community (E.C.S.C.), 596-7
European Economic Community, *see* Common Market
Evangelism, 748
Evolution, theory of, 284, 286-7, 779-80
Exceptional Laws (Prussia), 332
Existentialism, 735
Eylau, Battle of, 194

Fabian Society, 359-61
Fabricius, of Aquapendente, 87, 96
Factory Acts (England), 268-9, 350
Factory system, 253-66, 268-9, 716
Fair Deal (Truman), 604
Faraday, Michael (1791-1867), 280
Farnese, Alexander (of Parma), 7
Fascism, 496-504, 506, 528, 530, 543-9, 553, 622, 787-8
Fascist Parties: Italy, 499-505, 526; Spain, 546-7
Fashoda incident, 389-90
February Revolution (France), 237-8, 240, 249

Federal German Republic, *see* West Germany
Fenelon, 25
Ferdinand I, of Austria, 241, 243
Ferdinand II, of Sicily (1810-59), 312
Ferdinand IV, of Naples, 229
Ferdinand VII, of Spain, 229
Fermi, Enrico, 461
Ferrara, 174
Feudalism, 133-4, 142, 149, 210, 219, 227, 232, 243, 249, 251, 423, 777-9
Feuillants, 154, 157
Fichte, J.G. (1762-1814), 227
Fielding, Henry, 105
Fifth Republic (France), 594
Final Solution (Hitler), 528
Finland, 224, 466-7, 506, 534, 554, 611, 621, 641
First Empire (France), *see* Napoleon Bonaparte
First Estate, 128-9
First International, 302, 339, 616
First World War, 293, 344-6, 367, 372, 396-412, 437, 442-3, 467, 471-2, 474-5, 479-80, 495-7, 499, 504, 511, 542, 555, 704, causes of, 374-86; Peace of Paris, 412-19
Fiume, 496
Five Year Plans: China, 683; India, 667-8; Russia, 509, 511, 513-14, 599
Flanders, 162, 168
Fleming, Sir Alexander, 464
Foch, Marshal, 412
Fontainebleau, Treaty of, 204
Ford, Henry (1863-1947), 450-2
Foreign aid, 476, 478-9, 562, 594-5, 613-6, 618, 668, 709-11, 721-5
Fort Duquesne (Pittsburgh), 81
Fourier, Charles, 297-8
Fourteen Points (Woodrow Wilson), 413
Fourth Republic (France), 591
France, 2, 4-5, 8-33, 38, 46-7, 50, 52, 62, 65, 71-3, 80-2, 108-18, 123-211, 219, 224-6, 229-38, 281, 292, 295-6, 303, 305-11, 313-17, 322-7, 329, 332-3, 371, 374-5, 386-415, 418, 449, 453, 463, 467, 476, 479, 496, 517, 535-7, 541-4, 546, 549, 551, 554-9, 591, 594, 596-9, 612, 614, 616, 620, 625, 634-6, 644, 648, 651-2, 688-91, 693, 700, 741
Franchise, 236, 266, 271-3, 275, 293, 303, 305, 323, 327, 341, 346, 351, 354-6, 358, 466-7, 504, 601, 706
Francis I, of France (1494-1547), 72
Francis II, of France (1544-60), 10
Francis II, of Austria (1768-1835), 155
Francis Ferdinand, of Austria, Archduke (1863-1914), 397
Franco, General Francisco (1892-1975), 546-7
Franco-Austrian War, 306-8
Franco-Russian Alliance, 388, 390
Frankfurt, Treaty of, 338
Franklin, Benjamin (1706-90), 141
Franz Josef, of Austria (1830-1916), 243, 307, 314

INDEX 809

Frederick I, of Prussia (1657-1713), 36
Frederick II (the Great), of Prussia (1712-86), 38-9, 44, 46, 77, 81-2, 118-19, 123, 517
Frederick III, of Prussia (1831-88), 337
Frederick William I, of Prussia (1688-1740), 36-8
Frederick William II, of Prussia (1744-97), 155
Frederick William III, of Prussia (1779-1840), 189
Frederick William IV, of Prussia (1795-1861), 243-5, 249, 317-18
Frederick William (the Great Elector), of Prussia (1620-88), 36
Free French forces, 571, 581
Free trade 236, 330, 348, 352, 367-8, 372
French and Indian War, 80-2
French Revolution, 17, 80, 110, 143-69, 177, 180, 184, 198, 204, 208, 210-11, 219-22, 249, 300, 423; background to, 125-42, 775-9
Freud, Sigmund (1856-1939), 288
Frick, Wilhelm, 522
Friedland, Battle of, 194
Frondes, 23

Gabelle (salt tax), 13, 16, 134
Gagarin, Yuri, 754
Gagging Acts (England), 268
Galbraith, J.K., 724, 734, 737, 785-6
Galen of Pergamum, 94, 96
Galileo Galilei (1564-1642), 87-91, 98, 100-1, 770-1
Gambetta, Leon (1838-82), 309, 338, 341, 345
Gandhi, Indira (1917-   ), 670-1, 740
Gandhi, Mahatma (1869-1948), 469, 661-3, 667
"Gang of Four", 684
Gapon, Father Georgi, 431-2
Garibaldi, Guiseppe (1807-82), 245, 315-17
Gastein, Convention of, 322
Gaza Strip, 714, 718
General Assembly (U.N.), 645-6, 648-52, 655, 704
General Will (Rousseau), 116, 502
Genghis Khan (1162-1227), 40
Genoa, 63, 65, 174, 181, 223
Genocide, 528, 749
George III, of England, (1760-1820), 44, 266
George V, of England (1865-1936), 363
Georgia, 75
German Confederation, 223, 227-8, 233-4, 236-7, 240, 243-5, 249, 318, 323
German Democratic Republic, *see* East Germany
Germany (*see also* West Germany *and* East Germany), 17-19, 22, 29-30, 172, 189, 200, 208, 227-9, 281, 295-7, 327-38, 345, 371, 374-419, 438-9, 442-3, 453, 456, 467, 471-9, 486, 488, 494, 507, 530-2, 535-6, 539-45, 549-65, 573, 578-82, 594-5, 704, 754; post-war zones, 594, 611; unification of, 317- 26
Gestapo, 520
Ghana, 702, 707
Gibraltar, 81
Gilchrist, Thomas, 280, 347
Gioberti, Vincenzo, 312
Girondins, 153-5, 161-3, 166, 178
Giscard d'Estaing, Valery (1926-   ), 636
Gladstone, William Ewart (1809-98), 353-7, 369
Glorious Revolution (England), 61, 107, 267
Godoy, Manuel, 198
Goebbels, Josef, 520
Goering, Hermann, 520
Goethe (1749-1832), 213
Golan Heights, 714
Gold Coast, 701-2
Gold standard, 472-3, 513
Gordon, General Charles George, 369
Gothic, 213
Graham, Billy, 748
Gramont, 325
Grand Alliance, 568-9, 609
Grand National Consolidated Trades Union, 273-4, 295, 358
Great Britain, 200-1, 204-7, 223-6, 230-3, 251-77, 281, 292, 294-6, 303, 305, 322, 329, 337, 346-73, 375-80, 382, 386-415, 418, 453, 463, 466-7, 472, 474, 479, 486, 496, 517, 532, 535-43, 546, 549, 551, 554-62, 567-9, 590-1, 597, 599, 606, 612-4, 617, 619-20, 623, 625, 633, 636, 640, 642-3, 648, 651-2, 654, 663-7, 684, 693, 701-2, 706, 723, 732, 741, 750, 754
Great Depression, 470, 473, 479, 480, 483-90, 492, 495-6, 505, 604, 648, 785-7
Great Design (Sully), 13
Great Exhibition (1851), 346, 348
Great Leap Forward (China), 683
Great Protestation (England), 49
Greece, 227, 230, 376, 394-5, 409, 415, 533, 562-3, 612-3, 621, 634, 654
Grévy, Jules (1807-91), 341
Grey, Earl, 399
Grey, Lord, 272
Grotius, Hugo (1583-1645), 19, 22
Grouchy, Marshal, 206
Guatemala, 709
Guernica, i
Guerrilla warfare, 199, 315, 612, 616, 687, 689-94, 700
Guild system, 328-9
Guilt clause (Treaty of Versailles), 414
Guizot, François Pierre (1787-1874), 236-8, 293
Gypsies, 528

Habeas Corpus Amendment Act (England), 58, 61
Hague Conferences, 380
Haiti, 708
Halifax, 443

Hammarskjöld, Dag (1905-61), 647, 652-3
Hanover, 189, 323
Hapsburg Empire, 4, 17, 34-5, 46, 189, 242-5, 247, 249, 308, 312, 383-4, 466, 496
Hardie, Keir (1856-1915), 360-1
Hargreaves, James, 256
Harvey, William (1578-1657), 87, 96-8, 102
Heart's Content, Newfoundland, 281
Hegel, Georg Wilhem (1770-1831), 218, 300, 382, 502
Heine, Heinrich, 213
Heligoland, 224
Heliocentric universe, 85-6, 89
Hemingway, Ernest, 546
Henry II, of France (1519-59), 10
Henry III, of France (1551-89), 10-11
Henry IV, of France (1553-1610), 10-14, 72
Henry VII, of England (1457-1509), 73-4
Henry VIII, of England (1491-1547), 5, 49, 52
Henry of Navarre, *see* Henry IV, of France
Henry the Navigator, 68
Herzegovina, 384-5, 393, 395
Hesse-Cassel, 323
Himmler, Heinrich, 520
Hindenburg, Paul von, 521-4
Hindus, 661, 668-9, 749
Hiroshima, 585, 589, 602-3, 623, 674
Hitler, Adolf, (1889-1945), 30, 42, 218, 338, 382, 414, 456, 460, 478, 511, 518-28, 537, 540-4, 549-65, 567, 569, 571, 573, 580, 582-3, 623, 788-9
Hitler Youth, 493, 527
Ho Chi Minh, 689-94
Hoare, Sir Samuel, 539
Hochelaga, 72
Hohenlinden, Battle of, 181, 185
Hohenzollern family, 36, 236, 243-4, 249, 325, 466, 496
Holding companies, 481-2, 485, 492
Holland (United Provinces of the Netherlands), 7, 30, 52, 54, 69-71, 76, 162, 168, 172, 187, 194, 204, 224
Hollywood, 457
Holstein, 322-3
Holy Alliance, 225, 231
Holy Roman Empire, 17, 35, 381
Home Rule (for Ireland), 356-7, 364-7
Horizontal combination, 289, 292
House of Commons, 48-50, 53, 56-7, 271-2, 275, 313, 346, 353, 356, 362-3
House of Lords, 48, 54, 56-7, 61, 272, 346, 357, 362-3
Hua Kuo-feng, 684
Hudson, Henry, 70
Hudson's Bay Company, 75
Hugo, Victor (1802-85), 213, 305
Huguenots, 9-16, 32, 50, 61, 70, 72
Hundred Years' War, 218
Hungarian Revolution (1956), 628, 655
Hungary (*see also* Dual Monarchy), 4, 34, 120, 240-4, 304, 383-4, 410, 414-5, 475, 534, 551, 611, 614, 618
Hunt, Henry "Orator", 268

Hyndman, H.M., 359

Iberian Peninsula, 195, 558
Iceland, 621-2
Idealism, 213, 216, 218, 278, 304-5
Immigration, 473-5
Imperialism, *see* Colonialism
Incas, 69
Independent Labour Party (England), 361
India, 68-9, 73, 82, 187, 368, 410, 468-9, 567, 572, 661-71, 706-7, 722-4; Partition of, 666-7, 670-1, 740
Indian Mutiny, 368
Indo-China, 591, 634, 662, 686, 689-96
Indonesia, 662, 686-8
Industrialism, 102, 192, 208-12, 227, 234-7, 251-70, 278-84, 289, 292-3, 305-6, 328-30, 345-51, 425, 471, 474-5, 480, 509, 513-14, 667-8, 683, 720, 729
Inflation, 476-8, 484
Inquisition (Spain), 5
Insulin, 464
Insull, Samuel, 481-2, 485
Intendants, 16, 28, 135, 140
International Court of Justice (U.N.), 647-8
International Monetary Fund (World Bank), 649, 710
International Women's Year Conference (1975), 739
Iraq, 532
Iran, 684, 729, 732
Ireland, 54, 277, 372, 474, 599, 653, 749; Home Rule issue, 356-7, 364-7
Irish Church, 356
Irish Free State, 367
Irish National Party, 356-7, 362-5
Iron curtain, 612
Isabella, of Spain (1451-1504), 69
Islam, 686, 749
Isolationism (U.S.A.), 418, 603, 620-1
Israel, 651-2, 712, 732, 749
Italy, 4, 10, 34, 63, 172-4, 208, 223, 228-9, 233-4, 237, 245, 304, 307, 322, 336, 371, 394, 399, 413, 418-19, 456-7, 466, 474, 494, 496-504, 526-8, 530, 535-6, 538-46, 549, 562, 571, 596, 611-2, 614, 616, 621; unification of, 311, 311-17, 354

Jacobins, 153-4, 157, 161, 163, 168, 178-9, 183, 185, 219, 229, 339, 341
James I, of England (1566-1625), 47-50, 98
James II, of England (1633-1701), 57, 60-1, 81
James VI, of Scotland, *see* James I, of England
Jameson, Dr. Starr, 370, 372, 389
Jameson, Raid, The, 370, 388-9
Jamestown, 75
Japan, 184, 390, 392, 399, 410, 414, 418, 431-3, 466, 468-9, 472, 479-80, 504-5, 532, 534-5, 545, 547, 565-8, 572-3, 583-7, 601-3, 607, 648, 660, 672-3, 680-2, 684, 689, 716, 723, 731, 741

INDEX 811

Jaurès, Jean, 303
Jena, Battle of, 189, 205, 318
Jesuits, 100, 313, 332, 341
Jet propulsion, 732
Jews, 120, 151, 518, 520, 526, 528, 651, 745, 749, 788-9
Jingoism, 369-70
John XXIII, Pope (1881-1963), 744
John Paul I, Pope, 745
John Paul II, Pope, 745
Johnson, Lyndon B. (1908-1973), 696
Joint-stock companies, 65
Jordan, 712
Joseph II, of Austria (1741-90), 119-21, 123-4
Juarez, Benito, 308
July Monarchy (Louis Philippe), 232, 235-8, 249
July Revolution (France), 232
June Revolution (France), 238-40, 247
Jung, Carl, 289
Junkers, 36, 318, 330, 521
Jupiter, 755
Jutland, Battle of, 409

Kant, Immanuel (1724-1804), 218
Karlsbad Decrees, 228, 233-4
Kashmir, 669, 688
Kay, John, 256
Keats, John, 213
Kemal, Mustapha, *see* Ataturk
Kennan, George F., 589, 615-6, 638, 730
Kennedy, John F. (1917-63), 629, 632-3, 659, 696
Kenya, 701
Kenyatta, Jomo, 701
Kepler, Johann (1571-1630), 87-8, 90-2, 100-1
Kerensky, Alexander (1881-   ), 441, 444-5
Keynes, John Maynard (1883-1946), 491-2
Khartoum, 369-70
Khrushchev, Nikita (1894-1971), 600-1, 627-33, 685
King George's War, 80
Kingsley, Charles, 294
Kirov, Sergei, 509
Kissinger, Henry A., 638, 716
Kitchener, General Herbert (1850-1916), 370
Kléber, Jean-Baptiste, 177
Korea, 431; South, 696
Korean War; 603, 625-6, 649-50, 659, 691, 693, 696
Kornilov, General Lavr, 444-5
Kossuth, Louis, 241
Kosygin, Alexei, (1904-   ), 601, 633
Kruger, Paul, 389
Krupp Company, 289, 329, 376
Kulaks, 515
Kulturkampf, 331-2
Kuomintang (*see also* China, Nationalist), 672-4, 676, 680, 682
Kurds, 532

Kuwait, 729, 732

La Vendée uprising, 163, 182
Labour Party (England), 296, 358-64, 590
Layfayette, Marquis de (1757-1834), 131, 141, 148-9, 153, 158, 161, 232
Laibach Congress, 227, 229
Laissez-faire, 116, 136, 212-13, 263, 267, 286, 349-50, 360-1, 372
Lamartine, Alphonse de (1790-1869), 238
Laos, 689, 691, 694
Lateran Accord (Italy), 502, 526
Latin America, 466, 468, 708-11, 720, 723-4, 741
Latvia, 418, 466, 554
Lausanne, Treaty of, 415
Laval, Pierre, 539
League of Augsburg War, 80-1
League of Nations, 231, 413, 415, 418, 505, 514, 530-7, 540-2, 545, 547, 552-3, 587, 606, 639, 641-2, 647-50, 677, 704
League of the Three Emperors, *see Dreikaiserbund*
Legion of Honour, 183, 343
Legislative Assembly (France), 150, 152-61
Leipzig, Battle of, 204, 228
Lend-lease, 562, 616
Lenin, V.I. (1870-1924), 166, 428, 430, 433-5, 442-7, 497, 506-8
Leningrad (St. Petersburg), 506, 564
Leo XIII, Pope (1810-1903), 294
Leonardo da Vinci (1452-1519), 96, 103
Leopold II, of Austria (1747-92), 123, 155
Lesseps, Ferdinand de, 342
Liberal Party (England), 351-8, 361-4, 373
Liberalism, 210-13, 218, 221-2, 227-34, 243-9, 277-8, 294, 297, 302-4, 320, 323, 326, 423
Liebknecht, Karl, 516
Ligurian Republic, 174
Limited liability, 289
Lister, Joseph, 287
Literacy, 123, 292, 468, 667, 701, 724
Lithuania, 418, 466, 533-4, 554
Livingstone, David, 371
Lloyd George, David (1863-1945), 362, 413, 418
Locarno Treaties, 481, 536, 540
Locke, John (1632-1704), 107
Lombardy, 173-4, 223-5, 307, 312-14
Long March (Chinese Communists), 677, 678
Long Parliament (Charles I), 52
Lorraine, 280, 329, 338, 345, 376, 381, 396, 399, 413, 475
Louis XIII (1601-43), of France, 14, 22
Louis XIV (the Sun King), of France (1638-1715), 2, 4, 22-33, 44, 46, 57, 61, 72, 80-1, 125-7, 135, 140, 162, 381, 528
Louis XV, of France (1710-74), 126
Louis XVI, of France (1754-93), 126, 129, 138, 140, 142, 145-52, 162, 205
Louis XVIII, of France (1755-1824), 204-7, 232

Louis Napoleon, *see* Napoleon III
Louis Philippe, of France (1773-1850), 235-8
Louisbourg, 81-2
Lovett, William, 275
Low Countries, 4-5, 172, 398, 496, 557, 559
Lucca, 223
Ludendorff, General Erich von, 410, 520
Lusitania, 409
Luther, Martin (1483-1546), 83, 86
Lutheran Church, 13, 22, 119, 527, 746
Luxemburg, 4, 381, 544, 557, 596
Luxemburg, Rosa, 516
Lvov, Prince Georgy, 441, 444
Lyell, Sir Charles, 284
Lytton Commission, 535

MacArthur, General Douglas, 601, 625-6
McCarthy, Joseph, 604
Macedonia, 395, 533
Machiavelli, 499
McLuhan, Marshall, 734-5
MacMahon, Marshall, 341
Magellan, 69
Magenta, Battle of, 307
Maginot Line, 543, 556-7, 567
Magna Carta, 51
Magyars, 240-3, 249, 324, 384, 415, 418
Mahan thesis, 378
Majuba Hill, Battle of, 370
Malaysia, 684-5
Malawi, 705
Malaya, 473, 572
Malik, Adam, 688
Malta, 187, 224
Malthus, Thomas, 284
Manchester, 262, 265, 268, 271
Manchu Dynasty, 674
Manchurian Incident, 505, 534-5, 545, 547, 553, 650, 674
Mandated territories (League of Nations), 642, 648, 701, 704
Manhattan Island, 70
Mantua, 173, 178
Mao Tse-tung (1893-1976), 674-684
Marat, Jean Paul (1743-93), 158, 160-1, 164, 168
March Revolution (Russia), 440-3
Marconi, Guglielmo (1874-1937), 284, 454
Marcuse, Herbert, 734, 736-7
Marengo, Battle of, 181, 204, 209
Maria Theresa, of Austria (1717-80), 34-5, 38-9, 44, 46, 119-20
Marie Antoinette (1755-93), 126, 137, 152, 155, 162
Marie Louise, of Austria, 200, 223-4
Marlbourough, Duke of, 81
Marne, Battle of, 402
Marseillaise, 157, 167
Marshall Plan, 591, 613-6, 618, 620, 622
Marx, Karl, (1818-83), 166, 218, 286, 298-302, 340, 359, 780-1
Marxism, 298-302, 330, 339-40, 427-30, 435, 511, 530, 618, 676-7, 684, 739, 745, 780-1
Mary Stuart, Queen of Scots (1542-87), 47
Maryland, 75
Mass production, 106, 201, 253-7, 450-3, 495, 756
Masséna, 176, 181, 189
Mathematical Principles (Newton), 92-4
Matteotti, Giacomo, 500
Mau Mau society, 701
Mauritius, 224
Maximilian, Hapsburg Archduke, 308
Maxwell, James Clerk, 280
May Laws, (Prussia), 332
Mayflower, 75
Mazarin, Cardinal (1602-61), 22-4, 26, 29
Mazzini, Guiseppe (1805-72), 245, 312-13, 315
Mead, Margaret (1901-1978), 742
Mechanization, 255, 265, 450, 453, 515
Medicine, 94-8, 463-5
Meir, Golda (1898-1978), 716, 742
Memel Statute, 534
Mendel, Gregor, 288
Mendeleyev, Dmitri, 280
Mendès-France, Pierre, 691
Mensheviks, 428-30, 433-5, 440-2, 447
Mercantilism, 30, 68-76, 116-17, 231, 257-8, 367-8, 764-6
Mesopotamia, 382
Metternich, Prince (1773-1859), 220-30, 233-4, 240-1, 312, 326
Mexico, 69, 307-8, 324, 509, 708
Michelangelo (1475-1564), 83
Michelet, Jules, 775-6
Middle Ages, 17, 83, 85, 103, 106, 168, 271, 722
Middle class, 9, 125, 131-6, 148, 151, 182-5, 210, 212, 227, 232, 234-6, 238, 244, 247, 266, 270, 273, 297, 346, 348-9, 355, 520
Milan, 4, 63, 229, 242-3
Militarism, 501, 504-5, 528, 530, 540, 565, 567
Mill, John Stuart (1806-73), 352
Mir, 423, 425-6
Mirabeau, Comte de (1749-91), 144-5, 152-3
Mixed economy, 667
Modena, 223, 312, 314
Mohammed VI, Sultan, 415
Molotov, Vyacheslav, 614
Monarchism, 2-40, 210, 222, 320, 338, 341-3; constitutional, 150-5, 157, 233, 244, 304, 316, 466
Mongolia, 40, 534
Montesquieu (1689-1755), 110-11, 113, 116-17, 131, 149
Montgomery of Alamein (1887-1976), 571, 580-1
Monnet, Jean, 596
Montreal, 82
Moreau, Jean Victor, 181, 185
Morgan, J.P., 483

INDEX 813

Morgan, Thomas, 462
Morocco, 390-1, 698
Moscow, 201, 433-4, 564-5; Declaration, 642
Moslems, 34, 63, 96, 230, 306, 661, 666, 669, 745, 749
Mount Palomar, 458-9
Mountbatten, Lord Louis, 666
Mountain Party (France), 153, 161
Mouvement Républicain Populaire (France), 591
Mundt, Wilhelm, 288
Munich Conference, 551, 606
Murat, Marshal Joachim, 178-9, 202, 204
Mussolini, Benito (1883-1945), 218, 456, 497-504, 523, 526, 538-41, 543-4, 546, 549, 551-3, 571, 582, 787-8

Nagasaki, 585, 602-3, 674
Namibia, 704-5
Nantes, Edict of, 12, 32
Naples, 4, 174, 176, 181, 189, 227, 316
Napoleon Bonaparte (1769-1821), 30, 42, 119, 169-209, 219, 222, 224-5, 228-9, 308, 311, 343, 422, 518, 528, 554, 558, 563; achievements of, 184-5, 208-9; Austrian campaigns, 172-4, 200; Battle of Austerlitz, 190; becomes Emperor, 185-6; Continental System, 193-4, 198, 200-1; Egyptian campaign, 174-7; exiled to Elba, 204; internal policy, 182-5; One Hundred Days, 205-7, 224; Russian campaign, 201-3; seizes power (*Brumaire*), 177-80; Trafalgar, 191-2, 195; Waterloo, 206
Napoleon III (Louis Napoleon) (1808-73), 247-8, 304-11, 313-17, 322-5, 345, 368
Napoleon, Joseph, 194, 198
Napoleonic Code, 184-5, 195, 200, 208, 232, 467
Napoleonic Wars, 172-7, 181, 187-204, 267, 370, 608
Narodnici, 426, 434
Nassau (Germany), 323
Nasser, Gamal Abdel (1918-1970), 650-2, 714
Natal, 372
National Assembly (France), 142, 145-52, 245, 247-8, 338-41, 591; (Germany), 244-5, 249
National Black Feminist Organization, 742
National Conservative Party (Germany), 330
National Convention (France), 158, 161-3, 168-9
National Guard (France), 148-9, 169, 238, 339
National Health Insurance Act (England), 361-2
National Industrial Recovery Act (U.S.A.), 493
National Liberal Party (Germany), 330, 523-4
National Socialist German Workers' Party, *see* Nazi Party

Nationalism, 208, 210-11, 213, 218-19, 221-2, 227-34, 236-7, 240-5, 249, 278, 286, 303-4, 311-26, 353, 374, 380-6, 467-9, 495, 505, 546-7, 601, 614, 651, 660-718
Nationalist Party (China), *see* Kuomintang
Nationalization, 359-60, 590, 599, 651-2
Navarino, Battle of, 230
Navarre, 10-11
Nazi Party, 478, 511, 518, 520-8
Nazism, 506, 515, 520-8, 543-4, 553, 749, 788-9
Nazi-Soviet Pact, 554, 562, 606
Necker, Jacques (1732-1804), 126, 141, 146
Nehru, Jawaharlal (1889-1964), 661, 667-70, 688
Nelson, Sir Horatio (1758-1805), 175, 191
Netherlands (*see also* Holland), 4-8, 17, 65, 81, 227, 232, 234, 557, 596, 619, 686-7; Austrian, *see* Belgium
Neuilly, Treaty of, 412, 415
New Amsterdam, 70
New Deal (Roosevelt), 490-4, 604
New Economic Policy (Russia), 513
New England, 75, 81-2
New France, 72-3, 75, 82, 140
New Guinea, 369
New Netherland, 70
New Plymouth, 75
New World, colonization of, 70-82, 473
New Zealand, 368, 467, 693, 696, 723
Newcomen, Thomas, 255
Newfoundland, 71, 74-5, 81-2, 281, 284, 562
Newton, Isaac (1642-1727), 87, 91-4, 100-2, 106-7, 458, 461; laws of motion, 94
Ney, Marshal Michel, 205-6
Nicaragua, 704
Nice, 162, 174, 307, 315
Nicholas I (the Iron Czar), of Russia (1796-1855), 230, 233, 306, 422
Nicholas II, of Russia (1868-1918), 380, 430-42, 507
Nietzsche, Friedrich, 782-3
Nixon, Richard (1913-   ), 633
Nkrumah, Kwame, 702
Nobility (*see also* Privilege), 2-3, 10, 12, 16, 23, 26-8, 44, 48, 115, 119-24, 129-36, 144-5, 148, 183, 205, 220, 266, 275-7, 318, 421-6
Nobles of the robe, 130-1
Nobles of the sword, 129
Non-alignment, 646, 668, 687
Normandy, Battle of, 578-81
North Atlantic Treaty Organization (NATO), 604, 620-2, 628-9, 634, 636-7, 654, 706, 715
North German Confederation, 323-4, 327
North Vietnam, 740
Norway, 224, 467, 557, 621, 732
Nouveaux riches, 130
Nova Scotia, 72, 81-2, 443
November Revolution (Russia), 445-7
Novi, Battle of, 177
Novum Organum (Bacon), 98
Nyasaland, 705

Oberkommando der Wehrmacht, 525
O'Connor, Feargus, 275
October Manifesto (Russia), 434, 439
Ohain, Hans von, 754
"Oil Weapon", 730, 732
Oil, "See Energy Crisis"
Old Age Pension Act (England), 361
Olmutz, 245, 317-18
Olympic Games, 380
Omdurman, Battle of, 370
On the Law of War and Peace (Grotius), 22
One Hundred Days (Napoleon), 205-7, 224
On the Revolutions of the Heavenly Spheres (Copernicus), 83, 86
On the Structure of the Human Body (Vesalius), 94-5
Orange Free State, 370
Order Number One (Russia), 441-2
Organization of American States, 709
Organization of Petroleum Exporting Countries (OPEC), 716, 731, 733
Origin of Species (Darwin), 284
Orlando, Vittorio, 413
Orthodox Church (Russia), 40, 44, 121, 306, 421, 424, 746
Osler, Sir William, 463
Ostpolitik, 638
Otto, N.A., 450
Ottoman Empire, 230, 306, 367, 369, 375, 382, 384, 415
Outer Space, 750-7
Owen, Robert, 273-4, 295, 358

Pacific War, 565-9, 572-3, 583-6, 607
Pakistan, 661-71, 693
Palestine Liberation Army, 712, 716
Palmerston, Viscount (1784-1865), 353-5, 368
Panama, 708, 711
Panama Affair, 342-3
Panama Canal, 281, 342
Pan-American Union, 709
Pan-Germanism, 242-3, 381
Pan-Slavism, 242-4, 382, 385-6
Pankhurst, Mrs. Emmeline, 363
Panmunjon Armistice, 626, 650
Papal Infallibility, 783-4
Papal States, 174, 223, 233, 312, 315-17
Papen, Franz von, 521-2
Paris, Congress of, 306, 325; Peace of, 412-19; Treaties of: (1763) 82, 140; (1814) 205, 224; (1815) 224
Paris Commune (1871), 302, 339-40, 343
Park, Mungo, 371
Parlement of Paris, 12, 46, 142
Parliament, English (*see also* Reform Bills, England), 47-58, 110-11, 266-77, 362-3; French, *see* Estates-General; Russian, *see* Duma
Parliament of the Protectorate, 55
Parma, 223, 312, 314
Parnell, Charles Stewart (1864-91), 356-7
Party system (England), 351-7
Pass system (South Africa), 703

Pasteur, Louis, 287
Paul V, Pope, 89
Paul VI, Pope, 745
Paulette (income tax), 13
Pavlov, Ivan, 288
Peace Corps (U.S.A.), 711, 724
Peaceful coexistence, 627-33, 638, 685
Pearl Harbour, 565-8, 572, 603, 607
Pearson, Lester, 652
Peasantry, 12, 16, 44, 119-25, 128, 131 133-5, 142, 148-50, 157, 163, 182, 205, 229, 238-45, 247, 251-3, 421-7, 435, 443, 469, 513-15, 681, 775-9; emancipation of serfs, 243, 424, 427
Peel, Sir Robert (1788-1850), 257, 269, 277, 352
Penicillin, 464
Peninsular War, 190, 195, 198-200
Pennsylvania, 138
Penny post, 276
People's Charter (England), 275
People's Republic of China (*see also* China, Communist), 682
People's Will society (Russia), 424
Perry, Commodore Matthew, 480
Peru, 711
Peter I (the Great), of Russia (1672-1725), 41-4, 421
Peter III, of Russia (1728-62), 44
Peter I, of Serbia (1844-1921), 385
Peterloo Massacre, 268, 274
Petition of Right (England), 50-1
Petrograd, *see* St. Petersburg
Phalansteries, 297
Philip II, of Spain (1527-98), 1-8, 10-12, 61, 76
Philippe Egalité, 232
Philippines, 5, 69, 82, 545, 567, 583, 686, 693
Philosophes, 108-23, 126, 128, 131, 138, 151, 211, 747-51
Physics, 83-94, 457-62
Physiocrats, 116-17
Picasso, Pablo, 546
Piedmont, 172-3, 187, 227-8, 245, 249, 307-8, 312-17, 395
Pig War, 385
Pitt, William (the Elder) (1708-78), 82
Pitt, William (the Younger) (1759-1806), 187-8
Pius VII, Pope (1740-1823), 182
Pius IX, Pope (1792-1878), 245, 294, 312-13, 683
Pius XI, Pope (1857-1939), 502
Pizarro, Francisco, 69
Plain Party (France), 153, 157, 161
Planck, Max, 459
Planning, 725-6
Plehve, Viacheslav, 431
Plekhanov, George, 427-8
Plombières Agreement, 307, 313
Pocket boroughs, 271
Poincaré, Raymond (1860-1934), 396, 542
Poland, 42, 163, 172, 194, 201, 216, 224, 226, 233, 386, 413, 418, 424, 466, 475, 506, 531, 551, 554-6, 582

INDEX 815

608-11, 618, 643, 692; partition of (1772), 44, 123, 224
Police state, 228, 234, 424, 501, 509-11, 523-8, 667, 681
Polish Corridor, 413, 534, 554
Pomerania, 224
Pompadour, Madame de, 108, 126
Poor Law (England), 269
Pope, Alexander, 102
Populations, 9, 76, 82, 240, 253, 277, 284, 292, 348-9, 473-5, 495, 667, 671, 720-26
Populists (Russia), 426-7
Portugal, 5, 65, 68, 70, 76, 176, 181, 195, 198-9, 224, 474, 620
Pot walloper voters, 271
Potsdam Conference, 611
Prague, Treaty of, 326
Presbyterians, 49, 54, 57, 746
Price index, 454
Princip, Gavrilo, 397
Privilege (*see also* Nobility), 33, 125, 134-6, 142, 341, 351
Progressive Party (Germany), 333
Proletariat, dictatorship of, 300-3, 526
Protestants (*see also* Huguenots), 9-17, 22, 151, 745-9
Protopopov, Alexander, 439
Proudhon, Pierre, 297, 339
Provence, 9
Provisional Government (Russia), 441-6, 506
Prussia, 34-40, 46, 81-2, 118-19, 123, 155, 189, 194, 203-4, 206, 223-6, 231, 233, 236, 243-5, 307-11, 317-38, 383
Purges: Germany, 526; Russia, 509-11
Puritans, 49, 53, 57, 75
Pyramiding, 481-2, 485

Quadruple Alliance, 225, 231
Quebec, 72, 82, 184, 467
Queen Anne's War, 80
Quesnay, 116
Quintuple Alliance, 225, 389

Racism, 605, 633
Radar, 560, 581, 750
Radical Party (England), 267, 269-72
Radicalism, 153, 157, 237-8, 330, 343-4, 352-4, 358, 497, 516, 739
Radio, 454-7
Railways, 235-7, 259-60, 280-1, 305, 329, 347, 349, 382
Rasputin, Gregory, 436-7, 439-40
Rationalization of production, 453
Realism, 278
Realpolitik, 304-5, 307, 315, 320, 326
Red China, *see* China, Communist
"Red Guards", 684
Reform Bills (England): First, 272-3, 276, 351, 354-5; Second, 355, 358; Third, 356; Parliament Bill (1910), 362-3
Reformation, 103, 210, 228, 744

Reichstag, 303, 323, 327-8, 338, 378, 517-8, 521-3
Reign of Terror (Robespierre), 163
Reinsurance Treaty, 336, 387
Relativity, theory of, 459-61
Religious toleration, 12, 16, 22, 102, 106-7, 113, 119-21, 123, 138, 149, 182, 211
Religious wars, 9-22, 651, 661, 666-9, 749
Renaissance, 103, 106
Reparations, from Germany, 374, 414, 476-9, 488, 521, 616; from Japan, 602
Republicanism, 155, 157, 161-9, 245, 305, 308, 312, 315-17, 338-45, 546
Revisionists, 302, 685
Revolutions of 1848, 234, 237-44, 304, 324
Rhee, Syngman, 625
Rhineland, 19, 162-3, 181, 224, 325, 414, 418, 511, 540-2, 545, 553, 557, 582; Confederation of the Rhine, 189, 208, 223
Rhodes, Cecil (1853-1902), 370
Rhodesia, 702-06
Richardson, Samuel, 105
Richelieu, Cardinal (1588-1642), 14-17, 22-3, 26, 50, 72
Riddell, Dr. W. A., 539
Rivoli, Battle of, 173
Robespierre, Maximilien (1758-94), 153, 163-9
Rochdale Pioneers, 294-5
Roehm, Ernst, 526
Romagna, 314, 497
Roman Catholic Church, 5, 8-13, 17, 22, 46, 49, 57, 60-2, 73, 75, 89, 119-20, 129, 151, 182-6, 195, 205, 210, 220, 232, 293-4, 306, 330-1, 343-5, 502, 527, 546, 744-6
Romanesque, 213
Romania, 395, 399, 409, 415, 453, 555, 611, 614, 618, 634-7
Romanians, 240, 383-4
Romanovs, 320, 466, 496, 509
Romanticism, 211, 213-18
Rome, 174, 245, 247, 316-17, 502, 572
Rome-Berlin Axis, 540, 545-9
Rome-Berlin-Tokyo Axis, 545, 553
Rommel, General, 571
Ronvray, Louis de, 760
Roon, Count von, 320-1
Roosevelt, Franklin D. (1882-1945), 456, 490-4, 561-2, 565, 568, 604, 607-10, 615, 639-43, 708
Rosetta Stone, 175
Rothschild, 369
Rotten boroughs, 271-2
Roundheads, 53
Rousseau, Jean-Jacques (1712-78), 110, 113-17, 124, 138, 166, 502, 738, 773-5
Royalists, 168, 177-8, 185, 341-3
Ruhr, 476, 478, 521, 581
Rus, 40
Russell, Lord, 355

Russia (see also USSR), 34, 40-6, 82, 120-2, 163, 172, 176, 187-90, 194, 200-4, 223-6, 229-33, 266, 292, 298, 306, 322, 325, 333, 336, 338, 367, 376, 382-410, 419, 453, 462, 466, 469, 474, 476, 479, 486, 506-16, 521, 530-2, 534, 537, 541, 546, 554-5, 582-3, 585-6, 594, 599-601, 606-20, 623, 626-33, 636, 638, 641-5, 649-51, 653, 655, 659, 684-6, 697, 706, 712, 722-3, 731, 739; invaded (by Napoleon) 201-3, (by Hitler) 561-7, 569-71, 599, 607, 640
Russian Revolution, (1905) 433-5; (1917) 266, 439-47, 453, 474, 506, 531; role of intelligentsia, 426-30
Russian-Japanese War, 392, 431-3
Russo-Turkish War, 369
Ruthenians, 240, 383
Rutherford, Lord, 461

Saar, 413, 534
Sadat (el-), Anwar (1918-   ), 716
Sadowa, Battle of, 323
St. Bartholomew's Day Massacre, 10-11
St. Germain, Treaty of, 412, 414
St. Helena, 200, 207-8
St. John's Newfoundland, 284
St. Petersburg, 44, 121, 433-4, 439-40, 442-3, 445-6, 506
St. Pierre and Miquelon, 82
Saint-Simon, Comte de, 297
Salons, 137-8
Salt March (Gandhi), 663
Salvation Army, 294
San Francisco Conference, 643-4, 647
Sarajevo, 397
Sardinia, 223, 228-9
Sartre, Jean-Paul, 735-6
Saturn, 755
Satyagraha (passive resistance), 660-1
Saudi Arabia, 729, 732
Saxony, 82, 224
Schacht, Dr. Hjalmar, 526
Schleicher, Kurt von, 522
Schleswig, 322
Schlieffen Plan, 398-9, 402
Schuman Plan, 596
Schutzstaffeln (S.S.), 526
Science, 83-108, 278-94, 457-65, 727-57, 769-71
Scientific method, 105-6, 108; of Bacon, 100
Schmidt, Helmut (1918-   ), 636, 730
Scot and lot boroughs, 271
Scotland, 48-9, 52-4, 351
Scott, Sir Walter, 213
Sea power, 7-8, 66, 68, 75-7, 81-2, 181, 188, 191-3, 337, 362, 378-81, 386, 388, 409, 537, 543, 558-60, 572
Seasons society, 237
Sebastopol, Battle of, 569
Second Empire (France), 247-8, 305-11
Second Estate, 128-31
Second International, 302-3, 332, 616

Second World War, 18, 456, 462, 471, 475, 479, 506, 515, 525, 530, 553-87, 623, 666, 682, 754; cost of, 589-90
Secretariat (U.N.), 645-7, 654
Security Council (U.N.), 642-7, 649-55, 704, 712, 716
Sedan, Battle of, 308, 333, 345
Selassie, Haile, 539-40
Self-determination, 413, 418, 608, 645, 666, 686, 700-01
Senegal Company, 73
Serbia, 240, 383-6, 392-7
Serfdom, *see* Peasantry
Seven Weeks' War, 322-4
Seven Years' War, 80-2, 118, 140
Sèvres, Treaty of, 412, 415
Shaftesbury, Lord (1801-85), 263, 269
Shaw, George Bernard, 360
Shelley, Percy Bysshe, 213
Shintoism, 505, 601
Ship money tax, 52
Shipbuilding, 260-1, 329, 347, 379, 396, 472
Short Parliament (Charles I), 52
Sian incident, 680
Sicily (*see also* Two Sicilies), 4, 315-16, 571
Siemens-Martin open hearth process, 280
Siéyès, Abbe (1748-1836), 144-5, 153, 166, 177-80
Silesia, 34-5, 38, 81
Sinai, 714
Singapore, 470, 567
Sino-Indian conflict, 670, 688
Sino-Japanese War, 547, 680-1
Sino-Soviet dispute, 632, 684-6
Six Acts (England), 268, 274
Six Day War (1967), 714, 716
Slave trade, 73, 370, 423
Slavs, 40, 240, 242-3, 384, 393-5, 410, 528, 564
Slovaks, 383-4, 614
Slovenes, 383-4, 410
Smith, Adam (1723-90), 117
Smith, Ian, 706
Smith, Sir Sidney, 176
Smuts, Jan (1870-1950), 410, 415
Social contract (Locke), 107
Social Contract, The (Rousseau), 115
Social Democratic Federation (England), 359, 361
Social Democratic Party (Germany), 303, 330, 332, 338, 521, 523; (Russia), 427-8, 433-4
Social Revolutionary Party (Russia), 434, 441
Social Security Act (U.S.A.), 493
Socialism (*see also Marxism*), 211, 213, 237-8, 247, 249, 278, 286, 294-303, 332, 346, 358-64, 372, 374, 490, 497-9, 508, 513, 590, 667, 739
Socialist Party, (France) 303, 542, 591; (Italy) 499-500
Solferino, Battle of, 307

INDEX 817

Somalia, 708
Somme, Battle of, 410
Soong T. V., 676
Sorel, Julien, 502
South Africa, Republic of, 372, 648, 702-06
South America, 5, 69, 231, 292, 315, 371, 453, 474, 724
South Seas Company, 257
South-East Asia Treaty Organization (SEATO), 693
South-West Africa, 648, 704
Sovereignty, 3, 36, 107, 116, 219, 517
Soviets, 412, 433-4, 516
Spain, 1-8, 10, 17, 49-50, 52, 55, 65, 68-71, 73, 76, 162, 172, 191, 195, 198-9, 224, 227-9, 231, 308, 474, 496, 531, 545-7, 621
Spanish Armada, 7-8
Spanish Civil War (1930's), 545-7, 606, 617
Spanish Crusade, 4-8
Spanish Succession, War of, 34, 80-1
Spanish-American War, 545
Spartacists, 516, 521
Spee, Admiral von, 409
Spinning jenny, 256
Spirit of the Laws (Montesquieu), 110
Sputnik, 732
Sri Lanka (Formerly Ceylon), 740
Stalin, Joseph (1879-1953), 507-11, 515, 528, 554-5, 562, 565, 569, 571, 582, 600-01, 606-11, 615, 617, 626, 642-3
Stalingrad, Battle of, 569-71, 607
Stalinism, 600, 614, 618
Stephenson, George, 260
Stolypin, Peter, 435-7
Storm Troops (S.A.), 520, 523, 525-6
Strategic Arms Limitation Talks (SALT), 633
Stuarts, 47, 51, 61
Sudan, 369-70
Sudetenland, 549
Suez Canal, 281, 342, 369, 563, 571, 714
Suez Crisis, 628, 650-1, 712
Suffragettes, 363-4, 467
Suharto, General, 687
Sukarno, Achmed, 687
Sully, Duke of (1559-1641), 13, 16
Sun Yet-sen, Dr., 672-3
Suvorov, General, 122
Sweden, 17, 224, 463, 534, 558, 621, 653, 741
Switzerland, 174, 187, 224, 496, 558, 621
Syria, 175-6, 712, 731

Taff Vale decision, 361
Taille (direct tax), 16, 134
Taiwan, 655, 682, 684, 685
Talleyrand-Périgord, Charles Maurice de (1754-1838), 225-6
Tannenburg, Battle of, 402, 438
Tanzania, United Republic of, 701

Tartars, 40, 420
Taxation, 3, 5, 8, 13, 16, 27-32, 35, 46, 50, 52-3, 77, 120, 124-5, 131-6, 139-42, 145-6, 150-1, 236, 362, 476, 678
Tax-farmers, 139
Taylor, General Maxwell, 694
Technology (*see also* Science), 280-4, 449-57, 495, 528, 727-57
Teng Hsiao Ping, 684
Tennis Court Oath, 145, 150, 152, 177
Tereshkova, Valentina, 739
Terrati, Filippo, 497
Terriers (legal documents), 133, 148
Terror of 1793 (France), 177-8, 339
Test Act (England), 57, 61
Thailand, 684, 693
Thant, U, 647
Thatcher, Margaret (1905-   ), 741
Thiers, Adolphe (1797-1877), 338-9, 341
Third Estate, 128, 131-6, 144-5, 177
Third International, 616
Third Republic (France), 338-45
Thirty Years' War, 17-22, 34, 77
Tibet, 670
Tillich, Paul, 747
Tilsit, Treaty of, 194
Tiran, Strait of, 714
Tirpitz, Admiral Alfred von, 378
Tithe (church tax), 134-5
Tito, Marshal (1890-   ), 617-8, 637
Tocqueville, Alexis de, 209, 777-9
Tojo, General, 567
Tordisillas, Treaty of, 68
Tories, 57, 61, 266-73, 351-8
Toulon, Battle of, 163, 169-70
Townshend, Lord "Turnip," 252
Trade unions, *see* Unionism
Trades Union Congress (England), 296, 358, 361
Trading companies, 65
Trafalgar, Battle of, 191-2, 195
Transportation, 259-60, 280-1, 348, 449-53, 466, 480, 725
Transvaal Republic, 370, 389
Treitschke, Heinrich von, 328, 382
Trentino, 383
Trianon, Treaty of, 412, 415
Trieste, 611-2
Trygve Lie, 647
Triple Alliance, 336, 388, 390, 399, 409
Triple Entente, 390, 399
Troppau, Congress of, 227
Trotsky, Leon (1879-1940), 430, 433-4, 442-7, 506-9
Truman, Harry S. (1884-1972), 604, 610, 613, 620, 622, 625, 643, 693, 696
Truman Doctrine, 613-4, 620
Trusteeship Council (U.N.), 647-8
Tudors, 47-8, 73, 251
Tull, Jethro, 253
Tunisia, 336, 698
Turgot, Baron (1727-81), 116, 124, 126, 140
Turkey (*see also* Ottoman Empire), 40, 44,

119, 175-6, 181, 230, 392-5, 399, 409-10, 415, 466, 468, 506, 532, 613, 621, 634, 654-5
Tuscany, 223, 312, 315
Two Sicilies, Kingdom of, 223, 229, 312, 315-16
Tyrol, 383, 418

Uganda, 701
Ukraine, 40, 506, 554, 562, 564, 582, 600
Ulm, Battle of, 189-91
Ulster, 365, 367
Ulyanov, Alexander, 428
Union of Soviet Socialist Republics (U.S.S.R),(See Russia), formation of, 507
Unionism, 273-5, 278, 294-6, 302-3, 345-6, 349, 358-64, 504, 526
United Arab Republic (1958-71), 712
United Church, 746
United Nations, 231, 562, 568, 604, 609 611, 613, 619, 621, 625-6, 633, 639-59, 669, 685, 703-5, 712, 742; Organization of, 644-9; Emergency Force, 650-51, 714, 716,; Voting, 642-4, 650-1, 654-5
United Republic of Egypt, 712
United States, 117, 140, 194, 281, 368, 371, 399, 409-19, 442, 450-8, 463, 470-94, 505, 537, 539, 543, 553, 561-2, 565-86, 597, 603-34, 638, 640-4, 650-l, 659, 669, 682, 688, 691, 693, 696, 708-11, 715, 730, 741, 754-5; foreign aid, 476 478-9, 562, 594-5, 613-6, 618, 668, 706, 709-11, 722-3
Uniting for Peace resolution, 646 650-l
"Untouchables", 671
Universe, theories of, 83-94, 458
Upper Silesia, 534
Urbanization, 261, 292-3, 346, 349-51, 453, 465-6, 474, 725-6
Utilitarianism, 267
Utopians, 298, 301
Utrecht, Treaty of, 72, 81

Valmy, Battle of, 161-2, 219
Vatican, 173, 502, 744
V-bombs, 581, 623, 754
Venice, 63, 65, 173-4, 189, 242-3
Venetia, 223-5, 307, 312-17, 322-3
Venus, 755
Verdun, Battle of, 410
Verona, Congress of, 227, 229, 231
Verrazano, Giovanni, 72
Versailles, 23, 26, 28, 33, 115, 141-2, 146, 149, 152, 297, 326, 339, 345; Treaty of (1919), 412-15, 475, 481, 491, 496-7, 520, 530-1, 537-8, 540, 553, 643, 672
Vertical combination, 289, 292
Vesalius, Andreas (1514-64), 87, 94-6
Veto (U.N.), 642-4, 650-1, 654, 719
Victor Emmanuel II, of Piedmont (1820-78), 245, 249, 312-17
Victor Emmanuel III, of Italy (1869-1947), 500
Victoria, of England (1819-1901), 355, 363, 369, 376, 390
Vienna, 120, 173, 241, 247
Congress of (1815), 206, 211, 219-20, 222-4, 232, 234, 311, 326
Viet Cong, 694-6
Viet Minh, 689-94
Vietnam, 696
Vietnam War, 604, 638, 687-97
Vikings, 40
Villafranca, Treaty of, 307, 314
Vimy Ridge, Battle of, 410
Vingtième, (tax), 134
Virginia Company, 75
Vitamins, 462
Volgograd (Stalingrad), 40
Voltaire (1694-1778), 110-21, 124, 131, 136, 138, 722-3
Voting Rights Act (1965), 605
Voyager I, 755

Wagram, Battle of, 205
Waldheim, Kurt, 647, 716
Wall Street, 483-6
War Communism, 511-12
War guilt (German), 374, 414, 542
Ward, Barbara, 722
Warfare, methods of, 66-8, 77, 80, 199, 536-7, 555-8, 581, 585, 623, 639, 662 719, 754
Warsaw Pact, 628, 637
Washington, George, 81, 140
Waterloo, Battle of, 190, 206-7, 209-11
Watson-Watt, Sir Robert A., 560, 750
Watt, James (1736-1819), 255, 258-9
Wealth of Nations, The (Adam Smith), 117
Webb, Sydney and Beatrice, 360
Weimar Republic, 516-18, 521, 594
Wellington, Duke of, 204, 206, 247, 275
Wells, H. G., 360
West Bank (Jordan River), 714
West Germany, 594-6, 616, 618-20, 621, 636
West Indies, 69-70, 73-4, 76, 82
Westphalia, 194-5; Treaty of, 17, 22, 35-6, 328
Whigs, 57, 61, 266-73, 351
Whittle, Frank, 754
William I, of Prussia (1861-88), 320, 323, 325-6, 332, 337, 345
William II (Kaiser Wilhelm), of Prussia (1859-1941), 337, 376-9, 382, 387-9, 391, 397, 399, 412
William IV, of England (1765-1837), 272
William of Orange (1533-84), 5, 7, 61, 81
Wilson, Woodrow (1856-1924), 413, 415, 418, 466, 491, 607, 621
Women's Roles, 738
Women's Social and Political Union, 363
Women's Trade Union League, 359

INDEX 819

Wordsworth, 213
Worker's Educational Association, 295
Working class, 157, 235-6, 238, 244, 261-6, 268-70, 272-7, 294-303, 331-2, 346, 349-51, 355-6, 358-64, 423-5, 427, 497
Workmen's Compensation Act (England), 350
World Council of Churches, 746, 748
World Health Organization, 649, 723
Wright Brothers, 281
Wurtemburg, 189, 323

Yalta Conference, 607-9, 615, 642

Yezhov, N. I., 509
Yom Kippur War (1973), 714, 730
Yorktown, Battle of, 140
Yoshida, Shigeru, 602
Young Italy, 311-12, 315
Young Plan, 478-9
Yugoslavia, 384, 393, 410, 415, 418-19, 496, 563, 611-2, 616-8, 637, 684, 709

Zambia, 705
Zemstvos, 424
Zola, Emile, 343, 396
Zollverein, 236

AUTHORSHIP

While the authors of *Modern Perspectives* generally share collective responsibility for the contents of this book, the specific division of materials is as follows:

CHAPTERS 1-4   John Trueman
CHAPTERS 5-7   H. J. P. Schaffter
CHAPTER 8   V. P. Seary
CHAPTERS 9-16   R. Stewart
CHAPTER 17   V. P. Seary
CHAPTER 18   D. Scollard
CHAPTERS 19-16   T. Murray Hunter
CHAPTER 27   Pages 712-718, 719-725, 729-733, 738-744 and 750-757 T. Murray Hunter
                  Pages 725-729, 734-738 and 744-749 D. Scollard

The authors and publishers would like to thank Mr. John Burbidge and Mr. Daryl Sharp, whose advice and assistance were invaluable.